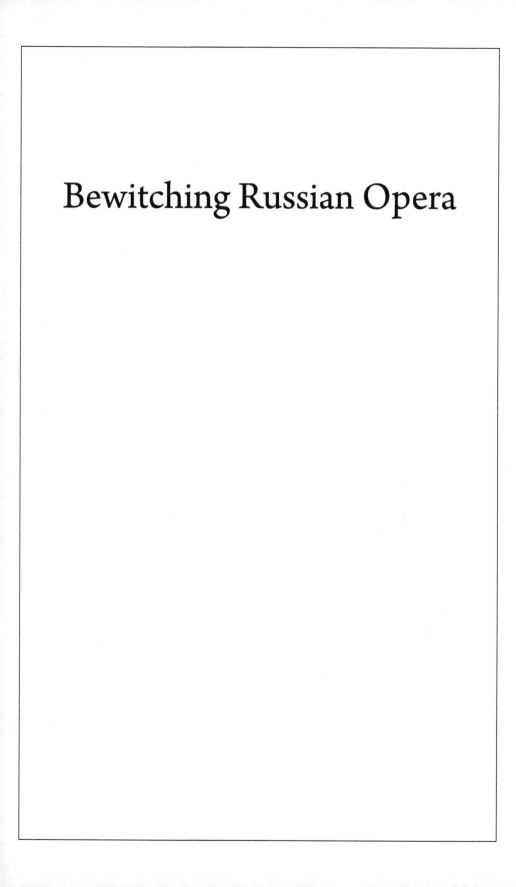

Bewitching Russian Opera

Bewitching Russian Opera

The Tsarina from State to Stage

Inna Naroditskaya

OXFORD
UNIVERSITY PRESS

OXFORD
UNIVERSITY PRESS

Oxford University Press, Inc., publishes works that further
Oxford University's objective of excellence
in research, scholarship, and education.

Oxford   New York
Auckland   Cape Town   Dar es Salaam   Hong Kong   Karachi
Kuala Lumpur   Madrid   Melbourne   Mexico City   Nairobi
New Delhi   Shanghai   Taipei   Toronto

With offices in
Argentina   Austria   Brazil   Chile   Czech Republic   France   Greece
Guatemala   Hungary   Italy   Japan   Poland   Portugal   Singapore
South Korea   Switzerland   Thailand   Turkey   Ukraine   Vietnam

Published by Oxford University Press, Inc.
198 Madison Avenue, New York, New York 10016
www.oup.com

Library of Congress Cataloging-in-Publication Data

Naroditskaya, Inna, 1955-
    Bewitching Russian opera : tsarinas from state to stage / Inna Naroditskaya.
        p. cm.
    Includes bibliographical references and index.
    ISBN 978-0-19-534058-7 (alk. paper)
1. Opera—Russia—18th century. 2. Opera—Russia—19th century.
3. Empresses—Russia—History—18th century. 4. Women opera
producers and directors—Russia—History—18th century.
5. Kings and rulers in opera. 6. Women in opera. I. Title.
    ML1737.N37   2011
    782.10947'09033—dc22   2011007497

9 8 7 6 5 4 3 2 1
Printed in the United States of America
on acid-free paper

To Oktiabrina-Zhenia-Zhenechka Golik
and *Pavlik Naroditskiy* you are my world

ACKNOWLEDGMENT

This book gave me the precious gift of learning from, interacting and collaborating with, remarkable scholars and thinkers on Russian music and culture on the both sides of the Atlantic. Andrew Wachtel informed the frame of the book as a literary scholar. A colleague and friend (and incidentally one of the busiest people I have encountered in the academic world), he read the manuscript twice, leaving his incisive remarks throughout. The work owes its existence to the everlasting patience, continuous encouragement, and tireless editing of my life partner, James Borland. His intellect and inquisitiveness, his pointed questions guided me in writing. The number of times he read every chapter, page, line, and footnote is a secret I share only with my computer. He now knows about the subject as much as I do. Nick Naroditski, who perused the volume, enjoying the opportunity of passionate criticism and equally passionate praise of his mother, translated several poetic excerpts and edited others. In our daily lives, he made sure that I keep an ironic distance between myself and the regal heroines of the volume. I am looking forward to the next collaboration with him.

Whether knowingly or not, the contributors include Richard Wortman, whom I recently met and who continues to inspire me; Boris Gasparov, whose interdisciplinary writing served for me as a model; and Richard Taruskin, whose writing reshaped the field and certainly my understanding of it. The excitement of working with recent Russian scholarship on music, theater, and cultural history was complemented by personal contacts with authors who through the past seven to nine years generously shared their works, donated their time, challenged and were challenged in our engaging ongoing discussions in Moscow and St. Petersburg: Maria Shcherbakova, Natalia Ogarkova, Polina Vaidman, Liia Lepskaia, Liudmila Starikova, and the late Viktor Varunts. Emma Rassina and her assistants opened to me the archives of the Taneev' Research Library of the Moscow Conservatory. Together with Rassina, my musicology colleague Svetlana Sigida hosted a preliminary presentation of my research at the Conservatory. John Roland Wiley and Glenn Watkins read and commented on parts of this work; Judith Becker as always supported and advised me in my research choices. The illustration for the book were generously provided by the State Hermitage Museum, St. Petersburg; the State Tretyakov Gallery, Moscow; and the Harvard University Library. I appreciate the assistance of my Northwestern colleagues Jesse Rosenberg and Thomas Bauman, as well as the enthusiasm of my former and current graduate students (particularly their help with musical examples): Natalia Zelensky, Rebecca Bennett, Megan McFadden, Rachel Maine, Jennifer Myers, and Brian Oberlander. The volume would not be possible if not for the support of Northwestern University Research Grant Committee and leaves afforded by the NWU School of Music. The project developed within the interdisciplinary atmosphere of the university, particularly the Alice Kaplan Humanities Institute. As a Harvard University Davis Senior Fellow in 2005, I enjoyed (almost around the clock) the treasures of Harvard's many libraries and drew on the wisdom of scholars such as Loren R. Graham, Julie Buckler, and John P. LeDonne. Fortunate to complete this manuscript during a Rockefeller Foundation Bellagio Scholarly Residency, I was treated as royalty in this princely setting, the affairs of the estate conducted by Pilar Palacia, who became a dear friend and who warmed my writing. I presented parts of my research at various conferences, most notably at the Russian State University for the Humanities and at a conference on "The Imperial Nation" at the University of Michigan organized by Olga Maiorova. The idea for the book, which germinated one fall day in a conversation with Gayle Sherwood, has developed in collaboration with my editor and friend Suzanne Ryan.

Моему самому дорогому на свете человеку, бесконечно щедрой, любящей, требовательной, храброй моей маме, которая уже не сможет увидеть этой книги! Дважды иммигрантка, герой войны и врач, всегда гордая, предельно честная, с высоким чувством достоинства, ты и сейчас ведешь меня. И моему отцу, инженеру, глубоко разбирающемуся в изобразительном искусстве и литературе, который, слушая мои музыковедческие "байки" на русском, дал мне столько полезных идей. Их любви, интеллекту, этике я обязана всем.

To the dearest person of my life, endlessly generous, loving, demanding, courageous: my mother, who will not touch this book. Twice an immigrant, a war hero, a doctor, proud, honest, always guided by a sense of integrity, you lead me still. And to my father, an engineer who knows art as I never will and who, listening to my endless chatter about this book in Russian, gave me the most precious ideas.

I owe everything to your love, intellect, and ethics.

CONTENTS

INTRODUCTION

A ball-masquerade. Costumed pairs of courtiers proceed in a majestic polonaise, the tsar of dances and the dance of tsars. Guests dressed as Arcadian shepherds sing and dance a pastoral. Excitement reaches its peak when the master of ceremonies announces the arrival of Her Imperial Majesty. Everyone joins in a cantata-polonaise "*Slavsia sim, Ekaterina!*"—Glory to Catherine the Great.

The scene takes place in the middle of Tchaikovsky's *Queen of Spades*. At the close of the nineteenth century, the composer brings the silent shadow of the eighteenth-century empress on stage. Why would Catherine appear in this and two other Tchaikovsky operas? Why would she emerge as well in Rimsky-Korsakov and Cui? No other Romanov monarch inspired composers to flout the imperial decree forbidding operatic portrayal of the ruling dynasty. One might suspect that the composers were prompted by the centennial of Catherine's death (1896). Possibly. But my contention is that the shadow of the empress and the idea of the power she stood for had always been present in nineteenth-century operas, appearing in various guises, changing, evasive, residing in the world of magic and fairy tales.

Weaving history and opera, this volume explores two interconnected stories. One is *her* story, which belongs to the Russian "women's kingdom," a phrase coined by Michelle Marrese to describe an era not only ruled by tsarinas but in which women of a certain class enjoyed legal and social privileges far beyond those in Western Europe. Catherine the Great, as a central figure, emblemizes the chain of four vigorous tsarinas who dominated Russia for three-quarters of a century. The other is *his* story, that of nineteenth-century Russian literati who contributed to the restoration of patriarchal rule, converging masculine ideals with nationalism. Both stories began with a break from the preceding age. *Her* era started when tsarinas emerged from the ruins of the demolished *terem*, an architectural and social construction that until the beginning of the eighteenth century segregated tsars' wives, sisters, and daughters from public life. *His* century, the nineteenth, began four years before its chronological date, on the day the last empress, who during her thirty-four-year reign never lost her tight grip on the empire, passed away. The dialogue between the two stories is traced here through operas.

Eighteenth-century empresses devised their court as theater and made theater a part of their court. Imported and assimilated, opera served as *the* imperial genre. Consistent with the notion Harsha Ram identifies as the "imperial sublime," operatic choruses praised the empresses as Olympic gods and heroes, Eastern armies on the stage symbolically submitted to empresses' power, ritualistic weddings signified the blessed Russian folk, and the tsarinas' surrogates—operatic monarchs—exemplified the rulers' virtues and benevolence. Folk songs, weddings, heroic ventures, and final choral "Slavas" were passed to the nineteenth century, becoming major elements of Russian nationalist opera. As real tsarinas disappeared from Russia's political stage, a number of magical tsarinas materialized in Russian fairy-tale operas. In their enchanting gardens (replicas of the imperial park in Tsarskoe Selo) or in their aquatic kingdoms (like the waterways the empresses were proud to acquire), entrancing female queens tried to allure, hunt, or trap Russian heroes. Champions' victories over the magical tsarinas were celebrated as a triumph of the nation; their defeats led to the destruction of the folk or at least the disappearance of the folk chorus from the operatic stage.

While preserving and expanding upon elements of eighteenth-century operas, nineteenth-century Russian intellectuals demeaned and discarded the culture of their predecessors. Claiming new beginnings, however, they never escaped in their operatic tales from formidable tsarina-sorceresses, never broke the ties. A number of marvelous nineteenth-century operas, viewed in relation to male contempt and nostalgia for the tsarinas' age, illuminate an anxiety of nineteenth-century Russian male artists. Crossing political and artistic realms, as it always does, opera in Russia bridged the two centuries and linked the two stories. Thus *his* story (in opera) rewrote and refashioned *hers*, while *hers*, casting a shadow and woven into his story, defined *him*.

Events lived through and times past belong to imagination, turning into fictional narrative that includes history. Even historical chronology, the establishment of recognized events and dates, reflects a particular set of values, an angle of perception. Everyone knows, for example, that the history of Russian national music begins in 1836 with Mikhail Glinka's *Life for the Tsar*. The premiere of Glinka's first-born opera, however, marked the hundredth anniversary of the first Italian opera troupe's arrival in St. Petersburg and the fiftieth year since Yevstigney Fomin's *Boeslavich, Champion of Novgorod*, on a text by Catherine II. Both dates vanished behind national dithyrambs to the first, the founder, the "father" of Russian national opera. If Glinka is indeed a "father," how does one account for the hundred-some operas staged in the late eighteenth and early nineteenth centuries? Why would historians largely ignore the nobility's obsession with theater, when nearly every courtier, and a number of provincial aristocrats, engaged in theatrical ventures—versifying, composing, acting, staging dramas, collecting folk tunes, and establishing their own theaters? What about the emergence of professional composers, librettists, and actors? How did the operatic "folk" —a defining factor of the Russian musical self—become disconnected from the real folk, serf actors, who constituted a major performing force in early Russian theater? The folk songs these peasant actors belted out on rural and urban, public and private stages were overlooked in favor of a grand beginning of Russian opera crafted by the aristocrat and serf owner Glinka, whose ears were sensitive to peasant songs. Yet what Marina Ritzarev terms the "Glinka-centric conceit"[1] is only now being questioned; discussing Glinka's *Ruslan and Liudmila*, Marina Frolova-Walker writes that "shedding the nationalist inheritance is even more difficult than was the shedding of Marxist-Leninist aesthetics a few years ago."[2]

Even scholars who extend the history of Russian opera to pre-Glinka times, and even those who have produced remarkably rich works on eighteenth-century musical Russia, weave their prose with an ongoing apology for Russian artistic insufficiency and mimicry of the West. The dismissal of early theater and opera and the separation of the two centuries by cultural historians reflect particularities of Russia's past. Patriarchal Russia, encompassing gender prejudices of both West and East, has found it difficult to deal with the cultural memory of more than seventy years of female rule during Russia's formative period. The biggest problem was Catherine —a monarch, woman, and foreigner, also a prolific fellow Russian writer and historian, a creator and producer of early operas. Her historical semi-operatic *Early Reign of Oleg*, a transitional work that falls between Italian *opera seria* and native heroic operas such as Gavrila Derzhavin's *Dobrynia* and *Pozharsky*, laid the path for famous, cherished nineteenth-century nationalist historic operas. Catherine's operatic tales—including a *bylina* (old native epic), a magical opera, a satire, and a moral tale—prefigured the nationalist opera-*skazka*s (tales) that blossomed in the next century.

Looming over romantic artists and perhaps fueling their craving for nationalist male primacy, the shadow of the empress(es) materialized in a number of operas in two ways. One was the creation of vicious royal operatic women. Though differing in their appearance, character, and functions, these formidable women share common characteristics. They are often foreigners, whether Italianate virtuosos or Eastern seductresses. These women of supernatural power express themselves in a musical lingua infected by chromatic, whole-tone, or octatonic gestures, which sets them in contrast to diatonic Russianness. Several of them are silent or deprived of elaborate vocal parts. Instead they are linked with dance or accompanied by an entourage of fleeting, graceful, tempting, or dangerous female dancing choruses that represent "others" in the domain of the opera. Bearing royal, princely, or elevated titles, these women, devised to represent multifaceted otherness, challenge and combat operatic male leads. Male victories precipitate folk/nation celebrations in the final scenes of Glinka's *Ruslan and Liudmila* and Nikolai Rimsky-Korsakov's *Sadko*; the defeats of other protagonists are associated with the demise of the folk, flooded in *Mlada* and replaced by laughing female shadows in Dargomyzhsky's *Rusalka*. In neither case is there a celebration for a female protagonist—a dead soul that in the afterlife turns into a royal water spite, an aerial spirit, or, in Tchaikovsky's *Queen of Spades,* a dreadful ghost. How would psychoanalysts following Freud or Jung address this nightmarish resurrection of the female ghosts navigating between past and present? How might literary scholars Harold Bloom and Michael Roth interpret the anxieties shared by generations of Russian male authors? Analyzing the operas named above, I contend that the supernatural tsarinas, tsarevnas, and countesses, if examined in their historical and intertextual context, can be viewed as a manifestation of Russia's nineteenth-century nationalist ethos—or its psychosis.

Second, the empress's shadows also revealed themselves in essential elements of Glinka's operas and of post-Glinka nationalist works. Despite all the "forgetfulness" or active disparagement, nineteenth-century Russia expanded patterns characteristic of operas before Glinka, including Catherine's. Despite their acclaimed primacy, nineteenth-century national operas reiterated familiar (if often forgotten) precedents and conventions: the genres of historic-heroic opera and opera-skazka; ritualistic weddings equating lovers' vows with the bonds between folk and crown; monumental choruses representing the folk; choral "Slavas"; princes and nobles as lead characters; the multifaceted East welcoming and acceding to omnipotent Russia; the use of folk tales and songs; colossal productions reminiscent of the huge casts engaged in the empresses' court theater; the imperial polonaise; ancient Greek modes represented as authentic Russian sound; lyric songs (*protiazhnaia*); and musical otherness. This catalogue suggests that the issue at stake was not a break between centuries, but rather an unspoken conflict over the ownership of the nation and national lore. As power and ownership shifted, the image of bygone empresses underwent metamorphosis; after their demise, tsarinas returned in the guise of enticing dangerous supernatural operatic heroines.

This subject matter invites a combination of three "*inter*" approaches—interdisciplinary, intertextual, and intergeneric. Interdisciplinarity is a common thread in American scholarship about Russian culture, which has produced a constellation of works such as those of Richard Taruskin in music, Boris Gasparov in music and literature, and Richard Wortman on Russia's cultural history and performativity. In Russia today, scholars including Liudmila Starikova and Natalia Ogarkova have produced revealing intertextual readings of theater history. As an analytical method, the intertextuality identified with the semiotics of Yurii Lotman and Boris Uspenskii is inherent to Russian intellectual tradition. Throughout history, Russian literati have engaged in intertextual exchange as an intellectual and political game, transmitting their ideas via references to one another, commenting on events, targeting politicians, creating a densely coherent body of literary works. Intertextuality in Russia encompasses not only literature but also music, theater, and opera. At their very base, such close readings require intergeneric dialogue, which, according to Andrew Wachtel, illuminates a specific period "through multiple competing narrative perspectives."[3] The principle of intertextual and intergeneric dialogue applied to sources in different genres, ranging from memoirs to historical documents and musical scores, coincides with methods of historical ethnomusicology that, according to Joseph Lam, allow one to "probe ideologies, aesthetics, and methodologies with which people interrelate their musical past and present into musical and intelligible realities."[4]

This inquiry, dealing with issues of gender, involves female authorship and performance on one hand and the operatic treatment of female characters on the other. It leads me to question the historiography of the Russian female monarchs, the empress-dramatist, and historic female performers ranging from noble dilettantes to serf actresses. Like the writings of female authors elsewhere in Europe, Catherine's literary works were posthumously dismissed as "lacking wit" and overall "mediocre," "worthless."[5] Written by the monarch, they were also disparaged for deluding and corrupting citizens. Such scornful remarks have not typically required evidence. Jacky Bratton, in a feminist study of theater that recovers names and works of "lost" female dramatists and artists, calls for a form of "archaeology." While dealing with largely unknown works of the female monarch, the inquiry here requires both archeological and anthropological approaches. What specific circumstances determined the value of a female author's works?

The topic of gender also involves the study of a certain type of female character produced in nineteenth-century Russian operas. Reflecting and commenting on the eighteenth century, nationalist artists engaged European romantic tropes, subjecting their native heroines to the "undoing" successfully fostered in the West. Catherine Clement's classical work on how operas deal with their heroines provides a basis for analyzing the story lines, situations, characters, voice types, and vocal parts. Carolyn Abbate delved into voice as an acoustic and social phenomenon. Both addressed a wide-ranging repertoire spanning national borders and traditions. Indeed operatic theater presents a significant body of shared gender prejudices—on stage, backstage, in libretti, music, and performers' stories. This book, proposing a connection between historical figures and the repertoire of Russian fairytale operas, addresses and situates gender in a specific historical and national, operatic and extra-operatic context.

What led me to pursue this research was the rather surprising discovery of Catherine II's operas, of which I, trained as a musicologist in the former Soviet Union, never knew. It was only when I returned to attend a conference at the Moscow Conservatory as an American ethnomusicologist that I found, merely by chance, the published libretti and scores of Catherine's *Oleg* and *Fevei*. The lack of attention to half a dozen of Russia's earliest operas is puzzling and telling. More than two hundred years after Catherine's death, in the vein of post-Soviet revision of imperial cultural history, the encyclopedia *Musical Petersburg* finally acknowledged Catherine among the "pioneers of traditional Russian fairy-tale opera"—a recognition briefly mentioned in parentheses. The first volume analyzing Catherine's dramas in recent times was produced not in Russia but in the United States, by Lurana Donnels O'Malley. Having the copies of Catherine's operas on my shelves for a few years while teaching nineteenth-century Russian fairy-tale operas, Glinka's *Ruslan and Liudmila*, Dargomyzhsky's *Rusalka*, Rimsky-Korsakov's *Mlada* and *Sadko*, Tchaikovsky's *Slippers*, which I have known and loved for many years, made me see these operas in a new and quite different light.

The book consists of two parts. The first part raises the curtain on the theatricality of the eighteenth-century court, scripted, staged, and conducted by empresses. Opera seria and early comic opera functioned within the courtly social repertoire, bourgeoning in the culture of imperial masquerade, in which theater permeated society, from nobles to serfs. The analysis of Catherine's operas, her collaboration with native and foreign artists, and the political purpose of the productions aims to reconsider her role as a highly influential political playwright during the formative period of modern Russian society, literature, and theater. The second part of the book consists of five chapters each focusing on a nineteenth-century opera; four of them are magic tales and one a ghostly opera that connects an eighteenth-century imperial tale with late-nineteenth-century symbolism. Although selected to demonstrate issues traced through the book, each opera is a world of its own that entices and absorbs one as a spectator and as a writer. I found the operas taking over my writing, each demanding prose that would befit its watery, phantasmagoric, wicked, or witty magical world. It has been exciting to trace the genealogy of these operas back to the age of tsarinas, and to the monarch-librettist and producer who had at her disposal the best artists as well as unimaginable resources. By establishing links between Glinka's *Ruslan* and Catherine's *Oleg*, between her *Boeslavich, Champion of Novgorod* epics and Rimsky-Korsakov's *Sadko*, by grappling with the anxiety of her cultural progeny, and by seeing her shadow in Tchaikovsky's *Queen of Spades* and Rimsky-Korsakov's *Christmas Eve*, one can't help recognizing the irony that the Russian nationalism we now know, patriotic and patriarchal, was built on a foundation created by foreign matriarchs.

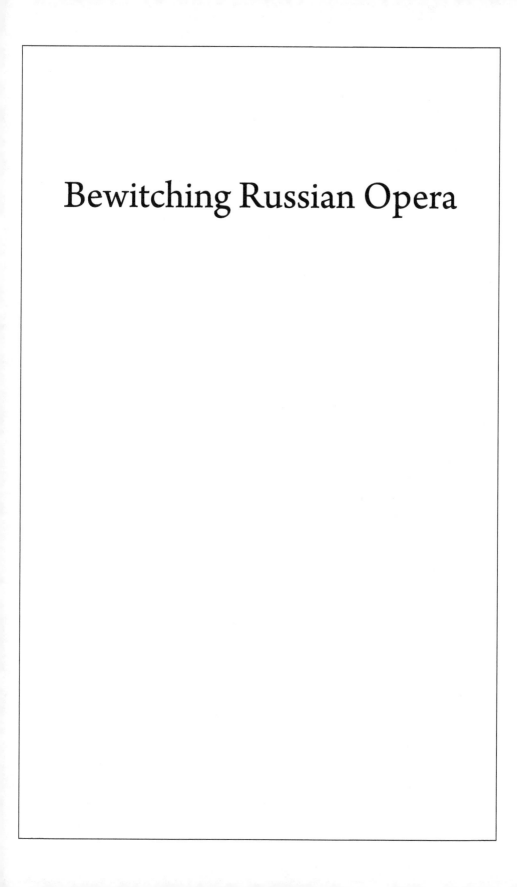

Bewitching Russian Opera

OVERTURE
RUSSIA'S IMPERIAL PRIMA DONNAS

A magical tsarina changes into a mighty river at the end of Nikolai Rimsky-Korsakov's *Sadko* (1897), while a folk chorus praising the opera's hero for bringing prosperity to Novgorod sings a "Slava" that had long been a hallmark of Russian national opera. Sadko's accomplishments rest on his marriage to two women: one a suffering, submissive, and nearly forgotten Russian Christian wife, the other the Sea Princess who provided his fortune and, when no longer needed, sacrificed herself for his convenience, bequeathing herself as a river to benefit his fellow citizens. A predecessor of Sadko, the male lead in Pushkin's poem and Dargomyzhsky's opera *Rusalka* (1855) is likewise split between two women. Seducing (and in the opera impregnating) a miller's daughter and afterward marrying another woman, his equal, *Rusalka*'s protagonist is haunted first by the bodiless voice of his deceased lover and then by her ghost, a deadly water sprite. Unlike Sadko, he is incapable of becoming a people's hero—not so much because of the moral dilemma but because in his guilt-ridden vocal solo, one of the most poignant vocal parts in Russian operatic literature, he shows himself vulnerable to the magic vengeful tsarina who in the end vanquishes him.

Fairy-tale operas like *Sadko* and *Rusalka*—a distinct brand of national operatic literature—have been analyzed, contextualized, and conceptualized in terms of musical language, ties with folklore, literary sources, and intertextual connections, but rarely through the lens of gender theory. Folk tales lent a sense of authentic, untainted Russianness to Russian operas,[1] which have been seen as a manifestation of nineteenth-century national aspirations. Their stories and characters, even when borrowed from early sources, have been examined in relation to historical and social issues of the nineteenth century. But never in the plethora of musicological scholarship has there been an attempt to connect the operatic magic tsarinas, princesses, and dangerous women of power with the unprecedented chain of formidable tsarinas who had ruled Russia a scant century earlier: Catherine I (1725–1727), Anna (1730–1740), Elisabeth (1741–1762), and Catherine II (1762–1796). These historical tsarinas championed theater and opera, acting as patronesses, authors, actresses, critics, and ardent spectators—their robust commitment to theater interlaced with the acquisition and exposition of supreme power. Though referring to four empresses, this study focuses mainly on Catherine II (Catherine the Great), the last and the longest-ruling female monarch, who also wrote in various literary genres, including libretti, and produced operas. Establishing her unique and powerful persona, as did the female monarchs before her, Catherine distanced herself from her predecessors.

Beginning under Anna and increasingly in the courts of Elisabeth and Catherine II, operas, as a part of imperial ceremonials, mirrored regal weddings and coronations, echoing monumental church choruses and resounding military salvos—elements inherited by nineteenth-century historic and fairy tale operas. Pronouncing Mikhail Glinka the founder of national opera—a status unchallenged by native scholars to this day—his contemporaries and followers, much like Sadko discarding the tsarina-donor while enjoying her gifts, cast aside eighteenth-century Russian opera and spectacle. Reuniting nineteenth-century operatic tsarinas with eighteenth-century female monarchs offers the tempting possibility of reading nineteenth-century operas as a commentary on eighteenth-century history, and eighteenth-century operas as a shadowy precursor to nineteenth-century historic aspirations.

The four eighteenth-century female rulers, appearing in the guises of Eastern princesses, Aegean shepherdesses, and triumphant victors, crossing gender, social, and ethnic lines, staging masquerades, surrounded themselves with a cast of costumed courtiers. Also impersonated on stage as ancient heroes, tsars, and goddesses—long before Russian fairy-tale tsarinas appeared on the operatic stage—the empresses became characters in their own dynamic absolutist production. Not at all domesticated, doleful women, they shaped their courts and waged wars while probing, polishing, and disseminating their social and political agendas in highly politicized theater. The performativity of state and stage converged.

The discussion of Russia's imperial court as a theater owes its direction to the works of Richard Wortman, who views the history of imperial Russia through the lens of mythologized drama; and Natalia Ogarkova, who explores theater as an organic part of dramatized spectacular court rituals. Wortman terms this mythologized social repertoire Russia's "scenario of power": "The sumptuous, highly ritualized presentations of Russian monarchy, produced at enormous cost of resources and time, indicate that Russian rulers . . . considered the symbolic sphere of ceremonies and imagery intrinsic to their exercise of power."[2]

Tracing the transformation of historical empresses into supernatural operatic (anti)heroines requires one to begin with the Russian triangulation of eighteenth-century female rulers, state, and opera. Drawing on Wortman's reconstruction of Russian imperial history as an ongoing scenario of power in which each ruler enacted a multifaceted play of absolutism, this study addresses Russia's empresses as stars and *régisseurs* of the political-theatrical show. The empresses' reigns manifested "the doctrine of the exemplary center" that Clifford Geertz, studying Balinese theater in relation to the "nature of sovereignty," defines as "at once a microcosm of the supernatural order—'an image of . . . the universe in smaller scale'—and the material embodiment of political order."[3] Peter Burke, applying the Geertzian concept of the "theater state" to his study of Louis XIV, suggests that the king and his contemporaries "were accustomed to see the world as a stage,"[4] and that metaphors of theater were widely used in descriptions of the court. Ogarkova delves into both Russian state rituals and theatrical productions, discussing the ritualistic function of theater and applying stage metaphors to major rituals and imperial celebrations.

Each empress combined two roles—grand master of the empire and mistress of the court. Enacting both parts, they defined courtly éclat, fashions, and entertainment, while simultaneously advancing their military projects, political agendas, and social reforms. While court ceremonies appear highly theatrical, scripted, staged, and rehearsed, Russian theater, which emerged during this period largely at the initiative of the same empresses, frequently mythologized the state and female rulers. With empresses and their imperial casts enacting their roles—their images reciprocated and magnified in numerous odes, staged cantatas, celebratory operas, and ballets—they fostered what Ram calls the "imperial sublime," which he terms "a specifically Russian tradition of relating poetics, rhetoric, and politics," embodying "the connection, within an autocratic state, between authority and authorship."[5] Translating immediate political aims into timeless diachronic mythologies, theater fashioned the imagery of the imperial sublime, traversing spatial, temporal, and cosmic domains and identifying the heads of state with Olympic gods, classical heroes, and native champions.

New Rituals, New Mythologies, New Images

Luminous eighteenth-century court rituals and spectacles—anniversaries of the empress's birthdays, coronations, weddings, and national victories, as well as endless carnivals scripted and led by the prime actress/monarch—were mirrored in playful scaled-down theatricals. What Wortman defines as an "ongoing theater of power" required charisma bordering on enigmatic supernatural appeal combined with secular authority and imperial iconography; all of these rested on the supreme performance of the Russian empresses. Embodying sacred, military, and legislative authority, they were the central figures in multiple ritualistic acts and day-to-day performances, receiving foreign ambassadors and maintaining networks among the native nobility. Not only did they need to enact the role of a paramount leader with conviction but also, in the course of performance with their cast of nobles, they constantly shaped and revised the underlying scenario of power.

Beginning with Peter I and continuing with his female followers, eighteenth-century rulers refashioned Russia, a remote, Asiatic vastness into a European state. They fully appropriated European mythology and mapped it into poetic and architectural constructions manifested by the cities of Moscow and, particularly, St. Petersburg. An earlier concept of Moscow as the Third Rome[6] bourgeoned in the eighteenth century. Counterbalancing the religious impurity of pagan Rome and Muslim-conquered Constantinople, Moscow was the center of the "true faith" (*Pravoslavie*, Eastern Orthodoxy). So profound was Moscow's historical legacy that, residing in recently built Westernized St. Petersburg and deriding provincial Moscow, every Russian monarch nevertheless went for ritualistic investiture to the old capital. Moscow endowed Russian rulers with the mission of defending Orthodoxy; one eighteenth-century Russian monarch after another masterminded a "Greek project"[7] and waged consistent wars against the Ottomans.[8]

Peter had founded St. Petersburg as the "new [fourth] Rome," a Russian capital in which "holiness . . . [was] not a governing factor, but subservient to the state."[9] St. Petersburg, laid out by major Italian masters as a perfect city, with its Peter and Paul Fortress and Cathedral semiotically connected to St. Peter's Basilica in Rome, became not just another enduring imitation of antiquity but a rival of Rome (also contesting the city of canals, Venice, and the architectural counterpart of Peter's city, Paris). Thus St. Petersburg signified the connection of Russia with Rome, the Russian eighteenth-century ruler with Augustus, and Russian mythology with the Roman classics. Along with Roman antiquity, Russian rulers, like other major European dynasties— the Habsburg, Valois, and English Stuarts—claimed "direct descent from the ancient imperial stock of Troy."[10] Orthodoxy enabled Russian rulers and the court literati to trace the myth of their origins via Constantinople-Byzantium to Greek antiquity, thus fully adopting and expanding upon the eighteenth-century Western notion of majestic autocracy.

Territorial conquest as the defining basis of power—intriguing when linked with sublime femininity—was extolled in omnipresent forms of imperial representation. Triumphal arches, spectacles, odes, fireworks, illuminations, and engravings—products of individual homage and collective aspiration—fostered the allegorical association of heroic female-tsars with bygone Russian heroes, Greco-Roman mythology, and modern imperial narrative. In his "manifest" on the coronation of his spouse, Peter

I announced his intention to follow the model of the Byzantine emperors Julius, Justinian, and Heracles, who all crowned their wives.[11] Increasingly throughout the century, the empresses were identified with Olympic goddesses, most frequently Minerva and Astraea. As Judith Ginsburg observed in her study of female power in the Roman and Hellenic worlds, "the attribution of the names of deities and of nonhuman characteristics to their rulers made it easier for the subjects of the eastern empire to make sense of . . . the ruling power."[12]

Riding on the ticket of modernity and propelling the Westernization of Russia, each of the empresses, women and mostly foreigners, adhered to the traditions of "*her*" native Russian fatherland.[13] Progressively through the century, the more European Russia became, the more insistently its rulers asserted Russian identity. The foundation of Russian theater, the encouragement of native literature, the translation of foreign texts into Russian, and the collection of folk tales and songs were all linked with the image of Mother Russia, bonding old Rus' with the empresses.[14]

The Four Empresses

Framed by the thirty-some-year reigns of the two Greats, Peter I and Catherine II, the Russian empire was ruled by women for more than two-thirds of the eighteenth century—arguably the age of the most significant territorial expansion, as well as radical social and political modernization, and Russia's enlightenment. The four empresses, their reigns interrupted briefly by Peter's unfortunate grandsons and by the tragic shadow of his grand-nephew,[15] endorsed Westernization and planted the seeds of Russian nationalism.[16] The acquisition of imperial power coincided with the increasingly extended tenures of the empresses—Catherine I reigning for two years, Anna for ten, Elisabeth for twenty, and Catherine II for thirty-four. Only a few decades separated these women from their female royal predecessors—generations of tsars' sisters and daughters who, too alienated from the outside world to acquire foreign royal suitors and not allowed to stain the tsar's blood by union with his subjects, were destined to pass their lives in monasteries. There they lived "like hermits, seeing little of the world and little seen by it."[17] Secluded in their terems,[18] an institution not unlike harems, the tsars' royal consorts and female relations were surrounded by wandering nuns, god's fools, and cripples.

The four empresses broke through at least two significant and long-standing barriers: gender and ethnicity. Unlike their predecessors, they were foreigners by blood or formative experiences: the two Catherines were of Germanic descent, Elisabeth was half Russian, and pure-blooded Anna spent much of her life in the Germanic Duchy of Courland. They were also strangers to the antiquated culture of terem Russia. Obtaining and holding absolute power, they committed themselves to fostering the imperial scenario initially drafted by Peter, while developing, acting, and perfecting their roles as sublime female rulers, in Wortman's words "exemplars of both cathartic force and disarming mildness and love."[19]

The first Russian emperor to ascend the throne in a spectacular imperial coronation was Catherine I.[20] Peter himself directed the ceremony, establishing a model for future Russian emperors. The path of Catherine, a Lifland (part of the Baltic region) peasant girl—enslaved during the Russian-Swedish war and like others sold and exchanged; serving as a *portomoia* (laundress) for Field Marshal Boris Sheremetiev; noticed and confiscated by Alexander Menshikov for his pleasure; passed on to Tsar Peter; and in the end becoming the first Russian empress—attests not only to this woman's shrewdness but also to her performing abilities.[21] Typically dismissed by historians as evidence of Peter's eccentricity, Catherine was able to tame his temper, share his hardships, and secure his loyalty.[22] Many times she saved her ally Menshikov from Peter's rage. But she stood firmly by her husband, soothing his pain as he tortured and executed Aleksei, his son from the first marriage. Obliteration of the rightful heir to the crown secured her marriage and her future prospects. Her role in the Russian court in its formative period cannot be overlooked.

After the long isolation of the Russian ruling family from European marital alliances, Anna was the first princess given in marriage to a foreigner—Frederick William, Duke of Courland (1710).[23] Widowed before reaching her husband's duchy, she spent nearly two decades there, pouring out tears in her letters to her imperial Russian relations and to every important statesman in her homeland. Russia's Highest Privy Council, an early attempt at collective oligarchical rule, "knowing Anna for her religiosity and obedience,"[24] selected her as an easily controllable candidate for the throne, crafting "conditions" that would limit her power.[25] Thirty-seven days after signing these conditions, however, Anna theatrically ripped up the paper at her public début in Moscow, beginning a new act in the spectacle of absolute power. During the following nine years, professing to be "grateful" to the Dolgorukovs[26] and Golitsins who had promoted her to the throne but who also intended to limit her power, Anna gradually and ever more brutally dismantled their clans. In the case of the Dolgorukovs, she first stripped them of their titles, then sent them into exile, relocating some to jails and finally executing several by drawing and quartering, and then cutting off their heads and tongues.[27] Torn more than her successors between archaic Russia and modernized Europe, Anna gathered around her the personages of her mother's terem, including widows, pilgrims (*strannitsy*), and six court jesters, several of them members of the high nobility. At the same time she invited the first professional theatrical troupes to Russia, founded an imperial theater, and established the first Russian acting schools.

The half-Russian Elisabeth, in order to assume the crown, dethroned the lawful heir, one-year-old Tsar Ivan VI, along with his mother Anna Leopol'dovna—the regent and Elisabeth's cousin—and exiled the entire family. With these acts, "the rightful daughter of Peter the Great," "the bearer of his spirit and vision,"[28] ascended to power, transforming the heavy, forceful imperial scenario of her predecessor (Anna) into a celebration of joy—the spirit of a swirling masquerade overlaid with monumental state events, weekly balls, and theatricals. Elisabeth cultivated visual magnificence, commissioning palaces with the same gusto she ordered dresses—fifteen thousand gowns made of precious fabrics imported from Europe. Princely salaries lured the best European architects, composers, singers, dancers, and adventurers to the Elisabethan capital.

Catherine II, with no tinge of Russian blood but married to Peter's grandson, had to be a most gifted imperial dramatist and convincing actress to ascend the throne and assert her role as the Mother of the Russian Fatherland, the Protectress of Eastern Orthodoxy. Brought to Russia as a fourteen-year-old princess—the niece of Prince Karl Augustus of Holstein-Gottorp, who had died shortly after his betrothal to Elisabeth—Catherine endured two decades of tutelage as Grand Duchess. Coming to the throne after disposing of her husband, she continued the celebratory tone of Elisabeth while artfully forging her role as the leading actress in the Petrine imperial scenario. She arranged for the impressively cumbersome transportation of a mammoth natural rock that served as the pedestal for the Bronze Horseman, a monument to Peter, bearing the dedication in Russian and Latin "Петру Первому Екатерина Вторая, 1782" (To Peter I—Catherine II). The emperor on the rearing horse salutes her.[29]

The creator of the sculpture, Frenchman Étienne Maurice Falconet, discussing the project in detail in a letter to the empress, referred to the Horseman as "a monument to Peter and to You."[30] Alexander Sumarokov, who saw the model but died before the completion of the monument, wrote the poetic inscription "Peter gave us being, Catherine—soul."[31] Derzhavin likewise enthused in his "On the Statue of Peter the Great":

Екатерина,—Росс чтоб зря благоговел,	Catherine—for Ross [Russians] to revere [You]
Воздвигла зрак его. Ея сей образ дел.[32]	Erected his figure. Her deeds this image is.

While engaged in significant territorial expansion, Catherine II acquired, with stereotypical Germanic pedantry, rare libraries and artistic collections[33] and nurtured the native intellectual elite in her enlightened Russia.[34] However, Pushkin wrote:

Catherine supported the enlightenment, yet Novikov, spreading its first rays, was transferred from Shishkovsky's hands (the domestic persecutor of shy Catherine) to a prison cell, where he remained till his death. Radishchev was exiled to Siberia; Kniazhnin died under the whips, and Fonvizin, whom she feared, would not have avoided the same destiny had it not been for his great popularity.[35]

Though Pushkin's references are an exaggeration,[36] the empresses indeed were not docile wives but indomitable monarchs, whose gender was a weakness to reverse, whose battle for political power (thus physical survival) would be stopped by no considerations, and whose excessive presentation of power was equated with actual omnipotence.

The Lead Actress as a Man

Each female tsar, evincing different strengths, built on the accomplishments of her predecessors while at the same time carefully dissociating herself from them and crafting her own nonpareil image and power. Displaying "the superior qualities of a being entitled to rule,"[37] the prima donnas of Russia's imperial play devised a concept of the empress's gender. Remaining single, the four rulers toyed with gender ambiguity by exhibiting male traits, encouraging the circulation of court gossip, legends, and traveling notes that confirmed their ability to rule. Traversing the binaries of West and East, modernity and traditionalism, they also traversed gender boundaries.

Personal strength, whether physical or intellectual, that matched and exceeded a man's became a part of the mythology of the majestic feminine. Early eighteenth-century volumes on Russian history by John Mottley referred to Peter's half-sister and rival regent Sophia as a "Woman of a masculine Spirit, and great policy, [who] got the administration of the government into her own hands."[38] Catherine I, whose "manly persona was observed by everyone,"[39] demonstrated her physical strength by "picking up with her one extended hand her husband's heavy marshal's mace, which could not be moved by either the tsar's orderly or the Austrian envoy."[40] Accompanying Peter in his military campaigns, Catherine I has been credited with exhibiting unwomanly smarts, saving her future spouse from defeat and capture by sending all her jewelry to the Ottoman grand vizier,[41] and thus acting, according to one observer, "as a man and not a woman."[42] In state rituals, Her Majesty in magnificent costumes led a group of her ladies-in-waiting, wearing the same colors and dresses as she, the Amazon.[43] Anna, an avid hunter[44] who exercised and shot daily, was recalled by Countess Sheremeteva née Dolgorukov[45] as very big, a head taller than the cavalier guards in her retinue and as heavy.[46] The image of the empress in the frontispiece of the published description of her coronation emphasized the grandness of her figure.[47]

Catherine II's unwomanly bravery and composure were communicated in various accounts. The French diplomat Louis-Philippe, comte de Ségur, for example, recalled the empress's request during her journey in Tauride (1787) to be guarded by "Tatars, hateful of women, enemy of Christianity, recently occupied by the empress—her exhibition of trust proved successful—as every courageous exploit."[48] Advancing the age of Enlightenment, Catherine II produced abundant literary and legislative works, exhibiting her unnatural "manly" reason and creativity, which were validated by her most distinguished correspondents, Voltaire, Grimm, Diderot, and Marmontel. ?

Known for her "spirit [that] was firm, masculine, and truly heroic," Catherine was at the same time derided for displaying the characteristics of her sex.[49] O'Malley and Brenda Meehan-Waters cite a number of examples showing how contemporary descriptions of Catherine's masculinity were tempered by criticisms of her feminine qualities.[50] James Harris, First Earl of Malmesbury, observed, "Her Majesty has a masculine force of mind, obstinacy in adhering to a plan . . . forbearance in prosperity and accuracy of judgment, while she possesses in a high degree the weaknesses vulgarly attributed to her sex—love of flattery, and its inseparable companion, vanity."[51] According to the Chevalier de Corberon, "This astounding princess, legislatrix, and warrior, successively, but always woman, offers the strange and inconsistent mingling of courage and weakness." Karamzin found that Catherine, "a great statesman at principal state assemblies—proved a woman in the minutiae of royal activity. She slumbered on a bed of roses."[52]

Enacting masculinity, the Russian empresses ventured into gender cross-dressing performance. In Mottley's *History*, issued in 1744, an unattributed portrait of Catherine I depicted her "in the Habit in which She appeared at the Head of her own Regiment."[53] Grand Duchess and future Empress Catherine II commented on the cross-dressing *kurtags* (masquerades) fancied by Empress Elisabeth: "Truly and unquestioningly beautiful in a male outfit was only the empress, because of her height and full-figure; the male attire fit her marvelously. . . . She danced with remarkable grace in both male and female clothing."[54] About Catherine II, Lord Buckingham, a British envoy, wrote that "a man's dress is what suits her best . . . she wears it always when she rides on horseback. It is scarce credible what she does in that way, managing horses, even fiery horses, with all the skill and courage of a groom."[55] Borrowing a Preobrazhensky military uniform from one of her guards, Catherine rode ahead of a twelve-thousand-man army when she dethroned her husband;[56] her perfect equestrian posture astride Brilliant on this triumphal occasion is memorialized in a huge canvas painted three years later by Vigilius Eriksen.[57] A number of portraits depicted Elisabeth and Catherine riding in military uniforms (Figure O.1). "In Oranienbaum," wrote Catherine, who

Figure O.1: Georg Christoph Grooth (1716–1749). *Portrait of Empress Elizaveta Petrovna on Horseback Followed by an Arab Boy.* 1743. Oil on canvas. 85 x 68.5 cm. Tretyakov Gallery, Moscow.

enjoyed a man's saddle, "I was again ahorse all the time, and wore male attire except Sundays."[58]

From the moment of their political ascent, the empresses proclaimed and nurtured intimate ties with their armies, imperative for their enthronement and sustainability. Both Catherine II and Elisabeth acquired the crown by staging a revolt and leading loyal regiments. Threats posed by the Imperial Guard to wrangling oligarchies ended feuds and secured the accessions of both Catherine I and Anna. "Swearing to keep the 'conditions' to her death" and in accordance with one of seven points relinquishing her control of the army, Anna at the same time announced herself a captain of the cavalier guards and a corporal of the Preobrazhensky regiment, "which trembled with admiration" as she distributed vodka.[59] Elisabeth, on the day of her revolt, declared the Preobrazhensky guards noblemen, presenting each soldier with a village and serfs. Battling for their crowns, all the empresses claimed to accept the throne, like Anna, "at the request of their devoted subjects, especially the regiments."[60]

To their armies, the empresses appealed as wife (Russian *zhena* means both wife and woman), as *dshcher'* daughter (in the case of Elisabeth), as *matushka* (mother) of all Russia, and, in coronations, as the bride of the Russian Fatherland. Simultaneously enacting their multiple parts, these ruling women assumed manly roles by commanding the army, conducting parades, venturing wars, and accepting praise for victories. Though none of the empresses appeared on the battlefield, Russia's triumphs were attributed to the "female eagles"—Anna, "before whom the enemy shivers, unable to battle the strong tsarina,"[61] and Catherine II, who, "the equal of great men,/holds a cross in one hand, / and a burning torch in the other / spreading flares over the Bosphorus,"[62] and whose "sword and arrows instill fear in enemies"—another "She-eagle protecting her nestlings.'[63] The imagery of the empress as commander, tailored to the symbolic military leadership of the female rulers, was exulted in state celebrations, ceremonies, and dramatic productions venerating the empresses' heroism.

Supporting Actors: Politics and Romance

With empresses adopting masculine attributes while not rejecting their feminine selves,[64] the "chivalric conception of women as symbols of weak and oppressed territories rescued by the king's conquest"[65] was replaced by the reality of the imperial *she* and her conquest of "well-kept" favorites. The empresses' sexual exploits stirred anxiety that significantly increased in the aftermath of their rule, becoming perhaps the most publicized, discussed, and remembered markers of each woman's reign. Yet, beyond their personal desires and cravings, the institution of favoritism, an intimate circle of lovers and courtiers, served practical and performative functions instrumental to women's rule.[66]

As female absolute monarchs, the empresses, like several of their counterparts in other lands and times, had to deal on one hand with the stigma of being unmarried, and on the other with the awesomeness and singularity of power that elicited the devotion of every subject to the ruler. Not sharing their absolute power, rising above the gender binary, they probed different types of intimate relations. Anna's monogamous bonds with Ernst Johann von Biron (monogamous on her part; he was married) and his critical role in governance clouded her reign and provoked strong distaste in her subjects.[67] Elisabeth and Catherine, by contrast, exhibited strong sexual appetites and fostered a line of favorites, most of them aiding both the empress and the empire. Wortman writes about Catherine's "chosen on occasion" (lucky) young men:

> The empress's favorite played an important role in training the noble elite in genteel con-
> duct. Like Louis XIV she used her current favorite as an ornament of power; he rode in
> her carriage and stood at her side at important functions. In this respect, her amorous
> attraction was to be displayed as another attribute of her supreme power. But the favorite
> also was a tutelary image. Catherine sought out lesser noblemen from the provinces,
> whom she had turned into paragons of cosmopolitan grace. She thus repeated and
> reversed the transformation that Peter had wrought with Catherine I, turning a creature
> of the opposite sex into a symbol of civilization and progress.[68]

Beyond the aphrodisiacal aspect of the empresses' relations, there was an element of theatrical decorum through which the empresses' power (political and sexual) and desirability were asserted—the splendid appearance of a mighty actress adorned by her supporting actors, handsome men of enormous physical strength (Orlov, Potemkin), stupendous appearance (Razumovsky, Potemkin), exquisite attire (Mamonov), and taste in the arts (Shuvalov, Potemkin, Razumovsky, Lanskoi), with many others loitering about, enviously watching and competing for the role.

Thus demonstrating prowess on personal and political levels, Russian empresses navigated between the symbolic images of England's "virgin queen" Elizabeth and of European queen mothers. Anna arranged the marriage of her niece and namesake Elisabeth at her coronation presented her "adopted" heir Peter III, and Catherine II at her succession endorsed the ambiguity of her role as an empress and regent for her son Paul and later groomed her grandsons as future tsars.

Patronesses

At the dawn of the eighteenth century, Peter's half-sister Sofia (the stepdaughter and rival of Peter's mother) opened the doors of her terem—literally[69]—staging a public debut, herself leading a flock of female captives to the burial of their brother and nephew, Tsar Fedor. Sofia demolished the terem gates politically when assuming the regency (1682–1689). A tenacious reformer later defeated by Peter, the tsarevna-regent has often been referred to as an author and translator of the plays staged in her female quarters. The grandmother of the nineteenth-century literary figure Prince Alexander Shakhovskoi was nicknamed Tat'iana Large Eyes by Peter I for playing the title role in *Ekaterina velikomuchenitsa* [Catherine the Martyr], a play attributed to Sofia and staged in her terem.[70] Nikolai Karamzin included Sofia as "one of the greatest women" in his "Pantheon of Russia's writers."[71] The legendary actor Ivan Dmitrievsky claimed to have seen Sofia's translation of Molière's *Le Médecin malgré lui* (*Lekar' prinuzhdennyi*) performed for her birthday.[72] Pushkin, in a letter to a fellow writer, suggested crafting a tragedy in eighteen acts, as Sofia did.[73]

Tsarevna Natalia, who, unlike her half-sister Sofia, enjoyed close relations with Peter, built her own private theater and was credited with writing sacred and secular tragedies and comedies. Indeed, some historians attribute Sofia's plays to Natalia. Following Peter's fast-fading infatuation with drama and the short-lived public theatrical enterprise of Kunst and Furst, Natalia acquired their stage props, costumes, and scripts, establishing the first known private court theater in Russia, to which she "admitted everyone." Friedrich Christian Weber, residing in Russia in the second decade of the century, wrote:

> The princess Natalia once had the Direction of a Tragedy. She had caused a large empty House to be fitted up, and to be divided into Pit and Boxes. The Actors and actresses were ten in Number, all native Russians, who had never been abroad, so it is easy to judge of their Ability. The Tragedy itself, as well as the Farce, were in Russian, and of the Princess's own Composition, being a Compound of sacred and profane History. I was told that the Subject related to one of the late Rebellions in Russia.... The Orchestra ... of 16 Musicians, all Russians, whole Performance was suitable to that of the rest. They are taught Music, as well as other Sciences, by the Help of the *Batogs* [rods for beating].[74]

Generations of Russian writers and historians were enticed by the notion of early tsarinas as writers and promoters of theaters.

Peter's household consisted almost entirely of women (his son Aleksei avoided his father's habitat). Peter's sisters, his widowed sister-in-law Tsarina Praskovia (1664–1723), his wife Catherine I, and a flock of daughters and nieces were collectively transplanted from Moscow to St. Petersburg, where their remarkably consistent involvement in theater became apparent to diplomats and foreign visitors. Friedrich Wilhelm von Bergholz refers several times to spectacles launched by Peter's niece, the Duchess of Mecklenburg. On October 11, 1722, her ailing mother, Tsarevna Praskovia, surrounded by members of the Synod, including the archbishop of Novgorod and the archimandrite of St. Trinity, waited for her younger daughter's sign to move into the home "theater," where before "a large number of women and men . . . the curtain went up, showing an elegant stage, though the costumes were not good. . . . The Duchess of Mecklenburg conducted everything."[75] Three days later, another spectacle occurred, during which the Duchess apologized for her "childish" production, unworthy of cultured spectators, and left her guests for the backstage, herself "directing the performance, which without her would stop."[76]

What could be seen as an amusing pastime for women of the imperial household became a state affair for ruling empresses. Hardly two weeks after Anna's coronation, a stream of letters went to the Saxon Court requesting King Augustus II[77] to assist in choosing and dispatching a troupe to the court of Her Majesty. After half a year of intense correspondence, the Russian court welcomed a professional *commedia dell'arte* company, including "a couple of lovers, one Doctor, one Pantaloon, and one Harlequin,"[78] as well as an "apartment [court] singer," Ludovica, who would entertain the empress in assemblies with celebratory cantatas.[79] This first Italian acting group and Araia's operatic troupe, arriving four years later, began the long-lasting history of Italian opera in Russia.[80]

Anna's court witnessed three *opere serie*; under Elisabeth the production of opera seria became a frequent event. A "band of French comédiens" had been brought to Russia at Anna's behest; Elisabeth further cultivated French theater. Twice a week, every Tuesday and Friday, her court was presented with dramas by Racine and Corneille and comedies by Molière.[81] A German "free company"[82] seeking Elisabeth's attention staged celebratory prologues that, like Italian productions, were populated by Muses, allegorical Virtues and Sins, mythological heroes, and parading Roman, Persian, and Armenian kings and queens.[83] Elisabeth, known for her love of choral singing, had her own music stand in the small female choir rehearsing in her palace. She also significantly expanded the size of the court chapel chorus. Joining with an Italian troupe, this court *cappella* performed at balls, dinners, operas, and state events, with the empress bestowing aristocratic titles and estates on her most diligent and long-serving singers.[84]

Anna, whether on the spur of the moment or according to a set schedule, was entertained in her parlor by her guards and their wives performing Russian *khorovods* (circle dances), with some exceptional dancers among them.[85] A few months into her reign, "upon Her Majesty's *ukaz*, choreographer William Igins was hired to teach dancing to her courtiers, pages, and cadets."[86] Elisabeth, a remarkable dancer, endorsed ballet and engaged noble military youths—the St. Petersburg Imperial Infantry Cadet Corps (*Shliakhetnyi Sukhoputnyi Kadetskii Korpus*)—in imperial productions. Later when she established the provincial Yaroslav acting troupe as the "first Russian theater," she enrolled several members in the Corps.

If Elisabeth's ardent love of music, dance, balls, and entertainments infected and energized her court, Catherine II lifted the culture of theater and theatricality to a different level. She endorsed native theater as a means of education for her people. Claiming to lack musical abilities, she launched the creation of a Russian operatic repertoire. Downplaying her literary "exercises," in addition to legislative documents she penned plays, some battling Russians' distaste for Shakespeare and others introducing social satire a là Molière or Beaumarchais, or channeling the empress's political ambitions. In the literary journals she founded, she provoked, adhered to, and rebuffed the idea of European liberalism, also providing early examples of literary and theatrical criticism. Under Catherine—this insurmountable paragon of power—theater became no longer merely a pastime at the court. Writing, staging, acting, playing in the orchestra, singing in the chorus, commissioning plays, music, providing the best European or native music tutors for children, and establishing private troupes became as much a part of an aristocrat's life and persona in the late decades of the century as their titles, houses, and dress codes. The magnitude of literary activity, music, and theatrical productions at the end of the century is mind-boggling.

During Peter's reign, a dozen-piece ensemble borrowed from the Duke of Holstein-Gottorp had sometimes performed the function of "court chamber ensemble."[87] Anna established a court chamber orchestra; Elisabeth fostered her ninety-member court chapel chorus. Under the empresses' patronage, the visual and musical spheres were predominantly entrusted to European masters; literary genres that would serve the crown, however, called for native voices. Vasilii Trediakovsky (1703–1769), acknowledged as Russia's first court poet, wrote and possibly sang his verses to Anna. Mikhail Lomonosov (1711–1765) adulated Elisabeth, the high style of his lofty odes matching the regal beauty of the architectural ensembles erected by Bartolomeo Rastrelli (1700–1771) and resonating with the choruses coming into fashion in St. Petersburg. Catherine immersed herself in literary exercises and published in a variety of literary genres, from legislative papers to journal articles, historical essays, children books, plays and philosophical writing. Her bevy of literati were led by Russia's greatest eighteenth-century poet, Gavrila Derzhavin (1743–1816).

Mirrors, Reflections, Magnified Lenses

Adopting the pen name and the persona of his supposed predecessor, Tatar Murza, in a series of poems Derzhavin addressed Catherine as Felitsa—the Kirgizian Princess. Borrowing both Felitsa and Murza from Catherine's own *Tale of Khlor*, the poet initiated a playful, intimate literary/political correspondence with the empress. Featuring the imagery Catherine chose for her literary alter ego, Derzhavin lauded Felitsa as goddess, tsarina, and heroine in an "oriental fairy tale."[88]

Кто ты? Богиня или жрица?"-	Who are you?—Goddess or Priestess?
Мечту стоящу я спросил.	[I] Asked the appearing dream.—
Она рекла мне: "Я Фелица!"	She spoke: "I am Felitsa."
Рекла - и светлый облак скрыл	She spoke—and a bright cloud veiled
От глаз моих ненасыщенных	From my yearning hungry eyes
Божественны ее черты [Видение	Her divine countenance [Vision of Murza]
Мурзы[89]]	

The exalted image of the empress-actress was magnified in the reflective lenses of the visual arts (triumphal arches, coinage, paintings, printed maps), venerated in literary and musical works (odes, three-part *kants*, celebratory cantatas, choruses), and enacted in theater, the last often an addendum to state spectacles. The theatricality of Catherine II's representation is apparent in her many portraits. Vigilius Eriksen depicts Catherine II before a mirror as a gentle, graceful figure turning to face a spectator, with a tilted head and soft oval face, one hand folded lightly on her chest and the other extended, holding a fan. The seemingly "inaccurate" reflection in the mirror, as clear as the figure itself, projects a strikingly different image. Although the empress looks directly into the spectator's eyes, the mirror depicts a strong, uncompromising Roman profile and a solid, stationary posture. If the live figure is associated with a playful fan and a freely unfurled scarf, the two crowns seem to belong to the reflection (Figure O.2).

The double imagery in the painting paralleled the poetic mythology of Catherine as both the heroic empress/goddess and the pastoral Dushen'ka in the poetic tale of Ippolit Bogdanovich (1743–1803). While Derzhavin appeals allegorically to Raphael, asking him to fill the canvas with Catherine's "heroism, so that her eyes would express the greatness of her soul,"[90] Bogdanovich lauds "not Achilles' rage and the siege of Troy"[91] but the sweetness of his Dushen'ka-Chloe as an idyllic version of the empress. The theater, employing metaphors and vocabulary cultivated in these visual and literary forms, explored various aspects of empresses, identified with victorious ancient emperors and heroes and by the end of the century with Russian history and still-unfolding Russian mythology.

In the course of a complex semiotic exchange between absolutist politics and celebratory arts, each empress perfected her role as a reflector of her multiple representations. Performing her part in ceremonial events and in private carnivalesque festivals, she acted as her own surrogate—the impersonator of her imperial self in various guises. For example, at one of Naryshkin's balls Catherine appeared costumed as Tsarina Natalia, the mother of Peter the Great.[92] Reversing times, in a peculiar twist, Catherine appropriated the parentage of the emperor whom she claimed as her model and direct imperial precursor.

Figure O.2: Vigilius Eriksen (1722–1782). *Portrait of Catherine II in Front of a Mirror.* Between 1762 and 1764. State Hermitage, St. Petersburg.

The empresses elevated themselves above the gender divide, not conforming to any convention and encompassing all possibilities by mastering their own "imperial gender." Along with gender, they established ownership of Roman-Hellenic mythology, and at the same time combined the Western enlightenment with baroque splendor and Russian antiquity. They waged wars to defend Eastern Orthodoxy and stripped the Russian church of its traditional power. Comfortable with these contradictions, they enacted allegorical battlefield conquests on the inlaid floors of their ballrooms and theaters, and endlessly shaped and perfected their professional acting roles.

Unlike actresses in the theater, the empresses' performances were not limited to several evening hours and were not demarcated by the perimeter of the stage. The ongoing imperial *spettacolo* comprised a number of theatrical acts—the once-in-a-lifetime event of an imperial coronation, annual ceremonial state events, victory celebrations, private gala productions, and theater itself. Like an actress impersonating different characters, the empress played many parts, while enacting *one* multifaceted and complex role with the skill and conviction that would manifest her sublime power and secure her survival.

1

RUSSIAN MINERVAS STAGING EMPIRE

In the course of the eighteenth century, the Russian imperial court developed into an arena for spectacular performances. An array of social genres—masquerades, coronations, weddings, and imperial operas—reveal remarkable fluidity, constituting a unified continuum. Theater, enjoying close kinship with court rituals, emerged under strong monarchial patronage. Opera, introduced as part of imperial celebrations, replayed grand events on a smaller scale, contributing elements of mythology and a sense of absolute, universal authority. The imperial sublime, realized in odes, theater, and architectural wonders, reached a hyperbolic level that suggested possible ironic subversion, a subject of later chapters. The grand mistresses of Russia approached theater as seriously as they staged coronations, fashioned courtly conduct, defined modern absolutist Russia, and shaped their own public personas. An examination of state rituals and a culture of masquerade illuminates the conventions underlying the operatic representation of monarchs and their domain, no matter how direct or veiled the association.

Masquerades

In the fall of 1790, after the end of a war with Sweden, Catherine II, according to her secretary Alexander Khrapovitsky, occupied herself with staging two events. One was the premiere of the empress's own operatic spectacle, *The Early Reign of Oleg*,[1] the other a staged ball-masquerade. The empress was actively involved in choosing actors, costumes, and scenery for her *Oleg*. Several rehearsals were played before Her Majesty; she corrected the actors' interpretations,[2] discussed the music for the play, and read Giuseppe Sarti's thesis on Greek music, later included in the published libretto.

The day after the premiere of *Oleg* in the Hermitage Theater, the sixty-one-year-old empress deigned to do something she had rarely done in recent years: "danced a Polish [polonaise], remained for the ball, the games, and an after-supper comedy."[3] The following evening, after another well-received performance of *Oleg* (in the Kamenny Theater), Catherine entrusted to Khrapovitsky her secret project, a surprise masquerade.

The empress approached the masquerade's production with the same attention she had lavished on *Oleg*. She requested costume designs, tried on a sample dress, and was apparently pleased.[4] She also meticulously drafted a plan.[5] The masquerade comprised multiple levels of re-dressing, including gender, social, and ethnic. Men dressed as women, while female guests put on male attire. Professional actors, distributing costumes, switched roles with noble guests. In the wake of the ending war with Turkey and in the mode of imperial appropriation of the East, the empress and her nobles appeared in the "costumes des premiers ministres de l'Egypte."

Throughout the eighteenth century, the empresses' desires for amusement were never divorced from their political and social agendas. Masquerades, often with a political subtext, were held in the court weekly and also organized for special occasions. The participatory spectators—a vast number of courtiers traversing the divide between reality and game, ritual and theater—were trained to obey and to improvise, kaleidoscopically changing acting roles as dictated by the head of the state, herself an amalgam of triumphant Minerva and idyllic shepherdess. Within this theatrical dominion, aristocrats in their palaces and estates produced events that imitated and rivaled imperial masquerades. Dressing, cross-dressing, acting, and directing, they exposed themselves to a "play of possibilities," further discussed in the next chapter.

In 1739, Anna held a masquerade wedding in an ice castle as both a public amusement and an exemplary punishment for Prince Mikhail Golitsin, the protagonist and lead actor. Having displeased his empress by acquiring a poor Italian wife and converting to Catholicism, Golitsin was promoted to the position of the empress's court fool.[6] Anna annulled his marriage and selected another woman for him to marry in a ceremony of her design. After the grand celebration, the bridal couple was accompanied to the specially constructed Ice Castle, placed in an ice bed with pillows, blankets, and frozen sheets, kept there by guards to "chill" through the night.

In early 1763, a half year after Catherine's installation, in a series of continuing celebrations, Moscow witnessed "Triumphant Minerva," a grand three-day pageant in the spirit of Venetian carnival adapted to the culture of the enlightened Russian She-Monarch. Choruses by Alexander Sumarokov and Mikhail Kheraskov rang out in the winter soundscape of Moscow. Fedor Volkov, founder of the first Russian professional theater, planned, rehearsed, and conducted the festive procession of three parts, each with many "quadrilles."[7] (In celebratory spectacles, this term referred to a group of masques; it was also applied to a military unit in chivalrous tournaments and a dance in courtly balls and stately weddings.[8])

"Triumphant Minerva" hinted at recent events and was imbued with political allegory. The first act, introducing Satanic masques—Chimera, Deceit, drunkards, and witches, all led by the god of mockery, the ill-spirited Momus—alluded to the vices of Peter III's half-year reign. Large kettledrums accompanied the infernal choruses. Sumarokov, "exhausting his imagination, expressed all possible human blemishes in pungent satire."[9] In the second act, mighty Vulcan and Cyclops were played by the Orlov brothers—Grigory, Catherine's lover at that time and a possible marital prospect, and gigantic, athletic Aleksei—both principal characters in deposing Peter III. Armed with storms and fire, expelling the preceding groups, they "cleared the way" for Jupiter, who signaled the beginning of the third part. Entitled "the Golden Age," the final procession consisted of Virtues introducing the central figure, Triumphant Minerva, unquestionably identified with Catherine. The Golden Age of Astraea was proclaimed already restored during the first six months of her rule. Like Anna's mock wedding, Catherine II's street masquerade functioned as the empress's "lesson" to warn her courtiers, especially those who had recently supported Peter III.[10] Catherine simultaneously appropriated the Elisabethan image of Astraea[11] and dissociated herself from her recent predecessors, thus establishing her imperial persona.

Russian tsarinas favored identification with Minerva, claiming the goddess's military prowess, wisdom, and patronage of the arts. Celebrating Anna's proclaimed victory over Ottoman Turkey (1735–1739), Vasily Trediakovsky depicted her as "Minerva in a shining helmet ... fearsome even without a shield ... a goddess in all her features."[12] Lomonosov's Elisabeth was "the daughter of Russian Zeus / Minerva in everything, the harmony of goodness."[13] Catherine II, portrayed as the helmeted goddess,[14] was famously venerated as the Northern Minerva by her court poets and as Semiramis by Voltaire.[15]

Five years after "Triumphant Minerva," its stock figures, conflicts, idioms, and title were revived in an allegorical ballet by Domenico Angiolini (1731–1803).[16] This *Triumphant Minerva*, dedicated to the smallpox inoculation that Catherine II underwent with her son Paul (Pavel), dramatized the empress battling medical prejudices and saving her people.[17] In the ballet, the characters fall into two conflicting groups, one represented by the personified Spirit of Knowledge and several heroes surrounding tearful Russia and the other by Ignorance, Superstition, and a dancing army led by Chimera. A Russian Minerva helps to defeat Chimera and consoles Russia, who brings her son for vaccination. A Trojan obelisk erected by Russia is inscribed to "our All-Merciful Monarch . . . a redeemer of human kind." Thus Catherine, identified with both Minerva and Russia, embodied the ruler and the state, the mythological past and the modern present.

Figure 1.1: Catherine II as Minerva. 1789. Agate-onyx and gold; cameo. State Hermitage, St. Petersburg.

Some members of the aristocratic elite staged exuberant masquerades with multiple theatrical entertainments, hosting the empress. On July 29, 1772, Prince Lev Naryshkin,[18] an avid devotee of music and theater, held a fête on one of his estates near St. Petersburg for more than two thousand people.[19] The monumental production began with the empress's arrival and ended with her departure, lasting from seven in the evening to three in the morning. Like ceremonies and theatricals of the time, this gala masquerade consisted of several autonomous genres—celebratory operas, ballets, choruses, and incidental events—folding into the general adulation of Her Majesty.

According to the *Description of a Masquerade*,[20] the first act began in an ideal pastoral meadow. As the empress approached, an island with mountains, rivers, and grottos was filled with the sounds of trumpets and drums. Seated on a bench at the foot of the mountain, the empress was joined by two shepherdesses played by Naryshkin's daughters, who strewed flowers on her path; as the harmonious trio proceeded toward a hut on the artificial mountain, the mountain erupted, revealing a temple inside.

Genius, enacted by the host's son, presented the empress with a tiara. Accompanied by cannon salvos, the empress stepped into the temple to see trophies and paintings of Russian triumphs in battles over Ottomans and Tatars.[21] Next, the *Description* narrates two paired scenes. In the first, Naryshkin's majestic visitor and guests come to a "Chinese domain with houses, gardens, and bird-homes with various birds, all in Chinese style, and with inhabitants in Chinese garb, playing different Chinese musical instruments." Crossing a little bridge to the next "scene," the empress hears songs of jubilant villagers and sees beautiful pastures, fields, and the homes of rich and happy Russian peasants. The illumination spectacle in the evening features a vision of Astraea holding scales and a cornucopia. A thousand rockets, shot into the night sky, light up the figure of sunlike Phoebus on a chariot bearing the empress's name, beneath him an image of a bowing Indian Brahmin. In the finale, an obelisk of Siberian marble is unveiled to reveal an imperial eagle holding Her Majesty's monogram. An ode inscribed on the column evokes Catherine's recent victories on the Black Sea and links her with mythological deities and the Russian folk.

This allegorical production demonstrates the fluidity of temporal and spatial planes (from ancient Greece to modern Turkey). The bucolic idyll, with princesses dressed as shepherdesses, coincided with the advent of French comic operas that introduced streams of heroines in disguise. [22] The image of the empress—central to this and many other productions—was magnified in abundant imperial symbols: eagles, insignia, engravings, and allegories. According to the script, the empress playfully enacted Her Majestic self. Sitting at the foot of the mountain in the company of the shepherdesses, she (if one believes the *Description*) enacted surprise at the moving mountain and lush landscape. Parts of the *Description* were written as if through the eyes and ears of the empress as she walked along the path to the "dark forest" and listened to "the echo of shepherds' pipes."[23] She was to be followed by all the guest-spectators, her cues observed at every point. The trope of the lively empress getting lost in picturesque pastures, dark forests, and grottos reemerged in Bogdanovich's antique tale in verse, *Dushen'ka* (1775–1783),[24] which the empress enjoyed as an invocation of herself.[25]

Featuring victorious Russia against multiple Orientals, Naryshkin's spectacle constituted an all-encompassing image of the native imperial sublime—controlled and beautified nature, military triumphs, remote ethnicities, and Greco-Roman mythological figures identified with the empress. These elements were consistently recycled in theatricalized courtly rituals and ritualized theatricals. A Chinese village, a kneeling Brahmin, and defeated Turks, all enclosed within a single Russian estate, emblemized appropriations of the East and manifested an appetite for conquest. Russian Orientalism, magnifying Russia's military expansion in the East, likewise revealed itself in Catherine's operas, followed by others, including Glinka's *Ruslan and Liudmila* (on Pushkin's text), in which the title hero (his name signifying Russia) gains the hand of the princess over Eastern and Western rivals[26] and achieves victory over a "Blackmoor" and his Arabic, Turkish, and Caucasian servitors.

A wide spectrum of eighteenth-century courtly genres explored the hegemony of Russian imperialism over global diversity. Preparing the infamous Ice Castle wedding, Anna requested the Academy of Science to provide a "roster of different ethnic groups in four parts of the world with the general description of peoples and their animals, their traditional food and dress."[27] The procession following the newlyweds included ethnic couples dressed in native costumes, playing native musical instruments, and riding on sledges harnessed to deer, dogs, bulls, donkeys, pigs, and camels.[28] During the festivities, the guests were fed their local food and performed folk songs and dances. According to Manstein, "the empress, in giving this entertainment, had a mind to see how many different kinds of inhabitants there were in her vast dominions."[29] This festival also displayed Anna's supremacy over her multiethnic dominions to her courtiers, foreign ambassadors, and anyone else witnessing.

Constantly exploring different performative venues to endorse Russian imperial valor, in 1766 Catherine held a *carousel*—a staged equestrian tournament. Not unlike masquerades, carousels combined re-dressing with military exercises. The Russian carousel drew on ancient Olympic games, medieval knightly contests, and also on a magnificent Grand Carousel that had been staged a century earlier by France's Louis XIV, the Sun-King (1662). The Russian carousel consisted of four quadrilles dressed as Slavs, Romans, Indians, and Turks. The empress introduced women as participants and competitors in the carousel, revivifying the myth of the Amazons.[30] Identifying with brave Spartan maids, Catherine II assumed the role of chief of the Slav quadrille and directed rehearsals of her team.[31]

A cannonade from the Admiralty Building signaled the beginning of the carousel. Streaming in orderly fashion from four directions, the glittering festive quadrilles met at an amphitheater specially erected on Hermitage Square before the Winter Palace.[32] Each quadrille was led by a herald and an orchestra playing tunes of the represented nations.[33] Poet Vasily Petrov wrote exultingly:

Я странный слышу рев музыки!	I listen to the strange musical bellow!
То дух мой нежит и бодрит;	[It] soothes or energizes my spirit
Я разных зрю народов лики!	I see it in different peoples' faces!
То взор мой тешит и дивит;	Which both pleases and amazes my eyes;
В порфирах Рим, Стамбул, Индия	In porphyry [are] Rome, Istanbul, India
И славы под венцом Россия[34]	And Russia crowned with fame.

The aristocrats raced around the arena with perfect posture and manners, throwing javelins and cutting the heads off wax mannequins. Leading the Roman and Indian quadrilles were the Orlov brothers, who, equals in strength and military skill, won all the contests.[35] Derzhavin praised the Orlovs and Russia's Amazons:

На буйном видел я коне	On an unruly horse, I saw
В ристаньи моего героя;	My hero, in a tourney,
С ним брат его, вся Троя,	With him, his brother, and all Troy,
Полк витязей явился мне!	A company of knights appeared to me!
Прекрасных вслед Пентесилее	Behind Penthesilea, beautiful
Строй дев их украшали чин. . . [36]	Maidens stand in ranks, decorating them. . . .

Neither Petrov nor Voltaire, who also wrote an ode to the carousel, saw the spectacle. Cross-referencing Petrov's pompous rhymes, subsequent generations of poets fostered this carousel as a subject of ironic subversive discourse. Fifty years after Catherine's original carousel, Pushkin, a lyceum pupil in Tsarskoe Selo, poked fun at his aged fellow poet Derzhavin and simultaneously ridiculed Petrov, "a famous poet of ours."

О громкий век военных споров,	Oh thunderous century of warriors' quarrels,
Свидетель славы россиян!	Witnesses of Russian glory!
Ты видел, как Орлов, Румянцев и Суворов,	You saw how Orlov, Rumantsev and Suvorov,
Потомки грозные славян,	Descendants of the dreaded Slavs,
Перуном Зевсовым победы похищали;	[With] Zeus's Perun, they snatched their victories.
Державин и Петров героям песнь бряцали	To them, Derzhavin and Petrov jangled out an ode,
Струнами громкозвучных лир.[37]	On the strings of rackety lutes.

The winner of Catherine's carousel, Countess Natalia Golitsyna (née Chernyshova), is considered the prototype of Pushkin's countess in *Queen of Spades*. Her daughter, Lady Nocturne, praised by Pushkin, and her husband, Prince Apraksin, held the last lustrous carousel in 1811. The recipient of a special prize as the youngest and most elegant participant was Alexander Vsevolozhsky, whose son Ivan years later, as the director of the Imperial Theaters, convinced Tchaikovsky to write the opera *Queen of Spades*—a history woven into familial networks, honors, and ridicule.

Like masquerades, carousels occupied an intermediate position in the performative continuum ranging from state ceremonies to theater. The empress, supported by her courtiers' cast, appeared in various guises. Enacting androgynous roles, dressed as generals, Spartan maids, Persian princesses, Egyptian ministers, and picturesque native shepherdesses, the female monarchs remained recognizable as their majestic selves.

Coronations

Российско солнце на восходе. . .	The Russian sun on the rise,
В сей общевожделенный день	On this all-desired day,
Прогнало в ревностном народе	Expelled from hard-working people
И ночи и печали тень.	The shadow of darkness and night . . .
Так ты, монархиня, сияешь	That is how you, she-monarch, shine
В концы державы твоея . . .	To all ends of your domain . . .
От славных вод Балтийских края	From Baltic waters
К востоку путь свой простирая	To the East, your paths are laid. . . .

—(Lomonosov, Ode, 1752 [38])

A centerpiece of the imperial theater of power was the coronation spectacle, which adhered to the Aristotelian "unities" of time, place, and action. Lacking the conflict of classical drama, coronations directed all the performers' and spectators' energies to the ritualistic passage of "a body in transition, from subject to monarch and from mortal to divine."[39] For the performer of the starring role, the spectacle was a one-time-only premiere. A cast of thousands—from the imperial entourage to massive crowds, including native counts, foreign princes, church choristers, cannoneers, and tableau painters—doubled as performers and spectators. As elsewhere in Europe, this regal ceremony culminated in the solemnized wedding of the ruler and the state. The Russian *venchanie* (crowning, from *venok*, circlet, wreath), signifying an Orthodox marriage ceremony and a coronation, cemented both unions till "death do them part."

The day of coronation was followed by a week (for Catherine I) or several months (for Catherine II) of ceremonial dinners, masquerades, and fireworks. Coronations established several elements essential to Russian theater. Held in multiple settings, extending beyond the primary cast to massive crowds, the coronation established staging as an all-consuming business. [40] Though based on the solemn Orthodox ceremonies of old Russia, eighteenth-century coronations were engendered with excesses fostered in Renaissance and Baroque Europe. Russian state rituals valorized the godly imperial domain epitomized by the theatrics of absolute monarch Louis XIV.[41]

The coronations of the four empresses took place during forty years between 1724 and 1762—a period also marked by the advent of theater in Russia. At the time of Catherine I's coronation, European-type theater hardly existed in the empire. Anna, as mentioned earlier, invited the first troupes. Elisabeth conditioned the date of her investiture on the construction of an opera house. Catherine II utilized theater as an educational institution, an occupation for her aristocrats, and her own literary and political platform. In the early eighteenth century, gala state spectacles such as coronations occupied a void later filled by professional theater. As the apex of state and dynastical rituals, the coronation drama laid the foundation for theater and established a channel of exchange between state and stage performances.[42]

Similarities and divergences in design, scenery, soundscape, and acting in the four coronation spectacles reflected changing historical contexts defined by the female leads. Sandra Logan, writing about the English Elizabeth's coronation, acknowledges the "problem of history … in the theatrical representation of mediated and immediate experiences," where "the text/event, with its particular interests and agenda, has displaced and come to stand in for the event itself."[43] The interpretation of the Russian empresses' coronations relies largely on the officially published *Descriptions*,[44] which, like the ritualistic acts themselves, elevated the notion of the sublime and shaped historical memory. The dispatches of foreign ambassadors who observed and partook in coronations echoed these descriptions. Similar to scripts of theatrical productions, these manuals included details of setting, stage design, and identified actors (statesmen, foreign diplomats) by name and qualification. Indicating the appearance, entrance, grouping, and positioning of participants, the scripts also offered fragments of spoken text and references to sound effects. A comparison of the first three coronation *Descriptions*—written for Catherine I, Anna, and Elisabeth[45]—demonstrates increasing theatricality and a sense of competitiveness from one coronation to the next. Progressively, each expanded the imperial entourage, enlarged the "stage," and extended the length of the celebration.

The *Description* of Catherine I's investiture portrayed the decoration of the streets, the imperial couple's progress, and the ritual of the coronation itself. The *Description* of Anna's enthronement, repeating elements of the previous manual, added visual illustrations of the empress's crown and mantle, the layout of the church, and celebratory illuminations. Although the *Descriptions* of these two coronations focused inside the Kremlin, the script of Elisabeth's investiture referred to a broader Moscow setting and timeframe encompassing the triumphal entry of the empress into the city, the coronation three months later, and subsequent banquets, masquerades, and festivities. The accession of Catherine II is memorialized in the *Description of the All-Joyous Entry of Pious Empress Catherine into the Holy Trinity Sergey Cloister*,[46] where clergymen praised their "desired *mati* (mother)," and their celebratory kants[47] asserted her right to the crown that had fallen from the head of her murdered husband.

Though following the tradition of investiture in the old capital, the empresses inherited Peter's disdain for "antiquated Moscow," which he "emptied" by ordering "all the famed nobles, including widows and their unmarried daughters, to move to St. Petersburg."[48] Moscow's lethargic, rumor-mongering provincialism and its continuous conspiracies—"much stupidity there," Catherine opined, ". . . all this recalls the beards of our ancestors"[49]—led the eighteenth-century monarchs to increasing estrangement from this castaway capital that nevertheless served as the place of coronations, affording the rulers historical and religious legitimacy. The monumental entries of the empresses—accompanied by the St. Petersburg elite, with guards and cavalry parading through the city, its auditory space filled with military music and shooting, and with the Preobrazhensky, Semenovsky, and Izmailovsky regiments lining the streets—could have been seen as invasions of Moscow or enactments of triumphal conquest.

The old Russian capital served as a backdrop for displays of imperial imagery, entwined with historical, biblical, and mythological themes. The spectacles unfolded in three settings: Kremlin streets during entry and procession, the stage of coronation in the Assumption Cathedral, and the ceremonial banquet in the Faceted (Granovitaia) Palace. The cortège that accompanied Anna consisted of seventeen colorful groups. The number increased to forty-two in Elisabeth's ritual, and to fifty-one in Catherine II's. Persian carpets bedecked the Kremlin to greet the Russian ruler. Specially constructed wooden paths covered with red cloth lined the pathway from the Tsar Palace to the Cathedral, and to the Church of Saint Michael.[50] Along the empresses' progress to the Kremlin, Moscow erected triumphal arches—three for Anna, four for Elisabeth, and seven for Catherine II.[51] Each crowned empress was portrayed leading personified Mercy, Wisdom, Chastity, Truth, and Bravery, as well as Greco-Roman gods and heroes. The combination of piety, militaristic attributes, and the equation of the "virgin queen" with the She-Eagle protecting her children defined the mythology of the eighteenth-century Russia women's kingdom.

The Description of the Allegoric Illumination Shown at the All-Most-Joyous Coronation Day of Catherine II[52] was published side-by-side in Russian, German, and Latin. The illuminations at Moscow University displayed a portrait of the empress on a pedestal. Below her, Russia, kneeling, presents a scepter to Catherine; from above Eternity and Hope bestow the crown on the empress's head, as a Muse gives her a celestial globe. A smaller panel on the right side of the canvas pictures Nymphs holding vessels with imperial insignia.

The personified Virtues depicted in triumphal arches and odes were animated on the theatrical stage. Together with choruses, ancient heroes—Alexander, Tito, and Scipion (Scipio Africanus)—extolled each empress, as nymphs, naiads, rusalkas, zephyrs, and cupids danced.[53] Notably, choruses and dancing water sprites became characteristic of nineteenth-century fairy-tale operas, which, despite their purported association with the folk, featured almost exclusively the royal and princely domain.

Eighteenth-century Russian coronations stood in stark contrast to the past. During the venchanie of Fedor (1584), "amazing silence accompanied him." A description of Tsar Mikhail Fedorovich's procession (1596–1645) reads: "Silently he walked. . . . As he entered Assumption Cathedral everyone stood without noise."[54] Newly anointed Aleksei Mikhailovich (1645) approached silently, "walking with a tsar's majestic splendor."[55] The church treated music with suspicion, and Peter's father, Tsar Aleksei, in "his joyous days, forbade *zurnas* and trumpets. Instead of trumpets and organs, the sovereign ordered his state chorus of deacons to sing at his banquets. . . . And upon his, the tsar's wise and righteous thinking, there was to be silence. . . ."[56]

By contrast, if eyewitnesses of eighteenth-century coronations had not been blinded by the glitter of the red and gold decoration or stupefied by the parade of luminaries, they would have been deafened by the sonic "symphony"—an indiscriminate composition of musical and nonmusical ensembles, including church bells, cannons, and rifles[57]; military "signaling music" (trumpets and drums); church choruses; and in the evening, expanding from one coronation to the next, dancing music, brass and chamber groups, and operas. The sound palette represented three power centers: artillery fire epitomized military conquest; bells and church choirs conveyed the religious aspect of the ceremony; and orchestras and Italian cantatas signified the European court. Two days prior to Anna's coronation, twenty-four heralds, officers, and grenadiers in uniform, along with "twelve trumpeters and kettledrummers wearing rich golden tassels," rode "with much éclat" throughout the city announcing the day of investiture.[58] The night before Elisabeth's coronation, in the Assumption Cathedral and in other churches, monasteries, and chapels in the Kremlin, Moscow, and the provinces, bells tolled, signaling night vigils. At six o'clock in the morning of the following day, cannons began. In the case of Elisabeth, the ritual included 101 cannons together with rifles of all regiments.[59]

In the course of the empress's progress, along with the bells and cannons, church choruses sang Russian kants. "Who did not hear [kants] himself," wrote Jakob von Staehlin, "can't imagine how rich and magisterial this church music is, performed by large, trained and selected choruses."[60] In the evening the acoustic mix continued as the empress dined with a hundred close associates at a ceremonial table placed under a canopy on an elevated stagelike platform, while listening to "the Imperial music in the built-up great Theater [stage]."[61] A culminating point of the weeks of festivities was the premiere of *La clemenza di Tito* in an opera house that seated five thousand.[62] The birth of official Russian musical culture can be traced through and understood in the context of eighteenth-century coronations.[63]

The most prominent Russian "patricians"—the marshals of the ceremony—conducted the well-rehearsed productions, visible at all times close to the empresses. Every element of the coronation spectacle, like the entry of the English Elizabeth, revealed the politically sensitive social structure of the government apparatus: where one rode in relation to the monarch and one's fellow courtiers was of pointed significance, signaling the favor of the monarch and indicating one's potential influence on her as well.[64] The participants' positions, presence, and elevation on the cathedral platforms as well as their placement at the banquet—within the horizontal and vertical dimensions of the space—translated into their standing in the state hierarchy.[65] This dynastic structure made them into a sort of professional acting guild, honing and passing on the art of performance in the gala imperial spectacle. The court elite facilitated the transition from one lead actress/leader to the next and from one imperial drama to another by providing a sense of continuity and tailoring the production to the strength and ambitions of the main performer.

During the coronation of Catherine I, the imperial couple shared the spotlight. In the morning procession, the emperor walked behind members of the highest elite, displaying French regal colors in his "summer sky-blue caftan, adorned with silver, red silk stockings, and a hat with a white feather.... Behind him, Her Majesty the empress approached in a most opulent robe of purple taffeta with rich gold needlework made in Spanish fashion . . . and in a headdress encrusted with most precious stones and pearls."[66] In the cathedral, Catherine's future son-in-law Charles Frederick Holstein-Gottorp escorted her to the emperor, who helped the empress walk up the twelve steps to the *chertog* (tsar's place). There, on Peter's call, the archbishop blessed Catherine and she knelt on "the pillow placed before her."[67] She knelt a second time when Peter, accepting the crown from the archbishop, placed it on his spouse's head. Tears streamed down her face. After the mantle was laid on her shoulders, the empress knelt for a third time and tried to kiss Peter's feet. This threefold kneeling, Catherine's own emotional improvisation representing the Orthodox trinity,[68] demonstrated the empress's adept handling of theatrical effects.

Anna observed Catherine I in the prime role, and six years later she enacted her own interpretation in her coronation. She did not kneel to receive her crown. As both secular and religious attendees in the cathedral bowed in reverential silence, Anna alone stood tall above the assembly. Walking with heavy steps, she crossed the threshold to the altar—a holy place where women were not permitted and where Fedor, the elder brother of Peter I, had become the first ruler to follow the archbishop for communion (1676).[69] Peter's daughter Elisabeth likewise did not hesitate to breach either gender or religious traditions when applying her personal sense of the dramatic. At an appropriate moment after the prayer, she pointed to the crown, which the chancellor gave to the Novgorod archbishop, who presented it to Her Majesty.[70] She herself, like

Napoleon a half-century later, placed the crown on her own head. Catherine II fortified all her predecessors' ritualistic innovations by magnifying the scale of her entourage, the opulence of the scenery, and the expanding soundscape. She proceeded,
surrounded by the brothers Razumovsky and Orlov. The favorite/husband of the late
Elisabeth, Aleksei Razumovsky, carried the crown "studded with 75 large pearls, 2,500
diamonds, and 5,012 other precious stones." It was indeed "the most opulent thing . . .
in Europe."[71]

Both the nobility's involvement and the imagery of Catherine II's coronation were
captured in a painting by Stefano Torelli. At the center of his canvas portraying the
Assumption Cathedral, the empress stands on the imperial chertog at the top of the
staircase; her proud posture and crown make her taller than everyone in the painting,
including the metropolitan archbishop and a few selected companions next to her.
Near Catherine, at the apex of a pyramid, its sides formed by lines of courtiers, are
Westernized nobles in wigs and sky-blue caftans matching the colors of the empress's
dress; clergymen in rich, colorful, gold-embroidered robes kneel in the lower right
side of the painting. The bottom left depicts a darker group of bearded men, some
looking away and one in the forefront turning his back to the empress.

No matter how talented the lead actor was or how well trained the troupe, as in our
day, state "stardom" impelled an enormous multifaceted artistic production. Several
dozen participant-spectators constituted an empress's immediate entourage, and other

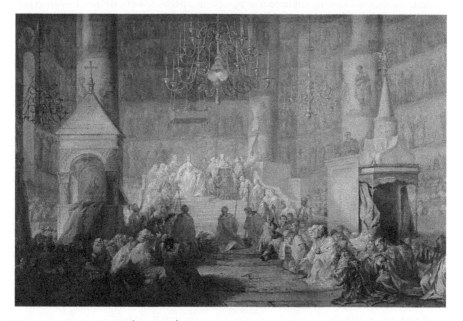

Figure 1.2: Stefano Torelli (1712–1784). *Coronation of Catherine II, September 22, 1762.* 1763. Sketch.
Oil on canvas. 84 x 126 cm. Tretyakov Gallery, Moscow.

prominent statesmen and courtiers followed in their splendid equipages. Thousands more would catch a glimpse of the gold-purple taffeta of her dress, the back of her majestic carriage, or the tail of her entourage from afar. For the crowd, the coronation would be associated with wine spurting from fountains, with roasted bulls stuffed with different meats, with deafening cannonades and illuminations. The empress would be remembered through visual portrayals in arches, paintings, and engravings, surrounded with theatrical props—globes, flags, cannons, trumpets, and curtains. Constructed also of words and tunes, the royal image was fostered in verses sung, repeated, and memorized from church sermons and published texts. Occupying the public domain, the empress also became her subjects' personal possession. Pushing through the crowd, the lucky ones might have caught and later caressed in their pockets their treasure, a coin with a regal profile—whether Anna's (heavy), Elisabeth's (beautiful with a low-cut neckline), or Catherine II's (in her Minerva helmet)—which provided the enduring pleasure of intimate physical contact with their empress.

The coronation was a grand spectacle that unfolded at the intersection of immediate experience and mediated inscription, with the lead character situated between the presentation of self and her multimedia representation. If the triumphal arches, Kremlin walls, and multiple processions lent an architectonic definition to the "stage," and the thick sound layering defined its acoustic space, the published text, recycled productions, and exuberant anniversaries shaped historical memory. Between the one-time act of coronations and the annual ceremonials reenacting the empresses' inaugurations, the imperial sublime was upheld in operas, ballets, orchestras, and choruses performed by amateur and professional troupes.[72] Enjoying unlimited human and financial resources, employing the best Russian and European artists, and relying on successful historical models, the coronations of Russian empresses were serious drama. They were staged by highly professional courtiers/actors who performed roles daily in spectacles of various genres that served as the prototypes for operatic theater, emerging at this time as a subset of Russia's imperial drama.

Weddings

Амуру вздумалось Психею,	Amour thought of Psyche,
Резвяся, поймать,	Playing, to catch [her],
Опутаться цветами с нею	To tangle in flowers with her
И узел завязать.	And tie the knot.
Она зовет своих подружек.	She called her friends,
Чтоб узел развязать,	To untie her knots
И он ь крылатых своих служек,	And he, his winged servants,
Чтоб помоць им подать.	To give them help.

Ни крылышком Амур не тронет,	Not a wing would Amour move
Ни луком, ни стрелой;	Not his bow or arrows
Психея не бежит, не стонет,	Psyche doesn't run, or groan
Свились, как лист с травой	They're entwined like a leaf with grass.
Так будь чета век нераздельна,	Thus is the couple! forever undivided,
Согласием дыша:	Breathing in agreement,
Та цель тверда, где сопряженна	That chain is hard that yokes
С любовию душа.	The soul with love.
(Derzhavin, "Amur i Psikheia"[73])	

Derzhavin's poem links Amour and Psyche with Catherine II's beloved grandson Alexander and his bride, Princess Elisabeth of Baden.[74] With their respective entourages, both couples—poetic and princely—held hands performing a ritualistic Russian game, *"Zapletisia pleten'"* ("Weave the Wattle"), during which they "became so entangled with ribbons that they had to be cut."[75] Both the game and Derzhavin's poem are identified with a Russian khorovod—a folk song and circle dance (*khor*, chorus and *vodit'*, to lead by the hand)

> during which the circle is broken at one end, with [two people] raising their arms to form gates through which everyone from the opposite side walks holding hands; the second person, making the gates turn around, grabs the hand of the third person over his shoulder; the game continues until all are entangled.[76]

Written for the celebration of the *sgovor* (engagement) of the ducal couple, with music composed by Vasily Pashkevich, the song was performed before the empress at the betrothal on May 10, 1793. Nearly half a year later, the ballet *Amour et Psyche* became part of the couple's wedding celebration.[77] Premiered in Catherine's Hermitage Theater, this five-act production engaged a European team, French choreographer Charles Le Pique, Spanish composer Vicente Martín y Soler, and Italian designer Pietro Gonzaga.[78] The cast of characters and choruses demonstrated the magnitude of the production. The gods—Venus, Jupiter, Mars, and Apollo—were surrounded by the allegorical figures of Sadness, Sorrow, and Disquiet, and joined by three Graces and four animated Winds. Dozens of tritons, cupids, zephyrs, and shepherds accompanied Amour and Psyche.

The "entwining" of the Russian heir and the German princess linked European decorum, Russian ritualistic elements, and hybrid conventions developed in the eighteenth-century Russian court. Beyond native and Western symbolism, folklore and courtly etiquette, the zapletisia, as a metaphor, wove different genres and entangled the performances of both imperial and theatrical actors. The princely couple, having played the game, later watched its reenactment on the stage.

Historically, a Russian tsar seeking a spouse for a brother or kinsman "ordered all of his boyars and princes to bring their daughters to the tsar's yard" for the ruler to select the bride.[79] The tsar's wedding, lasting for several days, involved a prescribed cast of characters: svakhi (women attending the bride and at some points the groom, knowledgeable about the wedding sequence, and central to several procedures), the bridegroom's druzhki (friends), tysiatskie (men leading the ritual[80]), and surrogate mothers, fathers, and sisters. Identified by name (in early Descriptions), noblemen were assigned various chores: to collect the bride, follow her bridal sledge on foot, hold the ceremonial cups, perform ritualistic hair brushing, oversee the venchanie or crowning, make the bed of seven mattresses, stand by the head of the bed, carry the "three-times-forty sables," fan the bride, prepare the bath, and accompany the groom to his ritualistic washing. In the Assumption Cathedral, the marriage was sanctified with the deacons' chorus accompanying the service. After a feast at the Faceted Palace, the procession led the newlyweds to a bedchamber. The following days were strictly defined in terms of diet, bathing, gender-divided festivities, and visits. (Several elements—the ritualistic figure of svakha, the segregation of the bride, and traditional wedding songs—were included in Catherine's Oleg.)

Some tsars held weddings with music—"to increase the tsar's joy, the surnas and trumpets would play day and night, and nakras would be struck in the palace."[81] Others, like tsar Aleksei Mikhailovich, who walked silently in his coronation and ordered deacons to sing at his wedding, forbade the use of musical instruments.[82]

Among the eighteenth-century rulers, only Peter the Great married after his accession to the throne. However, he celebrated his matrimony not as a tsar and an emperor but as Admiral Petr Mikhailov.[83] Although a line of secret husbands and paramours streamed through the eighteenth-century Russian imperial household, none of the empresses undermined their sublime wedding to the Fatherland by marrying a man. Instead, they engaged in choreographing wedding spectacles for their courtiers and relatives.

With kinship and marital alliances binding the aristocracy,[84] rulers authorized and directed marriages among their courtiers throughout the eighteenth century. Catherine I and her husband staged weddings routinely. Anna was called by Anisimov "the matchmaker of all Russia."[85] Under Elisabeth, according to Catherine II, "weddings at court upon the empress's permission might take place several years later, because Her Imperial Majesty herself set the dates."[86] The monarchs arranged court marriages in much the same way aristocrats wedded their serfs—at their whim. In her memoirs, Catherine II described the selection of a bride of "her liking" for longtime friend and associate Prince Lev Naryshkin, who "while falling in love with one maiden, his mother preparing to engage him to another [second], instead married a third one, of whom neither he nor anyone else had thought three days before."[87] Each empress led the ritualized dressing of a noble bride, directed the couple in the church, organized a ceremonial ball, accompanied the bride to the bedchamber, and bestowed on the couple jewelry, orders, titles, villages, and serfs. Even when sick, Catherine, upon Elisabeth's order, had to dress a court bride.[88]

Acting as marshals and mistresses of these ceremonies, Russian monarchs treated weddings as a space for entertainment and experimentation, probing and defining imperial etiquette and social relations. Catherine I designed the wedding of her daughter Anna to the Duke of Holstein-Gottorp (1725).[89] The marriage ceremony of their son, Peter III, and Catherine II was staged by Elisabeth (1745); Catherine II masterminded the weddings of her son Paul and her grandchildren. The tradition of political marriages between Russian and European princely houses, reintroduced in the wedding of Princess Anna and her short-lived spouse, the Duke of Courland (1710), prompted the rapid Westernization of court wedding rituals.[90] Not sledges but a parade of fifty boats began the wedding ceremony of the future empress. With a wind orchestra cruising ahead of sailors wearing uniforms encrusted with imperial eagles, the aquatic procession was led by Tsar Peter, the bride's uncle. At the ball, the Courland orchestra played a polonaise—the dance that would open imperial balls throughout this and the following century and would become a convention of imperial representation in nineteenth-century opera.[91] When Peter, with his sense of the spectacular, cut the cakes, two dwarfs jumped out and danced a minuet.[92]

Describing her ten-day wedding celebration, Catherine II recalled that "among other events, there was a masquerade of dominoes in different colors, dancing quadrilles, each composed of twelve couples":

> ... the first quadrille, in rose and silver, was the Grand Duke's; the second, white and gold, was mine; the third one, my mother's, was of a melting blue and silver; the fourth, yellow and silver, was my uncle's ... the quadrilles were not to intermingle; rather, each should dance in its allotted corner of the room.[93]

In these colorful quadrilles[94] the ducal couple reenacted the theatrical idyll that emulated the wedding pair and simultaneously offered an idealized model. The circular energy seemed to float freely among performative genres and across social boundaries.

This wedding engineered by Elisabeth exhibited what her court knew best: ceremonial dinners, masquerades, and a sequence of theatricals including illuminations, stage cantatas, ballets, and specially commissioned *opere serie*. A few hours after the wedding ritual, the empress and the ducal couple proceeded to their seats in the theater. Three ballets presented by "French comédiens" depicted the triumph of love. *The Princess of Elis*, about the heiress of an imaginary kingdom who renounces love for hunting (reminiscent not only of mythological Diana but also of Russian empresses), ends with a triple wedding of the princess and her two sisters. In the *Ballet of Flowers*, produced by Rinaldi, Rose, the queen of an animated garden, is nearly ruined by the storm Borei, but rescued by her beloved wind Zephyr; the couple celebrates their union in the "dancing" garden. In *Zeneida*, a young princess at her birth receives a blessing from a benevolent enchantress but is also cursed by a malicious witch. Eventually a prince from afar breaks the spell, wedding the princess at the end (a plotline echoed by Tchaikovsky's *The Sleeping Beauty* a century and a half later; 1888).

And the sequence of celebratory theatricals continued. Three days after the French ballet, the royal family "deigned to attend" a production of *Scipion*, an Italian opera seria by composer Francesco Araia and librettist Giuseppe Bonecchi, created on Her Majesty's wish with the empress attending the rehearsals.[95] Throughout the opera, choruses recited praises to the operatic heroes as well as to Her Imperial Majesty and the ducal newlyweds.[96] One of the ballet intermissions in *Scipion* added to the parade of theatrical weddings another version of Amour and Psyche (*Le nozze di Psiche e Cupido*).

Embracing the domains of the royal, mythical, natural, magical, native, and foreign, these theatrical events entwined the couple's bliss with the majestic power of a central player. A firework spectacle designed by Staehlin, with pyrotechnic effects developed at the Russian Science Academy, displayed the busts of tsars with Elisabeth and Peter I at the center of a sculpted group on a large decorated barge floating on the river before the Winter Palace.[97] Nereids, Tritons, and Cupids rode the dolphins; in the midst of this merry aquatic company, King Neptune stood on a chariot harnessed to sea horses, Venus on a carriage borne by doves. Lomonosov's ode, created for the event, venerated the "young couple's radiant *lik* [canonized image]" and praised the image of "Herself, looking at them with marvel. . . ."[98]

This state wedding functioned as a spectacular affirmation of the empress's role. The parts of the celebrations echoed, reiterated, and succeeded one another in a uniform design. The range of genres and forms—from ceremonial to masquerade to majestic illumination and fireworks, and to opera and ballet—mixed the imperial with the imaginary. In *Soedinenie Liubvi i Braka* (*The Union of Love and Marriage*, 1745), a staged cantata-panegyric by Araia on a text of Bonecchi, Venus is portrayed accompanied by the three Graces.[99] The goddess glorifies "this great day that unites [personified] Love with Marriage." The allegorical duo, vowing peace and harmony, blesses the ducal couple. Identifying with Catherine and Peter III on the stage, the Olympic couple expresses their "fervor before the empress who reigns in these countries, so that everyone would please Her, whose mercifulness supplants even Her beauty." Hymeneus calls "blessed people . . . to sing, exalting the empire of HER Augustan MAJESTY." As the scene ends with blissful union, "suddenly the trumpet and drums are heard," signaling the advent of "Mars, the god of war and Minerva, goddess of wisdom." But instead of hurling thunderbolts, the two rush to join the celebration. In the merriment of the second scene, Mars, promising future victories to the "beautiful couple," professes that "people always give in to force, but even the best warriors rarely win over people's hearts, as does the pleasant She-Sovereign, the tsarina of her peoples' hearts." Minerva, revering the empress's benevolence, pledges to double her support for the Russian ruler. Now Venus, gaily abandoning Pathos and Cyprus, wishes nothing more than to reside in "this [empress's] gleeful house." Love and Hymeneus join the procession of "all people of kingdoms and provinces, living happily under HER IMPERIAL MAJESTY." The cantata ends with a mass ballet.

Half a century after these matrimonial festivities, the wedding celebrations of Catherine II's grandson (1793) were likewise populated by gods and goddesses, virtues, new versions of Amour and Psyche. The fireworks for Alexander's wedding, resembling those for Catherine's, portrayed beautiful "gardens decorated with cascades, flowerbeds . . . that showed the prosperity of all-Russia, the peace in the empire represented by a large palm tree with the illuminated AUGUSTAN NAME OF HER IMPERIAL MAJESTY! . . . Hymeneus uniting the two burning hearts at the altar of love."[100]

Idyllic gardens and princely weddings served as a prominent feature in Catherine's comic operas. Russified Arcadian gardens also became part of a literary tradition that extended from eighteenth-century odes, operas, and illuminations to nineteenth-century poetics—for instance, the magical gardens of Pushkin's "esthete dwarf Chernomor."[101] The figure of Hymeneus in illuminations and a number of wedding spectacles would be evoked at the end of the next century in the *intermedi* of Tchaikovsky's *Queen of Spades* (1891).

Needless to say, however convincing the ceremony and theatricals depicting royal domestic bliss, rarely did the weddings result in successful marriages.[102] After the death of their "protector" Elisabeth, the glittering wedding of Catherine and Peter III ended up with a game of elimination in which Catherine won freedom and the empire. Two years after the slaughter of her husband, at the Christmas festivities in 1764, Catherine played the *zapletisia pleten'* with Grigory Orlov, her lover and one of Peter III's executioners.

Beyond the politics of representation, these weddings portrayed the prime imperial actors, the exemplary center—not so much as they were, but as they wished to be seen.[103] The theatricals staged as reflections of the matrimonial spectacle produced an idealized version of unions, thus identifying the shift of the exemplified center from the imperial to the theatrical domain, in which, fused with abstract imagery and allegory, it reinforced "ideal" monarchial representation.

Music was an intrinsic part of state celebrations. By the second half of the century, the imperial court in St. Petersburg enlisted some of the leading European composers, who created operas, oratorios, and quadrilles for endless court events. Soon they were joined by the first generation of Russian composers. Undergoing drastic revision in the early eighteenth century from the mock ceremonies staged by Peter and Anna, the wedding as a refined Westernized institution was polished and perfected by both Elisabeth and Catherine II. Operas and musical dramas staged for imperial weddings were no longer an occasional extension but a significant part of the state spectacles. From the very beginning of Russian theater, and particularly from the marriage celebration of 1745, the sequence of weddings on the theatrical stage shone in various colors and genres, embracing the worlds of ancient heroes, gods, and fairies. The word *wedding* appears in many operatic titles;[104] wedding scenes occur in Catherine II's operas. Staged in tsar's palaces and picturesque villages, involving princes, shepherdesses, and urban merchants, wedding scenes came to represent native culture. Although courtly ceremonial weddings displayed rapid Westernization, Russian operas of the end of the century, including Catherine II's, featured traditional native marriage celebrations, bridal rituals and songs as national markers; the wedding, crossing the threshold of the century, would become a characteristic of Russian nineteenth-century operatic repertoire.

The Genealogy of Russia's Celebratory Opera

Throughout the eighteenth century, an array of theatrical genres—staged cantatas, serenatas, ballets, illuminations, and opere serie (also known as *dramma per musica*)—emerged as vehicles for representation of real empresses. Attending the spectacles, the dedicatees of these musical and dramatic tributes sat in their lavish stage-balconies, while allegorical characters temporarily enacted monarchs on the stage. As elsewhere, perfectly trained actors and singers "stood in as royal figures, heroes, counselors, generals, and confidantes,"[105] their voices aligned with the imperial sublime. This section focuses on a specific segment of Russia's burgeoning eighteenth-century theater: opera seria productions adapted, commissioned, and produced for state events, and thus termed here *celebratory* theater.

Created predominantly by European composers, musicians, and performers in the service of the crown,[106] Russia's opera seria was largely discarded by later generations as foreign. In her recent monograph, Ritzarev, reviewing the literature on the subject and challenging the nationalistic-romantic mode that bashed eighteenth-century opera, states that the moment one tries to analyze stylistic features in order to separate the borrowed from the native (or what had become native by the eighteenth century), one becomes trapped either in exaggerated nationalistic pretensions or in total rejection of native elements, throwing out the baby with the bath water.[107] Yet even Ritzarev, pointing out the "condescending contempt" toward the eighteenth century's "quaint mélange of copied foreign models and vernacular self-expression," gravitates to the prevailing Russian focus on national music and native composers.

What might be interesting in this "foreign" culture—largely dismissed by Russian scholarship—is *how* the borrowed imperial libretti, operas, and ballets were adjusted, revised, and refashioned to fit Russian tastes. In the near absence of musical scores, research into Russia's opera seria depends on published libretti, which include, along with text, detailed descriptions of stage designs, musical numbers, solos and ensembles, ballets, lists of performers, addressees, and events for which they were produced. This relatively forgotten repertoire reveals a lineage that led to nineteenth-century nationalist heroic Russian opera.

Celebratory theater—the operatic affirmation of sovereign bodies, "reactualized as a force that is primordial, timeless, and sacred"[108]—was developed and polished in European courts long before reaching Russia. In St. Petersburg's court, opera seria and other court musical theatricals were entwined and shaped by densely knotted social and artistic processes: (1) the four tsarinas' embrace of operatic genres as a major agency of their social, gender, state, and global politics; (2) the meteoric transition from seventeenth-century tsardom to dynamic Western empire and a European-style court;[109] and (3) the introduction of opera and a quest for Russian theater that matched and rivaled its Western counterparts. Adapting and intending to surpass ceremonial theater developed in European capitals, the Imperial She—both Russia and the empresses—extended Her expansionist trope to include the European cultural terrain.

Opera seria, "a school for the nation" and kings[110] that exemplified the sublime world it represented and idealized, reached Russia during Anna's rule. The empress, with one foot in the European enlightenment and the other in the tsarina's terem, favored Italian comedy. Intermedi such as *The False Cuckold, The Successful Deceit, The Husband Gambler,* and *The Wife Prude* resembled Anna's home entertainment: multiple mock beatings enacted by her fools and scenes such as one with the buffoon Padrillo, upon the order of Anna, bedding a goat.[111] During the first years of her reign, the Russian court was introduced to fifty-four spectacles, of which forty-two were comedies.[112] Nevertheless, the Italian operatic troupe Anna rushed to request from the King of Saxony in the first month of her reign finally arrived and staged Russia's first opera seria, *La forza dell'amore e dell'odio,* by Francesco Araia, in 1736.

For five months in 1738, eighteen issues of the *St. Petersburg News* educated the Russian court with a newspaper serial called "Opera and Its History."[113] Situating opera seria as "the best entertainment . . . honored at great courts and famous republics," the author differentiated the genre from tragedy and from comedy, the latter "sometimes showing people of the lowest conditions. . . . "[114]

> Besides gods and brave heroes opera [seria] permits no one [on stage]. Everything in it is noble, majestic and astounding. Presenting past times and the innocent bliss of a human king, it shows happy shepherds and joyful shepherdesses.[115]

From one issue to the next, the paper covered operatic productions in all European courts, concluding the series with a discussion of *La forza del amore*, presented for Anna's birthday.[116]

The next two operas that Araia composed for Anna, followed by Adolf Hasse's *La clemenza di Tito* staged for Elisabeth, signaled the midcentury achievement of harmonious union between imperial ceremony and opera. As in other European capitals, the events of the monarch's birth, name day, the marriages of her relatives, victories and state anniversaries, and most important coronations were marked by operas, some of which are listed below[117]:

La forza del amore e del odio/ *Sila liubvi i nenavisti*	Araia	Anna's birthday, 1736
Il finto Nino, ovvero La *Semiramide riconosciuta/* *Pritvornyi Nin ili* *Uznannaia Semiramida*	Araia, Metastasio (rev. F. Silvani)	Anna's birthday, 1737
La clemenza di Tito/ *Miloserdie Tita*	Hasse, Metastasio (Dalelo/Madonis)	Elisabeth's coronation, 1742 Elisabeth's birthday, 1742
Seleuco/Selevk	Araia, Bonecchi	Elisabeth's coronation anniversary, 1744 Peace with Sweden, 1746
Bellerofont	Araia, Bonecchi	Elisabeth's birthday, 1750 Elisabeth's coronation anniversary, 1753
Scipion	Araia, Bonecchi	Wedding of Catherine II and Peter III, 1745 Elisabeth's name day, 1746
Alessandro nell'Indie	Araia, Metastasio	Elisabeth's birthday, 1753 Elisabeth's birthday, 1755 Elisabeth's coronation, 1756 Anniversary of wedding of Catherine II and Peter III, 1759

L'Olimpiade	Manfredini, Metastasio	Catherine II's coronation, 1762
	Manfredini, Metastasio	Catherine II's name day, 1762
	Traetta, Metastasio	Catherine II's name day, 1769

Mastered by Pietro Metastasio, dramma per musica used stock characters and followed formulaic plotlines. Stripping the formula to its basics, one finds in the operas listed above a cast of characters, typically six: a king or counsel (of Persia, Syria, India, or various Greek city-states); two young couples, including a set of siblings, often a sister and brother (the king's heir); and another male figure, the ruler's associate, possibly duplicitous. The king, misled by circumstances, wrong advice, or his own passion, disavows the couples. The four young lovers, faced with moral dilemmas and physical challenges, are thrown into an emotional tempest aimed to arouse anxiety in the spectators. Recurrent contemplation of suicide and threats of execution keep the audience in suspense, but nobody takes anyone's life and one rarely ends one's own, unless after exhausting all ploys he is left with only one alternative, to exit life (and the stage) heroically (*Selevk*). Love stories, though central to the plots of the imperial operas, relate to significant conflicts involving the king's pride and honor (*Bellerofont*), filial revenge (*Selevk, La forza*), political ascendance or military victory (*Alessandro nell'Indie*). Young female characters are often associated with Arcadian gardens (*L'Olimpiade*). Even when heroic and strong, they are often controlled by their fathers and brothers. Conflicting loyalties are an engine of the drama. With moral obligations directed "ever upward from lovers, friends, counselors, and confidantes, to fathers, brothers, and sisters, and finally to kings," this drama of loyalty and devotion constitutes what Martha Feldman identifies as "scalar movement," with the king [empress] "at the apex" of public concerns, embodying the same idealized hierarchy enacted in imperial ceremonies.[118]

After magnificently staged battles, weddings, sacred rituals, multiple imprisonments, clever disguises, and cross-dressing, the couples reconcile at the end—most often with the king showing clemency, to his and everyone's delight. Ballets inserted, in the tradition of opera seria, after each act fall into several categories: ethnic vignettes (Japanese ballet in *La forza*, a ballet of the world's people in *Selevk*), portrayals of nymphs and zephyrs, mythical scenes (*L'Olimpiade*), and semi-independent stories. Stage sets—regal palaces, thrones, city squares, courtyards, and temples—frame magnificent coronations, weddings, sacred rituals, and Olympic games, typically at least two kingly settings per opera.[119] Thus opera seria clearly drew a parallel between a real ruler and operatic kingship. The universal imagery was flexible enough that, with some tweaking, it could be identified with a specific monarch or empress. Presenting an elevated moral drama, the opera's formula could be tailored to time-and-place-specific situations. Attuned to the Russian imperial scenario, the operas were supplied with staged prologues, which, like the processional "Triumphant Minerva," implied political circumstances and imperial agendas. The ballets featured battles and the conquests of ethnic, often Oriental others; portrayed antique or magical domains; and mirrored imperial celebrations, for which those operas were produced. Operatic choruses entwined the name of the ruling empress with an Arcadian heroine. Praising the powerful and merciful king, the choruses equated him with the Russian Majesty, turning to and addressing her on an alternative stage. The operas thus reciprocated the empresses' dual gender role of triumphant monarch-warrior and virtuous mistress.

Operatic spectacles in the court were state events. Ordered to attend productions as "their duty,"[120] courtiers, along with foreign ambassadors, waited for Her Majesty Elisabeth's entrance. Like state parades and official ceremonies, the play took place only when attended by the empress (or, in the second half of the century, by the ducal couple). The schedule of theatrical productions (by Italian, French, German, as well as Russian troupes), the time, the dress code, and the seating arrangements were dictated by the empresses themselves.[121] From the first year of Anna's reign and on her order, the programs of commedia dell'arte and later Italian operas and other theatricals were issued in Russian translation along with the language of the original. The opera programs resembled Russian *Descriptions* of imperial coronations, weddings, and private masquerade spectacles. The abundant choruses in opera seria produced in Russia echoed religious and secular kants sung to monarchs during accession ceremonies and state events.

Differing in their personalities, governance style, and personal fancies, yet with the vigor they displayed in diplomacy and warfare in both East and West,[122] the Russian empresses instituted their theaters. Like monarchs elsewhere in Europe,[123] the Russian Majesties frequented rehearsals—Elisabeth coming to a newly built theater "through specially constructed corridors directly from her room."[124] They dressed, critiqued, and befriended actors, the glitter of regal roles played by both sides perhaps creating a peculiar invisible bond between them.

Entering the theater, an empress enacted two major roles: lead actress and exemplary spectator. The events on stage were symbolically and allegorically connected to her and her empire. Affirming the intrinsic ties between ceremonial and spectacular, political and behavioral, she perfected courtly etiquette. The noble audience observed her every move, smile, nod, fluttering fan, departure—her responses to events on the stage followed by fellow spectators. Thus, with the lead actress in an imperial balcony not unlike the stage, the spectacle had two foci. Across from the stage—featuring a heroic king at times played by a female actress—sat the empress, situated in a majestic frame, the two engaged in a play of reflection. As a common practice, at the order of the monarch the spectators attended operas in masks and costumes, expanding the performative space beyond the stage, converging stage and state. Voices of ineffable beauty filled the performance arena, as Olympian characters loaned their acoustic power to Russian empresses.

The connection of singing king and real empress extended beyond the symbolic level. In the course of the spectacle, singers referred to the empress, she herself becoming a character in the play. For example, *Le Rivali* by Lodovico Lazzaroni and Vincenzo Manfredini,[125] a staged cantata for the third anniversary of Catherine II's investiture, unfolded as a rivalry between Minerva and Venus in Jupiter's quarters, while the performance itself took place in the empress's magnificent residence at Tsarskoe Selo—doubling as Jupiter's palace.[126] Apollo's attempt to resolve the dispute inspires the first vocal solo of self-praising Minerva, "Goddess of Arts, Science and the Hope of Heroes, . . . who leads the warrior's hand for him to be brave on the battlefield."[127] Jupiter, emerging when Venus sings her self-promoting air, ends the argument between his peevish daughters by asking Apollo whether there is "anyone in the human race endowed with the virtues and rare gifts of both goddesses?" Delighted, Apollo immediately responds that "the whole universe reveres the Great Heroine that reigns over (*vsevladychestvuet*) the Russian empire . . . In her alone shine the majestic beauty and supreme virtues of all the gods."[128]

Minerva admits Her Majesty's superiority and Venus does not "risk competing with Her." Next, Jupiter sings an air, beseeching everyone to turn eyes to the "divine perfection of EKATERINA"—the noncompeting winner of the Olympic contest, and the only name capitalized in the program. The cantata announcing the four singers in fact engages five actors, Her Majesty's salient role attesting to the power of silence in musical performance.[129] She "bears the image of Jupiter himself," and the final chorus resounds in adulation: "O Father of Gods, we adore/In Her the image of yours we glorify."[130]

Emblemizing both masculine and feminine elements, the empress was in some operas identified with more than one character. For instance, the opera *Bellerofont* by court poet Bonecchi and composer Araia,[131] produced for an anniversary of Elisabeth's enthronement (1750), equated her with the title hero. A young orphan prince, deprived of his father, his bride, and his state and betrayed by close kin who usurped power and plotted his destruction, Bellerofont rises above all challenges to regain his kingdom. The story of the operatic hero reflected Elisabeth's path to the Russian throne. Unveiling the true identity of the hero, the libretto points out that "the chorus, in an allegorical way, under the name of Bellerofont, sings praises to Her Majesty."[132] Battling both Chimera and furies, Bellerofont entreats the help of Minerva, who descends from the clouds as a *deus ex machina*. Everyone on stage joins in the choral accolade to "Her Goodness," adulating Elisabeth. Thus the image of the empress imparted via her acting surrogates embraced terrestrial and celestial, male and female dominions—the "She" that she crafted by cross-dressing in masquerades.

The operatic stage allowed the empress to be identified with and simultaneously rise above Russia. For Elisabeth's coronation, Hasse's *La clemenza di Tito* was shown with a prologue by Staehlin entitled "Insulted But Again Rejoicing Russia."[133] Ruthenia (the personification of Russia), in the midst of darkness and disaster (alluding to preceding reigns),[134] "recalls the blissful times of Peter the Great" and pleads for "Peter's blood," Russia's only savior, Elisabeth. As the horizon lights up and the sun rises, from the clouds Astraea/Elisabeth descends with the "high name of Her Imperial Majesty on her shield," surrounded by a chorus of her Majesty's Virtues. Below from the four corners of the theater/world come groups of Europeans, Asians, Africans, and Americans—all singing praises to their empress.[135] Thus the prologue was enacted by three female leads: Ruthenia and Astraea on stage and Elisabeth in the balcony. Ruthenia unveils a monument to Elisabeth—"Mother of the Fatherland, Joy of mankind, and the Tito of our times"—as the international chorus links Elisabeth and Tito:

Титова, когда рука Римский скиптр держала.	Tito, whose hand held the Roman scepter.
Образ коего и мы зрим на троне ныне	Whose image we see on the throne now
И того днесь похвалы сплетем богине.[136]	And from this day [we'll] weave praise to our goddess.

The operatic setting is a "supremely prosperous city square, decorated with many arcades and showing a chorus of citizens [on the stage], . . . patricians, senators, and guards."[137] The emperor-hero, enacted by the female singer Giorgy, reflects the luster of the real empress. Elisabeth remains the one and only *authentic* performer of Her Imperial Self, present in the sight of everyone attending the spectacle.

Despite its generic plot, an opera seria chosen for a celebration befitted the occasion and pointed to specific events in Russia. Bonecchi/Araia's *Selevk*,[138] for example, was produced for a double event: an anniversary of Elisabeth's coronation and the "eternal peace" between Her Majesty and the Swedish Crown. The peace treaty with Sweden (1743) was conditioned on Russia's choice of the next Swedish king; Elisabeth chose Adolf Frederick—an elder brother of her late betrothed prince. She also announced Peter III as her own successor and wedded him to the future Catherine II. Like the operatic Vologez from *Selevk*, Elisabeth secured the two crowns. Besides political reasons, her decisions were motivated by her sentimental fealty—also not unlike noble Vologez. At the end of *Selevk*, "from the sky descends a machine picturing the temple of glory, inside which, among the orderly placed depictions of gods and heroes, is elevated a portrait of Her Imperial Majesty. The final chorus is a harbinger of nineteenth-century Slavas"[139]:

Не можем ТЯ ИМПЕРАТРИЦА,	[We] can't compare YOU, EMPRESS
Героям прежним уподобить	with past heroes
ТВОЕ ВЕЛИЧЕСТВО и храбрость,	YOUR GREATNESS and courage
ТВОИ победы и щедроты	YOUR victory and generosity
Их честь и память омрачают	Eclipse their memory . . . .
Гласит ЕЯ вселенной имя	To sing HER universal name
Краса! Краса всея природы	Beauty! Beauty of all the nature
Пример живых и честь бессмертных . . . .[140]	An example to the living and honor to immortals . . . .

The choruses proliferating in celebratory operas signified the omnipresence of the empress. For example, in *Scipion*, staged at the wedding of Peter III and Catherine II, the chorus "under the names of Scipion [the king], Sifaks and Nirena the regal couple, recites praise to Her Majesty and the wedded ducal couple"[141]—both entertaining the audience and asserting Russian court hierarchy.

The prominence of choruses, unusual for Italian opera seria by Metastasio, who exhibited "little interest in ensembles,"[142] became a trademark of Russian opera. Staehlin's account makes Elisabeth responsible for choruses on the Russian stage; learning that in the coronation performance of *La clemenza di Tito* the emperor was to sing praises to himself, Elisabeth ordered the court cappella to sing these lines as a chorus. "Italian words written in Russian letters" were distributed among the four-part chorus of fifty selected singers.[143] Indeed the longstanding tradition of Russian church singing, secular choral panegyrics, and cantatas laid the foundation for the "inimitable" operatic choruses that after *La clemenza* "were used in operas as well as in court festivals and chamber performances."[144] Just as classical emperors stood for the Russian empress, the singing crowd represented the Russian folk and foreign observers, glorifying operatic surrogates of the female monarch.

Unlike many operatic renditions of *L'Olimpiade*, two Russian versions, one by Vincenzo Manfredini for Catherine II's coronation (1762) and the other by Tommaso Traetta (1769) for Her Majesty's birthday, were interspersed with choruses, the second opera including seven choral episodes.[145] One of "Metastasio's subtlest and most beguiling" texts,[146] *L'Olimpiade* presented its spectators with a plethora of excitement. Framed by large-scale majestic scenes—Olympic games and a ritualistic sacrifice, the latter disrupted and swiftly replaced by a double wedding—the opera dealt with four possible suicides and one attempted, the execution of a hero on a sacred altar, and endless disguises, as well as double-talk and multiple confusions. The spectators find themselves more acutely aware of situations than do the lead characters wrapped in a web of mutual misunderstanding.

A particularly interesting image is Argena, an aristocratic woman redressed as a shepherdess (and also a nymph), accidentally appearing in the suite of noble Aristea. Argena fuses high drama with an element of teasing and irony, a precursor of comic heroines that captured the Russian audience from the last quarter of the century onward. The noble maiden redressed as an Arcadian shepherdess, a bijou of French and French-like Russian plays and operas, linked drama with comedy; navigated among Italian, French, German, and Russian theater; bridged myth and fairy tale; and set the standard for female leads—a peasant acting as a princess, dressed as a picturesque rustic girl playing a nymph. But before that, in the later years of Elisabeth's reign, comic operas and heroic pastorals became a part of the celebratory repertoire; Baldassare Galuppi's *Il filosofo di campagna,* on Carlo Goldoni's text and Francesco Zoppis's *La Galatea,* on Metastasio's libretto (1760), were performed at Her Majesty's name days.[147]

Although comic opera in Russia appeared more appetizing to courtly audiences than serious opera, by midcentury Italian opera seria was prospering on the Russian imperial stage. French and German troupes likewise flourished in the capital, when Elisabeth became enticed by the Russian tragedies created by Sumarokov. "She was never tired of seeing these tragedies"—wrote duchess and later empress Catherine II—"she took care of the costumes, herself applied rouge, and one could see how the whole troupe, dressed for a spectacle, came directly from Her Majesty's private quarters."[148] Sumarokov's first plays, officially approved by his professors Lomonosov and Trediakovsky, were enacted by his fellow students before Her Majesty—in her palace,[149] in the opera house, and the theater at Peterhof. Written and performed in Russian, Sumarokov's tragedies, several of them dealing with Russian history and mythology, closely followed the Metastasian operatic model.[150] One of Sumarokov's early plays, *Semira* (1751), invoked an association with her namesake in the Metastasian *Artaserse.* Though Sumarokov's play refers to Russian historical figures, the plot has no relation to historical events. Instead, the Russian *Semira* matches typical Metastasian plots, "oscillating continually between the demands of public duty and private desire."[151]

Recycling and Russifying *Seria*

From one celebratory production to the next, the operas, cantatas, and ballets replayed the formula of European majestic representation, increasingly adjusted to the Russian imperial scene. Not only did Italian seria function as a decoration for the Russian crown and affirm the Russian monarch's radiance; the plots and characters, as remote as they were, served the immediate political and social goals of the empire. In doing so, celebratory productions began to usurp operatic images of East and West to match Russia's imperial lore. Characters traveled from one opera to the other, woven into revised libretti conveying complex cross-referential associations. A few connected pieces of repertoire briefly introduced here lead from *Artaserse* (1738) to *Semira* to Domenico Angiolini's ballet *Semira* (1772), and to Catherine's *Early Reign of Oleg* (1791), and from Metastasio's *Alessandro* (1725) to Bogdanovich's *Slaviane* (1787). Cross-textual allusions, an essential element of the nineteenth-century literary realm, are discussed in later chapters and continue as the core of twentieth-century Russian literary and operatic experiences. Like other libretti of Metastasio, *Artaserse* was adapted by a number of European composers. In St. Petersburg, an *Artaserse* created by Araia was staged during Anna's reign and published in Russian.[152]

The plotline of *Artaserse* that Feldman draws in her analysis closely resembles the drama of siblings and lovers in Sumarokov's *Semira*.[153] The heroine in both is caught between two young men (Rostislav/Artaserse and Oskol'd/Arbace) tied to different clans—her relatives' and the ruler's. In *Semira*, a devoted sister (of Oskol'd) and a passionate lover (of Rostislav) fluctuates between the two: her assiduous support of her brother endangers her lover, and her subsequent remorse and aid for her lover lead to her brother's fall. Like her Metastasian counterpart, the Russian Semira belongs to a family that, though related to the king, occupies a subordinate social position and battles for power. The rightful ruler, representing a just cause, is the Russian prince Oleg. Feldman writes that "there is always a mythical sovereignty that is Ours and other less legitimate ones that are Theirs. Who exactly Ours is is not important."[154] The question of Ours and Theirs is significant in *Semira*, which deals not with symbolic distant heroes but with Russian historical figures. The images of the merciful and stoic ruler Oleg and his earnest son Rostislav (literally, Growing-glory) contrast with those of Oskol'd and Semira, the bearers of non-Russian names and identities. Could Semira, foreign to the cast of Russian heroes, imply the otherness of Western drama to Russian theater? At the end of the play, the expiring Oskol'd gives away his sister to Rostislav as Sumarokov appropriates the Metastasian dramatic formula. Just as Semira becomes assimilated into the tsar's family, foreign drama was adapted to Russian culture.

Some twenty years after Sumarokov's play, Angiolini used it as the basis for his tragic ballet pantomime. The victories of Oleg and his image as a forefather of modern eighteenth-century Russia, continuously invoked in historical and literary works and in drama and ballet during the last decades of the century, would reappear in Catherine's *Oleg* (which will be discussed in Chapter Four). Freeing itself from "theatrical rules"[155] and from the formulaic plotline of seria (omitting Semira or Rostislav), Catherine's opera pageant[156] focused on the heroic ventures of Oleg, who liberated old Russia's capital Kiev and afterward led a massive fleet to Byzantium. When victorious Oleg enters the city in Catherine's opera, the Byzantine king treats him with Olympic games (*L'Olimpiade*) and a production of a fragment from the classical *Alceste*. If Sumarokov's *Semira* adapts foreign heroine/drama, Catherine's *Oleg* appropriates native history and forges contemporary heroic opera. As shown in the following chapters, Oleg joins the khorovod of mighty Tito, Scipion, Jupiter, Minerva, Astraea, and Alessandro— surrogates of the Russian empress, the only authentic ruler.

The dichotomy of European and native elements in late-eighteenth-century Russian theater reveals some intriguing patterns. For example, one of the most enduring European myths—the painted, woven,[157] and sung tale of Alexander's victorious voyage to India,[158] dramatized by Metastasio and adapted by at least twenty-five composers over some fifty years (1730–1784[159])—was also favored in the Russian court, especially under Elisabeth.[160] Dainty Bogdanovich, Catherine's court poet, the author of idylls, love poems, sacred cantatas, fairy tales, and plays very much in the fashion of the day,[161] rewrote Metastasio's *Alessandro nell'Indie* into his *Slaviane*—an opera with choruses and ballet, both discussed in Chapter Four.

In *Alessandro*, the Macedonian emperor, defeating the Indian ruler Por and falling for his beloved princess Cleofide, honors her commitment to her lover Por and finally stages their wedding. In *Slaviane*, the manipulative Cleofide is replaced by Dobroslava (Kind-glory), a Slavic princess, who appears in the modest and dignified terem-like company of her maid (Milogliada, "Nice-look") and an older peasant woman (Potap'evna). In the course of Bogdanovich's drama, the female Slavic trio, placed against a trio of Greek men of fame, demonstrates the superior qualities associated with the "Slavs' kindness, simplicity, and loyalty requiring no commands."[162] As in the case of Triumphant Minervas—the masquerade and ballet—different theatrical productions formed dialogical relations, which conveyed their intertextual meaning.

Slaviane, dedicated to a quarter-century of Catherine's rule, concludes with a monumental festival: Genius accompanies operatic Alexander and his people offstage to the "right side of the amphitheatre for him to see [the spectacle]." The setting—the Greek emperor and his suite across from the real empress—forms a two-sided mirror with the two lead actors doubling as spectators. When the chorus of "famous Slavs," filling the space of the theater and following Ruslan and Dobroslava, sing the "Slava" to Catherine, the performing space rotates; the empress becomes the lead, with the emperor "observing."

By the late 1780s, not only did European Greco-Roman heroes come to duplicate, replace, venerate, learn from, and submit to Russian empresses, but native mythology and opera thrived under and against the influence of European theater. Catherine's birthdays, name days, and coronation anniversaries were celebrated with operas of her own creation.[163] The celebratory productions of the late century also revealed another strand, a playful and sometimes ironic replay of "high style" in a pastoral setting such as Bogdanovich's *Radost' Dushin'ki* [Joy of Dushen'ka],[164] a one-act "lyric comedy" with ballet. Attended by Her Majesty (1786), it was a doubly playful remake of Bogdanovich's own poem *Dushen'ka* dedicated to and introduced as a pastoral invocation of the empress in the style of la Fontaine's *Amour and Psyche*.

From the early nineteenth century and throughout the socialist era, Russian literary luminaries, musical critics, and scholars commonly disregarded eighteenth-century operatic theater. Even when acknowledging early Russian theater as the forerunner of the esteemed national opera of the next century, writers focused on comic and folk themes largely modeled on disguise comedies and Arcadian pastorals. The operas promoted and staged in the court and by the empresses along with a number of foreign composers were disavowed as merely imitative. Compiling an impressive list of European composers who lived and worked in eighteenth-century Russia—"leased [mail-ordered] for court service together with French chefs, barbers, Italian decorators, costume-makers, and bakers"[165]—later generations of native scholars proclaimed them "the creators of palatial operatic art . . . abstract, virtuosic, pompous, and cold."[166] Yet exploring the political and cultural dynamics of eighteenth-century Russia one might conclude that the inferiority complex toward the West and the battle against it became a trope of nineteenth-century intellectuals. By contrast, the contextualization of operatic productions in relation to imperial ceremony shows that operatic theater, much like the policies the empresses pursued, manifested a culture of conquest: taken by storm, adapted and adjusted to Russian taste, Italian opera and its ancient gods and heroes gave Russians a model for native mythology subservient to Russia's imperial sublime.

Exploring the circle of major state rituals, parades, masquerades, and theatricals makes apparent not only the ties between these social genres but also a reciprocity between state and stage. Emerging as an extension of imperial celebration, serious opera from its inception in Russia became part of political narrative. Abstract libretti and allegories were attuned to Russian concerns, distant plotlines revised and adjusted to native history, as the operatic royalty impersonated the ruling empress.

Spectators recognized Her Majesty in foreign emperors, princesses, gods, warriors, and Arcadian heroines—a fact little explored in post-eighteenth-century literature. Young or old, man or woman, kingly or idyllic, her identity was signaled by various shared codes; she could be identified with gardens, with Russian nymphs and water pools, with the conquered Orient, adulating choruses, the polonaise, and indeed with the leading role.

Audience recognition of empresses as a part of spectacles, so critical to eighteenth-century serious operas, leads to a question: What happened to these imperial figures and their flamboyant musical soundscape in the rising nineteenth-century operas? So extreme was the representation of Russian imperial sublime, so exuberant the praise! Nothing seemed enough to match *her* glory, and yet there seemed to be nothing new to add—besides irony, which, sprouting in the eighteenth century, blossomed in the nineteenth.

2

THE PLAY OF POSSIBILITIES
SERFS ENACTING ARISTOCRATS, COUNTESSES PLAYING PEASANTS

Анюта на себе алмазов не имела,

Но души попленить смотрителей умела.

Анюта выросла, сказали мне, в лесах.

Неправда, выросла она на небесах

Aniuta wore no diamonds,

But spectators' souls she could beguile.

She grew up, I was told, in the woods;

It's a lie, she grew up in the skies.

(Alexander Sumarokov, "*Aniuta*"[1])

"White-milky round-faced"[2] Aniuta became a darling of eighteenth-century Russian comic opera. Disguises, traversals, and surprises, though quite different from opera seria, matched the spirit of masquerade reigning in the Russian court and culminating in the age of Catherine II.

Aniuta, emblemizing a play of possibilities, appeared as the title character of Mikhail Popov's *Aniuta* (1772) and the lead in Iakov Kniazhnin and Vasily Pashkevich's *Misfortune from a Coach* (1779), Ivan Krylov's *Coffeegrounds-Reader* (1784), and Alexander Ablesimov's *The Miller—Wizard, Cheat, and Matchmaker* (1779).[3] Approaching her wedding in the finale of one opera, Aniuta launches into a new romance in the next. In her love affairs, the peasant girl shows a consistent preference for love over money—except when her beloved is a local nobleman, Victor, in Popov's opera. Then again, full of surprises, in another opera she appears as the long-lost heiress of a distinguished aristocrat. In yet another, she is half-noble and half-peasant, her identity debated by her parents—her mother an impoverished noblewoman and her father a peasant, each anxious to marry her within their own class (*The Miller*). Aniuta and her counterparts who populated comic operas get kidnapped and tricked, their lovers nearly sold or recruited into the army. She battles for her lad, using her wits, cleverness, and biting tongue. She speaks in crude, folksy language but gives inklings of noble bearing. She sings folk songs, urban romances, and fashionable airs.

Quintessentially a Russian heroine from an obscure native village, a bearer of common sense, peasant wit, and rustic sentiment, enticing and faithful Aniuta was actually borrowed from French *opéra comique*.[4] Staehlin recalled that

> in the summer, several courtiers—men and women—learned the French comedy *Le Philosophe marié honteux de l'être* and the comic opera *Annette et Lubin*, aiming for a performance during the winter carnivals in the theater of Count Stroganov. The project came to hand when in November the court and the city celebrated the happy outcome of the Empress's and Grand Duke's smallpox inoculation. . . . In the comic opera, countess Bariatinskaia as Annette and count Buturlin-Lubin both played with ease and dexterity as if they had spent many years on stage. The orchestra of native noble dilettantes . . . , approximately thirty of them, played various instruments, mainly violins, flutes, and cellos. The most distinguished were the Princess of Courland, baroness Cherkasova—harpsichord; the brothers Naryshkin, Count Stroganov, Senator Trubetskoi . . . and the officers of the imperial guard.[5]

Charles-Simon Favart's *Annette et Lubin*, introduced at Catherine II's court (1764) and soon refashioned into the Russian *Aniuta*, began a stream of native comic operas. Five years after the début of *Annette* in the Imperial Court Theater, *Aniuta* premiered in the empress's theater in Tsarskoe Selo. The heroine's original partner Lubin/Lubim (literally "beloved") took on a love life of his own four years later in Nikolai Nikolev's *Rozana and Lubim* (1776).[6] *The Miller* likewise premiered in the court theater.

Like opera seria, comic opera enjoyed the patronage of the head of state and the aristocratic elite. But while serious opera displayed majestic figures entangled in complicated lofty plotlines, comic opera introduced characters that teased and toyed with disguised social identities. Opera seria elevated, above all, the image of radiant omnipotent emperors—though in the Russian context, they were identified with the monarchical She. Comic operas starred a female heroine, whether a Russian version of an Arcadian shepherdess or a Russified French Annette. In the last decades of the century, comic opera heroines evolved from lighthearted Aniutas to tearful Ninas, leading to the dolorous, devoted native maidens or wives who would populate the operatic stage in the next century. These sentimental peasant love stories, which hit a soft spot with Russian aristocrats, were performed by professional companies and private theaters, by permanent and touring Italian, French, and German troupes along with Russian actors who resided in St. Petersburg and Moscow.

This chapter focuses on private theater involving two poles of Russian society: aristocratic dilettantes and serf performers. The comic and sentimental opera they performed featured social traversal. The playful countesses and picturesque peasants in comic operas were enacted by aristocrats on their home stages, or by real peasants in private serf theaters. On stage, an operatic peasant girl suddenly discovering her aristocratic origin could be portrayed by a countess dressed like and imitating her servant, or the part of a countess could be played by a serf girl impersonating her mistress. The traversal of social roles written into the libretti of comic operas involving dressed-up or dressed-down actors made comic opera an experimental performative space that simultaneously defied and solidified the class structure. Also, in the carnivalesque spirit cultivated in the Russian women's kingdom, social re-dressing as a breach of class boundaries—from a shepherdess to a countess, and from a prince to a fool—sometimes provoked transgressions that spilled beyond the theatrical stage. At the intersection of multiple transgressions lies the playful operatic story of a heroine such as Aniuta and the intense social drama of the serf prima donna, the central figure in every serf troupe.

Social Cross-Dressing: Making Serf into Tsarina, Countess into Peasant

The comic operas produced in private theaters point to several types of social/operatic cross-dressing. The first, contained in the texts and plots of the operas, involves the social class cross-dressing of operatic characters—a countess disguised as a peasant, for instance, or a peasant who turns out to be a countess. Writing about masquerade during the French enlightenment, Amy S. Wyngaard uses the term cross-dressing to identify a kind of social class transgression. She suggests that "clothing" becomes a "highly charged symbol . . . of social codes and hierarchies," and "the (il)legibility of clothing emerges as a dominant theme in literary and theatrical representation."[7] A rustic girl exhibiting noble sensibilities or reemerging in the course of the opera as an aristocratic maiden offers intriguing possibilities.

In the Russian context, a second type of cross-dressing happened between the performers and the characters they enacted. A princess or a countess might play French Aniuta in the language of the original, or impersonate a Russian rustic girl by imitating local peasant dialects, using a few strong colloquial words, imitating manners, singing songs, and jeering at the nobles' life style. A number of illegitimate offspring bearing the abridged names of the highest aristocratic elite—usually with first syllable omitted, such as Betsky from Triubetskoi, Temkina from Potemkin, Remeteva from

Sheremetev and many others with no names or recognition[8]—could remind the noble spectator of cross-dressed Aniuta. When Princess Bariatinskaia appeared as a peasant girl, she charmed an audience that was well aware of her social standing. Meanwhile, in the serf theater that belonged to the family or neighbor of an aristocratic dilettante, a serf girl, turned at her owner's whim into an actress, might perform her own peasant "self" with a touch of noble finesse, exploring all the possibilities of the character to better satisfy her master's fancy.

Though providing assurance of the existing order, comic opera also hints at social mobility. With female characters traversing the class divide, and their performers occupying opposite extremes of the social spectrum, the prominence of operatic cross-dressing raises hypothetical issues about the inversion of social norms and roles. Wyngaard writes about the potential peril and "subversive nature" of temporary exchange of identities.[9] Penny Gay, researching theater in early modern England, likewise finds "danger" to an audience in being exposed to a "play of the possibilities" that could be transgressed in life.[10] What might cross the mind of an aristocratic spectator when a serf girl, whom he could bed any day or whip, sell or give in marriage, exposes on stage feelings not unlike those of his sisters, daughters, wife, or mistresses? Her acting role could extend offstage.

In the domain of Russian serf theater, the danger—the third type of social transgression—occurred when, inspired by operatic fictional pastorals and romances, real people enacted comic operatic plots in their own lives, intentionally or accidentally crossing extreme social boundaries. Not scripted by a librettist or composer, such cross-dressing might not have the happy ending of comic opera. In real life, the play of possibilities was constrained by social hierarchies. The dichotomy of transgression and reinforcement was especially tangled in Count Nikolai Sheremetev's theater, where a romantic operatic scenario was replayed in real life by the count and his famous serf star. Their love story epitomized the artistic paradigm and social danger in the last decades of eighteenth-century Russia. Inevitably, cross-dressing in this context forced the issue of entangled gender-class relations, which were probed and continuously revised in a reflective exchange between life and theater.

Aniuta as a Culture Guide

The clear plots and Aniuta's relatively simple nature enable multiple transgressions and reversals. In the French *Annette*, the pregnant heroine and her cousin Lubin, disobeying the laws of consanguinity, achieve a blissful marriage with the help of their *seigneur du village*. Russian versions, breaching no legal system, situate the heroine in a perfectly common domestic frame, within which her happiness is decided among three men: her father, her lover, and an alternative suitor. The heroine's father, consistent with Claude Lévi-Strauss's "rule of the gift," exchanges the object-gift-bride with the receiver; however, a girl's feelings in eighteenth-century comic operas are typically taken into consideration.[11] The libretto of *Aniuta* features a dispute between a father and a couple; the daughter's suitor (incidentally a wealthy aristocrat) arranges a different type of exchange, bribing the father. Typically a blissful path to marriage is disturbed by a third man, an irritator, who surfaces in the plot. Developing an appetite for the girl, he, a local supervisor or owner himself, creates a conflict that drives the libretto. In *The Miller*, there is no alternative "suitor;" the canny title hero—who on his own merit, like Aniuta, parades from one opera to another—gives the groom two identities, befitting the conflicting inclinations of the heroine's socially unequal parents. In the operatic finale the riddle with which the Miller introduces the groom— "himself a landlord and a peasant, himself a serf and owner"[12]—leads to a happy resolution. The Miller and his counterparts, the Fool (in *Misfortune*) and the Coffeegrounds-Reader (*Coffeegrounds-Reader*), much like the doctor-pretender in Molière's *Le Médecin malgré lui,* spin an intrigue and eventually arrange the heroine's wedding.

Aniuta's operas exude humor and trickery. For example, drawing on various French sources,[13] Russian comic operas, in an ironic twist, exposed and ridiculed native Gallomania. In *The Coffeegrounds-Reader*, Aniuta's matron, Novomodova ("New-fashion"), is appalled by the "foolish Russian habit of calling each other by name and patronymic." In France, "everyone is called madam or damsel—only our Russian fools can float so infinitely adrift." When in *Misfortune from a Coach*, Aniuta's lover Lukyan faces the threat of being sold in exchange for a French coach desired by his landlord, the rustic pair suddenly remembers a few French words that win over their "sophisticated" owner, who exclaims, "Parbleu! I would never have believed that Russian people could love that affectionately, I am stunned! Am I not in France?"

With her fellow peasant friends Aniuta jeers urbanites—incidentally her spectators in Moscow, St. Petersburg, and other cities:

Да ведь я не горожанка,	I'm not a city girl
Чтоб стыда-то мне не знать	For me not to know shame.
(*Kofeinitsa*)	(*Coffeegrounds-Reader*)

Aniuta is a striking hybrid of idyllic shepherdesses à la Rousseau, the shrewd servants of Pierre Beaumarchais, the flock of maids who led directly to Mozart's Suzanna, and serf girls from the Russian provinces. In Vasily Kolychev's *Futile Jealousy or the Coachman from Kuskovo* (1781), specially created for the Sheremetevs and featuring as a main player their Kuskovo estate, rustic Aniuta reconnects with her original partner Lubin. The scenery on the open-air stage reflected the park, lake, river, and overall perfectly designed landscape of the estate—a metaphor of theater as a mirror enacted literally. A singing gardener leads a tour of "a beautiful grotto . . . of spiral shells, the orangery . . . the Hermitage and the Dutch house, the Italian house, all the gazebos and the birdhouse near the pond."[14] At the end of the opera, the gardener recites his important line: "our life's happiness was to see our empress here." Responding to the mention of Her Majesty, a big chorus sings, an orchestra plays, and cannons discharge—the comic opera echoing state rituals and serious operas.

Aniuta, a peasant of possibly noble origin, may fight for her beloved like Argena, the noblewoman disguised as a shepherdess in *L'Olimpiade*. A heroine of "drama with voices"[15] as opposed to *dramma per musica*, the multiplied Aniuta and her lovers mock the threat of heroic sacrifice that permeates opera seria. Popov's Aniuta delivers oaths to die if separated from her swain, viscount Victor. Her pedestrian language turns despair into comedy:

Я жива скорей не буду,	I'd rather not be alive,
Все мученья претерплю,	I'll bear all of the pain,
Нежели тебя забуду	Should I forget you
И другого полюблю.	And fall for someone else.

Victor, learning that Aniuta's father promised her to his peasant-assistant, responds with comic outrage:

Victor:	Что! За этого страмца, за	What! For this lowlife, for this pig
	этого скотину	This will cut short my life. . . .
	сие мне жизнь первет . . .	
Aniuta:	И я свою покину	And I will leave my own.
	(*Aniuta*, Act I, Scene 6)	

Their shared desire to die for each other is echoed in a no less harmonious adieu in *Misfortune*:

Я с тобою погибаю;	I die with you;
Я тебя на век теряю.	[If] I lose you forever.
Ах! навек, навек прости!	Akh! forever, forever, forgive!
Можно ль, можно ль то спасти?	Can we, can we somehow be saved?
(Act II, Scene 3)	

The empty melodramatic threat is amusing, and until Karamzin's poor Liza (1792) and her suicide come to overshadow jovial Aniuta, she gets her way at the end of the opera, celebrating her love union. So powerful was life-loving Aniuta that Vasilii

Fedorov, adopting Karamzin's Liza for a stage production—*Liza, or the Consequences of Pride and Seduction* (1803)—refashioned her destiny in the manner of comic opera, saving the heroine from suicide, establishing her noble origin, and marrying the girl to her frivolous lover.[16]

The authorship of eighteenth-century comic operas, frequently with preexisting music, was often identified with playwrights or librettists. Published libretti in verse or mixing prose dialogues and song lyrics at times indicated the tunes of the songs; the music rarely appeared in print. Like French opera comique, Russian comic opera consisted of spoken and sung episodes. In Paris, *Annette et Lubin* (1764) marked the historical amalgamation of the theater companies Comédie-Italienne and Opéra-comique, which signaled a transition from the compilation of popular tunes in *comédie en vaudevilles* to the composed *comédie mêlée d'ariettes*. Some Russian operas had no written scores, employing native tunes or borrowing music from French comique and Italian operas. *The Coachman from Kuskovo*, for example, used an overture by Gaetano Pugnani. The score of *The Miller* mixed folk songs and composed pieces;[17] ten tunes from the opera thirteen years later appeared in *A Collection of Russian Folk Songs* by Ivan Prach and Nikolai L'vov.[18]

Musically, Aniuta and her operas stand at the intersection of oral and written musical traditions. At a time when fashionable ariettas, popular urban songs, and folk tunes brought from the Russian provinces existed in numerous manuscripts and later in published collections circulated among aristocrats, comic opera with folk "voices" (tunes) represented perhaps the most democratic musical form. Despite the social divide, it made counts and princesses learn, perform, and enjoy songs borrowed from their servants in the cities and from the peasants on their estates. At the same time, serf actors memorized French songs and fashionable ariettas, adapting them to local-native color.

The Miller: The Singing Matchmaker
Bewitching Aristocrats

After a bright courtly overture woven from several folk songs, the curtain goes up and the spectators see a miller chopping wood and humming a wordless tune. He stops and, probably winking, tests his spectators—"What is this song? . . . Yep, 'What an evening we have since midnight'"[19]—presumably, a folk song familiar to the audience (Example 2.1). In his self-introduction, Ablesimov's Miller sings about his ability to cash in on the villagers' superstitious belief that millers deal with devils. Playing on the audience's auditory expectations, the Miller in this perfectly syllabic quick-paced melody repeatedly syncopates, stretching one word: "bluff" (that is, he is a bluffer; Example 2.2).

Example 2.1

Mel'nik: Kakaia bish' eta pesnia? . . . Da, -- "Kak vechor u nas so polunochi". . . Tak . . .
Miller: (Polishing the piece of wood, and humming then says): What is this song? . . . Yes, -- "As evening till the midnight". . . So . . .

Miller: What an evening we have since midnight

Example 2.2

Miller: [He] Who is able to live by bluffing, is called by everyone a Gypsy

Peasants' fear of and need for his witchcraft, as well as his own cunning, afford the Miller a comfortable income. In the course of the opera, he receives double pay for helping lovers in the first act, cajoles gifts and drinks separately from Aniuta's well-bred mother and her peasant father in the second act, and is paid and publicly praised in the third—a good self-advertisement, especially when he sings, accompanying himself on the balalaika, and leads the opera's chorus.

Filimon, Aniuta's swain in this opera, enters the stage and, mixing rustic and sexual metaphors, bemoans the loss of his never-fed, never-watered horses. Aniuta, a desired maiden and a lucky bride, is missing in the first act of *The Miller*. Appearing in the opening of the second act, she utters two tearful songs, "In my youth I see no joy" and "If in my youth I could be sure,"[20] that convey the heroine's boredom and sexual craving. Her pained descending melody with stretched syllables in the beginning of the first song leads to an anxious accentuated rise with a thinly veiled allusion—"everything

Example 2.3

Ka - by - ia, mla - da, u - ve - re - na - by - la,

shto druzh - ku svo - mu khot' chut' - chut' ia mi - la

Anyuta: If in my young years I could be sure that my lad likes me at least a little bit

dries, everything destroys me at every hour." Her subsequent spoken dialogue with Filimon shows the couple's comic "love play," with each enunciating revealing remarks aside, to themselves. In her second song, Aniuta ventures into wide leaps in the verses and short tearful slides in the refrain, even when the wording is somewhat more hopeful: "I would see him every day a little, at least through a window, then would live without boredom" (Example 2.3).

In the third act, Aniuta, unaware of the felicitous resolution, delivers her last vocal solo, ending with "Dreadful is my life!" During the rest of the opera, she has only one brief spoken remark, before everyone else—including the maiden's chorus, the pacified parents, and the groom—joins the choir echoing the self-praises of the tipsy title hero. Although the opera finally arrives at its predictably happy ending, this Aniuta foreshadows Karamzin's poor Liza and operatic Nina.[21] The crafty drunken miller captured the imagination of operagoers across social lines, and the opera became one of the few eighteenth-century comic theatricals that survived into the nineteenth century. The final act features a sequence of three wedding songs—one of the first examples of the folk wedding repertory that permeates late eighteenth-century opera and continues as a major feature of nineteenth-century nationalist operas.

Catherine's Contribution
to Social(istic) Parody

Existing scholarship on operatic Aniutas (Rozanas, Lubims, Filimons, and others) stems from literary criticism that emerged in the nineteenth century, significantly expanded on by Soviet ideologues. Innocent peasant love stories ridiculing plutocrats, whose only worry is "to drink, to eat, to walk, and sleep . . . and to sock away money," were viewed as attacks on serfdom, "targeting despotism, abuse of landlords and defending the rights of peasants."[22] *The Miller,* in this context, was seen as an "ideological compromise," featuring a hybrid half-peasant half-lord.[23] Perhaps operas and comedies about peasants and servants might be linked to satirical journals and were, however tangentially, connected with peasant revolts;[24] but one name is lost in most scholarship on the early comic operas.

The year that introduced the Russian *Aniuta,* the matriarch of eighteenth-century peasant plays,[25] was also marked by a bouquet of five comic plays issued by the head of state, Catherine.[26] The historical bias surviving even today against the empress's works—"she takes a compromising position . . . refuses [to use] caricature, satire and direct moralization"[27]—is invalidated by the plays themselves. Their acute and pointed humor matches the tone of emerging native comic operas. Her unsympathetic depiction of noble domesticity dissects the laziness and emptiness of poorly educated landlords "obsessed with superstition, drenched in gossip and mindlessly mimicking everything foreign."[28] Beside them, Catherine paints a gallery of quick, clever, and resourceful servants (the female servant is often Mavra and the male servant Trofim).[29] Had these plays been written by anyone else, Russian critics would have applied an entirely different analytical approach, celebrating these comedies as forerunners of the anti-absolutist movement. Unable to reconcile biting social criticism with the position of the author of the plays, they preferred to ignore these works, while lauding social criticism in plays by other eighteenth-century figures.

In Catherine's *Invisible Bride,* love unions are rearranged. A suitor undesired by the bride marries her aunt instead; the daughter, a phlegmatic young maid, in turn weds her sweetheart; the father of the promised bride is confused; and all of this happens at the design of a female servant, who along the way cooks up her own wedding. At the very beginning of another comic play, *The Birthday of Madam Vorchalkina* (from *vorchat'*, "to nag"), which Catherine conceived with musical intermissions, the housemaid mocks her mistress, who wakes up at midday and spends "no more than four hours before the mirror."[30] The maid's suitor, also a serf, offers his philosophy of owner-serf relations:

At Nevezhdov's [*nevezha,* "ignoramus"], serfs are whipped every day whether for nothing or for something big, and all [the serfs] are robbers or drunks. . . . By contrast, our owner rarely uses beating . . . and we are all-handsome, merry, and honest.[31]

The serf couple sorts out their owners' marital projects entangled in a web of greed. At the final curtain, the housemaid announces that everything is over, "fools with their vices are punished and gone, all virtues rewarded, which pleases" her immensely—such a Figaro-in-a-skirt! The matron in this play exclaims, "Oh, oh, oh, Times!" cross-referencing another of Catherine's comedies, *O, Times!* The marriage projects, nailed down with the maids' help, constitute, as in comic opera, the canvas and the final outcome of the comedies.[32]

Fashioning her social parodies, the head of the despotic regime employed biting vernacular language—expressions that she likely learned from her servants (the empress asked her literate footman to read her operatic *Fevei* and check the authenticity of her folk expressions).[33] The names of her noble characters fall into two categories: indicative (Ignorance, Penny, Dreaming) and foreign or foreign-sounding (Christiana, Merimida, Olimpiada). Native names are given to serfs (Maria, Antip, Egor). Adding to her collection the caricatures of a Frenchman, a German nobleman, and a Turkish aristocrat (*Vestibule of a Renowned Statesman*), the empress-author, much like creators of comic operas, adapted and assimilated French models while ridiculing Russian subservience to French fashions. Nearly twenty years later, Krylov, the author of one of Aniuta's operas, similarly evokes the ambiguity of his aging Russian/French peasant/aristocrat heroine by tying her to French couture (1793):

Нежна *Клоя, Флоры* друг,	Sweet Chloe, friend of Flore,
Воздыхая — и сквозь слезы,	Sighing—through her tears,
Видит побледневши розы,	Sees the fading roses,
Так тебе, Анюта, жаль,	That is how much Aniuta pities,
Что французски тонки флёры,	That French gauze is so thin
...Легки шляпки, ленты, *шаль,*	...Light hats, ribbons, shawls,
Как цветы от стужи, вянут —	Like flowers languish from freezing—
Скоро уж они не станут	Soon they will no longer
Веять вкруг твоих красот[34]	Frame your beauty

Despite the likeness between the servants in Catherine's comedies and peasants in comic operas, and although three of the Aniuta operas premiered and others were shown in imperial theaters, one can hardly suspect Catherine of planting the seeds of social revolution. The empress's motivations complicate the question of Aniuta's appeal in aristocratic circles. Perhaps the presence of serfs on the imperial stage embellished the image of an enlightened monarch Catherine cultivated, especially in the first half of her reign. Also, her Russian remakes of characters and situations from French comedies or Shakespearian dramas were part of the empress's design for the nation and national culture.[35] Viewing theater as a piece in a social and political jigsaw, Catherine employed the comic stage as a model of society in which the empress-playwright explored and exposed human mores, rehearsed and played out social relations and different class roles.

Beyond that, the empress, approaching the end of her third decade as grand duchess and monarch in the early 1770s, may have become tired of the "sublime" presentation. Dismissing the original plan of a 1775 peace celebration, Catherine expressed herself with perfect clarity:

> All the usual stuff: temple of Janus, temple of Bacchus, temple of whatever else devil, all the foolish, unbearable allegories, besides everything in such immense size, with such an extraordinary effort to produce something absolutely meaningless.[36]

While revising yet preserving "state allegories, grandeur, and extraordinary effort" in the domain of official culture, the court indulged itself with these operas about peasants—a part of the Russian courtly masquerade. In this "life-as-theater"[37] culture that evokes Bakhtin's definition of carnival as "not observed but lived through, and lived by everyone . . . as an alternative reality,"[38] the empress becomes a libertine, a French *paysanne* turns into a Russian serf, a maid into a countess, a prince courts a peasant girl, and a character is at one moment a serf, the next an owner. It was the "festive life" of comedy that permitted the Russian elite—led, inspired, and curtailed by their female rulers—to experiment with liberal ideas while simultaneously solidifying, with a tint of flirtatious self-deprecation, the social stratum of classes and powers.

Poor Nina

Some twenty years into successful production of fairly simple stories about Aniutas, Russian operatic aficionados discovered pleasure in the more finessed and challenging possibilities of a new type of opera comique. Nicolas Dalayrac's *Nina* premiered in Paris (1786) and was staged in Russia three years later; the same year, Giovanni Paisiello composed his *Nina* (1789)—"one of the greatest hits of the century."[39] Dalayrac's opera captivated Russian audiences. Ivan Dolgorukov exclaimed: "Who did not know this opera? Who did not admire it from Paris to our glacial rivers? Who did not sing something from it?"[40]

The opera's heroine is another young maid whose betrothal to her beloved, once approved by her father, is broken by him in a favor of wealthy groom. After a duel between the two suitors, the father fabricates news of her lover's death, causing Nina to lose her mind. The psychological breakdown of the heroine, cured when she is united with her beloved in the operatic finale, parallels the sudden loss and return of the maiden's voice in *Le Médecin*. Like Nina, Molière's young protagonist-bride recovers her speech after reuniting with her swain.

In another comic opera, *The Pretended Madwoman* (*Pritvorno sumashedshaia*, 1787), which preceded *Nina* on the Russian stage by two years, Kniazhnin fashioned his image of a deluded bride.[41] In this opera, the old goosey guardian of the young heroine, much like Paisiello's Bartolo (composed for the St. Petersburg court in 1782), plans to marry his ward. Ordering her windows and doors barred, the geezer delivers lines that immediately invoke Molière's forester-doctor:

Лучше всякой мне музыки!	Better than any music for me,
Звук приятный: ток! ток! ток!	The pleasant sound: tok! tok! tok!
О дрожайший молоток! . . .	Oh, dearest hammer! . . .
Вы слесари,	You're carpenters,
Не лекари! (Kniazhnin)[42]	Not doctors!

Unlike Lucinde in *Le Médecin* or Rosina in *Il barbiere di Siviglia*, Kniazhnin's heroine takes the matter into her own hands by staging her insanity. She parades as a warrior dressed in her guardian's uniform and toting his corroded spear; later she appears as a hundred-year-old woman, snatching in the course of her pretended madness a hundred gold coins from her warden-jailor. Despite the short and insignificant life of Kniazhnin's opera, the names of the beau couple—Liza and Erast (Greek, "lover"), adopted like *Aniuta* from French theater[43]—would enjoy fame and longevity in Russian culture. Although the flow of cross-dressing shepherdesses and amorous French and Russian couples continued in Russian comic operas late into the century, the merry tricks and feigned madness faded significantly with the arrival of Dalayrac's genuinely unhinged, delirious Nina.

The plot of the French opera is absolutely static. The story of Nina's happy days with her Germeuil, her father's sudden breach of his promise, "so cruel . . . so repugnant,"[44] the duel, her beloved's supposed death, and her derangement—all before the beginning of the opera—is narrated by Nina's governess. During the five scenes before Nina's first appearance on stage, the mingling of characters accomplishes two goals. One is to establish two social domains: the aristocratic, represented by Nina's grieving father the count, and the rustic, populated by peasants and servants. The other goal is to gradually escalate the audience's anxiety, aroused by an ongoing exchange about Nina's behavior and condition—in the absence of the heroine herself. The rest of the opera is a poignant exposé of different states of the heroine's delirium. The text of Nina's first spoken words is permeated by irregular punctuation—multiple exclamations, dashes, sighs, pauses: "Ah! no! Ah! no!" Oblivious of spectators, Nina undergoes a psychological journey from one state to another. Swinging between the profound happiness of waiting for her beloved and the extreme fear of his not arriving, she comes dangerously close to self-destruction—a threat conventionally made by heroines of comic as well as serious operas. In her fragmented interaction with her governess, it becomes apparent that Nina recognizes no one. A group of children whom Nina greets with gifts and tears makes the scene especially moving. She asks them to sing a song she made up for Germeuil. As she teaches the kids to sing, she herself forgets the verses and pleads for them to teach her back. Not recognizing her father, poor Nina later fails even to identify her beloved. Arriving, Germeuil—now embraced by Nina's father, who calls him a son and seeks his help—has to gradually replay for Nina their courtship and betrothal. Drawn deep into delirium, Nina treats Germeuil as a messenger and then as an imposter; only at the very end does she come to her senses as a chorus of peasants celebrate their marriage.

Confused about her own identity throughout the opera, Nina also confuses her spectators. Once a count's daughter, she loses the memory of her aristocratic self and, wandering with loose hair and in her simple garment, bonds with peasants. Not recognizing anything or anyone, Nina is a blank slate, presenting both spectators and performers with a play of possibilities beyond comic operas with charming Aniutas. Absorbing the image of a simple rustic heroine and introducing spectators to the painful pleasure of witnessing her dementia, at the end Nina retreats to a wonderfully familiar, safe wedding. Karamzin admired the touching mad scene played by Louise Dugazon, the first Parisian performer of Nina. A few years later, a peasant girl hurt and deranged by failed love would be driven to a different, fatal ending in Karamzin's short novella that redirected the path of Russian literature and operatic theater. Kniazhnin's Liza, pretending madness, and converging with both peasant Aniuta and deluded Nina, turned into *Poor Liza*, which ended with suicide (Figure 2.1).[45]

In Count Stroganov's private theater, organized by Prince Dolgorukov, *Nina* was staged (1789) with the prince's young wife (Evgeniia Smirnaia) playing the title role "before a large selective audience, . . . aristocrats and foreign ambassadors attending the spectacle." Composer Dmitri Bortniansky conducted the orchestra, with the choruses sung by court chamber singers. The proud husband, Dolgorukov, enacting the role of Nina's father, wrote that "after she sang the famous air 'Quand le bien aimé reviendra,' the victory was hers. . . . From this time on in society my wife was called 'la princesse Dolgorukov Nina.'"[46] Her performance of the melancholic Nina, who, even in "extreme delusion preserved dulcet softness and simplicity," was rivaled by other aristocratic actresses. Dolgorukov critiques the performance of Nina by one of his relatives, Countess Dolgorukova, who, "intending to show all her beauty and charm, . . . played not deranged Nina, but a court belle stepping on the stage." Nelidova's tumultuous Nina exhibited rage and fury and had to be stopped and held by her supporting actors.[47] *Nina* was also played in public and private theaters by aristocratic and serf actors, traversing social divides not only in the domain of theater but between stage and life.

Figure 2.1: Orest Kipresnky (1782–1836). *Poor Liza.* 1827. Oil on canvas. Tretyakov Gallery, Moscow.

At the request of Count Sheremetev, Dalayrac's *Nina*, directed and played on his stage by the Dolgorukovs, was shown for Sheremetev's favorite serf actress so that she could learn the role by observing princess Dolgorukov's acting (1790).⁴⁸

The Prince-Forester, the Count-Lackey, and the Servant's Tsarevna-Spouse

Generations of the aristocratic elite, whether they enjoyed it or not, put up with lengthy, noisy, and glittering coronations, no less ostentatious weddings, and bombastic parades; they might suppress a yawn while dozing during a long opera seria.

Living in invigorating yet dangerous proximity to the monarch, partaking in state spectacles in which they displayed both their elevated positions and their servility to the head of the state, the members of the native elite extended their acting skill to the home stage. In private spaces, the members of the same dynasties, as well as rulers and their families, counterbalanced tiresome state decorum by seeking pleasure in staging and acting in scaled-down, sometimes naughty comic sentimental plays that poked fun at their own court culture.

The institution of Russian private theater can be traced to the terem of Tsarevna Sophia, where groups of nobles entertained their mistresses with games and theatricals. In *Le Médecin malgré lui*, these amateurs played comic roles contrasting with their social bearing: Prince Dolgorukov (a predecessor of Ivan Dolgorukov) in the leading part as a comic forester; Princess Khovanaskaya his quarreling wife; Count Vladimir Golitsin, Sophia's favorite, the forester's neighbor; and, among other nobles, Countess Sheremeteva as a servant's wife.

In *Le Médecin*, the forester's beating of his wife—French opera comique borrowing from the Italian commedia dell'arte—spurs her revenge. When a group of men arrives seeking a physician, she points to her husband. As a consequence of her puckish gesture, he, a lazy forester, finds himself posing "against his will" as a world-famous doctor, a stock character from Italian comedy. Brought to the suddenly mute daughter of a wealthy local nobleman, the doctor-imposter offers his patient a cure in the form of her beloved but poor suitor, ejected from the house by her father but reappearing dressed as the doctor's assistant—an element of Beaumarchais's *Le barbier de Séville*,[49] in which a chain of disguises, including a fake doctor, leads to the happy union of a young couple. In Molière's finale, clinching a socially unequal yet happy union, the underprivileged groom suddenly comes into a fortune at his uncle's death—social normality reestablished as in *Aniuta, The Miller*, and elsewhere.

Descendants of the same Golitsin and Sheremetev families, as well as other court celebrities, played a half-century later for the birthday of Elisabeth. Decades later, in the early winter of 1765, the *St. Petersburg News* announced several performances of Néricault Destouches's facetious *Le Philosophe marié*[50] (five acts in verse, 1727), staged at the marvelous Millionaia Street palace of Peter Sheremetev, the senator and decorated general. A descendant of Princess Khovanaskaya, featured in Sophia's terem, appeared in the lead role, the "philosophizing" young aristocrat Ariste, while the host's daughter, Anna Sheremeteva, portrayed Ariste's wife. [51] Two sisters, the countesses Chernyshov, played frolicsome characters: the wife's sister and a servant. Several other counts filled the remaining roles; Nikolai Sheremetev, for example, appeared as a lackey, a minor character.

Like *Le Médecin, Le Philosophe marié*, imbued with trickery, misconstrual, and disguise, enjoyed longevity on the private Russian stage.[52] In Destouches's play, one protagonist, affluent Demont, pretends to be poor to test his beloved, whom he eventually marries; the other, the philosophe Ariste, a resolute adversary to matrimony but already hitched, conceals his marriage. His loyal wife, obeying her husband's wish to keep it a secret, has to accept the amorous advances of his noble friend. The husband in his turn—his name, Ariste, recycled in Russian literature as Erast and Arist (eventually becoming Pushkin's Gherman[53])—comes dangerously close to bigamy by nearly signing marriage papers with his rich uncle's daughter.

The spectacle was planned, staged, enacted, and advertised; tickets were distributed and guests ushered in. Count Ivan Chernyshov directed the play, Prince Trubetskoi was in charge of the orchestra, and other noble patrons handled publicity. Catherine II saw performances of the "troupe." The same winter (1765), fourteen-year-old Nikolai Sheremetev also "attended in the imperial palace the rehearsals of a children's ballet . . . and danced with Paul à-la-Russian."[54] The involvement of the highest elite in staging and acting in private spectacles reached its pinnacle in the last decades of the eighteenth century and was sustained through the following century with dynasties such as the counts Sheremetev holding family spectacles into the early twentieth century.

One can imagine the delight with which Prince Dolgorukov stepped into the role of the lazy drunkard forester in Sophia's *Le Médecin*, or a young Prince Beloselsky explored the privileges of an aristocrat in disguise chasing after flirtatious maids—a situation he would elaborate forty years later in his frivolous, politically scoffing comic opera *Olin'ka*.[55] In the carnivalesque atmosphere of private theater, nobles and their serfs could be paired as amorous couples; peasants were expected to beguile owners, noble partners, and spectators by playing counts and princesses. In his diary, Bergholz recalled how the niece of Peter I, the lovely Duchess of Mecklenburg, who directed several plays in the imperial household, once told a story about a serf actor who received two hundred lashes because, as he followed the Duchess's orders to deliver posters in the city, he also tapped people for money. Some two hours after the beating, the same man appeared on the stage with "the countesses and noble matrons . . . the marshal's daughter playing the wife of the whipped king."[56]

By mixing serfs and aristocrats in the operas with multiple disguises and class cross-dressing, Russian comic opera toyed with possibilities of social fluidity, an adventurous social rollercoaster. Dolgorukov, a prince, playwright, actor, and memoirist who provided a first-hand account of himself as an actor-aristocrat, writes:

> *O tempora! O mores!* Well, whenever did it not happen? Menshikov sold flapjacks! Razumovsky sang in the church corner! Sivers was a foot-messenger! Why wouldn't Kutaisov be a count? He skillfully shaved Pavel's beard? Not a trifle![57]

Not a trifle indeed. As illusory as social fluidity could be in highly polarized hierar-chical Russia, such social transgressions resonated with real eighteenth-century stories: the captured Turk Ivan Kutaisov elevated to baron by Paul I, a Ukrainian chorister named Razum becoming the most influential prince, a peasant girl from conquered Lifland crowned as empress, a stateless princess from a distant province rising as Catherine the Great.

Titled Dilettante

Life and theater converged in the histrionic persona of Ivan Dolgorukov, whose memoirs were filled with references to the private aristocratic spectacles of the late eighteenth century. A distant heir of Moscow's founder and a member of the most luminous Russian clans—Sheremetevs, Stroganovs, Rzhevskys, Apraksins, Skovronskys, Menshikovs—Dolgorukov inherited, along with a ringing name, a family history entangled with eighteenth-century monarchial drama. His namesake grandfa-ther, Ivan Dolgorukov, as a young man had been the best friend of Peter II. Both youths were betrothed, the teenaged tsar to Dolgorukov's sister and Dolgorukov to the daugh-ter of the legendary Field Marshal Boris Sheremetev. The family ties did not material-ize, and the princely power of the Dolgorukov clan abruptly ended with the sudden death of the teenage ruler. Empress Anna, a couple of weeks before her enthronement, ordered their extended family into exile; seven years later, two of Dolgorukov's men, including Ivan, were broken on the wheel, their uncle beheaded, two other male rela-tions drawn and quartered,[58] and the women forced into Siberian monasteries. So ghostly was the family's destiny that, returning from exile with her two little sons, the widowed Princess Dolgorukov née Sheremetev got very little help even from her rela-tives, as if the dreadful curse were contagious.

Two reigns and two generations later, with his restored titles on the one hand but a slim inheritance and constant financial struggles on the other, Prince Dolgorukov regained access to the highest privy circles as a connoisseur of theater and an actor. According to the prince's memoirs, he played in a Moscow private theater belonging to the widow of Catherine's natural son, Alexis Bobrinsky.[59] The twenty-year-old prince appeared in aristocratic spectacles staged in the Grand Ducal residence and in the theaters of Russian patricians.[60] Proudly, Dolgorukov recalled how Senator Strekalov—the official in charge of imperial entertainment—seeing him on the stage lamented that because of Dolgorukov's princely title he could not offer him a lucrative salary at court.[61] The prince appeared on private stages in the capitals and provinces, in ducal palaces, and at modest small-town gatherings. He shared the stage with aristocrats, serfs, and professional actors, playing in both comedies and operas.

In his memoirs, he created a literary gallery of people he had encountered throughout his life, most of them involved in theater.

Aristocrats established private houses for their own entertainment and for their growing daughters, who, because of their fashionable upbringing, would "know music, sing pleasantly, dance with skill, and succeed in the theater." The daughters and cousins of General Stepan Rzhevsky, according to Dolgorukov, constituted a most harmonious troupe, whose comedies during several winters gathered the Moscow elite. In Volkonsky's theater, along with the daughter of Field Marshal Saltykov, Dolgorukov appeared in the lead role of *Le barbier de Séville*. On Shakhovskoi's stage, he played *Serva Padrona* with countess Gagarina, who "could neither sing nor play, [in a] theater [that] could seat under a hundred-fifty people, . . . three hundred tickets were distributed, . . . a crushing throng, noise, screams—everything amused her immensely."[62] Princess Baryatinskaya had a troupe whose comedies were staged by an actor of the Imperial French Theater and Dolgorukov's private acting teacher.

Dolgorukov also described his cross-dressing appearances on and off stage. For example, during an à-la-Venetian masquerade he played Cleopatra in a comedy of the same title, and, according to the prince, elicited sustained laughter.[63] In the company of the Stroganov family's French governess, who was wearing a nun's habit, Dolgorukov, dressed in beauteous women's attire, attended a court masquerade in which, remaining incognito, the merry duo tricked and annoyed Potemkin.[64] The divide between life and theater, if it existed, appeared blurred. The grandson of a prince executed on the wheel and the son of a convict, Dolgorukov, a "patched figure," was known to wander about the streets "dressed in the oddest manner in clothes half military, half theatrical, taken from costumes of the parts he himself had played."[65]

The prince's first wife exemplified the amateur yet well-trained noble actress appearing in many private theaters. She was a "Smolianka"—a graduate of the Smolny Institute, a counterpart of the St. Petersburg Infantry Cadet Corps (Shliakhetskii Korpus), which, founded under Anna, throughout the century produced Russian playwrights, actors, and dancers. Under Catherine, the Smolny Institute became largely an acting school for young noble women, trained to dance, sing, and play musical instruments. Portraits of Smoliankas in theatrical costumes by Dmitry Levitsky decorated the walls of the empress's Hermitage.[66] Grand Duke Paul courted one of the Smoliankas, Nelidova, with whom Dolgorukov played in a number of spectacles.

Although the performers in private theaters occupied polar-opposite social positions, they mingled at times on the stage and enacted characters that traversed social divides. What would this do to an actress who performs consistently, diving in and out of her social space, and returning—whether immediately after every spectacle or a few years down the road—to the barn, field, or servant chores?

Serf Actresses, Russian Odalisques

Serf theater—performing troupes of peasants and servants owned by nobles—reached its zenith in the last quarter of the eighteenth century after Catherine gave her nobility unlimited power over their serfs while liberating the aristocrats themselves from the mandatory service imposed by Peter I.[67] Consequently, starting in the 1770s, the most affluent statesmen of the empire, such as counts Iusupov, Sheremetev, Apraksin, and Vorontsov, retired from the imperial service and left St. Petersburg for their estates near Moscow or the Russian provinces, where they immersed themselves in art and theater.[68] Significantly, most serf theaters were owned by men, even though female aristocrats took a strong interest in theater and frequently participated in productions.

The primary data on serf theater, which was popular until the third decade of the nineteenth century, are scattered among diaries of contemporaries attending serf productions, as well as in records of theater owners. Vivid descriptions of theaters, plays, and operatic productions come from a number of memoirs; however, one has little hope of finding first-hand accounts by serf performers, who were largely illiterate and consumed by their jobs. Their stories are inferred from the roles they played, the budgetary records of costume costs, scattered and impersonal references penned by spectators, literary accounts of traveling writers, and the highly politicized literature of following generations. Most of the scholarship on serf theater produced during the Soviet period approached it from an ideological platform, as a system of class exploitation on the one hand and as evidence of the genius of the simple Russian folk, forebears of the Soviet proletariat, on the other.[69]

Erecting palatial private theaters reminiscent of the one at Versailles, and sometimes creating their own courts composed of serfs who could magically turn into counts, courtiers, or peasants, Russian aristocrats competed with each other and with the monarch herself. The best serf troupes rivaled those of the professional theaters of St. Petersburg and the provinces. Maddox, the director of the Moscow Public Theater, repeatedly complained that Sheremetev's productions were taking audiences away from public theaters.[70] Serf theaters became an arena where many aristocrats realized their personal and political ambitions.[71] Providing native Croesus with a quick, cheap, and abundant supply of performing forces, serf troupes impelled the development of native theater.

Serf actors were inherited, borrowed, sold, and exchanged. Some were included in dowries, presented as gifts, and won or lost in card games. In *Soroka-Vorovka*, Herzen recounts how, after the sudden death of the "kind owner" of one of the "best" Russian actresses, the troupe was sold wholesale on the public market.[72] One area of competition among the most distinguished serf theater owners was musical theater, which required special training for singers, dancers, and musicians. The actors and actresses in these operatic troupes had a high commodity value—an ordinary young female serf in the provinces could be sold for two and a half rubles, while a singer in Moscow could cost eight hundred. The newspaper *Moscow News* (1797) contained advertisements of serfs—for instance a "'special bargain' on a sixteen-year-old maid with a nice voice, successful in singing and acting theatrical roles, also cleaning well and making delicious food."[73] Count Kamensky exchanged one of his villages with two hundred inhabitants for two musicians he desired.[74] Perhaps the best-known operatic troupes formed at the end of the eighteenth century belonged to Nikolai Sheremetev and Alexander Vorontsov.[75]

Though both male and female serfs appeared on the private stage, actresses brought more distinction to the troupes than actors. Both pioneers and victims in a gender performance, they were caught between operatic plots and social realities. Catherine Schuler discusses serf actresses as "doubly oppressed by class and a rigid set of largely unreconstructed medieval gender conventions."[76] Senelick states that if "the playing houses were . . . saturated with sexual allure, then private [serf] theaters offered even greater incitements and greater opportunities for consummation."[77]

The girls selected for the theater ranged from children under ten to young women in their late teens. They were the daughters of servants, *dvorovye* (working in a *dvor*— court-yard),[78] and peasants. The main criterion for selecting girls was their appearance. Depending on the owner, the theaters where these girls performed could represent a momentary whim, a fashionable pastime, or a serious theatrical venture. When not on stage, serfs may have carried out their regular agricultural or household duties. In more permanent troupes, actresses were placed in special quarters where, caged in their cells, they were kept separate from fellow actors and from other serfs, including their families. Evreinov writes that actresses were supervised by matrons who accompanied them during rehearsals and performances, kept them in their dressing rooms, and prevented them from talking with male partners.[79] Liubov Onisimovna, the heroine of Leskov's novella *The Toupee Artist*, recalls that the landlord purposely chose matrons with children. The female wardens, well aware that an actress's misbehavior would be taken out on their children, acted as harsh jailors. Even the most liberal aristocrats, such as the Sheremetevs, kept their actresses under tight surveillance in their quarters and under the supervision of matrons, the exception being their attendance at Sunday services at the count's own church.[80]

Physical punishment was a conventional method of training. After a spectacle, a serf actress could be sent back to the barn, flogged for her mistakes, or locked in her small cell. Old Count Kamensky, the owner of two theaters in Orel, known even among his peers as a despot and a madman, usually attended his troupe's performances with a special notebook in which he recorded inaccuracies and imperfections.

During intermissions he used his whip, "punishing the guilty, whose shouts and cries frequently reached the ears of audience."[81] Only one troupe owner, Count Vorontsov, was known to have abolished corporal punishment.

Because of their visibility on stage and their presence in the landlords' household, serf actresses were especially vulnerable to their owners. Because of the special attention of their landlords, these actresses were also exposed to the jealousy of fellow serfs and house servants. Brought to the stage, these women no longer fit the traditional role of serf; nor did they become professional actresses. They fell into a social gap, trapped in an indeterminate space open to experiments not of their making. Ironically, although visible and vocal on the stage, they remained socially inconspicuous and voiceless. Like the Tunisian-owned singing slave girls, described by L. JaFran Jonce, who were purchased along with "other cultural artifacts" during "shopping expeditions to Baghdad,"[82] Russian serf actresses were simply the property of a male owner. Like those singing slave girls who "contributed significantly to the cultural brilliance of Cordova" and North Africa,[83] serf actresses played an important role in developing Russian artistic traditions.[84]

Some serf girls were simply yanked from the field or collected from the barn or kitchen and made to memorize a couple of French sentences or a short song. They were powdered, dressed in hoopskirts, draped with jewelry—worth more than the price of the girls themselves—and thrown on stage to play the part of a countess, princess, or picturesque shepherdess. Writing about serf theater, Emmanuel Beskin tells about the uneasy process of transforming two peasant daughters into actresses for Count Gruzinsky's theater. For four weeks, the two serfs, Dunyasha and Parasha, scared by the stage, could not memorize their lines and finally were whipped to stimulate their learning. Following the flogging, the text was memorized quickly. In the spectacle, the girls played idyllic versions of themselves:

> As the curtain rose . . . , from one side of the back stage comes the beautiful shepherdess Dunyasha—a weaver's daughter, with made-up hair, decorated with flowers, a *mushka* [mole] on the cheek, dressed in a hoop-skirt (pompadour), carrying a branch with blue-pink ribbons. Next Parasha comes dressed as a shepherd. The two will begin talk about love and about their sheep, then sit next to each other and hug.[85]

By contrast, the best native and foreign theatrical pedagogues were hired to train the leading actresses in the private serf theaters of Sheremetev, Vorontsov, Iusupov, and Apraksin, teaching the girls to understand music and poetry and to speak French and Italian. For example, the Italian Franz Morelli, a dancer of the St. Petersburg Court Theater and later an instructor at Moscow University, worked with Sheremetev's troupe. Singing was taught by Italians, dancing by Italians and French, and acting

by Russians. Count Sheremetev junior frequently participated in rehearsals and prac-
tices.[86] Some serf actresses from an early age served members of noble families, from
whom they were to learn genuine aristocratic manners; others were taught in schools
for free professional actors.

Enacting princesses and shepherdesses, serf actresses stimulated the social and
sexual imagination of their spectators, creating the same "circulation of erotic energy
between actors and audience" that Gay finds in Elizabethan English theater.[87] Sexuality
enacted on the stage commonly led to sexual performances afterward, as demanded by
the owner. A Frenchman living in Russia described a landlord who surrounded himself with "serf actresses [who] were at the same time his maidens, servants, and seam-
stresses, . . . also his mistresses, wet-nurses, and the babysitters of the children they
bore him."[88] Unidentified nobleman "B." had a sort of seraglio consisting of serf
actresses, mistresses, dancers, and cooks. The master loved traveling with this harem
from one village of his estates to another. During frequent stops, two tents were set up,
one for the nobleman with his "favorites" and the other for his musicians—about
twenty people pleasing the master with singing while he occupied himself with his
mistresses.[89]

Exploiting his actresses, keeping them for his sole use, a master controlled women's
sexuality outside his bedchamber. Actress Piunova recalled that in Count Nikolai
Shakhovskoi's theater, "female performers were ordered not to talk with any male
member of the troupe."[90] Filipp Vigel adds in his memoirs that in the same theater
touching actresses was prohibited even on the stage, "a precise distance prescribed
between the male and female actors."[91] Matrimony was also controlled by the male
owner. "When a woman reached the age of twenty five," writes Piunova, "the owner
gave her in marriage, which was a simple process. He called in all the unmarried male
actors and asked who would wish to marry the available bride, after which he informed
the actress of the groom and wedding arrangements, with the owner himself blessing
the wedded couple, supplying them with a dowry and giving the man a raise."[92]

Despite differences in treatment and professional training, serf actresses shared one
common feature. These women—simultaneously serfs and performers—fit neither
role, occupying a marginal space in which they were subjected to the unique institution
of serfdom, the specific customs of the trade, and the gender bias of Russian society.

Traversing Theatrical and Social Spaces

A Russian serf actress, crossing the stage, turned into an elegant noble princess.
Re-dressed Dunyasha and Parasha are reminiscent of Shakespeare's disguised heroines—"boys pretending to be women pretending to be men."[93] The *gender* cross-dressing
of Parasha, who appears as a young man, is secondary to her (and Dunyasha's) *social class*

cross-dressing; to rephrase Kaplan and Rogers, each girl can be seen as a peasant pretending to be a noble (man or woman) pretending to be a shepherd(ess).

Perhaps an aristocratic spectator in a serf theater would experience feelings similar to Goethe's watching castrati singing: "the double pleasure is given, in that these persons are not women, but only represent women."[94] Here the observer would see elegant women on the stage, knowing them to be serf peasant girls. This process of "dual recognition" explicitly extended the drama beyond the theatrical space into a territory offstage. Vigel, recalling his visit to Esipov's estate in Kazan, describes how at dinner he was astonished by the appearance of a dozen attractive, elegantly dressed young women, who were rather too docile and accommodating with a governor. These high-society women, played by Esipov's serf actresses, sat at the table among the men, providing them a wide range of services, accompanying the food and drink with passionate kisses, cuddles, and songs.

In such cases, theatrical roles were displaced from the stage to the household, confusing the distinction between theatrical role playing and social role playing, which together defined the liminal space occupied by serf actresses. Not only actresses but also their owners became involved in the act of re-dressing. A provincial nobleman, Ivan Shepelev, conducted the rehearsals of his female chorus in his house à la Turk, himself parading in a Turkish robe, trousers, and a fez woven with gold.[95] For an aristocrat who appeared as an enlightened European in public while impersonating a sultan in private, served by harem singers and dancers like a "tsar sitting in his prefecture,"[96] his own state/estate/serf theater was his re-dressed court with subjects over whom he—a ruler with absolute power—exercised his own justice, meting out punishment and reward. Actresses, the glory of the theater/court and the owner's prize, were instrumental to his power.

What explains the obsession and enormous power drive of male aristocrats with serf theater and serf actresses? Seeking the source of fascination with theater in early modern England, Gay writes that "one consistent feature of Shakespearian drama . . . is that it proceeds by way of *inversion* of the norms of behaviour," providing "the exhilarating sense of freedom which transgression affords."[97] In Russian serf theater, although the pleasure of transgression was triggered by the cross-dressing of a serf girl, an "exhilarating sense of freedom" was achieved when the theatrical "playground" was extended to a dreamland "in which people [aristocrats] did things that they could not or would never dare do."[98] What they could not or would never dare do with real countesses, they were able to do with their theatrical surrogates. Thus theater offered owners the invigorating pleasure of exercising and exhibiting their power over (made-up) noblewomen. Unlike the singing slave girls documented by Jonce, Russian serf girls were of the same ethnicity as their owners.[99] Their physical features, figures, faces, hair, and eye color were no different from those of the countesses, patronesses, and princesses surrounding the nobleman in his social circle. These Russian girls also spoke the same language, perhaps (because of their training) even better than some noblewomen. Furthermore, selected for their youth and beauty,[100] the actress girls may have been more attractive than their titled counterparts. With their natural beauty, refined tastes, education, trained voices, movements, and understanding of music and poetry, these actresses were expected to be submissive in an age when the traditionally patriarchal upper-class Russian male elite was "subjected" to female rule and the emergence of noblewomen in the public arena.

Perhaps the obsessive fascination of noblemen with theater and actresses represented the dangerous possibility of reversing theatrical and social roles. Marjorie Garber, investigating gender dress codes and social differences, sees theater as a generator of "deep-seated anxieties about the possibility that identity was not fixed, that there was no underlying 'self' at all."[101] The plot of opera comique to some degree probes this notion by making a peasant girl a concealed countess; by extension, the identity of the serf actress may be seen as nonfixed.

The Serf Countess

What if the operatic plot spills off stage and becomes a life story? This took place between the legendary serf actress Praskovia Zhemchugova (1768–1803) and her owner, theatrical patron, and husband Count Nikolai Sheremetev (1751–1809).[102] He belonged to the thirteenth generation of a dynasty descended from Prussian kings; in the course of their glorious history, the Sheremetevs had assisted Alexander Nevsky; founded major Russian dynasties, including the Romanovs[103]; and consistently held a prominent place in the tsar's court. Tsar Peter's favorite field marshal, married to the widow of the tsar's uncle, was Nikolai Sheremetev's grandfather. Nikolai's father, named after Tsar Peter, was among the most influential figures at the courts of both Elisabeth and Catherine. He was a close friend of Aleksei Razumovsky, once a singer and later Tsarina Elisabeth's morganatic husband. Following the fashion of "masquerades, choruses, orchestras and theaters inspired by Razumovsky,"[104] Peter Sheremetev established his celebrated *capel* (choir), his famous *rogovoi orkestr* (horn ensemble), and later a serf theater. The heir of one of the wealthiest and most influential Russian aristocrats, Nikolai Sheremetev refused court and military careers, devoting his life to the arts, music, and theater. Zhemchugova was the star of the troupe.

During her short life, the actress acquired six names that illuminate her story. Gorbunova (from *gorb*, "hunchback") identified the physical defect of her serf father. He was likely a smith, and she carried the name Kuznetsova (from Russian *kuznets*, "smith"), and its Ukrainian equivalent, Kovaleva. The stage name Zhemchugova (*zhemchug*, pearl) was chosen by the Sheremetevs, who gave their actresses the names of jewels and precious stones: Anna Izumrudova (emerald), Arina Iakhontova (sapphire), sisters Fekla and Mavra Biriuzovas (turquoise), Avdotia Ametistova (amethyst), and ballerina Tatiana Granatova (ruby). When the count sought to legitimize his love for a serf actress, he ordered a genealogical search of her family roots; the name Kovaleva was turned into Polish Kovalevsky, with the implication of impoverished, lost, forgotten noble origin—invented in the style of operatic libretti. The marriage of the count and his serf star and mistress of twenty years, blessed by the patriarch of the Russian church but unsanctioned by the tsar, remained a secret, her name and the title of countess unacknowledged.

Zhemchugova the actress and star was admired by Catherine II, who ordered her secretary to present the actress with jewelry; she was applauded by Tsar Paul, Tsar Alexander, and the Polish King Stanislas Poniatowski. However, the funeral of the "made-up" countess Sheremeteva, the brightest star of the eighteenth-century Russian theater, was attended only by a few servants and by the architect of Catherine's Hermitage Theater, Giacomo Quarenghi (1744–1817).

The image of Zhemchugova, her fame, and her dramatic story continue to stir the imagination of Russian musicians, historians, writers, and readers. In the introduction to a recently issued monograph on the actress, Douglas Smith notes a paucity of sources, which leads him to infuse her biography with the "breath of fiction." Mythologized, the persona of the actress is hidden in the shadow of her theatrical roles as a noble shepherdess, disguised princess, and devoted lover. On and off stage, the peasant and actress, serf and countess Zhemchugova lived an operatic story that unfolded from simple jovial Aniuta to sentimental ambiguous Nina, crossing the threshold of the century from mischievous to tragic Liza.

Conclusion: Masquerade—Empresses and Actresses

Two poor young women, living in different times, married royal men and became powerful tsarinas. Both of them changed their Germanic names to Catherine. Both were major players in Russian history, Catherine I as the wife of Peter the Great and Catherine the Great as one of the most powerful Russian rulers. The two Catherines marked the beginning and the end of women's rule over the Russian empire, which included four tsarinas. All of them were involved in acts of re-dressing. The masquerade was a political and cultural engine of early modern Russia, in which social and gender roles were formulated, questioned, and reformed. The process reached its culmination under Catherine the Great, who ruled for more than a third of the century.

One can picture an ornate theatrical auditorium. On one side, in a special balcony designed for royalty, sits Catherine the Great. Across from her, on a stage level with the royal balcony, is Zhemchugova, leading a chorus of two hundred (dancing) soldiers. In the finale she appears in a royal chariot.[105] Perhaps more than any other woman, Catherine could understand the transformation of a serf girl into a singer performing the role of the heroic Eliana, who, against societal and gender rules, declares her love and, when needed, cross-dresses as a soldier, defending her people, saving the commander, and winning the battle as a woman.

For a short moment, the paths of the two crossed, their life stories revealing paradoxical similarities.[106] Seven-year-old Parasha Kovaleva was taken away from her serf hut; the impoverished fourteen-year-old German princess was brought to Russia. The first was taught music and dance as well as French and Italian; the second assiduously studied Russian, dance, court manners, and Orthodox doctrines.[107] Zhemchugova, from an early age, appeared on the stage in a wide range of operatic roles. Catherine also enacted various roles during seventeen years of a miserable marriage under the harsh observation of Elisabeth. Both Zhemchugova and Catherine loved theater; one made the stage her empire, the other approached her empire as a theatrical arena. Both came from a social background that provided neither a basis nor preparation for the head-spinning traversing of roles and crossing of the theatrical/social/political spaces. Steven Greenblatt suggests in his writing on Shakespearian theater that "the boundaries between the theater and the world were not fixed, nor did they constitute a logically coherent set: rather they were a sustained collective improvisation."[108] These two women, Catherine II and Zhemchugova, represented opposite ends of a social spectrum in which social actors traversed territories of state and stage, testing, demarcating, and solidifying social, class, and gender roles. The two female types—one a formidable tsarina, a woman of frightening vigor and power, and the other Russia's own doleful bride or wife, who, like her stage heroines, surrendered herself to her lover—together entered a cast of characters in nineteenth-century fairy-tale operas.

3

CATHERINE THE EMPRESS(ARIO)
MAKING TALES INTO PRINCELY OPERAS

Мы не греки и не римляне;
Мы не верим их преданиям; . . .
Нам другие сказки надобны;
Мы другие сказки слышали
От своих покойных мамушек.

We're not Greeks and not Romans
We don't believe in their stories
We need other tales—
The tales we listened to
From our deceased mothers [nannies]
(Karamzin, unfinished poetic tale *Ilya Murometz*)[1]

Once upon a time the Russian *skazka* (tale) branched into the operatic tale.[2] Populated by triumphant Russian heroes, evil dwarves, devoted brides, daunting magical tsarinas, and folk choruses venerating the Motherland, these operas became a manifestation of Russian national culture. Traditionally, scholars associate the emergence of operatic skazka with the bourgeoning culture of nineteenth-century Russia, rarely acknowledging the operatic fairy tales produced in the last third of the eighteenth century.

During this era, Russian aristocrats became increasingly Europeanized. The Russian elite imported from enlightened Europe the idea of "nation" as inherently connected with the folk.[3] Though the folk and folklore remained largely foreign and imaginary to Russian aristocrats, they nevertheless gradually developed a longing for their lost

Russian identity and sought its roots in the folk. The European concept of nation, however, provided no formula for dealing with Russian complications such as ethnic diversity, the vastness of the empire, and the great cultural and linguistic disparity between Russian aristocrats and peasants. In an introduction to the memoirs of Princess Dashkova, Catherine's associate, friend, and intellectual rival, Jehanne M. Gheith poses a question that can be applied to most of the aristocratic elite of the day: "Given that Dashkova spoke very little Russian until she was married, to what extent is she 'Russian'?"[4]

Catherine II, propagating Westernization, demonstrated herself to be more Russian than the Russians. She adopted the role of defender of Russian Pravoslavie (Orthodoxy). She learned the language, promoted Russian translations of European literary works, supported research and publications on Russian history, encouraged collection of songs and tales, and bestowed gifts and intimate friendship on native intellectuals and her fellow writers (at least those propagating her agendas). Among her various projects, she explored the combination of native tales and opera. Robert-Aloys Mooser wrote that the ultimate support of Russian comic opera came from Catherine II, "who several times set aside politics to write comedy, anonymously."[5] She may not have been the first to create fairy-tale spectacles with music, but she did pioneer the opera-skazka as both author and empress-patroness. Although the empress labeled her operas as comic, they are quite distant from the comic operas discussed in the previous chapter. What Mooser refers to as her *opéras-comiques russes*[6] were in fact opera-skazkas. Catherine supported the collection of folklore and adapted several tales in her operas. Exploiting the allegoric potential of tales to speak about real and contemporary political goals, she fostered a sense of Russian history and laid out guidance for future monarchs. Using choruses to represent the Russian folk, featuring Slava-like choruses and Russian folk songs, and portraying wedding scenes, the empress with her many collaborators laid out a genre of fairy-tale opera and its elements.

Nikolai Fendeizen, who is kinder to the empress than many of his Russian and Soviet musicology colleagues (partly because, writing in the early Soviet period, he may have faced fewer political restrictions), stated that Catherine "foresaw the necessity of Russifying the theater" and encouraged introduction of folk traditions and music into the court. Fendeizen added parenthetically: "Would this [her advocacy of Russian folk topoi] not explain the emergence of *Aniuta* in the court theater in 1772?"

The "discovery" of the folk in Russia took two major directions, one associated with portrayal of picturesque peasants and serfs and the other with literary adaptation of oral repertoire, particularly folk songs and skazkas fancied by aristocrats. The multidimensional repertoire of oral skazka (from *skazat'*, to tell), in Russia as elsewhere, served as a repository of historical memory and a prescription for dealing with nature and human relationships (daughters, stepmothers, in-laws, owners, and neighbors). Skazkas also offered a diversion from daily problems, drawing listeners into a world of hopes, dreams, and heroic ventures.

The images, stories, and language created by noble writers and the Russian literati were distant from folk models. Nikolai Nikolev (1758–1815), the author of *Rozana i Lubim,* wrote that he chose not to depict characters who employed the "low and hideous speech of the Russian mob; as for example, the dialect of laborers and peasants from the steppes."[7] Vasily Levshin (1746–1826), a pioneer of the Russian literary skazka, while claiming to "preserve our antiquity and . . . to create a bibliothèque of Russian tales," admitted that he "used as a model the French Bibliothèque Bleu as well as German collections."[8] The question of the writers' intentions in assimilating folklore to literature and their methods of "improving" the originals are discussed in a number of works.[9] This chapter explores how the skazka converged with folk songs in Russian operas.

In the last decades of the eighteenth century, skazkas permeated the Russian literary world. They were written, translated, dedicated, read, enacted, and sung. Many-headed dragons, kidnapped princesses, gigantic snakes breathing fire, rusalkas (mermaids) laughing in the darkness, wicked magicians craving sexual and military conquests, and brave, handsome native champions appealed to both children and adults. They taught moral principles, introduced geographically remote and nonexistent places, and mixed history and magic. Late eighteenth-century skazkas fall into three groups: (1) tales translated from various foreign sources, (2) collected (and revised) folk tales, and (3) authors' literary tales. Yet there is no clear-cut division among the three, because most of the same authors who collected and translated tales also wrote their own novels and plays. From its inception, the literary skazka had strong links with both theater and folk song. Launching into his acting career, Mikhail Chulkov (1744–1792) published a song collection and his tales in the same period.[10] Mikhail Popov—who shared the stage with his brother and with the legendary Fedor Volkov, a protégé of Tsarina Elisabeth[11]—issued a collection of ancient Slavic tales in approximately the same year he completed *Aniuta.* Vasily Levshin collected tales and created vaudevilles and comic operas. In one of his tales, he included a fragment of musical notation of a tune performed with folk lyrics.[12]

There were also translated tales. Prince Lev Naryshkin, Catherine's chamberlain and close associate, presented the *Skazkas of the Fairy* (each with a moral) to his daughter. Countess Viazemskaia received—translated from French and dedicated to her—the tale *Krasota (Beauty).*[13] Along with French and other European stories referred to as skazkas, there were Arabic tales such as *Khalif Vatek* (1792), likely adopted from French sources; the Persian *Magic Palace* (1792), purportedly a translation of its native source; and the Chinese *Benefactor and Wizard* (1788). The skazka was not limited to the realm of the magical. An unknown amateur, Roman Kulikov, left a manuscript, *Skazka or Archaic Reality*, in which the author depicts a somewhat porno-graphic scene attributed to an unidentifiable past. In very careful and meticulous handwriting, Kulikov portrays a couple courting and experimenting with multiple cross-dressing, disguises, and appetizing erotic games.[14]

The literary skazka, like its oral forerunner, overlaps with the domain of history; as aristocratic Russians drafted the nation's history, their tales wove historical events with magical adventures.[15] One of Levshin's tales, for example, portrays the historical Prince Vladimir, who, assisted by two folk champions, Dobrynia and Ilya, triumphs over the Polish Marina, associated with the wife of Dmitry the Pretender (anachronistically, since she and Dmitry lived six hundred years later), a woman endowed with magical power.[16] Collected, borrowed, or newly created, the eighteenth-century Russian liter-ary tale could be several stanzas or a hundred pages long. Chulkov's *Story of Siloslav* (*silo*, strength; *slav*, glory) comprised a reading sequence for twenty-two nights, echoing the tales of the *Arabian Nights*.

In the early collections, skazkas overlapped with fables and novels.[17] Tales were written as poems, prose narratives, and dramas. The repertoire, not yet restricted by genre definition,[18] seemed boundless. It freely mixed subjects and styles, referring to foreign knights and native tsarinas, contemporary landscapes and remote antiquity; it blended political topics with gossip from aristocratic salons and stories from the peas-ant's hut. Juxtaposing high and low, the skazka became one of the first democratic liter-ary genres, crafted by an intelligentsia emerging from the unprivileged classes; Chulkov, for example, was a soldier's son, orphaned at an early age.[19]

Although Chulkov, Popov, and Levshin worked in the inherently connected domains of skazka, folk songs, and theater, none of the three concocted a fairy-tale opera. It was enterprising Catherine who endorsed opera-skazka by creating four operatic tales and aligning their production with affairs of state and the concept of nation. Several tales had surfaced on the stage earlier. Nearly forty years before Catherine's first operatic tale, on the occasion of Empress Elisabeth's birthday, some nobles staged *Kharabryi i smelyi bogatyr' Sila Bober* (*The Brave and Bold Power-Beaver*, 1747), a comedy with singing and various dances, adapted from ancient Russian tales by Kolychev. In fact, the title of this play anticipated one of Catherine's magic operas, *Khrabroi i smeloi vitiaz' Akhrideich* (*The Brave and Bold Knight Akhrideich*, 1787). Magic elements had also appeared in various operas, including works by Galuppi and Goldoni, favored by the Russian court. Later in the same year that Catherine created her first opera-skazkas (1786), Prince Dmitry Gorchakov collaborated with Mathias Stabingher in his operatic skazkas staged in Moscow. His two operas, *Schastlivaia Tonia* (1786) and *Baba-Yaga* (1788), containing magical elements, were essentially situation comedies. Gorchakov's third opera tale, *Khalif for an Hour* (1786), retold an

Arabic tale. Within two decades, a number of operatic skazkas, created by Russian literati, told and retold stories about the triumphal adventures of Russian princes.

Turning a Short Tale into an Imperial Operatic Production

Catherine's venture into opera-skazka was akin to her military and political campaigns. Within about a year she wrote three libretti; during a four-year period she completed and produced four opera-skazkas. The theatrical destiny of these works was not helped by their difficult names: *Novgorodskoi bogatyr' Boeslavich* (*Boeslavich, Champion of Novgorod,* 1786), *Fevei* (1786), *Khrabroi i smeloi vitiaz' Akhrideich* (referring to Ivan-Tsarevich as Akhrideich[20]), and *Gorebogatyr' Kosometovich* (*The Woebegone-Champion Kosometovich,* 1789).[21] The music for these operatic tales was composed by two natives, Vasily Pashkevich (1742–1797) and Evstigney Fomin (1761–1800), as well as the Czech Arnošt Vančura (1750–1802) and the Spaniard Vicente Martín y Soler (1754–1806), one of the most popular European composers of his time, whose operas were produced in Vienna twice as frequently as Mozart's.[22]

Free to choose among the best living artists in Russia and Europe, Catherine not only wrote libretti but immersed herself in operatic production: selecting composers, choosing actors for lead roles, attending rehearsals and performances, and suggesting costumes. As in her political and military ventures, for which the empress assembled highly trusted teams and delegated tasks to individuals who were simultaneously experts, personal associates, and often favorites, in the realm of musical theater she undertook the creation of operas as a highly collective affair.[23] In her choice of composers, Catherine frequently sought advice from and confirmed her choices with the passionate music lover Potemkin as well as with Alexander Mamonov and Platon Zubov; her favorites were connoisseurs of music, theater, and drama.

Catherine's comic operas combined spoken dialogue with songs, orchestral intermissions, dances, and choruses. The libretti of these operas included prose text and song lyrics. It must be noted that none of Catherine's own lines were actually put to music because the empress did not write poetry.[24] For example, she produced extensive handwritten sketches of *Akhrideich,* but according to Khrapovitsky's detailed account she requested that he write verses; the empress read and edited his airs, while he copied the final version of her text.[25] She devised the plots, outlined the operatic structure, and wrote the spoken parts for her operas, but the lyrics of the songs, arias, and choruses—though defined and approved by her—were selected, written, or solicited by Khrapovitsky, who, in his spare time, finessed a couple of comic operas of his own.[26]

In her role as empress and entrepreneur, Catherine was conscious of her plays' reception, repeatedly questioning Khrapovitsky about the reactions of readers and spectators. To verify her use of Russian folk idioms in *Fevei*, she handed the script to her peasant-servant Christian Brazinsky. By bringing together people of different social groups, occupations, classes, languages, and nationalities, Catherine stimulated her courtiers' involvement in theater. Among the close associates whom Catherine convinced to write a play was Princess Dashkova, herself a dramatic figure who, some twenty years earlier, borrowed officers' uniforms and galloped through the night with Catherine to orchestrate her enthronement. Beginning in 1782, Dashkova occupied the post of director of the Academy of Science. Complying with the empress's request to write a play, she beseeched Catherine to "read the first two acts, correcting them" and to tell her "frankly whether they ought to be thrown in the fire."[27] Nearly all Catherine's courtiers and associates wrote plays with music and comic operas. The empress herself, while gathering and adapting the input of others, disseminated her ideas defining theatrical and operatic fashions.

Catherine's striking theatrical productivity, especially in 1786, related to the "inauguration" of her newly built Hermitage Theater, the "Little Hermitage." Designed by Quarenghi, the theater emulated the "fameux Teatro Olimpico de Vicenze, oeuvre du Palladio."[28] Its novel semicircular open interior, accommodating 150 spectators, had no privileged seats (but indeed a privileged audience). Adjoining the Hermitage Museum in a wing of the Winter Palace, the Theater, intended for the empress's inner circle, would introduce a repertoire created by the empress herself and her associates.[29]

Catherine's operatic tales, first staged and polished in the public Kamenny Theater, were repeated several days later in Catherine's Hermitage for specially admitted diplomats, the highest native elite, the empress's intimate friends, and the royal family.[30] Though often played for an intimate circle, the lavish productions involved hundreds of performers—a large ballet, choruses, and an orchestra—as well as lavish scenery and mechanical effects. Count Victor Esterházy, attending *Fevei* at the Hermitage, wrote:

> The setting is splendid. The scene takes place in Russia in ancient times. All the costumes are absolutely magnificent. . . . It features a legation of Kalmyks, singing and dancing in the Tatar manner; . . . I have never seen a spectacle more varied nor more magnificent; there were more than five hundred people on stage, while there were hardly fifty of us spectators, even though the little Grand Dukes and the four little grand Duchesses were there with their governors and governesses, so exclusive is the Empress in granting admission to her Hermitage.[31]

Cherishing her role as a grandmother, Catherine created operatic tales and compiled a nine-volume collection for her grandsons and heirs.[32] In addition to operas, she wrote an ABC book, tales about distant lands, and descriptions of ethnic and national customs and traditions.[33] For example, *Za-pis-ki* (Notes), written in very light, engaging prose as a chain of short sections, describes distant lands—China, Siam, Africa—and the recently erected city Kherson in the Crimea. The empress used the stories to familiarize her grandsons with geography and the concept of empire and simultaneously to provide a wider audience with a historical argument for imperial expansion, thus keeping focus on her political agenda. Introducing these nations, the Augustan author depicted the customs and portrayed the characters of various classes, from the emperor to a craftsman telling moral tales. "The allegory of Minerva and Telemachus"[34] that Richard Wortman applies to Catherine and her grandsons stresses the empress's belief in improving the monarchy by "training better monarchs" and simultaneously reveals the image of the empress as "the enlightened ideal—the monarch as philosopher and pedagogue [and playwright], uplifting her people."[35]

As Catherine's tales turned into an imperial enterprise and her spectacles into state events, the theatrical space became dominated by its spellbinding actress-author. Sitting in the theater and embodying the highest level of visibility and performance, Catherine signified the coexistence and overlap between two performative dominions, the theater and the empire. The little children's tales reveal the complexity of the age—what would today be seen as a contradictory set of values: enlightenment and intense imperial expansion, education and serfdom.

Figure 3.1: Brown, William, and Charles. *Catherine II Instructing Her Grandsons.* 1790–91. Agate-onyx and gold; cameo. State Hermitage, St. Petersburg.

Princely Tales for Royal Heirs

Several common threads run through Catherine's four operatic tales. The title hero in each is a teenage prince who matures over the course of the spectacle by overcoming obstacles and temptations and by achieving victory in a battle, either real or simulated (as in *Gorebogatyr'*). Along with bravery and strength, the plots test the princes' moral virtues, their patience, their obedience to parents, and their devotion to their future purpose. In two operas, *Gorebogatyr'* and *Boeslavich*, widowed mothers raise their sons. (A pattern of single parents and orphaned protagonists would later characterize the works of Alexander Pushkin, with the gender combination often reversed. In Pushkin's fairy tales, short stories, and poems, some adopted for the operatic stage, with several exceptions, including *Eugene Onegin*—mother and daughters—fathers raise their daughters.[36])

From the time of the ancient Slavs, the widowed mother of a son assumed a special social status. Identified as *materaia vdova*, she, unlike a childless widow or a mother of daughers, would become an owner of her husband's property, the head of the household, stepping into a man's role, exhibiting masculine character, and shaping the male heir.[37] In Catherine's operatic tales, single mothers are much stronger than their married counterparts. Wortman writes about Catherine: "Like Minerva disguised as Mentor, she sought to replace the absent father and teach her pupil to be a better man and a good ruler."[38] Sympathizing with her single mothers, herself acting as a materaia vdova, the empress drew the problematic images of their sons—the untamed boisterous Boeslavich and the silly meek Gorebogatyr'. The mothers, however, taking a strong position with their sons, lead them to successful finales.

The tales may have had a personal overtone; the satiric Gorebogatyr', seen as a caricature of Swedish King Gustav III, also hinted at Paul.[39] Taken away from his mother as a boy by Empress Elisabeth and growing up surrounded by whispers that his father had been deposed by Catherine and slain by her supporters, Paul was never able to overcome the shadow of his illustrious mother; during his short reign, he was simultaneously feared and ridiculed. The birth of Catherine's first grandson Alexander (the future Alexander I) revived the empress's "hopes for future. She doted on Alexander."[40] The focus on a young man in these stories highlights the preoccupations of the grandmother-monarch, who intended to groom Alexander as a powerful military leader and enlightened monarch. As she did twice with her son, the empress arranged her grandsons' marriages to foreign princesses from the Germanic kingdoms that had provided an endless supply of brides for Russian tsars. In all her comic operas, as the respective heroes accomplish their tasks each is awarded a prize: a beautiful bride. Surfacing on the stage only in the last acts, all of the brides but one (in *Boeslavich*) are foreign princesses, three chosen by parents (except in *Akhrideich*).

Although Catherine's four operas share a basic outline, each with its own story represents a distinct genre of operatic skazka that would evolve during the nineteenth century: *Fevei* is a moral tale, *The Brave and Bold Knight Akhrideich* a magic tale, *Gorebogatyr Kosometovich* a satiric opera, and *Boeslavich, Champion of Novgorod* a bylina or Russian heroic epic in verse. All the operas in various ways instilled the traditional imperial virtues of Truth, Devotion, and Patience that were depicted in triumphal arches, pageants, and coronations. Preserving the spectacular aspect of these productions, Catherine dressed lessons on imperial virtues in the guise of comic operas. The princes presented in these operas range from the refined Alexander-like Fevei to brave Akhrideich, forceful (even violent) Boeslavich, and the hapless Woebegone-Champion. Demythologizing the images of champion and ruler (especially in the case of Gorebogatyr'), Catherine humanized her teenaged princes and, perhaps most important, transformed the mythologized monarchial abstraction using distinctly Russian imagery rooted in native tales, songs, and folk epics.

Operatic Tales as Lessons

Two operas, *Fevei* and *Gorebogatyr'*, are based on the empress's own prose tales. *The Brave and Bold Knight Akhrideich*, closely related to a European chivalric epic, is her remake of one of Levshin's skazkas.[41] The plot of Catherine's *Boeslavich* draws on Levshin's adaptation of one of the best-known Novgorod bylinas.[42]

Catherine's original skazka *The Tale of Prince Khlor* (1781), the source of *Fevei*, was reprinted annually in Russia for several years and appeared in English translation in London under the title *Ivan Tsarevich, or the Rose Without Prickles That Stings Not.*[43] The story tells about a little prince the same age as Catherine's four-year-old grandson Alexander. At the beginning of the tale, Khlor's royal parents have left the country, entrusting their son to nannies. Similarly, in real life, when Grand Duke Pavel (the future Paul I) and his wife went on a European tour, Alexander remained in Russia with his royal grandmother. Surrounded by seven skillful nannies, Khlor is shielded in a city that, as described by Catherine, reminds one of the most tasteful and elaborate eighteenth-century Russian estates: "behind the palace there were gardens with fruit trees, ... ponds filled with fish, and gazebos in the styles of different peoples, ... and a view of far-reaching fields and meadows."[44] When the curious boy disobeys an order and steps beyond the guarded gates, a Kirgizian Khan kidnaps him, putting him to the test of finding the rose without prickles. During his journey, Khlor is directed, guided, and assisted by wise Felitsa, who warns him against dull amusements and meaningless praise and who teaches him that working peasants are as worthy as tsars and tsarinas. This social message, ignored by democratic and socialist Russian scholars, adds some complexity to the long-sustained view of the empress as the unapologetic autocrat and supporter of Russian serfdom.[45] Accompanied by Felitsa's son Rassudok (Reason), Khlor finds that the rose with no prickles signifies royal virtues: Goodness, Honesty, and Humility.

The equation between Catherine and Felitsa was well-known. Within a year of the publication of *Khlor*, Derzhavin began his poetic cycle on Felitsa, "the godlike Tsarevna of Kirgizian hordes whose unmatched wisdom guides Khlor."[46] Twenty years later, the same Derzhavin wrote the ode "To Tsarevich Khlor," addressing the new emperor Alexander. Derzhavin's verses would soon be read and admired by another young man, Alexander Pushkin (born in 1799).

Meanwhile, the empress issued a new tale whose main protagonist, a teenaged version of Khlor, is fifteen-year-old Fevei. Four years later this tale would serve as a foundation for Catherine's opera of the same title (1786). Felitsa is no longer present. The royal couple, having no travel plans, is fully involved in the life of their son Fevei. Unlike the tale, the libretto explores the theme of youth's amorous fantasy. At the beginning of the opera, Fevei is sleeping, dreaming of a beautiful maiden who appears on stage as a ballerina. As he wakes, the vision fades away. The dream of a desired woman would become very popular in nineteenth-century Russian operatic literature, whether the dozing man is a young prince (Rimsky-Korsakov's *Mlada*) or a foolish old tsar (Rimsky-Korsakov's *Golden Cockerel*). Restless Fevei craves travel and adventure, worrying his royal parents. In the course of the spectacle, without departing from his kingdom, he stands up to Kalmyks and is embattled by Tatars. Exhibiting bravery and saved by his guards, he submits to marriage with a princess from afar chosen by his parents, only to realize as he removes the bridal veil that she is the subject of his dream.

Roses (without prickles) frame the cover of a 1789 edition of *Fevei*, confirming a parallel between Catherine's two tales and her opera, as well as between Khlor/Fevei and the real prince Grand Duke Alexander.[47] However contrived and distant from reality, the opera permits a glimpse of a highly idealized royal family, much like modern-day footage of a presidential candidate's household during an election. The little prosaic tale can be seen as a teaching tool for Alexander and her second grandson Constantine. By imbuing her protagonist/heir with certain qualities, Catherine endorsed a moral code that stressed filial obedience, devotion, and honesty. Complying with his parents' wishes, submitting to an arranged marriage, and refusing gifts from Kalmyk emissaries, Fevei exemplifies the ideal monarch.

As her short moral tale turned into a spectacular production to amuse the St. Petersburg aristocracy and European diplomats and travelers, Catherine was already occupied with other literary pursuits. She aimed to "translate" the early Russian history of somber and militant Ruriks into a modern dramatic trilogy that would be educational, easily grasped, engaging, and related to current events. In the time she had to spare from foreign politics and internal reforms, court intrigue and love affairs, the empress researched historical sources for another sort of operatic project: the reinvention of the heroic and noble Russian past.

Less than two months after the premiere of *Fevei*, Khrapovitsky wrote in his diaries: "Ordered to make a copy of the comic opera *Khrabroi i smeloi vitiaz' Akhrideich*."[48] The opening scene of the opera—a garden with a limpid stream, where the tsar's two daughters listen to "singing nightingales"[49]—portrays the pastoral harmony of a tsar's family. The Arcadian vignette is disrupted by a sudden windstorm and a descending cloud that sweeps away both princesses. This combination of a thunderstorm and a kidnapping, much relished in eighteenth-century operatic tales, foreshadows the beginning of Pushkin's and Glinka's *Ruslan and Liudmila*. In Catherine's opera, it is not the groom but a devoted brother, Prince Ivan (Ivan Tsarevich), who undertakes the search. (In his initial libretto, Glinka included Ivan Tsarevich as Liudmila's brother.) Catherine's hero encounters magical personages; fighting, outwitting, and charming his opponents, he finally finds a Tsar-Maiden who becomes his bride and helps him liberate his sisters. As the tsar's entire family rejoices, a Russian folk chorus muses: "What else is there to wish for? . . . All the tsars are blissful in skazkas."[50] The irony of the last lines makes the typical choral accolade to the tsars into a kind of caricature, which, though not written by Catherine, was approved and perhaps appreciated by her.

The moral message of patience and familial loyalty relates *Akhrideich* to *Fevei*, but the language and the tone of this comedy are much lighter and more humorous. For example, after the first scene, the remainder of the act is a chain of exaggerated recountings of the kidnapping to every new character entering the stage, each version accompanied by added details and new bursts of emotion. By the end of the act, the tsar, concerned about his spouse, who has lost weight and whose beauty has faded ("her body sticks to the bones . . . the beauty falls from her face"[51]), suddenly steps out of his role as grieving father and comments: "Though it is difficult to think like that, / . . . there are a hundred examples / [of kidnapping] one finds in magic tales." Similarly, upon the author's direction, Ivan, who is in the midst of various magical tasks and busy with his rescue mission, dives out of character by pulling out a watch and commenting that it is getting late.[52]

The only magic tale among Catherine's operas, *Akhrideich* catalogues phantasmagoric creatures and devices of Russian folklore and includes all the "seventeen transformations" Mikhail Druskin finds in early nineteenth-century magic opera.[53] The young hero, departing from home, immediately encounters an arguing pair of *leshiis* (mischievous Russian wood-goblins). Tricking them, Prince Ivan, much like his folk counterpart Ivan the Fool, manages to receive a flying carpet, a magic hat that makes him invisible, fast-walking boots, and a tablecloth that when unfolded produces food and two dozen servants who turn into a chorus if needed. As the prince proceeds in his task, combining charm and cleverness, he solicits the support of the typically wicked Baba-Yaga, befriends Bear-Man and Sea Wonder (his sisters' kidnappers), and wins a battle with a twenty-headed Snake. The text of the opera refers to visual effects, changing scenery, colorful magical characters, striking costumes, ballet scenes, and choruses.

The swiftly finished libretto of *Akhrideich* would not premiere for another year and a half. During that time Catherine managed to complete yet another opera-skazka. *Boeslavich, Champion of Novgorod* is the first-known operatic adaptation of a Russian bylina, though Russian musicologists praise Rimsky-Korsakov as a pioneer of the operatic bylina—his *Sadko,* created over a hundred years later (1897). Catherine adopted the plot of *Boeslavich* from *Russian Tales* by Levshin, who himself probably borrowed it from Novgorod bylinas included in the collection by Kirsha Danilov.[54] In the copyright-free eighteenth century, the stories, much like those in the realm of oral culture, could be endlessly repeated and elaborated. In the case of *Boeslavich*, the story, extracted from a short tale buried in some thousand pages of Levshin's ten volumes of skazkas, is turned into an opera lavishly produced by Catherine.

The main protagonist is another teenager, who, possessing enormous physical strength, repeatedly gets himself into fistfights—a traditional pastime among Russian youths in ancient Novgorod. Unable to manage the son of Novgorod's deceased ruler, a group of wealthy city merchants approaches Boeslavich's mother with precious gifts, asking her to tame the youth. To confirm the peace, they invite the young champion to attend their gathering. Drunk, bragging, and boasting, they trick the young man into a "topping" contest, which ends with the two sides challenging one another. Learning about the conflict, the worried mother rushes her son to a "deep cellar" and sends costly gifts to the merchants, who refuse her gesture of reconciliation. In the morning, the people of Novgorod surround Boeslavich's palace. Without armor, the awakened youth meets the "thousands," yanks an oak tree out of the ground, and races a mob through the streets to the river Volkhova (a name that resurfaces as a Sea Princess in Rimsky-Korsakov's operatic bylina). At this point, the gift-giving procession again reverses its direction; now the merchants beg the champion's mother for forgiveness and assistance. With great difficulty (strangers and pilgrims die in the folk versions), Boeslavich's family and friends manage to calm the champion, who accepts lavish presents and fees in return for the oath of his former opponents to cede to him "all the Slavic lands and Old Russia." Many renditions of the oral bylina about Boeslavich are quite crude and portray not a hero but a troublesome character who, crushing, breaking, and slaughtering everyone in his path, often ends up killed.[55] Following Levshin, Catherine further softens the story and manages to save the hero. Moreover, she also successfully marries off Boeslavich and ennobles her champion by making him a protector of his family rights, as well as a forgiving victor and a somewhat tender spouse.

Swinging between different operatic reincarnations of her young princes—whether invented, borrowed from folklore, or adapted from literary sources—Catherine created yet another type in her last operatic tale, *Gorebogatyr'*. The title character of this opera is a mocking portrayal of the Swedish King Gustav III, a son of Her Majesty's maternal uncle and the ruler of neighboring Sweden, who had fashioned operas of his own. During the summer of 1777, under the name Count Gotlandsky, Gustav visited the Russian imperial court and spent a festive month with his cousin attending many balls, artistic affairs, and operas.[56] The two reconvened in June 1783 and parted, exchanging assurances of friendship and trust. Catherine, writing to Potemkin, talks about Gustav's preoccupation with his clothes and remarks on his prohibition against courtiers appearing in military attire: "It displeased me since there is no more honorable attire than a uniform."[57] The last remark is a bit ironic, considering that in midsummer 1788 Gustav ordered a theatrical tailor to make Russian uniforms, and dressed as Russians, a group of Swedish soldiers enacted an assault on their own borders (a tactic Peter I had used against Swedes in 1704[58]). This gave the king a "legitimate" reason to attack Russia, which at the time was immersed in a war with the Ottomans and preoccupied with the French revolution.

While the two armies faced each other's fire, an operatic-type battle continued in the royal salons. Swedish ambassadors delivered to the empress what Khrapovitsky referred to as "a crazy note" with an impossible ultimatum; the Russian envoy, cultivating internal opposition among the Swedish aristocracy, sent an open letter announcing to "everyone in the nation who participates in ruling, that Her Imperial Majesty wishes nothing more than mutual peace between the two countries."[59] Catherine was enraged by Gustav's promise to treat Copenhagen ladies to breakfast in St. Petersburg and by his continuous boasting about his victories: "Let him brag all he wants, he makes himself a nuisance to objective eyes."[60] In the stressful autumn of 1788, while closely following events at the front, dealing with political unrest in Europe, and listening to rumors about the boisterous king, Catherine herself made sure that Gustav III was seen as "a nuisance." So she conceived an operatic tale about a character initially called Fufliga ("a pimple, pustule; a petty and undersized person, driveller"[61]). Consulting with her favorite Mamonov, Catherine renamed her main character Gorebogatyr' (Catherine's portmanteau word combines *gore*, woebegone, and *bogatyr'*, champion). At her request, Khrapovitsky wrote an aria for the protagonist that would begin with an anagram of "Gustav": "Geroistvom naduvaias'" (swelling with heroism).[62]

The introduction to the opera, probably written by Catherine herself, announces that the tale of Gorebogatyr' was "rewritten word by word from a manuscript kept in the capital city in storage and inside an old bag." In this story, another boy of fifteen, raised by his mother, has decided to have a heroic venture. Unlike his counterparts in the other operas, he is short, physically unfit, hardly educated, also boisterous and stubborn. The text reflects the silliness of the protagonist. When his whim for traveling fails to meet his mother's approval, the hero throws himself on the floor. His loud crying exhausts the female companions and his mother, who finally grants his request:

Куда ты хочешь поезжай	Go wherever you please
Лишь только лоб не разбивай	Just don't break your forehead on the floor
И потоком слез из глаз твоих	And with the pouring stream of tears
Ты не мочи ковров моих.	Do not wet my carpets.

The second act takes the hero to a barn, where he attempts to find himself a horse. Scared of the first horse, a thoroughbred; failing to mount the second; and thrown by the third, the hero finally manages to straddle an old mare. He also intends to carry his familial armor but can neither lift an iron club nor wear the large and ponderous breastplate. His involuntarily assigned assistant Krivomozg (Crooked-brain) convinces the "champion" to wear paper armor colored with metallic paint and to use a papier-mâché cap instead of a heavy helmet. Finally leaving home in the third act, the hero covers a short distance when, feeling hungry, he decides to attack a little hut and its owner: an old man with no arms, whom Khrapovitsky equates with the superintendent of a real fortress in Nishlot, near the Swedish border.[63] Not threatened by the hero, the brave old man chases the Woebegone-Champion out of his yard. The hero's companions, failing to teach him anything and constantly getting him out of trouble, stage a counterfeit battle (much as Gustav III himself did) by stirring up dust on the road. This persuades the hero to return home, and they all agree to tell the same story of the champion's victorious journey. In his palace, the hero is awaited by his bride, Gremila Shumilovna (Thunder, daughter of Noise), who naturally finds pleasure in thunder, storms, whistling, and various noises. The two—large and loud Gremila and her short, pompous champion—constitute another happily wedded couple as the chorus sings a proverb about a tomtit who wished to set fire to the sea but, unable to ignite it, made a lot of noise instead.

The libretto was read by many in the court, including the young Grand Dukes, who enjoyed the production and sang the opera by memory. Shown in the Hermitage in the midst of the Russian-Swedish war, the opera, at the insistence of Catherine's most trusted associates, did not appear on the public stage. Instead, the indefatigable empress sent the score to Moscow's best private troupe belonging to Count Nikolai Sheremetev, who successfully produced other operas by Catherine.[64]

Music Bridging Folk and Court Cultures

At a time when tsars and queens reigned on the stage of opera seria with baroque magnificence, Catherine moved royalty into the realm of what she called "comic opera," written in colloquial language and with a strong folk element. In so doing, she disturbed the boundaries of theatrical genres and forged a genre of her own as she also poked fun at and humanized the domain of the powerful. The relations between tsars and their successors, and between mothers and sons—central to the empress's libretti—are wrapped in humorous situations and folk details. The protagonists, outlined graphically according to their functions in the simple plotlines, are free of complexities.

Announcing that her operas are "compiled from the worlds of *skazkas*, Russian songs, and various other things," Catherine fulfilled her premise by saturating the operatic text with folk expressions, by using folk and popular songs, and by recreating on stage many elements of characteristically Russian games and rituals. Drawing on a long-existing tradition of tale telling, Catherine's tale uses the poetic epithets typical of the real and imaginary folk: "white-stoned palace," "merry wide yard," "gold-headed *terems*," "red [maiden], eyes of a falcon, brows of a sable, gaits of a pheasant, breast of a swan.[65] The characters address each other in barely translatable old Russian: "udaloi molodets" (daring fellow), "liubeznoe chado" (amiable child), "otets—svetlyi mesiats" (father—bright crescent).

One can dissect Catherine's operatic libretti, questioning which lines were written by the German-born tsarina, which suggested by her secretaries or edited by her many assistants. Most important, however, behind each word of her tales and libretti was Catherine's intention to sculpt Russia as a cultural entity. The same intention led her to encourage and support Dashkova's projects—the establishment of the Russian Academy of Science and the compilation of the first Russian dictionary. She also underwrote a significant grant for Russian translations of European classics, wrote various educational works in Russian, and jokingly penalized Petersburg's aristocrats for using foreign words when visiting her "Little Hermitage." She championed Russian theater as both Westernized and distinctly native, and—embracing a European concept of nationalism—envisioned and advocated Russianness as rooted in the folk.

Though in a number of her nonmusical comedies Catherine created a gallery of Beaumarchais-like shrewd maids who save their matrons' romances,[66] the personages of her comedies did not make it into her operatic tales. Neither did the re-dressing of noble characters into idyllic peasants (and vice versa), a convention of contemporary comic opera. Instead Catherine brought folk elements into operatic princely palaces and advanced the concept of Russianness by absorbing various literary and musical ingredients, ranging from urban folklore to native light classics.[67]

The song lyrics in *Fevei* unite two main streams of Russian songs; one comprises collections of folk repertory and the other composed sentimental airs (a genre that in the early nineteenth century would come to be known as "romance"). Six songs woven into the libretto of *Fevei* are identified with Chulkov's anthology, *Collection of Various Songs* (1770–1774). Typically viewed as a repository of folk verses, this collection also included theatrical arias and masquerade songs. Vocal numbers composed for Catherine's operas (especially the tunes by Pashkevich) later reappeared in various folk song anthologies. A noteworthy example is the *Collection of Russian Folk Song* by count Nikolai L'vov and Ivan Prach—the compilation perhaps most frequently drawn upon as a source for folk songs by nineteenth-century composers. The L'vov-Prach collection came out around the same time as the publication of Catherine's two operas, *Fevei* and *Gorebogatyr'*. The title pages of both operas bear the name of Prach as responsible for "arrangement for voices."

If Pashkevich (whose name does not appear in the score) was indeed responsible for the music of *Fevei*,[68] the reason Catherine chose him to compose the music for her first opera seems apparent.[69] Pashkevich was one of the busiest musicians in the capital. For several years preceding *Fevei*, he served as musical director of the St. Petersburg public theater of Kapnist-Dmitrievsky,[70] conducted the court ball orchestra, coached the court chapel chorus, and taught voice at the Academy of Arts. Letters of his contemporaries attest that Pashkevich also sang in his early operas.[71] Exposed to Italian, French, and Russian operatic traditions as well as to the culture of the Russian court, Pashkevich seemed a perfect candidate for the job: a man capable of creating and organically uniting disparate musical elements, from Italian light classical opera to opéra comique, Russian song, and early Russian music portraying the Orient. His multifaceted musical experiences may explain the remarkable balance between styles and musical idioms in *Fevei*, even though Russian musicologists typically commiserate with Pashkevich for working with a hopeless libretto.[72]

The twofold Russian imagery implied in the text permeates the twenty-four musical numbers of the four-act opera, filled with tunes both expressive and melodious (no recitatives). On the one hand, the composer borrows and imitates folklike songs, with clear, wavy, balanced melodies and simple rhythmic patterns, mostly in major keys. On the other, Pashkevich's sentimental airs use short, often descending tearful motifs, sustained notes, frequent sighs, and at times peculiar melodic contours, predictably in minor keys.[73] The overture introduces both types. The opening theme in C major, energetic in a fast tempo, embraces full dynamics, wide range, and ends with bravura passages. The second theme, in a minor key and in much slower motion, consists of short motifs encircling sustained tones, repeated in sequence and ending with a dolorous, wavy gesture (Examples 3.1 and 3.2).

Example 3.1

Example 3.2

Elements of the two themes recur throughout the opera. For example, at the opening of the first act, waking up as the image of the ballerina and the sounds of the overture fade, the teenage boy reiterates the melodic gesture of the second theme in his air (likewise in A minor), sighing repeatedly, "Ach! [come and] tell me, darling. . . Oh, [her] wondrous glance! / Oh, her pleasant looks." His whole tune—a sequence of short motifs, a falling tendency in the melody (balanced by a rising sequence), and then a long, winding melodic phrase—could serve as a model of the sentimental style (Example 3.3). The suffering of the hero throughout the opera is tinted with comedy. In the middle of his first air, for example, when the prince repeats in distress "I am losing you irrevocably! Can anything torment me more?" the melody changes to a light dance. The second theme of the overture defines the overall ambiance of this aria and recurs in other numbers sung by the grieving Fevei. The scene following the melancholy air of the love-struck hero portrays the joyful royal couple, yet untouched by parental worries. Their duet echoes the first energetic theme of the overture. The elements of two characteristic images introduced in the overture reappear throughout the opera; the initial theme sparkles in the female chorus from the middle of the second act, "Higher than all and merrier."[74]

The composer bridges the two Russian musical spheres thematically. Several numbers in the first act, for example, begin with nearly identical melodic gestures (Examples 3.3, 3.4, and 3.5). Drawing on the musical vocabulary of his time, Pashkevich also employs Italian operatic conventions, most remarkably at the beginning of the second act in the ensemble of the Tsarina and her maids, Mia, Naia, and Tina.

Example 3.3

Fevey: As you said to me in my dreams, Ach! [come and] tell me, darling, in real life, in real life, darling

Example 3.4

Tsarina: There was none as happy as me in the world; as much as I love my dove, he loves me in return.

To portray the women's agitation, he uses running passages, multiple repetitions of the same motifs, high ranges, and occasionally wide melodic leaps. A scene with voices imitating each other and joining in canon reminds one of Mozart's Quartetto in *Idomeneo*.[75] Pashkevich treats most of his ensembles in *Fevei* in a similar way, by first weaving voices consecutively into a continuous melody; then, gradually

Example 3.5

Fevei: I don't know what to say, and am afraid to embarrass myself; When appearing before you I know not what to say

branching off this melody, the voices begin echoing one another and joining in canon (Example 3.6). The gentle canonic entrances in the ensemble scenes are characteristic not only of this opera; Levashov notes the composer's repeated use of canons in *St. Petersburg Bazaar*.[76] From the beginning of the nineteenth century, and increasingly after the 1812 war, Russians forgot about Pashkevich. Neither Tchaikovsky nor his contemporaries seemed to know about the composer or his works. Yet, according to Levashov, some elements Pashkevich developed and polished in a number of his operas were imitated by his contemporaries and, "not disrupted, but instead, sustained, branching out," became conventions in the music of the forgetful nineteenth century.[77]

It is conceivable that Pashkevich both adapted from and contributed to a repertoire of songs circulating in published collections and personal manuscripts as well as in the realm of oral urban folklore. Embracing the light-hearted spirit of the tale, Pashkevich weaves folk tunes into comical situations. For example, when Mia and Naia, volunteering to divert Fevei from his travel plans, rehearse what they will tell the prince, Mia proposes to begin with one folk tune, "Ah, you—the father light crescent moon!" and Naia, immediately disagreeing, offers to address him with another, "Ah, you—the sun, red sun!" In Mia's song and several others, Pashkevich used asymmetrical phrasing, which in later Russian musical literature became identified as a characteristic folk element (Example 3.5). Among all the folk tunes used in *Fevei,* perhaps the most

Example 3.6

Mia: Listen, darling, one word
Naia: Beautiful like rose's light
Tina: My heart, my darling life!

familiar today is the song of Ledmir, which signals the beginning of the folk chorus, and the female khorovod at the end of the second act.

Constructing Russia Against Its Own Oriental Other/ness

Throughout the century Russia, undergoing internal reform, defined itself militarily, politically, and culturally, in relation to both West and East. Adopting and rivaling European culture, it repeatedly fought Ottomans and other nearby Easterners, fostering a culture that celebrated real and imaginary victories over the Orient. Thus Russia proclaimed itself a central player in global politics and internally a universe composed of the many ethnicities and nations that paraded before Anna during the Wedding in the Ice House and entered the stage in Catherine's operas. Eastern exotica occupied the political and artistic mind in Western Europe, whose interaction with the East in the years before the Napoleonic ventures was mostly related to the Ottoman Empire.[78]

Aiming to create a "self-consciously Russian idiom"[79] and understanding that construction of a strong Russian identity required contrasting "others," Catherine fostered the dichotomy of Orient-Occident. The third act of *Fevei* introduces dramatic and musical imagery that fully blossoms in nineteenth-century opera as the Russian portrayal of the Orient. Russia, itself viewed by Westerners as exotic, conquered and constituted its own Orient. Although the Oriental theme in the opera is not a novelty on the Russian stage, the representation of the Orient in *Fevei* is rather specific and historical: Catherine portrayed Kalmyks and Tatars, two neighboring ethnic groups living in the lower part of the Volga within the Russian empire. In the course of constant war and negotiation, Russian courtiers had observed the princes and messengers from these khanates not in operatic but real settings.[80] By portraying musically only the Kalmyks, Pashkevich maintains a clear distinction between Russian and Eastern musical imagery, "curiously foreshadowing," in the words of Taruskin, "the technique of certain nineteenth-century Russian masters."[81] The musical cluster depicting the Kalmyks consists of a sequence beginning with Ogliad's description of the visitors ("young men," "big foreheads," "fur coats"), followed by a quartet of the tsar and three messengers, a Kalmyk unison chorus and Kalmyk dances interspersed with solos, and a three-part chorus at the end of the scene. Pashkevich's choice of musical elements for the Kalmyks appears more closely informed and accordingly more nuanced than the operatic portrayal of the Orient by his contemporaries.

One finds in Pashkevich's East the seven elements Thomas Bauman identifies with oriental imagery in Mozart's *Die Entführung aus dem Serail* and other Oriental operas of its day.[82] In his Kalmyks' chorus Pashkevich applies intricate and specific dance rhythms (typically in 6/8) with abundant syncopations. While working several years earlier on one of his operatic hits, *The Tunisian Pasha*,[83] Pashkevich had likely discovered the monophonic style of Eastern vocal music. Accordingly, in *Fevei* he stripped the choral parts of harmony, placing the vocal lines an octave apart and writing nonintrusive accompaniment that consisted of a drone in the bass and a simple rhythmic formula. The dancing choral sections alternate with a solo, in which a shift from major to minor keys and rhythmic flexibility imply an element of improvisation typical of various Eastern musics (Example 3.7).

Recent research on Orientalism, exploring the dichotomy of "us and others," defines a basic tenet: the necessity of oriental "otherness" for the establishment of one's own modern, occidental, national self. In *The Early Reign of Oleg*, discussed in the next chapter, an Oriental scene is placed between and in drastic contrast to two Russian ones. In *Fevei*, preceding the entrance of Eastern guests, maidens dance and sing in the khorovod; a protective father orders young women to get home before the arrival of Kalmyk and Tatar warriors. Following the scenes with the Oriental visitors is a large celebratory Russian wedding. Both khorovod songs and wedding rituals would become emblems of Russianness in nineteenth-century national operas.

Russian elements generally thought of as the exclusive province of nineteenth-century nationalist composers are also characteristic of the text and music of Catherine's two other operas, *Akhrideich* and *Boeslavich*. Neither of the two scores was published, except for the overture of *Akhrideich*, which like the overture of *Fevei* introduces folk tunes. The empress assigned the music of *Akhrideich* to Arnošt Vančura (1750–1802), who, living in Russia for many years, established a reputation as a theater enthusiast, theatrical entrepreneur, and composer.[84] *Boeslavich*,

Example 3.7

Chorus: On that rock, A Kalmyk woman was consuming *kaimak*, *suliak*, and *turmak*
Soloist: To her came a little Kalmyk, asked for *kaimak*, *suliak*, and *turmak*

rooted in old native epics, was entrusted to Fomin (1761–1800). An orphaned son of a cannoneer, Fomin benefited from "charitable institutions set up by Catherine II,"[85] first undergoing musical training in the Academy of Arts and later sent to study with Padre Martini in Bologna. Back home the debut of Fomin's *Boeslavich* was followed in the remaining years of his short life by some thirty works for the theater. The score of *Boeslavich* was not published, and the manuscript has not survived. Taruskin suspects that "Fomin's effort . . . failed to please his royal collaborator."[86] Perhaps by the time of the production of *Boeslavich* on November 22, 1786, Catherine's mind was occupied by the historical triptych she intended to realize in opera, by a politically important half-year trip, and by anticipation of a war that broke out the following year.

Besides the "Russian tales and songs" promised by the author, the libretto of *Boeslavich* introduces ethnographic features such as the *kulachnyi boi* or fistfight. "One-on-one" or "wall-to-wall," these street fights were known as a popular (though dangerous) entertainment in ancient Novgorod. Starting with a small cohort and rapidly spreading, a local feud could ignite an entire city crowd. The resulting dreadful fights and murders were random and pointless. Catherine, an enlightened monarch and educator, significantly underplayed this violence in her opera.

Another ethnographic element of early Novgorod culture is the traditional *pokhval'ba* or bragging contest, which Levshin referred to and Catherine's plot expanded in verses sung by Novgorod's self-praising merchants.

Мой конь красоты невообразимой, . . .	My horse is of unimaginable beauty . . .
Из ноздрей огонь мечет	Fire comes out of its nostrils
Жена моя боярыня,	Wife of mine
Родом она болгарыня,	Is Bulgarian
Черноброва,	Dark-brows
Черноглаза	Dark-eyes
Черноволоса	Dark-hair
Где копьем верну,	Where [I] turn a spear
Тамо улица	There is a street;
Где копьем махну,	Where [I] swing a spear
Нету тысячи.	Thousands disappear

While appropriating much of Levshin's language, permeated with folk idioms, Catherine—well acquainted with the theater—transformed his short tale into a fast-paced spectacle. By breaking up and distributing lines among characters, she replaced the anonymity of several secondary figures with the brightness and familiarity of *lubok*-like characters.[87] The group of Novgorod merchants, for example, includes Sadko (here Satko), who, making his debut in Catherine's opera, would reappear a century later as Rimsky-Korsakov's title hero.

The Wedding as an Operatic Finale

From the wedding masquerades of Petrine times to the ice–castle marriage organized by Anna, weddings had served as a primary entertainment and performative milieu for the Russian aristocracy. The theatricality of the court and the role of the theater in court rituals, discussed in Chapter One, identified the wedding as a locus of intriguing overlap, convergence, and reversal of the theatrical and the royal. The time-consuming process of matchmaking, engagements, wedding arrangements, and performances— as evidenced by notes and diaries of the time—made marriage ceremonies one of the main occupations of courtiers. Nuptial agreements signed between the highest Russian families were celebrated in wedding ceremonies that defined the boundaries of high court society and culture. At the same time, in these weddings even modernized courtiers, like their noble (or non-noble) predecessors, adhered to some ancient folk traditions. By employing folk elements, those performing imperial and noble weddings asserted both their connection to the historical past and their ties with native roots. In addition, these massive celebrations, held on a grand scale—with food provided and money tossed to the massive crowd gathering around decorated palaces—allegorically bridged the worlds of the opulent Westernized court and the native folk.

A junction between real life and performance, ritual and entertainment, the wedding ritual entered the realm of Russian opera from its beginnings.[88] Several native scholars suggest that wedding games were a source of native opera, referring to a number of early operas that portray marriage rituals as signifiers of Russian culture and character.[89] Catherine incorporates weddings in all four opera-skazkas and her historical pageant *Oleg*. In the opera-skazkas the wedding serves as a grand operatic finale in which a massive chorus celebrates the happiness of a future heir. These choral auguries allude to and playfully reenact real courtly weddings, which themselves included operas created and performed for regal events. Final operatic choruses were often directed not to theatrical characters but, as discussed in Chapter One, to a wedded couple sitting in the royal balcony.

In *Fevei*, the wedding scene in the second half of the fourth act is preceded by a musical portrayal of the Kalmyks, central to the third act and the music-free action scene at the beginning of the fourth. Singing a short air in Act III, Ogliad reports the arrival of the Kalmyks, and in the last act he sings about the approaching bridal wagon, "All horses shiny black [*voronye*, raven], all carriages of gold." A prince's wedding is a state event, and no one knew this better than the libretto's author. The tsar assumes a commanding role, briefly ordering Fevei to "go home: prepare to meet the bride," and questioning Vulepul', "Is everything ready for the marriage?" While the tsarina—in her incurably teary manner, her nervousness expressed in the racing triplets of the accompaniment—"sweetly prays" to her husband for a beautiful spouse for her son, the tsar opens the window and looks for the arriving bride-to-be. Next, Vulepul' reports to the tsar (and the audience) that the wedding celebration will follow the sequence of the tsar's own wedding "with small exceptions [considering] the [different] times." Vulepul' offers a comical account of the mythological procession flavored with Grecian and Roman references: "on both sides there are many cupids, air vibrating with the sound of their wings, . . . all exclaimed together accordingly . . . hei! But more amusing than everything was when Apollo appeared with a violin."

The wedding of the teenage boy is delightful and timely. Fevei's restlessness, which today would be attributed to hormones, was perceived in Catherine's time as a discomfort curable by war and marriage, themes that belonged not so much to the realm of the tale as to a reality intimately familiar to the spectators of *Fevei*. The trumpeting sound of the orchestra opens a chorus that praises the beauty of the bride. The chorus encircles a love duet led by Fevei and concludes the opera with a jubilant song:

Играй, о сердце сердцем нежно,	Play, oh heart with heart tenderly,
Теки, о время безмятежно,	Stream, oh time serenely
В забавах чрез весь наш век.	In games throughout our days.
Ею мы благополучны, . . .	Through her we are blessed,
Дай судьба дни неразлучны.	Give us, destiny, many days together

The text expresses the crowd's emotional investment in the happiness of "her," the bride; the folk's inherent link (*nerazluchny*) is not with the tsar's heir but with the bride's blissful future. "Through her we are blessed" points to Catherine, identifying the empress with the bride (of the Russian Fatherland) and life with the theater.

A meticulous description of the wedding in Catherine's hand constitutes part of her draft of *Akhrideich*. The text begins with the arrival of the rescued sisters and the royal parents via air chariot. The next section of the libretto is a sketch of Russian weddings that, stripped of any relation to this particular plot, presents ritualistic personages such as druzhki, svakhi, and tysiatskie and also points out the *kika*, a headdress for the bride that signifies the change of role from maiden to matron. The ten-section wedding description is remarkably close to a precise ethnographic outline of a wedding. Though not included in this opera, the detailed wedding ritual was staged in *Oleg*. Around the same years in which Catherine devised her operatic weddings, she also planned the marriage and wedding celebrations of the real imperial heir, Alexander, and his bride, the Grand Duchess Elizabeth (Luise Marie Auguste of Baden). In that ceremony, like Catherine's operatic princes, the ducal couple led a Russian ritualistic *zapletisia pleten'*.

In Catherine's adaptation of *Boeslavich*, the plot is happily resolved by the final wedding of the hero and young Umila (derived from *mila*, nice), a name that places the heroine in a long line of Miloradas, Milas, and Ludmilas. Though the daughter of the leader of the opposition, the young woman first attempts to defend the hero and then shows respect to and gains trust and support from Boeslavich's mother. Throughout the play, Umila has somewhat clumsy encounters with the champion. When he takes her by the hand, for example, the girl says that she burned her arm:

Boeslavich: How?
Umila: By fire.
Boeslavich: Where?
Umila: Everywhere around.

And then she modestly escapes.[90] This reference to fire and burning is as close as Catherine comes to depicting actual romance. By the end, Umila's father, defeated by Boeslavich in battle, happily contributes his daughter along with other gifts to his now pacified son-in-law. Moreover, the author actually manages to wed not one but two couples. Listening to the dialogue of Boeslavich and Umila, the groom's friend Foma begins "twisting [another] girl's arm"[91] and "pinching" her, finally admitting that he too wants to get married.

This double wedding might bring to mind the final episodes of a masterpiece of twentieth-century cinematography, Sergei Eisenstein's *Alexander Nevsky*. Among the main characters in the screenplay by Petr Pavlenko and Eisenstein are two Novgorod champions in love with the same girl.[92] Having defeated the Teutonic Knights, they arrive, seriously wounded, at Novgorod. One of them, Vasily Buslai (Vasily Boeslavich)—a direct reincarnation of the champion of the old bylina—nobly insists that his friend-rival marry their beloved Olga. In the last scenes of the film, Buslai, after a colorful exchange with his mother (Amel'fa, as in the *bylina*s and Catherine's opera), proposes marriage to the girl-warrior Vasilisa in the style of Catherine's heroes. None of the recorded versions of the bylina, including Levshin's tale, end with a wedding.[93]

Constructing a comical layer in his film, Eisenstein portrays Novgorod's champion with the light humor Catherine used in her comic opera. The layout of the film, interlacing music and drama, vocal and spoken episodes, and choreographed scenes, quite overtly points to eighteenth-century comic opera. Moreover, the film's producers emphasize choral episodes over vocal solos, following the Russian musical tradition that stemmed from eighteenth-century court culture and specifically from *partesnoe penie*—the heterophonic choral (three-voice) singing associated with court celebrations and ceremonies. Notably, Catherine used folk choruses in operas.[94] It is not impossible that in researching the history and mythology of old Novgorod, Eisenstein and his creative team found Catherine's opera and in this betrothal scene drew on ideas of an empress.

Catherine's Heroines: Mothers and Brides
in the *Terem*

Although they are distant from elated or suffering classical heroines enunciating their exhausting monologues, Catherine's operatic female characters also differ from the witty figures of fashionable comic opera. Russian nobles who learned to appreciate the elegant French operatic shepherdess used her as a model for their own Russian serf peasant*ress*. As described in Chapter Two, so outstanding was the aristocrats' delight that the act of re-dress was endlessly repeated and replayed in various ways. The roles, names, costumes, and places of French opera were adapted to the Russian landscape, and native peasant actresses were expected to act on stage as coquettish damsels in the comic operas. No adapted French, Italian, or Russian comic opera ever disappointed its spectators by failing to match in the operatic finale a graceful rustic heroine with an appropriately noble lover, whether a carpenter or an undisclosed aristocrat.

Catherine's operatic tales focus on young princes. The female characters are bound to the domain of supporting roles; rarely diverting attention from their main task, they appear monochromatic. The "outwardness" of the protagonists in the fairy tale operas and the use of character-symbols that "bear elements of epic naïveté bordering on amusement, with purposefully playful and showy features, stylization of emotions of love," which Komarnitskaia points out in nineteenth-century operatic tales, can well be applied to Catherine's personages, especially to her women.[95]

The women in Catherine's operas fall into three categories: tsarina-mothers, princess-brides (or sisters), and indistinguishable nannies and matrons who cluster around the mothers, echoing, supporting, and reflecting the tsarinas' concerns. The married mother-tsarinas in *Fevei* and *Akhrideich*, in no way relevant to the course of operatic events, function as an emotional barometer. Swinging from jubilation to tears and confined to the harmonious, carefree domestic space fostered by their royal spouses, they exhibit happiness in their married life. Disturbances related to children—the only son's possible departure (*Fevei*) or the daughters' disappearance on a cloud (*Akhrideich*)—leave the tsarinas helpless. Although they exhaust themselves and others with a flood of tears throughout the operas, they recover in the final wedding scene, providing a good model for the young royal couples.

Catherine-the-author seems somewhat more sympathetic to her widowed mothers in *Boeslavich* and *Gorebogatyr'*. In the former, she dismisses references to a "mindless *starukha*" (hag, in Danilov's version) and a *baba staraia* (old crone, in Levshin). By contrast, Catherine refers to Boeslavich's mother Amel'fa as "not a young woman" and an "honest widow." In Levshin's text, she marches with gifts to the city merchants who humiliate her and throw her out; Catherine, on the other hand, consigns Amel'fa to the security of her palace, giving her the company of a devoted male servant. The author stresses the importance of filial loyalty to the mother of Novgorod's champion, who, threatening everyone else, admits that though he "is not afraid of merchants, and Novgorod's people do not scare him, he is afraid of his mother's parental talk" (Act I, Scene 6). Unlike the bylinas, where Boeslavich on a whim throws a violent party, in the opera he seeks his mother's permission to gather his friends, consistently accedes to his mother's power, and often echoes her words. Invited to the merchants' feast, he publicly turns to his mother for advice: "Bude matushka blagoslovit k vam itti, to budu" (If mother gives me her blessing to go, then I will; Act I, Scene 7). Seeing her son drunk, Amel'fa simply locks him in the basement, fortifying the door with many "iron bolts" and piles of sand. After defeating his opponents and calming his temper, the champion directs the merchants to his mother, telling them that "without her blessing [he] won't accept" either their gifts or the offer of peace that they signify.

Even the silly, obstinate Gorebogatyr' avoids disobeying his mother. Instead he throws an emotional tantrum, hoping to convince her to give him permission for the journey. He also promises his mother's companions, who support his request, to bring expensive gifts of "black sable and marten, red fox, velvet and satin." He vows that after conquering the ocean, he will throw a grand feast "on the ocean-sea," serving them the "champion's own sweet food" and feeding them "by his own hands"—a reference perhaps to Gustav's boasting pledge to feed Copenhagen's ladies in St. Petersburg. Like her counterparts in Catherine's other operas, Gorebogatyr's mother, with her maids-in-waiting, is situated in a "white palace" decorated with carpets and reminiscent of a pleasant version of the terem.

The brides in the operas display a variety of female types: the beautiful and silent Danna; the Tsar-Maiden, herself a ruler; the doubly loud Gremila Shumilovna, towering over the undersized champion; and the clever Umila, who bridges the conflicting camps in *Boeslavich*, and who, though respectful to her father, cultivates filial-parental ties with the champion's mother. In addition to the brides, there are typically young women who surround the mothers. Unlike the secondary male characters, these maidens form an undistinguished group often with no individual characteristics or names. Even when given names, they sound alike (Mia, Naia, and Tina in *Fevei*). Indispensable to the plays yet projecting only a group identity, these women define both the feminine space and its anonymity.

Like the terem tsarinas, the women in these operas are stationary. None of them exhibit a desire to travel, to move, or to explore as princes do. The only female figure who arrives—or is, rather, delivered—is a bride who, accompanied by her mother and nannies, appears at the request of a prince's mother or both parents. Ivan Akhrideich's sisters, kidnapped by a Bear-Man and a Sea Monster, accept their fate by pleasing their captors. Even his bride Tsar-Maiden, who possesses magical powers that are supposedly stronger than those of all the wicked, malicious, and forceful spirits and monsters, does nothing but strike a bargain with the obedient jinn she holds in captivity. In the same story, Baba-Yaga attempts to patronize Ivan and later two leshiis. Still she admits to Ivan that, lonesome, she has lived in the same place and not seen anyone for forty years.

Thus the plots, confining women to limited (private) domains, and stressing the primary female function as nurturer of royal heirs, invoke an association with the terem. The operas were designed for Catherine's Little Hermitage, which physically linked the realm of theater with the empress's private space. Both the familial topics wrapped in the phantasmagoric or moral skazkas and the semiprivate space of the empress's theater appropriately matched the terem. Years earlier, as described before, in real terems wandering strangers, pilgrims, and *skomorokhs* (professional street entertainers) had narrated tales before the tsarinas, who were attached to their private quarters and thus invisible and abstract—hence virtuous to outsiders. Nearly one hundred years separated Catherine from Peter's legendary sister, Sofia, who created, translated, and staged plays in the royal terem.[96]

Why would Catherine, the breaker of all rules and the maker of her own, draw on anything related to the terem? The image of Catherine as a sexual libertine seems in no way translated into her moral "terem" tales. This is deeply disappointing to readers and critics who have sought in Catherine's operatic tales and other theatrical works traces of her own dynamic personality and the feminine role she chose for herself. Perhaps the mighty woman, who never ceased to astound and challenge her contemporaries— kings, poets, nations, and the whole world—in the third decade of her reign, marked by multiple wars, reformation, and continuous public self-display, felt tired, craved some momentary withdrawal and wondered about the bygone place of refuge for tsarinas.[97]

The terem also implies secrecy, concealed details, and veiled messages. The allusions of the opera to the terem suggest the possibility of alternative interpretations and implications that might well escape today's reader. In *Fevei*, for example, the author borrows the name, character, and even parts of the text of Vulepul', a secondary character from Trediakovsky's tragedy *Deidamia*. "The first general" and master of ceremonies in both works, Vulepul' organizes royal assemblies by giving orders to everyone—to go faster, step with "the speed of wings," run, fetch, place (chairs and tables), and then leave and join the rest of the group, which is organized in order of rank—all of this a light parody of court ceremonies. In her lines for Vulepul' Catherine directly quotes Trediakovsky.

In *Deidamia*, a great warrior Pir, dressed as Pirra, is placed near Tsarina Deidamia. The same Vulepul' who orders Pirra next to the tsarina in Trediakovsky, in *Fevei* directs Mia:

Благополучно к вам	It is proper for the Tsarina to step a
Царине стать поближе	bit closer [to the Tsar]
Долги Мии быть при ней однако	The duty of Mia to be near her
довольно ниже...	but lower ...
Сим образом весь бок девицами	This way the maidens would adorn
скрасится	this side
Но стража поперек иль одаль да	The guards situated across and
вместится....	around....

Trediakovsky's Pirra is in fact the cross-dressed Achilles, lover of Tsarina Deidamia. In the ceremonial order, next to Pirra is Nephalia, another companion of the Tsarina. Nephalia is in love with Achilles and jealous of Deidamia; the characters form a dramatic triangle. Lacking details of the production of *Fevei*, one may ponder whether, along with text and characters, Catherine borrowed from Trediakovsky the cross-dressing and an intriguing triangle as a subplot. Also, considering Catherine's love of parody and the sharp sketches in which her associates frequently recognized familiar persons and events, it is conceivable that by implying the parallel between the two duos—Deidamia-Pirra and Tsarevna-Mia—the author alluded to contemporary court rumors and adventures.

The last scene of *Fevei* is also peculiar. It begins with a chorus that glorifies the bride, who, "ready to be wed," is "*krasneisha* / more beautiful than the sun and radiant stars, dressed in a silver garb according to the wedding order." Strikingly, while the chorus venerates the bride and the love union and while Fevei recites his sentimental love confession, the bride herself sings only four lines. In response to Fevei's overly emotional air, echoing one of his dreams at the beginning of the opera, the princess answers, "nothing more can [I] add" and explains that she has things to conceal. On Fevei's insistence—"Tell me at least, dear / That you are mine forever"—the princess-bride soothes Fevei somewhat nonchalantly: "Enough to suffer and to endure / I ought (*ia dolzhna*) to love you till death." After this short, ambiguous admission, Fevei rejoices, proclaiming that "all troubles have passed, no sadness is left," and that the one who ignited his soul belongs to him now.

Catherine used Trediakovsky's *Deidamia* and his translation of semi-erotic poems[98] not only in *Fevei* but in *Akhrideich* as well. Also, at the empress's request, Khrapovitsky delivered to her a copy of Trediakovsky's work as she was creating *Gorebogatyr'*. Does this connection with the now little-known Trediakovsky imply subversive ideas concealed from later readers? Could it be that the interplay between the imagery of the virtuous terem on the one hand and Trediakovsky's island of love on the other reflect Catherine's view of gender?

Complex and controversial, Catherine's attitude toward women's social roles is reflected in her continuous promotion of women as well as women's legal rights, and simultaneously in her support of traditional feminine roles. Indeed Catherine herself, not submitting to any gender categories, played her own perplexing role as mistress of her subjects and Mother of the Fatherland.[99] Rising to a position of enormous power unprecedented for a woman, playing a major part in the political arena occupied by kings, emperors, and sultans, Catherine, as usual, wanted it all: to project solid masculine stamina and along with it the feminine virtues (terem) and domestic graces of both antiquated pre-Petrine and operatic rulers.

The Shadow of the Tale Teller

Catherine and her works belonged to an age of musical dilettantism that, predictably, would be sneered at by the proud professionals of the coming centuries. Yet there is something intriguing about the daily engagement of nearly all intellectuals in literature and theater. Life events and situations fashioned into plays—serving as idealized models of courtly behavior and noble sensitivity—defined the fluidity and interchangeability of the realms of theater and court. There is something appealing (or threatening) about high administrators and officials who write not only policies but also playful comic operas, and about imperial autocrats who, waging wars and refashioning society, create operatic tales. Catherine belonged to a group of enlightened rulers (among them Frederick of Prussia and Gustav III) who dabbled in drama and opera. None was as prolific as Catherine, whose literary heritage includes plays, musical spectacles, and complete operas, which she not only wrote but also produced. Her operatic *Akhrideich*, *Fevei*, and one-act *Fedul* remained in the theatrical repertoire throughout at least the first quarter of the nineteenth century.[100] Coming from "such a height," created in collaboration with established European and homegrown musicians, Catherine's opera-skazkas, according to Mooser, "incited an outbreak of analogous works."[101] An incomplete published collection of her works issued in the early twentieth century consists of twelve volumes. A few names of female royals who likewise produced musical and theatrical works have been gradually restored to history.[102] None, however, played a role comparable to Catherine's as monarch, political player, and zealous writer.

Catherine's prose and theatrical works, acclaimed during her monarchy, were soon after rejected with vehemence. Something in her plays must have been demeaning to her masculine royal and literary successors, who battled her image as a powerful, victorious monarch and also denied her creativity as a writer. To a large degree dismissing Catherine, subsequent generations craved for the colorfulness and theatricality of her age. Pushkin, for example, unsympathetic to the empress, nevertheless consistently situated his protagonists and plots in her time. Even when dealing with his contemporaries in *Queen of Spades*, his story is drawn into the previous century.

The ease with which Catherine approached her own theatrical works and their production somehow belittled her literary posterity. Male writers and poets of subsequent generations, competing, intriguing, and feeling unappreciated, totally devoted their lives to the play of words, while for the empress writing was an occupation on the side. Nineteenth-century romantic authors seemed unable to write without experiencing personal suffering, longing, and disillusionment. The shadow of Catherine, the female stallion whose feats would have been notorious even for a male ruler, disturbed them all—her literary, theatrical, and political heirs. But as this chapter has shown, an exceptional number of the devices that would come to be accepted as typical for Russian national opera had their debut in Catherine's work, leading us to suspect that for all the public dismissal, her literary and musical heirs remained under her spell.

4

OLEG AT THE ROOTS OF RUSSIAN
HISTORICAL OPERA

Tsarina Catherine as a Greek Goddess . . .

By the sea-washed shore, near a broken Grecian column, dressed in a free-flowing Greek toga, a royal mantle, and a crown—the empress extends her royal hand, holding a banner with the two-headed Russian imperial eagle. A caduceus of two-winged snakes is carried by Hermes, next to her, his hand mimicking her gesture. Behind her rise victorious flags; cannons, barrels of gunpowder, military drums, trumpets, and rolled-up maps lie at her feet. Time has collapsed, linking eighteenth-century Russia with Greece—the cradle of antiquity, the motherland of Eastern Orthodoxy, and the precursor of Ottoman Turkey, all three embodied in a tantalizing city on the Black Sea—Byzantium/Constantinople/Istanbul. Perhaps Hermes, wrapped in clouds, is acting as the messenger of victory in Catherine's first war with the Ottomans. (The engraving appears on a 1776 map that marks Russia's territorial acquisition; Figure 4.1.) In a similar map of 1787, pointing toward the water and the fleet, Hermes seems to call for action just as the second Russian-Turkish war erupts (1787–1791). Another map of the same year, shown below, portrays the tsarina as bare-breasted Demeter with a cornucopia and the Russian blazon, traveling to Tauride, where across the sea, far on the horizon, Orthodox churches rise on the Ottoman shore (Figure 4.2).

The cartographic documents attest to the construction of a Russian imperial mythology of conquest, and also to the role of the ever-young Catherine. She is simultaneously Mother Russia, a Greek goddess, the champion of Eastern Orthodoxy, and its defender against the Ottomans—a highly ritualized image that Catherine herself helped to sculpt.

Figure 4.1: Engraving on a map of Catherine's traveling to Kiev and Taurida, 1787. Harvard University, Map Library.

. . . And as Prince Oleg

What happens when the long-reigning ruler of the Russian empire, besides "making" history by waging wars and reshaping world politics, takes up her pen to shape national mythology? By creating and producing the historical spectacle *The Early Reign of Oleg*, Catherine wove politics and theater into a coherent narrative. In the same way that Catherine's opera-skazkas anticipated major elements of well-known Russian nineteenth-century fairy-tale operas, *Oleg* directly or indirectly led to creation of Russian historical opera, a genre that came to emblemize the rise of Russian musical nationalism.

Ascending to absolute power, and known as a prolific writer and producer, Catherine was mythologized during her lifetime. After her demise, she was stripped of

Figure 4.2: Engraving on a map of Russia 1776. Harvard University, Map Library.

much of her historical and literary legacy and dismissed as a writer, her dramatic works and operas nearly forgotten. A wave of post-Soviet Russian historical revisionism has revitalized interest in the eighteenth century in general and Catherine in particular. Andrew Wachtel traces the intertextual dialogue between Catherine's prose histories of Russia and her "Shakespearian" historical dramas. Maria Shcherbakova, a musicologist and the director of archives of St. Petersburg's Mariinsky Theater, writing about Catherine's *Oleg*, focuses on a phenomenological interpretation of *Oleg*, a work Catherine defined as a historical *predstavleniie* (show), or what Taruskin terms a pageant. Shcherbakova suggests it was the empress's intention to create a syncretic genre that would integrate elements of drama and opera and at the same time extend beyond the theatrical frame. Similarly, Lurana O'Malley refers to *Oleg* as metatheater, relating "the central plot (Oleg's attack on Constantinople) to the context of Catherine's 'Greek project' and the Russo-Turkish War of 1787–91."[1] O'Malley explores Catherine's use of various literary models, including Shakespearian historical plays. She also examines how Catherine emphasizes Greco-Russian connections in the context of her own policies toward Ottoman Turkey. O'Malley's analysis of the play is complemented by her rich and detailed account of the original production.

The present chapter examines the creation of *Oleg* not only as a play connected with historical events but also as a strategic script for Catherine's political actions. A historian might note that after completing the draft of the play, the royal author began enacting her plotline in real life by setting up a long journey that followed Oleg's route to the Black Sea. Creation of the play in 1786 can be seen as a prelude to an actual war, and the opulent premier of *Oleg* in 1791 became part of a spectacular celebration of the proclaimed victory.[2]

Weaving together spectacle and politics, Catherine shaped her perception of Russia in two dimensions, temporal and spatial. She drew a temporal vector by recreating and appropriating the historical past, and a spatial vector by dramatizing her conquest of extensive territories. At the same time, she appropriated literary sources ranging from Shakespeare and Euripides to the odes of Mikhail Lomonosov. The rich intertextuality of *Oleg* also rests on the integration of high, popular, and folk cultures. Exploring the plot, structure, and language of *Oleg*, this chapter, challenging conventional views of Russian musical history, identifies this musical spectacle as a forerunner of Russian historical heroic opera. Although the ample iconography of the time portrayed Catherine as a Greek goddess, in the empress's own historical spectacle she is represented by Oleg, the Russian champion.

The Plot of *Oleg*

On August 9, 1790, Catherine wrote to Prince Potemkin:

> We've pulled one paw out of the mud. Once we've pulled out the other one, we'll sing Hallelujah. *A propos de cela*, Platon Aleksandrovich [the brother of Alexander Zubov, her current lover] gave me Sarti's choruses. Both are very good, and the "Te Deum" is the most masterful of all. It is a pity that it can't be sung in church because of the instruments. Thank you for sending the music. "Oleg" is now being prepared for the celebrations of the northern peace-making, because of which we have achieved a cessation of military operations and, consequently, have saved men and money.[3]

This letter fragment raises a curtain revealing Catherine's political consciousness—the mind of a historical dramatist who can entwine issues of war, state, church, and theater with personal affairs in a short, coherent text. Potemkin was her advisor to his last day, a person whose zeal for life, pleasure, and power matched hers.[4] Sharing a strong affection for theater and music, the two maintained magnificent orchestras at their respective courts, staged theatrical productions of great magnitude, and led highly theatrical lives. The *Te Deum* Catherine referred to was composed by the Italian Giuseppe Sarti (1729–1802), whom the empress had invited to St. Petersburg and who at the time of the letter was working with Potemkin's orchestra. Sarti was one of three composers Catherine engaged to collaborate on music for *The Early Reign of Oleg*, which she calls simply "Oleg." The first "paw out of the mud" was the Russian war with Sweden, the other an anxiously desired victory over Turkey.

The five-act *Oleg*, based on Catherine's libretto, reenacts historical events in ninth-century pre-Christian Rus' and portrays Princes Oleg and Igor, who were among the founders of Russia's longest-reigning dynasty.[5] The play is the second part of a dramatic trilogy dealing with the history of early Rus', specifically the Rurik dynasty. *Oleg* was the only one of the three produced with music (largely choruses) and is often referred to as an opera.[6] At a time when classical Aristotelian drama still governed the stage, Catherine's historical epic not only broke the dramatic unities, unfolding in different places and stretching over time, but (re)produced historical events.

The title character Oleg—Prince Igor's uncle and advisor—directs political and military operations, aiming to unite pre-Christian Russia and protect its pagan beliefs by defeating Christian Tsargrad ("Tsar-City," Constantinople). The plotline and the structure of the spectacle continuously refer to a map of the Russian territories. Flouting the dramatic unities of time and place, Catherine situates the first act near Moscow, the second in Kiev. The third act portrays a royal wedding, also in Kiev; the fourth depicts the Russian army at the Bosphorus, and the fifth unfolds in Byzantium.

The play begins at the intersection of three rivers—the Moscow, Yauza, and Neglinny—where Oleg holds rites celebrating the foundation of the new city of Moscow. He is surrounded by nobles, a crowd of ordinary people, and torch-bearing priests. Messengers from Kiev bring grievances against Igor's vassal Oskold, the sovereign of Kiev. Having battled his neighbors and gathered fellow Slavs, Oskold, ahead of his fleet of two hundred vessels, descended the river Dniepr to the Black Sea. Keeping Tsargrad under siege and bringing back with him captured Greeks, Oskold has become spellbound by the new religion—Eastern Orthodoxy. A hundred fifty years later, Russian rulers would embrace Christianity, but at the time of Oleg, Oskold's fascination with Christianity would have been seen as disloyalty to the native faith, the Grand Prince, and the Russian people. On his return to Kiev, Oskold congregates with captured Christian Greeks and consequently abandons Kiev's old ritualistic hills and denounces the pagan priests. Listening to the messengers' complaints about Oskold's betrayal, Oleg muses about the strong appeal of the fast-growing religion spreading among the Dutch, French, Swedes, Bulgarians, and Czechs. Moving his army to Kiev, Oleg approaches but does not enter the city. Instead, he sets up camp on the bank of the Dniepr and entices Oskold to come out to greet his Russian overlords. Outside the city walls, Oleg takes Oskold under guard, avoiding bloodshed between Slavs and peacefully restoring order in Kiev. In the version of "merciful" Catherine, her equally merciful predecessor Oleg does not murder his adversary (as the Russian *Primary Chronicle* reports) but merely strips him of power.[7]

After the next scene, which portrays the wedding of Igor and Prekrasa (Beauty), renamed Olga (890–969),[8] Oleg undertakes a military campaign against Constantinople. His fleet of two thousand vessels and eighty thousand warriors, made up of many ancient Slavic tribes—"Varangians, Slavs, Russes, Kriviches, Drevlians, Radimiches, Polanians, Croatians, Dulebs, and Tverians" ("who," Catherine remarks, "still need to be united"[9])—moves down the Dniepr to the Black Sea. There, before the panorama of Tsargrad, Oleg prepares for battle but shrewdly avoids combat by staging a demonstration of his superior military power in full view of his rivals. In dialogue with his associate, Oleg comments, "Though the enemy blocked the Bosphorus with a thick iron chain, seeing our army landing from the ships and ready to attack Constantinople, [they] will quickly send people to negotiate peace."[10]

Indeed the Greeks submit to Russian power, and Oleg levies taxes and sets other conditions benefiting Rus'. Curious about Constantinople and its new religion, he accepts an invitation from the Greek emperor Leon to visit the city. Leon orders that "in honor of such a famous guest, nothing will take place but endless games, singing, dances, joy, and magnificent feasts."[11] In the grand finale, the Greeks present Euripides' *Alkestis*. Before departing from the city, Oleg places the shield of the Russian Grand Prince on a pole of the Hippodrome "for future generations to see it here." Leon, bowing farewell to him, praises Oleg's wisdom and bravery.

Writing a Play as a Narrative of Conquest

To promote her political plans and gain the support of her subjects (what could now be seen as public relations), Catherine chose a charismatic historic hero. As O'Malley suggests, "the connection between Oleg's staged spectacle and Catherine's own political projects . . . was hardly illusory."[12] The hero, Prince Oleg, was admired by Catherine's courtiers and intellectuals who were coming to view history as a defining factor of Russian identity.[13] Oleg's aspirations, notably restoration of Russian rule in Kiev and military campaigns in Constantinople, embodied ideas that, according to Igor Losievsky, "guided Catherine throughout her reign."[14]

For Catherine's contemporaries, Kiev, the ancient capital of Rus', signified long-term Russian military and political maneuvers in Poland and the Ukraine that were intensified and completed under Catherine.[15] She had installed her former lover, Stanislas Poniatowski, as King of Poland and, continuously supporting (and using) him, exploited the Polish kingdom as a bargaining chip in her negotiations with Western partners. Partitioning it repeatedly, the empress absorbed much of Poland into the Russian empire. Throughout her reign, she gradually imposed administrative and social regulation over the vast territory on both sides of the Dniepr (the east bank, known as Little Russia, was under Russian rule; the west bank was under Polish control) and over the southern lands, populated with Cossacks, bordering the Crimean khanates.[16]

One of the primary political goals Catherine had inherited from Peter the Great was a desire to defeat Ottoman Turkey and capture Constantinople/Istanbul.[17] According to Catherine's plans, Constantinople, the cradle of Orthodoxy, was to be a capital for her aptly named grandson Constantine.[18] Khrapovitsky quoted the empress as saying: "Let the Turks to go wherever they wish. The Greeks might construct a monarchy for Constantin Pavlovich."[19] The triumphal arches erected along Catherine's progress through recently conquered Tauride read: "Sent Fear and Brought Peace" and "Mother of these Lands."[20] Poets likewise supported the imperial mission. Derzhavin called on Russians, "destined / ... to clean Jordanian waters, / ... to return Athens to Athenians, / the city Constantinople to Constantin."[21] Elsewhere the poet wrote:

Россия наложила руку	Russia put its hand
На Тавр, Кавказ и Херсонес,	On Tauride, the Caucasus, and Kherson
И, распустя в Босфоре флаги,	And, raising its flags on the Bosphorus,
Стамбулу флотами гремит: ...	The fleet threatens Istanbul: ...
Магмет, от ужаса бледнея,	Muhammad, pale with horror,
Заносит из Европы ногу,	Withdraws his leg from Europe
И возрастает Константин![22]	And—Constantine rises up!

Over the course of repeated assaults against the Ottomans during Catherine's thirty-four-year rule, Russia acquired significant territory, including the fertile and strategically significant Crimea (Tauride), thereby gaining access to the Black Sea, which stimulated creation of a naval force.[23]

As O'Malley notes, Catherine's *Oleg*, written before the beginning of the second war and staged upon the declaration of peace, presents an intriguing opportunity to study a play as a historical and political document. The interplay between theatrical and historical texts reveals the sense of theatricality that guided Catherine's political choices.[24] Written a year before Russia entered multiple wars and five years before these wars ended, the play reflects the empress's readiness for military conquest. Yet her actions show that, like her politically astute protagonist Oleg, Catherine sought non-military ways of achieving her ambitious goals. Between the completion of the play and the beginning of the war, Catherine took a half-year voyage, a piece of her grand plan, her political/theatrical plot.

Catherine Enacting the Voyage of Oleg

Finishing *Oleg*—Khrapovitsky's note on November 1, 1786, affirms near completion of the script[25]—Catherine switched her role from regal author to regal actor, herself impersonating the hero and enacting his journey (Figure 4.3). Two months later, in the first week of January 1787, in the midst of a freezing Russian winter, Catherine left St. Petersburg, beginning her extensive journey. With her entourage, Catherine traveled in fourteen warm, lavishly decorated carriages (each pulled by eight to ten horses), accompanied by 124 sledges carrying servants—a voyage elaborately "staged" from beginning to end. After a month of traveling, the cortège arrived in Kiev, where the empress remained until spring.

While Catherine devised the overall scenario of her cavalcade, Prince Potemkin made all the travel arrangements, acting as the director and "stage manager" of Catherine's spectacular production. He built grand scenery: majestic palaces, ships, and carriages. He staged massive military games, processions, fireworks, and theatrical productions. After the Russian acquisition of Crimea, Potemkin Tavrichesky (of Tauride) continuously communicated with the empress, sharing his ideas about developing Crimea and receiving her approval. He erected throughout the region new modern cities, picturesque villages, and immaculate peasant huts situated along the imperial route. Ségur, traveling with Catherine, found these "cities, villages, mansions, and sometimes simple huts decorated with flowers and elaborate paintings and gates . . . magically created, an illusion." According to another member of the party, Charles Joseph, Prince de Ligne, these were merely "theatrical settings—towns [that] lacked houses, and houses lacking roofs, doors, and windows."[26] These scenic constructions, which came to be called "Potemkin villages"—whether stage settings or actual dwellings—obscured the lines between life and theater.

In the course of the grand tour, Catherine played two roles: critical spectator and star actress. She brought along with her a superior cast consisting of the native elite and major European players, so that "one's astonished eyes beheld at once a splendid court, a victorious Empress, rich and warlike nobles, counts and princes [often from conflicting European parties]."[27] Catherine was attended by Joseph II of Austria, the Polish king Stanislas Augustus, and the Princes Nassau and de Ligne. Among her

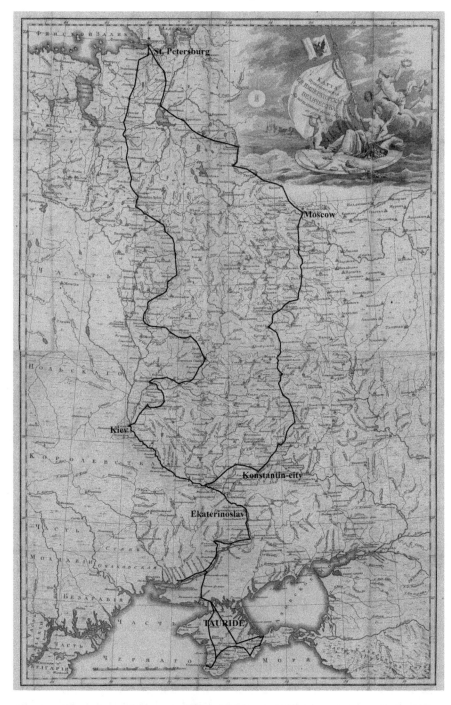

Figure 4.3: Map of Catherine's traveling to Kiev and Tauride, 1787. Harvard University, Map Library (names of major cities in English and the route of Catherine's journey added by the author).

permanent companions were Ségur,[28] the English ambassador Fitzherbert, and the Austrian minister Count Ludwig von Cobenzl.[29] The empress, paying all expenses, treated her companions in a princely fashion.[30]

During her stay in Kiev, Catherine (like Oleg) staged elaborate receptions for local aristocrats, governors, and foreign emissaries from adjacent and distant lands. She keenly remarked to Ségur that she wished to be accessible to her people, open to their grievances and concerns: "This is a purpose of my journey: to make known my good intentions."[31] According to Ségur,

> [Catherine] admitted clergy, governmental persons, and representatives of the nobility . . . merchants with long robes and huge beards, officers of all the regiments; famous Cossacks of the Don River in their lavish Asiatic cloth, Tatars, the past masters of Russia now vassals of a woman and a Christian, the Prince of Georgia bringing to the foot of Catherine's throne gifts of his land, several emissaries from numerous tribes of Kirgiz— fighting nomads, who could often be defeated, but never conquered, finally wild Kalmyks. All the East gathered there to see the new Semiramid.[32]

Such collective veneration of Russia by East and West, ritualized in eighteenth-century narratives including her own, became a tradition in Russian nationalistic operas of the following century.

Meanwhile, with orchestras in each of four flower-garlanded galleys (among the musicians was Sarti, who would later compose music for *Oleg*), followed by eighty ships with three thousand sailors and marines[33] (a number more realistic than the ones she cites in her operatic plot), Catherine continued her travel on the Dniepr, closely following Oleg's route to Constantinople. Along the way, she visited newly built settlements and cities.

A few months before, in the fall of 1786, as Catherine was working on her play, Potemkin wrote several letters to her about his project for construction of a city carrying Catherine's name: Ekaterinoslav (Catherine's Glory).[34] He sent her his plans for "a magnificent temple, an imitation of St. Paul's outside Rome, . . . a court of law resembling ancient basilicas, state chambers . . . in the style of Greek and Roman buildings, and a university complete with an academy of music and a conservatory" in the Venetian style, under the direction of Sarti.[35] At approximately the same time that Potemkin began planning the city, Catherine wrote about the ritualistic foundation of Moscow, which priests foresee as "the place of people's refuge and unification," auguring "wealth and prosperity to the city."[36] In her journey in spring 1787, Catherine frequently complained about Peter's choice of the capital—too far north, too close to the borders, and away from the center of Russia.[37]

The foundation of Moscow in *Oleg* parallels celebrations in the newly founded city of Catherine's Glory, attended by the two emperors, Catherine and Joseph II of Austria.

The association between Moscow and Ekaterinoslav invokes a parallel between foreign Ruriks (Varangians-Vikings) and German-born Catherine; one established ancient Rus,' the other erected cities and fashioned the Russian nation and empire.[38] Descending via the Dniepr, Catherine reached Tauride, where, according to Ségur, cited in an earlier chapter, Catherine chose to be guarded by "Tatars, spiteful of women and infidels," their land recently annexed by the empresses. Her gesture of trust was reciprocated by their respect and cooperation.[39] Her continuing route lay toward the Black Sea. Triumphal arches erected along the way read "This way to Byzantium."[40] Despite strong European opposition to Catherine's military plans in Turkey, the empress and her entourage observed extensive military parades and large-scale naval spectacles staged on the Black Sea not far from the Ottomans.[41] Perhaps all of this was designed to achieve the bloodless victory described in *Oleg*. However, in real life, within a few weeks after Catherine's monumentally theatrical return to St. Petersburg, Turkey declared war against Russia. The two plotlines, historical and operatic, diverged.

Catherine Revising History

In the play, Oleg exhibits his forces before Byzantium and takes the city without bloodshed. Catherine, after her military parades in Tauride in the view of Ottomans, found herself at war. Recognizing a significant deviation of reality from the script, the author-autocrat put *Oleg* aside. During the following two years, though occupied with wars and perilous political affairs, she continued to fashion new plays and operas. *Oleg*, however, seemed forgotten until a drastic turn in the war in late summer 1789. After two weeks of a Russian offensive against the Swedish fleet, Catherine set into motion preparations for the premier of *Oleg*, scheduled for late 1790.[42] At this point the empress assumed the role of producer.

The political climate through most of 1790 remained extremely tense. While Russia battled Turkey, Prussia publicly announced a peace treaty with the Ottomans. Austria, fearing a Prussian invasion and seeking stability after the death of Catherine's admirer Joseph II, likewise sought communication with Turkey. Left without allies, Russia faced multiple enemies alone: Turkey, Sweden, Prussia, Poland, and Britain.[43] Until the summer of the same year, the Russian situation seemed desperate; then, after a war of attrition between the Russian and Swedish fleets,[44] the Swedes initiated a peace agreement. There followed a series of victories over the Turkish navy and then peace treaties with multiple players. The timing of the lavishly staged *Oleg* was perfect.[45]

What motivated Catherine to launch the production in late 1789? Had Catherine, a political visionary and an astute planner, anticipated, despite all the losses during the previous year, a successful end to the wars? Or did she, ordering her secretary "to pull out the costumes, get money, and prepare the play for the end of the next year [1790]," set the date for a military victory that she, a meticulous planner, intended to achieve?[46]

Christopher Pye, exploring the dynamics between sovereign and theater discussed by Shakespeare's contemporary Thomas Hobbes, writes that "Hobbes shifts theatricality from an instrument of affective enforcement to a vehicle for abstractly conceptualizing the authorization of power."[47] Following Hobbes's logic, and discussing the possibility of exchange and convergence between theatrical and historical or political spaces, Pye likewise traces a "transition from 'authorship' to 'authorization,' from fictional to legal representation."[48] Catherine assumed three roles: autocrat, author, and actor. She negotiated between theatrical and political arenas like Queen Elizabeth I, who wrote: "For we princes, I tell you, are set on stages in the sight and view of all the world duly observed."[49] Recognizing the power of her spectators' gaze and echoing Elizabeth, Catherine, speaking through Oleg, appeals to her contemporaries and to posterity:

> From ancient times, it is an affair of the Peoples' Sovereigns to tolerate peoples' contempt patiently. But knowing me by face, everyone judges me by my own sense and habits; [I] cannot and will not defend myself against all, because I am by myself, alone; but [I] will leave it to posterity [for them to] to refer to me without bias, gladly and in detail.[50]

Appropriating Literary Sources

Catherine modeled her historical spectacle on Shakespeare, the master of chronology plays and the portrayal of regal characters. O'Malley writes that if the empress had been only a playwright choosing to imitate Shakespearean drama, she "might have done well to dramatize the scandal of her own accession to the throne, the intrigue surrounding her husband's death, the murder in prison of Ivan Antonovich (Ivan IV), and the endless parade of her own favorites—events certainly rivaling the Wars of Roses."[51] But Catherine thought and wrote as a monarch, her actions as well as her writing serving her political ambitions and aspirations.

The script and score of *Oleg* do not bear the name of Catherine.[52] Instead, the line on the cover below the title reads: "an imitation of Shakespeare, not observing customary theatrical laws."[53] To most Russian readers at the time of *Oleg*'s publication, the name of Shakespeare was hardly known; it was not mentioned, for example, in the first Russian rendition of *Hamlet*.[54] The few Russians familiar with his works, mostly from abridged prose versions in French and German,[55] commonly shared Voltaire's view of Shakespeare as a brilliant yet uneducated playwright who rejected the rules of classical theater.[56]

The empress may have originally heard about productions of Shakespeare's plays from Russians who visited England, among them Princess Dashkova and one of the first stars of the Russian stage, Ivan Dmitrievsky.[57] It is known that the empress ordered twenty volumes of Shakespeare in French for her library in 1775 and read Shakespeare in German ten years later.[58] In 1835, Vissarion Belinsky would praise Nikolai Karamzin's translation of *Julius Caesar* (1786), eulogizing Shakespeare's "independent mind and [his] ability to go against general opinions and beliefs in spite of the mighty and powerful gods of their times such as Voltaire." It should be noted that Karamzin turned to *Julius Caesar* the same year Catherine created four plays explicitly evoking Shakespeare.[59]

The chain of Shakespearean dramas in Russia extends from Catherine's *Oleg* to Pushkin's *Boris Godunov* (1825). Modeling on Shakespeare, Pushkin wrote, echoing the empress: "I structured my tragedy following the system of our father Shakespeare and sacrificed to his altar two classical unities."[60] Even if the empress did not introduce Russians to the English playwright, she may have stimulated an interest in his works and set an example by claiming to imitate him. In any case, by modeling her historical plays on those of the little-known Shakespeare, Catherine, who pioneered in nearly all her pursuits, liberated herself from the rules of neoclassical drama.

In Shakespeare's time, the standing crowds gathering in theaters on the south side of the Thames "outside the jurisdiction of the aldermen and mayors"[61] were enthralled by intimacy with charismatic royal figures and magnetized by the power of kings. Spectators could identify with ambitions, celebrate victories, and conspire in royal deceits and abuses. The elevated language of Shakespeare's kings and queens coexisted with street talk familiar to commoners. Shakespeare thus embedded subversion in these plays; the audience was dazzled by royal power but simultaneously witnessed it slandered, mocked, weakened, and eradicated. In close proximity to royal palaces and yet in a space external to the elevated and abstract aura of monarchical power, the kings in Shakespeare's historical dramas were commanded, manipulated by and subservient to an author/actor and at the same time scrutinized and evaluated by the public. The artistic and financial success of these plays depended on a reversal of power in the theatrical space.[62]

Such subversion did not match the authorial goals of the Russian empress-writer. Catherine staged her opera inside her court; the premiere took place in the Hermitage Theater that she had designed as an extension of the imperial palace, a part of the magnificent architectural complex at the heart of St. Petersburg. Not at all concerned about profit or loss, the empress enjoyed unlimited resources for production of her work. Catherine's audience, attending by imperial invitation, consisted of the native aristocratic elite, European ambassadors, and royal guests. Staging the spectacle in her royal space and for her courtiers, on the one hand Catherine ignored neoclassical rules, but on the other, in a sense she preserved and controlled the unities of place, time, and action for her spectators. Watching Catherine's *Oleg* with the empress as a central protagonist, they were situated in a play-within-a-play within the carefully staged drama of her court.

She conveyed the notion of unquestionable absolute power by devising a clear, positive, and straightforward plot that disseminated her vision of Russian history, enlightening her subjects and asserting her educational agendas and political goals. She assumed control over the representation of royalty, the vision of history, and the dramatic narrative.

Choruses

The fifth act of *Oleg*, starting from the moment Oleg disembarks in Tsargrad and continuing throughout the regal feast honoring the Russian hero, is framed and shaped by four choruses based on odes by Lomonosov (1711–1765). The choice and positioning of the choral episodes are significant. As Leon—the emperor of Constantinople—and his wife, Zoe, with their courtiers welcome Oleg, the chorus sings odic "Glory."

Коликой славой днесь блистает	What glory this day shines upon
Сей град в прибытии твоем! [63]	This city at your coming!

When the noble company gathers at the festive table, the chorus sings a second ten-line ode by Lomonosov associating king and kingdom with joy and peace. The poetic line subtly shifts from abstract to specific imagery, identifying the happiness of villages and the security of cities with "*you*, worthy and beautiful" (*ty polezna i krasna*). The Russian feminine (-a) endings here curiously define the royal *you* as female. In the following lines of the ode, the gender of the ruler is no longer stressed. Instead the imagery shifts to "vessels full of treasure." This maritime motif, essential to Russian eighteenth-century narrative, refers to the emergence of Russia as a naval empire. While "daring fleet" implies prosperity and power, the endearing *you* who spreads *your* wealth over the whole land simultaneously embraces intimacy and grandeur in the portrayal of her imperial majesty.

Царей и царств земных отрада	Tsar's and Kingdom's earthly joy
Возлюбленная тишина,	Beloved tranquility
Блаженство сел, градов ограда,	Bliss of the villages, delight of towns
Коль ты полезна и красна! . . .	With *you*, worthy and beautiful!
Сокровищ полны корабли	Vessels full of treasures
Дерзают в море за тобою;	Chance the Sea in your pursuit
Ты сыплешь щедрою рукою	*You* spread with your generous hand
Свое богатство по земли.[64]	*Your* wealth over the world.

Next, in contrast with the stately chorus, a group of nymphs and zephyrs entertains the royal company. An exchange between Oleg and Leon during the Grecian military games serves as a cue for the third chorus, which affirms the people's duty to protect their cities and restore peace. A reference to the military is echoed by the sound of trumpets that signal the beginning of the Grecian games. The fourth chorus opens with the word "war"[65] and ends with a great army of brave men led by a no-longer-concealed *she* who enters the theater[66] as the theatrical space converges with the surrounding world.

Российска повесть тем полна.	Russian history is thus full.
Уже из тмы на свет выходит,	Already from the dark to light appear
За ней великих полк Мужей,	The great army of men after her,
Что на театр всесветный взводит	Enters the theater of the whole world
Одетых солнечной зарей.	Dressed with the rays of the sunrise.[67]

Included within a single act, the choruses on Lomonosov's odes form a separate layer in the play.[68] Having no direct relation to the plot, the four choruses create a sequence linking Oleg's victory to the abstraction of royal power and to the supreme empress. Thus in these choruses the victorious Oleg, through a series of subliminal messages, turns into Catherine herself.

By choosing odes created by Lomonosov for Elisabeth,[69] Catherine adds various strands to the cumulative tapestry of her political, historical, and literary power.

Figure 4.4: Stefano Torelli. *Allegory of Catherine's Victory over the Turks.* 1772. Oil on canvas. Tretyakov Gallery, Moscow.

She appropriates both the image of Elisabeth and the aura of Lomonosov, the most influential Russian scholar and intellectual of the eighteenth century. A fisherman's son from a village on the White Sea, driven by a desire to study and thus traveling on foot to the imperial capital, Lomonosov became a paramount figure in Russian science, history, and literature.[70] As a writer and poet, he generated a comprehensive chronology of Russian history, created dramas, and wrote works on Russian grammar, literary pursuits later taken up by Catherine. Drawing on European poetic forms and simultaneously generating a national literary style, Lomonosov combined the old Slavonic and Russian languages, "naturalized the iamb . . . as corresponding to the 'innate properties' of Russian," and devised his poetic verse as an emblem of lofty Russian lyrics.[71]

Throughout the eighteenth century, the elevation of language and poetic forms was linked to rising state and imperial power, a combination Lomonosov championed in his celebratory odes. For the poet, the "lofty ode and upbeat iamb" became a vehicle for literary construction of the "imperial sublime." Ram, exploring the Russian poetic representation of imperial power, connects Lomonosov's poetics with the politics of the state. According to Ram, to an extent unknown to his European fellow writers Lomonosov embraced the notion of double submission—"the poet surrenders more completely, and passively, to his inspiration, just as he will submit more abjectly to his vision of Russia's conquering rulers."[72] Flying on Lomonosov's poetic wings, the empress writer (though neither a poet nor quite a rightful empress) ascends to prophecy, asserting the sublimity of the state and herself as its ruler. In the operas of the nineteenth century, this glorification often becomes the climax of the production, with the final Slava simultaneously lauding the heroic figure of the male protagonist and the Russian state.

Euripides and the Play of Substitution

Catherine's *Oleg* does not end with Lomonosov's odes. The final act falls into two halves; in the second, Oleg, invited by the Greek emperor (like Catherine herself sitting in her theater) becomes a spectator of scenes from Euripides's *Alcestis*. The Euripides play had been adapted to Russian opera by Sumarokov and Hermann Raupakh (*Al'tsesta*, 1758), who preceded Gluck's *Alceste* (1767) by seven years. The former was staged in private and imperial theaters, the latter rehearsed by Count Sheremetev's serf troupe.[73] Perhaps Catherine relied on her audience's familiarity with the complexity of a play that involved multiple exchanges and substitutions.[74]

The three scenes Catherine chose from the Greek play parallel the first half of *Oleg*'s final act—the arrival of Oleg and his retinue in Constantinople, where the defeated emperor Leon greets the Russian prince regally. In the play within a play, Hercules enters the house of mourning Admetus, king of Pherae, who hides his grief by showing hospitality to his guest. The choral odes of Lomonosov in the first half of the act are mirrored by the final choruses of *Alcestis*, the former venerating kings and the latter glorifying Olympic heroes.

The introduction of *Alcestis* (438 BCE)[75] into *Oleg*—already remote from Catherine's time by nine centuries—extends the time frame of the empress's plotline by another thirteen hundred years. O'Malley writes, "One has only to raise a curtain to be drawn into ninth-century Byzantium, and to raise another curtain to be transported to ancient Greece."[76] Russian intellectuals of Catherine's time believed ancient Greece to be the cradle of Russian culture and music. Thus by citing Euripides, Catherine asserted Russia's historical lineage in an effort to justify her claim to Byzantium/Constantinople/Istanbul.

Although Alcestis is the title heroine of Euripides' tragedy, she is absent from Catherine's play (no competition for the empress in the theatrical space). The episode the royal author includes in *Oleg* portrays Admetus, who welcomes his distinguished guest appropriately, concealing his wife's death. Mourning and festivity coincide, emphasizing the virtue of hospitality. The scene from *Alcestis* extends the encounter between Oleg and Leon, transposing *Oleg* from the historical realm to the mythological. Like Admetus, who lost his wife, Leon, defeated in Tsargrad, overcomes his sorrow by treating his Russian guest honorably as did his ancient counterpart.

By incorporating the episode from *Alcestis*, Catherine constructs yet another layer to the dramatic space. In this chain of replacements and exchanges, Hercules adds a mythical dimension to Oleg, further emphasizing Catherine's royal ambitions. Thus identifying herself with Oleg, the empress, called the Minerva and Semiramis of the North, established her ancestral ties to both Russian antiquity and Olympian myth, just as she asserted her regal lineage by erecting the monument to "Peter Primo." Moreover, if the male duo of Oleg and Leon parallels Admetus and Hercules, then Alcestis herself is an allegory of Byzantium, captured (thus liberated) by Oleg and craving to be revived by Catherine. The image of the empress as one who breathes life into a city had been nurtured since the early days of her reign; Lomonosov and Kheraskov attributed to Catherine the soul of St. Petersburg.[77]

Почтенья к тем святым словам я ввек не рушу.	Reverence for these holy words I'll never lose.
Петр Россам дал тела, Екатерина душу (Kheraskov, 1768)	Peter gave us body, Catherine soul
Прославя Россиян богатством наградил Петр дал нам бытие, Екатерина душу (Sumarokov 1770)	Bestowing Russians with wealth and glory Peter gave us being, Catherine soul.

The figure of Hercules, appearing in Catherine's Oleg, is also significant in Russian and European imperial mythology. The Pillars of Hercules frequently appeared in triumphal arches. Carl V of Spain adopted the Pillars as a symbol of his expansionist politics. Figures of Hercules decorated triumphal arches upon the victorious entrée of Peter the Great after his capture of Azov.[78]

Wedding and Choruses Celebrating the Union of the Russian Folk, God and Tsar(ina)

Assimilating wide-ranging literary sources (European, native, and ancient classical), Catherine weaves another element into the dense intertextuality of her play: the ritualistic Russian wedding. The matrimonial scene of *Oleg*, situated between the hero's voyage to Kiev and his military campaign in Byzantium, occupies the third act of the production. The discussion of courtly ceremonies and rituals in Chapter One contended that wedding ceremonies became significant both to the self-imagination of Russians (as being Russian) and to the life of the imperial court, where weddings served as a prime area of performativity and entertainment. Mixing court fashions with old folk customs, wedding rituals—specifically the devichnik (maid's gathering)—entered the realm of Russian opera from its beginnings.[79] Unlike male playwrights and composers, Catherine recreated these women's wedding rituals as an insider. She herself prepared, dressed, and decorated the brides.[80] Not only does the wedding in *Oleg* follow the ritual; the author pens an ethnographic account of costumes, describing traditional wedding personages (svakhi, *boyare*, and druzhki) as well as the roles and the behavior of various ranked participants.

The wedding consists of two scenes. The first is the devichnik, in which, as Catherine emphasized, "not a single man is present" and "only maidens dance." The royal author graphically outlined the number and position of the participants on the stage: "Two *baryni*-svakhi holding Prekrasa by the hand guide her to the chamber, . . . and to the oak table; then svakhi sit down on a bench, four on one side [of the bride] and four on the other. Standing maidens sing." Catherine meticulously described the preparation of the bride: "Svakhi and maidens adorn Prekrasa in Russian garb [and, while adorning her, sing], covering her with a cloak, above it putting a veil decorated with pearls and golden beads."[81]

The scene echoes accounts of native and non-native attendees of Russian weddings. Adam Olearius, traveling through Russia in 1634–1636, left a colorful picture of the wedding rituals:

> The bridegroom having taking his place, the Bride is brought in most richly Clad, having a Veil over her face. She is seated by the Bridegroom, but to prevent their seeing one

another, they are separated by a piece of Crimson Taffeta. . . . The Bride's *Suacha* [svakha] comes to the bride, paints her, ties up her hair in two knots, puts the Crown on her head, and dresses her in all things like a married woman. . . . The other *Suacha* paints the Bridegroom, and in the mean time, the women get up on the benches and sing several foolish songs. . . . The *Suacha* having covered the Bride's face again. . . in the church where Benediction is given, the part where the couple walks and stands is covered with Red taffeta. . . ."[82]

The second scene portrays Kiev and the wedding procession from the Grand Prince's palace to the church. Two merchants observe the procession; their dialogue is a comprehensive commentary and explanation of the order of the ritual, the arrangement of participants according to rank, the number of people in each group, and the festive clothing according to social hierarchy. This detailed description and the opulent wedding procession are distant reflections of the real royal weddings and coronations discussed in previous chapters, in which Catherine participated as Grand Duchess, bride, empress, and imperial mother-in-law.

By creating a rich though laconic text for the wedding, Catherine-the-dramatist minimizes use of language in favor of songs, which play a critical role in the devichnik scene. Thus the empress's libretto presents a model for many famous wedding scenes depicted in nineteenth-century operas.

Catherine as a Musical Impresario

Rejecting the use of music as decoration in her play, Catherine employs it as a functional element. In particular, she incorporates music in settings where it would be played in real-life events, namely weddings, victory feasts, and plays (within rituals). Thus music, though an integral part of the spectacle, is used only in the third and fifth acts. The following section analyzes the role of music, particularly the issue of folk repertoire and the significant role of choruses—two elements essential to *Oleg*.

Catherine's admission that she lacked musical talent and interest in music (at times she also referred to her literary pursuits as capricious and unworthy),[83] supported by several witty remarks of her courtiers, has been quoted for more than two centuries. Yet these remarks seem inconsistent with the abundance of musical events in her court, her fascination with opera, and in the case of *Oleg* her active involvement in the musical aspects of production.[84] Although Catherine indeed composed no music for *Oleg*, she devised the overall musical concept of the production by selecting the composers and identifying the placement of music in the libretto.[85] For instance, dissatisfied with the choral music composed by Domenico Cimarosa for the final act, she redirected the task to Sarti.[86] Her dramatic setting entailed the convergence of two operatic types discussed earlier, one associated with operas or "dramas with voices" that recycled preexisting rural and urban folklore and popular tunes, and the other with specially composed operatic scores consisting of arias, ensembles, choruses, and instrumental interludes.

For *Oleg*, Catherine assembled a group of three composers, each assigned a particular task. Carlo Canobbio (1741–1822) composed the overture, march, and entr'actes; Vasily Pashkevich (1742–1797) handled the songs for the Russian wedding scene. Sarti wrote the music for the last act. Except for the orchestral overture, entr'actes, and several short melodramatic episodes in *Alkista* (in the second half of the fifth act), the score of *Oleg* consists of choruses, which leads native musicologists to refer to the play as a choral opera. By the time of the production, the Venetian Canobbio had had eleven years of experience as a composer and as first violin of the St. Petersburg Imperial Theater; his musical choices were defined by the fashions of the Russian court and by the tsarina's own musical tastes and desires.

Pashkevich, one of the first native Russian opera composers and "the only one among native composers loved by the empress,"[87] was also employed in Catherine's court and collaborated with the empress in two operas besides *Oleg*.[88] His earliest existing work with Iakov Kniazhnin's *Misfortune from a Coach* (1779) premiered in Catherine's Hermitage.[89] Tamara Livanova, a major Russian scholar, defines Pashkevich's early operatic style as "neutral," modeled on the popular Italian style of Galuppi, Piccinni, and Paisiello.[90] His style changed in the 1780s, which is apparent in his work with Mikhail Matinsky on *The St. Petersburg Bazaar* and in three operas on Catherine's texts. In *Fevei*, Pashkevich used folk tunes to compose wedding choruses in the Russian style.[91] Apparently pleased with his work, Catherine invited him to create the wedding music for *Oleg*. The most remarkable of Pashkevich's wedding scenes, and perhaps of all Russian operatic weddings, is the musical ethnography in the second act of *St. Petersburg Bazaar*.[92] Whether or not the version of *St. Petersburg Bazaar* we know today appeared before or after Pashkevich's weddings for Catherine's plays, the fact remains that the empress was among the first operatic authors to foster theatrical enactment of ritualistic weddings.

At least six musical numbers from *Oleg* are traditionally compared with tunes included in Nikolai L'vov and Ivan Prach's *Collection of Russian Folk Songs*. The figure of L'vov is important. An aristocrat, architect, poet, and leader of a prominent intellectual circle in eighteenth-century Russia, he collaborated with and assisted many writers and composers.[93] It is believed that L'vov was the primary author of the *Collection*. He and Prach may have been the first to use the term "folk songs" (*narodnaia pesnia*) in their title; other authors addressed the collected tunes as "various" or "simple" songs.[94] L'vov's anthology came nearly two decades after several others published in the 1770s.

Four of the five orchestral numbers contributed by Canobbio correspond to tunes found in the L'vov-Prach volume. Somewhat curious is Canobbio's overture, based on a song from the rich oral repertory about Sten'ka Razin, the leader of a peasant revolt in the seventeenth century (Example 4.1). The image of Razin was popular among the Russian folk and paralleled that of Emelian Pugachev, who, proclaiming himself Catherine's long-dead husband Peter III, led a powerful Cossack insurrection during Catherine's reign (1773–74). Soviet scholars such as Livanova assumed that the Italian Canobbio and by extension Catherine could not have known the context of the song. Livanova attributed the inclusion of this song in various anthologies to the social consciousness of the collectors and pointed out that it was L'vov who suggested the song to Canobbio.[95] Needless to say, Soviet scholars gladly acknowledged the class consciousness of the aristocratic L'vov and the court *guslar* Trutovsky.[96] Yet both L'vov and Trutovsky used this song about Razin with a text that praised Tsar Peter the Great: "Oni khvaliat velichaiut pravoslavnogo tsara, pravoslavnogo tsara, imperatora Petra" (They praise, glorify the Orthodox Tsar, the Orthodox Tsar, the emperor Peter; Example 4.2). It is hard to imagine that Catherine neither knew the song nor was alerted by anyone about its implication. It seems plausible that, fostering native mythology as manifesting its roots in the folk, she appropriated, along with the tune, the image of the folk hero to support Peter's cause and her own.[97]

Example 4.1

The tunes Canobbio employs in his entr'actes before the second and the third acts have in very different ways enjoyed striking longevity and prominence in Russian music and culture.[98] The first corresponds to "Zain'ka, popliashi" [Rabbit, dance] in the L'vov-Prach collection (Examples 4.3 and 4.4). Although this song does not appear in any anthology compiled before Catherine's *Oleg*, it has surfaced in various publications since and remains a popular children's song included in instrumental collections

Example 4.2

Chto po - ni - zhe by - lo go - ro - da Sa - ra - - to va

A po -vy -she by - lo go - ro - da Tsa - ri -tsy -na.

What lay below the city of Saratov
And above the Tsarcity.

Example 4.3

Allegro

Example 4.4

Za - in' - ka po -ska - chi s rin' - koi po - plia - shi

kruzh -kom boch -kom po - ver - ni - sia kruzh -kom boch -kom po - ver - ni - sia.

Example 4.5

for beginning music students. The melody from the entr'acte to the third act (Example 4.5) was also used by Glinka in *Kamarinskaia* (1848), a symphonic poem that became an emblem of musical Russianness.[99]

The melodies and keys of Canobbio's overture and entr'actes correspond to tunes from L'vov-Prach, but the composer infused the simple songlike themes with dynamic contrasts, changes of texture, wide ranges, melodic sequences, and frequently bravura endings. The entr'actes, based on folklike melodies, create the underlying unity of the spectacle. This folk canvas leads to and culminates in several ritualistic wedding choruses. Thus the music conveys and embodies the image of the Russian folk (*narod*).

Pashkevich likewise uses folk tunes, but in a different way. Unlike Canobbio, he does not directly quote existing folk songs, but two of his three wedding choruses in *Oleg* are clearly similar to tunes from the L'vov-Prach collection. The text of the first chorus invokes imagery characteristic of the traditional wedding lament: *rasnoe solnyshko* (red sun), *zvezda zakatilas'* (falling star). The song tells about a bride's tears as she begs her parents not to give her away to a *moguchii velikii bogatyr'* (mighty, great champion). The melodic contour and poetic expression remind one of its counterpart in L'vov-Prach. The composer designed a three-part chorus in a traditional Russian folk style. Characteristic of wedding songs are the six-measure sentences in the beginning (Example 4.6).

Example 4.6

Chorus: Rolling red sun / Good is our cohort / Sitting at the oak table with the festive tablecloth

The changing tone of the wedding is reflected in the second chorus, its text corresponding to the *pliasovaia* (folk dance tune) from L'vov-Prach but its melody closely related to another song from the same collection (Examples 4.7 and 4.8).[100]

The text of this song in the collection praises God and the tsar. In the opera, the same melody, employed as a wedding chorus, draws on marriage as an allegory for the union of God and tsar with the Russian people. This message and the tune became a

Example 4.7

Chorus: In the chamber [a young maiden] paced, walked

Example 4.8

symbol of nationalism in the operas of Glinka, Mussorgsky, Rimsky-Korsakov, and Tchaikovsky:[101]

Уж как слава Тебе Боже на	Glory to you our God in the heavens!
небеси! Слава!	Glory!
Государю нашему на сей земле!	To our Tsar on earth!
Слава!	Glory!

The last wedding chorus, though idiomatically connected with several songs in L'vov-Prach, does not seem to have a direct counterpart. Considering the close link between the music of *Oleg* and that of the L'vov-Prach anthology, the general view of Russian scholars has been that the song collection served as a source for the music of the spectacle. Ignoring the fact that both the production of *Oleg* and L'vov-Prach's publication took place in the same year, scholars such as Livanova claim that "probably, L'vov handed over to Canobbio the songs that were already completed for his collection."[102] Yet Brown, after Fendeizen, points out that the 1790 edition of L'vov and Prach contained only text and no music.[103] Taruskin, having no sympathetic ties to Russian and socialist musicological traditions, boldly suggests that "although the assumption has always been that the collection was the source from which the composers of the stage works drew the tunes, most of the stage works in fact predate the first edition of the collection, and the relationship between borrower and lender is more likely the reverse."[104] Livanova, recognizing that "in almost every eighteenth-century Russian opera one finds the same popular melodies as in L'vov-Prach," proposed that "if some operas came out before the collection, then L'vov's group perhaps knew these songs well."[105]

Early song collections typically included romances, arias, and popular urban songs, many borrowed from personal manuscripts. The division between composed and folk tunes was blurry even for the collectors of the songs. In his introduction to the collection, L'vov wrote, "Since the authors of these songs are unknown, they belong to all the *narod*." Further, L'vov suggested that the creators of these songs might be Cossacks, soldiers, marines, coachmen, or laborers, therefore setting wide ethnic, professional, and regional frames for his folk songs.[106]

Whether these tunes belonged to the folk, composed, or popular realms was not clear at the time and indeed remains unknown to us today. This was an age when tunes, even more than the oral tales discussed in the previous chapter, were unrestricted by copyright and flowed in open space—serfs in Muscovite villages sang melodies from operas on their landlords' stages, and playwrights adapted street songs for their operas.

One can view the connection between *Oleg* and the L'vov-Prach *Collection of Folk Song* from another angle. Published the same year as the production of *Oleg*, the L'vov-Prach anthology linked Canobbio's and Pashkevich's tunes with folklore. Notably, Catherine's spectacle and L'vov's anthology not only shared the same songs but also reached the same audience: courtiers who attended court spectacles and purchased the newly published collection of songs. Thus the tunes exchanged among Canobbio, Pashkevich, and L'vov, chosen with or without Catherine's personal involvement to match her tastes and preferences, became identified with Russian folklore. In short, to some extent, Catherine herself directly or indirectly fostered the musical representation of the narod, mastering a model and a source for nineteenth-century composers.

For the author of *Oleg*, however, the musical imagery of the Russian folk was not an end in itself. Catherine's design of the last and most musical act of the spectacle led Sarti to devise two musical strands, one associated with Lomonosov's odes and the other with *Alkista*. No more references to folk culture. Unlike the wedding choral suite by Pashkevich, the chain of choral odes, accompanied by a large orchestra with a brass ensemble and four drums, forms an oratorio-like composition.[107]

By composing all the choruses in a major mode, Sarti creates a celebratory tone. The shared keys and thematic similarity of the first and fourth (last) choruses bring unity and symmetrical completion to the choral cycle. The virtuosity, the massive instrumental and vocal texture, the full harmony created by the (as many as) seven-part choir, and the shifts between soloists and the choral/orchestral *tutti* are reminiscent of *concerti grossi*. They are also found in Sarti's Russian oratorios such as *Tebe Boga Khvalim*, composed for a double chorus and large orchestra, including a uniquely Russian rogovoi orchestra, bells, and special effects such as cannon shots.[108] It is conceivable that the *Tebe Boga Khvalim* performed on Alexander Nevsky Day (1789) to honor Potemkin's victory in Ochakov (1788) as well as the *Te Deum* composed for the Russian conquest of Bender (1790) also served as points of reference for the same audience that listened to the Sarti-Lomonosov choruses in *Oleg* honoring another set of victorious Russians. This connection between the two compositions was instrumental in the creation of this metahistorical national musical narrative.

"Majestic and brilliant," as suggested by Rabinovich, an expert on the musical culture of pre-Glinka Russia, Sarti's choruses for *Oleg* represent a perfect "equivalent of the celebratory poetic ode of the eighteenth century." According to him, the musical odes from *Oleg* embody the austere style of St. Petersburg classicism, akin to the city's buildings designed by Quarenghi.[109] Drastically different from the "folk" tunes used early in the opera, the combination of Lomonosov's lofty odes and Sarti's "dazzling, courtly" oratorio style signifies the high culture of Westernized Russia. "In contrast to all his Russian contemporaries as well as secondary foreign composers, Sarti . . . had a perfect command of vocal-instrumental ensemble," wrote Fendeizen. In his study of eighteenth-century Russian music, Fendeizen emphasizes the importance of Catherine's choice of Sarti as a master of choral music.[110]

In Sarti's music for *Alkista*, the first Russian opera to use the harp, the composer experiments with Greek modes, melodies, and musical instruments. Here, in contrast to the other choruses in *Oleg*, Sarti uses unison singing; the heroes speak their lines between short instrumental fragments of two-or-three-measure chord sequences for harp and strings. The composer claimed that his score harmonized an ancient melody from an ode by Pindar, which Vsevolod Cheshikhin called charlatanism.[111] Sarti's "Explanation" mentions the "use of a fragment from a Greek song," referencing L'vov's folk song collection. L'vov, on the other hand, in his introduction, scrutinizes the melody of Pindar, finding "to his surprise" that "we in our *narodnoe* (folk) singing inherited" some characteristic elements of ancient Greek music. The circle is complete! *Alkista* not only extends the historical frame of Catherine's spectacle from modern Russia to Byzantine Constantinople to Greek antiquity; the shared lineage between Russians and ancient Greece is confirmed by musical ties. Further, the complex familial relationship with Greece sanctifies Catherine's war of liberation from the Ottomans.

These cross-references show that various independent and yet interrelated texts used by Catherine addressed the same audience and formed a body that was much larger than a single play, even one as monumental and lavish as *Oleg*. By delegating creation of music to three composers, Catherine defined three musical layers that represented Russian folk song, the elevated style of Russian classicism, and (according to Sarti and L'vov) special ties with Greece, the cradle of European culture. The juxtaposition of these three areas signified Catherine's most significant creation: the concept of the Russian nation. Nineteenth-century nationalism owed the genre of Russian historical opera to the pioneering work of the empress. In this as in her skazka operas, she likewise fashioned the Russian chorus, which is cherished in the history of Russian music as the most recognizable signature of nineteenth-century nationalistic opera.

From *Oleg* to *Slaviane,* Constructing Theater, Hero, and Nation

Catherine, author and autocrat, created Russia as a narrative and her citizens as spectators of her political-theatrical drama. Creating the image of the hero and promoting the concept of nation, she fashioned literary and theatrical forms. At a time when the Russian stage was characterized by neoclassicism, tearful lyric drama, and opéra comique à la Rus', the empress fostered a complex intertextual theatrical genre. The direction Catherine pursued was continued by such celebrated court poets as Derzhavin and Bogdanovich. In his essay on opera, the poet Derzhavin, perceiving *Oleg* as an opera, argued the significance of this genre as a political mechanism: "Catherine the Great knew it perfectly. We [poets and spectators] observed and listened to the effect of *Oleg* created by Catherine."[112] Writing about the genre Catherine pioneered in her *Oleg*, Shcherbakova suggests that the empress, seeking to unify a number of stylistic elements, drew on opera. At the same time, the genre of opera seemed to Catherine to lack the "common sense" and strong effect of drama.[113]

Catherine's experimentation with the genre of *Oleg* generated a number of historical productions by other writers, operas as well as dramas with choruses and dancing. Perhaps the reason Catherine and her followers favored historical productions with music is explained by Derzhavin in the introduction to his *Pozharsky or the Liberation of Moscow* (a "heroic production with choruses and recitatives"):

> In order to make this solemn production, serving the welfare of the Empire today and not a boring and grave spectacle like tragedy, I adorned it with a splendor typical of operas,

providing it with changing scenery, music, dances, and even magic. On the other hand, in order not to lose in glamour the heroic importance and power of some characters [I] devise fairly emotional prolonged monologues without any singing and dancing, which in turn are assigned to ballet, choruses, and recitatives.[114]

Bogdanovich, another of Catherine's court poets, dedicated to her both a poem and a drama about Dushen'ka, which Catherine received with expressed satisfaction, encouraging him to write *Slaviane* (1787), a "drama with music and a ballet in three acts."[115] Etymologically the name belongs to a group of words including the river Slavena and, near the river, the legendary city Slaviansk, the first capital of the ancient Slavs. Commenting on Bogdanovich's use of these words, Zorin adds that "the river Slavena is simultaneously a little brook Slavianka running into the Tsarskoe Selo, associated with Catherine the Great."[116]

In the play, two secondary characters—Pansophii, a Greek philosopher, and Milorada, a Slavic maid—debate their views of theater.

> Pansophii: Spectacles in our theaters bring our minds into complete reverie; they present delight to everyone's eyes; music and dance rise beyond everyone's imagination. This requires . . . a regulated combination of acts limited in time and place, . . . a finale that according to Athens' taste, brings everyone to sadness, horror, and shivering.
>
> Milorada: Why such distress for no reason? Our smart people create plays not for sadness, but for kindness and merriment [Act II, Scene 2].[117]

In a lengthy debate, the Slavic maid's common sense appears more convincing than the argument of the cultured Athenian scholar; a woman ascends above a man, an uneducated servant rises above a Greek thinker, and by implication Slavic theater supersedes classical drama. Following Catherine, Bogdanovich used Greek imagery to proclaim the superiority of Slavic (Russian) over classical theater. Thus, by appropriating Greek imagery, Russian theater proclaimed its own character and destiny.

Slaviane is an interesting case study. In his play, Bogdanovich retold Metastasio's story of *Alessandro nell'Indie*, one of the most popular operatic plots, which, with music by the Russian imperial court composer Araia, had been successfully staged in St. Petersburg as a part of royal celebrations: Elisabeth's birthdays (1753 and 1755), anniversaries of Elisabeth's coronation (1756), and the marriage of Peter III and Catherine II (1759).[118] In Metastasio's drama, Alexander the Great encounters an Indian princess. She loves his rival and uses her charm and shrewdness to spice up the military contest between the two heroes with a romantic rivalry. Eventually she convinces Alexander to restore peace and save his opponent.

In *Slaviane*, the Indian princess is replaced by a Russian tsarina, Dobroslava (*dobro*, kindness, and *slava*, glory), who, unlike her Indian counterpart, exhibits uncompromising devotion to her country and her beloved Ruslan (from Rus', the old name for Russia).[119] Falling under the spell of Dobroslava's beauty and won over by her integrity, Alexander finds himself willing to "follow the chariot" of the Russian tsarina, who "exudes goodness." Consequently realizing that it is "not praiseworthy for a hero to attack those who prevail over others by virtue and integrity," he calls off his military campaign.[120] Unlike the Metastasio/Araia finale that venerates Alexander, *Slaviane* ends with celebration of the union of tsarina Dobroslava with Ruslan; Alexander admits that he prefers "this [Slav] feast over many Athenian pageants."[121]

In the last act of *Slaviane*, Alexander meets Ruslan, his rival on the battlefield and in romance. The two discuss the connection between the state of arts and theater in connection with the people's mores.

Alexander: Who instilled such integrity in you?

Ruslan: We had a kind and smart Tsarina who based her law on the best Greek wise men as well as our own. She had a benevolent and merciful mind: she decorated our lives with beautiful buildings; developed our minds with free scientific thinking; extended the borders of her regions, not so much with the power of arms as by caring about her subjects.[122]

Here the superiority of Russia is proclaimed on two levels, moral and cultural. *Slaviane* ends with a festival—a short version of the final scene from *Oleg*. In the midst of the brightly lit stage rises a tall pyramid with a large sign: "25 years." Emerging from the pyramid, the "Genius of time" calls to the stage twenty-five Slavic women and as many men, and signals the beginning of a dance. The choir sings "Glory [Slava] to all-mighty God in the sky, glory. To the benevolent She-Monarch honor and glory." Celebrating a quarter-century of Catherine's rule, the spectacle proposes to set a tradition for all "Slavs to celebrate each twenty-five years of her rule by a solemn reestablishment of all her institutions that will never vanish from the memory of our successors."[123]

Defining both temporal (historical) and spatial (territorial) vectors of Russia, the authors of *Oleg* and *Slaviane* establish the descent of Russian culture from ancient Greek literature, mythology, and music. By using classical Greece as a point of reference, Russia claimed cultural roots shared with advanced European nations. Russia's special affinity with Constantinople as a center of Eastern Orthodoxy enabled Westernized Russia to set its culture apart from Europe and to assert its own cultural distinctiveness and sophistication. But if in *Alessandro nell'Indie* Russians identify with Alexander, in *Slaviane* Alexander yields to the moral eminence of Slavic Dobroslava. Thus between the two spectacles establishing historical (*Oleg*) and moral (*Slaviane*) victory over Greece, Russia—the defender of antiquity and Orthodoxy (Catherine's own campaigns against the Ottomans)—attains moral and cultural superiority over Greece, over the East (Ottoman Turkey), and, by extension, over Western Europe.

Postlude: What Came After Catherine's Opera-Skazkas and *Oleg*

Both *Slaviane* and *Oleg* manifested a new aesthetic. Catherine's historical plot, divorced from the realm of classical drama, was written in modern Russian. The situations described in the play and enacted on stage were not too distant from the spectators' own life experiences of weddings, military campaigns, managerial issues with officers, and lavish imperial celebrations. Tackling everyday tasks, the play projected a very clear political message. Though judged by critics of the following centuries as dull and mediocre, it stands as a well-conceived popularization of Russian history, capable of reaching and educating the Russian aristocracy beyond the intellectual circles already invested in creating historical chronology. *Oleg* "was one of the most lavish, expensive productions ever seen in Russia," writes O'Malley. It was staged in Catherine's own Hermitage and several times in the Kamenny Theater: "The cast contained six hundred supernumeraries from several field regiments." She cites Arapov: "Witnesses to the 1795 production said 'that in the first act of this play the public went into raptures in the scene of the founding of the city of Moscow, and when the eagle flew, they burst into thunderous applause."[124] Among the spectators were Russians and foreigners, aristocrats and intellectuals.

Contrary to Livanova's statement that no Russian writers followed Catherine's lead in historical opera,[125] Livanova herself compiles the list of now largely unknown historical operas that surfaced after Her Majesty's, establishing the lineage of Russian historical opera. All of the operas she lists surfaced after Catherine's *Oleg*: Fomin composed choruses for V. Oserov's *Iaropolk and Oleg* (1798); Derzhavin created the unstaged opera *Pozharsky*, followed by the oratorio *Minin i Pozharsky* by Degtiarev; and after Derzhavin's *Groznyi*, Shakhovskoi and Cavos' *Ivan Susanin* came to life.[126]

Similarly in the realm of opera-skazka, discussed in the previous chapter, scholars typically discard operatic works before Glinka. Olga Komarnitskaia, for example, writing about the "operatic dramaturgy of epic and magical spectacles of Glinka, Borodin, and Rimsky-Korsakov," outlines such traits of opera-skazka as (1) the suite-like sequence of scenes in which dramatic conflict is replaced by pictorial contrast (the very quality that Rabinovich and others criticized in Catherine's operatic works); (2) aesthetic appreciation of "every single [colorful] moment" in a tale-opera; (3) the epic hero portrayed as a simplified "one-dimensional" type; (4) "the 'cult' of the people" and "collective imagery;" (5) the closeness of the tale to old legends, bylinas, and songs; (6) again the central role of a bogatyr (champion); and finally (7) lack of "seriousness" in the narrative of the operatic tale (Catherine's comic operas), in which the "themes of nation, patriotism, heroism" are tied to "satire, grotesquery, and hyperbole."[127] Though the elements mentioned above clearly relate to Catherine's opera-skazkas, rarely do Russian scholars bother to mention her works. For instance, even today Inna Bulkina, reconnecting Pushkin's *Rusalka* with "bogatyr' epics" and tracing the lineage of his *Ruslan and Liudmila* back to Krylov and Cavos's opera *Ilya Bogatyr'* (1806), fails to recognize the link between *Ilya* and Catherine's operatic bogatyr' *Boeslavich* and *Akhrideich*.[128] Recently Shcherbakova, exploring the empress's comic and historical works for musical theater, writes that Catherine's "theatrical innovations should be recognized today as one of the most productive phases in the history of native drama and musical theater."[129]

Several major streams in nineteenth-century Russian operatic theater evolved from Catherine's rarely acknowledged historical-heroic *Oleg*. One line leads to nationalistic *heroic* operas such as *Ivan Susanin* (the first version composed by Cavos, 1815; the second by Glinka, 1836). Another is a lineage of operas representing Russian *historical* personae: a hundred years separate Catherine's Princes Oleg and Igor and their historical and operatic progeny, Borodin's *Prince Igor* (1890). The monumental scenery and massive, hundred-piece choruses in *Boris Godunov* (1874) echo the splendor of Catherine's set portraying Constantinople; the Polovitsian games, choruses, and dances observed by Prince Igor bring to mind the gladiators, dancers, and monumental oratorical choruses of the Byzantium feast honoring Oleg.

In the aftermath of the theatrical *Oleg* and throughout the remaining years of Catherine's rule, the image of the hero of ancient Rus' converges with the mythological representation of the empress. Echoing the map iconography at the beginning of this chapter, Derzhavin lauds Catherine as victorious Oleg ("Ode on the Capture of Izmail," 1790):

. . . златая колесница	. . . a golden chariot
По розовым летит зарям;	Flies over the rosy sunrise;
Седящая на ней царица,	Sitting there the Tsarina,
Великим равная мужам,	Equal to the greatest men,
Рукою держит крест одною,	Holds a cross in one hand,
Возженный пламенник другою,	A blazing torch in the other,
И сыплет блески на Босфор;	Spreading sparkles over the Bosphorus;
. . .	. . .
Не вновь ли то Олег к Востоку	Is it not again Oleg to the East
Под парусами флот ведет. . . ?	Leading his sailing fleet . . . ?

The image of Oleg attaching his shield to the hippodrome of Tsargorod attained an important place in nineteenth-century Russian literature, a story told and retold by Karamzin and L'vov, Ryleev and Pushkin. Comparing and cross-referencing various texts about *Oleg*, they forgot—much as their fellow composers did—even to mention his eighteenth-century counterpart: the female, the foreigner, and the author-autocrat.

INTERLUDE

TO PATRIA AND NATION

Among the *rusalka*s there arose *Ilya Bogatyr'* [*Ilya the Champion*], a magic opera that Krylov was importuned to write. He created it casually, jokingly, but so keenly, so successfully, that his hero unintentionally killed the sorceress-German [rusalka], who, to seduce the Russians, had turned herself into their co-citizen.[1]

The dilettante memoirist Filipp Vigel in this witty, ironic Aesopian fragment[2] reflects on the reception of two major operatic hits. One was *Ilya the Champion* (1807)[3]; the other, featuring the "German sorceress," was a four-part operatic series of *Rusalka*s drawn from the Viennese singspiel *Das Donauweibchen* (1798).[4] Relocated to the river Dniepr and stocked with Russified main characters, the *Rusalka*s assimilated to the Russian operatic stage.[5] Obsessed with and dangerous to mortal men, the rusalka—a native pagan sprite—converged with the European siren. From one sequel to the next,[6] foreign traces were erased and references to the Germanic source eliminated. However, the capacity of the pseudo-Russian sorceress to control and manipulate a man was perhaps not forgiven, her foreign origin not forgotten; neither was the recent history of a German princess who "seduced Russians, turning herself into their co-citizen." "I wanted to be Russian so that Russians would love me,"[7] the empress once wrote.

Krylov's *Ilya* won over its competitors, the multiple *Rusalka*s; Ilya, an operatic character retrieved from native mythology, defeated the Eastern enchantress Zlomeka. Russia's proclaimed triumph over East and West had been well explored in operas before *Ilya*, but the new element was that Russia manifested its superiority over foreign dominions often represented by female characters; nationalism converged with masculinity. The final chorus of *Ilya*, celebrating the Russian victory and proclaiming death to the enemies of righteous Rus', notably echoes the famous cantata-polonaise "Grom pobedy" (Thunder of Victory) by Kozlovsky and Derzhavin.[8]

In the late eighteenth century, Derzhavin's cantata-polonaise had become virtually a national hymn; the chorus from *Ilya* inherited this status.[9] Derzhavin's lyrics extolled Catherine, reiterating her name and pledging devotion to "our dulcet mother." (So seminal was the association with Catherine that a hundred years later Tchaikovsky, preparing for a ceremonial appearance of Catherine, used the same lines in his *Queen of Spades*.) In *Ilya* the chorus, redirecting "victories" to the Russian epic hero, engaged cultural memory and retuned it to identify nationalism with masculinity, paired as one.[10]

The Russian nationalist lore that emerged around the time of the Napoleonic wars has been celebrated for nearly two hundred years as aligned with the native peasant folk, democratization, and anti-absolutism. Russia's nationalism also associated itself with patriotism, military power, and cultural superiority—a vision of victorious Russia conflating the "Russian soul" and "Russian soil." Whether glorifying, theorizing about, or defining Russianness, the nationalist discourse successfully avoided the issue of gender. Yet Russian nationalism in all its facets was (and is) profoundly and militantly gendered. Acquiring European gender biases and fashions, Russia's anxious reflection on its own recent past as a female kingdom surfaced in various artistic forms, including five operas analyzed in the following chapters.

The combat of a Russian champion and a royal sorceress, often a foreigner, may reflect the overpowering shadow that Catherine, a signifier of the empresses' age, cast on her male political and literary progeny, stirring remarkably consistent nineteenth-century anxieties. The Germanic descent of Catherine and her predecessors only reinforced the anomaly of female monarchy in patriarchal Russia. Neither overarching contempt nor simultaneous nostalgia for the glitter of the empresses' era freed the Russian romantic man from the past, which troubled him till the end of the nineteenth century, resurfacing in the realms of fairy tale, opera, and short fiction, mixing real and supernatural. The century that began with Ilya the Champion "killing" the formidable German heroine ended with Tchaikovsky's Russified German/Gherman relocated to Catherine's era, in which he, desperately searching for the secret of instantaneous success, much like *Ilya*, murders a countess—"unintentionally."

Patria, Nation, and Founding Fathers

Tracing the dynamics of power in the eighteenth-century Russian empire, Wortman points out a gender trajectory from Peter, who fashioned Russia "in female form that epitomized the refined and civilized image of empire," to Catherine II, who aimed to shape "a future monarch into an exemplar of a male ruler."[11] Perhaps it did not turn out quite the way she envisioned it. The day Catherine died marked the restoration of Russia's patriarchy, which required a recasting of the immediate past. This was done in several ways: by disgracing, appropriating, and putting the memory of female rule to sleep. Paul I (reigned 1796–1801) assaulted Catherine's body and her memory by exhuming and reassembling the remains of his father and by burying his mother next to him as the emperor's consort—after her thirty-four-year solo reign.[12] Aiming to diminish or prevent the possibility of female rule, Paul lost no time laying out at his coronation the law of the "male primogeniture of succession, with women following in line only in the absence of a male heir."[13] The law specifically denied the monarchical crown to an emperor's spouse, which years earlier would have prevented Catherine's rise.

For several decades, the empress's memoirs were kept a secret—outlawed, burned, destroyed by her imperial successors, her son, and her grandsons (but hand-copied and published abroad[14]). The diaries of her courtiers were likewise banned from publication; the poetic adulation of the empress's living court poets became muted.[15] Paul's loathing rejection of everything associated with Catherine, the brief revival of her legacy in the early reign of Alexander, and the serendipitous amnesia and legal prohibitions under Nicholas I—all indicated that the magic, marvel, and excesses of the eighteenth-century court were gone. Along with multiple losses, a new generation of ambitious men found themselves deprived of the embarrassing yet alluring institution of favoritism. The nineteenth-century emperors feared and forbade any reference to the empresses' promiscuity, particularly in the case of Catherine II. Her sexual conduct, threatening to stain the façade of dynastical morals, also raised the question of the emperors' descent and rights to the crown. Thus the heirs of daunting Catherine imposed laws of secrecy and also limited and in opera prohibited the portrayal of the Romanov family, specifically the empresses.

Everything praiseworthy about the eighteenth century was attributed to Peter, as if the nineteenth century had begun in 1725 and nineteenth-century emperors and poets with no interruption had continued the Petrine patrilineage.[16] Drawing on eighteenth-century lore of conquest, the Russian nation established itself not only as a strong player in relation to West and East but also as an imperial power within its own West (earlier acquired parts of Poland and Ukraine) and its own East (the Crimea, Caucasus, and, later, Central Asia). Even literati who battled the autocracy embraced nationalism, defined by and against ethnic otherness, thus equating nation with imperialism. Dostoevsky wrote:

> Our Russian land is a universe. . . . If one wishes to understand our history of post-Petrine reforms, you will find traces of these ideas . . . in the character of our communication with

European tribes, even in our state politics. Alas, what else did Russia do during the last two centuries in its politics if not serve Europe, perhaps much more than [it served] itself?[17]

None of the ingredients of literary nationalism were new: Orthodoxy as an ideology of conquest; Russianness defined against the East conquered in military or imaginary terms and modeled on, then surpassing, the vision of the West; absolute power invested with a sense of global and universal destiny; the folk associated with late-century collections of tales, bylinas, and songs; and the native language and literature endorsed by the last empress and her associates. Thus early-nineteenth-century literati gave both a name and an ideological definition to what was already there, filing their patent and assuming their ownership of the nation and its history. Nationalism and Russianness defined the value of an artistic work; in an interesting way, once proclaimed national, a work would then constitute a model and source for others to follow. Having written his frivolous chivalric poem during his student years, Pushkin some eight years later added to his *Ruslan and Liudmila* a famous prologue that reintroduced his tale as the quintessence of "Russian soul and Russian odor." Though found by Belinsky to be "as much Russian as German or Chinese,"[18] and its operatic version "neither Italian, nor German, and at the same time not Russian,"[19] *Ruslan* has been gradually elevated to signify Russian spirit and serve as a matrix for national expression. What initially began as a passionate critical discourse about *Ruslan's* language, eroticism, and characters landed in the debate about nationalism. "A light and fanciful narrative poem in eighteenth century taste"[20] was recognized as bearing the stamp of true Russianness,[21] its author pronounced, by fellow writer Gogol, "a phenomenon of Russian spirit."[22]

The craving for self-assertion and new horizons posed a need for founding fathers. There were a number of aspiring candidates in music—opera in particular—as if no operas had been produced on the Russian stage before. Alexei Verstovsky's *Pan Tvardovsky* (1828) was seen as a "new, comforting event we did not see yet on the Russian stage. It is ours, our first Russian opera."[23] Several years later, Verstovsky himself called his *Vadim* "the first opera in Rus."[24] By the middle of the century his *Askol'd's Grave* (1835) successfully rivaled operas by Glinka. Perhaps, besides his unquestionable talent, Glinka's decision to create an opera without spoken dialogue elevated him to the role of "the founder," the "Columbus of Russian music."[25] Or perhaps his two operas, as opposed to Verstovsky's six, presented Russian literati with a more manageable entity around which to define the basis and establish the direction of nationalistic opera. Two friends and later rivals, composer and critic Alexander Serov and critic Vladimir Stasov, neatly divided between them Glinka's two operas, the historical *Life for the Tsar* and the epic *Ruslan and Liudmila*, each privileging one opera over the other. Taruskin demonstrates how their decades-long, passionate dialogue shaped Russian musical taste, laid the groundwork for national music criticism, and carved out their own ambitious space in the nineteenth-century cultural landscape.[26]

Glinka's statement that "music is created by the [Russian] folk, and we composers only arrange it" became a manifesto of Russian musical nationalism.[27] With its meaning shaped by the following generations, this phrase became segregated from its historical context. The sentence in fact reflects the practice of early Russian operas and vaudevilles made up of folk songs and urban romances, "arranged" and at times combined with composed music. Thus whether created by native or foreign composers, late-eighteenth-century operas laid folk repertoire as the foundation for the nineteenth-century operatic tradition.[28]

Pushkin the Great

Pushkin, born in the last year of the eighteenth century, missed Catherine's Golden Age—a fact that likely captivated him as a pupil of the Lyceum recently opened in Catherine's favorite residence, Tsarskoe Selo. He was too young to participate in Russia's war with Napoleon. Banished from St. Petersburg by the emperor, he could not join the Decembrist Revolt; his drawings showed a gallows and the heads of hanged men with the curious inscription "And I could have been there as a joker. . . ." Missing the major historical events of his time, Pushkin was obsessed with history.

One primary area of infatuation and a target of his wit was the era that immediately preceded his birth. Like his fellow literati of the early nineteenth century, a tight social circle, Pushkin lived in a cultural sphere filled with spoken, unspoken, permitted, and ever-more-thrilling once-forbidden references to the age of Catherine. Despite the tsar's prohibition, Pushkin copied and kept in his possession Catherine's memoirs. After the poet's death, Nicholas I, looking through Pushkin's library inventory, discovered and acquired a copy of his grandmother's recollections.[29] Pushkin collected anecdotes of Catherine's surviving courtiers, attended their salons, and nurtured personal relations. One of the poet's romantic muses, Anna Kern (the mother of Glinka's lover, Catherine Kern), wrote about the extravagant devotion of her grandmother, Agafokleia Shishkova, to the deceased empress.[30] On the wall of her boudoir, Shishkova ordered two full-length portraits—the Savior and Catherine II—and, after the empress's death, was known to wear only Her Majesty's blouses.[31] Another of Pushkin's paramours, Princess Elizaveta Vorontsova, was a grand-niece of Potemkin. Simon Montefiore contends that "her Potemkin connection was surely part of the attraction to the poet: he [Pushkin] knew Potemkin's nieces and noted down the stories they told."[32] His wife's aunt, Countess Natalia Zagriazhskaia (1747–1837) was the favorite niece of Prince Aleksei Razumovsky and one of Catherine's trusted ladies in waiting.[33]

Zagriazhskaia's genealogy reminded aristocratic insiders about once-existing opportunities that brought the handsome Ukrainian chorister Razumovsky to fortune and his family to the highest aristocratic elite. Enchanted by Zagriazhskaia's anecdotes and the language of the teller, Pushkin wrote them down.[34] A large part of "Table-Talk," a collection of short vivid sketches about Catherine's courtiers, is dedicated to Prince Potemkin, his peculiar attire, expressions, and dialogues; Catherine speaks and is commented upon throughout the collection.[35] As Renato Poggioli points out, "Pushkin merged within himself the traditions of two centuries, which in a sense were at war with each other."[36]

In his many works, Pushkin entwined courtly gossip with archival research. Drawing on historical and poetic narratives and consistently using the literary expressions of his predecessors, Catherine's court poets, Pushkin produced a new hermeneutic that not only changed the meaning of lines that he placed in new contexts but also destabilized the literary sources and their meaning. Writing about history in the language he transformed into his own, and imbuing his visions of history with passion and wit, he fashioned the past as it has been perceived by his followers ever since. Thus Pushkin appropriated the past we know now.

Russian *Inoskazanie*

Much like Lomonosov before him, Pushkin mapped nineteenth-century nationalism between two vectors: temporal/historical and spatial/territorial. If Lomonosov used these vectors as the basis for his lofty language of the sublime, Pushkin recast them with outrageous irony and mockery, flying above the imperial obelisks (in his "Monument"), expelling the air from whatever sublime there was. Because of imperial censorship, Pushkin and his fellow nineteenth-century literati could not engage with the age of the empresses, whose glitter and memories filled early-nineteenth-century aristocratic salons and boudoirs. Instead, literary youths learned to convey their anxiety about the past in codified images, ironic covert language, and plentiful allusions. Disseminated across texts and artistic media, these subversive keys, intended for their contemporaries, easily escape "decontextualized" readers and spectators. The eighteenth century, for example, had been accustomed to the allegorical, mythological, idyllic, gender-crossing presentation of empresses and their family on the operatic stage, whether Elisabeth-Tito or Catherine's own Alexander-Fevei. Both extending and disrupting that operatic tradition, even before Nicholas introduced a law prohibiting the portrayal of the Romanov family in operas (1837), the operatic stage in the early nineteenth century became populated by fairy-tale royalty, patriotic and *almost* innocent.

While appropriating and reshaping the recent past, nineteenth-century literati obsessively separated themselves from the cursed monarchial "sorceresses" and their temptations; generational and gender tensions entwined. Generational relations in literature can often exhibit a struggle that Harold Bloom explored in his *Anxiety of Influence*. For him, "influence . . . is a metaphor, one that implicates a matrix of relationships—imagistic, temporal, spiritual, psychological—all of them ultimately defensive in their nature."[37] This defensiveness could lead to denial or aggressive rejection, which Michael Roth, studying the "amnesia" symptomatic of cultural anxiety in late-nineteenth-century France, associates with the "use and abuse of its past."[38] For Russians in the early nineteenth century, the "anxiety" that led them to renounce the influence of the previous era was associated not only with a generational break and their wish for an independent voice but also with their desire to define if not defend their maleness—individual and collective. Individual identity aligned itself with literary idiosyncrasy and collective identity with the nation (of men/Ruslans), both suffering insecurity in the aftermath of the reigns of the female rulers.

Nineteenth-century Russians had it two ways: they developed amnesia with respect to the past and simultaneously experienced anxiety by remembering it. Manifesting a new nationalistic/collective masculine beginning and discrediting everything before them, whether by critiquing, ridiculing, or conveniently forgetting, the literary men also maintained continuity. One of the literary modes they inherited and extensively developed reflected the Russian anxiety of "remembering forgetting"—*inoskazanie*, a style of narrative that literally means "other than it tells."

Inoskazanie implies the coexistence of several texts in one, triggering in readers textual and extratextual associations. This textual pluralism aligns inoskazanie with allusion, parody,[39] Aesopian language, and allegory. In Russian literature, allegory and inoskazanie are viewed as overlapping, the two terms at times used interchangeably. Breaking the division between a writer who says something other than he appears to say and a reader who understands what has not been said, allegory charges textual metaphor with extratextual associations.

From the early eighteenth century, the same Russian poets who mastered elevated encomium also cultivated allegoric irony.[40] A master of celebratory odes dedicated to sublime mistresses or to members of the aristocratic elite, Lomonosov also indulged in parody, allegory, pungent sarcasm, and implied profanity; his former student and academic secretary Ivan Barkov still retains fame as the most profane of Russian poets.[41] Derzhavin, in his ode on the triumphal siege of Ochakov (1789), praising Potemkin as "Russia's only Mars," urged Golitsin to "rush home with olive laurels" to his golden-locked wife and to tell her about the "heroic ventures of her uncle and father." (Potemkin, the uncle and self-inaugurated father of Golitsin's wife, was known as his niece's former lover.)[42] Poetic irony was at times used to deconstruct the language of pomp and power, even poetry the court poets themselves created. Inoskazanie could also bear a subversive political message. An anonymous early-twentieth-century poet wrote a pun on the tsars' dynastical name Romanov (*roman* also means "novel"):[43]

Но молвлю, правды не тая:	But [I] say, not concealing the truth:
Я не люблю твоей семьи романов	I don't like your family of novels [*romanov*].

Inoskazanie involves a complex dialogical poetic discourse consisting of bits and pieces of literary allusions. Russians fostered special appreciation of veiled textual allusions as a mark of refined poetic style and intellectual prowess. Losev cites Herzen: "In allegorical discourse there is perceptible excitement and struggle: this discourse is more impassioned than any straight exposition. . . . Implications increase the power of language."[44]

Citational exchange can give an innocent text a subversive layer of meaning. Recycled outside its initial context, a brief expression illuminates an "unsaid" association within its new poetic surrounding, but it is also capable of commenting on, targeting, and transforming the meaning of its initial source. Thus a short, playful, two-or-three-word phrase clipped from a poem of praise can turn into a double mockery of both the "singer" and the subject of the singer's veneration.

Inoskazanie relies on the hermeneutics of intertextuality. Submerged in the poetry of the time, one realizes that citations and allusions in a seemingly light poetic line may convey jolting commentary capable of initiating literary duels or poisonous critical attacks that span numerous texts and poets. Permeating Russian literature from early fables[45] to the literary underground of Soviet times, inoskazanie requires an intimate, almost inbred communion between a writer and an educated reader—an ability Russians cultivate from childhood. Marina Tsvetaeva described how, at seven, she became acquainted with the "fairy-tale *inoskazanie*" of Pushkin's Pugachev (*The Captain's Daughter*):

The proverbs, I did not understand and did not attempt to understand, besides the fact that he [the guide, Pugachev] speaks—about something else, the most important. This was my first in life inoskazanie—about this most—in these words, other words—about other [things].[46]

By definition, inoskazanie functions as a literary masquerade whose veiling can be inviting, triggering, possibly risky, and also intangible, evasive. Teasing intertextual connections from Pushkin's *Gavriliada* (his second mock-epic after *Ruslan and Liudmila*), Maria Rubins delves into "sophisticated metaliterary subtext and multitargeted parody"—in other words, inoskazanie. Alexander Ivanitsky, discussing a network of allusions in his essay on Bogdanovich's *Dushen'ka*, explores the notion of "mythological and language masquerade."[47]

Bogdanovich's poem, employing an array of historical allusions, formed close ties between lofty celebratory odes and light-hearted erotic pastorals.[48] The author weaves the beginning of *Dushen'ka* with concrete details of Catherine's coronation, specifically the theatricalized imperial street procession, to which he contributed parts of the text. Ivanitsky carefully traces Bogdanovich's use of citations that identify the surroundings of the title heroine as Tsarskoe Selo. The nymphs and zephyrs serving Dushen'ka are referred to in a long poetic, visual, and theatrical depiction of the empress's mythological entourage. Bogdanovich's Dushen'ka (from *dusha*, soul), masked as a princess and Arcadian shepherdess, suffering and erotic, humanizing and softening the imperial mythology, pleased Catherine, who, according to Ivanitsky, recognized Dushen'ka as a "compliment to herself."[49]

Conceiving his playful, sensuous Dushen'ka as a recognizable persona, in his opera *Slaviane* Bogdanovich mythologized the moral convictions of his heroine (and the original).[50] Derzhavin, in a short poem "A Stroll in the Tsarskoe Selo," echoed Bogdanovich's description of the gardens in *Dushen'ka*. Naming the location in the title of his poem, Derzhavin also reaffirmed the equation of Bogdanovich's idyllic garden with Tsarskoe Selo. Derzhavin himself forged multiple images of Catherine as a "God-like Tsarevna," a female warrior, and the wise mentor of Khlor (her grandson and a character in her tale).[51] Whether involving single or multiple literary texts, allegory, much like masquerade, veiled the subject to reveal it.

The rising generation of nineteenth-century literati, contrary to their proclaimed independence from and sometimes scorn for the past, evinced a strong sense of literary genealogy. The idiosyncrasy of one's style became nearly inseparable from fluent engagement with both contemporaries and predecessors through a network of allusions and covert ironic commentaries. Thus inoskazanie suggested possibilities of intertextual and extratextual interpretation. Although poems, tales, and operas conveyed individual meaning and represented shared conventions, they also offered the possibility of reading between texts, as if the words and their meanings came though a stack of transparent pages of different authors at times superimposed one above the other. For example, Lomonosov's sexual allegory connecting beard with phallus ("Hymn to the Beard"), not lost on his poetic followers, might contribute to a reader's interpretation of Pushkin's Chernomor, the dwarf whose long beard was a source of his magical power. Pushkin's playful Liudmila, as will be shown later, echoed Bogdanovich's Dushen'ka, while his Ruslan followed the path of Ilya the Champion. Crossing genres, the three tales shared plotlines and characters, an ironic narrative style, and most importantly poetic clues, expressions, and hints open to literary insiders.

A Champion Crossing into a New Century

Writing his champion poem *Dobrynia* (1796), a predecessor of *Ilya*, Nikolai L'vov, proclaimed that the "Russian spirit in Rus' is no longer an illusion . . . in Peter(sburg), yesterday I saw Boeslavich."[52] L'vov had apparently attended a production of Catherine's *Novgorodskii Bogatyr' Boeslavich*, which he acknowledged as an existing model for his champion and a stream of others coming to the nineteenth-century operatic stage.[53] Only a few years later, the new generation of ambitious early-nineteenth-century literati, continuing yet denying what was before them, expressed the urgent need for a mythological or historical Russian champion as a manifestation of new nationalist literature and truly Russian opera.[54]

Much as Catherine's *Oleg* was her transgendered and historically distanced self-portrait, early-nineteenth-century literary and operatic champions emerged as the ideal impersonators of their male authors and their aspirations. The champions displayed stupendous physical dexterity, ventured into impossible (magical) encounters and contests, and, overcoming all obstacles, were glorified by the folk. The poetic images of male operatic heroes were not far from the excessive eighteenth-century presentation of the triumphant "She."

A string of champions and operatic stories about a remote, half-historical, half-legendary Slavic past evoked native tales and bylinas that affirmed the authenticity of these operas.[55] The heroes, though defeating supernatural forces and creatures, related to historical figures.[56] In a pair of heroic operas, for example, Derzhavin featured quite similar champions: Pozharsky, a historic figure[57]; and Dobrynia, a character from a bylina. The plots, characters, and literary tropes in operatic and poetic tales were developed and polished by the time Zhukovsky wrote his *Twelve Sleeping Maidens* (1817) and Pushkin produced his *Ruslan and Liudmila*. An army of champions permeated the literary horizons in the early century, as if poems and operas had become the field of male conquest.

Pushkin's and Glinka's *Ruslans* had organic connections with their literary and operatic predecessors, particularly with *Ilya the Champion*.[58] The plotlines of operas with champions evolve around kidnapped and liberated Russian princesses, whether Vsemilas (nice-to-everyone), Vseslavas (all-fame), Milolikas (nice-face), Gremislavas (great-fame) or Liudmilas, (nice-to-people).[59] The operatic hero, lulled to a short sleep by foreign and magical seductresses, tends to avoid their temptations. A captured heroine, on the other hand, is put into a deep, lethargic sleep, as if her withdrawal affords security and prevents her and her hero from experiencing dangerous surprises. In *Ruslan*, Pushkin pokes fun at Zhukovsky's ballad *Twelve Sleeping Maidens*: their "hearts moved by love of / their soft silent sleep, their silent imprisonment."[60]

Pushkin's heroine, sleeping throughout most of the tale, appears most animated and energetic in the magic gardens of her kidnapper Chernomor.[61]

In their pursuit of the maidens, Russian heroes fulfill multiple tasks and celebrate triumphs as they encounter exuberant foes, magical and oriental. Glinka may offer the largest and, in the words of Taruskin, the most "self-indulgently promiscuous"[62] gallery of foreign others: Tatars, Persians, Turks, Caucasians, Arabs, Khazars, and Finns. His multiethnic parade typified nationalistic imperial lore, reminding one of *Oleg*— Catherine's manifesto announcing her expansionist plans and achievements—and also her *Fevei*, which introduced the Orient within a globalized Russia. Wedding scenes, an indispensable part of these operas, continued the tradition of eighteenth-century ceremonial and operatic nuptials.[63] In *Ilya* and *Ruslan*, a ritualistic operatic wedding at the beginning of the opera reconvenes in the final scenes with a massive choral "Slava," as if the exciting adventures, virtuosic arias, ensembles, dances, pantomime, military events, battles with endless monstrosities, and multiple transformations were a mere disruption, reinforcing the equation of wedding with national triumph.

Glinka's narrator Bayan is aligned with other operatic bylina tellers, including his namesake in Verstovsky's *Vadim* (1832) and Topor in *Askol'd*.[64] These "Bayans," mythologizing the native past and foreshadowing operatic plots, embody authenticity and pave a path for a large ensemble of fellow storytellers in Rimsky-Korsakov's *Sadko*, whose title hero, like his predecessors, strikes the antique *gusli* (harp or piano).

Formidable women challenging male champions likewise become essential to nineteenth-century Russian operas. Sorceresses and seductresses surrounded by their dancing minions have strong ties with the East: Zlomeka (from *zlo*, evil), a daughter of khan Uzbek (*Ilya the Champion*), and *Naina* with her Persian beauties (*Ruslan*). At some point in the fable, the champion, his associate, or the two together find themselves diverted from their victorious march by the seductresses—flying, dancing, and trapping a hero in a magic never-land. A bevy of Eastern beauties, for instance, alluring Ilya's assistant Russian Torop, praise him as "amazing Khán / Torop the wise and famous!" to which he responds with the wish to "live a bit longer like a khan."[65] Pushkin's Ratmir, khan of the Khazars (an ancient powerful kingdom that collected tribute from the Rus' in the lower Dniepr River until the tenth century), once a rival and later a friend of Ruslan, is also captured by a flock of dancing maidens "with dozing languishing eyes down, / themselves enchanting, half-naked, / indulgent and numbed."[66] Pushkin's emphasis on fluid graceful movement sets the stage for dancing choruses in Glinka and other operas with floating and often voiceless nymphs in Dargomyzhsky and Rimsky-Korsakov.

The rise of a native champion demanded forces against which he would demonstrate his power and celebrate victories. The formidable sorceresses populating the fairy tales fulfilled the purpose. Quite different from an ordinary folk witch (Baba-Yaga), these magical women, often revealing noble traits and high status, and accompanied by dancing entourages, bear some resemblance to the stubborn inescapable empresses. Two female roles in *Ruslan and Liudmila,* the virtuous title heroine and the aged sorceress Naina, both carry some allusions to Russia's female kingdom as manifested by the last of them, Catherine. Such female doubles, contrasting but rarely sharing the stage or facing each other, became a suspiciously recurring element in Russian nineteenth-century opera.

5

RUSLAN AND LIUDMILA
THE PRINCESS, THE WITCH, AND THE DWARF

Pushkin + Glinka

The opera *Ruslan and Liudmila*, created by the two "founding fathers" of Russian national culture and revered as "the inaugural work of a new epic-opera genre,"[1] has typically been analyzed in the context of what came afterward. *Ruslan*, however, exhibits strong connections with the Russian past. Not only does it share characteristic traits with Krylov's *Ilya*, but the two title bogatyrs (champions) inevitably recall their counterparts in Catherine's four opera-skazkas, most closely *Khrabroi i smeloi vitiaz' Akhrideich*. *Ruslan* shares with *Akhrideich* a similar plotline: a kidnapping, heroic ventures, encounters with magic beings, rescued princesses, and a wedding. Moreover, in his original draft of the libretto Glinka featured Ivan Tsarevich, the namesake and twin of Catherine's Akhrideich (Ivan-Tsarevich). Had Glinka followed his initial plan, his Ivan, the brother of Liudmila, would have rescued her, much as Catherine's Ivan Tsarevich aided his three sisters, kidnapped by monstrous suitors.[2] Thus the "first" epic opera might not be the first after all.

Pushkin constructed his poem as six songs. Like *Akhrideich*, it is replete with choruses, dances, and musical allusions: the "lyre" of his "windy capricious muse," his "noisy waves," "gaily sounding clouds," "hushed hills," "invisible harp," "singer of mysterious visions," and his "companion . . . Northern Orpheus." Whether or not young Pushkin envisioned a musical spectacle when he conceived the poem, his dancing sprites inspired the creation of a ballet in 1821, a scant year after the poem was published.[3] Four years later, Prince Alexander Shakhovskoi staged the theatrical trilogy *Finn*, based on a subplot and a character in Pushkin's tale.[4] Glinka wrote that the same Shakhovskoi suggested the project of the opera *Ruslan*, which the composer and Pushkin discussed at one of Zhukovsky's literary gatherings. Pushkin died the same year, and the creation of the operatic *Ruslan* stretched on for some five years, its libretto fathered by a band of six literati: Nestor Kukol'nik, Valerian Shirkov, Mikhail Gedeonov, Konstantin Bakhturin, Prince Shakhovskoi, and Nikolai Markevich. "Folk wisdom tells," wrote Kukol'nik, "that with seven nannies, the child ends up losing an eye! . . . But the genius of Glinka will cover our transgressions."[5]

The opera turned Pushkin's light, teasing poetic tale into a monumental spectacle, a Russian version of serious opera that, mixing a myth with a tale, conflating a fantasy about the archaic past with a web of allusions, might trigger allegorical interpretation. The sizable cast falls into two groups. One includes human characters: the lead couple, Liudmila's father, Ruslan's two rivals for Liudmila (Ratmir and Farlaf), Ratmir's lover Gorislava, and Bayan, a singer of bylinas. The other part of the cast comprises supernatural beings: beneficent Finn, the gigantic Head, the witch Naina, and the kidnapper Chernomor. Each group is associated with massive choruses of dancers and singers. Luxuriously dressed folk—not native ragged peasants but rather a couple hundred or so courtiers masquerading in native costumes—take part in a ritualistic wedding in the first act and a grand finale in the fifth. Their counterparts are choruses of dancing enchantresses and animated singing flowers in magical gardens. Except for Finn, the rest of the magical company engages in combat with humans. Yet the supernatural characters are disadvantaged. Although possessing magical powers, they are old and expose a variety of physical limitations. The gigantic Head has no body; Naina, looking like an eerie ghost, has to deal with her overwhelming sexual cravings, rejection, and thus humiliation; the kidnapper Chernomor is a buffoonish dwarf with inflated desires but no voice (and no longer any activity in another body part!). Disturbing the divide between the two terrains, Chernomor relocates Liudmila to his land, which brings the two worlds into conflict. Youth wins over the aged contenders (a metaphor for the struggle between literary generations). The Russian champion rightfully regains his bride, who, as argued later, is tamed in the course of the adventures. Defeating his enemies, Ruslan collects their magical gardens, palaces, and kingdoms and in so doing expands his Russia. The opera's first and last acts portray the mighty and prosperous ancient Kievan Rus'. The internal acts depict the domains of the supernatural beings: the captivating palace-park of Naina in the third act and another architectural ensemble, Chernomor's magical garden and chateau, in the fourth.

The story and main characters of *Ruslan* are strikingly similar to Mozart's *Die Zauberflöte*, immensely popular in Russia since its publication and premier in Russian (1794) and its production in 1818 just as Pushkin was writing his *Ruslan*.[6] In both operas, a kidnapping is the starting point of a clash between magical and human. Both Naina and the Queen of the Night attempt to use a young heroine to avenge a former suitor. The haunted forest in *Die Zauberflöte* parallels the magic gardens in Ruslan. The role of Mozart's moor Monostatos, who repeatedly refers to himself as "black" and lusts after Pamina, is enacted by Pushkin's Chernomor (*cherno*, black; *mor*, plague) creeping up to sleeping Liudmila. Rescuing their brides, both Ruslan and Tamino demonstrate devotion and heroism; the unions of the young princely couples in the finales double as communal celebrations of Kievan Rus' in one opera and the brotherhood of the Masonic Temple in the other. In Mozart, the successful resolutions affirm a paternalistic message:

Ein Mann muß eure Herzen leiten,	A man must lead your hearts,
Denn ohne ihn pflegt jedes Weib	For without him every woman lacks a guide
Aus ihrem Wirkungskreis zu schreiten.	To step out of her sphere.

Die Zauberflöte has been perceived as a covert attack on the autocratic figure of Maria Theresa, allegorically associated with the Queen of the Night.[7] A detailed comparison of the two operas, though extremely compelling, is left for another time. However, it is important to note that *Ruslan and Liudmila*, echoing the story line of the Viennese opera, may have inherited its hermeneutics: a patchwork fairy tale masking political allusions, references, and historical characters—elements corresponding to the "cultural atmosphere of St. Petersburg, [its] spiritual psychological ideals, . . . poetics of hints, allegory and shared memory"[8]—i.e., inoskazanie.

The abundant scholarship on *Ruslan and Liudmila* includes monographs and essays analyzing the structure of the opera, the sources of its multiethnic musical palette, its modal language and harmony, and the reception of its many productions. Nearly all the literature inevitably arrives at the topic of musical nationalism. The Russianness of Ruslan, at least for Russians, remains unshaken, even after Taruskin lambasted the mindlessly repeated assumptions of this opera's Russianness as a "normative criterion," and even after Frolova-Walker shredded, point-by-point, Ruslan's glorified Russianness as a composite of "Stasov's hasty speculations, Odoyevsky's misdirected erudition, and Laroche's polemic."[9] *Ruslan*, in fact, offers an anthology of otherness, which goes beyond ethnicity and the supernatural, toying with the otherness of recent history and historical figures. Discarding the mythologized lenses used in the nineteenth century and magnified in the next one, this chapter focuses on three characters—Liudmila, Naina, and Chernomor—by reconnecting them with their literary, artistic, and historical environs and by situating them in the context of inoskazanie.

Liudmila in Catherine's Tsarskoe Selo

Pushkin's title heroine, whisked away on her wedding night with Ruslan, finds herself in the magical gardens of the evil Chernomor. Three knights, former rivals of her husband—who did not have a chance to consummate the marriage—pledge to rescue Liudmila. Her royal father promises the heroine as a prize to her liberator. Ruslan, in the course of his journey, encounters a magical donor, Finn, who battles his former love, Naina, an ally of Chernomor. After plentiful encounters with supernatural and ethnic others and various knightly accomplishments, the tale reaches the expected jubilant reunion of the title heroes.

Both the poem *Ruslan and Liudmila* and the opera, situated in the midst of mythological and language masquerade, offer an exhilarating possibility of recognition. The title heroine, together with Bogdanovich's Dushen'ka and Ivan Dmitriev's Vsemila (*Prichudnitsa*, 1794), form a trio of Russified Psyches.[10] Each of the three beauties is kidnapped, delivered to an enchanting garden and magical castle, and entertained by a bevy of winged cupids, singing zephyrs, bathing nymphs, and other visible and invisible spirits. There each princess is put to sleep, is rescued by her lover, and ends up in a blissful union with her hero. Liudmila especially resembles Dushen'ka, and the plot follows Dushen'ka's story. Both contemplate suicide, and both are depicted enjoying their meals, being brushed and dressed, and experiencing nighttime encounters with their monstrous captors. Pushkin likely modeled his tale on *Dushen'ka*, whose "idyllic pan-pipe," according to Belinsky, charmed everyone more than the trumpets of the epic poems and lofty odes of Russian "Homers and Pindars."[11] Bogdanovich's poem begins with a prelude praising Chloe and immediately evokes the Olympic imagery of Russian imperial lore. Depicting a competition of goddesses, the opening lines echo the cantata *Le Rivali* (see Chapter One). Staged at the third anniversary of Catherine's enthronement, it portrayed a match between Venus and Minerva, with Jupiter choosing a victor possessing the virtues of both: Catherine. Likewise, in Bogdanovich's first verse, personified "Beauty and Benevolence / Argued for ages; / The World witnessed / Their rivalry and quarrels / Chloe unites the two."[12] Clearly drawing on mythologized imagery of the empress, the poet a few lines later continues with a nearly documentary and self-referential description of Catherine's coronation spectacle *Triumphant Minerva*.[13]

Identifying in his *Dushen'ka* the date, place, and event—"not long ago, in a Moscow masquerade, / During Shrovetide, in a ceremonial parade"—Bogdanovich narrates the sequence of a masked procession.[14] He further describes the routine of his idyllic heroine, who, according to Ivanitsky, "reenacts the lifestyle of Catherine in Tsarskoe Selo. Amours play for her concerts, operas and operettas."[15] Like Catherine, little Dushen'ka gleans knowledge of people and customs from "her library / among a mass of books, large and small." And in her "leisure, resting from all work, she observes the statues of major masters." Thus, whether wearing simple attire or masquerade dress, costumed as an Arcadian shepherdess or a Russian princess, Dushen'ka conceals her identity, only to reveal it later in its multicolored radiance.

Bogdanovich's stanza, which became a timeless Russian proverb, was recycled in the ironic "Solace to Aniuta" by Krylov.

Во всех ты, Душенька, нарядах хороша
По образу ль какой царицы ты одета,
Пастушкою ли где сидишь и в
    шалаше... (Bogdanovich)

In all attires, you, Dushen'ka, are beautiful,
Reminding [one] of a certain tsarina,
Even when sitting dressed as a shepherdess
    in a shack....

Не убором ты любезна,
Не нарядом хороша,
Всем нарядам ты—душа.
(Krylov, 1793)

'Tis not adornment makes you nice,
Nor does a dress define your beauty,
To all clothes you are—dusha (dushen'ka).

The allusions to the empress in multiple guises, including *dusha-dushen'ka*, are inescapable, her presence overwhelming, extending from odes to pastorals, from playful
poems and heroic operas to Aniuta, the peasant heroine in a number of native comic
operas.[16]

    In the first line of the dedication of *Ruslan*,[17] Pushkin curiously employs the words
dusha and *tsaritsa*, offering a poetic tribute to the "tsarinas" of his "soul."[18] The parallel
between Bogdanovich's and Pushkin's heroines becomes especially apparent as they
find themselves in the magical gardens of their respective kidnappers. Dushen'ka
observes a "myriad of wonders"; Liudmila, scared and depressed, nevertheless notices
the "enchanting place!" Both heroines walk along lush alleys of myrtle and palm trees.
"Roses cover the paths caressing the feet" of the first; "everywhere roses' branches live
and breathe along the paths" of the other. The location of the park, palace, and fountains is clear, especially when the two texts are read along with yet another poem,
Derzhavin's intimate "Stroll in Tsarskoe Selo" (1791), dedicated to Plenira (an endearing name he gave his young wife).[19] A few years later, the poet would mourn the loss of
"divine Felitsa" and Plenira, who "sings no more" ("Poet," 1801). The three poetic tributes employ not only the same visual iconography but also nearly identical poetic
metaphors.

Bogdanovich, *Dushen'ka*	Derzhavin "A Stroll in Tsarskoe Selo"[20]	Pushkin, *Ruslan and Liudmila*
Сквозь рощу **миртовых** [myrtles] и **пальмовых** [palms] древес		Аллеи **пальм** [palms] и лес лавровый, И благовонных **миртов** ряд [myrtles' row]
И всюду **розами** [roses] усыпанны дороги	Здесь **розы** [roses] воздыханье	Повсюду **роз** [roses] живые ветки Цветут и дышут по тропам

При токе **вод хрустальных** [crystal waters]	**Жемчужная** струя [pearl-like stream], **Кристалл** [crystal] шумел… стеклянны **воды**… [glassy waters],	**Жемчужной**…дугой Валятся, плещут **водопады** [pearl-like waterfall]
Фонтаны [fountains] силились подняться в высоту Каскады [waterfalls] и пруды И **Смехов** [laughter] и Утех, летающих вокруг	**Сребром** сверкают **воды** [silver-shining waters] И памятников вид [sculptures] Они где зрятся в **воды** Там эха **хохотанье** [giggle]; Тут шепоты ручьев И **соловей** [nightingale] сидит	Летят алмазные **фонтаны** [sparkling fountains] С веселым шумом к облакам, Под ними блещут истуканы [sculptures] С веселым шумом [gay noise] к облакам И свищет **соловей** [nightingale] китайский

This wide repertoire encompassing Dushen'ka and its literary relatives, as well as Catherine's *Akhrideich* and poetic invocations of Catherine's surroundings, found a way into *Ruslan*. How do these intergeneric and intertextual connections contribute to a possible interpretation of the poem? Do acoustic and scenic allusions—for example, recognition of Tsarskoe Selo—trigger an association between the tale's characters and historical personas?

Julie Buckler, exploring the poetic mapping of St. Petersburg and viewing its palace-parks as both a physically constructed space and a literary anthology, finds Tsarskoe Selo an especially potent body of cultural symbolism and historical allusion. She writes about the self-referential aspect of Derzhavin's "A Stroll" and another poem dedicated to the Tsarskoe Selo, "Ruins" (1797).[21] The first portrays a wondrous, romantic terrain; the second, written a year after Catherine II died and Paul abandoned his mother's favorite residence, is a nostalgic eulogy to the past glory of this place and the absence of its hostess.

Marveling over the "streaming wealth of Croesus, the gold and silver, the playing of harps repeated by the chorus," "sirens singing … enchanting hearts and minds," Derzhavin invokes the ambiance of *Dushen'ka* with "amours and cupids finding intimate refuge in shadowy grottos," in "theater and swings." The poet writes how "She" once walked in these "meadows and plains, … near waters, in the paths of roses, … to the pleasant music of pipes from afar."[22] Notably, Catherine's name is not pronounced; but her shadow remains in Tsarskoe Selo, where "She is no longer, the magical radiance is gone." Pushkin's line nearly replicates Derzhavin's: "Everything has vanished, the Great One gone!" There, in Catherine's forsaken residence, the two poets actually met, the student Pushkin reading to Derzhavin his "Recollection in Tsarskoe Selo." Perhaps *Ruslan's* magical gardens fused the poet's own youthful experiences of the place with the mythology of the empress's Tsarskoe Selo, poeticized by Derzhavin.

But the locus of Liudmila's captivity in his tale may also have an alternative address. Boris Gasparov points out that Pushkin himself compares Chernomor's castle with the palace-park of Prince Potemkin,[23] alluding to a very specific place and time: a legendary soirée Potemkin threw for Catherine in honor of Russia's victory over the Ottomans in Izmail (April 28, 1791). One might hypothesize that the poetic environs of *Dushen'ka*, recited in Catherine's circle, influenced the physical and artistic design of Potemkin's lustrous ball, or that Derzhavin's famous description of the fête made the palace and the ball into a historical myth, described in the same poetic tradition that he and Bogdanovich shaped.[24]

In the same way contemporaries and later generations mused about the past grandeur of Tsarskoe Selo, they could fantasize about Potemkin's former palace.[25] Its rather plain, long, one-story classical façade concealed a space once lit by "a hundred thousand candles," reflected in "golden chandeliers" and in "clear crystals spread everywhere." Under "hanging [platforms for] choruses, . . . decorated with Chinese vessels and two huge gilded organs," among monumental columns, guests traversed the indoor and outdoor spaces of the palace and orangeries. Between "live myrtle" and the "highest palms," Potemkin's guests and Her Majesty promenaded in "odorous meadows" with "glassy water pools" while listening, in the breaks "between the loud music," to "the whistle of a nightingale." Derzhavin expresses astonishment: "What glamour! Magic domains of Scheherazade!" Pushkin echoes him in his portrayal of Chernomor's palace: "no need for my / description of the magic house, / long ago Scheherazade / preceded me in this."

Potemkin devised for his imperial guest a sequence of dances, choruses, and theatricals. The nymphs entertaining Catherine invoke the musical entourage of Dushen'ka and foreshadow companions of Liudmila: the first, listening to the "sweet sound of musical instruments," could not decide whether she preferred "pleasant voices," the violin, the "harmony of harps, or flute"; the other was amused by "invisible harps."

Pushkin expresses no interest in introducing his heroine as anything more than a subject of male desire at the beginning of the tale. "Her groom, ecstatic and euphoric, / caresses in imagination / his maid's chaste beauty," anticipating sexual pleasure; the three unfortunate suitors engulf "the poison of love and hate." Liudmila becomes animated only when relocated to the magical gardens. If everything in the physical space and in the poetic invocations of Tsarskoe Selo conveys an association with the empress, Pushkin's recognizable gardens evince the character of his princess, whether idyllic, ironic, or comical. Her mood fluctuates between despair and capriciousness,

between the desire to die and the desire to eat, her trepidation and her playfulness—
"all night [thinking about] her destiny, in tears she wondered—and laughed." Pained
by separation from her beloved Ruslan and enduring intolerable suffering, she nevertheless turns to "high, clear mirrors," "reluctantly pulls up her golden locks,"
"carelessly" braids her hair, "accidentally" finds robes, sighs, and tries them on. After
Chernomor loses his magical cap, escaping from the shrieking princess grabbing him
by the beard, Liudmila tries it on, "turning it around, [putting it low] on the brow,
straight, and cocking it." The poet notes with delight that his heroine "is capricious,
/ So what?"

Pushkin concludes that she is *vétrena* (from *veter*, wind), a word that reminds
one of another heroine, Vetrana, the lead character of a poetic tale *Prichudnitsa* by
Dmitriev (1794). A poet of Derzhavin's generation, a master of allegorical tales and
fables, Dmitriev was respected in Pushkin's circles, his *Prichudnitsa* recognized as a
"precious pearl ... of the poet's laurels."[26] Pushkin himself used Dmitriev's expressions,
referred to his works, and possibly depicted him as an old man in *Eugene Onegin*.[27]
Commenting on the playful tone of both *Dushen'ka* and *Prichudnitsa*, Belinsky gave
preference to the latter. Glinka wrote a song on Dmitriev's lyrics.

Written several years before *Ilya the Champion*, *Prichudnitsa*, like *Dushen'ka*, does
not deal with a Russian hero and his victories. Instead it focuses on a heroine and her
adventures. Unlike playfully submissive Dushen'ka, Vetrana, as the poem tells, was
raised at the time when Russian boyars (nobles) stopped locking their women in high
terems, "permitting their freedom according to German fashion."[28] Thus in the very
beginning, the tale directly refers to two historical factors. The first is the dismissal of
terems and the consequent change in gender relations. The second is the story's surprising reference not to French influences in the Russian court and not to Italian
prominence in theater and the arts but to German vogue, perhaps commenting on the
chain of German, half-German, or German-groomed female tsarinas and by extension
to the operatic German sorceress defeated by Ilya.

Dmitriev's Vetrana, happily married and also enjoying liberties with her lover, has
all her desires fulfilled. But the capricious heroine becomes bored and annoyed. Like
her predecessor Dushen'ka and her later counterpart Liudmila, naughty Vetrana finds
herself transported to a magic garden. It is a familiar one—"all the rarity of nature that
is stuffed into Russian odes ... indescribable in *skazka*s, and unimaginable even in
dreams," appears in "Tsarskoe Selo, ... Armida's gardens or one in Peterhof."[29] In
Dmitriev's tale, the magical gardens, unappreciated by Vetrana, turn into a nightmarish witch-land where a wild rider snatches the heroine. Vetrana's flight, frightening
experiences, and subsequent prolonged sleep function as a moral lesson to a capricious beauty. Similarly, in the interlude to the "Third Song" of *Ruslan*, Pushkin, who is
about to picture Liudmila in Chernomor's kingdom, without any apparent connection

to the plotline addresses Klimena, a "victim of boring Hymeneus," whose "languid lowered eyes," tears, and blushes promise a "head decoration" for her husband.

Why would Pushkin, in the midst of Liudmila's horrid imprisonment, suddenly mention this woman's marriage-boredom? Will Liudmila undergo a lesson similar to Vetrana's? Are there traces of German fashion, libertine spirit, and domineering power that have to be weeded out of Pushkin's heroine?

Operatic Liudmila, or Inoskazanie in Music

Inoskazanie and intertextuality are not limited to literary texts. Music dialogues with other musics, acoustically and textually. Audible recognition of recurring melodies, motifs, and rhythmic patterns instills powerful associations; musically literate insiders share the appreciation of written musical text—the semiotics of keys, harmonic and enharmonic designs, codified tunes, visual allusions. A few listeners can instantly, by ear, appreciate Scriabin's "mystic chord"; others learn the beauty of recognition by studying the harmonic logic of Scriabin's scores, the visuality of the text affecting sonic appreciation. Music in opera, engaging its intermusical connections, also dialogues with the literary text, reinforcing, contributing to, or subverting its message for dramatic effect.

Although Pushkin's Liudmila remains largely unknown until her arrival in Chernomor's domain, Glinka introduces his Liudmila in the first act of his opera. Not a dulcet Russian princess she is but musically a foreigner, an assertive Italianate virtuosic soprano. In the wedding neither her father nor her chosen groom but rather Liudmila sings a solo. She addresses, one after the other, four men, first appealing to her father, then comforting her unsuccessful suitors, and finally singing to Ruslan. Preceding Liudmila, Bayan recites a ballad that foreshadows the story that is to unfold. Liudmila's cavatina is both framed and interspersed with a series of folk choruses; Bayan and the chorus sing syllabically. In the style of a ritualistic native wedding, the bride's lyric expresses the sadness of her separation from her parental home, her father, and the city of Kiev. However, the text is hardly discernible in her densely florid vocal part. Beginning with leaps on "sad it is for me" and ending with "my dear parent" in a playful fast staccato, the song to the father repeats the same melodic line, each time elaborated with increasing vocal ornamentation (Example 5.1). Thus it is she who introduces the light ironic tone of Pushkin's tale. The folk chorus "Don't suffer, darling child," syllabic and with vertical harmonic arrangement, emphasizes the drastic contrast between the heroine and the "folk." Choral episodes also separate the four parts of Liudmila's aria. Turning to the rejected Varangian prince Farlaf (*basso buffo*), Liudmila shifts from highly florid Italian *bel canto* to Italian buffo style (Example 5.2). Accompanied by pizzicato strings, she sings a lighthearted staccato tune with

Example 5.1

Liudmila: Sad it is for me, my darling parent! Like in a dream my days passed with you!
My song: Lado, oi, Lado!

Example 5.2

Liudmila: Don't brood, noble guest, that capricious love guides my heart to the other one!

syncopations and laughing passages. Her song to Farlaf defines his musical imagery before he delivers his famous rondo in the second act.

After another short choral interlude, the heroine approaches Ratmir, the Khazaran prince. Here our quite liberated and versatile tsarevna shifts to a new musical domain, introducing the first in a gallery of oriental images in *Ruslan*. Accompanied by lulling waves of violins floating among major, minor, and diminished triads and with soothing sustained sounds of winds and muted trumpets, Liudmila sings a dreamlike melody. She abandons wide leaps; her smooth, caressing vocal line, woven of stepwise mostly chromatic motion, paints the "lush southern skies and Ratmir's orphaned harem" (Example 5.3). While singing about his harem and his forgiving beloved, Liudmila repeats again and again the same phrase, adding alluring ornamentation and ending with a long, accelerated vocal cadenza. Immediately afterward, the heroine reiterates the tune of her jocular dedication to Farlaf, this time expressing her love to Ruslan. She completes her solo with another segment of brilliant vocal acrobatics alternating with a consistently syllabic even-paced wedding chorus. Glinka's Italian prima donna,

Example 5.3

Liudmila: Under the lush southern skies, orphaned is your harem.

satisfying the Russian operatic aficionado, befits the common comparison of Pushkin's tale with the chivalric Italian epics by Matteo Boiardo and Ludovico Ariosto, whose medieval knight Orlando defeats Tatars, Saracens, and Moors to win his bride. The Russian Ruslan, like Orlando, conquers the multifaceted East and magic in the name of a beloved; Liudmila establishes her Western persona in an obligatory fioritura that, Asaf'ev claims, overshadows "the lyricism and sincerity" of her cavatina.[30] Attempting to reconcile Liudmila's Russian origin with endless Italian roulades, Chernov comments:

> The cavatina is weak in drawing a moral image of Liudmila, who shares many general characteristics with Antonida from *The Life for the Tsar*. . . . The style of the aria is rather French-Italian than Russian.[31]

Thus Glinka's heroine, in the course of the first act, asserts her particular musical identity and her independence from the male characters. The coquettish bride, who chooses her groom and, in the midst of her antique "traditional" wedding, flirts with rejected suitors, is closer to fickle Vetrana than to Pushkin's heroine. Her kidnapping, offering the champion the opportunity for "manly" adventures, also gives the young tsarevna a preventive scare.

Locating the magic garden in the fourth act, Glinka begins with an orchestral intermission whose light dotted rhythm emphasizes the whimsical character of a march that fades away. After several measures of gently sighing violins, Liudmila launches into her second solo—the longest in the opera, a fifteen-minute scene and aria. Glinka does not use the poet's lyrics, depriving the heroine of Pushkin's edgy irony. Her lyrics are a straightforward expression of the heroine's expected despair. But Pushkin's irony finds its way into the music. In a fluid three-beat dancing frame, the poor bride, pondering "Why live?" dives into the head-spinning passages featured throughout the scene (Example 5.4).

Example 5.4

Liudmila: Why live? Why live on the earth any more? O, you, my passion . . .

Like the hostess of both the historic and the mythological Tsarkoe Selo, Liudmila enjoys choruses—water maids and animated flowers. After the spirits fail to console the girl, Liudmila sings "Ach! You, destiny" an aria seen as an affirmation of her Russianness. Our operatic heroine, however, appears full of surprises. Having fully established her solid and delightful Italianate musical identity, in the middle of the scene in the gardens she reveals another aspect of her persona. Her most famous aria, in the tradition of romance—a type of lyric song, traditionally accompanied by the guitar or piano—fools even skeptical Gasparov. He hears "a Russian woman—be it a princess or her maid—pouring out her heart through a quotidian but intimate musical medium."[32] But Liudmila's "unabashedly sentimental" aria resembles an urban type of romance tied with gypsy songs and gypsy musicians, who, playing in aristocratic salons, hussars' gatherings, and markets, had become in the early nineteenth century a prominent part of Russian urban culture.[33] In this aria Glinka, a master of some of the most refined romances, wove together three strands: the smooth romance melody with guitarlike accompaniment; the almost excessive expressiveness of gypsy song, especially in the duet with the violin; and the virtuosity of the operatic diva. As Liudmila sings about her doleful destiny, her melody leans to, winds around, echoes, and overlaps with a violin solo. The initially simple tune, often praised as a Russian folk type, gradually branches out into an intricate melismatic elaboration. The folkish "Ach" turns into an exposition of vocal hedonism (Example 5.5).[34] In the sensual melodic duet, voice and violin entwine.

Example 5.5

Liudmila: Ach! you destiny

A chorus of enchanted servants bridges to the next part of this aria, in which Liudmila, delivering a passionate rejection of the dwarf, falls asleep, exhausted. Whatever Liudmila is, she is a curious musical persona, whose identity floats in the discursive space between the lyrics and vocals.

Pushkin paints his sleeping beauty *à la naturelle*—wearing "the innocent and simple attire of our great grandma Eve." At some point, the bride, dreaming of her beloved, is attended by the dwarf. The poet exclaims: "What a horrid view!" continuing with rather graphic details of Chernomor's "droopy hand caressing the young body of Liudmila, his wilting mouth applied to her enchanting lips"; some of these lines were expunged after the first editions. The poet's contemporaries criticized Pushkin's treatment of Liudmila as an "inappropriate mockery of her sensibilities," along with his emphasis on her erotic allure.[35] By putting his belle to sleep, the poet makes her vulnerable to her assailant but also spares her from experiencing Chernomor's impotent attempts. Or perhaps Pushkin, lacking compassion for his heroine,[36] so playful and tricky in a magical land, makes her sleep to prevent Liudmila from repeating the actions of her namesake from a tale in verse by the poet's uncle, Vasily Pushkin. Written around the same time as *Ruslan, Liudmila and Uslad* (1818) pictures the young Russian couple traveling to Kiev.[37] The humongous wild Pecheneg—from an Oghuz Turkic tribe that attacked Rus' in antiquity—emerges before the couple and starts a battle for the Russian's bride. Equal in power, neither winning, the two men ask the girl to decide. This Liudmila quickly chooses the stranger and leaves with him, betraying her devoted knight. Glinka's Ruslan, defeating Chernomor and afterward finding his belle asleep, is consumed by suspicion. The waves of diminished harmonies and tremolos wash over, infiltrating his melody; the unison chorus rises in a chromatic scale, commenting on the hero's "fierce jealousy" (Example 5.6).

In the poem and the opera, sleeping through the battle between Ruslan and Chernomor, Liudmila remains dormant long after the evil dwarf is defeated. It is plausible that, "unsuitable as a Russian heroine,"[38] the young maid, relocated to a simulacrum of Tsarskoe Selo and treated to a décor that echoes Potemkin's fête, acquires an imperious identity that has to be pacified, cleansed, anesthetized, and ultimately subdued.

Example 5.6

Ruslan: Unknown fear tortures my soul! O, friends! Who knows whether her smile is addressed to me, and whether her heart trembles for me?

Like Vetrana, Pushkin's Liudmila, wondering if her long and vivid adventures were not an obscure dream, returns to her initial enigmatic self. In the mighty operatic finale that completes the wedding interrupted in the first act, the dazed operatic Liudmila rejoices in another spree of florid passages, which are promptly tamed, absorbed by the ensemble and massive chorus.

The stream of events from the disrupted wedding in the first act to the monumental finale, reconciling the bride and groom, the princely couple and the folk, completes the wedding (venchanie, "coronation") as a hymn to imperial Russia—a resounding "Slava" to the couple and to the "holy fatherland," Ruslan wedded to Rus'. With all the intricate inconsistency between Liudmila's lyrics, proper for a devoted Russian maid, and her flirtatious florid Italianate persona, she represented a good case for a Russian nineteenth-century nationalist to craft the girl as native epic heroine. Emblemizing Rus' as a bride, Liudmila, desired by West (Farlaf) and East (Ratmir), attacked by the magical composed East (Chernomor), is to be saved by her Russian hero. Ratmir, who acquires the respect of the title heroine and marries another Russian woman, echoes Bogdanovich's Alexander in *Slaviane*. Adapted from different operatic versions of Metastasio's plot, Bogdanovich's Alexander of Macedonia reveres the Russian maid Dobroslava and at the end befriends his rival Ruslan, the namesake of Glinka's hero.

Liudmila, "cast clearly as a soubrette,"[39] invokes intertextual connections that make her an interesting figure, playful, sensual, salacious, naïve—one of the various Dushen'kas whose identities are as evasive and concealed as they are revealed. Derived from foreign sources, fashioned into the heroine of a native poetic idyll and comic opera, adapted to Russian imperial mythology and literary masquerade, Dushen'ka/Catherine crossed (as Liudmila) into the nineteenth century. There she, tsarevna and operatic soprano, would be gradually reintroduced as a folk Russian character—which she is definitely not—both a captive and the mistress of the magical gardens of Tsarskoe Selo.

Naina

She is Liudmila's opposite. The princess is young, Naina old; the first is mortal, the other a sorceress; the first desirable and playful, the second desperately craving pleasure, her desire and her claim of power ridiculed. However, the two are not as different as they may seem. Once a beauty like Liudmila, capricious and proud Naina refused a lover, which at least partially causes her current fury. She belongs to a group of operatic females who are, in their own ways, involved in the young heroines' relocation and distress. For instance, Mozart's Queen of the Night aims to coax her kidnapped daughter to kill the queen's former lover; in *Dushen'ka*, Venus, jealous of the young title heroine, sends her far away; Vseveda (All-knowing), from *Prichudnitsa*, bears responsibility for the flight of her god-daughter Vetrana; and Naina, though indirectly, involves herself in the misfortunes of Liudmila by allying with the maid's captor. Whether closest kin, like Vseveda and Vetrana or the Queen of the Night and Pamina, the old and young female leads form intensely connected contrasting pairs. However wicked the sorceresses' actions, they eventually incite the development of young women into exemplary obedient brides and in the case of Vseveda's protégée into "a kind wife and children-loving mother, respected by all and herself happy."[40] Empowered by their magic, the aged women also share an overwhelming sexual appetite. Describing Vseveda's "wonderous power of unknown craft [and] her tricks unheard of in Russia,"[41] Dmitriev, for example, veers away from the plotline and tells about Bramberbas, a young military guard, used by powerful witches as a (boy) toy. Whatever the allegory may suggest, the poet refers to Vseveda as "some kind of witch," who, turning the guard into a cavalry horse, "worked his back through midnight till he lost his strength."[42]

In the opera, Naina is introduced by Finn. Now an old wizard, he tells how many years ago, as a young shepherd swayed by beautiful Naina, he tried to win her by becoming an adventurous sailor and fearless warrior, lavishing the maid with his devotion, victories, and gifts—rejected every time. Spending years among wizards, he cast a love spell on her, only to find out that time had turned the beauty into a decrepit old witch. Several scholars have pointed out similarities between the story of Finn and an old Skaldic saga about Harald III Hardrade (Hard/Severe, 1015–1066) and Elisaveta, the daughter of a Kievan ruler, Iaroslav the Wise.[43] Adopted in Russian by Nikolai L'vov and retold by a number of late-eighteenth-century poets including Bogdanovich, the story, which attained significant popularity, privileged the poetic longing of the Viking warrior over historical facts.[44] According to Russian versions of the saga, brave Harald sings about his love for the Russian maid, telling (like Finnish Finn) about his three victorious adventures, each time receiving the same response from the haughty tsarevna. The thrice-repeated phrase in Pushkin, "Hero, I don't want you," is a remake of Bogdanovich's threefold refrain, "The Russian lassie orders me to walk away home."[45]

Sympathetic to Harald's descendant the wizard, Pushkin severely punishes Naina by taking away from her the most precious gifts: youth and beauty. Although the old story ends with the beautiful stubborn maid repeatedly rejecting her suitor, Finn's tale, quickly moving beyond the romantic saga, portrays an old spiteful woman, not even a venerable aged dame but a ridiculous creature. Glinka found a musical equivalent for Pushkin's Finn in the genre of ballade and an authentic tune he learned from a Finnish coachman.[46] Glinka also contributes to the humiliation of his Naina by depriving her of the very essence of the operatic personage: vocal melody. Described by Finn and frightened Farlaf before entering the stage, Naina first materializes in a duet with Farlaf in the second scene of the second act—both characters musically treated as comic relief. The orchestral opening of the scene, with a sustained low B flat in trombones and bassoons and a light, "scared" flock of augmented and diminished triadic moves in flutes, portrays a dark haunted forest. Finding himself in the middle of this forest, Farlaf muses whether the pursuit and rescue of Liudmila are worth his discomfort. His recitative ends when the hero sees the "ugly old woman." A brief dotted gesture followed by an octave leap down in the strings and an accented second beat implies Naina's limping motion; the staccato jumps add a humorous element to the image. The accompaniment remains consistent throughout her singing. Her vocal part is most telling. She mumbles her orders on the same pitch with several shrieking exclamations, accompanied by a chain of limping,

Example 5.7

Naina: Believe me, uselessly you bustle

Example 5.8

Naina: So, learn - I am the sorceress Naina! But don't fear me!

dotted, downward motions and a giggling staccato of oboes and bassoons. Delivered in an absolutely static almost robotic vocal line, her promises and threats are mere bluff (Example 5.7). Mechanical elements in the musical portrayal of another of Pushkin's decaying females, in Tchaikovsky's *Queen of Spades*, are discussed in Chapter Nine.

Pushkin's Naina—"the chatterbox"—reveals to Farlaf the secret that she is a witch. With a smirk (indicated in the score), Glinka's Naina likewise proclaims that she is a powerful sorceress, repeating a single B flat, accompanied by the harp, trumpet, and trombones. The "scary" tremolo, moving by a tritone (F sharp-C natural-G flat-[B flat] C), gives her single-pitch melody enharmonic "variety" (Example 5.8). In the opera, Naina diverts Farlaf from pursuit of Liudmila. Though she seems successful at this point, her duettino is eclipsed by two longer scenes in which Ruslan encounters his benefactors; in the first scene of the act he receives instructions from Finn, and in the third, the Gigantic Head furnishes the champion with a magical sword. Thus from her very introduction, her actions are doomed; Naina is structurally tamed.

Stripping her of any drop of decency, Pushkin shows the old woman inflamed by suddenly awakened, overwhelming aphrodisiacal desire. Naina is also punished by experiencing the repugnance shown by the man she repeatedly refused and now lusts after. Finn, perfectly capable of projecting Pushkin's irony, switches from first to third person, imitating his old paramour:

Что делать,—мне пищит она . . .	What to do—she squeals to me . . .
Конечно, я теперь седа,	Indeed, I am grey-haired now
немножко, может быть, горбата;	A little bit, perhaps, crooked
. . .	
Она сквозь кашель продолжала	She, coughing, continued
Тяжелый, страстный разговор:	The heavy lusty talk:
"Проснулись чувства, я сгораю,	"Feelings awakened, I burn
Приди в объятия мои . . .	Come to my embraces . . .
О милый, милый! умираю. . . ."	O, darling, darling, I am dying. . . ."

Glinka unites Naina with Pushkin's "swarm of beauties," recast as Persian seductresses. They promise "nocturnal peace and *nega*"—a word suggesting sweet fragrant pleasures, according to Taruskin "a tender lassitude" and "a prime attribute of the orient as imagined by Russians"[47] (although not only by Russians). In the chorus of Persian maidens, Glinka uses Pushkin's text. Teaming Naina with the army of temptresses beguiling and destroying men, Glinka fashioned her into a rusalka type, foreshadowing Dargomyzhsky's title heroine and her magical kingdom, discussed in the next chapter. Dance sequences in both operas suggest a link between flowing, revealing bodies and formidable feminine magic.

Naina's dancers in the third act parallel the dancing chorus of water maids, which Asaf'ev calls sirens of Chernomor, in the fourth.[48] Both magical domains pose serious threats to the title characters and their associates. Ratmir, entering Naina's habitat, falls for a mixture of his own feverish hallucinations and a bewitching chorus of singing and dancing Persian maids, offering a full mélange: floating seductive moves, slow-motion quasi-Russian folk dance, and a sequence of classical French-Russian ballet episodes. Ruslan, who like Ratmir is trapped in Naina's forest, becomes in Frolova-Walker's words "temporarily three-dimensional . . . and nearly succumbs to the intensely erotic atmosphere."[49] Silent Naina is about to celebrate the victory, her beauties prepared to emasculate the Russian champions, when Finn's heroic tenor restores order. The quartet of Finn, Ratmir, devoted Gorislava (Blazing-glory),[50] and Ruslan concludes the third act.

If Naina's castle and park are a trap for men, Chernomor's enchanting garden is a prison for women. Naina's Persian beauties, mesmerizing Ratmir, recite their enticing "Come"; Chernomor's male slaves entertain Liudmila with a set of fiery Eastern dances. The events in two magical palace-park settings end with the defeat of their respective owners, Naina and Chernomor. If winning over Naina's female kingdom is a private affair completed by Finn, Ruslan's battle and victory in the finale of the Chernomor act is a public one, commented on and affirmed by a chorus of the folk. The two acts portray forces that encompass magic, eroticism, and the Orient, each curtailed locally in its respective finale and, in the overall operatic structure, "enclosed within the frame of majestic Russian scenes—a 'magic ring of Slavism.'"[51]

Musically, one intriguing element poses a link between Liudmila and Naina, the two not facing each other in either poem or opera. The theme of Liudmila's song to Ratmir in her cavatina from the first act is resonated in the Persian chorus, which, structured in the form of a variation, consistently recycles the same gesture (Examples 5.3 and 5.9). Moreover, the distant echo of Liudmila's Eastern theme can be heard in the chorus of invisible sirens in the fourth act (Example 5.10). Does Liudmila, initiating a musical reference to the East in the first act and foreshadowing Ratmir's path to the enchanting domain, define musical elements of the opera's Orient? Or perhaps seduction exhibits no ethnic or national bias and Liudmila has an inner link with the Persian beauties

Example 5.9

Chorus: Find refuge in our joyful *terem*! Here is nocturnal peace and *nega* [pleasure].

Example 5.10

Sea Maidens: Obey the call of destiny, O, beautiful princess!

and sirens? The connection may also warn of dangerous possibilities for a young girl deflected from a woman's path; after all, denial of a shepherd's pleasure turned Naina into a derided witch.

In his playful poem "Solace to Aniuta" (1793), appealing to his young capricious interlocutor, Krylov cautions her that soon she will not outshine the "glow of magical roses," her white breasts no longer rising under her shawl. In another dedication to Aniuta, "My Absolution. To Aniuta"[52] (1793), Krylov offers scary pictures of an old woman nearly identical to Finn's portrait of Naina.

Let Venus of hundred years of age	My gray-haired goddess
Drumming her false teeth	Was blazened by a novel passion
And pouting her faded lips	With the twisting smile of a horrid mouth
Damn me for	The sepulchral voice of the monster
My fault, that too critically	Mutters to me her love confession
[I] Glanced onto her toilet	
(Krylov)	(Pushkin)

Some years later Pushkin would revive the same portrait in prose, offering a no less horrid description of his countess in *Queen of Spades*. Pushkin's two old women, from unrelated stories in different genres, one a skazka and the other a novel with ghostly elements, reveal striking similarities. Even though their past beauty and bygone men's infatuation is conveyed by the male protagonists, the two women themselves appear as decrepit, repulsive hags, both possessing otherworldly power, both exposing their unfulfilled sexuality.[53] Pushkin's countess

was sitting before a mirror in her dressing-room. Three maids were standing round her. One held a pot of rouge, another a box of hairpins, and the third a tall cap with flame-colored ribbons. The Countess had not the slightest pretension to beauty—all that had faded long ago—but she preserved all the habits of her youth, followed strictly the fashions of the seventies.[54]

Later the same maids

undressed the countess, took off her cap trimmed with roses; removed the powdered wig from her gray, closely cropped head. The pins showered around her. . . . The silver-embroidered yellow dress fell at her swollen feet. Ghermann [like Krylov] was a witness to the disgusting mysteries of her toilet.[55]

Pushkin's unapologetic description of an aged countess echoes yet another Krylov fragment, also in prose (1792):

> Where is this enchanting beauty, . . . whose pink lips attracted a thousand kisses, her soft breasts inducing desire in young hearts and even most indifferent philosophers...?
>
> She sleeps, and all her beauty sorted out on the night table: her beautiful teeth lie orderly near the mirror; her head is as clean as a turnip, and her hair . . . is carefully hung on the mirror, her blushes in a jar prepared for the morning; meantime she recalls a mummy thrown on the bed. Her chest sticks to her bones.[56]

Krylov, a master of fables, comedies, and operas, developed a particularly pungent way of describing aged coquettes. Some find his mocked old ladies a form of political cartoon used to target the aging Catherine. Proskurina writes that Krylov's choice of the empress's private life and persona was a strategic one. Officials of the empire could not admonish him. To incriminate him, Proskurina suggests, would be to acknowledge the majestic original. Pushkin's countess in *Queen of Spades* is his contemporary, but her youth and memory belong to Catherine's age. His Naina, though belonging to fairy-tale timelessness, forged her own habitat in eighteenth-century palace-park architectural complexes. Glinka's melodic gesture illuminates a link between Liudmila and Naina's seductresses and sirens, while intertextual allusions may bridge Naina with the countess on the one hand and Krylov's coquette on the other—and beyond. By giving his anti-heroine the pleasant-sounding name Naina, echoing the French *nain*, Pushkin linked her not with dignified Finn but with the dwarf Chernomor.

Chernomor or the Prince of Tauride?

Forgotten in the two previous acts, Liudmila reappears in Chernomor's captivity in the fourth. The act falls into three parts: the first shows Liudmila surrounded by the garden's spirits, servants of Chernomor's pleasures; the second, Chernomor and his entourage; the third, Ruslan. In this magical garden, Liudmila, like Dushen'ka, will have a nocturnal visitor. In Bogdanovich's tale, Dushen'ka muses whether her invisible lover "with no name and age / without height and features," is a "spirit or a wizard," "a monster or a god." Liudmila's attendant . . .

Седую бороду несет;	Carries a silver beard;
И входит с важностью за нею,	And enters, behind it, puffed up with pride,
Подъяв величественно шею,	Stiffening his neck high and stately,

Горбатый карлик из дверей:	A hunchbacked dwarf, through gates:
Его-то голове обритой,	To his shaven head,
Высоким колпаком покрытой,	Covered with a pointed cap,
Принадлежала борода.	The beard belonged.

The beard invokes two associations. One is the vivid historical myth of Peter I applying gigantic scissors to the long beards of his boyars—the old male elite, who treasured their beards as a sign of traditional male-controlled Rus'. The other may draw on poetry equating beards with phalluses. Lomonosov indulged himself by scribing the "Hymn to the Beard," extolling male facial hair as "the root of impossible actions," "fertilizing it as a peasant his plow," and wishing the beard "to grow in lubricating wetness." The refrain reads:

Борода предорогая!	Beard most darling!
Жаль, что ты не крещена	Pity that you are not baptized
И что тела часть срамная	And that shameful body part
Тем тебе предпочтена. (1756–57)	For that is preferred to you

When the Synod reported Lomonosov to Empress Elisabeth, demanding a "public burning of such bawdiness" and the punishment of the author, the poet penned new (unpublished) verses on the topic, in which the beard "rises on crutches," "sits when others stand, scratched by someone's hand," and "revered for years, now lives in shame"[57]—the author fusing sexual and sacrilegious metaphors.[58] Pushkin hand-copied Lomonosov's verses to the beard.[59]

In *Ruslan*, the "joy-giving beard" (*blagodatel'naia*) serves as Chernomor's major attribute and the source of his supernatural power. The owner of the beard also possesses a magical terrain that doubles as (or according to Pushkin surpasses) the St. Petersburg residence of the Prince of Tauride. Gasparov, pointing out a geographic discrepancy with regard to the location of Chernomor's habitat, suggests a "spatial paradox with stinging implications."[60] What are these geographic paradoxes? Launching his rescue operation, Ruslan rides "far north" of Kiev to find himself southeast of the city. Liudmila in captivity discovers that she exists simultaneously in the midst of winter and summer. Through the window, she observes the wintry "monotonous whiteness dozing in eternal silence." "In tears," the prisoner runs to open the door and finds herself in a blossoming garden amid dancing and singing servants. The magical combination of snow through the window and blossoming spring behind the door is intriguing.

If Chernomor's garden can be equated with Potemkin's fête, one may find particularly interesting the notes made by the dedicatee of the grand ball. Catherine commented on the extraordinarily warm early spring of 1791 and suddenly a wintry cold and gloomy April 28, the day of Potemkin's fête. The empress also remarked on Potemkin's winter garden, some six times larger than her own, exceeding in fantasy anything the Prince had erected before.[61] The exotic orangeries and tropical gardens in Potemkin's palace in northern St. Petersburg reveal the combination of Western décor and Eastern aura the prince cultivated in his northern and southern residences, which he acquired during wars with Turkey on the Black Sea.

Although the name of Pushkin's dwarf is typically read as "Black-Plague" (*Cherno-mor*) or Black-moor, a no less plausible reading would be "Black Sea" (*Cherno-mor[e]*). Lying on the Black Sea, Tauride, which Potemkin annexed and built up for his empress, became a part of his title—Prince Tavricheskii (of Tauride)—and his kingdom. In "Waterfall," a tribute to the deceased Potemkin, Derzhavin sees the prince's spirit, his winged shadow flying above Tauride.

Какой чудесный дух крылами	What wondrous winged spirit
От севера парит на юг?	From North flies South?
Ветр медлен течь его стезями,	Slow winds stream along his path
Обозревает царствы вдруг	As he observes kingdoms around

A number of poets, painting Tauride as a place for imaginary flight and romantic escape, referred to a "shadow," alluding to Derzhavin's memorial verses to Potemkin. Viazemsky, for example, marveling about Tauride, used some of Derzhavin's key expressions and made an obvious double pun on Potemkin's name. Although the meaning of the specific verse below is quite obscure and puzzling, it emphasizes two words that resonate with the name Potemkin (*potiemok*, darkness; *potomok*, progeny).

Средь прохлады и **потемок**	Among the freshness and **darkness** [*potiemok*]
Древ, пресекших солнца свет,	Trees cutting the light of the sun
Допотопных гор **потомок**,	Antique mountains' **progeny** [*potomok*]
Камень—древний домосед.	Rock—ancient homebody.

Derzhavin questions: "Whose shadow rushes through the clouds in aerial mountain heights?"[62] Pushkin's dwarf sails into the sky to his mountains, flying above his magical kingdom as he battles Ruslan:

Чья тень спешит по облакам	Whose shadow rushes through the clouds
В воздушные жилища горны?	In aerial mountain heights?
На темном взоре и челе	In his dark gaze and his forehead

Сидит глубока дума в мгле	[Is] Written deep thought in a haze
(Derzhavin)	...
...	
Взвился, как вихорь, к облакам	Fly, like a windstorm, to clouds
Сквозь тяжкий дым и воздух мрачный	Through dark smoke and somber air
И вдруг умчал к своим горам	And suddenly took off to his mountains
(Pushkin)	

Pushkin's Ruslan, entering Chernomor's ambiguous habitat, encounters its owner dressed in Oriental style; Potemkin's contemporaries noted that he indulged himself with Oriental attire. Studying Eastern religions from his youth, infatuated with the traditions of the people he conquered, Potemkin adopted an Eastern demeanor, shaping his lifestyle at the crossroad of West and East, Russia and the Orient. Ségur wrote that, "luxuriously dressed in official ceremonies, with his speech, postures, and movement reminding one of a courtier of Louis XIV," in his private quarters Potemkin looked "like a Turkish or Persian pasha," confusing his uninitiated visitors, who imagined themselves "admitted to a vizier of Constantinople, Baghdad, or Cairo."[63]

Glinka, embracing the geographic ambiguity of Pushkin, further expanded the combination of Kievan and Oriental elements in the portrayal of his dwarf. Chernomor's scene in the middle of the fourth act falls into two parts: the famous March and a sequence of Oriental slave dances.[64] According to Irina Vyzgo-Ivanova, the March, despite its exotic color, derives from an old Ukrainian guild song, matching its melodic formula and characteristically Ukrainian "chromatic plagal mode."[65] The sequence of Oriental dances, complementing the "Ukrainian" March, completes the musical imagery of Chernomor, the combination alluding to an alternative persona, the "Grand Hetman" of the Black Sea and Ekaterinoslav Cossack Hosts.[66] In his soirée, Potemkin paraded before the imperial dame his captive "Ottoman pashas ... in the Asiatic splendor of their national dress"[67] and later entertained Catherine with the ballet *Le marchand de Smyrne*, which featured exotic dancing slaves; Glinka's Chernomor presents Liudmila with Turkish, Arabic, and Caucasian slave dances.

Revered even today as the "forefather of the Russian musical East" who opened this "genuine world unknown before him,"[68] Glinka in fact continued the eighteenth-century Russian operatic Orientalism fostered by Catherine in her operas. In *Fevei*, the empress used an "authentic" tune of the Kalmyks she conquered; Glinka's fiery Lezginka came from parts of the Caucasus that Russia annexed in the early nineteenth century. If the Oriental theme appears central to Potemkin's ball and to the overall eighteenth-century Russian court culture, the Orientalism in Russian nineteenth-century opera arguably signifies more than Eastern imagery. Edward Said's concept of

West-East relations, in which the Occident defines itself against the otherness of the Orient, seems to be layered in this opera with a collective self-identification vis-à-vis the recent eighteenth-century past. This "complex hegemony" is ever more complex because the past is "not merely *there.*"[69] The Orient in Glinka represents not only distant places and foreign characters but also a masqueraded past. With Glinka's two operas elevated to the status of manifestos of Russian nationalism, a scene like Chernomor's château became a model of tripled otherness—East, past, and otherworldly magic—a challenging subject of conquest and a test of Russian might.

If the portrayal of Chernomor hints at Potemkin, then the dwarf's sexual ambitions and abilities both comment on the Prince's scandalous reputation and invert his proclaimed sexual power—Pushkin repeatedly refers to Chernomor's "tall *kolpak* [a conic cap] covering the shaven head to which the beard belongs." The cap has magical power and is attended by Chernomor's entourage with care. Multiple descriptions of Potemkin's ball mention the splendor of the Prince's attire, focusing on his hat, which, "overlaid with many jewels, was too heavy, and a special aide-de-camp had to follow him round carrying the hat for him."[70] Pushkin toyed with his malicious dwarf by mocking his disproportionate figure—his long beard and short body; his tall, pointed, erect magical cap and his hanging features—all serving as a metaphor for his sexual appetite and his impotency. Scared of his beard, Liudmila "in tears wandered and—laughed," aware of his former horrid reputation and his no longer threatening abilities. Ruslan, lifted in the air when he grasps Chernomor's beard, "plucks [the dwarf's] hair from time to time."

Creating the operatic equivalent of impotency, Glinka deprives his dwarf of a voice. If Naina hardly sings, Chernomor has no vocal part. He is neither an operatic nor a ballet character. His musical portrait, the much-discussed whole-tone scale, is introduced in the overture by a fortissimo of trombones and resurfaces when he kidnaps Liudmila and conjures her to sleep. Repeated throughout the opera, this leitmotif is often preceded by a stream of chromatic scales manifesting the magical and anomalous. The whole-tone scale is absent in the March, the only number of the opera physically featuring the dwarf, melting into patterns of augmented triads, tritonic moves that turn into harmonic decoration of the melodic line, as if magic masks the character underneath.

The bombastic procession of the dwarf begins with a brass orchestra parading onto the stage. The punching accents, staccatos, and mechanical repetition of the same angular gesture reverse the effect of the militaristic thunderous brass, emphasizing the cartoonish aspect of the scene. The chromatic inflection, the stream of flats and sharps confronting each other in harmonic proximity, the uncertain gestures in the melody— all proposed by some and disputed by others as modal ambiguity—project the precarious figure of Chernomor. The military brasses can't obscure the indefinite, shaking melodic steps. When the strings in the regular pit orchestra add their pizzicato to the march of the onstage band, each pompous recurrence of the theme ends with a squeaking single note in the violins nullifying any effect of power. Furthermore, Glinka combined his heavy brass with a glockenspiel,[71] which, along with its idiosyncratic high-range magical timbre, may equate the fragility of glass with the comical feebleness of the kingdom and its soon-to-be-debearded (emasculated) owner. Pushkin's gardens may allude to Potemkin's fête, and so might Glinka's magical glockenspiel ("organs covered by multi-colored brightly lit glass vessels"), the harps, and choruses of invisible spirits, nymphs, and animated flowers, the "thunder" of trumpets and horns, the Oriental décor.

Once the suite of dances in Chernomor's domain reaches peak speed, dynamics, and energy, the trumpet calls the dwarf to the fight with Ruslan. At this point, Chernomor puts Liudmila to sleep with a tremolo in trombones walking down their whole-tone scale. In the upper register, with nothing between, the woodwinds, accentuating the weak second beat, fall an octave down in a dotted rhythm. This rhythmic figure, suddenly reminding one of limping Naina, is likewise repeated, moving convulsively up and down the whole-tone scale. This gloomy scale, resounding in distant registers, and the choral "will die, will die" a few measures later leave the dwarf no hope.

Ruslan returns with Chernomor's beard attached to his helmet as an emblem of his appropriation of sexual and magical prowess. Potemkin's grand soirée, for which he incurred enormous debts, made it clear that young Catherine's favorite Zubov had taken away his power and place in the court.

> The trap seemed to be closing on Potemkin. Most histories claim that, when the Prince finally left Saint Petersburg in late July, he had been ruined by Zubov, rejected by Catherine and defeated by his enemies, and was dying from a broken heart.[72]

Montefiore, though not sharing this view, acknowledges the impression that "the Prince, at the height of his dignity, now resembled a noble bear gnawed by a pack of dogs." Even Derzhavin, whom Potemkin defended over the years against the poet's enemies, "repaid Potemkin's decency with petty betrayal and poignant poetry."[73]

In the opera, after Ruslan's victory the chorus of Chernomor splits into two parts. The female chorus of spirits sings about an emptied kingdom and silenced harps, while low voices implore the brave knight Ruslan to take them—the Eastern nations introduced earlier in the act begging to join Russian Ruslan, much as they did in Catherine's operas.

Double Identities, or Literary and Operatic Masquerade

Did Pushkin endow the characters of his mock epic with traits of grand historical figures? His obsession with history, which permeated his works in various genres, and his unparalleled ironic wickedness often converged in the poet's acute *inoskazanie*. Situating his tale in a historically undetermined time (but not an undetermined place), Pushkin wove his narrative with allusions to multiple literary sources, which lent this fairy tale concrete, specific elements triggering a multitude of interpretations, including the possibility of reading the mock tale as Pushkin's playful commentary on the recent past. Glinka and his merry band of "seven fathers," who spent hours together sharing social gossip, edgy political anecdotes, and literary novelties, also likely vented multiple possibilities of adopting and expanding the "untold" aspects of *Ruslan*.

Russian authors have rarely provided testimonial explication of their *inoskazanie*. In recent times, a torrent of scholarship dedicated to political interpretation of Shostakovich's idioms led to multiple conclusions and clashing views. *Ruslan*, elevated on the pedestal of Russian national culture as the prime creation of Russia's "first" poet and "first" composer, requires, along with the study of the two texts, an intense integration of intertextual and contextual analysis. The creators of *Ruslan*, like those of other operas and poetic works discussed in the following chapters, engaged their readers and listeners in an exciting intellectual game of recognition and appreciation of deep-seated multiple meanings suggested and transmitted through layers of other texts. Admittedly, neither their contemporary literati and critics nor the following generation pursued the interpretation argued in this chapter, because they simply could not. Strengthening in the last years of Catherine's reign, Russian censorship under her male progeny made a significant leap for the worse. The possibility of intimate and somewhat collegial relations between court artists and their empress-patroness cultivated under Elisabeth and Catherine was eliminated. There would be no hope for another metaphoric duo like Murza-Derzhavin and Felitsa-Catherine. The array of official limitations and restraints accelerated after the Decembrist revolt; between the productions of the two Glinka operas, the genre was subjected to monarchical regulation. More important, the literati themselves were driven by an agenda quite different from discovering or acknowledging the traits of the recent past in the work of their iconic national and manly poet (duels, romances, defiance of authority). They yearned for and usurped the sense of origin in the name of nationalism, a concept that was in fact planted by their predecessors.

Crafting primacy, personal and collective, they lacked the ability to recognize the obvious. Instead they attributed to the texts they elevated a meaning that would befit their aspirations and manufactured public perceptions accordingly. For example, although Glinka employed some recognizable elements of pre-existing heroic and historic operas, in his first opera he also recycled the plotline of *Ivan Susanin* composed by his older colleague Cavos (1815). Entitled *A Life for the Tsar*, the opera was meant to please the ruling Nicholas I by depicting the reign of his distant predecessor, the first tsar of the Romanov dynasty. Moreover, Glinka's opera, focusing on the collective and individual Russian folk, endorsed their life purpose as total, unquestioning, selfless devotion to the crown. Unlike Cavos, who saved his Susanin, Glinka sacrificed his peasant hero, turning his "death for the tsar" into a monumental choral apotheosis. The music of the opera deserved all the praise it received. Amazingly, though, among his progressive democratically attuned circles the opera was perceived as a proclamation of the composer's deep social consciousness in relation to the folk, and decades later as an anti-tsarist action—and the title of the opera was appropriately changed to *Ivan Susanin*.

Asserting Pushkin's parity with Shakespeare, Cervantes, Schiller,[74] and Virgil, and Glinka's with Mozart, Gluck, Beethoven, Schubert, and Chopin,[75] Russian intellectuals confirmed the creation of a national culture. Once establishing that Russian culture matched that of the West, they proclaimed Russia's artistic superiority over Europe. In fact, operatic *Ruslan* exhibited the same sentiment; situated in terms of the plot and structure above all exotic and ethnic images, multiple Easts and Wests, Russia, in the course of the opera, encapsulates and absorbs all the parts of its self-proclaimed global empire. Whether Pushkin had Catherine in mind as he crafted a piquant portrait of his erotic Liudmila née Dushen'ka or ridiculed aged lustful Naina (the twin sister of Krylov's coquettes), and whether Glinka modeled his splendorous magical gardens on Potemkin's fête—the empress, emblemizing her monarchial female predecessors and their surroundings, became a significant part of nineteenth-century Russian mythology. Whether hermeneutically recognized or not, the formidable empresses and their female kingdom were written into and had a profound effect on nineteenth-century poetic lore. Determined to celebrate a new nationalistic beginning, the literati conveniently overlooked the fact that what proved to be successful, including *Ruslan,* owed much to the influence of European romantic opera on the one hand, and on the other it solidly relied on the conventions of the preceding century in Russia.

Wedding scenes featuring antique Slavic princesses, recycled from one opera to the next and praised for ritualistic and folk elements, descended directly from two eighteenth-century models: real weddings, which, designed by the empresses, combined European decorum and Russian ritualistic elements; and their operatic and ballet counterparts, produced as part of imperial matrimonial celebrations. Choral "Slavas"— the crown of nineteenth-century nationalist operas, manifesting Russianness (and liberation from formidable female rulers)—resonated with monumental oratorios by Sarti and majestic odes by Lomonosov dedicated to the empresses. Sarti choruses on Lomonosov's text in the finale of *Oleg* adulated Oleg-Catherine, the champion who in the nineteenth century lost her feminine aspect.

The chain of champions, from Ilya to Ruslan and beyond, represented an army of grown-up Feveis. Some in their patriotic zeal measured up to Oleg, who engendered two streams of historical and epic operatic nineteenth-century heroes. The portrayal of the Orient, the proclaimed hegemony over the West, the political allegories permeating both historical and fairy-tale operas—all of these constituted major traits of the nationalists' operatic repertoire. Reinventing authentic Russia, nineteenth-century artists, like their predecessors, drew on Slavic antiquity. Following the same path, they denounced the eighteenth century as polluted by Westernization and as distorting true Russia. However, the more they aimed to escape from the female century, the more they relied on and expanded its tropes.

For the nationalist male ego—masculinity masquerading as nationalism—the memory and image of formidable empresses was unbearable. She should be put to sleep and subdued like Liudmila, or ridiculed and defeated like Naina. The poetic dithyrambs, with each line trumpeting the empress's praises, had to be forgotten or intertextualized in a fashion that would turn the mighty empresses into magical characters existing in indefinite remote Slavic fairy-tale lands, causing problems and thus conquered, vaporized, or submitted to the good old institution of the tsar's terem. Asaf'ev, who took a shot at creative denigration of Catherine's operatic works and the musical culture of the pre-Glinka period, found that the ethics and humanism of nineteenth-century nationalist operas were reflected in the devotion and sacrifice of female characters. Offering a list of selfless heroines, he curiously added:

> There was also a need coming from a depth of the social psyche for the transformation of Russian feminine loving feelings (devotion) into a sensuous poison, to have a chain of images: the sorceress' seduction projected by Marfa in Musorgsky's Khovanshchina . . . in a mode of deep passion experienced like a flood; the fairy-tale seductresses: [Rimsky-Korsakov's] Kashcheevna and the tsarina of Shamakha, the ruthless heroine of [Prokofiev's] *Igrok*, and the cynical eroticism of [Shostakovich's] Catherine Izmailova.[76]

The "depth of the social psyche," unexplained by Asaf'ev, reflected various layers of the male artist's anxiety about formidable women. Nineteenth-century artists, mostly aristocrats knew stories about omnipotent women who freely traversed between female and male personas, who looked handsome in male military uniform, who toyed with arms too heavy for a soldier, who several decades away from the tsar's gender-segregated household chose their young lovers, and who, feared by European kingdoms, triumphed in many wars. Missing this all as they missed the opportunity of favoritism, artists such as Pushkin (despite the greatness acknowledged early in his life) could only dream about or envy the author of a little, possibly "mediocre," tale who had an imperial opportunity upon a whim to turn it into an opera, to produce it with the best composers, dancers, musicians, and to present it to a most receptive audience, fearing no critics or competition . . . during her life.

About *Ruslan*, Frolova-Walker writes:

> It was not because Glinka followed whatever was thought of as Russian that *Ruslan* was
> influential; rather, the prestige attaching to his ideas made others wish to adopt them as a
> national standard. . . . It was, in fact, this dialogue between *Ruslan* and the succeeding
> generation that played a large part in the creation of a Russian idiom recognizable in
> concert halls and opera houses anywhere in the world.[77]

Thus Pushkin/Glinka's *Ruslan* in fact serves as a bridge created by Russia's most
celebrated artists, a bridge that confirms the lineage of what constitutes nationalist
opera to the patronage, vision, and creative works of the formidable dame.

6

RUSALKA
WATER, POWER, AND WOMEN

The Russian rusalka—a cousin of sirens, lorelei, naiads, undines, and mermaids and a sister of Slavic rusalkas—is woven into Russia's history and culture.[1] There are two sirenlike creatures in Russia, the terrestrial woman-bird *sirin*[2] and the water-inhabiting rusalka. Carved at the base of columns on St. Basil's Bridge near the St. Petersburg Admiralty and leading sailors seaward from the prows of Russian vessels, the fish-tailed rusalka,[3] not the land-locked sirin, became a symbol of military expansion to the seas in the eighteenth century. In the nineteenth century, Russian male authors repeatedly invoked images of the rusalka, exploring, commenting on, and constructing links between gender and power, metaphorically connected with femininity and water.

Water

Though the turbulence and randomness of water imagery appealed to romantic poets elsewhere in Europe, bodies of water were especially reflective of the historical particularities of eighteenth-century Russia, whose military campaigns gave her enormously important access to the Baltic, Black, and Azov Seas.[4] Images of water—rivers, lakes, seas, clouds, and fountains—pervade the poetry of Derzhavin, a forefather of Russian classical literature: "steppes floating like seas," "streaming rivers of delightful tears," "swimming golden moon," the "last day of nature that spilled into a river of stars," and love that "poured into the soul." St. Petersburg, built on swamps along the Neva River, open to the Baltic Sea and near Lake Ladoga, carried the name of its founder and embodied the aspirations of his successors, venerated by Russian poets who linked water with royalty and power.

In Russian narratives of the late eighteenth and nineteenth centuries, water also became associated with female suicide. The gallery of heroines dying by throwing themselves into water includes Karamzin's Liza (*Poor Liza*); Ostrovsky's Katerina (*The Storm*, 1859); Leskov's Grusha, "swallowed up" by water (*The Enchanted Wanderer*, 1873); and Leskov's Katerina, who, "without removing her gaze from the dark waters," pulled herself and her rival into a river (*Lady Macbeth of Mtsensk*, 1865). Lev Tolstoy's Anna Karenina (1878), stepping in front of an approaching *steam* train, has a feeling "like that she had experienced, when preparing to enter the water in bathing."[5]

Bogdanovich's *Dushen'ka* and Karamzin's *Poor Liza* exemplify early Russian female suicide plots connected with water. In the Bogdanovich work, the sacrificial act ends unsuccessfully—animated singing pikes (actually naiads) save the heroine and carry her to shore.[6] Suicide is completed in Karamzin's story, when Liza, a peasant girl seduced and promised eternal love by an aristocrat, throws herself into a "deep pond" after he abandons her. Alexander Pushkin, of the next literary generation, creates a character reminiscent of Karamzin's unfortunate heroine in his drama *Rusalka*.[7] In his version, the tragic suicide is not the end of the story; in the afterlife, the peasant girl becomes the tsarina of a water kingdom, a powerful and merciless rusalka. The legend of Rusalka connects sacrifice with vengeance, reality with magic, classical poetry with folklore, and Christian Orthodoxy with paganism.[8]

The interplay of water, power, feminine sacrifice, and *volshebstvo* (fairy-tale magic)[9] became a major theme in Russian nineteenth-century operas. Although as dangerous to men as Homeric sirens, powerful magical heroines in some of these works perform self-sacrificial rituals, turning into a river (Rimsky-Korsakov's *Sadko*) or melting and evaporating into clouds (Rimsky-Korsakov's *Snow Maiden*) for the sake of their romantic lovers. Love and suicide turn Pushkin's and Dargomyzhsky's Natasha into a magical water sprite endowed with a desire to avenge herself on men. Rusalka belongs to a "particular brand" of heroine that Susan McClary analyzes, a nymph "fixated on memories of a lover who has abandoned her—who has awakened her sexually and has left her with no outlet for that excess."[10] She also matches what Ralph Locke identifies as a "primary [female] stereotype: the dangerous woman who holds no allegiance and thus disturbs the placid world of good bourgeois wives and husbands."[11] Locke ponders whether such dangerous women disturb social morality or reinforce it—an issue relevant to analysis of two *Rusalkas*, Pushkin's dramatic poem (1832) and Dargomyzhsky's opera (1855), which echoed and simultaneously moved away from the ideals of eighteenth-century Russia toward the nationalistic patriarchal nineteenth-century state. In the opera, a "discursive space" between narrative and music has the paradoxical effect Carolyn Abbate describes in Western European opera of the same period: the simultaneous empowerment and defeat of women. Another discursive space can be observed between Dargomyzhsky's opera and Pushkin's poem, on which the opera is based. Untangling the hermeneutic complexity that occurs within these spaces requires a study of many contextual facets[12] of the *Rusalka*s: the relationship of the poem and the opera to both European and Russian narratives; the poetic and musical conventions that reveal the interplay of gender, Russian history, and nationalism; and the dichotomies between drama and opera, opera and ballet, fire and water, female voice and muteness.

Who is Rusalka?

The Russian rusalka is "light like a nocturnal shadow, white like early snow" (Pushkin), dazzling like the "twinkle of a serpent" (Lermontov), with "shining eyes looking through dark-*rusyi* (reddish-blond) hair ... woven with seaweed" (Gogol). A beautiful maiden, she "plays, splashing in the waves, laughs and cries like a child" (Pushkin), is "joined by her sisters in a dancing-circle," and sings a lullaby to her knight, forever sleeping at the bottom of the sea.

Rusalka's complexity begins with her very name. One possible source of the word is *rusyi*, often the color of mermaid hair.[13] Dal' suggests an etymological link between *rusyi* and *russkii* (Russian).[14] Thus the word *rusalka* relates to Rus', the old name for Russia, and also to the archaic singular noun for a Russian person (*rus*). Some associate rusalka with *ruslo* (riverbed). In the literary world of Pushkin, Rusalka can be seen as a female counterpart of *Ruslan*. The image of the rusalka occupies an important place in the ancient traditions of various Slavic tribes and groups. The term is also linked to pre-Christian rituals called *rusalii*, which included celebrations, offerings, and exorcisms intended to remove the powers of a *zalozhnaia* woman (which means prematurely dead from suicide).[15]

The rusalka is closely connected with European mermaids—amazing, passionate creatures, half-fish and half-woman, who rise from dark water to play dangerous games with men, and whose power is linked to their voices. Through centuries of Christianity, these water sprites came to represent unrestrained and irresistible sexuality, illicit paganism, and the chaos of creation. Despite her kinship to European cousins, the rusalka is a distinct creature. Unlike many mermaids and undines, who yearn to exchange their voices, hair, and kingdoms for human feelings, rusalkas are half-magic and half-human, formerly mortal women inflamed by love and burned by betrayal. Though in their afterlife vengeful rusalkas are commonly associated with water, they also inhabit the forest, where they merge with another relative, the Vila, "a spirit known all over Russia and other Slavonic lands, ... the bride [who] continued to seek after death the joys of which she had been deprived."[16] Like a Vila, the rusalka may wear a bridal dress and flowery tiara. Or not. She may also appear naked wrapped in her wet hair or wear royal garb turning into a mighty tsarina.

The dreadful and playful Russian rusalkas despise living women and mesmerize or tickle men to death; kidnap children; steal clothes, milk, and bread; and swing by their hair in the depths of the forest, terrifying villagers and travelers with their laughter. At the same time, they may capriciously save children, and some believe that grass and wheat grow better in places where they dance.[17]

The versatile singing and dancing rusalka was attractive to poets and musicians. Her ability to draw on Western European, Slavic, and Russian mythologies and to mediate between folk and classical literature made her a potent image for nineteenth-century artists searching for a nationalist narrative. At the same time, her sensuality unleashed the male sexual imagination—the splashing waves of her hair, "waves tickling curved shoulders," the "dazzling emerald of her eyes" (Mai), "her feverish lips and flashing cheeks, eyes luring [men's] souls . . . herself burning with passion" (Gogol, "Strashnaia mest'"). This image of the rusalka or zalozhnaia affirms that eroticism, malevolence, and metamorphosis are inherent to female nature—a notion nourished beyond the tales of rusalkas by many romantic artists.

Literary Rusalka

The water sprites and rusalkas Pushkin created in several poems and four major works are closely related to other watery European heroines: Fouque's Undine (1811), Goethe's Melusine (1807), Heine's Loreley (1823), Andersen's Mermaid (1836), and Hoffman's Undine (1813–14). In Russia, Fouque's *Undine*[18] was read in French—the mother tongue of the native nobility—and in the poetic translation of Zhukovsky,[19] who issued his verse translation of *Undine* in 1830, a year before Pushkin began his *Rusalka*.[20] German counterparts were likewise well known. The operatic *Undine*, by the German romantic E. T. A. Hoffmann, was not staged in Russian theaters, but according to Norman Ingham the "remote Russians" were among the first (as early as 1822) to print Hoffman's works in translation. Ingham reflects that "from several sources we know that Hoffman had a vogue in the circles of Petersburg which Pushkin frequented, and that a manifestation of it was the improvising of fantastic tales."[21]

Though Pushkin brought native mythology and folk characters into the domain of Russian classical literature,[22] his heroine and his story echoed Kauer and Hansler's singspiel *Das Donauweibchen*. Successful in Austria, the opera was adapted by Russians who, following common practice of the day, russified the names and relocated the story from the Danube to the Dniepr, and accordingly changed the title to *Dneprovskaia Rusalka*.[23] Throughout the first half of the nineteenth century this four-sequel soap opera enjoyed extreme popularity and remained a stable part of the repertoire;[24] one or more sequels, shown annually, continued to stir the imagination of poets and musicians.[25]

Pushkin owned three volumes of *Dneprovskaia Rusalka* and knew it well enough to refer to it in *Eugene Onegin*.[26] The parallels between Pushkin's *Rusalka* and its Austrian-Russian predecessors are apparent: the birth of Rusalochka, the wedding, the appearance of the rusalka in the middle of the grand wedding celebration, and the depiction of the underwater kingdom. Using elements from European popular culture, Pushkin fed the Russian fascination with native tales and myths, which from the end of the eighteenth century were intensely collected and, as in Western Europe, aligned with national identity. Unlike her various European counterparts, Pushkin's heroine is mortal, and though possessing enormous magic power, she is driven by a woman's feelings and desires. In this, Pushkin and a number of his Russian contemporaries followed the same literary path, among them Orest Somov[27] in his short story "Rusalka" (1829) and Gogol in his portrayal of a rusalka zalozhnaia in *Evenings on a Farm Near Dikanka* (1831).

Pushkin's *Rusalkas*

Pushkin frequently referred to water sprites in his poems and wrote three major works about rusalkas. In his short poem "Rusalka" (1819), he describes encounters between an old monk and a rusalka who comes from the bubbling waters and sits on the shore, gazing at the monk, brushing her wet hair, and luring him into deep water.[28] In the same year that Pushkin wrote his "Rusalka," his friend and rival Zhukovsky issued a poetic translation of Goethe's "Fisherman" (1779), in which "the water rushes, the water swells" and "the gurgling waves arise; a maid, all bright with water drops" lures an old fisherman to "the misty heaven-deeps."[29] Five years later, a water sprite again emerges from the bottom of the river to meet the hero in another short poem, "Kak schastliv ia" (How Happy I Am; 1824). Nearly five more years pass before Pushkin begins his drama *Rusalka*, finished three years later. The heroine Natasha, the daughter of a miller,[30] is drawn into a romance with a *Kniaz* (prince or duke). She is deaf to the shrewd advice of her father, who wishes for a wedding or at least for some compensation from his daughter's wealthy lover. Faced with her pregnancy and the Kniaz's decision to marry someone else, Natasha is driven mad by despair. After the Kniaz's departure she throws herself into the Dniepr. The ritualistic wedding of the Kniaz and Kniaginia in the following scene is interrupted by a sad song performed by an invisible Natasha—the Kniaz recognizes her voice. As the years pass, the Kniaz, estranged from his wife, finds himself lured to the bank of the river and to the old oak where he used to meet his little "shepherdess." Meanwhile, Natasha, who in her afterlife has become tsarina of the rusalkas, masters a plan of revenge and retribution, enlisting the aid of her little daughter, Rusalochka. In the last scenes of Pushkin's drama, the poet portrays the bottom of the Dniepr, where Rusalka recalls herself as a "foolish and irrational girl" who turned into a "cold and mighty rusalka" dreaming of the vengeance to come. The Kniaz, drawn by his memory of "free, burning love," approaches the shore, where he is suddenly stunned by the sight of the daughter he never knew: "Otkuda ty, prekrasnoe ditia?" (Where are you from, beautiful child?). The poem ends with this question, leaving the fate of Rusalka and the Kniaz unresolved.

Though the dramatic *Rusalka* is considered unfinished, Pushkin later retold the same story in *The Songs of Western Slavs* (1834).[31] The setting is changed from the shores of the Dniepr to Moravia. The main characters are adapted to the new locale: the Russian Kniaz is replaced with Prince Ianysh, the Kniaginia with the Czech Princess Lubusia, Natasha with a neighborhood beauty Eliza, and Rusalka with Vodaniza (from *voda*, water), who "rules over all rivers and lakes."[32] This abridged poetic version of the dramatic *Rusalka* has a slightly altered outcome: here Pushkin moves a step further than in his dramatic *Rusalka* by beginning to narrate the encounter of the rusalka and her mortal lover. Vodaniza does not look forward to retribution, and it is the Prince who seeks reconciliation.

Dargomyzhsky's Rusalka

The water sprite's dancing and singing are mimicked in Russian poetry by water, itself full of sound and motion—"waves run, waves roar" (Zhukovsky), "racketing and whirling, the river quivered" (Lermontov),[33] and "boiling waves pacified suddenly" preparing for the rusalka's entrance.[34] Composers created images of sprites using musical conventions associated with water: wavy accompaniment, broken arpeggios, cascades of rising or descending passages that referred, aurally and visually, to "splashing, veiled, and caressingly smooth" waves (Examples 6.1, 6.2, and 6.3).[35]

Many songs and instrumental pieces, virtuoso solos, and symphonic compositions were dedicated to the water sprite.[36] But the artistic domain most suitable to her "natural" talents was musical theater.[37] Among the many operas based on Pushkin's drama[38] is a classic of the nineteenth-century Russian operatic repertoire: *Rusalka* by Dargomyzhsky.

Like Pushkin, Dargomyzhsky created several works featuring a water sprite, including the little song "Pesn' rybki" (Song of the Fish; 1860), based on Lermontov's poetry and musical sketches for *Prince Ianysh*.[39] In Dargomyzhsky's opera *Rusalka*, the heroine undergoes metamorphosis, appearing in three forms. In the first act, the peasant girl Natasha, a mortal woman and a sympathetic victim of betrayed love, commits suicide. In the second act, as in Pushkin's, she arrives at her lover's wedding as an invisible bodiless spirit. Absent in the third act, where dancing and singing rusalkas prepare for her entrance, she appears in Act Four as a powerful tsarina of the water kingdom accompanied by her little daughter Rusalochka.

Example 6.1: Balakirev, "Nad ozerom" (Over the lake), lyrics by Golenishchev-Kutuzov

Splashing, veiled, and caressingly smooth
In their swells there is much enchanting power

The character of the heroine is thereby fragmented into contrasting images: naïve peasant girl, passionate mistress, desperate woman, invisible spirit, and vengeful queen of the rusalkas.

The human Natasha, appearing only in the first act, remains largely undefined as a character; having no solo, she sings two duets and a trio with the main male characters, the Kniaz and the miller. Her expressive melodic lines in the dialogues with her "noble" lover and her father do not create a coherent portrait; instead, her musical episodes resemble unassembled puzzle pieces. In Natasha's first ten-measure solo episode, "Alas, passed the golden time," the descending vocal line is framed by a lilting waltzlike accompaniment (Example 6.4).[40]

Example 6.2: Borodin, "Morskaia tsarevna" (The Sea Princess), text by Lermontov

Come to me in the night, o young stranger!
Here under water, peace and repose.

At the departure of the Kniaz, she is stunned, disoriented, driven mad. In a duet
with her father, irony ("You know, a Kniaz is not free to choose his wife following his
heart's desire") gives way to sorrow ("O God, he left, forever abandoned me") in a
swift 6/4 episode reminiscent of Lucia di Lammermoor's "Spargi d'amaro pianto."
In this scene the Russian critic Serov finds the same mismatch between music and text
that McClary described in *Lucia*: the poetic text and music of the heroine's solo do not
cohere, and the spectator does not perceive "dreadful jealousy" in her vocal line.
Natasha's mad scene, like those in *Lucia di Lammermoor*, Bellini's *Il Pirata*, and *Giselle*,[41]
is public, witnessed and commented on by the chorus. Beginning with a folk song, the
chorus deplores Natasha's denunciation of her father, and later, learning about the
cause of Natasha's despair, expresses first sympathy with her, then fear mixed with a

Example 6.3: Rubinstein, "Ondine"

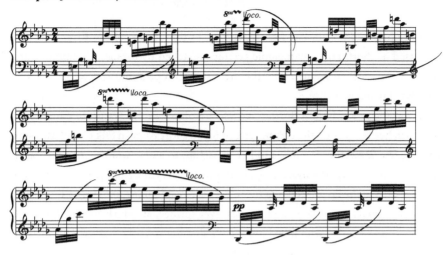

Example 6.4

Natasha: Alas, passed the golden time, how you loved me with all heart and soul. You used to have no other thought, no other wishes: only to be with me, no other joy, but in me alone!

desire to help her.[42] Natasha's frenzied appeal to the Tsarina of the River Dniepr is expressed in short, repeated melodic gestures matched by ostinato rhythmic figures and rushing scalelike sequences in the orchestra, European musical conventions for portraying madness.[43]

According to Keldysh, at the moment the heroine asks the Tsarina to embrace her and teach her vengeance, the composer employs a short Russian folk tune.[44] This song signifies her farewell to the folk and her departure to a new world—magical, pagan, and feminine. Natasha's physical separation from everything human and Russian is fully revealed in the lavish wedding scene. As an invisible spirit, she sings a short song, "Above the gravel and yellow sand the fast river springs," in which two small fish talk about a young maiden who killed herself, cursing her unfaithful lover. Although the words and metaphors of the song are reminiscent of Russian folklore, the short teary motifs with intense coloratura ornamentation echo European bel canto conventions (Example 6.5). Contrasting with the massive chorus praising the Kniaz and his new

EXAMPLE 6.5

Voice of Natasha/Rusalka: Above the gravel and yellow sand the fast river springs, in this fast river the two fishes swim

wife, the Kniaginia, the spirit's lonely song forebodes catastrophe. It powerfully expresses, musically and dramatically, the separation between the zalozhnaia woman and the choruses that represent the folk.[45]

In the beginning of the fourth act, the heroine receives a "Scene and Aria," a solo at last, her siren's song, in which she promises vengeance. However, the Kniaz is not even present, and the best she can do is teach Rusalochka how to lure him to the riverbank, even though the girl does not sing (this is a speaking role) and thus lacks the very instrument of a rusalka's power: a singing voice. This is the point where Pushkin's drama ends; Dargomyzhsky completes the remaining scenes. After her only solo in the opera, Rusalka once again becomes invisible; her last vocal lines are marked in the score as "Rusalka's Voice."

The heroine's name supplies the title for Dargomyzhsky's opera, but it is the Kniaz who receives a memorable and lyrical musical part. Like Natasha, he has no solo in the first act, and the second-act wedding celebration reveals little of his musical character. The intimate but uneventful third act, in the absence of both Rusalka and the mass choruses, establishes his presence as the male protagonist. In the cavatina "Unwillingly to these sad banks I am lured by a mysterious force" ("Nevol'no k etim grustnim beregam," Pushkin's verse), the Kniaz remembers the ruined mill, garden, and tree where he once met with Natasha. The hero mourns his forever-lost love in a graceful, beautiful melody (Example 6.6).

The wavy melodic line with its balanced, sequential rise and fall and light nostalgic intonation leads, at the end of the first part, to recognition ("Here is this memorable oak tree! Here she embraced me")[46] and an emotional awakening. But soon his expressive, wide-ranging vocal line and sequences, rising as he recalls the delight of their meetings and falling when he grieves "the delightful days passed with no return," lead to increased melodic agitation, which culminates in his recognition of guilt—"Did not I myself, a madman, lose my happiness." Starting as a dreamlike cantabile in ¾, with soothing accompaniment that further intensifies the poignancy of the Kniaz's part (Example 6.7), the cavatina turns into a dramatic (and thus operatically victorious) solo that is given additional energy by a series of orchestral passages. Emotional regret and lament are revealed in his duet with the mad miller, in which the Kniaz declaims repeatedly, "My heart is broken, my soul is full of pain. . . . Alas, it is I who am guilty of all these disasters." According to Abram Gozenpud, "The image of the Kniaz is ennobled and poeticized—he himself appears as a sufferer of the fated separation from his beloved."[47]

Sacrificing the hero, the composer undermines his main heroine throughout the opera by giving the live Natasha no distinct musical characteristics and then isolating this peasant girl from the folk, repeatedly disembodying her and musically failing her even as a rusalka. The separation of voice and body suggested by Pushkin in the

Example 6.6

Kniaz: Unwillingly to this sad shore I am lured by a mysterious force, familiar sad places!

wedding scene is repeated in the operatic finale and becomes a major dramatic device in Dargomyzhsky's version.

This Dangerous Game: Pushkin's and Dargomyzhsky's Finales

In Pushkin's *Rusalka*, the surface of the water is a passage into a world of shifted powers and conflated realities. At the end of the seemingly unfinished drama, the divide between the real world and the supernatural is about to be broken, blending the two irreconcilable dominions. At that moment of high suspense, Pushkin drops the curtain. What is the resolution? It is conceivable that Pushkin—the author of *Gavriliada*, famous for its explicit sexuality and for mixing the angelic and satanic worlds—would have led his characters and his readers across the boundary between acceptable norms and unrestrained, hazardous pleasures. But would the hero's *quick, wet death* satisfy the appetite of the underwater tsarina?[48]

Example 6.7

Kniaz: Everything brings back memories of the past and days of beautiful youth and freedom.

Drafting the conclusion of his opera, Dargomyzhsky thus faced several possibilities. Perhaps Rusalka could liberate the Kniaz from her spell and bless his mortal union. Natasha's suicide, forbidden by Russian Orthodoxy, might be justified only by the fact that her death makes possible a Christian marriage. Or Rusalka could sexually embrace the live Kniaz, making him the tsar of the water kingdom. Or she might follow through with her plan for revenge—the traditional rusalka's role.

At the beginning of the final act, Pushkin's rusalkas debate whether to frighten the strangers with their splashes, laughter, and whistles; Dargomyzhsky replaces this verbal exchange with a divertissement, an elaborate dance episode that ends with the entrance of the tsarina, who, after a brief instruction to the rusalkas, is left alone with her daughter. Their dialogue is colored by the harp, and a 6/8 waltzlike rhythm reinforces the association of the rusalka's realm with dance. Little Rusalochka does not sing, but speaks. Her voice has not yet developed a siren's perilous qualities. Teaching her daughter how to cuddle her father, her mother utters a curvy melodious vocal line, but ends with powerful, wide leaps: "I call on him and I wait!" (Example 6.8)

A long arpeggio on the harp signals the departure of Rusalochka and the beginning of Rusalka's most important solo in the opera. The opening recitative, Rusalka's recollection of herself as a foolish girl, is shaped into a peculiarly angular vocal line. In the following aria, long vocal lines give the singer no time to breathe, almost choking her. These extended vocal stretches alternate with short melodic sentences. The orchestra interrupts the vocalist's line, accentuating the weak beats, especially while she is

Example 6.8

Rusalka: I call on him and I wait! Tell him, my darling [*to Rusalochka*], tell him that I call and wait for him!

Example 6.9

Rusalka: The long-desired hour came! The fire of revenge and love burns in my blood!

holding long high pitches (Example 6.9). The vocal part and orchestral accompaniment are filled with chromaticism.

Serov describes the aria as "difficult in intonation and not very melodious, ... requiring an exceptionally strong mezzo-soprano."[49] He comments that Rusalka's music does not correspond to the dramatic task.[50] Similarly, McClary, commenting on *Lucia di Lammermoor*, writes about "the discrepancy between her [Lucia's] morbid text and her ecstatic dance music."[51] What is the meaning of this discordance in the text, the dramatic situation, and Rusalka's vocal part? Keldysh suggests that Dargomyzhsky was more successful portraying his heroine as a suffering and tormented victim than as a merciless rusalka.[52] Yet it seems unlikely that Dargomyzhsky—praised by Keldysh,

Serov, and other critics for his talent as an operatic dramatist and for his expressive
arias, recitatives, and especially for his melodic lyricism—failed in the portrayal of
his heroine. Could the discursive space between Rusalka's words and their musical
realization be attributed to the composer's intent to contest and undermine the
heroine's power? Not the cold and mighty rusalka of Pushkin's drama, she is rather
a jealous, madly loving, devastated woman. Dargomyzhsky uses Pushkin's words in
the recitative but writes different lyrics for the aria in which Rusalka's burning jealousy
and love make her repeat, "Alas, my proud, desired Kniaz, you are mine forever, yes,
forever!" (Example 6.10)

Example 6.10

Rusalka: Alas, my proud, desired Kniaz you are mine forever, yes, forever!

The Kniaz enters the stage singing the already familiar melody from his cavatina. He is mesmerized by his little water daughter, who intersperses his melodious lines with her spoken sentences. The Kniaginia, following her husband, now reveals her pain and despair and is soon joined by her compassionate companion Olga. As the Kniaz is torn between his wife and little Rusalochka, the girl announces that even if he does not believe her story, he must surely recognize Rusalka's voice. Invisible, Rusalka recites a melodic sequence with sentences gradually shortened and the tempo accelerated. The voices merge in a discordant ensemble, as another character joins the company; staccato dancelike steps precede the appearance of the miller, who calls the Kniaz his son-in-law. At the climax, the miller, inviting everyone to join the wedding of the Kniaz and his daughter, pushes the Kniaz into the river. The whole scene turns into a distorted replay of the wedding that was so lavishly performed in the second act. Offering no emotional release, the final scene shifts to the movement of silent rusalkas carrying the Kniaz to the feet of their tsarina in her watery kingdom.

Is the Kniaz's death in the *wetness* of the night a complete ending? Does this death satisfy the heroine? Or does the ending proclaim the lovers' reconciliation in some other world? Asserting that the dancing rusalkas impoverish the opera, Serov noted that in some second-rate productions this final scene became a series of banal divertissements and harlequinades, where the lovers reunite in Cupid's temple. But Pushkin's Rusalka is a symbol of power, and whatever dangerous game one imagines beyond the frame of the unfinished drama, it is governed by the capricious mind of a female monarch with unbounded power to play, to please, or to kill. By contrast, in the opera it is not Rusalka but her father who reunites his daughter with the Kniaz. The sexual desire of the heroine, suppressed for twelve years, leads the hero to his death, although the final point comes too quickly to give her much satisfaction. Not much satisfaction— not much singing. Throughout the whole scene, she is heard but not seen and in the end is visible but mute. Her victory is silent and thus anti-operatic. Dargomyzhsky overshadows the actual resolution of the drama with a mesmerizing picture of floating, shadowy, mute rusalkas.

The Romantic Context: Supernatural Female Dancers

From the very beginning of the romantic age, water sprites sang and danced in both opera and ballet. The same year Aliabiev completed his operatic *Rusalka* (1838), Russian audiences were introduced to another incarnation of the Danube water maiden: the ballet *La Fille du Danube* by the French composer Adolphe Adam and choreographer Filippo Taglioni.[53] Indeed in France as in Russia, in the first decades of the nineteenth century, opera and ballet—two not-yet-divorced genres—recycled the same stories,[54] with ballet employing operatic musical forms and dance "belonging comfortably with sung drama."[55] In Dargomyzhsky's *Rusalka*, ballet performs various roles, including ethnic tableaux: Slavic and Gypsy dances in the second act as well as the collective imagery of supernatural rusalkas.

In early ballets, ethnic and historic themes, referred to as "local color," coincided with the cult of the supernatural.[56] Cyril W. Beaumont suggests that the marriage between dance and the supernatural began in Meyerbeer's opera *Robert le Diable* (1831), where in the third act Duke Robert, visiting the ruined abbey of St. Rosalie, finds himself surrounded by the ghosts of nuns emerging from their tombs in a mystical mimed scene.[57] (The realm of the supernatural in ballet was limited to women; male leads were rarely associated with magic.) Within a decade, according to Théophile Gautier, the musical theater stage was occupied by Vilas who "fluttered here and there"; by Péri "skimming the ground without touching it"; by supple, sensual Bayadera with sorrowful languorous gestures"; and by the daughter of the Danube, "a shade, intangible."[58] In no time, ballets such as *La Sylphide*, *La Péri*, and *Giselle* were added to the core repertoire in St. Petersburg and Moscow.[59] *Robert le Diable* and *Les Huguenots*, both including large dancing scenes, were well known and widely discussed by Russian musicians and musical critics.[60]

Despite the closeness of the two genres, opera emphasized singing and literary text and was considered more sophisticated than ballet, which centered on the female body, moving, flying, fluttering, exposing, and offering itself to the eyes of spectators.[61] Felicia McCarren suggests that "in the course of the nineteenth century the dance becomes an art form uniquely attached to the female form, an art . . . in which the female body, feminine sexuality, and thus femininity itself, become the essential subject of the dance."[62] The costumes themselves, gauzy and revealing, with raised hemlines, were designed to inspire male patrons' daydreams and erotic reveries. Describing the Parisian ballerina Marie Taglioni, Gautier writes about her "slender legs . . . beneath billowing crowds of muslin, the rosy shades of her tights plunging you into dreams of the same hue."[63] The Russian critic Iurkevich, observing Marie Taglioni on the Russian stage, claims that "thoughts passionate and tender, which destroy and elevate the soul before us, wordlessly flash in her expressive, burning eyes. A winged, fascinating dream, elusive and undefined, plays and sports before your eyes."[64]

On the ballet stage, the female dancer, simultaneously veiling and revealing her body, was cultivated as an emblem of both sexuality and otherworldliness. The silent, ethereal ballerina seemed to combine innocence and eroticism, reality and the supernatural. Gautier, for example, commented on Giselle as "a paradigm for poetry; her dance can be seen not simply as the stuff of poetry, but as an image for the movement of poetry between realms."[65] Gautier claimed that "out of four lines of Heine"[66] he produced the libretto of *Giselle*, whose triumph and endurance on the Russian stage have been equaled by only a few spectacles.[67] *Giselle* conquered the Russian stage in the years preceding Dargomyzhsky's *Rusalka*.[68] "The original *Giselle* behaved like opera"[69]; Dargomyzhsky's opera incorporated elements of ballet.

The plot lines of the Russian opera and the French ballet are strikingly similar; a romance between a young peasant girl and a nobleman, followed by his betrayal,[70] leads the heroine to madness and death. In the afterlife each reemerges as a supernatural woman endowed with magic destructive power. Like Rusalka, Vila remains in her afterlife an ever-bride who will chase, seduce, tickle, and dance her male victims to death.

Ghostly brides appear late in both *Giselle* and *Rusalka*. In Dargomyzhsky's opera, the rusalkas emerge from the water singing in the second half of the third act and become absorbed in their dancing in the fourth. An orchestral interlude in the fourth act, with wavelike rolling octaves and "splashes" on the strong beats, echoes the Scène des Vilas from the second act of *Giselle*. In *Rusalka* the "watery introduction" has a melodious rather than a dancing character; in the following section the movement gradually gains energy and the speed increases, leading to an Allegro Vivace in 6/8 that explores syncopations reminiscent of *Giselle's* Vilas.[71] In the Allegro section of the divertissement, the rhythmic figure hints at Orientalized imagery. During this exotic orchestral interlude, the rusalkas' voices are raised only in laughter. A figure of native mythology and the title heroine, she becomes a shadow, a tsarina—a foreigner and an orientalized stranger.

Choruses and Nationalism

In both *Giselle* and *Rusalka,* the first acts are central to the portrayal of the folk. Though absent from Pushkin's intimate poem, the folk chorus plays an important part in Dargomyzhsky's opera, interspersing the duets of the two lovers and witnessing the heroine's demise. In the mass folk scenes, the mortal heroines of *Rusalka* and *Giselle* are rapidly introduced, loved, driven mad, and crushed. The wedding in *Rusalka* (second act) follows many Russian operatic weddings, echoing the one in Glinka's *Ruslan and Liudmila* (1838) and also several French productions, such as Meyerbeer's *Huguenots*.[72] The wedding rituals in Dargomyzhsky include two ethnic vignettes, one of them a "Gypsy Dance."[73] The massive choruses, dances, and special characters portrayed by Dargomyzhsky function as "genuine" rituals with a pan-Slavic and particularly boyar or noble character.[74] Thus even though the wedding in *Rusalka's* second act introduces several folk choruses, it departs from the folk and rustic into princely and urban space.

Traditionally the operatic mass scenes, choruses, folk or folklike songs, and the figure of the victorious hero (the Kniaz is an exception) typify the political, nationalistic spirit of Russian opera, which corresponds to Smith's association of opera with "public political" matters and ballet with "private affairs of the heart."[75] Dargomyzhsky's mass scenes explore elements of ritualistic, urban, and popular culture. Active participants in the drama, the choruses anticipate and comment on operatic events. For example, at the beginning of the first act, after the peaceful trio of the momentarily happy heroine, her noble lover, and the miller, the chorus sings on a sorrowful note, "Why are you, my willful heart, in such pain?" Similarly, a folk song and a khorovod with a mock fight contrast with and yet anticipate the troubled duet of the main characters before the tragic finale of the first act.

Not only is each choral scene significant by itself, but the sequence of scenes supports the dramatic process—the distribution and density of the choruses gradually decreases. The first act is replete with choruses representing peasants, and choral singing remains central to the wedding celebrations. After the end of the second act, however, there are no more massive folk choruses. In the third act, gender-segregated hunters (men) and rusalkas (women) replace the massive folk scenes. No choral singing takes place in the last act. At the same time, dances grow in importance, progressing from the women's khorovod song in the first act to the female Slavic and Gypsy dances in the second, to the rusalkas who conquer the stage in the fourth, framing the finale of the opera with their mute dance.

The reduction of the folk choruses coincides with gradual disintegration of the main characters. At the same time, the increasing role of dancing is associated, especially in the fourth act, with establishment of the magic realm. The operatic chorus and folk dances are linked with public male territory, while ballet represents an intimate, private female supernatural realm. Moreover, choral singing is associated with the live world, folk songs, the folk itself, and thus Russianness. Ironically, the nobleman whose class prejudice caused the destruction of the peasant girl becomes allied with the folk chorus in the second act and with the hunters in the third. It is the Kniaz's downfall, not the betrayed heroine's, that coincides with the gradual disappearance of the folk, who vanish completely at the death of the male lead, leaving the stage to the female dancers.

Though the rusalkas emerge from the water singing (third act), they soon dive back into the river and thereafter dance silently or laugh. The finale, with ghostly rusalkas floating across the stage, strongly contrasts with Russian operas before and after *Rusalka*. After Glinka's *Life for the Tsar* and *Ruslan and Liudmila*, nearly all operas, despite differences of plot and genre, culminated in a massive final choral "Slava" glorifying the bravery and victory of Russians led by a national (male) hero. What motivated Dargomyzhsky to conclude his opera with an unquestionably negative feminine ending, reversing the dynamics of gender and genre?

What Serov criticizes as the "weaknesses" of the score—an overabundance of folk choruses at the beginning, "too much counterpoint and too many voices" contrasting with the "cold and almost boring character of [the rusalkas'] ballet scenes"—is perhaps the essence of Dargomyzhsky's dramatic intent.[76] Replacement of Russian folk choruses with deadly female nymphs may constitute a clear warning about the dangers of being loved, controlled, and manipulated by powerful women—a bad omen expressed by the folk, from whom Natasha, the character most associated with native mythology and folk rituals, is separated by her suicide and her transformation.

The Historical Context: Pushkin's Precursors and Catherine the Great

Like their fellow European writers, Russian romantic authors were infatuated with the search for the feminine and for *volshebstvo* (magic); but, as discussed earlier, for Russians, unlike Europeans, the idea of female power was not an abstraction. Not only had the country been ruled by female monarchs for an extensive period, but eighteenth-century noblewomen enjoyed legal rights and control over property unequaled elsewhere in Europe. In her study of "the significance of separate property in practice" and the "the real scope of women's control of their fortunes,"[77] Marrese discusses the emergence of formidable women in public life, "peaking in the eighteenth century but dwindling after the reign of Catherine the Great."[78]

Considering Russian historical and cultural particularities, one might compare Pushkin's Rusalka with Dushen'ka, the title heroine of Bogdanovich's poem and lyric comedy, discussed in the previous chapter. In the poem, Dushen'ka is portrayed as a pastoral heroine whose magical encounters with an invisible lover are associated with water.[79] The first time she appears, Dushen'ka is guided to her bath by forty nymphs, with *amours* (cupids) bringing her dew instead of water. Bogdanovich's detailed poetic description of her bathing and her beauty is pregnant with sensuality.[80] A "little brook calls and guides her" along the "crystal water" of its clear streams to a grotto where, ever after, she spends "hours and days with her beloved spouse."[81] Losing her lover, the desperate heroine finds drowning to be the most "convenient" (*udobnyi*) method of suicide. Throwing herself into the water, she is miraculously saved by pikes—"in whom [she] recognized naiads"—and who lead the heroine to her beloved. As discussed above, Dushen'ka was perceived as a pastoral, humanized surrogate of Catherine II. Pushkin, who does not make Catherine the protagonist of any of his works, nevertheless continuously refers to her era, her rule, and her persona. The poet writes with nostalgia about the age of Catherine and recalls her marvelous palaces and parks; Catherine often appears as a formidable woman who, like Rusalka, eradicates men.[82]

Wachtel compares Pushkin's notes on eighteenth-century Russian history (1822) with his novel *The Captain's Daughter*, both invoking the era and the image of the empress, the first a work based on archival materials and the second a fictional first-person memoir of an accused traitor saved by a young woman who seeks forgiveness from Catherine. Wachtel's analysis of the two works leads him to define a "multiplicity of ways in which historical material could be codified" in the "intergeneric dialogue" that occurs "across the boundaries of separate texts."[83] The Russian literary scholar Berezkina, employing a similar approach to investigate Pushkin's language, claims that expressions such as "kartiny, mostik, luzhok" (pictures, bridges, meadows), used to describe scenery in *Eugene Onegin*, referenced the park that surrounded Catherine's palace in Tsarskoe Selo[84] and thus invoked the image of the tsarina herself.[85] Berezkina points out that in the margins of his manuscript of *Onegin*, next to the description of this scenery, Pushkin sketched the poem "Mne zhal' velikia zheny" ("I pity the great wife") about the aged empress.

How far can one go in searching for historical and literary cues, codifications, and commentaries employed in Pushkin's text? Though there is indeed no apparent connection between powerful Catherine and the tsarina-rusalka in Pushkin's tale, the story line of Pushkin's *Rusalka* parallels the queenly *Dushen'ka*. In Pushkin's drama, pikes do not save the heroine, as in the Bogdanovich story, but the song about two fish interrupts the flow of the wedding, signaling Natasha's mystical metamorphosis into an immortal queen, forever wedded to water. Bogdanovich's poem playfully explores the connection of the royal Dushen'ka with water, magic, and sensuality; Rusalka, transformed from a peasant girl into a tsarina, accesses the magic power associated with water and sexuality.

It is intriguing that Pushkin, referring to Bogdanovich in one of his drafts of "I pity the great wife," calls Catherine "tsarevna dushen'ka"[86]:

Мы Прагой ей одолжены	We owe her Prague
И просвещеньем и Тавридой	The enlightenment and Tauride
...	...
Царевной душенькой Кипридой	Tsarevna **dushen'ka** of Kypros.[87]

As noted in the previous chapter, the first line of *Ruslan* juxtaposes the same key words, "dusha" and "tsarina." In "I pity the great wife," Pushkin paints Catherine in the company of Derzhavin, who created the image of Catherine as the magic Felitsa, the navigator of an invincible fleet, an explorer, ruler, and voluptuous woman. In Derzhavin's verses, cited above, the sound of harps, the sirens' songs, and the khorovods the nymphs and cupids play all serve to "please the Goddess' eyes" (the Goddess is Catherine herself).[88]

Writing his tale of Rusalka, and elevating his zalozhnaia into a tsarina, Pushkin argu-ably comments on the image of the monarch nourished by his literary predecessors, as a formidable woman with an uninhibited appetite for power and sexuality. Considering the great attention paid to Catherine by the poet's predecessors, Pushkin's frequent references to and commentaries on their works, his strong interest in Catherine, and the rising fashion of literary tales, one might interpret Pushkin's Rusalka as an allusion not to historical Catherine but to a rich literary tradition related to her imagery.

The Literary Context: Gender in the Russian Skazka

Dargomyzhsky's rusalka is removed by several generations from the historical tsari-nas—no female monarchs would again be admitted to power in Russia—and she is equally distant from Bogdanovich's and Derzhavin's royal heroines.[89] Dargomyzhsky's rendition of the rusalka story reveals not only his adherence to Pushkin but also his great interest in the folktales that the French-speaking and foreign-educated Russian nobility saw as a revival of "the ingenuity and vehemence of the Russian soul."[90] At the end of the eighteenth century, the skazka or tale, a genre not yet defined, encompassed historical episodes and characters, events of real life, imaginary domains, and the underworld.[91]

In the mid-nineteenth century the fairy tale, recorded or created, came to represent a national mythology, with figures like rusalkas linking folk tales, pagan rituals, and Western mythology with romantic ideals. Rusalka, first as a mortal girl and later as a mythological figure, existed in two worlds, one real and the other ritualistic and fantastic—the two kingdoms that Vladimir Propp finds necessary for the composition of a magic tale. Dargomyzhsky's Rusalka resembles the character described by Propp in his typology of characters: "tsarina—*dusha* [dushen'ka] as a beautiful and faithful maiden, but also a wicked, vengeful, and nasty creature, always prepared to kill, to drown, and to harm her male partner, and the hero's main task is to suppress her." In Propp's typological plot, the aim of the male lead is "to remove her power. Then she is defeated and obeys the husband."[92]

Dargomyzhsky's Rusalka is affected by gender conventions developed in European operas and ballets. Female heroines were often destroyed; the stronger they were, the more intense and promising was the prospect of their subjugation to male power.[93] As shown above, Dargomyzhsky's opera celebrated the separation of the female voice from the body, manifested in the singing of the frequently invisible heroine and the dancing of the mostly silent rusalkas. When the male protagonist dies in the end, the heroine is victoriously mute. Her destructive power remains—she receives the body of her former lover from the arms of her fellow immortals. However, according to the national mythology examined by Propp, even though her submission could bring happiness to both female and male protagonists, the Kniaz's defeat gives Rusalka no satisfaction. Thus her victory makes impossible the traditional celebratory operatic ending with the heroine either surrendering to male authority or dying. Whether surrendering or dying, the operatic heroine should be a diva; instead, Rusalka is vocally undermined. The most romantic part is given to the Kniaz and the rounded melodious lines to Rusalka's rival, the Kniaginia. Pushkin's rusalka, transformed into tsarina, ascends to magic power; Dargomyzhsky's tsarina gradually fades away.

Conclusion

In nineteenth-century Russian narrative, the rusalka became an emblem useful in creating nationalistic mythology. As a folk-tale heroine, she was closely associated with ancient rituals, and her image as zalozhnaia endowed her with spiritual power. Living in various waters—from the Dniepr (rusalkas in Somov and Gogol), the Dniestr, and the Volkhova (Rimsky-Korsakov, *Sadko*) to the Aragva and the Kura in the Caucasus (Lermontov, *Mtsyri*) and the Bashkirian lake Aculu (Dal', "Bashkirskaia Rusalka")—the Russian rusalka served as a territorial marker of Russian imperialism and embodied a broad pan-Slavic identity.

On the other hand, Rusalka's paganism pitted her against Russian Orthodoxy. In his tale, Pushkin warns his fellow men about the frightening potential of women to control and destroy. Dargomyzhsky's Rusalka, created a quarter-century later, embodies both the qualities of Pushkin's water creature and a nineteenth-century European gender paradigm. Like Dargomyzhsky's mute but formidable woman, some other heroines were destroyed by nationalistic Russian operatic composers. In Rimsky Korsakov's *Sadko*, a successful version of the Kniaz is married to two women: the water spouse Tsarevna Volkhova and a mortal wife Liubava. Liubava spills rivers of tears throughout the opera; at the end the Tsarevna Volkhova turns herself into a river, benefiting Sadko and his city. This submission of women is celebrated in the finale of the opera by a massive choir glorifying the hero and the nation.

The rusalka, from whom writers and composers borrowed ritualistic power in the name of nationalism, is by contrast estranged from everything that is folklike and Russian. In her study of the connection between the image of women and national politics, Meyda Yegenogli argues that in different times and cultural contexts a woman "becomes the ground upon which nationalism builds its discourse."[94] The figure of rusalka, repeatedly invoked in Russian literary works from the late eighteenth century and into the second half of the nineteenth, shows the transformation of discourse about women and power—discourse that converges the processes of continuous Westernization, masculinization, and rising nationalistic extremism. Once a formidable woman, a threat to men's physical existence and memory, Rusalka was turned into a magical otherworldly creature whose singing and dancing codified her sexual and social challenge for the Russian romantic man.

7

MLADA AND THE SPELLBINDING FEMALE CIRCLE

... the mightiest of arts, Music, sings to us powerfully with the voices of the depth's nighttime Sirens. It raises us out of its vortex (as "chaos gives birth to a star") with the spiraling line of the sublime and returns us cleansed and invigorated to the earth with the good descent of Beauty.

(Viacheslav Ivanov, 1905[1])

In the middle of Rimsky-Korsakov's *Mlada*, a fantasy tale about ancient pagan Slavs, the spectators suddenly find themselves in the palace of Cleopatra.[2] The Egyptian scene exudes sensuality—exposed bodies, provocative poses, and voluptuous dances.[3] The seductress of all time, Cleopatra, and her graceful slaves ply their charms on the operatic protagonist and the audience. In addition to the orchestra, Rimsky-Korsakov places on stage tambourines, large drums, and specially made *tsevnitsas* (Pan's pipes), connecting the instruments aurally and visually with Cleopatra. The composer wrote:

> Among my musical impressions of Paris [at the World Exposition, summer 1889] I reflect on music in Hungarian and Algerian cafés. The virtuoso playing of a Hungarian orchestra on *tsevnitsas* gave me the idea of introducing this ancient instrument... during the dances at Cleopatra's. In an Algerian café, I was attracted to the beat of a large drum.... This effect I also borrowed for the scene of Cleopatra.[4]

Three years after the production of *Mlada*, in Rimsky-Korsakov's next opera, *Christmas Eve*, the chorus greeted another queen with a lofty cantata-polonaise, beginning with and repeating the words "*tsevnitsa* and drum," linking Cleopatra across operas with this unnamed tsarina.[5] However, the premier of *Christmas Eve*, set for November 1895, did not take place as planned. The composer noted in his autobiography:

> The Grand Dukes Vladimir Alexandrovich and Mikhail Nikolaievich came to the dress-rehearsal and both of them showed indignation at the presence (on the stage) of the tsarina, in whom they insisted on recognizing the Empress Catherine II . . . the Emperor has withdrawn his sanction for producing my opera.[6]

The grand dukes were not mistaken in recognizing their great-grandmother, who was named in the Gogol story on which the libretto of the opera was based. The ploy of "recognition" may have attracted Tchaikovsky and Rimsky-Korsakov to this particular tale. But neither of Tchaikovsky's two operas on Gogol's tale, *Vakula the Smith* and *The Slippers*, nor Rimsky-Korsakov's *Christmas Eve* succeeded in bringing Catherine II to the operatic stage. These three operas, as well as Tchaikovsky's *Queen of Spades* (1890), which relocated Pushkin's story to Catherine's era, featured the presence of the empress through her absence.

To circumvent prohibition of the operatic portrayal of Russian monarchs (1837)[7]—Catherine in particular—Russian composers developed certain operatic conventions and intertextual codes. Codes and conventions, though connected, are quite different things. Conventions invoke a shared semiotic vocabulary that gains clarity and strength through repetition. By contrast, intertextual codes—idiosyncratic, often partial, and spread throughout various texts—veil and conceal as much as they divulge. As discussed in previous chapters, coded intertextual clues were a product of a Russian literary tradition stemming from the eighteenth century as an intellectual game in which an author reached out to his or her readers by referencing various texts and relying on the readers' ability to detect and connect intellectual, and at times politically subversive, pieces. This tradition was shaped by an equally long history of Russian censorship, which aimed to shred any trace of suspicious implications and any hint of political irony. Thus Russian artists faced the remarkable task of simultaneously communicating and concealing their covert messages in the style of inoskazanie, while addressing two groups of literati: a receptive conspiring audience and the official censors. Accordingly, deeply seeded clues, displaced or misplaced from a single poem, drama, or opera, are "found" in citations, cross-references, and other suggestive semiotic gestures planted in other texts. Wachtel extends intertextual analysis from the study of Russian poetry to the analysis of drama, suggesting that "there are important ways in which the specificity of the medium impinges on and complicates intertextual practice."[8] Wachtel further elaborates that the participatory aspect of drama "can make the experience of the intertextual in the theatrical context more complex and interesting than in non-performance media."[9] In this context, operatic theater offers an additional set of texts and the possibility of intertextual connections between auditory and dramatic media, and intertextual communication across music, literary texts, and performance.

Working around the prohibition of the operatic portrayal of Catherine in *Slippers*, Tchaikovsky delegated her part to "His Lightness" (*Svetleiishii*) Potemkin, sung by a bass. His solution became a convention when Ivan Vsevolozhsky,[10] the director of imperial theaters, suggested that Rimsky-Korsakov follow the same path in *Christmas Eve* by replacing the tsarina with "His Most Serene Highness" Potemkin (a baritone). Rimsky-Korsakov found the solution "foolish" and "absurd" but, left with no options, conceded.[11] The principle of substitution opened intriguing possibilities, which will be further explored in Chapter Nine on *The Queen of Spades*. Another conventional way of depicting the empress and her surroundings was to enact long ceremonial processions paired with choral polonaises in the style of composer Josef Kozlowski, who was popular in Catherine's court.[12] The cantata-polonaise became a signifier of both her era and her physical absence on the nineteenth-century operatic stage.[13] Notably, Catherine's balls in the four operas named above occur in plots with supernatural elements, as if this specific historical age belongs to the world of fantasy, which leads one to seek intertextual connections and clues in magical operas.

The link between the silent dancing Cleopatra and the physically absent Catherine in Rimsky-Korsakov's operas may fall into the category of intertextual clues. The inkling of an equation between Catherine and Cleopatra suggested by the use of the *tsevnitsa*s had long existed in a corner of cultural memory. More than a hundred years before Rimsky-Korsakov composed his *Mlada*, young Krylov, a contemporary of the empress, wrote a tragedy entitled *Cleopatra* (1785). The manuscript was lost or burned, its exact contents unknown.[14] Yet its anti-Catherine political and sexual implications "raised no doubts, especially in the context of Krylov's other writings."[15] As discussed before, Krylov had a reputation as a satirist ridiculing excessive female coquetry, especially the sexual appetites of older women. Although many names and actual works have been forgotten, Krylov's non-existent *Cleopatra* remained in nineteenth-century cultural annals as a part of eighteenth-century myth—written, nonwritten, documented, intertextual. Proskurina writes that Catherine II was famous not only as "Russian Minerva" but also as "Russian Cleopatra."[16]

A recent production of *Mlada*[17] offers a double lens by locating the spectacle about ancient Slavs in the frame of the late-eighteenth-century court. Cleopatra and her Egyptian beauties dance, accompanied by an onstage ensemble of musicians wearing wigs and dressed in the fashion of Catherine's time. An intermusical connection can also be traced from Rimsky-Korsakov's Cleopatra to Catherine in César Cui's *Captain's Daughter* (1911). In *Mlada*, the Egyptian queen is enwrapped and rapturous in D-flat major, which Rimsky-Korsakov identified with "tonal power and splendor, . . . such succulence, velvetiness and fullness."[18] In Cui's opera, Catherine II finally appears and even sings a little song. And the moment Catherine steps on stage, the key content changes to D-flat major, to identify the empress—as Cleopatra.

From Ball to Sabbath

This chapter and the next primarily focus on Rimsky-Korsakov's *Mlada* and *Sadko*. *Christmas Eve*, as well as Tchaikovsky's three operas mentioned above, spotlight the omission of historical empresses; *Mlada* and *Sadko* display magical female royals as possible substitutes for the real thing. According to Rimsky-Korsakov, his group of three—*Christmas Eve, Mlada*, and *Sadko*—"in methods of composition" belonged together.[19] *Mlada* and *Sadko* can also be grouped with the composer's "water" operas.[20] Rimsky-Korsakov, once a young garde-marine sailing around Europe and North and South America and later vividly describing his naval journeys, created a number of operas connected with water.[21] Flowing, vacillating, ambiguous, water is an elemental force tied with the feminine and magic in these operas, as in *Rusalka*. Animated and identified with Rimsky-Korsakov's female protagonists, water both directs and distracts the plotlines of these operas, hypnotizing, seducing, and trapping the lead characters. Deceptively lucid, water is in fact reflective. Seemingly mirror-flat, it runs deep over craters and swallowing sands, all in constant unrest. Permeated with images and metaphors of flowing water, Rimsky-Korsakov's operas consist of capacious, picturesque tableaus in continuous motion that extend beyond the boundaries of one opera and stream into others, creating a semireflective operatic sequence akin to the overlapping tales of Scheherazade.

Mlada (1892) and *Sadko* (1897)[22] continued the tradition of Russian fairy-tale operas by combining folklore and fantasy, paganism and Orthodoxy, mass and intimate scenes, collective Slavs and diverse (Eastern and Western) others. Both operas feature magical tsarevnas (princesses) who inhabit nautical depths and control the nocturnal world of dreams and shadows, carrying on the rusalka's composite of the royal feminine, magic, and water. As discussed in previous chapters, the eighteenth-century Russian empire and imperial expansionist lore sought and celebrated access to the seas. Building on Peter's victories, each empress, in a chain of wars, acquired new waterways, developed the imperial fleet, and propagated her Russia as a naval empire. Odes, choruses, medals, and maps memorialized and lauded the four empresses, especially Catherine II, as mistresses of the sea.

In *Mlada* and *Sadko*, magical royals and feminine spirits form a khorovod—a circle-dance that within and across the two operas encircles a nonmagical male protagonist. In *Mlada*, the hero is trapped; in *Sadko*, the outcome is reversed.

The two operas present a contrasting pair: *Mlada* features a large gallery of powerful female characters; *Sadko* celebrates male fraternity and the victory of the title hero-musician.

Mlada is a hybrid opera-ballet based on the libretto of Stepan Gedeonov. Twenty years before Rimsky-Korsakov's opera, Gedeonov, then director of imperial theaters, envisioned *Mlada* as a collaborative project and commissioned the music to a group of four members of the Mighty Five—Cui, Mussorgsky, Rimsky-Korsakov, and Borodin—and ballet composer Ludwig Minkus.[23] Though some fragments were composed, a collective work never materialized. In 1879, Minkus produced his own *Mlada* as a ballet. Rimsky-Korsakov recalled that his interest in the project was rekindled at a gathering for the second anniversary of Borodin's death.

Sadko, like *Mlada*, remained in Rimsky-Korsakov's life for decades. He created a symphonic poem *Sadko* in his twenties (1867). Completing *Mlada* twenty-three years later, the composer reorchestrated his earlier *Sadko* (1891) and several years afterward ventured the opera of the same title. The plots of the two operas, though drastically different, reveal some similarity. Mlada is the shadow of a deceased tsarevna-bride, poisoned by her rival, another tsarevna Voislava. A silent ballerina, Mlada invades the dreams and visions of prince Yaromir (*yar*, bright, burning; *mir*, world); his earthly bride Voislava occupies him when he is awake. Both princesses receive aid from female goddesses who combat one another: Voislava secures the assistance of Morena (from *more*, sea; *mor*, death and darkness, as in Cherno-*mor*),[24] a goddess of water and a spirit of death[25]; Mlada is shadowed, guided, and protected by Lada. Each goddess appears with a massive otherworldly entourage. Torn between visions and reality, Yaromir in the final act avenges the death of Mlada by killing Voislava. After raging Morena floods the folk, Yaromir reunites with his beloved shadow in the sky.

In *Sadko*, the title hero also deals with two women. Married to Liubava, he is enamored with, supported by, and eventually weds the Sea Tsarevna Volkhova. Both his vacillation between paganism and Orthodoxy and his bigamy require an operatic resolution. Volkhova dissolves into a river, liberating her now-rich husband, providing his city of Novgorod with water routes and making her beloved a hero and legend among his fellow citizens. Here, in addition to the historical and operatic connection between powerful tsarinas and water, one finds the literary trope of water tied to female suicide. The intersection of the two contrasting ways in which women are linked with water— supreme power and suicide—is apparent in *Rusalka*, surfaces in Tchaikovsky's *Queen of Spades*, and threads itself through *Sadko*. In *Mlada*, the lead women draw their imagery and their power from streams of air (Mlada and Lada) and flows of water (Morena).

Monumental spectacles with complex plotlines, extensive casts, a combination of opera and ballet, a network of leitmotifs and intertextual connections, *Mlada* and

Sadko require separate analysis. The female cast of *Mlada* includes two tsarevnas, two goddesses, and Cleopatra, as well as witches, a ritualistic maidens' chorus, and market vendors with individual vocal lines. Mlada flows in aerial space; her smooth wavy theme emanates from entwined and overlapping arpeggios of flutes and clarinets in the first measures of the orchestral introduction. These streaming melodious arpeggios form a theme in flutes doubled by violins; both the waves and the theme pervade the spectacle (Example 7.1). Like Mlada, Cleopatra is a ballerina; her scene foreshadows the modernist works of Leon Bakst and productions of the Ballet Russes.[26] Lada, the goddess of love, descends from and returns to her habitat in the clouds accompanied by harp arpeggios. A mime role, she is "voiced" by the unison female choir, doubled by the flutes. Morena and Voislava are singing characters. Morena first appears on the stage in the guise of the old woman Sviatokha.[27]

Example 7.1

In addition to streams and flows, circles are metaphorically aligned with female imagery. Voislava opens the first act by spinning a wheel and weaving a ritualistic wreath.[28] Circles are later invoked in three *kolo* (wheel) dances: the "Folk Kolo," the "Fantastic Kolo" danced by shadows and spirits of the dead, and the "Infernal Kolo" by demonic forces. The semiotic expression of a circle is the khorovod of female heroines, who while rivaling each other form an inescapable tight ring around the male lead, Yaromir.

The men's group in the opera consists of Voislava's father Mstivoi (from *mstit'*, to avenge), the High Priest, and two episodic characters, Kashchei[29] and Chernobog.[30] The famous bass Fyodor Stravinsky (the composer's father) premiered the role of the father. The High Priest (baritone), a representative of the ancient militant god Redegast, leads double or triple choruses of pagan priests and worshipers.[31] The choruses voice the ballet roles of Kashchei and Chernobog, who, like Cleopatra, will reappear in later works by Rimsky-Korsakov and his pupils.[32] Lumir (alto), the leader of the Czech tribe, is another powerful episodic character.

The male protagonist is Yaromir, who finds himself in his dream world, and who spends a significant time on stage sleeping. He is not alone in Russian literature and theater. From the late-eighteenth and throughout the nineteenth century, dreams received ample attention. To name a few examples, Russian writer Alexander Radishchev (1749–1802), in his famous, politically charged *Journey from St. Petersburg to Moscow,* used night dreams as his message to an unnamed "world ruler" (Catherine II), whose morals he severely criticized.[33] Chernyshevsky's famous dreams in *What Is to Be Done?* also conveyed a strong political message. The chronically dormant Yaromir echoes the portrait of Goncharov's Oblomov. Wachtel, writing about a quintessentially nineteenth-century male protagonist in Lermontov's *Hero of Our Times*, points out the tendency of Russian literary works to encapsulate the experience of the entire generation. Linking a narrator with his protagonist, Wachtel identifies the extensive literary genealogy of Russia's superfluous men, "traditionally extremely intelligent and highly articulate but incapable of taking concrete and positive actions in the real world."[34] The type can be identified with the operatically articulate, yet sleeping, Yaromir. Thus *Mlada* portrays on the one hand a khorovod of active engaged feminine tsarevnas, a queen (Cleopatra), and spirits identified with water and magic, and on the other a lethargic hero.

Understanding an Operatic Plot?

Mlada introduces impossible characters, story lines, and orchestral colors. The operatic setting is an unleashed stream of phantasmagoric visions: dances of stars, temples with priests leading sacred white and black horses, a crowded world market, the seductress

Cleopatra with her female slaves, a witches' sabbath, and a final flood. The opera has a dreamlike quality, and rightfully so, since a good part of the spectacle unfolds in a nightmarish sleep with the characters acting out their dreams as if they were "sent by the gods in order to guide the actions of men."[35] The quickly changing scenes, the busy plot, the hazy margin between reality and hallucinatory visions, and music that combines vocal solos and choruses, orchestral episodes for ballet solos and scenes, and choruses "voicing" the dancing characters make the opera extremely complex. With an overwhelming and confusing plot, with endless reflections, with ideas recast from the past distorting the present and foreshadowing the future, the composer also makes a nonsinging character the title heroine of his opera-ballet. Is this a prank? Or is Rimsky-Korsakov defying operatic limits, challenging aficionados of the operatic diva? Having no voice, Mlada technically should not have a body either; she is a timeless, ambiguous, dancing shadow, projected from one's sleep. Insofar as it sees her, the audience is made to experience the hallucinogenic dreams, sexual reverie, and psychotic nightmares of poor Yaromir.

One can identify three plot elements in the libretto: a love triangle filled with consuming passion, death, and vengeance; a contest of untamed spectral forces acting in earthly and otherworldly domains, saturating the romance with a conflict between nature and magic, faith and mysticism; and a massive representation of the folk performing pagan rites and séances of exorcism. The plotlines for the most part remain nearly parallel, only at times intersecting—a flawed structure acknowledged by the composer.[36] The dramatic unfolding seems as unpredictable and capricious as the characters—their abundance, nearly incomprehensible in the frame of a single opera, could rival J. K. Rowling's endless cast in Harry Potter. Yet in typical Rimsky-Korsakov manner, a solid underlying structure and a "Wagnerian system of leading motives"[37] regulate the flood of plotlines and tableaus, and the overall tone of untamed magic.

Morrison's analysis of the intersection between operatic time and space in Sadko[38] applies as well to the masterfully clear framing of the otherwise maddening medley of fragments in Mlada. Each of the four acts is dedicated to one layer of the plot with some references to the others. The first act is given to the unresolved romantic trio, introducing Voislava at the beginning, the shadow of Mlada at the conclusion, and their beloved prince Yaromir in the middle. As the curtain rises, maidens weave floral wreaths, preparing for the celebration of the Ivan Kupala festival, which takes place at the solstice, the beginning of summer harvest.[39] Traditionally, every year, through the night till sunrise, around large fires burning in the forest and on ritualistic hills, lads and maidens sing and dance khorovods. The young unmarried women float their wreaths on the river; if a circlet sinks, the girl will lose her swain. In the opera, Voislava, surrounded by the maidens, feverishly spins a magic wheel.[40] Her first song, filled with tears and burning passion, repeats the maidens' chorus, shifting the melody from major to minor keys. Aware of Yaromir's infatuation with the deceased Mlada, Voislava gives herself as a slave to Morena, whose otherworldly power will secure Yaromir's affection. Yet when Yaromir, after a busy festive day with his bride Voislava, falls asleep, the shadow of Mlada, nocturnal like moonlight, visits him (along with Lada). In her dance, the deceased bride conveys to Yaromir how, during their wedding, her rival Voislava poisoned her. These dreams and visions vanish in the morning. The first act thus focuses on love, rivalry, and death, introducing the powerful female quartet that takes round-the-clock total control over Yaromir.

In the second act, Rimsky-Korsakov appropriately introduces and assembles a number of Slavic folk, while simultaneously establishing an equally diversified body of foreigners.[41] A string of scenes, each more colorful than the one before, includes solos and ensembles of traders; the arrival of exiled Czechs led by Lumir; a pageant of neighboring princes with dances and choruses; sacred witchery; worship of the pagan god-warrior Redegast; and finally, in an old-Slav Ivan Kupala festival, Lithuanian and Indian Gypsy dances, native khorovods, and ritualistic performances.[42] When the local Polabs join a fistfight provoked by a Novgorodian couple[43] (a century earlier, Catherine's opera featured a fistfight as the Novgorodians' favorite pastime), the arrival of Czechs escaping from German invaders[44] disrupts the hustle, bringing fellow Slavs together. A dramatic storyteller, the Czech Lumir delivers news about the German attack and pleads for help. (He is a reincarnation of Glinka's Bayan and a precursor of both Sadko and Nizhata, discussed in the next chapter).[45] The idea of Germanic occupation and marauding Teutons woven into the opera is consistent with Rimsky-Korsakov's comments on the advent of Wagnerianism.[46] Russia yielded to the musical dominance of the Germanic egomaniacal revolutionary, who, according to Rimsky-Korsakov, "took hold with St. Petersburg audiences . . . with the close of the Nineties."[47] Also, Rimsky-Korsakov, a prominent Russian orientalist, begins in this act to assemble his quasi-permanent set of foreign "guests." A Varangian and a Moor who sells Indian goods became his on-stage spectator-participants, soon reappearing in *Sadko*. The ornamented arabesque-like vocal lines of the Moor, marked *a piacere* in the score, foreshadow the character of the oriental Egyptian scene in the next act. The last scene of the second act brings on the stage the lead trio: the two brides and their beloved. The mortal Voislava aims to allure Yaromir, the shadow of Mlada dances between the two; the prince, disoriented, rushes away to his sleep.

The third act is a satanic domain of the feminine and magic. Even though Morena and Cleopatra act against Mlada, all three successfully keep the male hero possessed and paralyzed through most of the act. Mlada appears at the beginning (second scene), Cleopatra, close to the end (fourth scene). The two compete for Yaromir, both ballerinas and visions invading his psyche while he is asleep. After the fairly short first scene with shadowy spirits and a "Fantastic Kolo" on Three-Headed Mountain,[48] Yaromir appears following Mlada. Among the falling stars and dead souls in white ballet gowns[49] à la *Giselle*, he and the shadow glide about in the night skies. The two express themselves in different languages: he sings, trying to catch her shadow, and she dances, enticing him and yet moving away. The couple is a mismatch.

Example 7.2

The rest of the act is macabre, musically and pictorially the most memorable part of the spectacle. Morena, unable to get rid of Mlada, calls for a full parade of phantasmal forces: Chernobog (Black-god),[50] Kashchei, witches, the spirit of darkness, one after another trying their "charms" and powers on Yaromir. The chorus of underworld creatures, at times divided into eight parts, breathe out meaningless syllabic hexes now and again, bursting into a chain of forceful galvanizing vertical clusters, irregular, with unexpected, shifting syncopation and accents.[51] Twelve to sixteen tenors "voice" Kashchei, who according to the marking in the score accompanies "himself" on the gusli. The aphrodisiacal power of effeminate Chernobog is likewise "trumpeted" by twelve to sixteen basses singing through conical mouthpieces in throaty voices.[52] Whatever devices Chernobog uses—jumps, poses, choral whispers, screams, incantations of meaningless syllables: "Iida, Iida, kalanda, batana. Shikha, Ekhan, Reva, butz! . . . Begemot, Astarot, Shush, shush! Kopotso, kopotsam!"[53]—are to no avail (Example 7.2). The sleeping Yaromir remains out of his reach.

Astounded by his lack of success, chewing his hoof, the capricious Chernobog suddenly breaks into a confessional mode and in "his" (often a female dancer) choral voice admits that as a young man "even he" was seduced by a woman, who will be his next guest.

On the instantly changed stage, like a mirage of Fata Morgana, emerges the exotic habitat of Cleopatra and her slaves. Unavoidably referential to Naina's Persian beauties (*Ruslan and Liudmila*), they too try their charms on the immobile, mummified Yaromir, who is also attended by the shadow of Mlada. Cleopatra herself performs a solo that, as suggested by the composer, shifts from "impulsive movement" to "lazy and lingering" passionate gestures. (The ballerina who plays Mlada often also dances the role of Cleopatra, which further complicates the spectacle.) Cleopatra's dance is accompanied by sixty-four strings in unison, which like the dancer weave intricate melodic filigrees with long sustained sounds—dancing poses.[54] Subjected to the gala production, Yaromir is oblivious, untouched, impervious to frightening noises, wild dances, and the allure of Cleopatra. Indeed he turns out to be the worst spectator within the spectacle itself. In his paralysis, though present on the stage, he is thoroughly absent. A rooster's call signals the end of the night magic and the third act.[55]

The last act mixes the multiple layers. After talking to the high priest, Yaromir volunteers himself for yet another vision: a parade of three groups, matching the three-part performance of Kashchei, Chernobog, and Cleopatra in the previous act. Supposedly "positive" spirits urge Yaromir to slay Voislava, avenging Mlada's murder. When Yaromir kills his mortal bride, Morena sends wild winds, storms, and waters, flooding the land to the top of the witches' mountains, destroying everything and everyone. With little concern about the annihilation of the folk and the mortal protagonists, Yaromir and Mlada unite in the operatic finale. In the last scene of *Mlada*, the two rise above the water, greeted by the gods.[56] Meanwhile the flood disposes of the folk, who are no longer needed and thus destroyed. As in the last act of Dargomyzhsky's *Rusalka*, the stage is cleared for the magical sprites/shadows.

Shadow and Pairs

Morrison begins his essay on *Sadko* with optical terms he finds applicable to all fifteen of Rimsky-Korsakov's operas: "Kaleidoscope. Mirror. Prism."[57] The imagery of *Mlada*, even to a larger degree than *Sadko* and other operas of the Russian synaesthetic composer, involves plays of light, reflections, shadows, doubles. Mlada herself is a shadow. But a regular shadow has a source of light, as does a reflection. In life, an image in the glassy surface of a mirror or on water, as an exact repetition of an original, is an illusion. Reflection can play exhilarating and possibly dangerous games. Shadow, likewise dependent on its source, is even more capricious than reflection. It drains colors, casting darkness and distorting shapes. Not even a shadow can sap the colors from Rimsky-Korsakov's score, but it can form contrasting doubles of light and darkness, day and night, singing and dancing, elevation and descent, water and air—everything animated, changing, reversing.[58]

Mlada, with its shadows, is a domain of doubles. They obscure the plot, complicate the structure of the spectacle, direct and divert its dramatic flow, and define its musical language. They open and multiply the possibilities of interpretation. The composer employed two performing casts: full operatic and ballet troupes. The protagonists are paired. The two maidens compete for Yaromir, one a ballerina and the other a singer—night and day, spirit and mortal, smooth gliding orchestral melody and dotted, wide-leaping, desperate vocal themes. Each bride is connected with her magical assistant: Mlada and Lada belong to the dancing cast, Voislava and Morena are singers. Mstivoi is paired with the High Priest—a prince and a spiritual chief. The chorus voicing the god Redegast parallels the choruses singing for dancing Chernobog and Kashchei; two lilting couples of female and male vendors appear in the market; Moor and Varangian; the list continues. Cleopatra has no obvious counterpart in this spectacle. Her double will appear in a matching scene of *Christmas Eve*.

The characters belong to either daylight or nocturnal shadowy realms. The change from day to night becomes a critical factor in the dramatic plot. The shadow of Mlada for the most part belongs to the nighttime; Voislava seeks Yaromir's attention during the day, disappearing at night. Sleepy Yaromir leads a double life. All the events of the opera unfold in a sequence of three days and three nights, during which Yaromir experiences three types of dreams. Although night visions abound in romantic operas, the first dream of Yaromir is surprisingly reminiscent of the opening scene of Catherine II's *Fevei* (Chapter Three), which, along with other works by the empress, had been reissued around the centennial of her death (1896).[59] In Catherine's operatic tale, the title hero in his dream falls in love with the vision of a beautiful maiden, his imagined ballerina-bride dancing in the spectators' view. Yaromir may be dreaming the dream Catherine devised for her grandson. Asleep a second time, like Glinka's Liudmila,

Yaromir is transported to a magical dominion and put into a hypnotic paralysis. The apparitions of Yaromir's third night are prearranged by the high priest; in his vision the young man is attended by a delegation of princes and princesses from a remote past, forerunners of different Slavic tribes. Lacking an apparent double in *Mlada*, Yaromir can be seen as both match and antipode of Sadko, the hero Rimsky-Korsakov created five years later.

The layers of the opera are defined visually. The stage is figuratively and at times physically sliced into three horizontal levels: the upper part belongs to Mlada, Lada, the high priests, and the pagan warrior-god of the Western Slavs, Redegast, with his angelic chorus (the finale); the middle of the stage, populated by the folk, portrays their haggling, their ritualistic games, and their festivals; the lower part is inhabited by demonic forces. The story of love and death in the middle layer stirs a contest between the upper and lower domains. The divine and demonic (responsible for the love drama) use the middle layer as a battlefield, sandwiched between and infringed upon from above and below. The dancers and singers are divided into the three groups that are for the most part confined to their domains, with only a few perturbing the others' worlds. The nocturnal shadow of Mlada, seeking her beloved, materializes among the humans like a holographic image. Within this three-day, three-plane structure, all actions and characters are doubled, split, turned into reflections.

Duality in Russian music is defined by modal content. Set against everything non-Russian, foreign, and exotic, the native musical palette in the nineteenth century came to be associated with diatonic (and modal) scales and asymmetrical meters, which in *Mlada* identify the second, "folk," act.[60] The multiple *chuzhie* (strangers, aliens, possible foes)—Eastern imagery, underworld ghosts, dark spirits, and everything else extraneous to Russians and in this case their pagan Slavic forefathers—share chromatic, whole-tone, and octatonic scales, a palette significantly extended by Rimsky-Korsakov. These scales, featuring underlying tritones and augmented (whole-tone) and diminished (octatonic) triadic structures, dominate the third act. Rimsky-Korsakov ordered his tsevnitsas tuned to the octatonic scale. Spilling along the glissandi in flutes and diminished harmonies played by eight to ten lyres, with the tremolos of piccolos and the energetic pulsation of the tambourine, the whole-tone and octatonic collections manifest the alluring world of magical others.[61] The same elements also define the musical portrayal of Morena and everyone connected with her, which poses a problem for the only live Slavic tsarevna, Voislava. Non-diatonic color is an identifier of non-Russianness. It is a stain like a suspicious whisper in the communal apartments of Stalin's time—once tinted by any anti-diatonic scale, a character is unquestionably on the "other" side.

But what about Mlada? Does an air stream fit a modal scale? Is the sound of a wave diatonic? Or can it fluctuate between two musical worlds? Her short, melodious motif is spelled out in a minor triad with an added sixth, gracefully curving down. It is also an inversion of a half-diminished seventh leaning to diminished harmonies, craving for resolution, open to chromatic engulfing, yet tamed by the base that defines it within the dominant ninth, sliding through diminished chords before landing, for a brief, also arpeggio resolution (Example 7.1). In the underworld fest of the third act, as witches and serpents populate the stage spewing out short meaningless syllables, the strings and winds repeat again and again Mlada's line fused with chromaticism. Later this melodic pattern entwines quite comfortably with the theme of dancing Kashchei. Mlada is not seen on the stage, but her theme connects the beautiful ballerina with the chorus of masked witches and shaded, dark, odd figures. Is she a pristine fantasy aiming to protect Yaromir, or is she a deceitful temptress, her melody reminiscent of the rolling curved line of Saint-Saëns' treacherous Dalila, who caused the fall of heroic Samson?[62] (Example 7.3). Poetic Mlada, reminding one of Rusalka and echoing Dalila, may not be as innocent and harmless as she seems. With Mlada, the cascades of water, light, and motion, the flying arpeggios, glissandi, and chromatic runs, the ambiguous harmonies and suspended resolutions—all veil the shadow's identity and defy definition.

The heroine and the spectacle itself inspire multiple and contrasting interpretations, often embedded in music. As Yaromir first appears on the stage, he sings a happy and healthy song to Voislava. But his evenly paced, generous, long melody, directed to his bride, follows and fits the contour of Mlada's motif (Example 7.4).

Example 7.3

Example 7.4

Yaromir: Together with a decent clean hail [salute], beautiful maid, accept the gift of a youth's merriment

This poses the question of who shadows whom. Jung, who frequently writes about shadows, suggests:

> The meeting with oneself is, at first, the meeting with one's own shadow. The shadow is a tight passage, a narrow door, whose painful constriction no one is spared who goes down to the deep well.... [It is] a boundless experience full of unprecedented uncertainty, with apparently no inside or outside, no above and below, no here and no there, no mine and thine, no good and no bad. It is the world of water, where all life floats in suspension.[63]

Mlada may be Yaromir's meeting with himself. Notably, his wedding to Mlada, disrupted by her death, does not take place in "real" operatic time. It is enacted by spirits, and spectators learn about this betrothal through Yaromir's dreams. The shadow, as a visual projection of the actual subject negated by the lack of light, parallels dreams that, taking hold of us in sleep or nocturnal reverie, Freud writes, can "place us free from reality in another world and in quite another life-story."[64] Like shadows, dreams can be "complementary"[65] as well as displacing and distorting. The sleeping mind, having the capacity of "interpretation," may identify the dreamer with a specific existing person or a symbolic figure; it may also create composed and displaced images. In this context, Mlada emblemizes Yaromir's dream of himself in an alternative dream-life. Mlada can also be a projection of Yaromir's insecurities and fears of the union with forceful, sexually aggressive Voislava. Freud found an "intrinsic connection between dreams and psychosis, analogies pointing to their being essentially akin."[66]

Yaromir's ambiguous relation to his live bride (as if he fails to retain memory of her and others surrounding him), his perception of past events as if they occur in current time, and his deficient "sense of the temporal order" correspond to symptoms of a brain disease identified by a founder of Russian psychiatry, Sergei Korsakov.[67] Observing cases of this "extraordinary peculiar amnesia,"[68] Korsakov formulated the concept of confabulation (1887), the ability of a patient, unaware of memory loss, to fill memory gaps by conflating "past events in patient's life that did not happen, did not happen to him, or did not happen to him when he believes they did."[69] Around the time Rimsky-Korsakov began his *Mlada*, his namesake published and presented cases of his patients' "disorientation, particularly in regard to time,"[70] connected with amnesia and pseudoreminiscences[71]—syndromes similar to those experienced by Korsakov's operatic protagonist. Disoriented Yaromir becomes a character in his confabulated tale.

Russians certainly had their part in exploring psychosis in nineteenth-century literary works.[72] With its obsessive passions and its no less obsessive, constantly repeated theme, *Mlada* was created the same year as Tchaikovsky's *Queen of Spades*. These two operas, distant as they are, both deal with mysticism, shadows, psychotic fixation, doubles, and constantly repeated, penetrating, imprisoning leitmotifs.

Faith, Phantom, and Ego

Mlada offers an array of interpretations. A silent heroine of the operatic spectacle, she becomes a channel and embodiment of abstract music, with no words to detract from her perfection, no chatting, no vocal roulades that obscure text and no stretched vowels; all this is left to others in the opera. Inexplicable and unexplaining, a sweet seduction, the music and movement are akin to what Vladimir Jankélévitch calls *charme*. Carolyn Abbate explains:

> This word is difficult to translate because *charme* suggests an almost audible quality, a sound that comes into being and produces effects. But one must discard whatever implications either of hypnosis or niceness the word Charm may have in English, since *charme*—the summons made by enchantment, to which we react . . . , by being changed, changing ourselves.[73]

Mlada's musical line is a short melodic speck, spilling into a rain of stars or running tides. Yaromir can't hear the voice of his beloved shadow, and yet he pleads: "Tell me a word, a word of forgiveness, oh, beloved, tell me that [you] love me!" And when she "speaks"—the words of her pantomimic dance are actually written in the score—he begs her to repeat herself (Example 7. 5).

Example 7.5

Yaromir: O, repeat, o repeat, your love's confession!

When Jankélévitch writes about the enchanting interplay of music and night, he sees night "submerging all multicolored patterns into its great shadow" and music, "naturally nocturnal", capable of transposing "optic actuality into the nocturnal dimension of Becoming"[74]—"the dimension according to which the object undoes itself without end, forms, deforms, transforms and then re-forms itself."[75] Within this complex of ideas, the nocturnal shadow of Mlada may be neither maiden nor lover, but a transforming "dimension."

In his operas Rimsky-Korsakov consistently delves into different points of transition between paganism and Orthodoxy. The melody that the high priest recites in the second act recurs in the vocal exchange between Yaromir and the priest in the beginning of the fourth act. Associated with the godly realm, this theme resonates with Yaromir's first song and is thus also linked with the shadow's leitmotif, suggesting an inherent connection among Yaromir, the divine domain, and Mlada. Perhaps the spirit of Mlada—her motif fitting within his, his following hers—is a faith that guides him from within. After the trial of three days and nights, temptation by human and diabolic forces, ecstatic pagan festivals, the dreadful visit of arcane Slav spirits, and after he stabs his mortal bride, Yaromir, led by Mlada, is summoned to celestial paradise, where, father and son united, Orthodoxy absorbs paganism.

Or not. A gnostic spirit, Mlada could also fulfill her celestial mission by delivering the prince, tormented through the nights, to the skies where he belongs—Yaro-mir as Yarilo, a sun god of the ancient Slavs. Yarilo (spreading the shining light), instilling virility and strength, was imagined in various local traditions as a handsome blond youth, dressed in white and riding a beautiful white stallion.[76] Some identified Yarilo as a god of bacchanalias and debauchery, others as a patron of agriculture, procreation, and animal husbandry. A marker of Yarilo's figure was a sizable phallus. Around the time of the summer solstice, virile Yarilo, performing his mission of fertilizing the earth, had to die at Kupala to be reborn next spring.[77] Thus in the opera, Yaromir/Yarilo may be merely completing his annual cycle. Perhaps Yaromir's sexual and fertility mechanisms do not match Yarilo's potency, which leads the prince to withdraw from his bride/earth, to have visions and eventually to kill Voislava, whom he sees as the murderer of him/Mlada. He, whose amnesic symptoms intensify throughout the opera, acts under a command-hallucination. She, Voislava, is a victim of his acute psychic disorder.

Mlada's charms could also direct Yaromir to a different path. The various Slavs shown in the opera worship Redegast, who does not belittle himself by singing and, according to the score, appears high above in the clouds only at the very end. His representative, the high priest, conducts elaborate pagan rituals. In a "stentorian voice," as the composer indicated in the score, the high priest recites the god's fury with choruses of priests and priestesses resonating and magnifying his vocal line. Frightened, begging for forgiveness and for good fortune, calling the uneasy god by the endearing diminutive "Redegastushka," the folk chorus uses the same scalar motif again and again. Listening to the promises of rich offerings, the priest calls everyone to return to the temple three days later at sunset. In the final act, they reconvene at the priest's order; their ritualistic gathering ends with an apocalyptic flood.[78] The land and people are submerged in flowing water—while the violins repeat fragments of Mlada's theme merged with the descending chromatic scales that were heard in the sabbath. In the clouds above the devastated land resides the company of "blissful gods" headed by Redegast. When Yaromir ascends, with flowing ethereal passages, Lada, voiced by the chorus, greets the hero by bestowing on him the gift of happiness, love, and repose. In a caressing, "succulent," "velvety" key (D-flat major), Lada-chorus promises "tranquility and sweet dreams" while receiving Yaromir, a light-ghost (*prizrak*), forever.[79] In *Mlada*, D-flat major is the color of Cleopatra's scene and Lada's in the finale.

The basses and tenors voicing Redegast join Lada and afterwards split, echoing each other, spreading into a repetition of the slowly unrolling, ecstatic, forceful, hungry "Come!" Yaromir, after all, is a food offering to a bloodthirsty pagan god. Humanizing Yaromir, Rimsky-Korsakov opens the possibility of seeing the Kupala bacchanalia as preparation for his self-sacrifice, ever more poignant because it is wrapped into a love tale. The opera-ballet is both a reenactment of ancient rituals and a psychological case study.

Slavs, "Slava," VoiSlava . . . and Yaromir

Yaromir's alternative to union with a "godly father" above is earthly kinship to the fatherly Mstivoi, the "father of the bride," a traditional figure in Russian operas. Mstivoi fails on several accounts. His only heir is his daughter. He is unable to secure a husband for her or a son (in-law) for himself. In addition, he proves inadequate as a tsar, incapable of uniting the Slavs or extending his territory by wresting the state of Alkona from his withering son-in-law to be. A Slavic prince and ruler of the legendary state Retra, Mstivoi is the first in the opera to enter non-diatonic musical otherness. His melody, combining augmented and diminished triadic gestures, flirts with an octatonic scale (Example 7.6). Later, chromatic elements spread from Mstivoi to Voislava's vocal part, making the father and daughter musically distant from their folk.

The folk play a prominent role in *Mlada*, which would be expected in an opera by a leading composer-nationalist known for his profound understanding of folk tales, peasant songs, ancient pagan rites, and early Christian rituals. The portrayal of the folk falls into two types. The first comprises the maidens' ritualistic song, a vibrant market scene, and ethnic dances.[80] Rimsky-Korsakov also creates vivid, vocally memorable

Example 7.6

Mstivoi: (What did you promise in this fatal moment, when together we) presented Mlada with the precious poisoned wedding ring?

images of individual vendors, Lumir and his Czechs, and a variety of pagan rites. The second type continues the tradition of climactic choral "Slavas," whose abundance in *Mlada* is peculiar. In the first act, the chorus sings a "Slava" welcoming heroic Yaromir; another "Slava" is inserted in the encounter of Voislava and Yaromir, where he dotes on her beauty while she exaltedly praises Morena. In the second act, the folk choir dedicates a "Slava" to each dignitary in the princely pageant, resuscitating the "glory" many times in sustained, uneventful harmonies. Then without much of a break, a new "Slava" begins the rites dedicated to Redegast. In the final act, with the priest's affirmation of the god's good will, a triple chorus recites another "Slava" in the temple. The image of archaic Slavs happily trading, fighting, merrymaking, but also constantly kneeling, glorifying whomever they fear, willing to bargain over anything is not very appealing. The choral "Slavas" are recycled through the opera; their magnitude, rhythmic immobility, and harmonic squarishness subvert the very purpose (or at least the proclaimed purpose) of the folk "Glory" in Russian nationalistic operas.[81] These mechanical outpourings of "Slavas" may be seen as caricatures of the revered Russian nationalistic puppetry of folk representation. And the cartoonlike folk, despite so much beautiful music and dancing, go down drowning at the end.

Among the female lead characters, Voislava is the only full-blooded mortal Slavic woman. If Mlada, invading Yaromir's dream, reigns inside him, Voislava, an earthly princess and Yaromir's bride, remains extraneous to him, having to fight his dream or the shadow of his dream. Yaromir repeatedly escapes from Voislava to his Mlada, who always captures him in a shining, flawless realm inaccessible to Voislava.

But different as the two are, smooth alluring Mlada and impulsive blazoned Voislava are closely linked by music. Opening her mouth for the first time, Voislava nearly "re-sounds" Mlada's theme from the introduction, retaining the same key content (Example 7.7). Later in the same scene, her convulsive, spasmodic, burning leitmotif is yet another version of Mlada's sweet-rolling theme (Example 7.8). If the two, Mlada and Voislava, are in fact one (or perhaps mirror images?), whom and what does Voislava combat? Entering the stage for the first time, Yaromir sings a lean, smooth, rhythmically even, dignified greeting to Voislava: "Together with a decent clean greeting, beautiful maid, accept the gift of a youth's merriment." His pledge elicits a jubilant response from his bride Voislava. However, his melodic line follows the contour of Mlada's theme. The three lead protagonists are tied by the same shadowy motif that also penetrates the jungle of characters and contrasting scenes (Examples 7.1, 7.4, 7.7, and 7.8). The spectator, promised a fairytale, is instead trapped in the world of fin-de-siècle psychosis.

Yaromir's vocal part is both based on and frequently entwined with Mlada's. Melodious waves embody Yaromir as well as his dream of her—essentially himself. So arriving at the festival with a pledge of merriment, he escapes from the real girl to his somnolent reverie. Mstivoi, wishing his daughter married and satisfied, and aiming to boost Yaromir's desires and abilities, treats him with the Slavs' favorite fermented honey. The spell does not work, and neither does drink; the groom falls asleep to experience his autoerotic visions. Voislava's aggressive sexual games likewise produce no effect. In the sexually explicit kolo of the second act, when all the young couples

Example 7.7

Voislava: O, you, dark forest, inpenetrable forest

Example 7.8

Voislava: Love' s malice burned me with blistering fire, cought my heart as a snake

cuddle, nuzzle, and kiss, Yaromir gets close to Voislava three times, pushed toward her by the chorus-khorovod. But each time, the orchestra plays the theme and arpeggio of Mlada as her shadow surfaces between Yaromir and Voislava, causing him to withdraw at the last moment. His repeated refusal of any intimacy with his willing bride hurts and insults her: "O grief, shame, curse! He humiliated me, running away from me before everyone," she sings as he flees to his ethereal ballerina.

At the beginning of the third act, he soars with Mlada to celestial heights. Old Sviatokha-Morena, the mistress of all tricks and potions, administers a most radical treatment: since Voislava's charm does not arouse Yaromir, his libido has to be kindled by skillful, bewitching others—underworld creatures and Cleopatra's entourage. The instruments on the stage, including Pan's pipes and frame drums, bear sexual connotations physically and by association with ancient arts and rituals. Three waves of sweet placidity alternate with the carnal dance-attack; one dancer, then two, and finally Cleopatra herself approach the still-sleeping Slav prince. In this cascade of sound with a lulling "watery" rhythm, Rimsky-Korsakov uses his theme from *Scheherazade*, the two Oriental seductresses joining together. Enticing audiences even when played as a symphonic piece, serving as a model for Eastern musics, and offering both oral and optical pleasure, this scene of seduction leaves untouched only one spectator. Perhaps the tenor, occupied with his vocal part, catches a break before the intense final act. The Eastern beauty leaves him asleep and sexually dead. But wait: his "spirit livens and wavers . . ."—too late, a cock-a-doodle-doo signals the morning, and the vision disappears. Talking with the high priest about his everlasting love, quite surprisingly Yaromir muses about a "desired creature from a distant land," while the orchestra repeats the harp passages from Cleopatra's scene.

After another daylong cycle of encounters with the priest and nightly visions, Yaromir again faces the always desperate, desirous Voislava. Exhausted and confused between multiple dreams and realities, armed with Mlada's leitmotif he obliterates the source of destruction, his mortal bride. Liberated, Yaromir ascends to the cosmic space of eternal pleasure, where he is free from singing as well. Initially following Mlada's theme, joining hers throughout the opera, entwining with her like the flowers in a maiden's wreath, like a ritualistic zapletisia pleten', his theme leads him in the end to a silent dance in the sky, where, a beautiful Narcissus in full bloom, he embraces his libido-ego. This opera, entitled with a lovely sounding female name, is about a man, his sexual pressures, fears, failures, and spiritual substitutions, monomania, possibly his dreams of himself as Mlada (young) and Lada (good-looking). Yaromir is another hero who, for all his potency, is incapable of "positive actions in the real world." All the beautiful voices are subservient to his dreams, and all his perfectly delightful *balleting* shadows are reflections of his devotion to the only one he belongs to. The opera displays a bouquet of seductresses: the dulcet ballerina, the impassioned and seasoned

Voislava, the eternal Cleopatra, each accompanied by exotic female suites. Displaying contrasting styles, they offer themselves to Yaromir, charging the opera with sexual drive, tension, erotic potency or male impotency. The three heroines are royal women and, together with two goddesses, all form the ring or khorovod that defines him.

Mlada and *Rusalka*: A Siren Again and Another One?

"Water in motion drowns form, and night blurs its contours," writes Jankélévitch.[82] A sparkly rolling wave, touching sands, gyring gravel, leaves silhouettes only to have them redrawn by the next wave gliding over the shore, and then the next again, each delivering a line or a story immediately retold and revised. What is more enticing: the ever-changing contours, or the ever-repeated recurrent tides, or both together?

Mlada is a tale that retells itself in multiple ways; beyond the mélange of ritualistic, gnostic, erotic, scary, and psychotic stories, there is an old one with the familiar silhouette of a deceased bride, insatiable, stuck in a space between life and death, claiming her beloved. With her cascading arpeggios, trills, and smoothly flowing theme, Mlada comes from the place where the air and water blend, draped in dark velvet. A siren, a Slavic Vila, a Russian rusalka, a Sicilian ondine, and a French-Russian L'ombre,[83] Mlada is back to fetch her prince and also to retell the old story, relying on other models such as Pushkin/Dargomyzhsky's *Rusalka*. Rimsky-Korsakov had already fostered his image of rusalkas and their queen in *May Night* (1880), based on a different Gogol story (1831–32).

The first acts of both *Rusalka* and *Mlada* are about love and separation. In *Rusalka*, the love and death of the heroine are experienced on stage. In *Mlada* the romance is already history, retold in a ballet that echoes the end of *Rusalka*. The story of Mlada's death by poisoning frames the act, first raised by Mstivoi as the theme of the shadow (or the shadow of the theme) flits through his angular, anti-diatonic part, in which he curses both Mlada and his own daughter. Reciprocated by Voislava, the story returns at the end of the first act, this time replayed in Yaromir's dream, thus weaving together memory and imagination. Dreams about the past, exaggerating the sense of loss, spread a feeling of sweetly painful nostalgia.

Structurally, the folk festival of *koliada* in the second act is nearly a verbatim replay of the wedding in *Rusalka*. Mstivoi, the host of both the Kupala festival and his daughter's engagement, like the master of the wedding in Dargomyzhsky, calls ethnic dancers to entertain the engaged couple—in this case, Lithuanian and Indian gypsies. Following a wedding sequence, Mstivoi orders the maidens' khorovod. The folk celebrations are clouded by the intrusion of the ghost, an invisible, bodiless voice in *Rusalka* and a visible but voiceless spirit in *Mlada*. After the bewitching third act that seemingly veers away from the rusalka story, in the last act the ghost or a shadow of Mlada finally acquires her beloved. The ending in *Mlada* might be the least ambiguous thing in the opera. Pushkin's unfinished *Rusalka* and the ambivalence of Dargomyzhsky's last scene are resolved with full clarity and closure in *Mlada*. What a relief; the guilty party here is punished and gone. The shadow—sweet, shining, lustrous, wafted by the wind, with the water beneath her—sails through the celestial skies. The prince jubilantly joins his beloved; neither Voislava nor the thought of her overshadows his happiness.

While all this empyreal cuddling takes place above the earthly abyss, Yaromir's deceased bride down below, drawn into the fierce, foamy waters, may turn into just another ever-bridal rusalka. From the very beginning, Voislava, paired with her father (quite abusive by current Western standards, but in tune with the Miller in *Rusalka*), seems a perfect fit for another siren's magical Becoming. Like Natasha from *Rusalka*, she enters the stage longing for her beloved, torn by his coolness and breaking into tears. Her first song, a composite of Mlada's theme and the maidens' folk song, gradually submerges into the non-diatonic realm. Perhaps Voislava, as Robert Darnton argues in his semantic analysis of Red Riding Hood's literary self-consciousness,[84] is familiar with story(ies) of Rusalka. Perhaps because of her awareness of what's happening, Voislava rebels against her destiny, tries to save herself and her beloved. She refuses the urge to rush, like her prototypes in Karamzin, Pushkin, and Ostrovsky, to the dark waters. Instead, the militant, willful pagan princess attempts to change the sequence of events. Impossible—the story controls the girl.

The Miller's Natasha calls out to the Dniepr tsarina before jumping into the dark waters; Voislava gives herself to the Sea-Goddess Morena. The princess is not about to volunteer suicide, a custom of good Russian nineteenth-century heroines. Thus she has to be killed and then follow the usual course. In her last encounter with Yaromir, she frantically begins with a downward leap of a ninth, a fatal recognition: "I am here!" She confirms killing Mlada, in the heavily accented, distorted theme of her shadow-rival; she challenges Yaromir to kill her, then begs him to love her. Her gushing leitmotif, a neurotic distraught version of Mlada's, promises him happiness, love, and kingdom, and when he spews out the hateful "There is not a slave that I would not prefer to you," she offers herself as a slave. The murder of Voislava turns the opera full cycle, replaying the killing of Mlada. With one a shadow of the other, the tale of the siren or Russian rusalka ends to begin again; it interlocks with its repetition, retelling itself forward and backward.

When Voislava is done with, Morena enacts the role of vengeful rusalka by staging massive retaliation. Among the neatly divided characters belonging to one domain or the other, she is the only one who appears in two guises and has dual citizenship, remaining on stage throughout the opera, mixing with the folk in the guise of old

Example 7.9

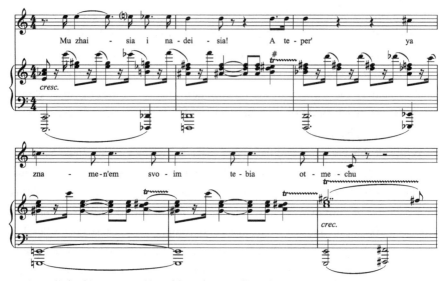

Morena/Sviatokha: Brave and hopeful! And now I will mark you with my flag.

Sviatokha and reemerging as Morena. Hers is not a dancing role and she does not have an elaborate or memorable vocal part. Her predominantly recitative-like part is filled with descending chromatic lines and octave-wide leaps downwards as if the vocal descents translate into her physical and visible association with the world below (Example 7.9). The function of Morena seems symmetrical to Lada; the two assist, double, and take the places of their respective maidens. Lada and Mlada (linked also by their names) are dancing shadows of one another. Morena acts more like a puppeteer, guiding and controlling Voislava. As Sviatokha, she offers the young princess her help and turning into Morena shames the maiden, who is terrified by the prospect of giving herself to demonic power. Like Glinka's Naina, she borrows beauty when needed—by welcoming lascivious Cleopatra.

Morena is well aware of the tale that she, a creature of the sea, an aged rusalka, may have lived once herself. Writing about old folk spirits and gods, Boris Rybakov suggests that Morena is connected with old Kupala songs about a girl drowned in a river and dissolved in nature.[85] As the only character remaining under the skies with everyone gone in the storm and flood she caused, she, the goddess of the sea, is the owner of the story and its teller—a literary persona, her identity concealed. When in the finale Lada, a speck of light, embraces the love duo, Morena destroys the temple and the city, both named and nameless characters, and merchants from far lands. With a final glottal "Ga!" all the people disappear under the water.

The deceptively exultant operatic ending, with a sweet, fulfilling love union and beautiful divine music lulling the spectators, is a trial of our common sense. Are we taken in by the finale, a moving union of two shadows that also doubles as the well-designed and executed sacrifice of a young man? The ending is in fact a magnified replay of Dargomyzhsky's last scene. There the shadowy flock of dancing water sprites takes the prince to their tsarina. The fading orchestral sounds, the rustling of the rusalkas' movement, their chilling whisper make it difficult for the audience to break into applause when the curtain falls. Here, in *Mlada*, as the sweetly poisonous shadow calls Yaromir to the sky and he, a Korsakov amnesic patient, follows voluntarily, dragged and drugged and soon comatose—the audience watches, perhaps as deluded as Yaromir. Were the image and the story of Mlada created close to our days, the hallucinogenic and ambiguous heroine could double as lulling, innocent Lucy in the Sky with Diamonds.

Did Rimsky-Korsakov fool his spectators, making them fall for a shadow with poetic moves and a heavenly sound, to be seduced by a siren, to follow forever-silenced Yaromir, to rise falling, to forget about the people—drowned Slavs—and to confuse the source with the reflection? Or was the composer himself deluded, seduced, intoxicated by the shadow who, though voiceless and thus by definition unable to seduce Odysseus, had no difficulties turning into a Siren, Rusalka, Cleopatra, or Morena? While the shadow-rusalka acquires her prince, Morena floods everyone else, the dead bride is about to come back, and Cleopatra is in the rusalka business; the opera seems to celebrate a khorovod of shadows emasculating a Slavic hero while destroying the Slavs.

It is remarkable that despite all the beautiful music the male lead acquires in the opera, the image and name of Yaromir rarely surface in musicological literature. Rimsky-Korsakov himself gave an extensive and detailed account of shortcomings in the premiere of the opera and subsequent productions and wrote about unfavorable and even hostile reviews. The opera did not inspire enthusiasm among musical critics. The composer listed multiple reasons, including the public's inability to deal with "all these gods, spirits, and devils" and its wish for drama and human characters.[86]

Perhaps the passive, dozing Slavic prince did not match the public's craving for a hero. Perhaps the sleeping protagonist also hit a raw nerve among nineteenth-century literati. Frolova-Walker (after Liah Greenfield) argues that in the nineteenth century Russian national character—read patriarchal nationalism—emerged from Russia's "existential envy of the West" via a convenient reversal of Western values.[87] However, to a larger extent the nineteenth century was also driven by an envy of the past, not the archaic distant past that nineteenth-century poets, writers, and composers had no difficulty relating to and utilizing, but more recent Russian history—the eighteenth century. Questioning their potency, feeling uncertainty toward both the West and the past, nineteenth-century Russian literati still at times acknowledged the existence and influence of the buzzing West, yet mocked and denigrated, or simply vaporized, Russia's eighteenth century. With all this, some of them found a refuge in dreams. The memorable Il'ya Il'ych Oblomov lay down "not because of necessity, like a sick person or one who wants to sleep, and not because of an accident, like one who is tired, and not because of pleasure, like a lazy man: this was his normal condition."[88]

Besides the longing associated with the age of European romanticism, Russian male protagonists and their creators were prone to mid-to-late-nineteenth-century psychosis, which, in part, reflected on the past, fictional and historical. The obsession of literati with Russia's history served as the basis of their national self-perception. The idea that their Russia had been shaped not only by Peter but more recently and more obviously by foreign female(s), haunted these men—both protagonists and their authors—who wished for Ruslans (and Olegs), often turning into dysfunctional sleeping Oblomovs or dazed paralyzed Yaromir, yet perhaps secretly hoping for the simple vision of sleeping Fevei.

8

SADKO
HE IS THE HERO!

Even after the completion of a rusalka story, with Mlada in full possession of her groom and Morena rejoicing over the flood, the swirling, swelling, untamed, murmuring waves still capture the composer, the water enchantress entices him, the story calls for repetition. Unable to resist, Rimsky-Korsakov finds an antidote to the magical maiden in the image of a fellow musician and sailor, Sadko.[1] *Sadko* reverses both *Rusalka* and *Mlada*. The hero, neither drowned in water nor allured to ethereal heights, prospers by subduing a Sea Tsarevna. Foreign and magical, she is not defeated by the Russian hero but rather, infatuated with him, willingly dissolves herself into a river. Sadko's blustery demeanor and his ties to Russian bylinas make him immune to nineteenth-century psychosis. He is a musician, a creator of songs, and a re-creator of his own destiny-by-lina, long known and sung. The composer casts the musician (and himself) as a hero; his Sadko is an artistic manifestation of national male character, energetic, drawing on his remote historical roots, enjoying female support, and free of the shadow cast by powerful heroines—historical or magical.

A hero of native epics, the title character is a virtuoso *gusliar* (a player of the gusli, a horizontal portable harp) related to several Russian musician-champions; the story of one of them, Solovei (Nightingale[2]), is recited within the opera. Russia's own Orpheus with a lyre or David with a harp, Sadko, magnifying his musical efficacy by drawing on his mythological predecessors, should be invincible in a musical match with a sea tsar-evna. Empowering his hero in an encounter with a rusalka tale, Rimsky-Korsakov relied on a team of literati—the young philologist Nikolai Shtrup, musicologist Nikolai Fendeizen, Vasily Iastrebtsev, Vladimir Stasov (long enthralled by the bylina), and Vladimir Belsky (his literary collaborator in operas to come)—to provide him with several drafts of the libretto.[3] Having yielded to feminine magic in *Mlada*,

Rimsky-Korsakov rebuffed it in this opera by interlacing the two stories, Sadko's bylina eclipsing, supplanting, and dominating the rusalka tale.

Symmetry and Women

A maritime singer, Sadko is one of two lead characters in the abundant bylinas of the city of Novgorod (New City). The other, Vasily Busalaevich, became the title character of Catherine's opera-bylina.[4] By inventing a wife for Sadko and giving her the patronymic Buslaevna, Rimsky-Korsakov suggests possible familial relations or at least a link between the two narratives.

Plentiful recorded versions of Sadko's bylina typically fall into three groups. In the first, "Meeting with the Sea Ruler," Sadko, from the Volga region, finds himself a guest in Novgorod. Whether carrying greetings from his Volga-Mother to her young brother Il'men Lake or calming the tempestuous Sea Tsar, Sadko gains sumptuous rewards from the masculine water host, who helps him win a bet with the Novgorod merchants and gain unimaginable wealth by netting golden-fin fishes from the depths of the lake. The second set of stories, "Sadko Boasting About his Wealth," or "The Argument of Sadko with the Novgorodians," pictures Sadko as a master of braggadocio, baiting the locals—"one brags of his gold, another of his steed, a silly one vaunts his young wife." Offending local merchants, not welcomed or invited to join their carousing, and thus losing his audience, Sadko regains his reputation among the Novgorod crowd after he displays gold from the bottom of the lake. With thirty-one newly acquired ships, Sadko sets off for trade and adventure. The third group of poems, "Sadko in the Underwater Kingdom," tells about Sadko the successful merchant who glides with his caravan over the sea; forgetting to pay due respect to his sea donor, he is consequently summoned to the underwater kingdom. Striking his gusli, the singer charms his angry host for a second time, and the Sea Tsar offers Sadko one of his (thirty) daughters. The wedding feast and wild dances of the water inhabitants disquiet the sea surface, and the rising squall swallows ships, taking Orthodox lives. St. Nicholas,[5] appearing to Sadko in a dream or vision, orders the musician to break the golden strings of his instrument to stop the sea storm. On Sadko's wedding night, the saint in several versions of the story advises him to neither kiss nor embrace his wife.[6] In the morning, Sadko wakes with his feet in the water (a sexual connotation?); the daughter of the sea ruler has turned into the Volkhova river running by the walls of Novgorod.[7]

The sailor's wedding in the wild water kingdom is central to the story, but his choice of bride and her identity vary. She may be the first or the last in a procession of the Sea Tsar's daughters, the most beautiful or the least attractive. She is insignificant and hardly discernible among her sisters, who marry mighty seas and give birth to streams and springs. She can also be a rusalka, "a tsarevna or a maid, or someone else, . . . a passing personage."[8] The role of the water bride changes in Rimsky-Korsakov's opera, in which orphic Sadko appropriates the traditional sirens' seductive voice to beguile the Sea Tsarevna Volkhova—a major character, the provider of his wealth, and his wife.

Sadko's seven scenes fall into two semi-independent parts. The first four scenes end in a massive apotheosis with resounding "Slavas" praising the victorious Sadko for fishing up the "uncountable" gold. The remaining three scenes, in which the victorious singer-sailor wins over the water kingdom and contributes a nautical route from Novgorod to the "blue ocean-sea," lead to a grand finale and another splurge of "Slavas." Typical of Rimsky-Korsakov, the sequence of scenes, their internal structure, and their external organization are symmetrical, the characters doubled. The first scene shows a fraternal gathering in bustling Great Novgorod. In the second, Sadko sings on the lakeshore as swans turn into nocturnal maidens; among them is the Sea Tsarevna, enamored with the songs and the performer. The third scene, which takes place in the daytime, depicts Sadko's quarrel with his earthly wife. In the fourth, mirroring the city crowd of the first scene, Sadko bets against the city heads, wins, and, adulated by the throng, foreign guests, and fellow entertainers, departs for an exciting journey. The fifth scene, with Sadko's ship stalled in the middle of the sea, is a transition to the underwater realm. The sixth scene, like the third act in *Mlada*, is dedicated to the exotic, entertaining, supernatural dominion, here also entwined with the ritualistic wedding of Sadko to Volkhova, the Sea Princess. The emergence of the young wedded couple from the water at the beginning of the seventh scene reverses Sadko's submergence in the fifth. The sequence of two duets, first Sadko and his siren-wife Volkhova and, immediately following, Sadko and his mortal wife Liubava, replays the second and third scenes. At the end of the seventh scene, a crowd mounts a massive celebration of Sadko the champion and the new river that opens trade routes to Great Novgorod. This finale, symmetrical to the beginning of the opera[9] and to the end of the fourth scene, completely washes away the ambiguous, feminine ending of *Mlada*.

The opera's structure, the succession and pairing of the scenes, has typically been associated with "the opposition of the folkloric and fantastic, pagan and Christian," mass and intimate scenes.[10] However, a never-mentioned and yet quite apparent factor in the scene sequence is gender, specifically inclusion or exclusion of female characters. A parade of male doubles—two city heads, two antique folk entertainers (the skomorokhs Duda and Sopel'[11]), two paternal godly-kingly figures (the Sea-Tsar and St. Nicholas), and two singers (Sadko and Nezhata)—counterbalances the profusion of female doubles in *Mlada*. *Sadko* has only two female protagonists. One, the Sea Tsarina, continues the operatic lineage of female royalty who wield supernatural power—Zlomeka, Naina, Rusalka, Morena, Mlada; the other, Liubava, belongs to a group of rather domestic, complaisant princess-wives, including

Gorislava, Liudmila, and the Kniaginia. Unlike in *Rusalka* and *Mlada*, in this opera the powerful magic heroine is conquered in the end, which allows the dominating male hero to achieve patriarchal happiness with his submissive earthly bride. In *Sadko*, the rest of the women constitute faceless female choruses: swan-maidens, naiads dancing in the water kingdom, and women joining the folk chorus in the fourth scene after the city space has been established as fraternal in the opera's all-male opening first scene.

Women are physically absent in the scenes that begin the two halves of the opera. In the first scene, Nezhata, a young singer and gusli player from Kiev, a trouser role, contributes *his* powerful contralto to the massive male ensemble. The scene in the middle of the sea, with no women on stage, ends with the short call of the invisible Volkhova, evoking the images of bodiless Rusalka and voiceless Mlada. Introduced in the amorous second scene, Volkhova is not seen again until Sadko's arrival at the sea bottom, even though her sublime incorporeal voice both guides Sadko and foreshadows her own dissolution into a bubbling, moaning, or rippling river. Her last appearance on stage as the wedded couple arrives on shore is in fact Volkhova's poignant farewell solo—with her husband asleep. Liubava first enters the stage in the third scene, which depicts her domestic quarrel with Sadko; she is not much seen afterward. Missing the excitement of her husband fishing the gold from the river, Liubava briefly runs onto the crowded stage at the very end of the fourth scene to see him departing and to sing one painful descending musical sentence; only in the last scene does she make a timely reappearance, after Volkhova's *liquidation*.

The two heroines belong to contrasting realms and enter the stage at different times, never facing each other. With their appearance and disappearance controlled by men on and off stage, one of them is musically locked into octatonic/whole-tone magical foreignness and the other is limited scenically to her domestic space. Once away from the house, Liubava's pleading in the midst of the jubilant crowd in the fourth scene is as foreign as Volkhova's bodiless non-diatonic voice.

It is quite scandalous that before meeting lovely Liubava and realizing that the operatic hero is already married, the spectators watch Sadko falling in love with the Sea Tsarevna. Moreover, the two women cater to his desires, competing with and completing each other in their service to the champion. Torturing herself with a self-deprecating introductory song, a perfectly simple folklike melody, Liubava waits for her husband and, seeing him, immediately ventures into an exultant F minor (Rimsky-Korsakov's own "inexplicable desire for this key" brought this heroine into existence).[12] She listens to or at least is present on stage during her husband's octatonic reveries, in which he muses about Volkhova: "Am I not your groom? Are you not my bride?" Immediately afterward, learning about his "travel" plans, Liubava pleads: "If I appall you or I'm guilty of something, bury me in raw soil, don't destroy yourself." But it is

Volkhova who, four scenes later, sacrifices herself, flowing into the "raw soil" in the name of *her* husband.

Powerful Princesses Across Two Operas

Moving away from ever-brides in *Mlada*, Rimsky-Korsakov created the two doleful wives in *Sadko*. Perhaps deflowering—a detoxification releasing female sexual anxiety—decreases or eliminates danger for a man, as if a woman's aggressive relentless energy is replaced by her multiple flows. In *Sadko*, one is a water creature finally turning into a river; the other spills constant tears. The champion himself makes a good pun of it when, lulled to sleep by one wife becoming a river during his sweet dreams, and waking up with the other, he questions, in manly fashion: "Who is crying here, like a pouring river?"

As if compensating for *Mlada*, with a male protagonist swayed, hijacked by mighty heroines, the composer made *Sadko* a distorted upside-down reflective mate of his opera-ballet. His Volkhova, uncharacteristically for a rusalka, behaves not as a dreadful temptress but as a magical donor. The roles reverse. Instead of enticing her victim, she, herself seduced, makes poor ridiculed Sadko a wealthy man and turns his dream of thirty-one ships and adventurous journeys into reality. When her fearsome father summons Sadko to the bottom of the sea, Volkhova, like Vassilisa the Wise, a daughter of the sea from another tale, abandons the safety of her environs to rescue her beloved. (But Vassilisa's tale ends with the wedded couple living ever happily together.)

Mlada, clinging like a traditional rusalka to Yaromir, carries him away from his folk; Volkhova, by contrast, delivers Sadko to the shore and to his people. Mlada takes her chosen away from his earthly bride; Volkhova leads her favorite back to his mortal wife. In contrast to the merciless flood orchestrated by Morena, Volkhova turns into a generous river; the Sea mistress Morena destroys all the people, while her relative the Sea Tsarevna supplies the Novgorodian fraternity with a better opportunity for doing whatever they do (drinking, fighting, boasting before one another, oppressing their women . . .). And yet, beyond all revisions and reversals, Volkhova is both a soft caressing rusalka and Mlada's twin.

However contrasting their actions may seem, their musical portraits offer some surprises. Morrison suggests that, flowing onto the stage with her naiadic consort, "Volkhova's hypnotic vocalize on a single vowel . . . recalls the ornate solos of the star soprano of Léo Delibes's *Lakmé* (1883)"[13] (Example 8.1). Perhaps it does. Volkhova's melodic phrases may also be Rimsky-Korsakov's "misspelled" enharmonic invocation of Wagner's Tristan chord (F, G-sharp, B, D-sharp), which is associated with unrequited love and desire. But most important, Volkhova's very first and oft-repeated rolling short arpeggio (E, G, B-flat, D, C-sharp/D-flat) is the opening of *Mlada*, which

Example 8.1

Example 8.2

introduces the theme of its ballerina (Examples 7.1 and 8.2). These two nearly identical arpeggios serve as the melodic and harmonic impetus for the rhapsodic waves that define the two heroines. The absence of words, and the open vowel in Volkhova's part, is a reminder of Mlada—her primary self as a wordless, ethereal ballerina. Morrison cites Rimsky-Korsakov's letter to Vladimir Belsky: "During the chorus of naiads, my Sea Princess vocalizes on the letter *a*. To new shores!!!"[14] But a meaning of the sentence may escape him. It is Mlada the composer welcomes to his new opera.

Mlada/Volkhova signifies yet another return of a rusalka, who in *Sadko* is tamed to fraternal delight; Volkhova's open *a* re-sounds not only the introduction to *Mlada* but also the flood thrown up by Morena, and the aerial arpeggio at the very end. The link (if not identification) between the heroines triggers cognitive musical associations across the two operas. Exploring Russian "harmonic sorcery" and focusing on Rimsky-Korsakov's use of the octatonic scale in the second scene of *Sadko*, Taruskin writes about "something extraordinary" that the composer does by "yielding an octatonic configuration in which the first interval is the tone rather than the semitone." Analyzing Rimsky-Korsakov's manipulation of modal facilities, Taruskin suggests that the whole tone is "much more useful melodically, since it was constructed far more like a diatonic mode. The scale beginning with the half step starts off as in the Phrygian mode. . . . The scale beginning at the second degree [the tone] . . . is congruent with the diatonic (i. e., minor) scale until the fifth degree is reached."[15] The same astute planning underlies the configuration and inversion of the chord that defines Mlada, Voislava, and Volkhova. Mlada's theme, introduced in the orchestral opening of the opera, follows the first inversion of the E half-diminished seventh, which accentuates the minor triadic base and, briefly sliding into a belated diminished triad, "cleanses itself" in a major triadic conclusion that matches the last descent to the upper C with a sustained C in the bass. Thus the chromatic diminished and half-diminished melodic waves ornament the underlying simple move from dominant ninth to the "watered-down" tonic. This is Mlada, a rusalka appearing as an innocent nocturnal shadow (Example 7.1). Voislava starts her neurotic dotted arpeggio flight with the first inversion of an E minor ninth chord (with a missing seventh), or alternatively the first minor triadic inversion. But she gets trapped in a diminished seventh; with a diatonic harmonic base held for some time, her vocal line, saturated with tritonic and diminished moves, expresses anguish rather than the otherworldliness of Mlada. Hence her introductory song keeps open the possibility of leaning toward either diatonic or non-diatonic domains, with the unresolved long-hanging diminished harmony at the end of her phrase (Example 7.8). In both cases, the line between diatonic and non-diatonic seems evasive, tricky, misleading a native listener accustomed (at least theoretically) to recognizing a clearly distinguished Russian musical "us" (diatonic) and foreign or magical "others" (non-diatonic).

Volkhova, who also reveals her ability or desire to fit a diatonic frame, in her first siren song is an unmistakably translucent, marvelous "stranger." Her prolonged wordless "Ah" is a zone of harmonic exoticism; swinging in the waves, washed in diminished orchestral "splashes," she herself repeats her half-diminished and augmented rises, followed by a chromatic descending gesture.

Although it is Volkhova who shines with the colors of all three heroines of *Mlada*, in *Sadko* the enticing and irresistible rusalka's song belongs to a male singer. Before dredging gold from the Il'men, he nets the royal water maiden, who affirms the reversal of their roles: "Your wondrous song captured my heart."[16] Introduced with a melody reminiscent of Mlada, Volkhova at this point changes her tune to a descending scalar melody with rolling triplets that echo Yaromir's impassioned appeal to his imaginary beloved.[17] Belonging to different operas, Yaromir and Volkhova are linked by their destiny, one ascending into the skies and the other turning into streaming water.

With the title character a bigamist whose two wives are used and forgotten, dismissed and dissolved, and with the fraternal crowd acclaiming him a national hero, Rimsky-Korsakov's *Sadko* may be the champion of misogynistic operas (although the competition is tough and there are plenty of candidates). But so profuse is the traditional operatic addiction to dolefully sacrificing female leads that *Mlada*, a challenger of this trope, has rarely been touched by researchers, the pairing of the two operas lost.

". . . Beware of the Charm"[18]

The traditional role of siren—sea sprite, singer, and seductress—in the course of the opera shifts to the title hero: a victim turned into a victor, a siren into a wave. Disquiet. Roiling sweltering water, attacking the sturdy, massive rocky waterbed and there breaking into sparkles; the waves race one other, licking the sand with large rasping tongues or swallowing it all, the stones, gravel, sand, and, suddenly running away, leaving little puddles afterwards—this is *Sadko*.

The opera opens with a nocturnal current; its leisurely harmony mixes diatonic and chromatic modes. In the beginning of the first scene, Nezhata plucks his gusli and sings an old heroic bylina about the Kievan champion Volkh, born in the blue sea. As he recites verses about stirring waters, about fish hiding at the bottom of the sea and birds high in the sky, running passages in violins followed by murky tremolos entwine with an arpeggio of harp and piano.[19] The pacified, glossy surface of water is what Sadko pictures later in the same scene when he dreams of his "necklace of ships."[20] Ever-changing, like an oral tale, water pervades this opera, but three scenes are devoted to it completely. The second takes place by a lake, the fifth portrays the ships on the sea, and the sixth is submerged in the azure waters.

What happens if, in the ebbing twilight, alone at the place where the forest meets the water surface, you, like Sadko, see a graceful swan (or a small duckling) riding lightly on the top of the wave or swimming into the shadow? Is it a promise of nocturnal magic, or danger, or nothing at all?

> Whoever looks into the water sees his own image [and Jung here is not mistaken about the gender of the looker], but behind it living creatures soon loom up; fishes, presumably, harmless dwellers of the deep—harmless if only the lake were not haunted.[21]

A young, ambitious, and unappreciated singer ridiculed by his drunken pals runs away in despair through the forest to the glittering waters—soft, widespread, sustained harmonies, the wind running downward and then upward through diminished arpeggios, then a slowly moving line in low strings setting the sound frame to be filled with an octatonic scale. In this secretive site full of shadows, the musician sheds tears, waking the lake, begging for a kind listener.

Young singers in various times and places have trained their voices on lakes, rivers, seashores, and mountains. Albert Lord wrote about learning to sing in the mountains during winter as a second phase for a singer-in-the-making.[22] The popular Soviet Azerbaijan bel canto Muslim Magomayev once revealed that he developed his voice by singing against the wind and the oily, riotous waves of the Caspian Sea. In any case, Rimsky-Korsakov's champion appears to be a lucky one, because with the light wind created by the strings, the trills (in the winds), and slow magical dotted octatonic rises, the lake is awakened. A flock of white swans, evoking the twenty-year success of Tchaikovsky's *Swan Lake* (1877), lands on the shore, turning as expected into beautiful maidens. The Sea Tsarevna is touched by the singer's song, whether finding his voice pleasant or simply feeling pity for a young handsome lad. She herself is a superior singer. Arriving, she ventures into a chain of flawless melodic filigree, framed by a harmonious maiden chorus echoing her voice with harp glissandos in the background. The sequence of Volkhova's phrases folds itself in melodic pairs of diminished and augmented arpeggios, curving like caressing waves.[23] Praising Sadko, she teaches him to sing beyond the ordinary diatonic palette. His stupefaction as he falls off the keys and slides within the tritone—"Marvel marvelous, wonder wonderous"—entices her.[24] Soothing the hero, she asks him for a different joyful song.

The perfect prescription for one aiming to win an audience or to get a girl is to begin with a sad Russian *protiazhnaia* (a type of traditional lyric song) and then break into a fast khorovod to engage graceful maidens in their favorite round dance. These two songs, representative of the Russian folk repertoire, should be delightfully exotic to Volkhova, who, both oriental and magical, is even more musically foreign than the foreign guests in the opera.[25] So while she is alien to him and supposedly to the operatic audience, he is alien to her. He is in her terrain. The waves shimmer in a harmonic sequence that Taruskin terms "triadic octatonicism";[26] she, in his element, sings for a short time in a diatonic frame. His songs are short—less is more. Proving the rule, by the end of the second couplet she enters his khorovod song. The two express divergent thoughts in matching tunes: his third verse pictures azure waves, moving, splashing, and whispering; she sings about a wreath of flowers she makes for a young man. Sadko promptly sends the Tsarevna's girlfriends away into the forest so as not to disturb the "good youth with a darling maiden."

The whole scene exemplifies Rimsky-Korsakov's mastery in displaying the mechanics of operatic falling in love. It begins with Sadko singing; intrigued, Volkhova sings back to him, then he sings at her request, and she weaves her own song into his. Afterward the two are ripe for a duet, so the third number in the scene immediately transports the couple into the "dark, warm, scarlet"[27] D-flat major (Example 8.3). He leads, and she, as if memorizing each sentence, repeats it four measures behind. The two four-measure well-balanced periods, with her following his tune, end with them singing together. The second time around, she begins and he happily repeats after her the melody she learned from him. Within the duet, she performs another brief solo, reciting the fatal admission that his song has captured her heart. Here is another example of Rimsky-Korsakov's astounding manipulation of diatonic–non-diatonic interlacing. Although Volkhova's melody appears perfectly diatonic, consisting of two two-measure sequences with the orchestral part also quite diatonic, the melody also hints at augmented elements (G-sharp, E, B-sharp and E, C, G-sharp; Example 8.4).

Example 8.3

Sadko: Your honey-braid shines with the dew, like pearls glow. Who are you, maiden? Who are you, marvelous beauty, who?
Sea Tsarevna: Sounding strings, artful fingers of yours. My darling, you! Tall, clean, and handsome!

Example 8.4

Sea Tsarevna: Your wonderous song captured my heart

Sadko breaks through her long-sustained sound with the much-repeated descending scalar line (within the tritone), now shifting the rhythm as he proclaims, "You I love and will love for ever!"

In the next episode of the duet the distance between the two shrinks. She begins and he rushes after her, following just a tad later in a tight canonlike episode, the two again aligned in jubilant D-flat. Now at the central point of the duet and the scene, suddenly the strings pulsate; the flutes and clarinets repeat the vocal melodies. The orchestra expands its rich palette of timbres, glittering in soft tremolos of magical widely spaced non-diatonic harmonies, when Volkhova sings yet another solo. She tells who she is, stripping all that was diatonic or semi-diatonic—everything that compromises her watery identity—instead reciting the full octatonic scale (Example 8.5).

After this self-revealing solo, Sadko and Volkhova complete their duet, both swearing mutual devotion. He briefly recalls: "I am married on land, but I will drop everything, to be with you," getting himself into another hollow tritone. Immediately the orchestral soundscape swells with non-diatonic, rising, running passages of two harps, as the flute, clarinets, and violins alternate, invoking the vocalize of Volkhova—an

Example 8.5

Sea Tsarevna: I am Volkhova, Tsarevna, daughter of the Sea Tsar the Great and Tsarina Vodianitsa the Wise

echo of Mlada's motif. Receiving Volkhova's magical "golden fish feathers" and accepting her vow of devotion and support, Sadko sees her departing at sunrise after she has saved him for the first time from her briefly appearing father, the Sea Tsar.

Was Volkhova there, or was it merely the deceptive, murky surface of the lake, a mirror that hides its depth? Referring to the old Russian tradition of calling a magic spirit or a beloved one in a mirror or in glassy water, Morrison suggests that "the Sea Princess' voice is a magic mirror in its own right."[28] Did Sadko listen to someone, or was Volkhova's voice just an echo in the night air, carrying his voice far and bringing it back, changed? Was he bemused by his own voice? Or perhaps the tipsy singer just fell asleep and heard the song in his dream.

By inventing this scene with the Sea Tsarevna, Rimsky-Korsakov changed the dynamics of the first two groups of Sadko bylinas. He imbued the old heroic epics with both a quintessentially nineteenth-century love story and his usual ambiguity. If there was no encounter, everything between the second and seventh scenes is Sadko's dream; he becomes the dozing twin of Yaromir, though not quite. Falling asleep at night after an upsetting evening, he awakes cuddled by his wife Liubava, who after the drunken party searches for her husband and finds him—not twelve years later but the next morning. Waking up, he becomes aware of the gift, the best gift a singer/composer can dream of: a new song that brings him instant success and stardom.

And if there was a magical encounter, was it a love scene or a competition between two mythological divas? So absolute and flawless is their duet that neither composer nor champion dares to complete what Orpheus did in his encounter with Siren. He learned her dangerous song and imitated her well; the copy worked better than the original. She, the Siren listening to Orpheus instead of killing sailors, herself plunged into swirling waters and drowned. But it is not the right time for Rimsky-Korsakov's tsarevna. By the end of the second scene, Volkhova has only stroked the ego of her favorite. The mistress of the marine kingdom has yet to confer high social status (as a hero, champion, legend) and most important to bestow on him unimaginable wealth to realize his most ambitious dreams while serving his state and people! Her siren-like disappearance in water comes later.

And good riddance to the sea creature, whoever she is, the doubly foreign Volkhova or the German rusalka! Well, Sadko might not be quite Russian either.

Does Sadko Know Who He Is?

The idea of Russia's historical ties to (if not ownership of) mythological, Orthodox, and Ottoman Greece, as discussed early in the book, thrived in eighteenth-century imperial operas. Linking his protagonist to classical, Eastern, and native mythology,

Rimsky-Korsakov crafts a late-nineteenth-century Russian prototype of the ultimate poet-musician. The association of Sadko with Orpheus enables him to appropriate not only the mythological laurels of his Grecian counterpart but also the operatic history of Orpheus in early European operas.[29] Besides his orphic identity, Sadko bore other streaks of non-Russianness—some recorded bylinas, for instance, refer to him as "a merchant from rich India."[30] Stasov, who took an active part in both of Rimsky-Korsakov's *Sadko* projects, drew a parallel between Sadko's submergence in the water kingdom and similar nautical adventures of several figures in Buddhist poems.[31]

The Indian theme surfaces in the opera in several seemingly isolated references and episodes. In the first solo number, Nezhata recites a ballad about Volkh, a champion whose birth to a Russian princess and an all-mighty snake-father caused the earth to tremble and shook the Indian Sea. "And when Volkh will reach twelve years," Nezhata continues, mixing tenses, reversing the time sequence, "gathered he a brave army and advanced to the famous Indian kingdom." Entranced by Nezhata's bylina, the folk chorus fills in details not mentioned in the singer's verses, intoning about Volkh's ability to turn himself into a wolf, a wild ox, and an eagle; Nezhata sings about Volkh's reign over an Indian kingdom, perhaps alluding to legendary Alexander and his conquest of India (*Alessandro nell'Indie* and *Slaviane*). Thus Nezhata's bylina implies familial ties between Volkh and Sadko, thus linking the three heroes. His tale about Volkh, the namesake of Volkhova, connects Sadko and the Sea Tsarevna before either enters the stage. While passing references to India surface in several places, the bearer of eastern imagery is an Indian guest, a singer, according to Taruskin, whose Russian roots stem from Serov's opera.[32] He is apparently Sadko's major rival—his song became by far the most independently popular number of the opera.

In addition to Greek and Indian connections, Russian Sadko or Satko,[33] according to a number of researchers, may be of ancient Jewish origin (Tsadok). Smirnov and Smolitskii suggest that the singers of bylinas would not have known the old Jewish name, an obvious mismatch to the image of the hero.[34] Indeed it is impossible to imagine Russians venerating a Jew as their national champion. Nevertheless, a Jewish contingent played an important role in ancient trade routes connecting Central Asia, Russia, and Europe. There is also another association. In the fourth scene, the group of old *kaliks* (sacred minstrels) ventures into a quite sudden incantation of fragments from the *Golubinaia kniga* (The Verse of the Dove Book[35]). A container of mystical wisdom, the book that fell from the stormy skies is incomprehensible to the folk and could only be interpreted by King David, a historical singer and harp player also equated with the champion of Novgorod.[36]

With these distinguished musical pedigrees, high ambitions, a ringing tenor, and good tunes, Sadko, entering the stage in the first scene, curiously receives no appreciation for his talent. Instead he finds himself a target of mockery and jeering from the same throng that reveres Nezhata's tale, enjoys the songs and jokes of skomorokhs, and later attentively listens to the singing of mystic pilgrims and foreign guests. Tales, songs, and stories saturate the opera; the stage is like a song festival attended by a wide-ranging variety of performers: singers, jesters, choruses, foreign travelers, old, young, drunk, sober. It's as if Rimsky-Korsakov's own pals from different times and intellectual circles gathered to perform in a *kapustnik* (from *kapusta*, cabbage), a theatrical hodgepodge of mocking songs and skits beloved by the Russian intelligentsia. Sadko, first appearing among his professional colleagues, singers and tale-tellers, despite having a marvelous vocal instrument, has nothing to say; besides his self-absorbed yearnings, there is no story for him to tell yet.

Here Rimsky-Korsakov again finds "something extraordinary," this time in the dramatic fabric of his opera. The oral Russian bylinas about Sadko had traditionally been circulated and delivered in several episodes, separate poems describing events varying in length and detail according to locale, performing lineage, and singer. Likewise in the opera, tales and fragments of tales—in genres ranging from ballades to mocking *chastushkas*, from chants to collections of nautical songs,[37] seemingly disconnected—nevertheless overlap, interact, and complete each other, like pieces of a puzzle falling into a single story, Sadko's. His story winds around him, a medley of clues planted by performers of various songs. Seemingly oblivious to others, he is the only one unaware of his own legend.

A peculiar creature, Sadko is both a teller and a tale. Rimsky-Korsakov gets to the heart of oral lore—always changing, retelling itself, ebbing and flowing like the tides. He makes his hero live a story that already exists and is performed (by others) in fragments. Nothing is more engaging than a personal narrative; but delivered by the one who lived it, the tale has already become passé, the edges smoothened, the suspense diminished, the outcome predictable. So Rimsky-Korsakov, himself a grand master of operatic tales, who in *Mlada* had three heroines enact various parts of the rusalka stories, in *Sadko* made a somewhat different dramatic decision that matched the very genre he employed. As Morrison notes, the tale "talks back to Sadko."[38] Recited by his colleagues, it guides, corrects, or steers him away, and near the end leads him to "create" the story anew—again. In other words, in the opera the bylina unfolds on four levels: recited in fragments by various singers, it is simultaneously experienced by the lead protagonist, who himself retells his personal tale, lending the composer who records and retells the story a sense of authenticity. Thus within the opera Rimsky-Korsakov replicates the very process of oral transmission. At the same time, while Sadko develops into a champion of oral tales, Rimsky-Korsakov doubles his hero by "championing" the transition from oral musical tale to composed opera.

Although Nezhata appears to know the bylina better than others, even the drunkards Duda and Sopel' are familiar with fragments of the story. Singing a mocking song about a foolish young fellow, Sopel' suddenly conducts Sadko to the Il'men' lake "to sit, to look into the depths, sing to golden fishes, earn money"—gabbing that proves providential. Volkhova, calling herself a sage, admits that her destiny is not to marry a blue sea but to wed a young lad. The fourth scene, where Sadko sets off for the voyage, is saturated with riddle tales. Nezhata's story of Volkh in India, delivered in the first scene, comes to life in the group of somber volkh warriors[39] who enter in the fourth. In the first half of the scene, the various parties, all singing their own heroic ballades and tales—the pilgrims with their mystifying *Golubinaia kniga*, Nezhata reciting praises to Novgorod, jesters invoking the bylina about Ivan Dunai (Danube),[40] volkhs proclaiming their transformative power—unite in a sort of psychotic chorus, pushing the story forward by reciting fragments of similar stories, foretelling events in the opera, and joining in anticipated glory. In the middle of the fourth scene, Sadko plays his trick by fishing up Volkhova's gold, and the crowd, entranced by Volkhova's chromatic slides and splashes, bursts into the expected choral "Slava." With his skill as a taleteller, Nezhata immediately makes a song, this time not a bylina but a fairy tale about the Nightingale, another Novgorod champion and singer who defeated the Sea Tsar. Nezhata's story arches back to the opening bylina about Volkh and also corrects the detour that Sadko eventually makes in his story by encountering the Sea Tsarina instead of the ruler of the ocean-sea.

The opera is thus an encyclopedia of bylinas, each a lesson for Sadko on his journey. Danube's bylina, for example, tells about a champion who finds his match in a woman warrior: "Defeated the first time they met, she, a Lithuanian Princess, wins over him as a woman" and becomes his wife. Later, bragging about himself as the first among heroes, Dunai challenges her to a fighting contest. When she wins, he shoots her dead and then himself, their bodies transforming into two rivers.[41] Their tournament parallels the song contest between Sadko and Volkhova; the allusions to Dunai forebode the end of the Sea Tsarevna, the champion's foreign wife. The name of Ivan Dunai, consistently evoked by jesters, is a covert coded message for Sadko.

The threads of allusions, subplots, and striking models for dealing with powerful or magic female tsarevnas are also woven into the songs of foreign guests: a Varangian, an Indian, and a Venetian.[42] This trio of guest consultants on Sadko's journey evokes a metaphor common in Russian fairy tales—a three-way intersection leading to death, challenges, or victories.[43] Like multiple Ivan-the-fools or Ivan Tsareviches, Sadko has to choose the direction of his journey. Shall he go to the unwelcoming waters of the Varangian, who, born near a severe sea, worships the (Wagnerian) Wotan? Or will Sadko be seduced by the sweet exotic aroma of an Indian song describing an ocean full of uncountable diamonds and inhabited by the "Phoenix bird with the face of a maiden and the voice that makes everyone forget"—another siren? Perhaps Sadko prefers the West and the free city Vedenets (Venice), praised by an

Italian merchant in a Russian-like tune with a typical wide native 6/4 meter. The Venetian's verse is about the free city. Its ruler, the Doge, weds the azure sea, the wedding symbolizing his marriage to the republic.[44] In the refrain, with a gliding-dreaming *barcarolle* accompaniment, the Venetian sings about their Sea Tsarina, above whom his "beautiful city reigns." Not only to study bel canto on Italian shores and not only because the Venetian's song is musically close to his own, but because of the tale about the tamed tsarina "kindly" ruled by the city, Sadko steers his naval caravan toward Venice.

Surprisingly, in the remaining parts of the opera there is a gap of twelve years and not a peep about which shores Sadko reached during this clearly established time frame. Did he even leave the lake?[45] In his introduction to the score, Rimsky-Korsakov remarks that his hero could travel toward the "far seas" only through the Volkhova River. But the river isn't there yet![46] Perhaps, like his counterpart in *Mlada*, seduced by the beautiful chromatic melody of their magical encounter, Sadko is merely asleep, his dream (unlike Yaromir's) a potent one.

What we spectators watch and listen to is Sadko's ship merely stalled in the middle of the sea. Floating there while reckoning, with "typically Russian cleverness,"[47] how to avoid leaving the ship, Sadko appears confused and expresses three somewhat conflicting sentiments. In his aria he first announces that "death came to me, a good youth," but then he utters hopefully, "Tell my young wife, god's will, I will return to embrace her." A full moon rising in the skies signals the presence of magic. A few moments later, descending to the waves, as tritonic and diminished configurations infuse first the orchestral part and then his melody, he recites, "My heart feels that the time has come for our reunion [his and Sea Tsarevna's]"[48]; his melodic canvas of even, long notes suggests his submergence.

He strikes the gusli (Example 8.6). A warm wave swallows the hero. A wide, half-diminished gusli-harp[49] chord and soon Volkhova's compressed melody, with pulsating alternation of diminished and augmented triads, carry him to deep waters like the riverbed where Rusalka finally received her Kniaz. The full, shining, glittering scale of colors, embracing chromatic, whole-tone, and octatonic scales with glissandi in between, indiscriminately combines diatonic and non-diatonic harmonies, which at the end of the nineteenth century were still associated in Russian opera with the domain of the magical—and magic it is.

S(adko) Is for Siren

What makes Sadko a champion: the appreciation of his musical gift, his heroism, or the affirmation of massive choral "Slavas"? A character derived from an oral bylina, the

Example 8.6

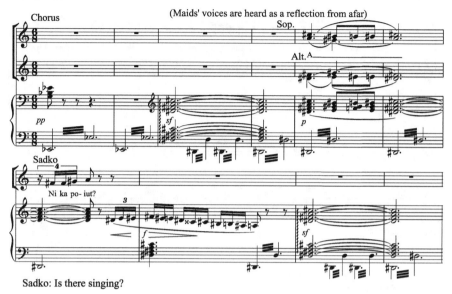

Sadko: Is there singing?

operatic hero is featured as a victor twice: first he wins his bet with the city leaders by fishing the gold from the bottom of the lake, and then when returning triumphantly from the underwater kingdom he brings to Novgorod the river Volkhova. Rimsky-Korsakov's protagonist, however, differs from his original, exhibiting a character of his own. In known versions of the bylinas, Sadko as a careless youth faces a frightful Sea Tsar, man-to-man. Staking his lungs against the all-mighty sea ruler, who can at any moment break into a swirling storm with raging waters, the singer intends to carry his tune over the crushing sky-sea.

In the opera, Sadko meets a different listener-competitor. In their initial encounter, she protects Sadko by warning him about the arrival of her father. Four scenes later, when Sadko is in the water kingdom, she disarms the fury of her parent, who, seeing Sadko, bursts out in a series of rising octatonic scalar fragments, each within the frame of a tritone. The violas repeat the song of the Sea Tsar; his voice and their racing lines overlap, recreating enduring octatonic waves rolling one after the other, with a long drone in low strings and bass clarinet. Changing melodic direction, the Sea Tsar enunciates in crisp slow motion the full length of the octatonic scale downward (Example 8.7), and when the orchestra, echoing him, gradually expands to full sound and arrives at a trembling augmented harmonic cluster, Volkhova—not Sadko—responds by echoing her parent's scale in a soothing, wavy melody. The fierce, yet loving, tsar-father suppresses his rage and fulfills his daughter's wish, ordering the musician to sing. Afterward the wedding celebration commences.

Example 8.7

Sea Tsar: Goi, the merchant, rich guest,
Many years you ran over the sea
[You] Did not pay me my due,
I waited for you, Sadko, for twelve years
Now you yourself came.

Invented because the composer undoubtedly needs both a good soprano and an amorous line, Volkhova transforms the bylina's champion. Setting the scene for his discussion of Orpheus and sirens, Jankélévitch writes:

> A woman who persuades solely by means of her presence and its perfumes, that is, by the magical exhalations of her being, the night that envelops us, music, which secures our allegiance solely through the Charm engendered by a trill or an arpeggio, will therefore be the object of a deep suspicion.

All is present: a woman, perfume, an enveloping night, music—"Charme!" So the water creature Volkhova allures the hero into a different tale, of a water sprite, a naiad, a siren, an aerial Mlada. Escaping from the city into a magical reflective lake, Sadko navigates himself into a story that should be finished not in the glorious fourth scene but in the following fifth, with the hero drowning in a flowing world of magic, embraced by his loving rusalka—Jankélévitch's "incantatory action of enchantment upon the enchanted in the form of an illicit relocation of the here-and-now to the Beyond."[50]

Sadko appropriately goes down, but this rusalka's story has a different finale. Its male protagonist is triumphant on at least three accounts. First, he survives the ordeal and returns from the place that proved fatal to all his predecessors in operas, folk tales, and literary stories—an army of princes, knights, and handsome village guys lulled by sirens into eternal sleep at the water's bottom. Second, *Sadko* becomes the spectator's goggles into a magical world that the Russian Orthodox folk knew about but did not dare to visit. The operatic portrayal of the rusalkas' domain was sketchy even in Rimsky-Korsakov's own *May Night* and Tchaikovsky's *Slippers*. Third, not only does Sadko enjoy himself down in the sirens' element, letting his spectators peek into a daunting terrain beyond human reality, but he returns to the shore, bringing two indispensable trophies: the river-wife and his own ingenious song, lived through and thus authentic.

What enables the hero to survive a rusalka's love and his visit to the water bottom is his musicianship and his character. Enchanted and himself enchanting, operatic Sadko exhibits in the presence of the Tsarina not a hint of the aggressiveness he exudes toward his earthly wife and even to his fellow citizens. Just the opposite: his songs are plaintive or cheerful according to the wish of his majestic audience in the water kingdom, his manner appeasing, his performance yielding and accommodating. For example, after the Sea Tsarina pacifies her parent at the beginning of the sixth scene, Sadko ventures into a *velichal'naia* or praising song to the Sea Tsar, revising the tune just sung by Volkhova in a diatonic fashion. However, offering a contrast to the splashing, intricate non-diatonic sound, he compromises. His vocal part, though diatonic, permits chromatic orchestral coloring. Sandwiched between Volkhova and her father in several trio episodes—all three accommodating each other's individual musical space and all introducing some flexibility—he seems comfortable with submersion in diminished harmonic sequences (Example 8.8).

Not a boisterous adventurous youth is he, but a smooth rusalka/siren. As such, by appropriating both the rusalka's song and her role, he becomes more dangerous than endangered.

Example 8.8

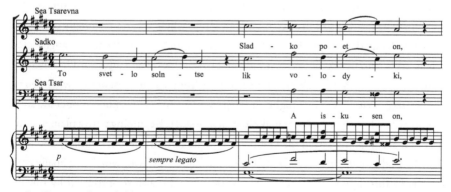

Sea Tsarevna: Sweet is his song,
Sadko: There is the ruler's face, light as the sun,
Sea Tsar: Skillful he is,

In the sixth scene, with oceanic majesties and wondrous sea inhabitants, there is also a wedding composed of several musical-dramatic layers: (1) folk songs and dances; (2) a nuptial ritual associated with a chorus of maids weaving flower wreaths, a wedding song, and dancing vignettes; (3) kingly splendor represented by trumpets playing on stage (behind curtains), a procession, and regal titles; (4) the "Slava" that Sadko sings to the sea ruler at the beginning of the scene and that the chorus repeats at the end; and (5) the magical realm that colors everything in the scene.

When Sadko returns from his exciting journey with Volkhova, the situation with the two wives resolves itself with the libretto's retreat to the bylina's path. In the bylina, the fact that the river-wife turns into water is logically consequential. The Sea Tsar hands Sadko one of his many daughters or maids in appreciation of the singer's musical talent. There is no love and no acquaintance between the wedded *étrangers*. By becoming a river, the bride fulfills a practical purpose for a singer-sailor and simultaneously attains (or rather, reverts to) her primary form. Rimsky-Korsakov's Sea Tsarevna, by contrast, is a lead heroine and a regal heir; the opera, imbued with the romance of Sadko and the Sea Tsarina, celebrates their marriage, confirmed by ritualistic, folk, and mythological elements. Although the question of bigamy troubled or at least concerned the team of literati pondering the libretto, neither they nor later critics questioned why the tsarevna, who requested and praised Sadko's loyalty, who waited for him for years and was jubilant about their union, suddenly ventures into a farewell song and afterward dissolves. In the end, Volkhova is not a siren who, outsung by Orpheus, in her outrage commits suicide by falling head-first into water. She is Sadko's wife, his generous benefactress, his supporter.

What happens on the wedding night is typically left out. In the opera, a gondola driven by swans carries the wedded couple over the glossy lake; the two utter several fairly brief amorous phrases, and the rest is obscured by nocturnal mist, veiled by the equipage's "closed drapes,"[51] and hushed by the rolling waves. In the rising sun, Sadko, perhaps exhausted, is sound asleep; Volkhova, overwhelmed and seemingly converted into a perfectly diatonic realm, sings a lullaby. Gradually, diminished and augmented triads, trills, and octatonic waves invade first the orchestra and afterward her melody. Whether faced with the inability to survive away from her element or overwhelmed by the sexual activity of the first night, she sings her last powerful solo—as operatic soloists do even while they expire or make love on the stage. Beginning with a plain melody and thin accompaniment in the first part of the lullaby, the heroine, audibly and even visually in the score, is overtaken by the increasing waves, with which she finally converges. In this liquid opera, sexual ejaculation may be well reciprocated by the all-consuming orgiastic flow into which the Tsarevna is drawn . . . passing on to her beloved her rusalka's sexual libido.

Perhaps tired by the laborious marriage adventures, Sadko wakes up on the shore and has a relatively brief private reunion with Liubava before the folk populate the stage. The chorus sings about Sadko's thirty-one ships sailing down the new river. At that point, the musician addresses his audience by retelling a bylina in the third person, conveniently adjusting his story: "For his song, the Sea Tsar gave Tsarevna Volkhova to Sadko-the-merchant." Astounded by multiple miracles—the river, Sadko's return with wealth and a song—the throng begins to repeat Sadko's words and comment on his accomplishments. Then Nezhata, leading the chorus of fellow entertainers and supported by the folk chorus, retells Sadko's story: "Knowingly with his song, Sadko snared the whole deep river for Novgorod's glory." Identified as a champion, Sadko formally greets the city and the people and sings his song.

For a musician, the most precious prize is a song/bylina—whether the product of his exciting journeys or his imagination—and a good night's sleep. Rendering a wide free-flowing melodic canvas in his "parlando-singing,"[52] he tells not about distant Nightingales, Volkhs, and other heroes but of himself and his adventures. Full of pride, Rimsky-Korsakov calls his hero's recitative an accomplishment of "an unheard of degree,"[53] and Sadko, having looked at himself in the water like Narcissus, recounts "far lands, beasts and birds coming together, grass and tree leaning, *tsarevna*s gathering" to hear his ringing songs. All the singers on the stage bow to the song champion. The Indian confesses that "the Phoenix's song is a mighty one, but Sadko's voice is sweeter." The pilgrims praise God, and the Russian champions Duda and Sopel' magnify segments of the singer's story. The folk chorus wraps the scene into an endlessly resonating "Slava" to the champion, the city, its saint protector, the Volkhova river (which like the sea in far Venice obeys the city and not the opposite), and the seas with the Sea Tsar locked in "dreary dreariness."

A "Glory" (Slava) must perpetuate glory, with no clouding questions and with all inconsistencies erased! How else to explain this permeation of choral "Slavas," from one scene to the other, from one opera to the next, repeated like an old broken record stripped of any comprehensible meaning, perpetuating some subliminal message of the folk's unquestioned subservience to power? How else to explain that for demanding critics, intellectuals of contemporary and following generations, these "Slavas" have been a representation of the Russian folk and expression of the national spirit? It's quite puzzling and yet revealing that even Soviet Russia, though dismissing the country's rich eighteenth-century choral tradition and discarding on an ideological basis most of the sacred literature of the nineteenth century, demonstrated high appreciation for the operatic "Slavas," despite the fact that they conveyed unweaving allegiance to monarchs—or perhaps precisely because of that! For one educated within Soviet culture but equipped with years of studying critical thinking outside the native ideological context, looking through Rimsky-Korsakov's nationalistic scores leads to a surprising revelation. The operas include abundant choral folk songs representing the people. But along with khorovods, wedding choruses, and folk tunes that give a multifaceted picture of the folk, there are these hallowed hollow "Slavas"—perhaps ironic, perhaps Rimsky-Korsakov's sadly truthful depiction of Russian throngs accustomed to break into a "Hurrah!" to any regime as their major duty on or off stage.

An Enchanted Kingdom in the Midst of St. Petersburg

"Fairytale geography can be frivolous, even bizarre, its placement of various lands and peoples capricious," writes Gasparov in discussing *Ruslan and Liudmila*.[54] Morrison similarly observes that in *Sadko* the Venetian song may be not about "the sinking, canalled city of the West, but St. Petersburg, the frozen, canalled city of the East."[55] Sadko travels not so much through space as through time, directing his ships to a city erected in the eighteenth-century future. Moreover, Novgorod's ternary of city, lake, and river, emphasized in the opera, also points to the ensemble of St. Petersburg, Lake Ladoga, and the Neva River. Thus enduring his many-year journey to remote places, navigating between terrestrial and aquatic, earthly and magical, Sadko progresses to the very place he started from: Novgorod, a simulacrum of St. Petersburg. Venice, the intended destination of Sadko's voyage, is the city that, washed in water, rules over the Sea Princess; St. Petersburg, a misty ambiguous fantasy city rising above marshes, was built by Peter and animated by Catherine. Her shadow, still reigning in this theatrical city, seduced artists and composers, who together with their protagonists traversed the temporal and spatial.

The magic gardens in Pushkin's and Glinka's *Ruslan* were imbued with the ambiance of Tsarskoe Selo and Potemkin's legendary eighteenth-century ball, itself "a powerful metaphor" of St. Petersburg[56]; these gardens set a paradigm for depiction of the magical and majestic in nineteenth-century operas. The splendor overlaid by Pushkin's irony and awe and by Glinka's marvel fused the royal domain with magical and Oriental imagery.

Glinka's enchanted garden shaped the Russian operatic magical terrain, its various inhabitants, and their musical lingo. Cleopatra's entourage, for example, resembles the dancing Eastern beauties that Pushkin and Glinka inherited from their predecessors in operatic and courtly stages. The fourth act in *Ruslan* progresses from Ludmila sharing her dismay with dancing sirens,[57] to the dwarf's procession, to the sequence of ethnic dances, and finally to the contest between Ruslan and Chernomor. The sixth scene in *Sadko* follows a similar structural pattern: the submergence of the title hero in the water kingdom, the pompous procession of the Sea Tsar, the exotic dance sequence, and the meeting/contest of St. Nicholas and the Sea King. The scene is awash in whole-tone, chromatic, and octatonic scales. Voiceless and wordless Chernomor has a memorable, mocking march; the Sea Tsar, a bass soaked in the octatonic realm, has no solo number of his own. Water, the orient, and wizardry are fused in the portrayal of the Sea Kingdom in *Sadko*—a scene with sounds transformed, pictures obscured by deep waters full of allusions.

Not only this magical kingdom but several operatic renditions of late-eighteenth-century balls drew on Pushkin/Glinka's enchanted garden. Tchaikovsky relocated Pushkin's *Pikovaia Dama* to the century before and created a ball attended by the empress herself. He also depicted Catherine's imperial palace in two operatic renditions of Gogol's *Christmas Eve.*[58] Half a year after Tchaikovsky's death, losing his major competitor and the only native musician of international reputation, Rimsky-Korsakov, emboldened, composed an opera on the same text.

Both Tchaikovsky's *Slippers* and Rimsky-Korsakov's *Christmas Eve* consist of four acts. As in *Ruslan, Mlada,* and *Sadko,* a magical terrain occupies the penultimate act. The third acts in *Slippers* and *Christmas Eve,* mixing real and surreal, portray the fantastic flight of a young Ukrainian villager, the smith Vakula, to the Russian capital. Unsuccessful in his amorous pursuits, Vakula—the son of a local witch—using power of his own harnesses the devil, and off he goes to an imperial ball. There he pleads to the empress of all-Russia for her "slippers," as a gift for Vakula's capricious sweetheart.

Tchaikovsky's third act falls into three scenes. The first depicts a dark, gloomy night in a riverbed, the second a lustrous imperial palace, and the third a ball, the latter colored by the bright color of E major. The orchestral intermission opening the third act is full of soft and mysterious whispers, chromatic splashes, short ripples, sustained pulsating air, and watery arpeggios to prepare for the appearance of familiar figures. A chorus of rusalkas, quite different from their usual laughing, plotting selves, instead moan about "dark darkness," "cold coldness," horrid and lonely imprisonment, as if they "lie in icy coffins." A grumbling leshii announces the arrival of Vakula. The sudden emergence of the devil makes the rusalkas spectators of haggling between Vakula and the fiend. The scene in St. Petersburg's imperial palace predictably begins with an orchestral polonaise and continues with its panegyric choral version and multiple incantations of "Slava to the wise tsarina."[59] Larosh wrote that the most essential scene in the opera is the kurtag (ball):

> The polonaise for a chorus and two orchestras, regular operatic and military . . . is one of the most inspiring pages ever written by Tchaikovsky. The grandness of motifs, iron energy of rhythms, shining richness of harmony, everything converges here to create the impression of grandness and power.[60]

A quadrupled "Hurray!"—another choral polonaise—signals the appearance of not the empress but His Lightness Potemkin. In *Christmas Eve*, Rimsky-Korsakov also featured a choral polonaise, and like Tchaikovsky he had to replace the empress, making His Lightness "an owner of Catherine's wardrobe."[61] In *The Slippers* Tchaikovsky identifies neither the prince nor the empress by name, but he offers explicit clues. His High Lightness ventures to sing an ode that venerates Russia's victorious naval acquisitions, reinforcing the connection between "triumphant Minerva" and water.[62] And as the scene in the imperial palace is about to end, the master of ceremonies invites the courtiers to the empress's private theater to see Catherine's comic opera *Prince Khlor or the Rose Without Prickles*.

Tchaikovsky and Rimsky-Korsakov devised their magical demonic night and the imperial ball each in his idiosyncratic way. Tchaikovsky set a striking contrast between a bleak winter forest with its magical inhabitants and the brilliance of the empress's ball with dances and choruses. As a master of magical episodes, Rimsky-Korsakov paid more attention to the aerial scene, composing sequences of phantasmagoric dances, races, and games in the sky.[63] The treatment of Vakula's flight in both operas is quite similar, employing repeated, short rhythmic figures. In Rimsky-Korsakov, the fifth scene (Act III) depicts the hut of the local sorcerer. The following scene shows the nocturnal skies (harp, triangle, and celesta); along with dancing stars, witches, and flying shadows populating the stage, a village sorcerer rides a mortar and Solokha flies on her broom. The dancing numbers culminate in a "Demonic Koliada."

A shift between aerial and demonic spaces and figures in the third act of *Christmas Eve* reminds one of the third act in *Mlada*, with Solokha echoing Sviatokha/Morena, the village sorcerer reminiscent of Chernobog. Both third acts feature demonic kolos. The overall structures of the third acts in the two operas are quite similar. They follow a close sequence: a magical, weightless, aerial ballet, a gathering of demonic forces, an explosive infernal dance. In the second half of the third acts, both suddenly shift to a radiant, royal space and all-mighty Majesty; in *Mlada* it is queen Cleopatra, in *Christmas Eve* an "unnamed" Catherine the Great. Rimsky-Korsakov creates his Eastern fantasy in *Mlada*, which could be inspired by Gogol's imagery of "ancient Egypt, stand[ing] on a still sea . . . , as enchanted as mummies . . . [;] untouched by time [and] jolly Greece, . . . priestesses young and lean, . . . reeds tied into *tsevnitsas*, timpanis."[64] The realization of this luscious musical imagery lends itself to *Christmas Eve*, on Gogol's text. At the end of the third acts in both operas, magic, dreams, or confused realities vanish with the rising sun, in *Mlada* signaled by the cockerel and in *The Christmas Eve* by the morning bells.

Mlada, Act III

Summer Festival of Ivan Kupala
Scene 1, Orchestral introduction, Ballet
one star
two stars
dance of shadows B major
Fantastic Kolo C major
Scene 2, Shadows of Mlada and Yaromir,
  Aerial Space

Scene 3, Chernobog, Kashchei, Morena,
  Sabbath
Demonic Kolo:
Chorus: Ugu, ugu, . . . chukh, chukh . . . !
Tso-po, ko-po, ko-po-tsa-ma . . .
Scene 4, Cleopatra D flat major, Ballet

"Scene is light, luxurious Egyptian hall,
  lit with golden-red light . . . on the rich
  purple sofa is Cleopatra; around her
  dancers and slaves. Black slave-girls
  with lyres and drums, black men with
  tsevnitsas."
Scene 5, Morning

Christmas Eve, Act III

Winter festival, Koliada
Scene 5, Duet of Vakula and Devil

Scene 6, Aerial space, Ballet
  (A) Games and dances of stars (mazurka and
    trio)
  (B) Procession of comets
  (C) Khorovod
  (D) *Chardash* and rain of the falling stars

Demonic Koliada
Chorus: "Atu, ego, uliu, liu, liu, liu . . . !"

Scene 7, Polish [polonaise] with Chorus
Chorus: "Glorify, trumpet, timpani, *tsevnitsas*,
    the light of mid-night lands. glorify/Mother
    of our good peoples!"

"Luxurious brightly lit hall in the palace, the
  procession of the courtiers in atlas dresses
  with long trails and men in military and
  civilian cloths decorated with gold."

Sunrise. Train of Osen' and Koliada. Vakula's
  flight back

The fête in the water kingdom of *Sadko* is not unlike Tchaikovsky's and Rimsky-Korsakov's imperial balls. In the sequence of a wondrous procession, choruses, and dances, one important courtly component appears missing in *Sadko*: the polonaise. But the attuned ear of an insider might recognize the rhythmic impulse of the choral "Polish" in the opening vocal line of the Sea Tsar, reciprocated by the Sea Princess.

He Is a Hero!

The magical operatic tsarinas and princesses—some recognizable, others obscure, magical, alluring, enticing, powerful, traversing domains of real and supernatural—formed a tight khorovod across a number of operas, reflective of and referencing one another, completing each other. Perhaps some poets and composers, notably Tchaikovsky and Rimsky-Korsakov, missed the empresses on the eighteenth-century stage, nostalgic about operatic Bellerofont equated with Elisabeth or Oleg as Catherine. Perhaps they fantasized about the operatic figures of ancient emperors, gods and goddesses, and idyllic shepherdesses, identified with tsarinas. Did the law prohibiting their portrayal in opera make the stage seem vacant? Did musicians and artists a century later still yearn for bygone intimacy with empresses—Tsarevna Elisabeth smitten and secretly married to a handsome provincial chorister, Catherine surrounding herself and showering unmatched favors on her artists and intellectuals? Or perhaps it is the opposite: Did the angst about the force of these women, their hunger for power, their unbounded appetites still cast a dark eerie shadow over nineteenth-century men, their psyches, their insecurities, their inferiority complexes, their self-nurtured Yaromir-like lethargy? Perhaps it was all of these together: the awe, nostalgia, and anxiety.

Sadko represents another type: relatively simple, clever, and healthy, tied to folk roots and free of nineteenth-century male complexes. Vakula tricks the devil, riding him to the imperial palace; Sadko appeases and thereby outsmarts the Sea Tsar, consequently leading to the submission of the powerful ruler. Vakula takes a magic aerial flight to get a gift from the tsarina. Sadko, transported to the sea's depths, gets a tsarevna as a gift. Both employ their folk wit and accomplish their goals. Sadko's return from the magical court is reminiscent of the flight of Vakula from the empress's ball in *Christmas Eve*, travel through space and perhaps through time.

Producing *Sadko* around the centennial of Catherine's death, Rimsky-Korsakov calls for a large chorus in the finale: free citizens and a group of professional singers and storytellers. If once upon a time *Mlada* began as a collective work, *Sadko* ends with a metaphorical gathering on stage of fellow musicians. All of them together glorify the hero for acquiring uncountable wealth from his tsarevna-rusalka and appropriating her sexual power and her song. To his fellow literati, Rimsky-Korsakov gave a champion who finally expunged the shadow of formidable female rulers and at the end of the romantic age gained freedom from nineteenth-century insecurities, psychoses, and self-doubts; thus affirming his sexual, social, and creative omnipotence.

9

THE INESCAPABLE QUEEN

Stealing through the gates of a palatial house in the heart of St. Petersburg, lurking in empty corridors near an unlit bedchamber, a young man freezes in front of a portrait on the wall. The air trembles. The midnight bells, "ringing in all the rooms one after another," merge with a rising, restless melody in the strings. Unable to move, the man whispers to himself:

> "Here she is! The Muscovite Venus! Some secret power tied our fates. I from you, you from me [are not to escape], as I feel that one of us will die at the hands of the other. Staring at you, I hate you, yet can't see enough of you! I wish to run away, but can't. . . . My eyes can't break away from the hideous and yet amazing face!"[1]

A few minutes later, accompanied by her maids, the Muscovite Venus herself enters the room. Through a gap in the curtain, the man observes her, registering every detail as she is undressed preparing for the night. Reading this fragment by itself, one might perceive the scene as a lover's obsession and jealousy, if not for the object of the young man's infatuation: his friend's octogenarian grandmother, the countess.[2]

This episode from *The Queen of Spades,* a short tale by Pushkin (1833) and an opera by Tchaikovsky (1890), could be viewed as the poet's imaginary encounter with Catherine II, had she not died two and a half years before he was born. Like his protagonist standing before the portrait of the eighteenth-century beauty, Pushkin was enticed by the glamour of the century, which he, born in its last year, did not experience. Sifting through every piece of Catherine's writing, hand copying her works, attending dinners and jotting down gossip shared by the relics of her time, envying the opportunities he missed, he found satisfaction in disparaging and satirizing the era and the woman. In the story, Pushkin's protagonist exposes his pistol, and the aged woman falls dead, a victim of his unused instrument. The sexual inference is apparent; the ironic death reminds one of Pushkin's lines elsewhere:

(на Екатерину II)	(on Catherine II)
Старушка милая жила	A nice old woman lived
Приятно и немного блудно,	Pleasantly and a bit wantonly,
Вольтеру первый друг была,	Voltaire's best friend she was,
Наказ писала, флоты жгла,	Wrote a Decree,[4] burned a fleet,
И умерла, садясь на судно. . . .[3]	And died, sitting on the john. . . .

In *The Queen of Spades*, the reappearance of the dead countess as a ghost is often seen as a turning point where the somewhat realistic story becomes a mystical tale. But in fact this may be the most revealing moment, showing a shadow of the empress that haunts the protagonist, the poet, and the nineteenth-century literati, who might fantasize about bygone mores, empresses' favorites, and instant fortunes and successes far beyond anything imagined at the gambling table.

Some fifty years before Pushkin wrote his story and a hundred years prior to Tchaikovsky's opera, a twenty-two-year-old officer, Platon Zubov, became a lover of the sixty-year-old empress Catherine. Zubov is believed to have been the last in the sequence of her "favorites," most of them officers in their twenties who competed for this prestigious position.[5] In her memoirs, Princess Dashkova, Catherine's younger friend, vehemently rejected court gossip that she had "groomed" her own twenty-one-year-old son as a candidate for the vacated role of Catherine's paramour.[6] The favorites were awarded titles, estates, palaces, and thousands of serfs, all of which they kept even after they were discharged. Though Catherine conducted these affairs as business matters, she loved her favorites, who claimed romantic reciprocity with her.[7]

Can supreme power instill passion that overcomes societal norms and values? In *The Queen of Spades*, the figure of the countess—a relic of Catherine's age—embodies for the protagonist Gherman[8] a prospect of future opulence and high status as well as ownership of an unattainable, enigmatic past, which magnetized both him and his creators. Though Pushkin pronounces the name of Catherine only once (when the countess recalls her youth as the empress's maid of honor), Catherine herself (almost) enters Tchaikovsky's opera. Pushkin's countess is an avatar of the empress's age; Tchaikovsky's, as argued in this chapter, coalesces with Catherine. The countess's youth is identified with the French court (an old song, "Vive Henry IV") and a French operatic air (Grétry); the old countess is aligned with German/Gherman. Her vocal persona consists of foreign tunes and, when she returns as a ghostly apparition, of a

Naina-like single-tone incantation. Her orchestral portrayal introduces angular dotted lines, chromatic and whole-tone scales—the sorceress's lingua. The paradigm of nineteenth-century literati dealing with eighteenth-century shadows continues from Pushkin's to Tchaikovsky's *Queen*, and from operatic gardens "better than Potemkin's" to balls in the style of Potemkin's. Pushkin's Gherman is his contemporary; his operatic counterpart slides between generations. A guest at a ball attended by the empress, Tchaikovsky's hero listens to an early-nineteenth-century song by Derzhavin, lives the passion and torment of the romantic midnineteenth century, and experiences the psychosis of Dostoevsky's gambler. The eighteenth-century Gherman, bearing late-nineteenth-century anxieties as well as the dreams and curses of Pushkin's generation, hunts his phoenix-fortune in different epochs, only to find that it is always gone. Pushkin's Gherman seeks to advance by acquiring a late-eighteenth-century secret; Tchaikovsky's Gherman, relocated to the eighteenth century, is still unable to gain the key to an instant fortune. Tchaikovsky wept at the death of his Gherman, who entered the world of Russian Symbolism that his creator foreshadowed but did not live to see.[9]

The Story

Pushkin's *Queen of Spades*, "at barely 10,000 words,"[10] portrays an old countess, once a famous beauty, who in her youth obtained the secret of three winning cards in the game of faro. Gherman(n), a poor, young military engineer obsessed with learning the winning formula, feigns a romance with Liza, the countess's ward. Liza offers herself to him, but instead of an amorous night with the beguiled young woman Gherman seeks a moment alone with the countess, reasoning, pleading, and finally threatening her with his unloaded pistol. She dies of fear. At the funeral, Gherman sees the corpse smirk; later, the ghost of the countess visits him, disclosing the secret of the three cards. When he finally plays the game, he wins on the first two cards but loses everything, including his mind, on the third.

Tchaikovsky's Liza is elevated to the status of the countess's granddaughter and heiress. The exchange of a note and a key between Liza and Gherman during the majestic ball is also the Tchaikovskys' addition. After the countess's death, Liza (unlike her counterpart in Pushkin's story, who in a short denouement marries "a very pleasant man") conforms to the fate of the romantic heroine by throwing herself into a river. Pushkin's Gherman ends up in an asylum. His operatic counterpart stabs himself, first addressing the countess's apparition and then the spirit of Liza.

Pushkin's plot can be read as an insider's malign gossip or a salon anecdote, as a story of unbounded passion and madness, a love drama, or a gambling novel. It has been investigated as a psychological or phantasmagoric text, as a numerological rebus, an allegory modeled on the game of faro, and an autobiographical sketch.[11] Is it a mystery to resolve, or a game that the author plays with his reader? In the words of Caryl Emerson, "Pushkin provides us . . . with fragments of codes, codes that tantalize but do not quite add up. He teases the reader with partial keys." Paraphrasing Emerson, Rosenshield writes that in this, "one of the earliest and most brilliant examples of deception in narrative prose, Pushkin not only encourages different interpretations but also purposely withholds sufficient proof for any one interpretation."[12]

The title refers to a playing card and suggests two very different connotations: gambling, in this case faro, and fortune telling. The two meanings constitute a complementary and conflicting pair. Faro, a game of chance, depends only on an unpredictable sequence of cards, defying either player's (punter's or banker's) control, calculation, or strategy; fortune telling signifies predestination, with the characters and their choices defined by fate. In either case, the game serves both as "a plot-propelling mechanism"[13] and as a model for the story, which in Lotman's words is dedicated to "man's struggle with Unknown Factors." In the opening scene of the opera, a spectator hears "I don't know her. . .," "You don't know me," and "Three cards"—all three sharing a nearly identical leitmotif.[14]

Example 9.1

Ia i-me-ni e-ie ne zna-iu   i ne kho-chu   uz-nat',

Gherman: I don't know her name and I do not wish to know

Example 9.2

Gherman: You don't know me!

Example 9.3

tri kar - ty, tri kar - ty, tri kar ty!

Tomsky: Three cards, three cards, three cards!

Drawn to the multiple riddles, the brothers Tchaikovsky (Modest, librettist) made the opera even more daunting than the novel. They extended the gambling metaphors codified in Pushkin's verbal and visual symbols. To Pushkin's exasperated hero, possessing the secret of the cards will *utroit* (triple, the net result of two winning rounds of faro) or *usemerit* (multiply by seven, the result of three winning rounds) his stakes. The numbers three and seven, dispersed through the opera, define its structure and leitmotifs. Consisting of seven scenes and three acts, the opera is opened and closed by two mass scenes—a pleasant spring promenade in St. Petersburg in the first and the emotion-laden atmosphere of a gambling salon in the last—both involving choruses and seven individualized characters. The romantic line of the opera weaves together three love triangles, two unfolding in real operatic time and the third performed in the *intermède*, a play enacted amid the ball scene. The phrase "three cards" is uttered some 130 times throughout the opera. The three-card leitmotif, formed of three segments of three-note motifs (a descending line with an upward leap and a step-down resolution), exudes madness and haunts both protagonists and listeners.

The words *igra*, *igrat'*, *vyigrat'* (game, to play, to win) constantly recur in the text of the tale. In the opera, before playing his third and decisive card Tchaikovsky's Gherman sings: "What is our life? A game," painfully rephrasing Karamzin's poetic line: "What is our life? A novel!" The opera is imbued with associative codes.[15] If in *The Slippers* Tchaikovsky points to the absence/presence of Catherine by announcing, before the curtain goes down, the beginning of *Prince Khlor*, in *The Queen of Spades* the countess leaves the ball that is attended by the empress. Entering her bedchamber, the countess recites "What times!"—an echo of "O times!" the title of Catherine II's comedy, a satirical play about a grandmother and her granddaughter and the protagonists' gambling habits.[16]

Intergeneric and Intertextual Associations

Long remote from its historical surroundings and from the literary and musical repertoire of which it was a part, *The Queen of Spades* is typically perceived as a unique stand-alone masterpiece. The story and opera, however, are filled with unspoken and unexplained codes, shared within close Russian aristocratic circles and family networks, which persisted from the eighteenth throughout the nineteenth century. The anecdote about a grandmother's mysterious cards was told in Pushkin's circles by Count Sergei Golitsin, a grandson of the possible prototype of the countess from *Queen of Spades*, princess Natalia Golitsina[17] (Figure 9.1[18]).

Another member of the luminary Russian dynasty, prince Alexander Golitsin, "a spendthrift, gambler and society wastrel, staked and lost his wife, Princess Mariia

Figure 9.1: François-Hubert Drouais (1727–1775). *Portrait of Countess Natalia Golitsina née Chernyshova (1741–1837), 1762.*

Grigorievna (nee Viazemskaia) to one of the most colorful Moscow grandees, Count Lev Kirilovich Razumovsky."[19] Fortunes won or lost at card tables, lives gambled in duels, and pens sharpened to scribble a love stanza or poisonous epigram as Gherman lights a candle and writes "his vision"—this is the world of Pushkin's literary and social chums.

Love and gambling overlapped. Pushkin, for example, once traveled a hundred miles to attend a ball in the hope of seeing a woman he desired, but "having arrived in the city, he sat down before the ball to gamble and lost the whole night right into the morning, so that he let slip all his money, the ball, and his love."[20] Under the famous malachite Green Lamp that gave the name to a well-known intellectual circle, Pushkin's associates read poetry, debated politics, and played cards. A possible model for the gambling setting in *The Queen of Spades*, this "generous retreat, refuge of love and free muse where around the [card] table sat equals"[21] belonged to a founder of the club, Nikita Vsevolozhsky.[22] It was his nephew Ivan Vsevolozhsky, the director of imperial theaters,[23] who seventy years later commissioned Tchaikovsky to write *The Queen*.

The composer himself, to a lesser degree, was a card player who occasionally confessed to his diaries both an affinity and a vexation with *vint* (Russian whist).[24]

Pushkin's *Queen* belongs to a large body of literature on gambling. Like E. T. A. Hoffmann's *Gambling Luck* (*Spielerglück*, 1819), *The Queen* is a story within a story. Both tales focus on protagonists obsessed with faro and destroyed by the Queen of Spades, and on young women sacrificed to the gambling passion.[25] In Nikolai Karamzin's *Poor Liza* (1792) gambling, though barely mentioned, is essential to the plot. Gherman's aristocratic counterpart Erast, attached to his peasant lover Liza, leaves her when called for military service.

> Instead of fighting with enemies, he occupied himself with gambling and lost his estate. After peace was declared, he returned to Moscow burdened by debts. The only way to improve his circumstances was to marry an aged wealthy widow.[26]

This seemingly insignificant passage about cards is a turning point in the love story. After encountering her beloved married to another woman, Karamzin's Liza throws herself into a lake.

Pushkin retells the story of poor Liza in various works, probing different endings. In his *Rusalka* the miller's daughter, betrayed by her noble lover, commits suicide near an oak tree by a river, returning in the afterlife as a vengeful tsarina Rusalka. Another incarnation of Karamzin's Liza is Pushkin's Lizaveta in *Baryshna Krestianka* (Noble-Maid), a noble's daughter who, dressed as a peasant girl, beguiles her aristocratic neighbor; she can't lose, being both a sweet, flirtatious serf girl and a wealthy heiress. In Pushkin's *Queen of Spades*, as noted earlier, Liza ends happily married; her counterpart in Tchaikovsky's opera follows the destiny of her namesake in Karamzin and the Miller's daughter in Pushkin/Dargomyzhsky's *Rusalka*.[27] But the role of powerful magical Rusalka is undertaken in *The Queen of Spades* by Liza's grandmother, whose ghostly apparition plagues Gherman.

Karamzin's "poor Erast" has his own literary history.[28] Nikolai Brusilov wrote *Poor Leandr* (1803) about a character who, infected by "the plague-like" "authorial spirit," entered a literary circle that doubled as a gambling salon.[29] One of Pushkin's card cronies, Ivan Velikopol'sky, an obsessive gambler and amateur poet, published *K Erasty: satira na igrokov* (To Erast: a satire on gamblers, 1828),[30] which stirred an ongoing poetic duel between him and Pushkin that preceded *The Queen of Spades*.[31] Another Pushkin associate, Prince Alexander Shakhovskoi, adapted and staged *The Queen* as a musical spectacle, *Khrizomania or A Passion for Money* (1836).[32] In its theatrical debut, German/Gherman was replaced by Jewish Irmus; Pushkin's Liza was split into two characters, Liza and Eliza (both names diminutives of Elizaveta), which introduced the possibility of doubles, fully blossoming in Tchaikovsky.[33] Liza, the counterpart of

Pushkin's heroine, is a servant girl; Eliza, a countess's goddaughter, foreshadows Tchaikovsky's Liza. The story of Shakhovskoi's noble Eliza has two endings. One is tragic, with Tomsky discovering Eliza's straw hat floating on the river Neva, suggesting her suicide. An appended vaudeville epilogue brings Eliza back from her romantic exile to celebrate her blissful union with Tomsky; this jovial conclusion, according to Liubov Kiseleva, was omitted after early productions.[34] Shakhovskoi's countess is also Elizaveta. The abundance of "Lizas" in the play is intriguing; the three of them make up a collective female image. The countess is acquainted with Voltaire, Marmontel, Diderot, Lomonosov, and Sumarokov[35]—Catherine II's pen pals and her court literati. Khrizomania had a long and successful staging history and was still performed at the time Tchaikovsky's Queen of Spades premiered.

In the middle of the nineteenth century Pushkin's tale, which had been translated and adapted by a number of librettists and composers abroad, promised to become a European operatic hit. The Parisian Opéra-Comique, which premiered La dame de pique (1850) by Frenchmen Fromental Halévy and Eugène Scribe,[36] "never had as resounding a success," wrote the hard-to-please critic and writer Théophile Gautier; "book, score, performance—everything has worked out beyond anyone's wildest dreams."[37] Less than a year after the Halévy premier, the Theater Royal Drury Lane in London staged The Queen of Spades (1851) with music by Henri Laurent.[38] The two European productions, devised as comic operas, included serfs with recognizably Russian first names, officers with Russian surnames, and counts and princesses bearing the old dynastic names. The game of faro defines the characters and plotline in both operas. The young princess disguises herself as her lame, deformed relative, the countess, and in the final scene shows up as a Queen of Spades impersonator. The real countess appears only at the end of the play, demystifying the legend by explaining that the three winning cards were a gambling trick of a woman who "had a mania for playing, but could not bear to lose"[39]: Her Majesty the Russian Empress Elisabeth. In these versions, the operatic imbroglio with political overtones gets resolved after Catherine (who never steps on the stage) deposes Peter III and herself rises to supreme power. Thus decades before Tchaikovsky's opera, European audiences saw several versions of The Queen of Spades set in the eighteenth century, depicting Russian princesses, countesses, and maids, and invoking the two empresses: Elisabeth introducing the card trick and Catherine restoring order in society.

Elements of the various versions seem to resurface in Tchaikovsky. The association with Elisabeth, for example, brings intriguing overtones to Tchaikovsky's chorus, which in the opening scene venerates the reign of Empress Elisabeth, when the "sun was brighter and the skies clearer." Her successor, Catherine, whose ascendance to the throne secured happy endings in the French and English Piques, is the majestic guest in Tchaikovsky's ball. The creators of the opera also used verses from the late eighteenth and early nineteenth centuries, most notably those of the creator of the mythological Felitsa, Derzhavin; Tchaikovsky's Liza and Polina together recite Zhukovsky's lyrics, and Polina sings her romance with lyrics by Konstantin Batiushkov.

Modest in St. Petersburg and Peter in Florence wrote the opera during a startling forty-four-day creative race in 1890; the latter was at times so impatient and impassioned that, unable to wait for the text, he would draft parts himself.[40] The mature composer relied on artistic choices that had proved successful in his previous works: regal and courtly domains, sumptuous eighteenth-century masquerade balls, "triumphal polonaises," protagonists writing and receiving letters, webs of simple, almost graphic melodic motifs, and a dense, poignant score. The harmonious female duets of Liza and Polina, echoing the opening duet of Tatiana and Olga Larina in *Eugene Onegin* (1879), contrast with the overlying vocal duet-duels of Onegin with Lensky and Gherman with Yeletsky.[41] Exploring the love dimension of *Queen of Spades*, which in Pushkin's version has little to do with romance, Tchaikovsky created the image of Prince Yeletsky, the fiancé of Liza and Gherman's rival, with some traits of *Onegin's* Gremin. By inventing Yeletsky, Tchaikovsky presented Liza with dilemmas beyond her literary counterpart and made her fail in not one but two romances—refusing Yeletsky in favor of Gherman, she is rejected by Gherman. The love triangle of Liza, Yeletsky and Gherman resembles two others in Tchaikovsky's operas based on Pushkin's texts: *Eugene Onegin* and *Mazeppa* (1884). In the finale of *Eugene Onegin*, Tatiana chooses to remain with the old noble Gremin, refusing Onegin, whom she loves; Maria selects aged Byronic Mazeppa over her childhood friend Andrew. The musical fraternity of the three male characters, Yeletsky, Gremin and Mazeppa, is apparent in their love arias. The choices Tchaikovsky probes with his three heroines lead to different outcomes. Dutiful Tatiana, rejecting Onegin upon his return, survives physically and retains her integrity. In *Queen of Spades*, as in *Mazeppa*, the heroine's love, superseding reason, leads to a fatal outcome. The dulcet Liza, charming the audience, holds no enticement for Gherman, his passion directed elsewhere.

Love of Liza or Fear of Passion for the Countess

The desires of the male protagonist echoed Pushkin's own passion for gambling, duels, and women and resonated with the poet's fate. His Gherman is trapped in the densely woven web of his craving for love and cards, the two conflated, conflicting, standing for something else. Both his passion and the subject of his infatuation are uncertain, shifting, perhaps misleading.

Of a Russified German family, Gherman is "secretive, ambitious, . . . overly frugal," and somewhat impoverished (Wachtel, examining his gambling stakes, concludes, however, that his financial standing was quite sufficient[42]). He proclaims to Tomsky that a union with his beloved, presumably Liza, is impossible because of her high stature. However, unlike Pushkin's low-status prototype—waiting for hours on the street to steal a moment with Liza by the countess's carriage—Tchaikovsky's Gherman, though "certainly not rich,"[43] is a friend of Tomsky, a guest at the imperial ball, and an officer.

At the beginning of the opera, boys playing guards march onto the stage, cheering for Empress Catherine II. Almost immediately after the departure of the boys' squadron, a group of grown-up officers takes their place on the stage. Boys grow fast, and so did their military ranking in the Russian imperial system. But promotion was meteoric once an older, powerful woman became involved.[44] Madariaga writes about Catherine's "main choices" of poor Guards officers: "Since all her favorites came from fairly obscure noble families, their rise thus reminded the nobility of the rewards that service (servicing the autocratrix, in this instance) could gain for an individual."[45]

Operatic Liza, an opulent heiress, could make Gherman, without any gambling victories, a very wealthy man. Although seemingly age-appropriate and socially plausible (despite his initial claim of low origin) and thus easily digested by readers and listeners, the love of the two is emotionally lopsided and no union takes place in either text. In Pushkin the protagonist, learning about the countess's secret of three cards, sends Liza a "letter containing a love confession: it was affectionate, respectful, and taken word for word from a German novel."[46] Charming her with skillfully copied lines, he then begins to write her every day "using language of his own, capable of expressing his unrelenting desires and disordered unrestrained imagination," directed beyond the figure of poor Liza.[47] After his unsuccessful attempt to wangle the code from the countess, leading to her death, Gherman faces Liza for the last time and tells her "everything. Liza listened to him with horror." Tchaikovsky makes Liza and Gherman see each other again. In the middle of her arioso, as Liza waits for him on a bridge, she sings "Ah dumoi sebia isterzala ia" (Ah, my thought wearied me; Example 9.4).

Accompanied by trembling strings and stepwise rising clarinets and bassoons, she utters a thrice-repeated, three-note descending motif that doubles "three cards"; the following melodic line echoes Gherman's love confession. Whether swayed by feelings toward Liza or by the powerful card/love theme, for a brief moment Gherman seems drawn into what could be a perfect romantic love duet but then suddenly pushes Liza away: "Who are you? I know you not! Get away!"

What is the problem with romance in this quintessentially romantic opera? In the opening scene, Gherman's confession of love for an "unnamed woman" precedes Tomsky's tale of the cards. The reversal of Pushkin's sequence might imply the protagonist's love for the young woman. Also before Tomsky's tale, when asked

Example 9.4

Liza: Ach, my thoughts wearied me
Where, where are you, my past joy?
Clouds arrived bringing the storm
Breaking my hopes!

about the "new passion" that keeps him all night *near* the card table, Gherman confesses that he "is lost, outraged by [his] weakness, incapable of self-control," suddenly declaring "I am in love!" This (con)fusion of love and cards, sown throughout the opera, poses the question of whether the three cards are themselves the object of Gherman's inescapable desire or a cover for something else. Tomsky's ballad, an anthology of the opera's leitmotifs opening with the "fate" motif of the Fifth Symphony (predestination in faro), introduces the theme of cards, which gives an alternative meaning to Gherman's recently sung love confession (likely still resonating in listeners' ears). Gasparov frames his musical analysis of the first scene: "This double musical perspective gives peculiar meaning to Gherman's refusal to name his beloved—was it indeed to the unearthly nature of his feelings, or was it due to the uncertainty as to her identity?"[48] Two variations of the same theme, the first expressing Gherman's desire for an unnamed woman and the second for unknown cards, point to his infatuation with one character: the countess (Examples 9.1 and 9.3).

The secret of the three cards, the key to success, the promise of enormous emotional, financial, and social (sexual?) reward—everything he seeks belongs to "another woman." She is the one he encounters in every scene. He runs away from her and is unable to leave, bound to her even after her death. Boris Gasparov bluntly poses a logical question: "Who is Gherman in love with?" Delivering the society anecdote, Tomsky dwells on the past beauty of the Muscovite Venus, loved madly by all Parisian men, herself a passionate gambler and a haughty aristocrat who paid one night of pleasure in exchange for the winning cards. Tomsky also sings about the curse: the countess will die from the "third, who, loving ardently and passionately, will come to force" her card secret.[49] Unable to control his passions (whatever those may be), Gherman muses about beguiling the countess and becoming her lover, adding that she may die soon.[50] His refusal to give his beloved an "earthly name," his attempt to restrain his "earthly passions," and his reiterated testimony of his "unearthly" yearning seem to foreshadow the (unearthly) appearance of the countess as a ghost. Repeatedly enunciating the curse of the "third [recipient of the cards' secret], burning with passion," Gherman by the end of the first scene is ready to step into the role of victorious lover/ killer: "vse *strasti* prosnulis' s takoi *ubiistvennoi* siloi" (all *passions* awakened with such *murderous* power).[51] As if he needs any more incitement, his pals' mocking advice and whispers ascribe the role of the third to him.

If Gherman's exacerbating confusion between love and cards attests to his disturbed mind, then his insanity could be responsible for his improbable, improper, and unbelievable affinity with the countess. As soon as he proclaims his passion awakened, the protagonist quickly moves from the expression of love to words of farewell and death; anger and horror creep increasingly into his lines. His dialogue with Tomsky ends with the words "anguish," "suffering," "horror," and finally "death." Paired in a duet with the happily engaged Count Yeletsky, Gherman's text is contaminated: "curse," "satanic," "chagrin," and "pain." Darkness and envy saturate his part even before he learns the identity of Yeletsky's bride. At the first entrance of Liza and the countess on stage, the word *strashno* (fear) spreads like a malign cancer; it is reiterated nineteen times during the quintet.[52] Invading a woman's space in the second scene, hiding on the balcony of the countess's palace, Gherman suddenly appears before Liza after her bridal gathering, proclaiming himself a "dying man" whose "verdict is death" and who seeks a "draught of her peerless beauty" before "death, and with it peace." He retreats behind the curtain when the countess briefly enters Liza's room and after her departure changes his dire tune. No longer wishing for death, he is exalted by a "burning passion" for winning in multiple games.

During the ball, the protagonist talks to himself, questioning and asserting his role as the fate-bearing lover "who is passionately in love, indeed . . . yes." Then escaping from a masked figure that points to the countess as Gherman's lover and crying in desperation: "I am scared! . . . Anathema! Alas, I am pitiful and insane!" Gherman is relieved to see Liza and rushes to proclaim his love to her. But when Liza gives him the key, it is not the joyful anticipation of their nocturnal meeting but the vision of the countess's bedchamber that exhilarates him to reach high G, immediately diving down ("to the bedroom, to her?" Example 9.5) and a minute later rising to a prolonged A ("Now it is not I, destiny itself wishes it, and I will know the three cards!")

Example 9.5

Liza: Here is a key for a secret door in the garden, there are the stairs,
for you to come to the bedroom of my grandmother
Gherman: What? In a bedroom to *her*?

In the Boudoir

Throughout the opera, Gherman's exasperated lines are inconsistent with romance, rather illuminating his madness or perhaps his horror of recognition—of *who* he actually desires. Then who does Gherman see when he looks at the countess, and what does he hear or listen to? The portrait of a young, proud beauty in the countess's dark boudoir, concealing the tantalizing secret of illicit games, challenges and entices Gherman, as the old countess returns from the ball. Analyzing the musical content of this scene, Vladimir Protopopov and Nadezhda Tumanina suggest that it is "built on the synthesis of the love theme [introduction], the aria 'Prosti nebesnoe sozdanie' [Gherman and Liza in the second scene], and Gherman's 'I don't know her name.'"[53]

After the crowded, busy ball in the third scene, the intimacy of the fourth fully dedicated to Gherman and the countess, the combination of the nearly empty stage, the murky night, two lonely figures, and music expressing extreme internal tension have inspired some extraordinary staging. In Dodin's production (Amsterdam, 1998), which relocated all the events of *Queen of Spades* to a mad house, the countess appears in this scene as "a woman of great subtlety, whose memories of youth rejuvenated her."[54] Meyerhold's countess (Leningrad, 1935) was "tall and slender, not bending, or shaking." During a rehearsal, Meyerhold himself took away her cane and replaced it with a large, expressive fan. "With the help of makeup, she makes herself attractive and this is the way she enters the stage, brushing off her maids' compliments."[55]

Before Gherman's eyes, the countess—praised by a chorus of maids for her ever-lasting beauty: "*krasavitsa*, . . . tomorrow you again will be *krashe* (more beautiful) than the sunrise itself!"—is undressed. Drawn into the past, she recalls her youth among Parisian luminaries, envisioning herself dancing with and admired by dukes and kings. The countess's vocal reminiscence "As if it were today" is as real to her as it is intoxicating to her invisible partner. Sending her maids away, the countess switches to a more intimate tone, singing a coquettish song borrowed from Grétry's *chérie doux Laurette* (*Richard Coeur-de-lion*, 1784). This dreamy, whispered song about the fear and excitement of a nocturnal encounter—*his* admission of love and *her* pounding heart—seems a hazy anticipation of a real encounter, as if the countess actually knows about her secret visitor. In Iury Temirkanov's production of *Queen of Spades* (St. Petersburg Mariinsky Theater, 1984), the countess (Liudmila Filatova) dozes and is nearly asleep after the first couplet of the song but suddenly wakes up, looks around, stares at the corner where Gherman is hidden, and then, rising in a slow dance motion, makes several steps toward him, repeating her little inviting song.

As the countess ends her reverie, her "pourquoi . . ." overlaps with the theme of cards/love in the bassoons, an otherworldly whisper in *ppppp*. In a few moments, with a swiftly expanding orchestral sound, the theme, fused with passion, is repeated in the cellos, only to be fragmented, distorted, and transformed into a critical leitmotif, which, as discussed later, is itself a conflation of opposite, contrasting movement.[56] Gherman is about to appear before the countess. Burning with the passion he himself fears, spellbound by the portrait, and draped in the curtain watching—or perhaps imagining—the countess's striptease (the poor light and the maids' hustle probably hinder him from seeing anything), caught in collapsing times and realities, smitten by the countess's list of French dukes, princes, and a king, and enticed by a playful love song, Gherman shows up asking the countess "for the happiness of his whole life."

He beseeches her in the name of love. He begs her as a wife, lover, and mother. Dodin's Gherman (Vladimir Galuzin) "became darker, but also softer, as he treated the Countess like a lover and then regressed into infantilism."[57] His demand for a secret—his libidinal desire—is further inflamed by his fantasy of the countess's "horrific sins, deadly pleasures, and satanic pacts." At the moment of his highest (emotional) arousal, he pulls the gun, and the countess is dead—a double sexual metaphor.[58] Elena Obraztsova, playing the countess with Plácido Domingo as Gherman (2001), made her heroine an "unfading beauty" who sees "Gherman as her lover. . . . They dance together; filled with joy and not noticing his threats, she dies in Gherman's hands."[59]

The midnight bell, which in Tchaikovsky's *Nutcracker* signals the shift to the world of fantasy, in *Queen of Spades* rings first in the countess's bed chamber and then again in the scene at the canal, also marking a liminal space. In three consecutive scenes unfolding in the dim light of the chamber, in the shadowy barracks briefly lit by the cold light of the moon, and in the dark night on the street, the images are blurred, the actions shady, and time crumples; the moon signals magic and menace here, mistaken identity and catastrophe in *Swan Lake*. The advent of the apparition in the fifth scene converts a fairly realistic anecdote into a phantasmagoria or a psychotic breakdown. Gherman, reading Liza's letter, is drawn into a "horrid dream and gloomy picture of the funeral as if it were alive," when, preceded by a strong wind and shadows, the countess's ghost enters the barrack. Pushkin's Gherman takes the woman in white for "his old wet-nurse." Tchaikovsky's libretto refers to the figure as a prizrak (vision, shadow, specter), an expression that evokes diverse associations: *strashnyi prizrak* (scary ghost) or *prizrak milyi, rokovoi* (lovely fatal vision), or *vezde so mnoiu prizrak milyi* (everywhere with me is the lovely vision).[60] What or whom does Gherman see in this lightless space under the transforming, secretive power of the moon?

The countess's spirit comes to the barracks against her will, discloses the three cards, and, in a recitation limited to a single unaltered F,[61] orders Gherman to marry Liza. Such revelations of the deceased were not taken lightly in eighteenth- and nineteenth-century Russia, as Vinogradov suggests in his intertextual analysis of Pushkin's *Queen of Spades*.[62] Gherman learns the secret of the countess's cards but breaks his end of the bargain about marriage with Liza. Afterward, in the final scene at the gambling table, he must make another choice, a simple one: picking from his own new deck the third winning card, the ace. For him, knowing the secret, faro is no longer a game of chance. Yet he messes up *(obdernulsia)*;[63] instead of the ace, the Queen of Spades is in his hands. According to Rosen, who examined a deck of cards from Pushkin's time, "the Queen and the Ace differ so much that a visual confusion of the two cards is out of the question."[64] At the moment of recognition, the silent countess's ghost materializes.

Like Vinogradov before him, Rosen suggests that for Gherman, the Queen of Spades merged with the "image of the dead old woman."[65] Or perhaps the figure on the card resembles the portrait of the young countess. The double image on the playing card (with the lower picture flipped and reversed) corresponds to the mirrored, confusing images in the countess's chamber. Rosenshield proposes that Gherman "must" select the Queen in his "pursuit of forbidden libidinal desires, the personification of which is the queen of spades, the queen mother, the ultimate object of forbidden desire."[66]

Appealing to the countess's prizrak in the final scene—his total failure making it utterly clear that the age of unmatched female patronage and young favorites has passed irretrievably—framed by the rushing triplets in the strings and a slowly, fatally descending whole-tone scale in clarinets and bassoons, Gherman begins with an octave-wide downward leap to a repeated F, which echoes the countess's night visit to the barracks, as her shadow is about to appear in this last scene. Following an augmented triadic path and falling again, now from F sharp, his vocal line climbs up, harmonically unsteady. With trembling strings and as if sounding from afar the love theme from the introduction softly played by clarinets, he, dying, appeals to the vision of Liza: "Beauty! Goddess! Angel!"

Spinning Time and Mixing Stories

The opera's deceptively straightforward libretto in fact consists of several semi-independent stories and comprises multiple temporal-spatial planes between which the characters find themselves lost, disoriented, and doomed. Pushkin's novel introduces two plots: the main story line set in his own time, as if the events took place around a card table he frequented; and his subplot (the countess's youthful adventure with the cards in Paris) evoking the eighteenth century, Catherine II's era. Pushkin renders pictures of the past in vivid detail, while the present surrounding the protagonists is vague and generalized. In contrast to a scattered exchange among officers about wins and losses, Tomsky's tale is filled with names, places, and historical figures, among them Richelieu,[67] who "nearly shot himself" because of the young Russian countess; the Duke of Orleans (Phillipe-Egalité), the man to whom the countess lost a big sum of money; and Casanova.

The richness of detail about the eighteenth century is echoed in descriptions of the old countess's bedroom. Here Pushkin's Gherman spends the nocturnal hours looking at paintings by Elisabeth Vigée Lebrun (1755–1842), a Parisian artist who, avowing an "irresistible desire to get a glance" of Catherine the Great, visited Russia[68] and painted forty-three portraits of noblewomen, including five women of the Golitsin family.[69] Other graphic visual details—"the clock of the celebrated Leroy . . . old images, a golden lamp, faded stuffed chairs and divans with soft cushions . . . in melancholy symmetry around the room, . . . porcelain shepherds and shepherdess, . . . roulettes, fans and various playthings"—make Pushkin's picture of the past more real, more palpable than the present. Like the poet, the Tchaikovskys provided a list of luminaries. The composer animated Pushkin's porcelain shepherds "sticking out from all corners" in his intermède, arguably affirming his own familial links to the eighteenth-century imperial domain: Tchaikovsky's great-grandfather Michel-Victor Acier, the artistic director of the Meissen porcelain factory, produced a large order commissioned by Catherine.[70]

The opera's main plot is moved to a spring in the early 1790s (April 1791 was the date of Potemkin's ball); the subplot could not have occurred before 1745, when Madame de Pompadour, named by the countess in her recollections, rose to stardom in the French court. Both time planes in the opera belong to the eighteenth century;

Tchaikovsky's countess, younger than Pushkin's, is approximately the same age as Catherine. The time lines in the story and opera overlap between the late sixties and early nineties, a period that coincides with Catherine's reign.

The chronological line in Pushkin is challenged by the broken, fragmented, and reversed sequence of events. For example, already after the fatal encounter between Gherman and the countess, Pushkin's reader sees the preceding ball and the countess (still alive) through the recollection of Liza. Tchaikovsky, establishing an eighteenth-century time-frame, includes period pieces, taking musical historicism, according to James Parakilas, "to unheard-of lengths: eighteenth-century styles appear in practically every scene of the opera, juxtaposed so disturbingly against Tchaikovsky's most modern styles."[71] The opera is a pastiche of borrowed and stylized music, its temporal scale extending from "pseudo-rococo inserts," translucent Mozartian sounds, and Wagnerian "expressionist heights"[72] to the tone of the postromantic *fin de siècle*—the "unexpected shift of the musical chronotrope is dizzying."[73]

Underlying this polytemporality is the opera's two-part design, the bright, crowded first half aligned with the eighteenth century and the second half with the late nineteenth century, dark, nightmarish, mystical. Scenes 1 through 3 constitute the female half of the opera, with a bridal gathering in the second scene framed by the throng venerating empresses in the first and courtiers in the third. With a little positive twist in the romance of Liza and Gherman, the luminous ball scene and the panegyric kant "Slavsia" to the empress could very well complete an eighteenth-century celebratory court spectacle.

The second half of the opera, stripped of eighteenth-century brilliance and instead flooded with postromantic shadows, visions, and hallucinations, is a sequence of three catastrophic duets: Gherman's rendezvous with the countess leading to her death (fourth scene), his fatal meeting with Liza (sixth scene), and in between Gherman's encounter with the apparition. Two frames reinforce the symmetry of the second half. One consists of Gherman's dramatic solos before the countess's portrait (fourth scene) and following his loss at cards (seventh scene). The second frame is composed of two choral episodes, the all-female chorus in the countess's chamber (fourth scene) and an all-male drinking song at the gambling table (seventh scene). In the first half the "last court composer" invokes the reality of eighteenth-century theatricals and simultaneously employs the conventions of nineteenth-century opera; in the second half he veers to the silver age of post-Tchaikovsky modernity.

In addition to the main and subplot lines, in the middle of the opera the Tchaikovskys unfold yet another inner plot, the intermède, "The Sincerity of the Shepherdess," that, conforming to late eighteenth-century court tradition, takes place during the ball. The bucolic heroine of this play-within-a-play, Prilepa (Charming/Chloe), undergoes the torment of deciding between two suitors, one young and poor, the other old and prosperous. When Prilepa chooses Milovzor (Tender Look/Daphnis), favoring love over money, Hymenaeus and Cupid bless their union; the shepherds and shepherdesses—re-dressed nobles, who, in the eighteenth century, would likely have mixed with serfs—dance and sing, celebrating the happy finale.

The image of the shepherdess, invoked throughout the opera, also surfaces in Polina's elegiac romance and in the French song of the countess. Seemingly out of place in the middle of a bridal gathering, Polina's shepherdess, "once living joyfully in pastures of Arcadia" and dying heartbroken, betrayed by a "golden dream and the promise of love," forebodes the destiny of Tchaikovsky's Liza. Personified by Polina, who sings in the first person, the deceased shepherdess becomes the opera's first ghost.

Tchaikovsky's *intermède* is also an idyllic enactment of Liza's situation, confirming her choice of poor Gherman over her "smart, handsome, and titled" groom. Observing the same pastoral, Gherman makes the opposite choice, selecting the old countess with mysterious cards over her granddaughter. In the next scene, completely forgetful of Liza, he stands bemused before the portrait of the young countess.[74] "The Sincerity of the Shepherdess," enacted by protagonists from the main plot, bridges pastoral heroes with courtiers. Likewise, the countess's French song, reflecting her nostalgic youthful reverie and evoking the image of a young country maiden waiting for her beloved, foreshadows the countess's meeting with Gherman.

The three shepherdesses evoked in consecutive scenes (second through fourth) form another subplot in *Queen of Spades* that unfolds backwards. The story of the shepherdess progresses from the countess's pastoral maiden—her "Je ne sais pas pourquoi!" ("not knowing why!" fourth scene) echoing Gherman's "not knowing"—to the intermède, in which the Arcadian heroine is united with her young, poor beloved (third scene), and to Polina's foreboding triple incantation "grave, grave, grave" (second scene). Musically, this internally unified story mirrors and relates to the outside plot: a descending melodic line, occurring in the middle of Polina's romance, the middle of Milovzor/Polina's song,[75] and the Countess' arietta, echoes Gherman's love/card motifs (Examples 9.6, 9.7, and 9.8).

Thus the mythological shepherdess fills the vacancy of Pushkin/Shakhovskoi's maid, completing a full spectrum of society from empress to picturesque peasant girl.

Dramatic Tensions Created by Doubles and Distortions

Falling between swirling time-spaces, trapped in what Gasparov calls *stereoscopic temporality*, caught within this nightmarish carnivalesque, a game with multiple

Example 9.6

Polina: In these joyous places? Grave, grave, grave!

Example 9.7

Milovzor: [I] won't be shy any longer, for a long time I concealed my passion

Example 9.8

Countess: I sense my heart beating, beating, I don't know why! Why are you standing here?

reflections and distortions, the characters are like card figures, symmetrical silhouettes tied together but placed against each other and facing in opposite directions.

The double images in the figured cards parallel what Taruskin calls "sinister doubles that haunt the opera on every level."[76] Gherman and St. Germain, for example, bear French and (Russified) German variations of the same name. Thus Gherman, a reincarnation of the countess's erstwhile benefactor, experiences the daunting, irresistible magnetism of the countess and her secret. Closely linked in the story and the opera, the two male protagonists extend a dialogue across the two texts. In Pushkin's story, St. Germain generously revealed the secret of three cards to the countess to save her honor; conversely, Gherman considers becoming her lover to acquire the secret cards. Gherman's idea of exchanging sex for cards, introduced in Pushkin, turns into the one-night bargain that the operatic St. Germain is said to have struck with the desperate Russian beauty.

The theme of Gherman's opening—"I don't know her name"—is magnified in the second half of his arioso "You don't know me!" The keys of the two-part arioso reiterate nearly the same scalar theme, separated by a diminished fifth (D to A-flat), at the end fused with chromaticism and tonal uncertainty. The descending melodic line, aligned with the doubled "don't know," vanishes in Gherman's duet/duel with Prince Yeletsky and is absent in the following chilling quintet with both Liza and the Countess. Soon it surfaces at the very beginning of Tomsky's scene and ballad.[77] Here in a refrain, the theme attains new power as the leitmotif of the three cards. Thus represented metaphorically by the descending theme itself, Gherman begins his downhill race, gripped by the desire of the triple unknown: love, cards, and self. At the pinnacle of his fatal chase, in the countess's chamber, he addresses her by echoing Tomsky's ballad about the Parisian adventure and about St. Germain, a man who had it all. Gherman's desires seem incomplete without his appropriation of St. Germain's (absent) role.

Along with Gherman doubling his temporally remote counterpart, the parallel pairing of Liza and the Countess, two generations apart, brings to mind other Tchaikovsky doubles, notably the two sisters Larina (*Eugene Onegin*) and Odette/ Odill (*Swan Lake*). At the beginning of the opera, just after Gherman confesses to Tomsky his love and his despair—the subject of his affection remains unknown—he sees not one woman but two enter the stage, Liza and the countess. The women sing together, uttering the same lines, sharing the fear—"Mne strashno!" (I am frightened!)—of the "mysterious and horrifying stranger," while Gherman is absorbed by "an ominous fire in the countess's eyes" (Example 9.9). Together the two likewise appear in the ball.

Is Gherman in love with the set of the two, the pair?[78] Does he mistake one for the other, or have a double vision? In the countess's palace, Gherman goes toward Liza's door but stops before the painting of the young Countess. The resemblance between granddaughter and grandmother implied, the portrait substitutes for Liza while the Countess enters the chamber. During Gherman's first duet with Liza, the countess enters the young woman's chamber; after the countess dies, Liza almost immediately surfaces in her room. The apparition of the deceased countess visits Gherman one night, and the next night Liza waits for him, all in black, in the moonlight, herself not unlike a ghostly figure. At a moment of extreme emotional tension, Gherman addresses

Example 9.9

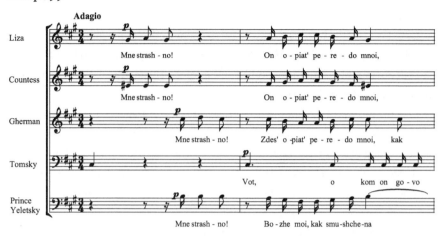

Liza: I am frightened! Again he is before me,
Countess: I am frightened! Again he is before me,
Gherman: I am frightened! Here before me, like fatal vision, appears the gloomy hag
Tomsky: Here the one he talked about. How baffled he is
Yeletsky: I am frightened! My God, how baffled she is! Why [do I have] this strange feeling?

Liza, "Yes, I learned from you the three, seven, and ace," confusing her with the countess. Dodin replaces the intermède with the trio of Gherman, Lisa, and the Countess;
Gherman takes the place of the shepherdess in the ball, staged as a game of *zhmurki*
(the Russian version of blindman's bluff). The three are blindfolded; drifting from one
to the other and choosing Liza, Gherman removes his blindfold finding himself caressing the Countess.[79] Is he disoriented, unable to separate the two and dreading his
madness?[80] The two blood relations, one old, the other young, the first concealing the
mystery of her past and the second open to and entangled in the drama of the present,
the countess and her granddaughter may represent two "displaced" halves of the same
heroine—a collage of multiple identities. Thus German's infatuation with the pair is

not entirely the product of his disturbed mind, but the operatic set-up, the trap in which he is caught.

Both Liza and the Countess are also cross-connected with the mythical shepherdess. The theme of Polina's romance (Example 9.10), initially assigned to Liza,[81] is a distant yet obvious match to the melodic contour of the shepherdess's happy song from the intermède (Example 9.11).

Like the mournful romance that arches across several scenes to Liza's destruction, the countess's little song from the fourth scene flashes back to the second scene—the night meeting of Liza with Gherman hiding on the balcony. Transposed down by a diminished fifth from Grétry's original, the melody of the countess's song matches the melodic contour of the sarabande (even though the former is in a minor key and the latter is in a major; Examples 9.12 and 9.13).[82]

Liza is also linked with Polina, who sings two duets with her, one at the bridal shower and the other in the intermède, where she appears in breeches as Milovzor

Example 9.10

Polina: Girlfriends, my dears, in my carefree playful [life]

Example 9.11

Prilepa: My nice little friend, darling shepherd

Example 9.12

Example 9.13

with Liza/Prelepa.[83] She and Tomsky are the two narrators, he in charge of the outer plot—his antiquated story (subplot) sets off the sequence of troubles (main plot)—and Polina unfurls the inner plot of the bucolic heroine. Tied to her mythical story and character, Polina, last seen in the pastoral, dissolves into the shadows of the Arcadian idyll. Considering the baffling doubles, it seems less surprising that, confused throughout the opera, the protagonist at the end picks the wrong card. The countess/apparition doubles as the Queen of Spades, the card itself as the countess's portrait (a rose in the young countess's hair frequently appears on the card), the portrait and countess with Liza, and both women with the shepherdess. This female khorovod is extended and empowered by one more person, a silent monarchial shadow at the falling curtain of the third scene; all the women eventually converge into a single composed image.

The Clash of Ascending and Descending Scales

Musically the drama unfolds in an array of mirrored, distorted, doubled musical leitmotifs. The introduction, which the composer created after he finished six scenes of the opera, pulls the spectator into a whirl of leitmotifs. Tomsky's ballad conflates the motifs, previously introduced and associated with separate numbers, turning musical themes into agents of dramatic process. Russian scholars traditionally identify the main leitmotifs with the old countess, the three cards, the love theme, the leitmotif of fear, and others.[84] By definition, leitmotifs afford some degree of stability, guiding one's ear through an opera's complicated design. In *Pikovaia*, the themes, injected with the germ of transformation, "tortured and skewed beyond belief (but not beyond recognition),"[85] divorce themselves from once-introduced extra-musical associative contents. Not following the Russian tradition of labeling leitmotifs, Taruskin and Morrison, considering the consistent permutation of themes, align them with the letters, x, y, and z. Morrison explains his use of the letters also by referring to Tchaikovsky's diaries, in which the composer chooses x and z to describe his emotions.[86]

Tchaikovsky's z and x, associated with playing vint, are entwined in a complex emotional knot: z is "less painful and perhaps more substantial than x—nevertheless more unpleasant."[87] The inseparable pair, z and x, is a metaphor for the dichotomy of two melodic gestures, ascending and descending, lying at the basis of the drama of *Queen of Spades*.

The genius of Tchaikovsky is that all the leitmotifs of his *Queen*, as well as the musical portrayal of its protagonists and the emotional content of the events, the mass and lyric scenes, the imperial procession and the storm—nearly all the extraordinary, rich thematic material of the opera—fall under one gesture or the other (z or x).[88] Against the descending scalar melody that governs the dramatic processes permeating the musical texture of the opera,[89] another group of themes, if condensed to their formulaic skeletal structure, can be associated with an ascending gesture. This broad category includes what Asaf'ev defines as the love theme from the introduction, the countess's chromatic rise, and the opening of Tomsky's ballad. The rising scale also links Liza's "moi devich'i slezy" (my maiden tears) from the second scene with her arioso "Ah, istomilas' ia gorem" (Oh, I am worn and drained) in her final appearance (Example 9.14).

Though sometimes this ascending gesture simply balances melodic curving,[90] in most instances—shifting, exchanging places with, shadowing and distorting the

Example 9.14

Ach, is - to - mi - las' ia go - rem...

downward line—it takes the part of the musical Other. The array of descending melodies for a while remains faithful to the diatonic realm; the ascending gestures immediately introduce their potency to fluctuate between diatonic and chromatic. In the
introduction, germinating the drama, a motif (a) borrowed from Tchaikovsky's Fifth
Symphony (and soon converted into the melody of Tomsky's ballad) is completed
with a thrice-repeated three-note triad-based descending motif (b). A new occurrence
of the motto of the Fifth leads to a triple sequence, a three-note *chromatic* ascending
line muscled up with a row of expanding, edgy harmonies (Example 9.15).

The two ascending and descending scalar gestures overlap, juxtapose, or coincide
throughout the opera, introducing a melodic counterpart of the card images, (quasi)
mirrored, symmetrical, and turned in opposite directions. For example, in the orchestral
opening of the first scene, which depicts a jovial spring promenade, the two contrasting
gestures, up and downwards, playfully counterbalance each other in a run of sixteenths.
The combination and confrontation of the two melodic directions pervade Tomsky's
ballad, first blended into the opening of his verse and then split and juxtaposed as a
rising chromatic "O, bozhe, ia vse by mogla otygrat'" (O, God, I could win everything)
and the already recognizable descending double Unknown—beloved and cards.

Extending from Tomsky's tale, the juxtaposition of chromatic rise and diatonic
descent infiltrates the short duet of Chaplinsky and Surin, and, magnified by a storm,
steals into the part of Gherman, who remains oblivious to the continuous tempest.[91]
The two melodically opposite gestures confront and subvert each other, yet clenched
together they emblemize the unbreakable magnetic bond between Gherman and
countess—"I from you and you from me, are not to escape."

Example 9.15

Example 9.16

(Directions in the score: Gherman comes out and stands before the Countess.
She wakes up and in horror moves her lips soundlessly.)

The repetition of the familiar descending theme (a) followed by its three-note motif (b) leads to yet another critical motion, which combines three-note descents with ascending leaps—an angular theme that pervades the fourth scene (c; Example 9.16). Tchaikovsky sketched it on the margins of the first page of the fourth act with a remark: "Intermission and beginning of the scene, chromatic whining."[92]

From the beginning and throughout the opera, entrusted to different instruments, conquering both orchestral and vocal parts, the descending theme undergoes rhythmic alteration and appears in different keys, forming a tight network and establishing flabbergasting links among the characters and between situations. After the first three scenes, the theme transcends the diatonic realm, to reappear in whole-tone spectral guises. In its overt form the theme last sounds in Gherman's "Da! Ia uznal ot teba pro troiku, semerku, tuza!" (Yes! From you I learned the three, seven, and ace!), a sentence that, confusing Liza with the countess, guides the former to suicide. Together with the destruction of the female protagonists, the theme in its discernible form vanishes. The fragments of the "Unknown," with a characteristic tearful intonation in the seventh scene, mirror the gradual crystallization of the theme(s) in the beginning of the opera.

Signifying contrasting temporal-spatial planes, this downward melody attains its exceptional gleam and brilliance in the very middle of the opera, in the majestic choral polonaise to the empress (Example 9.17).

Why Is She (Not) There, in the Second Act!?

Cupolas of azurite (stone), the ample dome held by eight pillars, . . . above hung circular [platforms for] choruses with railings, precious Chinese vessels, and two golden organs . . . Inside the oval hall . . . the myrtle and other trees of favorable climate zones are laden

Example 9.17

with flowers and fruits. In their shade, the velvet-like grass spreads around, . . . a medley of flowers; the sandy roads lie, hills rise and descend into valleys, the glassy pond glows. Under regnant spring, Art rivals the beauty of Nature. One's spirit swims in pleasures. . . . As the court arrives, the trumpets signal the beginning of the feast.[93]

Working on the libretto of *Queen of Spades*, originally commissioned to composer N. Klenovsky, Modest Tchaikovsky wrote in his diaries: "February 11 (1888). [I] Began the third scene, thus read Derzhavin."[94] Completed two years later by the Tchaikovsky brothers, the third scene draws on Derzhavin's description of Potemkin's fête.[95] Symbolizing the apex of the political and military power of Catherine's Russia and embodying the grandeur of the empress's court, unmatched by anything afterward, Potemkin's ball took place a hundred years before the production of the Tchaikovskys' opera. As mentioned earlier, Derzhavin wrote the lyrics of six choruses performed at the ball, and later, at the request of the host, penned an account of the spectacular event. In *The Queen of Spades*, references to Derzhavin create what Skvirskaia calls a "thematic interlacing," especially apparent in the language, use of poetic texts, and stage directions in the third ball scene.[96]

Music permeates Derzhavin's description of Potemkin's ball, filled with vivid auditory references to blasting trumpets and loud drums, an "orchestra and choruses of three hundred people," alternating with the "ringing song of a nightingale," "soft sounding-organs," and "angelic singing accompanied by celestial harmony."[97] The ball begins.

As the highest guests proceeded to the places prepared for them, music was heard . . .; majestic harmony flowed though the hall; out of the altar stepped a *khorovod* of twenty-four most noble and beautiful women and men. . . . This gala quadrille, composed of adolescent Grazias and young half-gods and half-Heroes, opened the ball with a Polish dance.

As in Potemkin's palace, the guests of the operatic ball appear in masquerade. One easily imagines the ambitions burning behind these festive masques and the sinister plots unfolding under cover of the imperial masquerade, the proximity to Russia's most powerful players promising love and fortunes to some and ruin to others.[98] Among the courtly throng, anticipating the arrival of the empress, there would be "many young whipper-snappers greedy for sinecures . . . almost all from the minor nobility and . . . [with] major ambitions. Each one hoped that his pretty face would attract the attention of the aging but unrepentant collector."[99] It is easy to imagine the vulgar comments whispered *sotto voce* by these masked Surins and Chekalinskys. In the operatic masquerade, between brilliant choruses and dances, Liza silently breaks her engagement with Yeletsky and rushes to give the keys to Gherman, whose masked cronies keep pushing him to the abyss.

At Potemkin's ball, the glow of a "hundred thousand lamps . . . everything covered with clear crystals filled with burning candles" is multiplied in "mirrors of unbelievable size!" They increase and amplify, distance and diminish the subjects. In the ball scene, everything is a reflection of something else. The play-within-a-play mirrors the theatrical space. Bridging the spectators on the stage with those in the auditorium, the intermède simulates the events of the "real" opera. Characters act as spectators; nobles impersonate peasants, Liza's girl friend becomes her boyfriend. Three love triangles, each draped in romance, pastoral, and late-nineteenth-century psychosis, go off-kilter in a head-spinning carnival. The excitement leads the lovers to make urgent bold decisions: Liza invites Gherman, Prilepa marries Milovzor, Gherman pursues the countess. On the margins of the libretto of the third scene following the intermède, Tchaikovsky originally wrote, "Countess walks and, seeing Gherman, shivers. Gherman looks at her intensely." Then the composer edited himself, "[Gherman] Turns. In front of him is the Countess. Both shiver as they look intensely at each other."[100]

Structurally, the operatic third scene is a pyramidal compilation of frames, one within the other. The scene opens and closes with a majestic polonaise with brass, tremolos recalling Derzhavin's "loud trumpets and timpani" with the same elevated orchestral tutti. The two choruses, linked with orchestral episodes at both ends of the scene, form what Taruskin calls "cantata-like choral panegyrics" and what Ogarkova identifies as a "celebratory choral cantata," a genre that came into fashion with the arrival of court composer Francesco Araia and flourished during Catherine's reign.[101] The text of both choruses in *Queen of Spades* is borrowed from Derzhavin.[102] The first chorus, "Gaily and merrily" (*Radostno, veselo*), was originally composed for a family celebration of Count Stroganov. The second and final lustrous cantata-polonaise, "Glory to you, Catherine" (*Slavsia sim, Ekaterina!*),[103] premiered at Potemkin's and became "virtually a national anthem."[104] The chorus of Tchaikovsky's "Slavsia" in three parts is faithful to the tradition of panegyric kants that typically "voiced" the state processions of empresses Elisabeth and Catherine.[105] Echoing the uplifting music of the promenade in the first scene, the triumphal final chorus from the ball also evolves from the now familiar descending theme.

Like the endless crystals radiating in Potemkin's fête, a shimmering D major illuminates Tchaikovsky's ball. A medley of Mozartian themes governs most of the scene.[106] D major, the key of the original choruses sung at Potemkin's ball, was favored by Josef Kozlowski and other composers of eighteenth-century Russian ceremonial music. Even when the first couple, Yeletsky and Liza, enters the stage and the pained Prince graciously returns freedom to his fiancée, his aria, changing color but not mode, remains in a major key (E flat). Although for the most part Yeletsky's air reminds one of Gremin's "Love defeats all ages," some melodic elements and the rhythmic beginning of the verse also echo Onegin's "Dreams and years are not to return." A mixture of Onegin's "love of brother" and the noble devotion of Yeletsky/Gremin leave Liza nearly silent throughout this duet; the Prince's melody, repeated by the clarinet with rushing syncopated low strings, crosses into the next number, where Gherman absorbs Liza's message, scared and enticed by the possibilities. Twice breaking through the jovial surface of the ball, Gherman leaps away from a defined key, drifting in a quasi-open tonal space saturated with chromaticism and lacking harmonic stability.[107] The spotlight, focusing on Gherman, momentarily shifts when the intermède begins, immediately returning to the D major colors.

Following the introduction, with the orchestra expanding to its full sound, the opening of the intermède mirrors both the beginning of the third scene and Derzhavin's remarks on Potemkin's ball: a "quadrille of the most famous and beautiful women, youth, and maidens dressed in shepherd dresses, comes to the meadow, playing games and dancing."[108] A central piece of the symmetrical design, the intermède is structured as a pyramid (within a pyramid), with sections or frames progressing toward an internal peak shortened in length and rising in pitch. In addition, the tonal plan emulates a fragment of a circle of fifths, first rising and then descending, in major keys: D, A, E (C), A, D.

Like the overall structure of the third scene, the intermède comprises multiple frames, mirroring each other and the ball. The opening sequence of dances—the quadrille, sarabande, and a chorus dance in between—parallels the beginning of the ball. The concluding frame—consisting of the two shepherds' choruses, with Eros and Hymenaeus leading the wedding procession and the dance—matches the end of the ball (a chorus of courtiers bedazzled by the prospect of seeing their empress, the orchestral part aligned with the ritualistic polonaise-procession of Catherine's entourage, and the final "Slavsia!").

The choral sequences in the intermède enclose a cluster of duets, beginning and ending with "Moi milen'kii druzhok," a Russian version of the Mozartian "Tender Looks."[109] Between the two recurrences of the duet, another smaller cycle unfolds with Zlatogor's "entourage, dancing [in the tempo of a minuet], as it brings precious gifts." The brief orchestral interlude and the subsequent duet of the two rivals, Zlatogor/ Tomsky and Milovzor/Polina, introducing all their gifts—"mountains of gold and precious stones" along with "birds, flowers, garlands, and ribbons"—reach the shining domain of E major. When Prilepa/Liza rejects wealth and comfort, choosing "heaven with [my] darling in a hovel,"[110] her brief solo, decorated with birdlike slides in the clarinet later joined by flutes, dives into the key of C major. Stripped of the key signature and tainted by chromatic inflections, with the harp spilling out a troublesome diminished arpeggio, Prilepa/Liza finds herself in Gherman's tonal space.[111] Albeit momentarily, the jovial duet, succeeded by the mythological company, with the dance-chorus hailing the "shining red sun, with nymphs and zephyrs in the sky," leaves no clouds in the playful pastoral. The picturesque wedding, which mixes shepherds, Olympic gods, princes and counts, and shepherds/serfs, is perhaps the most direct allusion to eighteenth-century court theater.

The rapid change from D major to B minor and then to a noncommittal, signature-free (C major) tonal space brings the focus back to Gherman, who, followed by murmuring, malicious masks, comes to meet Liza. Quite phlegmatic and nearly silent when walking with Yeletsky, the heroine is enlivened by her abundant singing as she plays the shepherdess; full of agility and conviction, she enters Gherman's tonal zone, already flooded with chromaticism, frantically racing upper strings, and a slow chromatic rise of vexing syncopated harmonies. This recognizable ascending scalar motif, first spun in the low strings, then permeates other orchestral groups, and as Liza disappears the low strings play an accentuated, troublesome third gesture, composed of x and z with swiftly increased fortissimo. Gherman makes his choice, as the master of ceremonies announces the arrival of the empress.

The whole scene unfolds as a gift-surprise in a sparkling colorful wrapper with plentiful ribbons. Under the paper there is another resplendent wrapper; the recipient/spectator peels one layer after the other, the suspense and anxiety growing as one approaches the prize—"the men bow low, and women freeze in a deep curtsy," the massive choral "Slavsia!" reverberates with the procession of pages, as the empress herself, the Mother of the people, is about to appear on the stage . . . but the curtain goes down—there is a puff, nothing at all inside the glossy covers, only a pile of shining colorful paper. The promised grand entrance of Catherine is a lustrous sham.

11.	12.	13.
Polonaise and Chorus	Aria	Scene
D major	Yeletsky/Liza	Gherman, Surin, Chekalin
C	Eb	**C**

14. Intermède

Sincerity of the Shepherdess

a.	b.	c.	Dance	Duet	Prilepa	Chorus
Dance and Chorus	Sarabande	Duet Prilepa/ Milovzor	Chorus Zlatogor	Zlatogor/ Milovzor	**C**	Dance Chorus
D	D	A	E	E		D

g. Finale	
Duet	Chorus
Prilepa/ Milovzor	Dance Chorus
A	D

15.		
Gherman	Gherman/	Chorus
Surin	Liza	Procession/ Chorus
D	(b)**C**	D

Tchaikovsky, *Queen of Spades*, Scene 3, Ball[22]

She Is There! Catherine in the Bedchamber

The "Slavsia" at the end of the scene, befitting the tradition of Russian operatic finales, is thus in fact another deception. Whether or not appearing on the stage (depending on the interpretation of the director), Catherine herself is a brisk, silent shadow, and the "Slavsia" concludes neither the opera nor even the second act. Instead the ball is paired with the scene in the countess's bedchamber. After the absence/silence of Catherine in the masquerade, the spectators and Gherman watch the countess returning from the ball.

The scene in the countess's bedchamber is a distorted replay-antithesis of the ball. The courtiers' frenzied anticipation of the empress's arrival in a way parallels Gherman's prolonged, anxious waiting for the countess in her palace—the pulsating strings marking the passing seconds, his rushing heartbeat, and rising agitation. A royal entourage precedes the entrance of the empress; a flock of maids accompanies the countess. A chorus of courtiers greets Catherine as their *matushka*; the maids address the countess as their "*blagodetel'nitsa* (benefactress, patroness), *svet baryshnia* (your lightness)." The countess's list of former attendees—the "duc de'Orleans, duc d'Auyen, the marquise de Pompadour"—substitutes for the glamorous company at the preceding ball. In the masquerade, the nobles dress up as shepherds; the scene in the bedchamber shows the undressing of the countess. The pastoral is replaced by the countess's song, the arietta of Laurette from Grétry. In Dodin's version of *The Queen* staged in Paris, the countess initially appears in an imperial bright green dress. At the end of the ball scene, it is she in place of Catherine who descends the imperial stairs into the crowd of courtiers and ancient classical statues. In the fourth scene Dodin uses the same setting for the bedchamber. Singing the little song, the countess dances gracefully imitating the poses of the marble figures. The countess-Laurette-empress reminds one of an episode that Varvara Golovina, Catherine's lady-in-waiting, recorded in her diary: "Catherine held her fan strangely. Cutting my glance, she asked: Don't I look little bit like Favart's Ninette, a peasant at the court, but the aged Ninette?"[113]

A shadow of the masquerade, the fourth scene, like the previous one, offers a sequence of three odd duos/ensembles, two of which take place with an absent but implied second party. The first duo involves Gherman, who stands stupefied before the portrait of the young countess. Fixated on the canvas and first referring to her image in the third person, he quickly shifts to addressing his two-dimensional interlocutor in the second person, his inanimate companion as silent as Liza with Yeletsky at the beginning of the previous scene:

Ah, here *she* is, Venus Muscovite!
Fate binds me with *her* by some secret force.
I am from *you*, and you from me.[114]

The second implied ensemble is the countess's little song. In this anachronistic "inserted novella,"[115] linked with the sarabande from the intermède, the countess actually voices two characters, a dreamy young shepherdess and her adoring suitor. Like the twice-repeated duet of Prilepa and Milovzor, the Countess sings the same verse twice. In between there is an echo of the descending "Unknown" line. Sensing someone else's presence in the chamber—the role of the "third, burning with passion" is now fully appropriated by Gherman—the countess wakes up between the verses. "She rose, leaned over the fireplace, and played a spectacle herself," reads Meyerhold's direction to the actress playing the countess. "There is almost nothing of old age. Use a strong confident walk."[116] The third duo, Gherman and the countess, actually involves the two physically present participants. But it turns out to be Gherman's solo. The countess's vocal utterance is desired but not granted. She is as silent as Catherine at the end of the ball scene.

The score of the second act is a densely woven configuration of thematic and key codes whose persistent meaning is not to be trusted, whose associations must be questioned and deciphered, their links and transference contextualized. The orchestral introduction to the scene in the boudoir is a medley of familiar and distorted themes. Before Gherman starts prowling around the chamber, violas begin their constant, rustling, running, toothache-provoking sixteenths, as all four sections of violins play a short, mournful, rising motif with descending closing leaps, while the symmetrical inversion of the melody is played simultaneously in the low strings. The repetition and the ascending sequence of this motif are balanced by a long descending motion that resembles its many variations—from what Russian scholars call the "love theme" in the introduction to a transfigured "Slavsia." Nothing is hopeful in this scalar descent calling for Gherman's appearance; the stumbling dotted rhythm echoes the polonaise and simultaneously reminds one of the similarly uneven, crumbling, syncopated, chromatic rise accompanying Gherman in the midst of the ball.[117] As he stands before the portrait, he is back in his tonal zone, and when later the countess begins, her voice slides into Gherman's key-signature-free space, where the two are interlocked.

The countess's first motif, a slightly adjusted version of the beginning of the "Slavsia," is immediately transmitted to bassoons, then to strings, and surfaces in the bass clarinet that overlays her reveries and the song, turning the echo of the polonaise into a macabre dance, or what Morrison (after Asaf'ev) coins a "funereal scherzo." Tracing the recurrence of the theme, Morrison suggests "it seems to touch on something more provocative."[118] Taruskin finds this consistent ostinato "the ticking time bomb."[119] The importance of time is signaled throughout the scene, in the running seconds in strings, the midnight bells, and the Countess's "What a time!" The wheel of time spins out when the events of one night, from the ball to the boudoir, turn into what Gukovsky calls a "montage" of the two epochs.[120] When the countess recalls the lustrous past and bemoans the current manners and tone—"Who dances? Who sings?"—to what ball and what age does she actually refer? Shifting from the splendor of the eighteenth century, the boudoir scene manifests Pushkin's nineteenth century, or rather the "rugged, negligent dark, gloomy" late nineteenth century, infected by the psychosis of Dostoevsky and Mussorgsky and all others denouncing the aesthetics of joy.[121] In his "new view" of Tchaikovsky, Taruskin positions the composer at the center of the historic clash of the eighteenth-century "Franco-Italian esthetic of enjoyment" and the nineteenth-century Germanic cultivation of self-torturing, nightmarish, driven-but-never-satisfied ego. In a letter to Modest, Peter Tchaikovsky wrote: "Before, music strove to delight people—now they are tormented and exhausted."[122] In *The Queen of Spades*, the Tchaikovskys personify the aesthetic conflict, the improbable duel between St. Germain and G(h)erman. An unwavering adherent of the Enlightenment, Peter Tchaikovsky replayed the aesthetic "split" in the second act of *The Queen of Spades*. The Mozartian intermède within Potemkin's ball, celebrating Derzhavin's "harmonious union of Arts and Nature," is succeeded by the "tormented, exhausted" reenactment of the previous scene, but with a lethal outcome.

There is one other invocation of Derzhavin in the final scene of the opera. Tomsky's song, its bawdy text borrowed from Derzhavin, resonates with the poet's third chorus in Potemkin's ball. Derzhavin in his description of the ball explained these playful verses by referring to loud music that glorified victories and aroused young men while venerating the beauty of young maidens. The sexual frivolity associated with "so many Nymphs and so pretty" and Cupid who "flies here and there and sits on the nymphs, on this and that and the other, like yellow bees sit on flowers in young fields"[123] is invoked in Tomsky's ditty.

Если б милые девицы	If pleasant maidens
Так могли летать, как птицы,	Could fly like birds
И садились на сучках,	And sit on twigs
Я желал бы быть сучочком,	I would wish to be a little (playful) twig
Чтобы тысячам девочкам	So that a thousand girls
На моих сидеть ветвях.	Could sit on my branches.

After the gradual demise and disappearance of female characters and in the absolute absence of women on the stage, the verses and the enthusiastic male choral response sound grotesque. Perhaps the song aligning women with "birds" invokes the prizraks, who like the Russian *sirin*, the woman-bird of death, claim the life of Gherman, leading to the final choral *panikhida* (requiem). Funereal sounds are woven into the musical texture of the opera, from the ostinato in the fourth scene to the vision of

Gherman in the fifth, the monumental tragic ending of the sixth scene, and the final *panikhida*-lullaby.

After the ball in the third scene, the funereal scherzo in the fourth rings the demise of the spectacular century. The transcending ostinato hammers into spectators' ears the "Slavsia" to Catherine; it entwines the image and reverie of the countess with the deceased mistress, the Germanic/Russified sorceress, the omnipotent empress whom she follows—to return as a ghost.

Conclusion: Spellbinding Shadow

It is intriguing that even though Pushkin makes no direct references to Catherine, Lotman, examining the story, brings to the center of his analysis favoritism in late-eighteenth-century Russia. Like Tchaikovsky, Lotman invokes Derzhavin by referring to the ode "To Fortune," suggesting that gambling is a model for the structure and dynamics of Catherine's court: "Depending on the caprices of fortune, vast amounts of money could be made overnight, in spheres of activity, which were very far removed from the normal course of economic affairs." Continuing, Lotman painstakingly chronicles the "fortunes"—the winnings—Catherine bestowed on her favorites: "the Orlovs received from the empress 17,000,000 roubles, Vasil'chikov 1,100,000, Potemkin 50,000,000, Zavadovsky 1,380,000, Zorich 1,420,000, Lanskoj 7,260,000 and the Zubov brothers 3,500,000."[124]

Staking all of his money—40,000 rubles—Gherman could come into instant possession of 320,000 rubles. In this context, the murky light in the bedchamber may conceal, distort, and confuse not only the identity of the old countess. Who is he, the seeker of the fortune, the one hiding behind the curtain? Is it the poet, Pushkin himself, mocking, jeering, and degrading the old woman, yet unable to escape the dream of past fortunes? Or is it the composer, who, sharing his protagonist's addiction to an eighteenth-century past, opened the possibility of an "encounter" with the very symbol of elapsed promises: the countess/empress? Gherman's craving and failure lead him to death and his operatic creator, according to his own admission, to continuous "weeping" "turning into a little hysterical fit."[125]

In this play of doubles, after the empress's momentary (almost) appearance at the very end of the ball, in the following chamber scene, the countess, still alive, becomes a ghost/*prizrak* of the empress.[126] Silent Catherine is actually omnipresent in Tchaikovsky's second act; she is present in the stately polonaise penetrating two scenes and in the little play whose bucolic Prilepa relates as much to Derzhavin's Prelepa as to Prekrasa from Catherine's *Oleg* (the score was reissued by Tchaikovsky's publisher and friend, Iurgenson, in 1891).[127] The strings, split into pain-impregnated harmonies, intone the "Slavsia" revised into slow, hard, heavily accented motion, as Gherman gazes at the countess's portrait. The rose in the countess's hair invokes the "courtly symbolism" connected with the image of "the rose without prickles" created by Catherine herself. Tchaikovsky employs the same allusion at the end of the ball scene in *Slippers*, when announcing *Prince Khlor or the Rose Without Prickles*. Puzzling is Pushkin's description of the portrait of a young beauty whose "aquiline nose" fits neither national traits nor Pushkin's own gallery of young, round-faced, white-armed, dark-eyed women. However, the aquiline nose as well as an open high forehead are distinct markers of Catherine, often referred to by her contemporaries.[128] Tchaikovsky's Gherman is unable to escape from the "hideous and marvelous face," but these words, taken from Pushkin's *Queen of Spades*, echo the poet's description of Catherine: "Her splendor has blinded, generosity chained, . . . the voluptuousness of this canny woman has fortified her rule." The circle of doubles—the countess, Queen of Spades, Liza, shepherdess—encloses a most enticing persona, Catherine herself.

Before giving up his dream of the Russian eighteenth century and Catherine/countess to Gherman(ization), Tchaikovsky, "the last of the great eighteenth-century composers,"[129] creates a ball, the brightest spot in the opera, with its glorious finale when the public, thrilled, spellbound, breathlessly waits for magic—the arrival of the majestic empress.

NOTES

Introduction

1. Ritzarev, *Eighteenth-Century Russian Music* (2006), 4.
2. Frolova-Walker, "On Ruslan and Russianness" (1997), 21–45, 21.
3. Wachtel, *An Obsession with History: Russian Writers Confront the Past* (1994), 7.
4. Lam, personal correspondence, July 2008.
5. Bratton, "Reading the Intertheatrical, or the Mysterious Disappearance of Susanna Centlivre" (2004), 1–24; see also Bennett, "Theater History, Historiography and Dramatic Writing" (2000), 46–59.

Overture

1. On the issue of the "folk" in these tales, see Chapter Five on *Rusalka* and Chapter Six on *Sadko*.
2. Wortman, *Scenarios of Power* (1995), 3.
3. Geertz, *Negara* (1980), 13.
4. Burke, *Fabrication of Louis XIV* (1992), 7.
5. The imperial sublime arose, according to Ram, as a "melding of the Baroque traditions of late Moscovy with newer literary codes and cultural fashions imported from France and Germany under monarchs Peter, Anna, and Elisaveta." See Ram, *The Imperial Sublime* (2003), 4–5.
6. Uspensky writes that in 1492 "the head of Russian church . . . proclaimed Moscow the new Constantinople," a city also equated with Jerusalem. Uspensky, *Semiotika istorii. Semiotika kul'tury* (1994), 87.
7. Madariaga, *Catherine the Great: A Short History* (1981), 383; and Alexander, *Catherine the Great: Life and Legend* (1989), 247. Catherine II explained her Greek project in great detail in her letter to Joseph II, September 1782. See Zorin, "Eden in Taurus" (2005), 229.
8. Peter fought the Turks in 1710–11; Anna waged a war between 1735 and 1739 that ended in significant gains and her veneration in multiple odes to the battle in Khotin; Catherine conducted two wars with Ottoman Turkey, 1768–1774 and 1787–1792. Wars between Russia and Ottoman Porte continued into the nineteenth century.
9. The notion of the fourth Rome disturbs the Christian trinity. Lotman and Uspensky, "Otzvuki kontseptsii Moskva—Tretii Rim" (1992), 201–12.
10. Strong, *Art and Power* (1984), 65.
11. *Opisanie koronatsii Eia Velichestva Imperatritsy Ekateriny Alekseevny* (1725), 33; Andreev, "Ekaterina Pervaia" (1869), 17–18.
12. Ginsburg, *Representing Agrippina* (2006), 98.

13. Princess Ekaterina Dashkova wrote in her memoirs: "if to a foreigner she spoke French rather than German, this was because she wanted people to forget that she was born in Germany. And, indeed, she succeeded, for I have often heard peasants in conversation with me refer to her as their countrywoman as well as their mother." Dashkova, *Memoirs of Princess Dashkova* (1995), 244.

14. Catherine I marched in her coronation procession wearing a magnificent royal taffeta dress embroidered with "such a number of golden two-headed eagles that the robe was thought to weigh a hundred-fifty pounds." Elisabeth, possessing the most fashionable and revealing European garments, instituted the custom of women attending her balls wearing traditional Russian attire. Catherine II was portrayed in lavish dresses covered with all the symbols of the empire, in a theatrical costume as Minerva, in the folds of a Roman robe as the mythological Legislator, and also in Russian attire that included a *kokoshnik* (traditional headdress). At the coronation of his spouse, two decades after the foundation of St. Petersburg, Peter bestowed on her a specially made Western crown that replaced "the cap of Monomachus," previously placed on the heads of Russian monarchs, which manifested a familial link to Byzantium emperors. In her monumental musical spectacle *The Early Reign of Oleg*, Catherine II, who wore Western-fashioned crowns and lived in her European capital, re-enacted the ritualistic foundation of Moscow, mythologizing the conquest of Byzantium before the birth of Monomachus, thus claiming Turkish territory and asserting Russian orthodox primacy. Roman and Greek mythology increasingly became an essential part of Russian imperial narrative throughout the century. Dynamic enactment of imperial power served the purposes of the state and of the woman with absolute and unquestionable power.

15. Peter I's grandsons included the teenage emperor Peter II (who ruled between 1727 and 1730), Peter III (who ruled between December 1761 and June 1762), and the infant monarch Ivan VI (who ruled between October and December 1741).

16. According to Richard Taruskin, it was "the earliest enlightened model of Russian nationalism purveyed by liberal aristocrats in the time of Catherine the Great." Taruskin, *Defining Russia Musically* (1997), 25.

17. Princess Zinaida Schakovskoy cited Grigorii Kotoshikhin, *O Rossii v tsarstvovanie Alexeia Mikailovitcha* (1840). Schakovskoy, *Fall of Eagles* (1964), 20–25.

18. Dal' defines "female terem" or "maid's terem" as a section of a house or palace designated for women isolated from the public and male domain. The terem, usually occupying the upper part of the structure and, often referred as "tall terem," was associated with the old nobility and the tsar's families. See Dal' (1989), 4:400. The institution of the terem, signifying women's segregation, began to decline in the last decades of the seventeenth century and ceased to exist under Peter the Great.

19. Wortman, *Scenarios of Power*, 86.

20. Peter adopted the title of emperor after ruling as a tsar for nearly a quarter of a century. He staged the imperial coronation for Catherine I; thus technically she was Russia's first crowned emperor. See Lotman and Uspensky, "Otzvuki kontseptsii," 201.

21. The first mention of Martha Scavronskaya appeared in correspondence of 1703. In 1704, she gave birth to the first of eleven children, though only three survived past childbirth. In 1707, she converted to Eastern Orthodoxy and was baptized as Catherine. In 1712, Peter and Catherine were married. Reading Peter's letter to Catherine, one notices his incredible tenderness to "*tetka*" and "*matka*," and "darling, friend Caterinushka"—a quality hardly

matching Peter's persona. See Peter I's letters, "Tsarina Ekaterina Alekseevna. Supruga Petra Velikogo, 1707–1713." In Andreev, "Ekaterina Pervaia," 1869, 3:1–26.

22. Ibid., 10.

23. Since the twelfth century, there had been no marriages between foreign princes and the daughters of Russian tsars. Anna was the middle daughter of Peter's brother and co-tsar Ivan, and Praskovia Saltykova, who was from one of the old boyar families.

24. Trachevsky, *Russkaia istoriia* (1895), 160.

25. The conditions prepared by the Privy Council included seven short but substantial points significantly limiting the ruler's power: (1) her legislative resolutions had to be approved by the privy council, (2) "she should not declare war nor make peace by her own authority," (3) "she would not lay down any new tax," (4) she could not order capital punishment without due process, (5) she could not confiscate anyone's property, (6) she had no right over the land belonging to the crown, and (7) she could not marry or choose an heir without asking the consent of the privy council. Manstein, *Contemporary Memoirs of Russia* (1773), 28.

26. The name of this old dynasty appears in different versions, as Dolgorukii, Dolgorukoi, or Dolgorukov. For example, the name of Prince Ivan D., an actor/writer is spelled differently in his two literary works. To avoid confusion, the name here appears consistently as Dolgorukov.

27. Kostomarov, *Russkaia istoriia v zhizneopisaniiakh ee glavneishikh deiatelei* (2003), 3:431, 446–51.

28. This wording and imagery pervades the coronation odes to Elisabeth by Mikhail Lomonosov, Vasilii Trediakovsky, and Aleksandr Sumarokov. See, for example, "To the Empress Elisabeth on the Day of Her Coronation" by Lomonosov (1748) http://www.infoliolib.info/rlit/lomonosov/elisav48.html.

29. The posture of the rider and rising horse is reminiscent of several engravings of Peter made during his life, including Alexei Zubov's "Peter I on the Horse" (1721) and "Battle at Poltava" (1714). See Alekseeva, *Graviura petrovskogo vremeni* (1990), 55, 140, and 142.

30. Proskurina, *Mify imperii* (2006), 125.

31. Sumarokov 's "ПЕТР дал нам бытие, ЕКАТЕРИНА душу" nearly repeats a line by Kheraskov: "*Петр Россам дал тела, Екатерина душу* / Peter bestowed Russians with body, Catherine soul." See Kheraskov's *Num Pompilii* (1768), and the discussion of the political and poetic equation, as well as rivalry of Catherine with the memory of Peter in Proskurina, *Mify imperii*, 111–31.

32. Derzhavin, *Sochineniia* (1851), 2:327–28. Unless otherwise noted, translations from Russian are the author's.

33. To name a few of Catherine's acquisitions, she "bought Pierre de Croizat's collection in 1772, that of the Duc de Choiseul in the same year . . . [and] swooped up the Houghton collection, built up by Sir Robert Walpole." Madariaga, *Catherine the Great*, 533. She purchased the libraries of Voltaire in 1779 and Diderot in 1765, as well as the book collections of Ivan Boltin (Russian historian and archival collector), historian Gerhardt Friedrich Müller, and Evgenii Bulgaris (Greek archbishop and Catherine's court librarian). See V. Fedorova, "Biblioteki Ekateriny II v Zimnem Dvortse" (1996).

34. Taruskin, *Defining Russia Musically*, 25.

35. Pushkin, *Polnoe sobranie khudozhestvennykh proizvedenii*, (1999), 916.

36. In fact, the vengeance against the named authors never reached the level Pushkin claims. Writer and publisher Nikolai Novikov (1744–1818) died more than two decades after

Catherine (see Levitsky's famous portrait of Novikov, 1797), and Kniazhnin (1742–1791), serving as an adjutant of the tsar's general, was punished for financial misconduct but soon forgiven. See Serman, *Poety XVIII veka*, 233; throughout his life Denis Fonvizin (1745–1792) kept attacking the Russian imperial rule and the empress. See Kantor, introduction to *Dramatic Works of D. I. Fonvizin* (1974), 22.

37. Wortman, *Scenarios of Power*, 8.
38. Mottley, *History of the Life and Reign of the Empress Catharine* (1744), 280.
39. Evgenii Anisimov quotes Peter I's speech at the award ceremony for the specially established order of St. Catherine to his spouse. Anisimov, *Five Empresses* (2004), 24.
40. Bergholz, *Dnevnik kammer-iunkera Berkhgoltsa vedennyi im v Rossii v tsarstvovanie Petra Velikogo* (1860), 3:19; Anisimov, *Zhenshchiny na rossiiskom prestole* (1997), 27–28.
41. Catherine's gift of her all jewelry to the Ottoman adversary of Peter was a significant contribution to the peace treaty on the Pruth. The vizier swiftly agreed to sign the peace treaty, which later cost him his life. Chizhova, *Piat' imperatrits*, 9.
42. Wortman, *Scenarios of Power*, 67.
43. Bergholz, "Dnevnik kammer-iunkera," in *Iunost' derzhavy* (2000), 28.
44. Catherine II, according to her memoirs, also hunted: "in Oranienbaum, . . . I got up at three o'clock, dressed myself from neck to toe in male dress; old gamekeeper waited for me with prepared guns." Catherine II, *O velichii Rossii* (2003), 539; see also Catherine, *Zapiski Imperatritsy Ekateriny Vtoroi* (1907), 331–32.
45. Ivan Dolgorukov, a close friend of Peter II, belonged to one of the most powerful families, constituting the majority of the Supreme Privy Council that devised Anna's "conditions." Soon after the coronation, she tried the family as regicides, stripping them of their rank, wealth, and lives. Ivan ended his life on the wheel.
46. Dolgorukaia, "Svoeruchnye Zapiski" (1990), 48.
47. *Opisanie koronatsii Eia Velichestva Imperatritsy, i Samoderzhitsy Vserossiiskoi, Anny Ioannovny* (1730).
48. Ségur, *Zapiski grafa Segiura o prebyvanii ego v Rossii v tsarstvovanie Ekateriny II* (1865), 208.
49. Meehan-Waters, "Catherine the Great" (1975), 293–307, 296.
50. O'Malley, *Dramatic Works of Catherine the Great* (2006), 14.
51. Meehan-Waters, "Catherine the Great," 293.
52. Ibid., 295–96.
53. Mottley, *History of Empress Catharine*, frontispiece.
54. Catherine II, *O velichii Rossii*, 571–72.
55. Buckinghamshire, *Despatches and Correspondence* (1900), 100.
56. Dashkova, *Memoirs* (1995), 110–11.
57. The portrait is a part of the Musee des Beaux-Arts, Chartres in France.
58. Catherine, *Zapiski*, 331; Christoph Grooth, *Portrait of Empress Elizaveta Petrovna on Horseback Followed by an Arab Boy* (1743, the Tretiakov Gallery, Moscow); Vigilius Eriksen, *Portrait of Catherine and Her Horse* (a double portrait of Catherine and her horse Brilliant; St. Petersburg: Hermitage, 1762).
59. Liria, "Pis'ma o Rossii" (1869), 3:27–132; Trachevsky, *Russkaia istoriia*, 161; Wortman, *Scenarios of Power*, 85.
60. Trachevsky, *Russkaia istoriia*, 181.
61. Mikhail Lomonosov lauded Anna on the victory over the Turks and Tatars and the conquest of Khotin in 1739.

62. Derzhavin, "On Seizure of Izmail," in *Sochineniia* (1851), 394.
63. "An Ode to Catherine II on her coronation upon her visit of the Seminary of the Holy Trinity-St. Sergius Lavra," in *Opisanie vseradostneishago vshestviia* (1762).
64. For an interesting current interpretation, see Gary Marker, "God of Our Mothers" (2003), 199.
65. Wortman, *Scenarios of Power*, 16.
66. Madariaga's chapter "Favoritism," in *Russia in the Age of Catherine the Great* (1981), 343–58.
67. Historical annals refer to Anna's reign as the "German Yoke" because Biron and his foreign clique were believed to govern Russia.
68. Wortman, *Scenarios of Power*, 132–133.
69. Semenkova and Karamova, *Russkie tsaritsy i tsarevny* (2001), 123, 128.
70. Pyliaev, *Staroe zhit'e* (2000), 173. Ilia Shliapkin shared Ivan Zabelin's view, attributing the play instead to tsarevna Natalia. See Shliapkin (1898), xi–xii.
71. Karamzin, "Panteon Rossiiskikh avtorov," *Izbrannye sochineniia* (1964), 2:159.
72. Ibid.
73. Pushkin's letter to Katenin, cited by Sergei Nikolev, *Literaturnaia kul'tura petrovksoi epokhi* (1996), 115.
74. Weber, *Present State of Russia* (1772–1723), vol. 1, 189–90.
75. Bergholz, *Dnevnik* (1858–1862), vol. 2, 219–20. See also Arapov, *Letopis' russkago teatra* (1861), 31.
76. Ibid.
77. King Augustus II was known to own at least five theaters. Starikova *Teatral'naia zhizn' Rossii v epokhu Anny Ioannovny* (1995), 18.
78. Starikova, *Teatral'naia zhizn' Rossii v epokhu Elizavety Petrovny* (2003), 144.
79. Ibid., 179, 182.
80. Ascending the throne, Anna came into possession of an Imperial Court Orchestra of about three dozen musicians, all foreigners except an unnamed *bandoura* player (a type of plucked Ukrainian lute/harp), and the only Russian name, curiously, is *arap* Fedor Ivanov. An arap (Arab) in the Russian context could mean a broad racial and ethnic category comprising Turk, Iranian, Easterner, or someone with curly hair and distinct features. Anna founded the first school of acting and established the School for Court Singers (1738), which provided the imperial court with singers and musicians. Fendeizen wrote about two major musical institutions she established, instrumental classes in St. Petersburg and the School for Singers in Glukhovo. The empress ordered to her court about twelve young Malorussians (Ukrainians), able to read music and taught to play instruments used in the orchestra. See Fendeizen. *Ocherki po istorii muzyki v Rossii* (1928), 2:18 and 29.
81. Arapov, *Letopis' russkago teatra*, 42.
82. Letter of Johan Christof Zigmund and Elizabeth Zigmund to Her Majesty, July 28, 1742. Starikova, *Teatral'naia zhizn', Elizavety Petrovny*, 665–66.
83. See the Prologue and Play for the celebration of the Russian-Swedish peace treaty (1743) and several others. Ibid., 674–88.
84. Petrovskaia, "Elisaveta Petrovna," 1:336.
85. Pyliaev, *Staroe zhit'e*, 199.
86. To name a few composers and choreographers arriving in Russia under Anna's initiative and patronage: Francesco Araia, the first Italian composer to have a long and fruitful residency in Russia; Jean Baptiste Lande, a choreographer and founder of the dance school bearing

his name; and the choreographer Igins. The empress apparently was physically present at the "construction of the theater" in the Kremlin, in 1733. Starikova, *Teatral'naia zhizn' Anny Ioannovny*, 42.

87. Bergholz describes the rare pleasure of listening to the "full orchestra," rehearsing and performing before sunrise with torches in honor of the birthday of Peter's spouse, Empress Catherine I. "The orchestra consisted of 17 or 18 persons, . . . 5 from the suite of his Lightness [Holstein-Gottorp] and 10 from the house of the Count Kaminsky." He also refers to Menshikov's ensemble as well as German and Swedish musicians in the eight-piece ensemble of Cherkasskaia. Bergholz, *Dnevnik* (1858–1862), vol. 1, 240–43; vol. 2, 71; vol. 3, 10.

Bergholz, "Dnevnik kammer-iunkera Berkhgoltsa vedennyi im v Rossii v tsarstvovanie Petra Velikogo, s 1721 po 1725 god.," 3.

88. On Derzhavin's "Felitsa," see Wachtel and Vinitsky, *Russian Literature* (2009), 53–56.

89. Derzhavin, *Sochineniia* (1851), 378.

90. Ibid., 400.

91. Bogdanovich, *Dushen'ka: drevniaia poviest v volnykh stikhakh* (1815), 1.

92. Sergei Glinka, *Zapiski* (1895), 228.

Chapter 1

1. Here, and throughout the book, Catherine's *The Early Reign of Oleg*—a historical production with music—is referred to as an operatic spectacle to avoid confusing it with other theatrical and social genres.

2. Khrapovitsky cites her suggestion to the lead actor, Ivan Dmitrievsky, who played "à contre sens. Oleg est un grand caractère, il est affecté de ce qui arrive, mais son jeu thèatral ne souffre pas d'emphase." Khrapovitsky, *Pamiatnye zapiski A.V. Khrapovitskogo* (1862), 232.

3. See Khrapovitsky's notes on *Oleg*, September 16, 26, 28; October 10, 11, 15, 16, 22–25. On the masquerade, see notes October 25, 29, 31; November 1, 5, 6, 10, 1790. Khrapovitsky, *Pamiatnye zapiski*, 231–234.

4. Ibid.

5. Catherine II, "Rasporiazhenie o pridvornom maskarade," *Zapiski* (1907), 668–69.

6. Starikova, *Teatral'naia zhizn' Elizavety Petrovny*, 95.

7. Volkov, overworked in the spectacle, died shortly afterward. Arapov, *Letopis' russkago teatra*, 73.

8. Zakharova, *Baly Pushkinskogo vremeni* (1999), 36–37.

9. Ibid., 74. The nine-part procession of negative forces included a wagon harnessed to tigers, satyrs riding goats, Ignorance on a donkey, Idleness and Slander shepherding a crowd of lazy people, a chorus of "Prevratnyi svet" (World of Perversion) wearing inside-out clothing, and an orchestra with a singing donkey and a goat playing a violin. See a detailed description in Pyliaev, *Staroe zhit'e*, 208–18.

10. Pogosian, "Lomonosov i Khimera" (2008), 11–24.

11. Wortman, *Scenarios of Power* (1995), 84–109.

12. Trediakovsky, "Oda torzhestvennaia o sdache goroda Gdanska" (1963), 129–34.

13. Lomonosov wrote, "Minerva po vsemu: v nei vsekh dobrot soiuz," 1761. Lomonosov, *Izbrannye proizvedeniia* (1965), 293.

14. Catherine II was portrayed as Minerva by Fedot Shubin, *Marble Statue of Catherine in the Guises of Minerva*; Stefano Torelli, *Catherine II as Minerva, Patroness of Arts*, 1770;

Dmitry Levitzky, *Portrait of Catherine II as Legislator in the Temple of the Goddess of Justice,* 1783; and I. G. Scharf, enamel medallion decorating a snuffbox presented to Grigorii Orlov. E. V. Sviiasov suggests that "in the 1770–1780s Minerva became nearly a twin of Catherine II." Sviiasov, "Evolutsia pronominatsii 'Ekaterina II-Minerva (Pallada)'"(1996).

15. Brikner, *Istoriia Ekateriny vtoroi* (1885), 630–54; Alexander, *Catherine the Great: Life and Legend,* 101; Gorbatov, *Catherine the Great and the French Philosophers* (2006), 109.

16. Angiolini, *Torzhestvuiushchaia Minerva ili pobezhdennoe predrazsuzhdenie* (1768).

17. After years of mistrusting treatments, Catherine invited British doctor Thomas Dimsdale to vaccinate her and Paul. Alexander, *Catherine the Great,* 144–47.

18. Lev Naryshkin was Catherine II's friend and a conspirator in her amorous adventures as the grand duchess. *Kamer-furierskii zhurnals* provide records of many musical events staged by Naryshkin's family. Livanova, *Russkaia muzykal'naia kul'tura XVIII veka* (1952), 2: 408.

19. Eighty guests dined with the imperial family in the specially decorated upper floor of the host's palace, and two thousand were fed in gazebos and tables set up in the meadows and gardens. See Liria, "Pis'ma o Rossii," 64–71.

20. *Opisanie maskarada i drugikh uveselenii* (1772).

21. Six victories were presented: the capture of Khotin (1769) and Bender (1770), the battles at the rivers Larga (1770) and Kagul (1770), the burning of the Ottoman fleet at Chesme (1770), and the conquest of Crimea/Tauride (1771).

22. Lev Naryshkin's daughters, Natalia and Katerina, performed Russian and Cherkess dances (Cherkess is a Turkic ethnicity in southeast Russia). Livanova, *Russkaia muzykal'naia kul'tura,* 2:408.

23. Ibid.

24. Bogdanovich created several versions of *Dushen'ka,* an antique poem in free verse.

25. Proskurina, *Mify imperii,* 253; Ivanitsky, "*Dushen'ka* I. Bogdanovicha i russkaia khvalebnaia oda" (1999), 34.

26. In Glinka's opera on Pushkin's text, Farlaf is a Varangian Prince and Ratmir a Khazar.

27. Starikova, *Teatral'naia zhizn' Elizavety Petrovny,* 650.

28. The wedded couple was placed in a cage on a live elephant. Another elephant, made of ice, stood in front of the frozen castle and spewed a stream of water twenty-four feet high. Ibid., 702.

29. Manstein, *Memoirs of Russia,* 250.

30. Twenty years later, Potemkin "surprised the Empress with a battalion of 'Amazons'—100 Greek women dressed in crimson skirts and gold-trimmed jackets." Alexander, *Catherine the Great,* 260.

31. Catherine herself conducted rehearsals in 1765. Ganulich, "'Pridvornaia karusel' 1766 goda i ee otrazhenie v literature i iskusstve" (1996), 234–36.

32. Antonio Rinaldi, an Italian architect favored by Catherine II, built the amphitheater.

33. Ganulich, "Pridvornaia karusel'."

34. Petrov, "Oda na velikolepnyi karusel'," in Makogonenko and Serman, eds., *Poety XVIII veka* (1972), 1:326–31, http://www.rvb.ru/18vek/poety18veka/01text/vol1/07petrov/226.htm.

35. Zakharova, *Svetskie tseremonialy v Rossii XVIII–nachala XX veka* (2001), 109.

36. Derzhavin, "Aphineiskomu vitiaziu" (1851), 1:535.

37. Gukovsky, "G. A. Petrov" (1947), 353–63.

38. Lomonosov, "Oda na torzhestvennyi den' voshestviia na Vserossiiskii prestol Eie Velichestva Imperatricy Elisavety Petrovny," *Izbrannye proizvedeniia* (1965), 142–43.

39. Sandra Logan writes about the coronation of Elizabeth I in England. Logan, *Text/Events in Early Modern England* (2007), 44.

40. Tokmakov, *Istoricheskoe opisanie vsekh koronatsii rossiiskikh tsarei, imperatorov i imperatrits* (1896), 66.

41. Wortman, *Scenarios of Power*, 13–21.

42. Ogarkova, *Tseremonii, prazdnestva, muzyka* (2004), 11–21.

43. Logan, *Texts/Events in Early Modern England*, 23, 35.

44. *Opisanie koronatsii Eia Velichestva Imperatritsy Ekateriny Alekseevny* (1725); *Opisanie koronatsii Eia Velichestva Imperatritsy, Samoderzhitsy Vserossiiskoi, Anny Ioannovny* (1730); *Obstoiatel'noe opisanie vshestviia Imperatritsy Elisavety Petrovny* (1744); *Opisanie vseradost-neishago vshestviia Ekateriny v Sviato-Troitskiiu Sergievu Lavru* (1762).

45. Catherine produced only the description of her coronation pilgrimage to the Holy-Trinity Sergey Lavra. Ibid.

46. The empresses and their secretaries oversaw the portrayal of coronations. Catherine II ordered the engravings for the *Description* to be made by the French artist Jean-Louis Voille; twelve engravings were housed in her palace. Several years later, she commissioned a painting of her coronation to the newly appointed court artist, Stefano Torelli. See Voille in Wortman, *Scenarios of Power*, 117.

47. Kants (or *cants*)—a tradition of three-part choral singing—encompassed both sacred and secular realms; they were closely linked to early songs and panegyrics as well as the poetry of Trediakovsky, Lomonosov, and Sumarokov. Vasil'eva and Lapin, "Kant" (1998), 2:20–37.

48. Bergholz, *Dnevnik* (1862), 4:68.

49. Alexander, *Catherine the Great*, 149. The empress's associate, Princess Dashkova, expressed a similar view of Moscow, "which scared me ever more because it reminded me of nothing to which I was accustomed. . . . I spoke poor Russian, and my mother-in-law did not know one foreign word. Her relations consisted of only old people." Dashkova, *Zapiski* (1987), 42.

50. Before Catherine I's coronation, everybody could access any place in the Kremlin including the Assumption Cathedral. Peter I and the rulers who followed him distributed tickets and controlled attendance according to strict regulation. Piatnitsky. *Skazanie o venchanii russkikh tsarei i imperatorov* (1896), 27.

51. For Anna's accession, the Spanish diplomat Duke Liria built and described arches in the Dorian style and twelve columns with Greco-Roman figures. Liria, "Pis'ma o Rossii," 3:65–69.

52. *Opisanie allegoricheskoi illuminatsii, predstavlennoi vo vseradostneishii den' koronatsii Ekateriny Vtoryia*, 1762.

53. Lazzaroni and Manfredini, *Le Rivali/Sopernitsy* (1765); Giovanni Battista Locatelli, *Ubezhishche Bogov* (1757).

54. Matvieev, *Kniga ob izbranii na tsarstvo Velikago Gosudaria, Tsaria i Velikago Kniazia Mikhaila Fedorovicha* (1856), 17.

55. Tokmakov, *Istoricheskoe opisanie*, 15, 51.

56. Novikov, *Drevniaia rossiiskaia vivliofika* (1772–1775, reprinted 1896), 1:198.

57. I. A. Chudinova writes about the "militarization" of both religious and state ceremonies. Chudinova, "Sakral'noe i mirskoe v tserkovno-muzykal-noi kul'ture Peterburga XVIII veka" (1994), 28, 32.

58. *Opisanie koronatsii Anny Ioannovny*, 3.

59. Ogarkova, *Tseremonii, prazdnestva, muzyka*, 36. On Russian taste for bells and cannons, see de la Messelière, *Voyage à Pétersbourg, ou, Nouveaux mémoires sur la Russie* (1803), 35–36.

60. Staehlin, *Muzyka i balet v Rossii XVIII veka* (1935), 60.
61. *Obstoiatel'noe opisanie Elisavety Petrovny*, 123–25.
62. Staehlin, *Muzyka i balet*, 98.
63. Ogarkova, *Tseremonii, prazdnestva, muzyka*, 35.
64. Logan, *Texts/Events in Early Modern England*, 35.
65. The same family names were recirculated through the four coronations and among other imperial rituals throughout the eighteenth and nineteenth centuries. They included state luminaries such as Counts Sheremetev and Saltykov and Princes Golitsin, Golovin, and Dolgorukov; all had plentiful opportunities to polish their roles as both actors and spectators of imperial theater.
66. Bergholz, *Dnevnik* (1858–1862), 4:50–51.
67. Ibid., 4:53; *Opisanie koronatsii Ekateriny Alekseevny*, 34.
68. During the coronation in Assumption Cathedral, the church chorus sang "Many Years" three times, with accompanying bells, cannons, and scattered gunfire after a proto-deacon announced the empress's full title. Then the religious clergy bowed thrice. Ogarkova, *Tseremonii, prazdnestva, muzyka*, 13.
69. Piatnitsky, *Skazanie o venchanii*, 25; Ogarkova, *Tseremonii, prazdnestva, muzyka*, 14.
70. *Obstoiatel'noe opisanie koronovania Elisavety Petrovny*, 53.
71. Wortman, *Scenarios of Power*, 115.
72. Ogarkova provides the list of operas, theatricals, cantatas, and other musical events taking place annually for the anniversary of imperial installation. Ogarkova, *Tseremonii, prazdnestva, muzyka*, 231–48.
73. Derzhavin, "Amur i Psikheia" (1793), and the poet's own commentaries in *Anakreonticheskie pesni* (1986), 12, 163, 402.
74. Luisa Maria Augusta of Baden (1779–1826), converted to Eastern Orthodoxy and renamed Elisabeth Aleseevna, was betrothed to the Grand Duke and future emperor, Alexander I.
75. See Derzhavin's commentary on his poem and the ritualistic games played by the princely couple. Derzhavin, *Anakreonticheskie pesni*, 86. Pashkevich used Derzhavin's lyrics in a choral song based on the folk tune "Zapletisia pleten."
76. Ostolopov, *Slovar' drevnei i novoi poezii* (1971), 472.
77. Multiple versions of *Amour and Psyche* also included the ballet pantomime by F. Hilferding and V. Manfredini (Moscow, 1762), a dramma per musica by M. Cantellini with music by Tommaso Traetta (St. Petersburg, 1773). Mooser, *Opéras, intermezzos, ballets, cantates, oratorios joués en russie durant le XVIIIme siècle* (1945), 9.
78. The name of the actor playing Amour in this ritualized game, known as *pleten'* (wattle), happened to be Pleten'.
79. Novikov, *Drevniaia rossiiskaia vivliofika*, 1:7–27.
80. *Tysiatskii*, from the word "thousand," was used to identify the head of an army of one thousand. The word also identifies the head of a wedding ritual.
81. Surna is an Eastern double-reed (*zurna* or surna); the nakra, likely a frame drum (*doira, davul, daf*) is used to accompany surna in Turkish, Azerbaijani, and other Turkic traditions.
82. Novikov, *Drevniaia rossiiskaia vivliofika*, 1:198. See also the descriptions of weddings by Mikhail Chulkov (1740–1793) in *Abevega ruskikh sueveriĭ* (1786), 41–43.
83. He used his patronymic as his surname. Anisimov, *Zhenshchiny na rossiiskom prestole* (1997), 21, 29.
84. Meehan-Waters, "Catherine the Great," 106–18.
85. Anisimov, *Zhenshchiny*, 102.

86. Catherine II, *Zapiski* (1907), 308.
87. Ibid., 401–3.
88. Catherine wrote that weddings in the court were so frequent that more than one could take place in a single day. Catherine II, *O velichii Rossii.*
89. Manstein, *Memoirs of Russia*, 1–2.
90. In the early second millennium, descendants of great princes (Kiev, Novgorod, Moscow) commonly married princes and princesses of Sweden, Byzantium, and other countries. This practice was abandoned for centuries until Peter gave his niece Anna to the Duke of Courland in 1710.
91. Polonaises in Tchaikovsky's *The Queen of Spades* (1890), *Cherevichki* (1885), and Rimsky-Korsakov's *Christmas Eve* (1895) are discussed in later chapters. See chapters on the polonaise in Druskin and Keldysh, *Ocherki po istorii russkoi muzyki, 1790–1825* (1956), 160–216; and Ritzarev, *Eighteenth-Century Russian Music*, 235–45.
92. Within a month, the tsar conducted his dwarf Volkov's mock wedding, which followed the plan of Anna's marriage celebration. Ogarkova, *Tseremonii, prazdnestva, muzyka*, 66 and 200; Zozulina, "Vremia peterburgskoi tantsemanii"(2003). Peter combined mock weddings with victory celebrations. A famous one, for prince Buturiline, part of the emperor's one-and-a-half-month masquerade, extended into a grand fete dedicated to the treaty with Sweden. Starikova, *Teatral'naia zhizn' Elizavety Petrovny*, 95.
93. Catherine also expressed her frustration with the arrangement since "there was not a single man who could dance. They were all between sixty and eighty years old." Catherine II, *The Memoirs of Catherine the Great* (1955), 99–100.
94. In the wedding empress Anna staged for her namesake and niece Anna Leopol'dovna, with Anton Ulrich Braunschweig-Lüneburg (1739), the princely couple, likewise dressed in dominoes, led several quadrilles. The bridal party was seated in a specially designed room decorated with moss, grass, and flowers.
95. Starikova, *Teatral'naia zhizn' Elizavety Petrovny*, 85.
96. The program notes for Act I, Scene 2 read: "two combined choruses of Romans and Numidians sing praises to her Imperial Majesty and Their Imperial Highnesses." Starikova, *Teatral'naia zhizn' Elizavety Petrovny*, 94.
97. The odes, read beforehand in the court, were written on large illuminated placards. The title of the allegory identified the place and the date of the event. *Iz"iasnenie i izobrazhenie velikago feierverka kotoroi po okanchanie torzhestv velikago kniazia Petra Feodorovicha i gosudaryni velikiia Ekateriny Alekseevny vseia Rossii v Sansktpeterburge na Neve reke pred Imperatorskim Zimnim domom predstavlen byl avgusta 1745* (1745).
98. Von Geldern, "The Ode as a Performative Genre" (1991), 930.
99. Bonecchi, *Soedinenie liubvi i braka* (1745).
100. Melissino, *Opisanie feierverka* (1793).
101. Asaf'ev, *Izbrannye trudy* (1952), 1:151.
102. In the case of Anna Leopol'dovna, the mismatch was apparent during the grand ceremonial production. Lady Rondeau (1699–1783), the wife of an English minister in the Russian court, attending the wedding events and accompanying the bride to the bed chamber, wrote: "And thus ended this grand wedding, from which I am not yet rested, and what is worse, all this rout has been made to tie two people together, who, I believe, heartily hate one another." Lady Rondeau Vigor, *Letters from a Lady* (1777), 206.
103. Burke, *The Fabrication of Louis XIV*, 11.

104. Fomin's *Nevesta pod fatoiu ili meshchanskaia svad'ba* (The Bride Under the Veil or the Merchant Wedding, 1791); Prokudin and Gorsky's *Svad'ba derevenskaia* (The Village Wedding, 1777); Fomin and I. Yukin's *Koldun, vorozheia i svakha* (Magician, Fortuneteller and Matchmaker, 1789); Aleksei Titov and Kniazhnin's *Devichnik ili Fedotkina svad'ba* (Bridal Gathering or Fedot's Wedding, 1809); Ivan Kerzelli's *Svad'ba gospodina Voldïryova* (Mr. Voldïryov's Wedding, 1793); and F. Kerzelli on the text by Aleksei Zheltov, *Tri svad'by vdrug* (Three Weddings Suddenly, 1794). The wedding rituals, such as maidens' *devichniks* (bridal gatherings), were staged in Vasily Pashkevich and M. Matinski's *Sanktpeterburgskiy gostinnyi dvor* (The St. Petersburg Bazaar, 1782), Fomin and L'vov's *Yamshchiki na podstave* (The Postal Coachmen at the Relay Station, 1778), Alexander Ablesimov's *Mel'nik—koldun, obmanshchik i svat* (The Miller—Wizard, Cheat, and Matchmaker, 1779).

105. Feldman, *Opera and Sovereignty* (2007), 31.

106. Among the foreign composers serving Russia's rapidly bourgeoning imperial theater, orchestras, and cappellas, Francesco Araia resided in Russia for nearly a quarter century (1735–1759), Giovanni Maddonis for more than thirty years (1735–1767); others included Vincenzo Manfredini, 1758–1769; Baldassare Galuppi, 1765–1768; Tommaso Traetta, 1768–1775; Giovanni Paisiello, 1776–1784; Carlo Canobbio, 1779–1822; Domenico Cimarosa, 1787–1791; Giuseppe Sarti, 1784–1787 and 1791–1801; and Vicente Martín y Soler, 1790–1794 and 1796–1806.

107. Ritzarev, *Eighteenth-Century Russian Music*, 2.

108. Feldman, *Opera and Sovereignty*, 33.

109. The proponents of Peter as a pioneer of reform should look to reformist actions of his elder sister Sofia and the somewhat nontraditional persona of his mother, Natalia Naryshkina.

110. Kimbell, *Italian Opera* (1991), 182–83.

111. Starikova, *Teatral'naia zhizn' Elizavety Petrovny*, 90.

112. Shcherbakova, "Puteshestvie v istoriiu" (2003).

113. Signed by the initials A. Sh. and attributed to Jakob von Staehlin, the articles appear in Starikova, *Teatral'naia zhizn' Elizavety Petrovny*, 532–76.

114. Starikova, *Teatral'naia zhizn' Anny* (March 9, 1738), 541.

115. Ibid., 533.

116. Ibid., 571–76.

117. Ogarkova compiled an extensive list of ceremonial repertoire. See Ogarkova, *Tseremonii, prazdnestva, muzyka*, 231–48.

118. Feldman, *Opera and Sovereignty*, 251–52.

119. Giuntini, "Throne and Altar Ceremonies in Metastasio's Dramas" (2006), 1:221–33.

120. Starikova, *Teatral'naia zhizn' Elizavety Petrovny*, 16.

121. Ibid., 109. See also *Kamer-furierskii zhurnal* (September 1745).

122. See, for example, Ségur, *Zapiski grafa Segiura*, 244–458, 266.

123. On Frederick the Great, who "exercised unprecedented control over every aspect of operatic production," see Bauman, "The Eighteenth-Century: Serious Opera" (2001), 61.

124. Karabanov, *Osnovanie russkogo teatra* (1849), 31.

125. Lazzaroni and Manfredini, *Le Rivali/Sopernitsy*.

126. Solo cantatas were performed during daytime or evening celebratory dinners, with libretti distributed among the guests. Ogarkova, *Tseremonii, prazdnestva, muzyka*, 52, 234.

127. Ibid., 12–13, 16–17.

128. Ibid., 18–22.

129. The same day the court enjoyed another Lazzaroni-Manfredini cantata for two choruses, *Minerva and Apollo*. Ogarkova, *Tseremonii, prazdnestva, muzyka*, 234.

130. Lazzaroni, *Le Rivali/Sopernitsy*, 24–25.

In LEI si veneri	Отец Богов! да обожаем
Di Te I'Immagine	В Ней образ твой, и прославляем.
Padre del Ciel	

131. The program, announcing the poet was from Florence and the composer from Naples, as in other cases emphasized the extent of the Russian imperial domain and cultural acquisition. The first Russian singer performing with an Italian troupe, Mark Poltoratsky, debuted in *Bellerofont* http://www.library.tver.ru/~shishkova/s05-p01.htm.

132. Bonecchi and Araia, *Bellerofont* (1750), 21.

133. Starikova, *Teatral'naia zhisn' Elizavety Petrovny*, 53; "Sankt-Peterburgskie vedomosti," 46, Monday, June 7, 1742.

134. The librettist depicts the "darkness . . . of a depleted country, in a deep forsaken forest . . . with some ruined and destroyed structures both on land and sea," as associated with the reign of Anna and the short regency of Anna Leopol'dovna. Her son Ivan IV, the legal heir to the throne, was destined to spend his life secluded and jailed throughout the reigns of Elisabeth, Peter II, shot at the beginning of Catherine II's rule in 1764. Starikova, *Teatral'naia zhisn' Elizavety Petrovny*, 55.

135. Ibid., 54–60.

136. Ibid., 60.

137. Ibid., 61, 64.

138. *Selevk* was symbolically relevant to the immediate historical situation in Russia. The mistrustful king Selevk revokes his eldest son Dimitrius's rights to the crown and turns against his ally Prince Vologez, his daughter Artemise's beloved. The maligned prince, displaying moral and military virtues, defeats Selevk, gives the crown to Dimitrius. Consequently the happiness of the two princely couples is restored. Bonecchi, *Selevk* (1744).

139. Bonecchi, *Soedinenie Liubvi i Braka* (1745), 52.

140. Bonecchi, *Selevk*, 52–53.

141. Bonecchi, *Scipion* (1745).

142. Bauman, "The Eighteenth-Century: Serious Opera," 54.

143. Staehlin, *Muzyka i ballet*, 60–61.

144. Ibid., 62; See also E. S. Khodorkovskaia, "Opera Seria," *Musykal'nyi Peterburg* (1998), 2: 289–90.

145. Traetta produced several versions of *L'Olimpiade*. Notably, his early productions in Verona (1758) and at the carnival in Pesaro (1759) had no choruses. According to Wilson, two years after Traetta's setting in Florence (1767), the number of choruses was expanded in the St. Petersburg production of *L'Olimpiade* (1767). Wilson, "*L'Olimpiade*: Selected Eighteenth-Century Settings of Metastasio's Libretto" (1982), 67–68.

146. Kimbell, *Italian Opera*, 250.

147. Galuppi's opera *buffa* was staged in 1758 and Zoppis's *La Galatea* in 1760.

148. Catherine II, *Zapiski* (1907), 180.

149. *Kamer-furierskii zhurnals* from February 8, 19, 24, and 29, 1750, cited in Starikova, *Teatral'naia zhisn' Elizavety Petrovny*, 801–3.

150. Sumarokov's *Tsefal and Prokris*—the first opera in Russian text—was staged for Elisabeth's name day of 1755.

151. Feldman, *Opera and Sovereignty,* 249, 250.

152. *Artaserse,* staged for Anna's birthday, was the third and the last *opera seria* during her reign. Metastasio's *Artaksers, drama na muzyke* (*dramma per musica,* 1738).

153. Feldman, *Opera and Sovereignty,* 251.

154. Ibid., 256.

155. The disregard for the "usual theatrical rules" is announced in the title page of the published drama and the score of Catherine's *Nachal'noe upravlenie Olega/The Early Reign of Oleg.*

156. Taruskin. "Catherine II," *The New Grove Dictionary of Opera.*

157. One finds, for example, the depiction of Alexander the Great's military campaign to India as part of the monumental tapestry "Arazzo di Alessandro Magno" (ca. 1460) in the Palazzo del Principe in Genoa.

158. Peter the Great's famous victory over the Swedes was celebrated with a large theatrical prologue to *Alexandr Makendonskii i Darii* [ruler of Iran] staged by Kunst's troupe in 1709. Arapov, *Lietopis' Russkago Teatra,* 24.

159. See Cummings, "Reminiscence and Recall in Three Early Settings of Metastasio's 'Alessandro nell'Indie'" (1982), 81.

160. The serenata "La Corona d'Alessandro Magno" by Bonecchi/Araia was staged for Elisabeth's birthday (1752–53); Araia's opera *Alessandro nell'Indie* on Metastasio's text was played for Elisabeth's birthdays (1753 and 1755), name day (1755), and accession (1756) and for the anniversary of Catherine II and Peter III's wedding (1759). Mooser, after Vsevolodsky-Gerngross, also referred to Angiolini's ballet pantomime *Alessandro* (*Liubov' Aleksandra, ili Veselie i Slava,* music by Gluck), staged in Moscow (1767). Mooser, *Opéras, intermezzos, ballets, cantates, oratorios joués,* 4; Gozenpud, *Muzykal'nyi teatr v Rossii* (1959), 213.

161. Sumarokov wrote *Hamlet* in 1750, and Catherine presented her *Oleg* as an imitation of Shakespeare in 1786. Kheraskov modeled an epic poem, *Rossiiada,* on Voltaire's *Henriade.*

162. Alexander himself acknowledges these qualities of the Slavs. Bogdanovich, *Slaviane* (1788), 5.

163. The opera *Fevei,* with music of Vasily Pashkevich, was shown at Catherine's birthday celebration (1786); *Novgorodskii Bogatyr' Boeslavich* (*Boeslavich, Champion of Novgorod*), music by Fomin, for her name day (1786); and *Khrabroi i smeloi vityaz Akhrideich* (*The Brave and Bold Knight Akhrideich*), music by Ernest Vančura, for the anniversary of Catherine's coronation (1787).

164. Bogdanovich, *Radost' Dushin'ki* (1786).

165. Cheshikhin, *Istoriia russkoi opery* (1905), 75.

166. Livanova, *Russkaia muzykal'naia kul'tura,* 2:118.

Chapter 2

1. Sumarokov, "Madrigal," *Polnoe sobranie vsekh sochinenii* (1781), 9:156.

2. *Aniuta* by Mikhail Popov, Act I, Scene 2. Ginzburg, *Russkii muzykal'nyi teatr* (1941), 34.

3. See synopsis and libretti of Kniazhnin and Pashkevich's *Neschast'e ot karety* (*Misfortune*), Krylov's *Kofeinitsa,* and Ablesimov's *Mel'nik—koldun, obmanshchik i svat* (*The Miller*) in Ginzburg, 37–41, 65–82; see analysis of these operas by Livanova, *Russkaia muzykal'naia kul'tura,* 2:126–50.

4. A. B. Zapadov suggested that the Russian audience was introduced to French comic operas in the fall of 1764, when a French operatic troupe touring Russia at the invitation of Catherine II staged Quétant's *Le maréchal ferrant* with music by Filidor. Zapadov, "Komicheskaia opera" (1947), 4:284–95. See also Karlinsky, "Russian Comic Opera in the Age of Catherine the Great" (1984), 320.

5. Staehlin refers to *Annette et Lubin* (1764) by Charles-Simon Favart (1745–1810). Staehlin, *Muzyka i balet*, 137–38.

6. Four years after *Annette et Lubin*, Framery's *Ninete et Lucas* continued the parade of naïve *paysannerie* on the Parisian stage—later adapted and adjusted as Aniuta and Lukyan/Lucas in the Russian *Misfortune from a Coach*.

7. Wyngaard, *From Savage to Citizen* (2004), 36–37.

8. A few enjoyed a high social profile. Betsky was a spokesman and close ally of Catherine; Temkina, a daughter of the empress and Prince Potemkin, was raised by members of his family. For the most part, illegitimate offspring lived among servants and serfs in nobles' estates.

9. Wyngaard, *From Savage to Citizen*, 42.

10. Gay, "The History of Shakespeare's Unruly Women" (1998), 43.

11. Lévi-Strauss, *Elementary Structures of Kinship* (1961), 481. See also Herman and Hirschman, *Father-Daughter Incest* (2000), 59–60.

12. The Miller calls the groom an *odnodvorets*, a rustic nobleman who, having no serfs, works on his land as a peasant.

13. Authors such as Nikolai Nikolev consistently denied the French sources. Nikolev, "Explanation," in *Rozana i Liubim* (1781), 3.

14. Elizarova, *Teatry Sheremetevykh* (1966), 144.

15. The expression *dramma s golosami* (tr. drama with voices, or tunes) identifying an eighteenth-century comic opera with preexisting tunes often appears in the title of libretti. See Nikolev, *Rozana and Lubin: drama s golosami*.

16. Schuler, "The Gender of Russian Serf Theatre and Performance" (2000), 36–38.

17. Authorship of the music of the opera is disputed. Two vocal scores attribute *The Miller* to different composers: Fomin and Ablesimov, *Mel'nik—koldun, obmanshchik i svat* (1956) and Mikhail Sokolovsky and Ablesimov, *Mel'nik—koldun, obmanshchik i svat.* (1984). Aleksei Finagin attributed the opera to Fomin. Finagin, "Yevstigney Fomin: zhizn' i tvorchestvo (1927), 94–95. Semen Ginzburg suggested that the score, composed by Sokolovsky, was later arranged by Fomin. Ginzburg, *Russkii muzykal'nyi teatr 1700–1835,* 65. Here and throughout the chapter I am using the score of Fomin (1956).

18. L'vov and Prach, *Sobranie russkikh narodnykh pesen* [*Collection of Russian Folk Songs*] (1987), 437–41; see also Fendeizen, *Ocherki po istorii muzyki*, 218–23.

19. "Как вечор у нас со полуночи."

20. "Во своей я младости вить не вижу радости," and "Кабы я, млада, уверена была." See Fomin and Ablesimov, *Mel'nik—koldun,* 28–29 and 30–31.

21. Ibid., Act II, 30–31.

22. Livanova, *Russkaia muzykal'naia kul'tura* 2:110; Vsevolodsky-Gerngross, *Istoriia dramaticheskogo teatra* (1977), 1:241.

23. Rabinovich, *Russkaia opera do Glinki* (1948), 53.

24. One of the first satirical journals, *Vsiakaia vsiachina*, was founded by Catherine; she also engaged in a passionate debate with Novikov, who established another journal, *Truten'*.

25. Vsevolodsky-Gerngross, *Russkii teatr ot istokov do serediny XVIII veka* (1957), 243.
26. "O, vremia!" (O, Times!), "Imeniny gospozhi Vorchalikinoi" (The Birthday of Madam Vorchalkina), "Peredniaia znatnogo boyarina" (Vestibule of a Renowned Statesman), "Gospozha Vestnikova s sem'ei" (Madam Vestnikova with Her Family), "Nevesta-nevidimka" (Invisible Bride) in Catherine II, *Sochineniia imperatritsy Ekateriny II* (1893).
27. Gus'kov, "K probleme zhanrovogo svoebraziia komedii imperatritsy Ekateriny II (1996)," 128.
28. Ibid.
29. O'Malley, *Dramatic Works of Catherine the Great* (2006), 58.
30. Catherine II, "The Birthday of Madam Vorchalkina," *Sochineniia Imperatritsy Ekateriny II*, (1901), 44–88.
31. Ibid., 54.
32. O'Malley, *Dramatic Works of Catherine the Great*, 46–47.
33. See Chapter Three, 85–86.
34. "Uteshenie Aniute" (Solacing of Aniuta), Krylov, *Polnoe sobranie sochinenii* (1945–46), 3:235–39. Philologist Vera Proskurina links Krylov's grotesque antiquated lustful coquettes to the aged Catherine. Proskurina, *Mify imperii*, 285–97.
35. See Chapters Three and Four on Catherine's operas.
36. Ogarkova, *Tseremonii, prazdnestva, muzyka*, 198.
37. Senelick's reference to Lotman in "The Erotic Bondage of Serf Theatre" (1991), 25.
38. Bakhtin, *Literaturno-kriticheskie stat'i* (1986), 297–98.
39. Castelvecchi, "From Nina to Nina" (1996), 92.
40. Dolgorukov, *Povest' o rozhdenii moem, proiskhozhdenii i vsei zhizni* (2004), 1:209.
41. Kniazhnin, *Komedii i komicheskie opery* (2003), 435–70. Premiered in 1787, *The Pretended Madwoman* was staged in the Moscow Bol'shoi Theater in 1795 and 1800. Fedorov, *Repertuar Bol'shogo teatra* (2001), 1:38, 50.
42. Kniazhnin, *Komedii*, 448, 450.
43. Kniazhnin's *Pretended Madness* was assumed to be a remake of J.-F. Regnard's *Les Folies amoureuses* (1704). See Kniazhnin, *Komedii*, 559. Elements of the plot remind one of an Italian opera with the same title, *La finta pazza* by Francesco Sacrati with a libretto by Giulio Strozzi (1641). It is interesting that the love story of Deidamia, central to Strozzi's opera, enjoyed remarkable popularity in Russia in Trediakovsky's tragedy *Deidamia* (1755). Catherine reread this drama while writing her plays.
44. Dalayrac, *Nina, or, The Madness of Love* (1787), 3.
45. Karamzin was well familiar with *Nina*, mentioning two performances of the opera in his "Letters of a Russian Traveler," *Izbrannye sochineniia*, 1:563.
46. Dolgorukov, *Kapishche moego serdtsa* (1874), 17.
47. Dolgorukov, *Povest' o rozhdenii moem*, 1:210.
48. Dolgorukov expressed strong disdain for his Sheremetev relatives. A generation back, the Sheremetevs deprived Dolgorukov's grandmother, returning from exile, of her family inheritance. The production of *Nina*, according to Dolgorukov's notes, gave him an opportunity for revenge. See details in Dolgorukov, *Kapishche*, 241.
49. The first operatic version of *The Barber* was composed by Friedrich Ludwig Benda in 1776. Bauman, "Der Barbier von Seville."
50. Elizarova, *Teatry Sheremetevykh*, 18.
51. Anna's premature death (she lived from 1744 to 1768) following the loss of her mother broke the heart of Sheremetev's father and son (Peter and Nikolai).

52. Staehlin wrote that the same noble troupe that staged *Annette* simultaneously rehearsed *Le Philosophe marié*. Also, some decades later, Ivan Dolgorukov, playing the lead part, confessed to nearly falling in love with his partner in *Le Philosophe marié*. Dolgorukov, *Kapishche*, 202.

53. See Chapter Nine on *Pikovaia dama*.

54. *Graf Nikolai Petrovich Sheremetev* (2001), 258.

55. The main character of *Olin'ka*, Prince Khlor, undoubtedly points to Catherine II's "Tales of Tsarevich Khlor" and her opera *Fevei*. In both, Khlor is identified with the empress's eldest and most loved grandson, Alexander I. Rumors about the production of the *Olin'ka* in Stolypin's private serf theater reached Emperor Pavel, and the text was promptly checked and revised. Guberti, *Materialy dlia russkoi bibliografii* (1966), 2:573–81.

56. Bergholz, *Dnevnik* (1902), November 15, 1722, 2:222–23; Arapov, *Letopis' russkago teatra*, 31–32.

57. After court theatricals, Kutaisov used to stitch and remove ducal diamonds from the acting costumes of Ivan Dolgorukov. Dolgorukov, *Kapishche*, 249.

58. Curtiss, *A Forgotten Empress: Anna Ivanovna and Her Era, 1730–1740* (1974), 256; Manstein, *Contemporary Memoirs of Russia*, 40; also Anisimov, *Five Empresses*, 117–120.

59. Bobrinsky was Catherine's son with Grigorii Orlov. Dologorukov's recollection of the theater in Bobrinsky's Moscow residency is found in his *Kapishche*, 192.

60. He appeared as a graybeard in Fenouillot de Falbaire's *L'honnête Criminel*. Since the Grand Duchess prepared the spectacle for her husband's birthday in secret, Dolgorukov hid in a palace room for a week, leaving only for late-night rehearsals. Dolgorukov, *Kapishche*, 21–22, 91.

61. Ibid., 176.

62. Ibid., 23, 55, 88, 204.

63. Ibid., 193.

64. Ibid., 43.

65. Prince Viazemsky's recollection is cited from Senelick, "Erotic Bondage of Serf Theater," 25.

66. See Levitskii, *Portrait of Ekaterina Khrushcheva and Princess Ekaterina Khovanskaya*. 1773.

67. Upon Peter's ukaz of 1720, "serf peasants and servants were assigned to serve 'aristocrats,' while the aristocrats themselves were to serve the empire until decease, death, the end." See Shepetov, *Krepostnoe pravo v votchinah Sheremet'evyh* (1947), 8.

68. Kurmacheva, *Krepostnaia intelligentsia Rossii* (1983), 17.

69. The works produced in the late nineteenth and early twentieth century include *Ostankino* (author unknown) and Baron N. Drizen, *Materialy k istorii russkogo teatra*, 1905. Soviet research on serf theater falls into three categories. One focuses on serf theater in general: Dynnik, *Krepostnoi teatr*; and Beskin, *Krepostnoi teatr*. The second group deals with serf theater within a larger frame of Russian theater: Evreinov, *Istoriia russkogo teatra*; Krasovskaia, *Russkii baletnyi teatr*; and Vsevolodsky-Gerngross, *Russkii teatr*. The third focuses on individual serf troupes: Kashin, *Teatr N. B. Iusupova*, on Iusupov's serf theater; on Sheremetev's troupe see Staniukovich, *Domashnie krepostnye teatry XVIII veka*; Sholok, *Ostankino i ego teatr*; Elizarova, *Ostankino*; and Lepskaia, *Repertuar krepostnogo teatra Sheremetevyh*.

70. Beskin, *Krepostnoi teatr*, 13.

71. More than forty serf theaters were functioning in Russia at the end of the century, almost half of them in Moscow, several in St Petersburg, and others in provincial cities and estates.

72. Herzen, "Soroka-Vorovka," *Izbrannoe* (1954), 234.

73. Beskin, *Krepostnoi teatr*, 6–7.
74. Ibid.
75. Vorontsov's theater, which existed between 1794 and 1805, was in the count's colossal estate in Vladimir province near the city of Tambov. Dynnik, *Krepostnoi teatr*, 251.
76. Schuler, "The Gender of Russian Serf Theatre and Performance" (2000), 217.
77. Senelick, "Erotic Bondage of Serf Theater," 25.
78. In the hierarchical scale among serfs, dvorovye held a place below household servants, whose closeness to their owners placed them at the "top" of serf society, and a step above peasants who worked in the fields and were separated from the landlord by a number of supervisors, mostly also serfs.
79. Evreinov, *Istoriia russkogo teatra*, 229.
80. Sholok wrote about the living conditions of Sheremetev's actresses, who were "kept under lock in humid cold cells, . . . were frequently ill, with cases of tuberculosis constantly increasing." Sholok, *Ostankino i ego teatr*, 40.
81. Beskin, *Krepostnoi teatr*, 25. Even one of the most liberal of aristocrats, Nikolai Sheremetev, ordered his assistant to punish young girls who studied acting by keeping them on their knees and limiting their food to bread and water. See Staniukovich, *Domashnie krepostnye teatry*, 15.
82. Jonce, "Tunisian Women as Professional Musicians" (1987), 71.
83. Ibid.
84. Especially considering that, at the end of the century, serf theaters constituted a significant theatrical venue: "Several types of theater existed in Russia. The leading was the St. Petersburg Imperial Court Theater, with regularly performing French, Italian, and German troupes. After 1780, urban public theaters were permanently established (Knipper in St. Petersburg, Medoks [Peter's Theater] in Moscow)." Lepskaia, *Repertuar krepostnogo teatra Sheremetevykh*, xvi–xvii.
85. Beskin cites I. M. Pylaev, who wrote down the recollections of a former *dvorovoi* serf of Count Gruzinsky ("Staroe zhitie"). Beskin, *Krepostnoi teatr*, 11–12.
86. Lepskaia, *Repertuar krepostnogo teatra Sheremetevykh*, 19.
87. Gay, "History of Shakespeare's Unruly Women," 45.
88. Evreinov, *Istoriia russkogo teatra*, 219.
89. Ibid., 220.
90. Vigel', *Zapiski* (2000), 239.
91. Ibid.
92. Evreinov, *Istoriia russkogo teatra*, 320.
93. Kaplan and Rogers, "Scientific Constructions, Cultural Predictions: Scientific Narratives of Sexual Attraction" (1990), 221.
94. Ibid.
95. The vivid picture of Ivan Dmitrievich Shepelev from Vyksa (Vladimir County) is offered by Vasily Sakhnovsky, *Krepostnoi usadebnyi teatr* (1924), 21.
96. This is how Beskin describes Count Sheremetev, whom his serfs referred to as "his majesty count-sovereign." Beskin, *Krepostnoi teatr*, 13.
97. Gay, "History of Shakespeare's Unruly Women," 43.
98. Ibid.
99. It seems paradoxical that the rise of nationalism coincided with enactment of the most restrictive laws with regard to serfdom during the age of Russian enlightenment.

Taruskin's revolutionary approach to the study of Russian nationalism in music has not yet been matched by a cultural study of nationalistic art in the context of slavery.

100. Similarly, Elizabeth Howe remarks on English actresses of the late 1600s: "The heroine's important quality was her beauty." Howe, "English Actresses in Social Context: Sex and Violence" (1998), 61.

101. Garber, "Dress Codes, or the Theatricality of Difference" (1998), 177.

102. See an extended discussion of Zhemchugova and Sheremetev in Naroditskaya, "Serf Actresses in the Tsarinas' Russia" (2005), 239–67.

103. Barsukov, *Rodoslovie Sheremetevykh* (1899), 5.

104. Elizarova, *Teatry Sheremetevykh*, 300.

105. The opera is *Les marriages Samnites* by Grétry. Today the carriage is still displayed in the Ostankino museum. Staniukovich, *Domashnii krepostnoi teatr*, 35.

106. Catherine's literary secretary wrote about his search for jewelry and gifts that Catherine wanted to present to Zhemchugova. Elizarova, *Teatry Sheremetevykh*, 303.

107. Catherine recalled in her *Zapiski* that, trying to win the sympathy of Tsarina Elisabeth and her courtiers, she secretly studied Russian at night, which led her to severe exhaustion and pneumonia. *Memoirs* (1859), 25.

108. Greenblatt, *Shakespearian Negotiations* (1988), 14.

Chapter 3

1. Karamzin, "Ilya Muromets," *Sochineniia* (1803–04), 7:202.

2. I am using the terms "opera skazka," "opera tale," and "operatic tale" for the most part almost interchangeably. Perhaps operatic tale brings more emphasis to the text of the operas, especially considering that Catherine was the author of the libretti.

3. Taruskin states that "Russian national consciousness was an aspect of Westernization." This, as well as his remark "that there was once such a thing as liberal nationalism even in Russia [under Catherine the Great]," kindled my interest in Catherine and her time. Taruskin, *Defining Russia Musically*, 3, 25.

4. Dashkova, *Memoirs*, 16.

5. Mooser, *L'opéra-comique français en Russie au XVIII siècle* (1954), 176.

6. Mooser, *Annales de la musique et des musiciens en russie* (1948–1951), 2:18.

7. Nikolev, *Rozana i Lubim*, 2.

8. Levshin, "Russkie skazki," from Chulkov, Popov, Levshin, and Kostiukhin, *Prikliucheniia slavianskikh vitiazei* (1988), 272.

9. To name a few, Propp, *Russkii geroicheskii epos* (1958); Lupanova, *Russkaia narodnaia skazka v tvorchestve pisatelei pervoi poloviny XIX veka* (1959); and Kaisarov, "Slavianskaia i rossiiskaia mifologia" (1993).

10. Chulkov's *Sobranie raznykh pesen'* was published around 1770, with the first two parts of *Peresmeshnik* issued in 1766. Fendeizen, *Ocherki po istorii muzyki*, 295; Stepanov, "Ob avtore *Peresmeshnika*" (1987) 337.

11. Volkov founded the first Russian professional theatrical troupe.

12. Chulkov, Popov, Levshin, and Kostukhin, *Prikliucheniia slavianskikh vitiazei* (1988), 314.

13. Nikolai, *Krasota* (1782).

14. Kulikov, *Skazka ili starinnaia byval'shchina*, written in the author's own hand (St. Petersburg, 1795). The original is in Houghton Library, Harvard University.

15. Kostiukhin, "Drevnaia Rus' v rytsarskom oreole" (1988), 5–20; Dereza, *Russkaia literatur-naia skazka pervoi poloviny XIX veka* (2001).

16. Chulkov, Popov, Levshin, and Kostukhin, "Russkie skazki," 272–75; Danilov, *Drevniia rossiiskiia stichotvoreniia* (1878), 70–72; Rovinsky, *Russkiia narodnye kartinki* (1881), 65–74, 79–82, 130.

17. There are primarily short fables in Ivan Khemnitser's collection of 1779, as well as in Ivan Dmitriev's anthology of 1797, both entitled *Basni i skazki*. See Khemnitser, *Basni i skazki* (1811) and Levshin, *Nravouchitel'nyia basni i pritchi* (1787).

18. The first attempts to define the genre of skazka occurred at the beginning of the nineteenth century in the works, for example, of Count Khvostov, himself an author of fables, moral stories, and tales. See references and citations in Dereza, *Russkaia literaturnaia skazka* (2001), 11–12. According to Khrapovitsky, Khvostov was the author of the opera *Ivan Tsarevich*. Khrapovitsky, *Pamiatnyia zapiski* (1862), 3.

19. See Stepanov, writing about Chulkov, "Ob avtore *Peresmeshnika*," 327.

20. A year before Catherine created this opera, "The Tale About Ivan the Tsarevich and His Beautiful Spouse Tsar'-Maiden" was published in the collection *Lekarstvo ot zadumchivosti* (1786). The plot and names of the characters, including Akhridei, Ivan's father, are the same in the printed story and the opera.

21. The translation of the two titles is borrowed from Taruskin, "Catherine [Yekaterina] II [née Sophie Auguste Fredericke von Ankalt-Zerbst]," Grove Music Online. The translation of the last operatic title is mine.

22. Waisman, "Introduction" to *L'arbore di Diana*, xxi.

23. See Moracci, "K izucheniiu komedii Ekateriny II. Problemy avtorstva" (2002), 12–17.

24. Mikhnevich, *Ocherk istorii muzyki v Rossii v kul'turno-obshchestvennom otnoshenii* (1879), 237.

25. Khrapovitsky's notes on November 22 and 23, 1788, *Pamiatnye zapiski*, 128; also Alexander Pypin (ed.), "Primechaniia," *Sochineniia imperatritsy Ekateriny II* (1901), 513.

26. In the eighteenth century, the "authorship" of an opera was associated with the author of its text; music could be compiled from existing songs or composed by unknown musicians. The composer's name, when acknowledged, was listed together with the names of choreographers, costume makers, and scenery designers or was referred to as "[drama] with music by. . . ." In many operas, the identity of the composer remains unknown or questionable. Accordingly, the authorship of the operas discussed in these chapters is most often associated with literary figures. For instance, Khrapovitsky wrote *Pesnoliubie* [Love of Songs] with music by Martín y Soler, 1790.

27. Dashkova, *Memoirs*, 235.

28. Mooser, *Annales*, 2:436–37.

29. The plays of Dashkova, the Comte de Ségur, and others were staged at the Hermitage.

30. Mooser wrote that *Fevei* was first shown in Kamenny public theater and three days later in Catherine's Hermitage; *Annales*, 2:439.

31. Seaman, "Catherine the Great and Musical Enlightenment" (2003), 132; see also Mooser, *Annales*, 2:442.

32. See Evgenii, Metropolitan of Kiev, *Slovar' russkikh svetskikh pisatelei* (1845).

33. Catherine's several short books written in the early 1780s were published in Russian with Greek translation, perhaps because of Catherine's desire for her second grandson, Constantine, to rule Constantinople, the capital of the Eastern Church. Among these

books are Catherine II, *Rossiiskaia azbuka* [Russian Alphabet] (1783); *Zapiski* (1782); and *Razgovory i rasskazy* (1782).

34. On the symbolic equation of Catherine with Minerva and other Greek-Roman goddesses, see the Overture, Chapter One, and Chapter Four. A marble statue of Minerva with shield and sword sat at the main entrance of the Kamenny Theater erected in 1784.

35. Wortman, *Scenarios of Power*, 145.

36. Among Pushkin's works featuring fathers and daughters are "The Captain's Daughter," "Dubrovsky," and several stories adapted to opera, including Glinka's *Ruslan and Liudmila* and Dargomyzhsky's *Rusalka*. The role of the father in several is enacted by the older husband.

37. Zabelin, *Domashniii byt russkago naroda v XVI i XVII st.* (1872), 75.

38. Wortman, *Scenarios of Power*, 158.

39. Brikner, *Istoriia Ekateriny vtoroi*, 728; Grech, *Zapiski o moei zhizni* (1930), 143.

40. Wortman, *Scenarios of Power*, 158.

41. Levshin, "Skazka o khrabrom i smelom kavalere Ivane-tsareviche," in *Ruskiia skazki* (1783), 5:75–87.

42. In an introduction to a volume of early tales collected by Danilov, Konstantin Kalaidovich wrote that "Levshin like Danilov depicts the heroic feats of young Boguslanovich. The hero's name differs in sources." Danilov, *Drevniia ruskiia stikotvoreniia* (with additional songs and musical notation 1818), i–xxxvi, xxii–xxiii. See also Levshin, *Ruskiia skazki*, 5:2–30.

43. In its British rendition, the "Tale of Khlor" came out under the title *Ivan Czarowitz, or the Rose Without Prickles That Stings Not*. In the introduction, the editor explains that the combination of letters [Khlor], so unusual in the English language, made him change the name Khlor to the more familiar Ivan. Catherine II, *Ivan Tsarevich, or the Rose Without Prickles That Stings Not* (1793).

44. Catherine II, *Skazka o tsareviche Khlore* (1781). See also operatic portrayal of Sheremetev's estate in Kuskovo in Chapter Two.

45. The term *samoderzhavitsa* (*sam*, self; *derzhat'*, to hold, possess, control) could be equated with the term absolute monarch. Unlike other absolute monarchs, a Russian monarch, *krepostnitsa* (*krepostnoi*, serf-owner), owned her people, especially the serfs. These two terms, frequently connected with Catherine, labeled her as the epitome of self-assumed power and as a ruler who turned peasants into serfs.

46. Derzhavin, *Sochineniia* (1845), 33–39.

47. According to Metropolitan Evgenii, Catherine dedicated *Khlor* to Alexander and wrote *Fevei* for her second grandson, Constantine. Other scholars favor the association of both tales and the opera *Fevei* with Alexander. Metropolitan Evgenii, *Slovar' russkikh svietskikh pisatelei*, 210.

48. The opera, music by Arnošt Vančura, is also known as *Ivan Tsarevich*. Both titles use the name of the main character, Prince Ivan, whose patronymic is Akhrideich.

49. The reference to the river and the nightingale as symbols of harmony surfaces in the lines of Uzhima [Mannered] in Krylov's "Pirog" (1801). See Krylov, *P'esy* (1944), 191.

50. Catherine II and Vančura, *Khrabroi i smeloi vitiaz' Akhrideich* (1787), 48.

51. Ibid., 6.

52. Ibid., 38.

53. Mikhail Druskin discusses characteristic elements of early fairy-tale operas by referring to pantomime, battles, parades, and seventeen magical transformations in *Kniaz'-Nevidimka*,

by Catterino Cavos (1775–1840), which premiered at the Imperial Court Russian Theater in 1805. Druskin and Keldysh, *Ocherki po istorii russkoi muzyki*, 267.

54. Danilov, *Drevniia rossiiskiia stikhotvoreniia.*

55. *Novgorodskie byliny* (1978), 2:13–17; 3:17–25; 5:32–40; 6:40–43.

56. According to Iakov Grot, Gustav watched several productions of *Zémire et Azor* in the Smol'nyi Institute, Oranienbaum. Grot, *Ekaterina II i Gustav III* (1877), 25–27.

57. Ibid., 47.

58. Odessky, *Ocherki istoricheskoi poetiki russkoi dramy* (1999), 61.

59. Brikner, "Angliia, Prussia i Rossiia, 1787–1791" (1887), 475.

60. Khrapovitsky, *Pamiatnye zapiski*, 75, 89.

61. Dal', *Tolkovyi slovar' zhivogo velikorusskogo iazyka* (1989), 4:540. The word *fufliga* shares the root with *fuflo*, a modern slang term for "unworthy."

62. Khrapovitsky, *Pamiatnye zapiski*, 139.

63. Ibid, 141.

64. Ibid, 170, 187. Sheremetev's theater produced elaborate stagings of *Fevei* and *Boeslavich*, both with ballets. *Gorebogatyr'* does not seem to have been shown in this theater. Elizarova, *Teatry Sheremet'eva*, 140–42, 160, 231–33.

65. "Merry wide yard," Akhrideich, 18; "breast of a swan," Boeslavich, 4.

66. Beaumarchais's *Figarova zhenid'ba* [The Marriage of Figaro] was published in Russian translation by a Russian philosopher and famous mason, Alexander Labzin (1787); *Evgenia*, translated by Boltin, was produced in 1770.

67. The line between urban folklore and classics, oral and written repertoire is very fluid. For example, Chulkov's collection of "various songs" includes verses of Sumarokov, Trediakovsky, and Lomonosov.

68. See Evgenii Levashov's "Introduction: the opera *Sanktpeterburgskii gostinnyi dvor i ee avtory*" in the revised score of Pashkevich, *Kak pozhivaesh' tak i proslyvesh ili Sanktpeterburgskii gostinnyi dvor* (1782) [*St. Petersburg Bazaar*], 466–91; see also Mooser, *Annales*, 2:55. Elsewhere Mooser discussed the composer of the music for *Fevei*, rejecting the candidacy of Briks and affirming the authorship of Pashkevich; *Annales*, 2:440–41.

69. Overall, Pashkevich collaborated with the empress on three stage works, including the historical production *The Early Reign of Oleg* (1790) and the comic one-act *Fedul and His Children* (1791). *Fevei* (1786) was the first and only opera that Pashkevich created without collaborating with other composers.

70. During the five years the public theater of Kapnist-Dmitrievsky existed (1779–1784), Pashkevich created *Misfortune from a Coach*, *The Miser*, *Tunisian Pasha*, and most likely *St. Petersburg Bazaar*, all of them staged in this theater.

71. Levashov, "Introduction" (1980); Porfir'eva, "Pashkevich" (1996), 2:342.

72. Livanova, *Russkaia muzykal'naia kul'tura XVIII Veka*, 2:154–56, 165–66, 171.

73. Pashkevich, for example, used a tune from *Sobranie nailuchshikh rossiiskikh pesen* [Collection of the Best Russian Songs] (1781), published by F. Meier, in the Tsar's song from Act II, Scene 3. See Keldysh, *Pamiatniki russkogo muzykal'nogo iskusstva* (1972), 91.

74. "Vyshe vsekh i veselei."

75. See Quartetto (no. 21) in W. A. Mozart, *Idomeneo* (1952), 195.

76. See Levashov, "Introduction," 483. The beginnings of Pashkevich's many canons bring to mind, for example, Tchaikovsky's duet of the sisters Larina in *Eugene Onegin*.

77. Ibid., 498.

78. See the chapter on oriental opera by Thomas Bauman, *W. A. Mozart: Die Entführung aus dem Serail* (1987), 27–35.

79. Taruskin, "Pashkevich, Vasily Alexeyevich," *Grove Music Online.*

80. The early eighteenth-century explorer Cornelius le Brun describes relations between Tatars and Kalmyks in the Astrakhan region of Russia in *An Abstract of Travels Through Russia and Persia to the East Indies* (1722), 2:371–432, 427–28.

81. Taruskin, "Pashkevich, Vasily Alexeyevich"; see also Guberti, Materialy po russkoi bibliographii (1891), 3: 700.

82. Bauman, Mozart: Die Entführung, 63–64.

83. Though the opera was extremely successful, the score has been lost.

84. Regarding all of Catherine's operas, including Akhrideich, see Seaman, "Catherine the Great," 133.

85. Taruskin, "Fomin, Yevstigney Ipat'yevich," Grove Music Online.

86. Ibid.

87. See the collection of luboks in http://tars.rollins.edu/Foreign_Lang/Russian/Lubok/lubok.html.

88. The central episode of the folk wedding ritual, the devichnik scene (girl gathering), may have appeared for the first time in two Russian operas premiered in 1779: *The Miller* and *St. Petersburg Bazaar*. The latter is better known in a version by Pashkevich, who used eight traditional wedding songs in his elaborate devichnik episode (Act II).

89. Rabinovich, *Russkaia opera do Glinki*, 38. A major historian of Russian theater, Vsevolodsky-Gerngross wrote that "ethnographers of the nineteenth and twentieth centuries have perceived the wedding as a dramatic act and referred to it as the 'wedding drama' [or *igrischa*]." Vsevolodsky-Gerngross, *Russkii teatr*, 14–15.

90. Catherine II, Novgorodskoi Bogatyr' Boeslavich (1786), 10.

91. Unlike Umila, this girl—often called chernoshechka (darky)—appears in most versions of the bylina, waking up Boeslavich, helping him, and doing various chores. Despite her small features, she often possesses enormous power. See twenty-six versions of bylinas about Vasily Boeslavich in Nikolev, Novgorodskie byliny, 5–147.

92. See Pavlenko, "Alexander Nevsky" (1953), 4:189–231.

93. Instead, a number of bylinas about Vasily Boeslavich end with the death of the protagonist. See Novgorodskie byliny.

94. Interview with Maria Shcherbakova, a musicologist and director of archives at the Mariinsky Theater in St. Petersburg, April 10, 2006. Also see Shcherbakova, Muzyka v russkoi drame (1997), 23–25 and the chapter on Oleg.

95. Komarnitskaia, "Drama, epos, skazka, lirika, v russkoi klassichdeskoi opere XIX veka" (1991), 14.

96. See the Overture and Chapter One on the terem and Chapter Two on female royal patronesses.

97. This interpretation was suggested in response to my lecture at Harvard by John Ledonne, a historian of the Russian empire.

98. Paul Tallemant, translated by Trediakovsky, *Ezda v ostrov lubvi* (1778).

99. On the image of an empress encompassing multiple roles, including *matushka* (mother) and bride, with respect to the Russian Fatherland, see the Overture and Chapter One.

100. Fedorov, *Repertuar Bol'shogo teatra*, 128, 136, 143.

101. "C'est ainsi que, de 1786 à 1791, elle se plut à fournir à des musiciens du cru ou établis en Russie, cinq livrets d'opéras-comiques russes: exemple qui fut déterminant pour l'avenir

car, venant de si haut, il ne valut pas seulement à celui-ci une faveur accrue dans les milieux de la cour; il suscita aussi, et bien naturellement, l'éclosion d'une quantité d'œuvres analogues." Mooser, *Annales*, 2:18.

102. Among them is Maria Antonia Walpurgis (1724–1780), Electress of Saxony, composer, singer, and patron. See Yorke-Long, *Music at Court: Four Eighteenth Century Studies* (1954), 73–93; James, "Her Highness' Voice: Maria Antonia, Music and Culture at the Dresden Court" (2002). Karen Britland writes that Maria de Medici "encouraged cultural interests in her offspring—all her royal children took part in French *ballet de cour*, and, in 1611, Princess Elizabeth was encouraged to stage a production of Robert Garnier's play." Henrietta Maria of France (1609–1666) "became the first recorded English queen to take a speaking and singing role in a dramatic production." Britland, *Drama and the Courts of Queen Henrietta Maria* (2006), 3, 6.

Chapter 4

1. Shcherbakova, *Muzyka v russkoi drame*; O'Malley, "Catherine the Great's Operatic Splendor at Court" (1998), 33.
2. Brikner wrote that the empress's "large drama *Oleg* illustrated the events of the war with Turkey"; *Istoriia Ekateriny vtoroi*, 728.
3. Smith (ed.), *Love and Conquest: Personal Correspondence of Catherine the Great and Prince Grigory Potemkin* (2004), 355.
4. Catherine wrote in one of her many letters to Potemkin fifteen years earlier, at the time of their most passionate romance: "Grishonok, priceless, rarest, and sweetest in the world. I love you madly, extraordinarily, my dear friend, I kiss and embrace you with all my body and soul, dear husband" (June 8, 1774). Half a year later, she concluded another letter to Potemkin: "Adieu, m'amour, mon coeur, husband dear, splendid, sweet, and everything nice, pleasant and clever that you can imagine" (December 8, 1774). Ibid., 38, 47. See also Montefiore, *Prince of Princes* (2000), 136–40.
5. Igor (845–945) was the young Grand Prince of all Russia.
6. Catherine intended to make an opera of the third part of the trilogy but eventually changed her mind, even though a large part of the musical score of *Igor* was completed.
7. In his introduction to Catherine's volume, Igor' Losievsky points out this and other examples of Catherine's "adjustments" of Russian history. The empress omits "horrific details" of Olga's punishment of the Slavic tribe of Drevlians who killed her husband, Igor. The empress symbolically reunites ancient Slavic tribes while in her political course she expands Russia to absorb provinces of Malorussia and Poland. See Losievsky, "Introduction: S perom i skipetrom" (2003).
8. A brief remark in Catherine's *Notes on Early Russian History* indicates that the bride was renamed for Igor's benefactor and adviser Oleg. Omeljan Pritsak, who wrote a provocative chapter on Oleg the Prince and Oleg the Sage, suggests the Scandinavian origin of the name "Oleg" derived from "a mythic institution called 'helgi,' that is, a succession of most noble individuals." According to Pritsak, Helgi reappears throughout European history, this time in Eastern Europe from Scandinavian sagas. See Pritsak, *Origin of Rus'* (1981), 1:163.
9. Catherine II, *Oleg*, 10.
10. Catherine II, *Oleg*, 16.
11. Ibid., 18.
12. O'Malley, "Catherine the Great's Operatic Splendor," 33.

13. See L'vov (ed.), *Letopisets Russkoi ot proshestviia Rurika do konchiny tsaria Ioanna Vasil'evicha* (1792); *Letopisets soderzhashchii v sebe russkuiu istoriiu* (1819; the author's initials N. L. may identify Nikolai L'vov); and L'vov (ed.), "Introduction," *Podrobnaia Letopis' ot nachala Rossii do Poltavskoi batalii* (1798–99). See also Lomonosov, *Zapiski po russkoi istorii*, including "Dushoi bluzhdaiu" by Losievsky (2003); and Lomonosov, *Kratkoi Rossiiskoi Letopisets* (1760).

14. Losievsky, "S perom i skipetrom," 43.

15. See fragment from le Compte d'Angeberg [Ghodzko], *Recueil des traites, conventions, et actes diplomatiques concernant la Pologne 1762–1862* (1862), 89–93.

16. The Cossacks presented an especially curious case. Carrying out military campaigns and serving as a strong buffer between Russia on the one hand and both the Tatar khanates and the Ottoman Empire on the other, they developed an affinity for and a claim to the land they resided on. With Russian acquisition of the Tatar khanate in Crimea, Cossack military power was no longer needed and in fact could be problematic. Catherine abolished the Ukrainian Hetmanate through a series of acts in the 1780s.

17. Iury Lotman believes that from the very beginning Peter's primary military goals were directed not to the Baltic Sea but to the Mediterranean. See Lotman, *Besedy o russkoi kul'ture* (1994), 290.

18. Khrapovitsky quotes Catherine: "Constantine is a good boy: in thirty years he will move from Sevastopol to Constantinople. We are now breaking their horns, and by then they will be broken already, for him it will be easy." Khrapovitsky, *Pamiatnye Zapiski*, October 9, 1789 (1862), 208. De Madariaga writes: "Under Potemkin's inspiration her [Catherine's] imagination was beginning to turn towards the realization of the so-called Greek project, namely the overthrow of the Ottoman Empire and the liberation of Constantinople." Madariaga, *Russia in the Age of Catherine the Great*, 383. On the Greek project, see Ol'ga Markova, *Rossiia, zakavkazskie i mezhdunarodnye otnosheniia v XVIII veke* (1958), 52–78. The connection between *Oleg* and Catherine's Greek project is explored by Seaman, "Catherine the Great," 134.

19. Khrapovitsky, *Pamiatnye Zapiski*, June 7, 1788 (1862), 66.

20. Khrapovitsky reports about the arches in the cities of Perekop, May 31, 1787, and of Kremenchug, June 4, 1787: ibid., 31–32.

21. Derzhavin, "Na vziatie Izmaila," *Sochineniia* (1851), 395.

22. Derzhavin, "Na priobretenie Kryma," ibid., 373.

23. The Russian wars with the Ottomans took place in 1768–1774 and 1787–1792; the takeover of the Crimea was completed in 1783. Basil Dmytryshyn cites *Polnoe sobranie zakonov russkoi imperii*. Dmytryshyn, *Imperial Russia* (1974), 97–107.

24. Igor' Losievsky points out that in the lines of the operatic *Oleg* one hears Catherine's characteristic voice. Losievsky, "S perom i skipetrom," 43.

25. Khrapovitsky, *Pamiatnye Zapiski* (1862), 16.

26. Ségur, *Zapiski grafa*, 185; Mansel, *Prince of Europe* (2003), 108.

27. Ségur, *Zapiski grafa*, 153.

28. In his notes, Khrapovitsky referred to the production of *Coriolanus*, written by Ségur, in the Hermitage Theater. See Khrapovitsky, notes of August 17, 1787; and Khrapovitsky (1862), 37.

29. According to Mooser, Cobenzl, who remained in the Russian court for twenty-one years, appeared in a number of private plays. With Princess Dolgorukova, he gave a remarkable performance of Paisiello's *Serva padrona*. Mooser, *L'opéra-comique* (1954), 150.

30. Ségur, *Zapiski grafa*, 155.
31. "Everywhere dissatisfied with formal welcomes, the empress questioned administrators, religious clergy, nobles and merchants about their situations, demands, and needs. This was how she earned the love of her subjects by seeking the truth." Ibid., 147, 155.
32. Ibid., 153–54.
33. Mansel, *Prince of Europe*, 102; Ségur, *Zapiski grafa*, 184.
34. Like the operatic celebrants in the first act of *Oleg*, Potemkin planned a city Ekaterinoslav "near Poland, Greece, the Walachia and Moldavia lands and the Illyrian people, so a multitude of youth will pour in to study, who will later return home with permanent gratitude . . . and with attachment to Russia." Letter to Catherine, October 13, 1786, in Smith, *Love and Conquest*, 164.
35. Letter in October 1786. Ibid., 163–64, 175; Brikner, *Istoriia Ekateriny vtoroi*, 611–16; de Madariaga, *Russia in the Age of Catherine*, 367–70. From the early days of her reign, Catherine engaged in systematic planning of the cities, which was enacted in practice by Potemkin. The two pioneered new architectural ventures advancing the planning of cities. Robert Jones, *Provincial Development in Russia* (1984), 163–68.
36. Catherine II, *Oleg*, Act I, 9.
37. Khrapovitsky records the empress saying, "To tell you the truth, Peter I made the capital [too] close [to the borders]"; June 28, 1788.
38. The question of the origin of Rus' in connection with the Varangian dynasty was debated in the mid-eighteenth century. Lomonosov, the most prominent intellectual and historian of his time, argued that the Varangians "descended from the Roxolans, a Slavic people, who with the Goths, also a Slavic people, migrated from the Black Sea to the Baltic shores; . . . they spoke a Slavic language, though somewhat corrupted on account of their association with the old Germans." Lomonosov, *Polnoe Sobranie sochinenii* (1952), 6:19–25. Maria Shcherbakova writes about "the increasingly popular idea of Nordic—Varangian and Scandinavian—origins of the Russian state system itself, and of 'Varangians' on the Russian throne. The Empress Catherine the Great was known to regard herself as one, and she was the author of well-known 'historical performances' dedicated to the legendary Varangian rulers of Old Russia—Prince Riurik and his descendants (*Riurik, Early Years of Oleg's Rule* 1786–1790)." Shcherbakova, "Ossian in the Late 18th and Early 19th-Century Russian Theatre" (2001), 93–94.
39. Ségur, *Zapiski grafa*, 208.
40. Troyat, *Catherine the Great* (1980), 285.
41. Seeing sixteen ships of the Russian Black Sea fleet in the harbor of Sevastopol, Catherine was overwhelmed and danced gleefully in front of de Ligne, laughing like a madwoman. Mansel, *Prince of Europe*, 106.
42. Khrapovitsky, *Pamiatnye zapiski*, July 7 through 24, 1789 (1862), 198–99.
43. In the first weeks of 1790, three years into the second war with Turkey, Catherine bestowed on Potemkin, already named the Prince of Tauride, another title—the Grand Hetman of Ekaterinoslav and the Black Sea Cossack Hosts—putting him in charge of both the Southern and the Western military arenas. In a letter of February 6, 1790, Catherine calls Potemkin "Sir Grand Hetman," the title given to him on January 10. See Smith, *Love and Conquest*, 332–33.
44. The Russian-Swedish battle of May 23, 1790, near the island of Kronstadt fifteen miles from St. Petersburg, was audible in the Russian capital. Khrapovitsky, *Pamiatnye zapiski* (1862), 221–22.

45. The celebration of the peace with Sweden took place on August 8, 1790. On August 16, the empress ordered the commencement of rehearsals of every act of *Oleg* in the Hermitage Theater. Ibid., 231.

46. Khrapovitsky' *Pamiatnye zapiski*, July 24 (1862), 1789. In September 1790, she attended rehearsals, conversed with the composer Sarti, and corrected the actor Ivan Dmitrievsky, who was playing Oleg. Ibid., 199, 232–33.

47. Pye, "Hobbes and the Spectacle of Power," in Greenblatt (ed.), *Representing the English Renaissance* (1988), 281.

48. Ibid., 286.

49. Elizabeth I, *Selected Works* (2004), 65.

50. Catherine II, *Oleg*, 10.

51. O'Malley, "Catherine the Great's Operatic Splendor," 42.

52. Though Catherine's authorship was known from the time of production of *Oleg*, the empress's name did not appear on the title pages of this or her other literary works.

53. Catherine II, *Oleg*, title page.

54. A Russian master of neoclassical tragedy, Sumarokov published his *Hamlet* in Russian without referring to Shakespeare.

55. See la Place, *Le theatre anglois*. 8 vols. (1746); and von Eschenburg (ed.), *William Shakespeare's Schauspiele* (1775). Some translations were done not from Shakespeare's plays but rather from the sources of these plays. See Alekseev, *Shekspir i russkaia kul'tura* (1965), 22–44.

56. References to Shakespeare as an important writer can be found in Novikov's magazine *Pokoiashchiisia trudolubez*. Alekseev, *Shekspir*, 48.

57. During his trip to London, Ivan Dmitrievsky worked with Garrick, a British actor famous for his interpretation of Hamlet and other Shakespearian roles.

58. In 1786, the empress wrote to Grimm (September 24, 1786) that she had "swallowed ten volumes" of Shakespeare's works. Alekseev, *Shekspir*, 34.

59. The cover pages of all four plays refer to Shakespeare: *Oleg*; *Vot kakovo imet' korzinu i bel'e* (*The Merry Wives of Windsor*), based on Shakespeare; *The Life of Riurik*, an imitation of Shakespeare; and *Profligate: A Free Adaptation of Shakespeare*" (*The Life of Timon of Athens*).

60. Alekseev, *Shekspir*, 173.

61. Greenblatt, *Will in the World*, 182.

62. See also Mullaney, *The Place of the Stage*.

63. Lomonosov, *Izbrannye proizvedeniia* (1965), 86.

64. Ibid., 121.

65. Here adoration of empire, state, and the blissful peace of nature is no longer abstract. It is Russia that throughout its history has produced famous heroes; the land, history, and heroes are combined with the might of *derzhava*—a term for the state rooted in the verb "to hold" and aligned with the "imperial sublime."

66. The intimate "you," addressing a different empress in Lomonosov's original text, is replaced with the distant "her."

67. Lomonosov, *Izbrannye proizvedeniia*, 172.

68. The sequence of these four choruses is included in a song collection; its cover page depicts a peasant lad sitting in the forest in front of a hut. *Novyi Rossiiskii pesennik* (1791), 50–51.

69. The first Lomonosov verse that the empress included in her play was written for Peter III, Catherine's unfortunate husband. The ode Lomonosov wrote for Catherine's inauguration actually displeased the tsarina, who issued an *ukase* to fire Lomonosov but later

withdrew it. See the notes accompanying the two odes Lomonosov wrote for Empress Catherine. Lomonosov, *Izbrannye proizvedeniia*, 527.

70. His wide-ranging activities included the founding of Moscow University, the discovery of physical and chemical laws, creation of mosaic artworks, development of various industries, and organization of fireworks and gala spectacles. Biliarsky, *Materialy dlia biografii Lomonosova* (1865). Lomonosov wrote works on geology and metallurgy, including *A Word on the Formation of Metals from Earth Tremors* (1757) and *On the Earth's Strata* (1763), and a paper on mineralogy, *Discourses on the Hardness and Liquidity of Bodies* (1761). Among his inventions was a self-propelled model of the helicopter "Aerodinamyc" in 1754.

71. Ram, *The Imperial Sublime*, 48.

72. Ibid., 55, 65.

73. In the 1764 production, D. Bortniansky, who would later become a celebrated Russian composer, performed *Admetus*; ten years later *Alkista* (text by Sumarokov, music by Raupakh) was staged in the palace of Prince Naryshkin S. K. with a rogovoi orkestr (a band of Russian horns). Fragments of Gluck's *Orpheus* were widely performed in Russian theaters; the first complete production of *Orfeo and Euridice* in Russia took place in 1782. Porfir'eva and Berezovchuk (eds.), *Muzykal'nyi Peterburg XVIII vek: Ensiklopedicheskii slovar'* (2001), 4:111, 125, 149, 169.

74. In Euripides' version, King Admetus is destined to die. Alkista, his wife, volunteers to die in his stead. Losing her, Admetus commissions a sculpted effigy to replace the original in his bed. He wishes for Orpheus' voice so that he might bring his wife back to life; instead Hercules appears—a third substitution/replacement. Hercules takes the place of Admetus in searching for his spouse and enacts Orpheus, who (in some versions) revives his wife. Indeed Hercules uses "force rather than Orphic song." The woman Hercules brings to Admetus at the end of the play is another striking substitution. She seems to be Alkista revived; but veiled and silent, she also doubles for her own effigy. See Euripides, *Heracles and Other Plays* (2003); and Segal, *Euripides and the Poetics of Sorrow* (1993), 38–40.

75. *Alkista* is the fourth play in Euripides' tetralogy.

76. O'Malley, "Catherine the Great's Operatic Splendor," 48.

77. Discussing the commission of the painting "Prometheus Makes a Statue at the Order of Minerva," Proskurina suggests that Prometheus making a figure of clay and Athena breathing life into his creation are allegorically associated with Peter and Catherine. Proskurina, *Mify Imperii*, 131.

78. Proskurina, *Mify Imperii*, 192–94.

79. See Chapter Five.

80. See Catherine, *Zapiski*, 114, 116, 147, 168–69; Khrapovitsky, *Pamiatnye zapiski*, notes of January 26, 1789 (1862), 216.

81. Catherine II, *Oleg*, 13.

82. Olearius, *The Voyages and Travels* (1669), 91–92.

83. In Part I of her memoirs dedicated to Countess de Bruce, Catherine recalls: "After seven years of worthless practice, she [her governess] announced that I have neither voice nor musical talent, and she was not mistaken in either case." Catherine II, *Zapiski*, 8.

84. Indeed her decisions were probably affected by the intellectuals that Catherine consulted; she would typically read a draft of a single act to her secretary Khrapovitsky, who afterward would copy it with corrections. Khrapovitsky himself wrote the operatic text for the *Pesnoliubie*, set to music by Martín y Soler. See Livanova, *Russkaia muzykal'naia kul'tura*, 1:306. Catherine also

consulted Potemkin, the grand master of productions, regarding both her theatrical and military ventures. Musical matters most likely involved count L'vov, who accompanied Catherine in the Crimean journey and translated Sarti's musical treatise written for *Oleg.*

85. According to Brikner, the empress nurtured personal relations with her famous court composers. Brikner, *Istoriia Ekateriny vtoroi* (1885), 730.

86. Khrapovitsky, *Pamiatnye zapiski* (1862), 204–05.

87. Porfir'eva, "Pashkevich," 340–44.

88. Catherine's *Fevei* (1786) and the one-act *Fedul s det'mi* (Fedul and his Children, 1791).

89. Pashkevich also sang in this opera. Levashov, "Introduction" (1980), 469.

90. On Catherine's invitation and with princely pay, Giovanni Paisiello spent seven years (1776–1783) at the St. Petersburg court, composing and directing the court orchestra and the opera company. Baldassare Galuppi visited Russia between 1765 and 1768, producing for Catherine's court the opera *Ifigenia in Tauride*, two cantatas, and fifteen Orthodox liturgical works.

91. See Chapter Three on Catherine's *skazka* operas.

92. This opera was first produced in 1782 by Matinsky; the second edition (1792), created six years after *Fevei* and two after *Oleg*, bears the name of Pashkevich. Recently some scholars have proposed that the music of the first version of *The St. Petersburg Bazaar* also belonged to Pashkevich, the musical director of the theater where the opera was premiered.

93. The group of intellectuals surrounding L'vov included such literary figures as Derzhavin and Kapnist (the three of them were married to sisters of the Diakov family) and composers such as Fomin, Pashkevich, Sarti, and others.

94. Chulkov, *Sobranie raznykh pesen* (1913); Teplov, *Mezhdu delom bezdel'e ili sobranie raznykh pesen* (1779); Trutovsky, *Sobranie russkikh prostykh pesen s notami*, 1776–1779 (1953).

95. Livanova, *Russkaia muzykal'naia kul'tura*, 2:21–23.

96. Vasilii Trutovsky was a court musician under Catherine II. He was known as a *gusli* player (a type of small horizontal harp, with strings attached to a resonating box in the shape of wings, a helmet, or other forms), as well as an early song collector and composer of pieces based on Russian folklore. The song discussed in the text was also included in one of the first Russian operas, *Lubovnik-koldun*, 1772. Rabinovich, *Russkaia opera do Glinki*, 40–41.

97. In her letters to Potemkin, it appears that Catherine, who had suffered from the insurgency of Pugachev, could also have some recognition of his heroism; she jokingly Potemkin Pugachev. Smith, *Love and Conquest*, 15.

98. The entr'acte before the fourth act corresponds to a Malorussian (Ukrainian) tune, "Oi, ne vidish mesats svetit," which the composer treats like his other orchestral episodes.

99. The appendix to *A Collection of Russian Folk Songs* indicates that before Glinka there were several other adaptations of this tune, among them Beethoven's *Twelve Variations on a Russian Dance* from Wranitzky's *Das Waldmädchen* and Cavos' *Ivan Susanin* (Act 1, No. 4), a direct predecessor of Glinka's opera of the same title. See Appendix, in L'vov and Prach, *Collection of Russian Folk Songs*, 439.

100. In the L'vov-Prach collection, this song is placed under the category of "*sviatochnaia*," folk songs sung by Russian girls to accompany their wishful rituals during the Christmas season.

101. Appendix, L'vov and Prach, *Collection of Russian Folk Songs*, 439.

102. Livanova, *Russkaia muzykal'naia kul'tura*, 2:75.

103. Brown, in L'vov and Prach, *Collection of Russian Folk Songs*, 7, 21.

104. Taruskin, *Defining Russia Musically*, 21.

105. Livanova, *Russkaia muzykal'naia kul'tura*, 2:74–75.

106. Brown, in *Collection of Russian Folk Songs*, 7.

107. Shcherbakova, *Muzyka v russkoi drame*, 23.

108. See Porfir'eva, Sarti (1997), vol. 3, 83–84.

109. Rabinovich, *Russkaia opera do Glinki*, 83.

110. Fendeizen writes that it was Catherine's understanding that "nobody here (in St. Petersburg) can combine [chorus and orchestra] as well as he [Sarti]." Fendeizen, *Ocherki po istorii muzyki v Rossii*, 2:250.

111. Cheshikhin, *Istoriia russkoi opery* (1905), 71.

112. Derzhavin, "Ob opere," *Sochineniia* (1845), 375.

113. Shcherbakova, *Muzyka v russkoi drame*, 19.

114. Derzhavin, *Sochineniia* (1845), 226.

115. Karamzin, *Sochineniia* (1804), 439. Bogdanovich draws on the imagery of Slav-Slaviane-Slavena-Slavianka in his two remarkable compositions, *Dushen'ka*, dedicated to Catherine the Great, and *Slaviane*.

116. Zorin, "Nezabvennaia Dushen'ka" (2002), 7–20. Perhaps Lomonosov was the first to identify Slavena with Slavianka; Catherine's palace thus signified the very birthplace of Slavs. Notably, on September 9, 1775, Catherine submitted to the Holy Synod a signed decree "Concerning the establishment anew . . . [of] a diocese under the name Slaviansk and Kherson." Batalden, *Catherine II's Greek Prelate Eugenios Voulgaris in Russia, 1771–1806*, 43.

117. Bogdanovich, *Slaviane* (1788), 40–41.

118. More than twenty-five eighteenth-century composers created works based on Metastasio's *Alessandro nell'Indie* (Alexander in India; 1730), among them Leonardo Vinci (Rome, 1730), Georg Frideric Handel (*Poro*, London, 1731), Johann Adolf Hasse (*Cleofide*, Dresden, 1731), Nicola Porpora (*Poro*, Turin, 1731), Baldassare Galuppi (Mantua, 1738), Christoph Willibald von Gluck (*Poro*, Turin, 1744), Niccolò Jommelli (Ferrara, 1744), David Perez (Genoa, 1744; Lisbon, 1755), Niccolò Piccinni (Rome, 1758), Johann Christian Bach (Naples, 1762), Tommaso Traetta (Reggio Emilia, 1762), Domenico Cimarosa (Rome, 1781), and Luigi Cherubini (Mantua, 1784).

119. The name Ruslan is known in association with Alexander Pushkin's famous poetic tale *Ruslan and Liudmila* and Glinka's opera of the same title based on Pushkin's tale. See Chapter Five.

120. Bogdanovich, *Slaviane*, 61–62.

121. Ibid., 87.

122. Ibid., 63.

123. Ibid., 69.

124. O'Malley, "Catherine the Great's Operatic Splendor," 38.

125. Livanova, *Russkaia muzykal'naia kul'tura*, 2:156.

126. Ibid., 1:169.

127. Komarnitskaia, "Drama, epos, skazka," 14–17.

128. Bulkina, "'Dnieprovskie rusalki' i 'Kievskie Bogatyri,'" *Pushkinskie chteniia v Tartu* (2007). The opera by Krylov and Cavos premiered in St. Petersburg in 1806 and remained in the operatic repertoire for at least two or three decades. See Fedorov, *Repertuar Bol'shogo teatra SSSR*, 147.

129. Shcherbakova, *Muzyka v russkoi drame*, 25.

Interlude

1. Vigel', *Zapiski*, 150.

2. Lev Losev writes about publication of *Aesop's Parables* in Russian and Latin by Ilya Kopievsky in Amsterdam in 1700. The expression "Aesopian language" came into wide use in Russian literature in the second half of the nineteenth century. P. Berkov traced Russian use of Aesopian language to the odes of Peter's archbishop, Feofan Prokopovich. See Losev, *On the Beneficence of Censorship* (1984), 1:4; Berkov, "Odno iz pervykh primenenii ezopovskogo iazyka v Rossii" (1971), 74–82.

3. *Ilya the Champion* was staged in 1806, published in 1807. In the words of the musicologist Boris Asaf'ev, Cavos, who composed music for Krylov's *Ilya the Champion*, attempted to "*russify* his style as none of the musical 'Varangians' has done in Russia before him." "Varangian" is an ironic reference to foreigners residing in Russia. Cavos lived in Russia for some forty-three years and there composed, among his many works for the theater, *Kniaz'-Nevidimka*, *Ilya Bogatyr'*, *Kazak-Stikhotvorets* (1812), *Ivan Susanin* (1815), and *Fire-Bird*. Asaf'ev, *Russkaia muzyka XIX i nachala XX vekov* (1968); Abramovsky, *Russkaia opera pervoi treti XIX veka* (1971), 25. Alexander Rabinovich considered Cavos as a nearly native composer, "growing into Russian culture." Rabinovich, *Russkaia opera do Glinki*, 147.

4. *Das Donauweibchen* was created by composer Ferdinand Kauer and librettist Karl Hansler.

5. Chapter Six focuses on operatic *Rusalkas*.

6. Stepan Davydov (1777–1825) was a major composer of four Russian *Rusalkas*. The Kapellmeister of Petersburg and Moscow court theaters, he was also a musical director of Sheremetev's private troupe. Davydov composed six numbers for the first *Rusalka*, collaborated with Cavos on the second *Rusalka*, and created music for both the third and fourth parts. The text of the first three operas was adapted/created by N. Krasnopol'sky, the fourth by Prince Alexander Shakhovskoi. Druskin and Keldysh, *Ocherki istorii Russkoi muzyki* (1956), 263–76, Rabinovich, *Russkaia opera do Glinki*, 120–56.

7. Catherine II, *Zapiski*, 61.

8.

Гром победы, раздавайся!	Гром побед и нашей славы
Веселися, храбрый Росс!	В ратных ты греми полях!
Thunder of Victory, Resound!	Thunder of [many] Victories and our Glory
Be merry, Courageous Russ(ians)!	Resound in the battlefields!
(Derzhavin)	(Krylov)

9. See more details on "Grom pobedy" in Chapter Nine.

10. For references to the choral "Victory!" (Pobeda) as the Russian anthem, see Druskin and Keldysh, *Ocherki istorii Russkoi muzyki*, 290; Abramovsky, *Russkaia opera pervoi treti XIX veka*, 19. See "Victory to a Russian hero! Death and shame to the enemy of Rus'!" in the finale of Krylov's *Ilya*. Krylov, *Polnoe sobranie sochinenii* (1945–46), 2:491–553, 525, http://www.rvb.ru/18vek/krylov/01text/vol2/01play/032.htm.

11. Wortman, *Scenarios of Power*, 149.

12. Wortman writes that in the funeral procession to the Cathedral of Peter and Paul, the imperial crown rested on Peter's coffin, while Catherine's was bare. Ibid., 173.

13. Ibid., 177.

14. Among intellectuals who copied her notes was Pushkin. Herzen issued his translation of Catherine's memoirs abroad. Catherine II, *Memoirs of The Empress Catherine II* (1859).

15. See Dixon, "The Posthumous Reputation of Catherine II in Russia 1797–1837" (1999), 654–55.

16. Ironically, the empresses forged the tradition of affirming a direct ascendance from Peter, each constructing her own link to Peter, unique and superior to those of her predecessors. Lotman wrote that Peter was above any criticism. Lotman, *Russkaia literatura i kul'tura prosveshcheniia* (1998), 233. Indeed some in the nineteenth century also considered Peter an anti-Christ and female monarchs his followers. In literature, the proponents of competing ideological and literary camps craved national identity. Schönle, *Authenticity and Fiction in the Russian Literary Journey, 1790–1840* (2000), 92.

17. Murav'eva, *Dan' priznatel'noi liubvi: russkie pisateli o Pushkine* (1979), 65–66.

18. Belinsky, *Sochineniia Aleksandra Pushkina* (1985), 559.

19. Frolova-Walker, "On *Ruslan* and Russianness," 22.

20. Poggioli, The Masters of the Past: Pushkin" (1987), 19.

21. Vilgel'm Kukhel'bekker, "O napravlenii nashei poezii, osobenno liricheskoi, v poslednee desiatiletie," 1824, http://az.lib.ru/k/kjuhelxbeker_w_k/text_0180.shtml.

22. Murav'eva, *Dan' priznatel'noi liubvi*, 7.

23. Abramovsky, *Russkaia opera pervoi treti XIX veka*, 51; see also Rabinovich, *Russkaia opera do Glinki*, 166.

24. Verstovsky's letter to S. Shevyrev, published in Livanova, *Opernaia kritika v Rossii* (1966), 327.

25. Stasov, *M. I. Glinka* (1953), 110–11.

26. Steaming right ahead with Russian musical nationalism and mixing aesthetic motives with personal ambitions, they engaged in what Taruskin refers to as a "game," each using some of the same arguments to privilege his favorite over the other's. Taruskin, "Glinka's Ambiguous Legacy and the Birth Pangs of Russian Opera," *19th-Century Music* 1:2 (1977), 142–62.

27. Livanova, *Glinka: tvorcheskii put'* (1955), 1:11; Iulii Kremlev, *Natsional'nye cherty russkoi muzyki* (1968), 14; Liudmila Nikitina, *Istoriia russkoi muzyki* (2000), 37.

28. See a number of eighteenth-century song collections listed in previous chapters.

29. Terebenina, "Kopiia 'Zapisok Ekateriny II' iz arkhiva Pushkina" (1969), 8–22

30. Extravagant Shishkova owned thirteen thousand serfs.

31. See Anna Kern, *Vospominaniia, dnevniki, perepiska* (1974), 111–12; see also Dixon, "Posthumous Reputation," 649. Kern draws a link between Pushkin and Glinka: "Once walking [in St. Petersburg Iusupov's Park] in the company of two maids and Pushkin, I met general Bazel, my good friend. He invited us for tea and introduced Glinka. . . . The young man, walking aside, made a step forward, made a graceful bow, and continued walking by Pushkin, whom he knew from before [1826]." Kern, 5.

32. Montefiore, *Prince of Princes*, 497.

33. Dixon, "Posthumous Reputation," 652.

34. Pushkin, "Razgovory s N. K. Zagriazhskoi," *Polnoe sobranie khudozhestvennykh proizvedenii*, 932–34. The literary critics considered Zagriazhskaia a possible second candidate for the model of Pushkin's *Queen of Spades*, favoring another contemporary and acquaintance of Pushkin's, Countess Natalia Golitsina.

35. Pushkin, "Table-Talk," *Polnoe sobranie khudozhestvennykh proizvedenii*, 923–35.

36. Poggioli, "Masters of the Past: Pushkin," 19.

37. Bloom, *Anxiety of Influence* (1997), xxiii.

38. Roth, "Remembering Forgetting: Maladies de la Mémoire in Nineteenth-Century France" (1989), 50.

39. Alexander Morozov suggests that literary parody was known to Russia from at least the time of Sumarokov, who endured a passionate poetic duel with Lomonosov. Morozov, "Introduction," *Russkaia stikhotvornaia parodiia* (1960), 10.

40. Trediakovsky adulated the "imperatrix Anna" and years later lauded the "long delayed" enthronement of Elisabeth. He also crafted *Telemakhida* (1766), a free adaptation of François Fénelon's diatribe, addressing an "allegorical" ruler: "Shame! what tsars are often tempted to do." Trediakovsky, *Izbrannye proizvedeniia* (1963), 338, http://www.rvb.ru/18vek/trediakovs ky/01text/01versus/12tilemachida/127.htm.

41. Though by no means do all verses attributed to Barkov actually belong to him. Instead, his name was attached to any unpublished verse that could get an author into trouble for its unacceptable content.

42. Varvara Golitsina, nee Engelhardt, was the second oldest among five sisters and Potemkin's nieces who after their mother's death were sent to their powerful uncle. The prince pronounced himself to be their father, which did not stop him from having four of the nieces as his lovers. Danilova, *Ozherel'e svetleishego* (2005), 290–93, 366.

43. The poem "Pisateliu Samozvanovu" (To the Self-Nominated Writer), issued in November 1905, was included in Dreiden and Chukovsky, eds., *Russkaia revoliutsiia v satire i iumore* (1925), 8. Losev cites the verses in *On the Beneficence of Censorship*, 115.

44. Ibid., 11.

45. See translated and original fables by Khemnitser, Kheraskov, and Krylov.

46. Tsvetaeva, "Pushkin and Pugachev" (1994), 5: 499.

47. Rubins, "Pushkin's Gavriiliada" (1996), 623–631; Ivanitsky, "*Dushen'ka* Bogdanovicha," 39.

48. In the beginning of his tale, Bogdanovich pays tribute to Lucius Apuleius and La Fontaine, "who adulated Dushen'ka in poetry and prose." Bogdanovich's playful tale also echoes Lomonosov's *Polidor* (1750). The short poem, dedicated to Elisabeth's favorite, Kiril Razumovsky, depicted a muse and a pastoral couple of a nymph and a shepherd praising another couple, a Goddess and her President (Elisabeth made Razumovsky president of the Imperial Academy of Science). Notably, the poet relocated the Arcadian idyll to a Ukrainian neighborhood along the Dniepr, interlacing elements of the local landscape in an abstract pastoral—specifics that will be discussed later in relation to Pushkin's and Glinka's Chernomor.

49. Ivanitsky, "Dushen'ka Bogdanovicha," 34.

50. Achieving success in one literary genre, poets rushed to adopt the successful formula, recognizable images, and self-references in other works. Issuing several editions of his poem-tale, Bogdanovich devised a play, *Radost' Dushin'ki* (1786).

51. In his poem "Winter" (1804–05), which the poet devised as a dialogue of a poet and his muse, evoking the model of his poetic correspondence with Felitsa, Derzhavin refers to Khlor. Derzhavin, *Stikhotvoreniia* (1957), 297–98.

52. "Russkii dukh v Rusi ne mereshchilsia, . . . / Sredi Pitera, v Novgorode, / Videl ia vcheras' Boguslavicha." The poet here refers to Catherine's opera-bylina about the Novgorodian Champion. L'vov and Lappo-Danilev, *Izbrannye sochineniia* (1994), 198. http://www.rvb. ru/18vek/lvov/01text/03poems/224.htm.

53. Abramovsky, *Russkaia opera pervoi treti XIX veka*, 37, 168.

54. Ibid.

55. Karamzin created a poetic tale "Ilya Muromets" (1795); Krylov wrote the opera *Ilya the Champion*; L'vov crafted his unfinished song "Dobrynia" (1706); Derzhavin completed an opera of the same title; joining this circle of champions was Zhukovsky's operatic title hero, *Alesha Popovich* (1805–1808), and a poem of the same title by Alexander Radishchev (1801).

56. Nazarova argues that the roots of Pushkin's *Ruslan* lie in Zhukovsky's unwritten *Vadim*, in which the author intended to connect imaginary elements with a "true description of custom of the time." See Nazarova, "K istorii sozdaniia poemy Pushkina 'Ruslan i Liudmila'" (1956), 216–21.

57. Prince Dmitry Pozharsky (1578–1642) is one of the heroic icons of Russian history. In the annals of Russian history his name is paired with Kuz'ma Minin. Both led the partisan resistance in 1611–12.

58. Abram Gozenpud suggests that *Ilya Bogatyr'*, representing the next step after *Rusalka(s)* (and *Kniaz-Nevidimka* by Lifanov and Cavos, 1805), "anticipated the images of Ruslan and Liudmila." Gozenpud, *Muzykal'nyi teatr v Rossii*, 295–96.

59. Vsemila in *Ilya the Champion*, Vseslava and Milolika in *Kniaz'-Nevidimka* by Lifanov and Cavos, and Gremislava in *Vadim* by Zhikovsky and Verstovskii.

60. Pushkin's lines in the Fourth Song read: "И сердцем тронутым любили/Их тихий сон, их тихий плен;/Душой Вадима призывали,/И пробужденье зрели их." Pushkin, *Polnoe sobranie khudozhestvennykh proizvedenii*, 159. Zhukovsky's *Twelve Sleeping Maidens* served as the basis for Verstovskii's opera *Vadim*.

61. Pushkin likely borrowed the name Chernomor from Karamzin's *Ilya Murometsa: A Champion Tale* (1794). Chernomor's counterpart, Black-boar (Chernyi Vepr'), surfaces in Verstovskii's *Vadim* (1832).

62. Taruskin, "Glinka's Ambiguous Legacy," 145.

63. See Chapters One, Three, and Four.

64. Glinka's famous Bayan recites a tune closely related to his predecessor in Verstovsky. Irina Vyzgo-Ivanova, *Opera M. I. Glinki "Ruslan i Liudmila"* (2004), 86.

65. Krylov, "Ilya," *Polnoe sobranie sochinenii*, 2:533.

66. Pushkin: "Потупя неги полный взор,/Прелестные, полунагие." Pushkin, *Polnoe sobranie khudozhestvennykh proizvedenii*, 160.

Chapter 5

1. Frolova-Walker, *Russian Music and Nationalism*, 117.

2. Stepanov, *Russkaia Starina*, 1871; see also Chernov, *"Ruslan i Liudmila," opera M. I. Glinki* (1908), 8.

3. The "magical-heroic ballet" *Ruslan and Liudmila*, on a libretto of choreographer Glushkovsky and with music by Friderik Shol'ts, was premiered in Moscow (1821); in St. Petersburg it was choreographed by Didlo (1824).

4. *Music by Cavos, choreography by Glushkovsky, 1825.*

5. *Chernov, "Ruslan i Liudmila,"* 10.

6. *Berezovchuk, "Mozart"* (2001), 2:240–41.

7. Sadie, Mozart and His Operas (2000), 102; Rushton, Mozart (2006), 224.

8. Ibid.

9. *Frolova-*Walker, "On *Ruslan* and Russianness," 27–28; Taruskin, "Glinka's Ambiguous Legacy."

10. Bogdanovich wrote that "Greeks called her Psyche / In other tongues, translated / she was Dusha, in the language of the wise, / and in stories of the ancient learned people, she was named Dushen'ka." Bogdanovich, *Stikhotvoreniia i poemy* (1957), 50.

11. Belinsky, "Dushen'ka, drevniaia povest' I. Bogdanovicha" (1979), v. 4, http://az.lib.ru/b/belinskij_w_g/text_0490.shtml.

12. Bogdanovich, *Stikhotvoreniia i poemy*, 45–46.

13. According to sources cited by Serman, along with Mikhail Kheraskov and Alexander Rzhevsky, Junior Lieutenant Ippolit Bogdanovich was to oversee the triumphal arches, emblems, and inscriptions as well as paintings. Serman, "I. F. Bogdanovich," in Bogdanovich, *Stikhotvoreniia i poemy*, 8.

14. "Ne v davnem vremeni, v Moskve na maskarade/ Kogda na maslianoi, v torzhestvennom parade," Bogdanovich, *Stikhotvoreniia i poemy*, 48, 51.

15. Ivanitsky, "Dushen'ka I. Bogdanovicha," 34.

16. See Chapter Two.

17. The poem was both complemented for and accused of drawing on and imitating sources that included Boiardo, Ariosto, and Voltaire. See, for example Olin, "Moi mysli o romanticheskoi poeme g. Pushkina 'Ruslan i Liudmila,'" 104–6.

18. Pushkin, *Polnoe sobranie khudozhestvennykh proizvedenii*, 143–73.

19. Derzhavin married sixteen-year-old Catherine Bastidon, whom he called Plenira, lauding her under this name in a number of his poems. The name echoes a group of female images: Prelesta in the works of Ivan Dmitriev (1760–1837), Nikolai Karamzin (1766–1826), and Alexander Rzhevsky (1737–1804); Prelepa in Derzhavin and later Tchaikovsky's *Queen of Spades*, and Prekrasa in Catherine's *Oleg* and Derzhavin. Imagery of Catherine is woven into the poem.

20. Derzhavin, *Stikhotvoreniia*, 173–74; Pushkin, *Polnoe sobranie khudozhestvennykh proizvedenii*, 496.

21. Buckler, *Mapping St. Petersburg: Imperial Text and Cityshape* (2005), 161–63; Golburt, "Derzhavin's Ruins and the Birth of Historical Elegy" (2006), 670–93.

22. Derzhavin, *Stikhotvoreniia*, 261–64.

23. Gasparov, *Five Operas and a Symphony* (2005), 38–39.

24. Derzhavin, *Opisanie prazdnestva u Potemkina-Tavricheskago* (1792).

25. Like Tsarskoe Selo, Potemkin's Palace was violated by Paul, who during his reign turned it into military barracks. Less than half a century after Glinka's *Ruslan*, when Tchaikovsky's *Cherevichki* incurred the wrath of the Romanovs over the possible portrayal of Catherine, the composer decided to end the scene instead with an announcement of the empress's opera *Prince Khlor or the Rose Without Prickles*.

26. See Viazemsky on "Prichudnitsa" in Viazemsky and Gillel'son, *Sochineniia v dvukh tomakh* (1982), 2.

27. Peskov, "Introduction," in Dmitriev, *Sochineniia* (1986); http://az.lib.ru/d/dmitriew_i_i/text_0090.shtml.

28. Dmitriev, "Prichudnitsa" (1967), 176–85; http://www.rvb.ru/18vek/dmitriev/01text/07tales/065.htm.

29. Ibid., 180.

30. Asaf'ev, *Izbrannye trudy*, 1:176.

31. Chernov, "*Ruslan i Liudmila*," 41.

32. Gasparov, *Five Operas and a Symphony*, 50.

33. Pushkin cried listening to his favorite Gypsy singer, Tania.

34. Glinka, *Ruslan and Liudmila* (1966), 275. Returning to the opening of the scene, she—the proud daughter of a Kievan prince—refuses Chernomor's gifts. Her melodic minor-major shifts and the key progression from B minor to D and B major sets the modal ambiguity that also identifies Chernomor's musical portrait.

35. Voeikov, "Razbor poemy Ruslan i Liudmila" (1996), 36–68.

36. Ibid., 57.

37. Vasilii Pushkin, *Sochineniia V. L. Pushkina* (1893), 24–25.

38. On Glinka's Liudmila, see Frolova-Walker, "On *Ruslan* and Russianness," 34.

39. Ibid.

40. Dmitriev, "Prichudnitsa," 185.

41. Ibid., 178.

42. Ibid.

43. Nikolaeva, "Ot Nikolaia L'vova do Nikolaia Gumileva" (2003), 3:82–94.

44. Harald, first a guard of Iaroslav and later king of Norway and Sweden, was denied but eventually married the daughter of the Kievan prince. Ibid., 83.

45. In his "Pesn' Khrabrogo Shvedskogo Rytsaria Garal'da" [Song of the Brave Swedish Knight Harald], Bogdanovich wrote, "A devka russkaia velit mne brest' domoi." Bogdanovich, *Stikhotvorenia i poemy*, 218–20.

46. Vyzgo-Ivanova, *Opera M. I. Glinki*, 127–135. Finn's empathy and aid to Ruslan is a nearly allegorical recasting of the Russian-Finnish alliance in a number of Russia's wars with Sweden, leading to creation of the Grand Duchy of Finland under the Russian empire (1811).

47. Taruskin, "'Entoiling the Falconet': Russian Musical Orientalism in Context" (1992), 259, 260.

48. Asaf'ev, *Izbrannye trudy*, vol. 1, 168–71.

49. Frolova-Walker, "On *Ruslan* and Russianness," 34.

50. The name Gorislava resonates with Dobroslava (kind-glory) from *Slaviane*.

51. Frolova-Walker cites and comments on the review of an anonymous O***. Frolova-Walker, "On *Ruslan* and Russianness," 39.

52. Krylov, "Aniuta," *Polnoe sobranie sochineniia*, vol. 3, 239–43.

53. On the countess, see Chapter Nine.

54. Pushkin, *Polnoe sobranie sochinenii* (1999), 419.

55. Ibid., 424.

56. Krylov, "Nights," *Polnoe sobranie sochineniia*, vol. 1, 284; see Chapter Two, 63.

57. See "Hymn to the Beard" (1756–57), 263–65, and "Gymn borode za sud" (Hymn to the Beard for the Court; 1757), Lomonosov, *Izbrannye proizvedeniia* (1965), 279–82 and 463–66.

58. Lomonosov's hymn targeted religious bigotry much in the vein of eighteenth-century secularization, which started with Peter and was continued by his daughter.

59. Pushkin, *Rukoiu Pushkina: nesobrannye i neopublikovannye teksty* (1935), 563–79.

60. Gasparov, *Five Operas*, 37.

61. Soloveytchik, *Potemkin, Soldier, Statesman, Lover and Consort of Catherine of Russia* (1947), 332.

62. Чья тень спешит по облакам / В воздушные жилища горны?

63. Ségur, *Zapiski*, 54.

64. See Sviridov's praises of Glinka, cited in Vyzgo-Ivanova, *Opera M. I. Glinki*, 150–57.

65. Ibid., 153.

66. Montefiori, *Prince of Princes*, 439.

67. Ibid., 469; Derzhavin, *Opisanie prazdnestva*.

68. Vyzgo-Ivanova, *Opera M. I. Glinki*, 158.

69. Said, *Orientalism* (1978), 1–28.

70. Soloveytchik, *Potemkin*, 332.

71. The march was one of the first numbers of the opera to be composed. According to Glinka, as early as in the summer of 1838 it was played by the serf orchestra of Tarnovsky. The bells in the score were replaced with wine glasses. Chernov, "Ruslan i Liudmila," 91–92.

72. Montefiori, *Prince of Princes*, 475–76.

73. Ibid.

74. Dostoevsky, *Polnoe sobranie sochinenii v 30 tomakh* (1984), 26:129–30; http://www.repetitor.org/materials/dostoevsky3.html.

75. Asaf'ev, *Izbrannye trudy*, vol. 1, 148.

76. Asaf'ev, "Opera" (1947), 23.

77. Frolova-Walker, "On *Ruslan* and Russianness," 32.

Chapter 6

1. Zelenin, *Izbrannye Trudy. Ocherki russkoi mifologii: umershie neestestvennoiu smert'iu i rusalki* (1995). Joanna Hubbs discusses rusalka in relation to Mother Russia and Great Russian Goddesses in *Mother Russia* (1993), 27–36. Ivanits writes on rusalka as a sorcerer and a nature spirit in *Russian Folk Belief* (1989), 75–82, 185–89.

2. The *ptitsa raiskaia sirin* (bird of paradise), symbolizing unearthly beauty and joy, often appears with another female bird, Alkonost, representing sorrow. See woodcut in Sytova, *The Lubok: Russian Folk Pictures, 17th to 19th Century* (1984), 58–59. Rimsky-Korsakov creates the bodiless voices of Sirin and Alkonost in his *Legend of the Invisible City of Kitezh and Maiden Fevroniya* (1903–1904).

3. The rusalkas on St. Basil's Bridge had wings as well as a tail.

4. See Lutz, *Crying: The Natural and Cultural History of Tears* (1999); and Kramer, "Little Pearl Teardrops," (2002), 59–60.

5. Tolstoy, Anna Karenina (1995), 760–61.

6. Bogdanovich, Dushen'ka (1815), 89.

7. Svetlana Slavskaya Grenier also suggests kinship between Karamzin's Liza and Pushkin's Lizaveta Ivanovna from *Pikovaia Dama* (*The Queen of Spades*). Grenier, *Representing the Marginal Woman in Nineteenth-Century Russian Literature*, 23.

8. When rusalka is used as a generic term, it is lowercased (and, in this volume, in italics only at the first occurrence in Chapter One); referring to the title of an artistic work, Rusalka is capitalized and in italics. As the name of a heroine, Rusalka is capitalized but not italicized.

9. Vladimir Propp writes on the history and classification of folktales in *Morphology of the Folktale* (1968), 3–18. Ivanits comments on the importance of magic healers in the Russian countryside, where healers were perceived as capable of lending assistance and "curing with the aid of God and the saints," but at the same time suspected of "dealing with the devil." Ivanits, *Russian Folk Belief*, 111.

10. McClary, Feminine Endings, 86.

11. Locke, "What Are These Women Doing in Opera?" (1995), 62.

12. Abbate, *Unsung Voices* (1991), 26.

13. The connections with both riverbed and hair color are emphasized in Zelenin, *Izbrannye trudy*, 39, 142.

14. See definition of "rusyi" in Dal', *Tolkovyi slovar'* (1989), 4:115.

15. Despite these Russian cognates, according to the *Etnahrafiia Belarusi* the word is derived from the Latin phrase *dies rosae*, which is associated with ancient rites surviving in various cultures. Shamiakin, *Etnahrafiia Belarusi: encyclopedia* (1989), 433. See also Reed, *The Rusalka Theme in Russian Literature* (1973), 3–4; and Vasmer, *Etimologicheskii slovar' russkogo yazyka* (1964), 3:520.

16. Heinrich Heine also suggested that the Vila "is not, by any means, invariably a deceased bride, but a being corresponding to the *fata, fay,* or life-size fairy, or to the peri of the East." Heine, "Elementary Spirits" (1906), v. 11, 139–40.

17. Zelenin, *Izbrannye trudy*, 207.

18. In the 1831 *Telegraph* (St. Petersburg), Frederich de la Motte Fauque is named among the most prominent European writers. See Ingham, *E. T. A. Hoffmann's Reception in Russia* (1974), 88.

19. Zhukovsky translated tales from several European languages. His original tales, such as *Sleeping Beauty,* were modeled on German fairy tales. See Lupanova, *Russkaia narodnaia skazka v tvorchestve pisatelei pervoi poloviny XIX veka* (1959), 299.

20. Mikhail Shemiakin comments on their common interests and competition in the correspondence between Pushkin and Zhukovsky during the time they created their works on rusalkas and undines. Zhukovsky published fragments from his *Undine* between 1835 and 1837, and Pushkin wrote his "Prince Ianysh" in 1833–34 before the drama *Rusalka*. Retsepter and Shemiakin, *Vozvrashcheniie pushkinskoi rusalki*, 62, 84.

21. Ingham, *Hoffmann's Reception*, 9, 139.

22. Propp, *Russkaia skazka* (1984), 71.

23. The text of the original *Das Donauweibchen,* turned into *Dneprovskaia Rusalka,* was translated and revised in Russian fashion by N. Krasnopolsky. C. N. Davydov added several musical numbers. Like *Das Donauweibchen,* the *Dneprovskaia Rusalka* was followed by three Russian sequels. The second and third, in 1804 and 1805, were generated by Catterino Cavos and Davydov. The fourth opera of the cycle was created in 1807 by Davydov (music) and Shakhtinsky (text).

24. Retsepter and Shemiakin, *Vozvrashcheniie pushkinskoi rusalki*, 74.

25. Between 1804 and 1825, *Dneprovskaia Rusalka* was shown in Moscow theaters every year. Three of the operas were performed in 1807, and all four in 1824. After a hiatus of nearly ten years, the operas were reproduced in 1845 and then remained a consistent part of the nineteenth-century repertoire. Fedorov, *Repertuar Bol'shogo teatra SSSR*, v. 1.

26. Pushkin, "Eugene Onegin," *Polnoe sobranie khudozhestvennykh proizvedenii*, 282.

27. In his critical writing, Somov repeatedly encouraged writers "to search for their romantic plots in native folklore." Cited by Semibratova, "Chudesnye rasskazyvaia tainy," in *Oboroten'. Russkie fantasmagorii* (1994), 330. Accordingly his "Rusalka" emphasized the folkloristic element more than the romantic plotline.

28. Pushkin, "Rusalka," *Sochineniia* (1985), 1:203–5.

29. Zhukovsky, "Rybak" (1988), 44.

30. According to Ivanits, "in the case of the miller, the proximity to water, an element commonly used in magic rituals," led to suspicion that he cast spells, or "whispered" over it, and that he lived in friendship with the water sprite (*vodianoi*). Ivanits, *Russian Folk Belief*, 111.

31. Curiously, though, Pushkin himself wrote that he borrowed most of his *Songs* from Mérimée, "the anonymous author" of *La Guzla, ou choix de Poésies Illyriques, recueillies dans la Dalmatie, la Bosnie, la Croatie et l'Herzégowine.* Pushkin, "Rusalka" (1985), 1:530. See also Eiges, *Muzyka v zhizni i tvorchestve Pushkina* (1937).

32. Pushkin, "Rusalka" (1985), 1:554.

33. "I shumia i krutias', kolebala reka"—"Rusalka" by Lermontov.

34. "Zakipeli volny/I prismreli vdrug opiat."

35. "Pleshchut, taiatsia, laskatel'no nezhnye," from "Nad Ozerom" (Over the Lake) by Mily Balakirev, lyrics by Arseny Golenishchev-Kutuzov.

36. Anton Rubinstein, study for piano "Ondine" (1842); cantata *Svitezyanka* by Nikolai Rimsky-Korsakov on the text of Mickiewicz (1897); and Lyadov's orchestral piece "Volshebnoe ozero" (The Enchanted Lake; 1909). Many songs were based on Lermontov's poems: Alexander Borodin, "Morskaia tsarevna" (The Sea Princess); Rubinstein, "Rusalka"; Mily Balakirev, "Pesnia zolotoi rybki" (Song of the Little Golden Fish); Mikhail Ippolitov-Ivanov, "Pesnia rybki" (Song of the Little Fish); Arensky, "Pesnia' rybki." Both Arensky and Balakirev composed songs called "Nad ozerom" based on Golenishchev-Kutuzov; and Rimsky-Korsakov, "Nymph."

37. Russian operas featuring a water sprite include Alexander Aliabiev's music for drama *Rusalka* (1838); Dargomyzhsky's *Rusalka* (1858); Aleksei Lvov's opera *Undine* (1848); and Tchaikovsky's *Undine* (1869); also Alexander Serov's *Undine* (1858) and *May Night* (1850); Rimsky-Korsakov's *May Night* (1879) and *Sadko* (1897).

38. The operas and music dramas based on Pushkin's *Rusalka* include works by A. Aliabiev (1825), Dargomyzhsky (1856), Mestr de Mexur (1870), A. Aleksandrov (1913). See Kikta, *Pushkinskaia muzikal'naia panorama XIX–XX vekov* (1999).

39. According to Mikhail Pekelis, a major biographer of Dargomyzhsky, though the existing fragments of *Prince Ianysh* were written as chamber music, the composer's remarks in the score indicate that it could be envisioned as an orchestral cantata.

40. Dargomyzhsky, *Rusalka.* Vocal score (1975).

41. *Il Pirata* by Bellini (1827) was shown in Moscow Bol'shoi Theater in 1837, *Lucia di Lammermoor* by Donizetti (1835) and the ballet *Giselle* (1841) by Adam in 1843.

42. Mary Ann Smart writes about Lucia's Mad Scene that "at least as important as Lucia's appearance is in fact that she is *observed* by the chorus throughout the mad scene." Smart, "The Silencing of Lucia," *Cambridge Opera Journal* 4:2 (1991), 125. McClary suggests that "the chorus of wedding guests . . . attempt in vain to lead her into a more suitable key. . . . Indeed, the wedding guests respond to and accompany Lucia very much as the trio of men did Monteverdi's nymph" (*Lamento della Ninfa*). McClary, *Feminine Endings*, 96.

43. McClary writes: "Whether in the semiotic service of grief, erotic transport, or madness, the ostinato is always associated with some obsessive conditions." McClary, *Feminine Endings*, 192. On the subject of musical portrayal of women's madness, see the selection of essays in. Nancy Jones and Dunn (eds.), *Embodied Voices* (1994); and Clement, *Opera: The Undoing of Women* (1988).

44. Keldysh, *Istoria russkoi muzyki* (1948), 456. See Pekelis, who suggests that this folk song was also introduced abroad in Benjamin Beresford's anthology *The Russian Troubadour*, published in London in 1816. Pekelis, *Dargomyzhskii i narodnaia pesnia* (1951), 122.

45. This song is the heroine's most intimate and individualized number in the opera. No longer connected with her people and recognized only by the Kniaz, she leads a bodiless existence that depends entirely on the male lead.

46. Among many invocations of an oak tree, there is a connection between one here and in the introduction and conclusion of Pushkin's *Ruslan and Liudmila.*

47. Gozenpud, "Pushkin i russkaia opernaia klassika," in *Pushkin: issledovaniia i materialy* (1967), 200–17.

48. Even in Pushkin's short poetic stanza "Rusalka," the voluptuous little water sprite plays with the old monk for three days before luring him to the water.

49. Serov, *Rusalka, opera A. S. Dargomyzhskogo* (1953), 147.

50. Ibid., 304, 330.

51. McClary, *Feminine Endings,* 92.

52. Keldysh, *Istoria russkoi muzyki,* 1:451.

53. Wiley, *A Century of Russian Ballet* (1990), 90–105.

54. For example, Glinka's first opera, *Ivan Susanin,* was preceded by the opera of the same title by Cavos/Shakhovskoi (1822), which was also adapted to ballet in 1826. Two decades before Glinka's second opera, *Ruslan and Liudmila,* Schultz composed a ballet pantomime, also based on Pushkin. Dargomyzhsky's opera *Esmeralda* (1841) was based on Hugo's *Notre Dame de Paris.* Several years later, Pugni and Perrot created the ballet *La Esmeralda.* Dargomyzhsky was also familiar with hybrid genres. Between 1843 and 1848 he created *Torzhestvo Vakha,* an opera-ballet.

55. Marian Elizabeth Smith, for example, writes about the "verbal aspect" of the music for ballet, which was "imitating the human voice in various ways and using so-called *airs parlants* (short snippets of melodies from folksongs or opera arias, which could introduce actual explanatory words into the viewers' minds)." Smith, *Ballet and Opera in the Age of Giselle* (2004), 6, 58.

56. Beaumont, *The Ballet Called Giselle* (1988), 13.

57. Tenor Adolph Nourrit, after experiencing the "accidental spiritualism" of the ghostly dance in his performance of Robert in Meyerbeer's opera, wrote the scenario for *La Sylphide.* Within a decade, opera theater became populated with ephemeral but powerful creatures that, according to Marian Smith, "fared particularly well in ballet pantomime." Marian Smith, *Ballet and Opera* (2000), 67.

58. See Théophile Gautier's reviews of ballets in the Paris Opéra in *Gautier on Dance* (1986), 49, 119. See also Smith, *Ballet and Opera,* 67.

59. *La Sylphide,* music by Jean Schneitzhoeffer, premiered in Russia in 1835; *La Péri* by Johann Friedrick Burgmüller, in 1844.

60. Serov, *Izbrannye stat'i,* 2:445.

61. Ibid., 1:311.

62. McCarren, *The Female Form* (1992), 3.

63. Gautier, *Gautier on Dance,* 37.

64. Iurkevich, "Bolshoi theater. Debut of Mlle Taglioni," *Severnaia pchela* (Northern Bee, 1837), as quoted by Wiley, *Century of Russian Ballet,* 84.

65. McCarren, *Female Form,* 20.

66. Gautier, *Gautier on Dance,* 13.

67. *Giselle* remains in the core repertoire of the Bolshoi Theater, performed annually throughout the last decade. In 1999, the Bolshoi celebrated its thousandth performance of *Giselle.*

68. Those were the years approaching the golden age of Russian ballet, which culminated in the works of Tchaikovsky and Marius Petipa. Before the legendary Petipa moved to Russia, his older brother Lucien appeared on the stage of the imperial Russian theater as the first Albrecht in the premier of *Giselle.*

69. Smith, *Ballet and Opera*, 167.

70. In *Giselle* he is already married, "not for the heart, but for social reasons." This line of Pushkin's Kniaz (v. 2, 491) reflects on male characters and situations in both plotlines.

71. Adam, *Giselle: ballet en deux actes* (1985), Act II, no. 1 and 7, 116–23, 166–68.

72. There is no wedding in *Giselle*. In Meyerbeer's opera (1836, first premiered in St. Petersburg around 1837–38), a Catholic wedding procession in the third act is interrupted by a Gypsy Dance.

73. The gypsy dances are idiomatically related and play similar roles in the dramaturgical plan of the two operas. Though apparently a French fashion, musical references to gypsies were also reflective of Russian urban culture, in which gypsies played a vital role. Pushkin himself traveled with a gypsy *tabor* (tribe), wrote a poem entitled *Gypsy*, and developed a particular fascination for the singing of the real gypsy Tania in 1831, the year he was completing his *Rusalka*. Eiges, *Muzyka v zhizni i tvorchestve Pushkina*, 228, 232–33; Glumov, *Muzykal'nyi mir Pushkina* (1950), 185.

74. Keldysh, *Istoria russkoi muzyki*, 451.

75. Smith, *Ballet and Opera*, 59–60.

76. Serov, *Rusalka*, 78, 102.

77. Marrese, *Woman's Kingdom*, 71–72.

78. Ibid., 1.

79. Bogdanovich, *Dushen'ka*, 55–57 and 36–38.

80. Ibid., 37–38.

81. Ibid., 55–56.

82. In *The Captain's Daughter*, on the other hand, Catherine reveals surprising benevolence.

83. Wachtel, *Obsession with History*, 71, 81.

84. Pushkin studied at the Tsarskosel'skii Lyceum, where he met his best friends and associates.

85. As discussed in the previous chapter, a young graduate of the Lyceum, Pushkin created the poem "Vospominania v Tsarskom sele" (Memory of the Tsar's Village; 1814), in which every step through the majestic palace reminds him of Catherine:

     ... со вздохом росс вещает:

     «Исчезло все, великой нет!»

     With a sigh Russia proclaims

     Everything has vanished, the Great One gone!

    In the *Captain's Daughter* the meeting of the heroine and Catherine also takes place in the Tsar's village.

86. Pushkin, *Polnoe sobranie khudozhestvennykh proizvedenii*, 1093. See also Berezkina, "Ekaterina II v stikhotvorenii Pushkina 'Mne zhal' velikiia zheny," (1999), 21:412–21.

87. Kypros or Cyprus, the birthplace of Aphrodite.

88. Also, in the poetic tale *Tsar'-Devitsa* (1812), based on a collected folk tale and one of the early examples of the convergence between Russian folklore and literary tradition, Derzhavin not only invoked an image popular in folk tales but created a vision of the "ideal monarch." See Lupanova, *Russkaia narodnaia skazka*, 61–62.

89. Nineteenth-century authors recast folk tales as "magic-knight poems." Savchenko commented on figures such as the Tsar-Maiden as *prishletsy* (comers, aliens), long ago assimilated in Russian tales. See Savchenko, *Russkaia narodnaia skazka* (1967), 278.

90. Alexander Turgenev as quoted by Lupanova, *Russkaia narodnaia skazka*, 7. Late-eighteenth-century collections of tales and folk songs include Chulkov, "Sobranie raznykh pesen" (1770–1774) and *Peresmeshnik ili Slavenskie skazki* (1789); Popov, *Slavenskie drevnosti, ili Prikliucheniia Slavenskikh kniazei* (1770–71); Levshin, *Ruskiia skazki* (1780–1783); and *Vechernie chasy* (1787). By the mid-nineteenth century, among many published compilations were the significant anthology of Dal' in two volumes (1832 and 1846) and Afanas'ev, *Russkiia narodnyia skazki* (1855–1864), as well as Avdeeva, *Ocherki Maslenitsy v Evrope, Rossii i Sibiri* (1849) and *Russkie skazki dlia detei* (1844); Bogdan Bronnitsyn, *Russkie narodnye skazki* (1838). Several scholarly works about the tale included a dissertation by Bodianskii, *O narodnoi poezii slavianskikh plemen* (1837); and Kostomarov's *Slavianskaia mifologiia* (1847), *About the Historic Importance of Russian Folk Poetry* (1847). According to the folklorist Propp, only two European languages, Russian and German, have a special term denoting this genre. Propp, *Russkaia Skazka*, 35.
91. Karamzin's "Poor Liza," for example, was considered a skazka.
92. Propp, *Russkaia skazka*, 182, 239.
93. See Clement, *Opera: The Undoing of Women*.
94. Yegenoglu, *Colonial Fantasies* (1998), 125.

Chapter 7

1. Ivanov, *Selected Essays* (2001), 11.
2. Rimsky-Korsakov, *Mlada*, Act III, Scene 4, is entitled "The Vision of Tsarina Cleopatra." The composer began orchestration of the opera with Act III, which was performed in a series of Russian symphonic concerts (St. Peterburg, February 1891). Asaf'ev, "Ot Redaktsii" (1960), ix.
3. The line in the score reads "Dances. Poses of dancers and slaves." Rimsky-Korsakov, *Mlada* (1959), 248.
4. Rimsky-Korsakov, *Letopis' moei muzykal'noi zhizni* (1909), 265. (Here I prefer my own translation.)
5. The chorus of courtiers recites "Slav' truba, timpan, tsevnitsa polunochnykh stran dennitsu, slav'!" (Glorify, trumpet, timpani, and tsevnitsa, the tsarina of nocturnal "mid-night' lands, glorify!") Rimsky-Korsakov, "Noch' pered rozhdestvom" (1951), 117.
6. Rimsky-Korsakov, *My Musical Biography* (1923), 302. Grand Duke Vladimir Alexandrovich was a son of Emperor Alexander II, and Mikhail Nikolaievich a son of Emperor Nikolai I.
7. Rimsky-Korsakov, *Letopis'*, 306.
8. Wachtel, *Plays of Expectations* (2006), 4.
9. Ibid.
10. Rimsky-Korsakov, *My Musical Biography*, 305.
11. Ibid., 303.
12. The polonaise or "Polish" opened Russian imperial balls from the time of Peter I. Josef Kozlowski was a composer in the service of Potemkin. See his famous cantata-polonaise "Grom pobedy razdavaisia!" ("Thunder of Victory, Resound!"; 1968), 428–31.
13. See Act III, Scene 3, no. 19, Polish [polonaise], Tchaikovsky, *Cherevichki* (The Slippers; 1951), 2:276; also Peter Tchaikovsky and Modest Tchaikovsky, *Pikovaia Dama* (2001), Scene 3.
14. Barsukov, *Zhizn' Pogodina* (1890), 3:348.
15. Proskurina, *Mify imperii*, 293, 95.

16. Ibid., 293.

17. The Bolshoi Theater presented this staging of *Mlada* in 1988, which was later recorded and issued as a DVD (2005).

18. Rimsky-Korsakov, *My Musical Biography*, 205; Wotton, "Drums" (1930), 793.

19. Rimsky-Korsakov, *My Musical Biography*, 307.

20. Rimsky-Korsakov's water operas also include *May Night* (1880) and *The Snow Maiden* (*Snegurochka*, 1882).

21. Rimsky-Korsakov, *Letopis'*, 19, 41–43, 47–48, 61.

22. The given dates are of first performances.

23. Gaub, *Die Kollektive Balett-Oper "Mlada"* (1998).

24. Vasmer also identifies the word "morena" with a fish. Vasmer, *Etimologicheskii slovar' russkogo yazyka*, 2:573.

25. According to Apollon Korinfsky, "In Malorussian (Ukrainian) villages, as late as in 1860 and 1870s, . . . during the celebration of Ivan Kupala held July 23–24, . . . the folk dressed a straw doll and placed it under a cut maple tree, named Morena—a goddess of death, which at the end of the Kupala ritualistic games was drowned in a river." Korinfsky, *Narodnaia Rus'* (1994), 242. In *Mlada* it is quite different; at the end of the opera and the Kupala celebration, Morena floods the folk.

26. See Leon Bakst's sketches of Ida Rubinstein in the role of Cleopatra (1909), the Egyptian costume for ballerina Tamara Karsavina, and images and costumes for the ballet *Scheherazade* (1910), *Afternoon of a Faun* by Nizhinsky (1912), and *Narcissus* by N. Cherepnin (1911).

27. Though her name is rooted in *sviat* (saint), it actually means the opposite and suggests irony: bigotry, pretended holiness.

28. As in Wagner's *Flying Dutchman* (1843), in Rimsky-Korsakov's score spinning is expressed in a sustained pattern played by clarinet and violas.

29. Nearly ten years after *Mlada*, Rimsky-Korsakov composed the opera *Kashchei Bessmertnyi* (*Kashchei the Immortal*; 1902).

30. Among the pantheon of old Slavic gods, Chernobog, a vicious fiend, is a counterpart and opposite of Belobog (White-god). According to Andrei Kaisarov, an effigy of the Chernobog was found in the temple of Retra. Kaisarov, "Slavianskaia i rossiiskaia mifologiia" (1993), 67.

31. A double chorus in Act II and triple in Act IV.

32. After Rimsky-Korsakov's *Mlada* and *Kashchei the Immortal*, Stravinsky created the image of Kashchei in his ballet *Firebird* (1910) and devil's dances in his suite from *The Soldier's Tale* (1919); Sergei Prokofiev likewise invoked the image of Chuzhebog and Pagan forces in the second movement of his *Scythian Suite* (1915). Prokofiev also wrote a symphonic suite called *Egyptian Nights* (1935). In their first season in Paris in 1909, Diaghilev's Ballets Russes presented the ballet *Cleopatra* with music compilation from Arensky, Glazunov, Glinka, Mussorgsky, Rimsky-Korsakov, Taneyev, and Cherepnin. Harris-Warrick, "Ballet" *Grove Music Online*.

33. In terms of intertextual connections, Radishchev chose the epigraph to his book from Trediakovsky's *Telemakhida*. Citing a poet known for poetic praise of Anna and also one Catherine used as a model and inspiration, Radishchev employed Trediakovsky's morbid portrait of a monstrous ruler, "Чудище обло, озорно, огромно, стозевно и лаяй" (Monstrously heavy, insolent, and barking). Radishchev, *Puteshestvie iz Peterburga v Moskvy* (1975), 44.

34. Wachtel, *Remaining Relevant After Communism* (2006), 169.

35. At about at the same time the composer was working on *Mlada*, Sigmund Freud referred, in the opening of his *Interpretation of Dreams*, to a long-existing belief that "dream-life" bears the "echo of the divine nature of dreams which was undisputed in antiquity. Nor are discussions of the premonitory characters of dreams and their power to foretell the future at an end." Freud, *The Interpretation of Dreams*, 63.

36. Rimsky-Korsakov, *My Musical Biography*, 307.

37. Ibid., 257. In *Mlada*, the composer also quadruples the group of woodwinds and accordingly increases the brass, which suggests the influence of Wagner's *Der Ring des Nibelungen*. Rimsky-Korsakov studied the score around the time he began thinking about *Mlada*.

38. Morrison, *Russian Opera and the Symbolist Movement* (2002), 261.

39. Preceding the Ivan Kupala festival is *rusalia* or rusalkas' week, from June 19 to 24.

40. The spinning here parallels the opening of the second act of Wagner's *Flying Dutchman*; spells, dreams, and visions play a critical role in both operas.

41. Slavic groups include Polabs (Western Slavs) ruled by Mstivoi; people of Alkona, Yaromir's city-state; exiled Czechs; and a couple from Novgorod, referred to as "Russians." In this opera Czechs, like Russians in Catherine's *Oleg*, are pagan, and in both spectacles they fight against the advent of Christianity. On Polabs, see Kulikov, "Polabskie i Pomorskie Slaviane" (1998), 77–78. The foreigners in the second act are represented by Lithuanians, Gypsies, and an Indian Moor.

42. The market scene with polychromic rhythmic and melodic combinations, and with the hustle of the marketplace, in a few years would be replayed in *Sadko* and some two decades later in Stravinsky's Shrovetide fair.

43. Catherine brought a Novgorodian fistfight to the operatic stage in her *Boeslavich, Champion of Novgorod*.

44. The theme of Czech-German conflict, sudden and by no means connected with any other lines of the opera, could be a quirky allusion to the Czech impresario Neumann, who brought to St. Petersburg a German operatic company to produce Wagner's *Ring*. Rimsky-Korsakov, *My Musical Biography*, 251.

45. Ibid., 309.

46. Rimsky-Korsakov comments on the advent of Wagnerism in Russia. Ibid., 251–53.

47. Ibid., 252.

48. According to Bazhenov and Kaisarov, Triglav or Three-head is a goddess of the soil, whose three heads signify sky, soil, and underworld; in her hands she holds a full moon. The gathering of shadows on the Three-Headed Mountain matches the character of the Kupala festival. Kaisarov, "Slavianskaia i rossiiskaia mifologiia" (1993), 78–79, and also Bazhenov, "Solnechnye bogi slavian" (1993), 3–16.

49. Rimsky-Korsakov, *Mlada* (1959), 198.

50. Ibid., 67.

51. The chorus of dark forces and "Infernal Kolo," with rhythmically sturdy chords, foreshadows Stravinsky's *Le Sacre du printemps*.

52. Rimsky-Korsakov wrote his directions in the score. See the vocal score of *Mlada*, Act III, Scene 3, "Infernal Kolo," Rimsky-Korsakov, *Mlada* (1959), 230, 37.

53. Episode with "*chookh*" from Rimsky-Korsakov, *My Musical Biography*, 266.

54. Rimsky-Korsakov, *Mlada*, Act III, Scene 4. Rimsky-Korsakov, *Mlada: An Opera Ballet in Four Acts* (1981), 106–7.

55. The rooster call would become central to the soon-to-be composed *Golden Cockerel* (1909). The motif in the piccolo answered by oboes in *Mlada* anticipates and reminds one of the cockerel's solo in trombones continued by oboes in the first measures of *Cockerel*.

56. The posthumous flight of the spirit-shadows would be echoed by the elevation of Petrushka's soul in Stravinsky.

57. Morrison, "The Semiotics of Symmetry, or Rimsky-Korsakov's Operatic History Lesson" (2001), 261.

58. Doubling characterizes the processes and structure of the opera. The quite spectacular metamorphosis of the mortal Sviatokha into the powerful, domineering Morena in the first act is counterbalanced by a flamboyant pagan ritual in the second. The grand fête of magical and foreign forces of the underworld in the third act is followed with another ritual in the temple and the parade of native archaic spirits in the fourth. A gay folk *kolo*—maiden khorovods, dances, kisses, and quite explicit pairings—is refashioned in the next act into two dances, a "Fantastic Kolo" and an "Infernal Kolo," saturated with eroticism.

59. Catherine's comic opera, issued in 1789, was reprinted in 1895 by Peter Iurgenson, a principal music publisher in St. Petersburg in the second half of the nineteenth century.

60. The nineteenth-century portrayal of a national "us" versus oriental "others" was not invented by Russians. In fact they successfully adopted European conventions, developing and proclaiming them their own. See Taruskin's works, in particular "Glinka's Ambiguous Legacy"; and Frolova-Walker, "On *Ruslan* and Russianness," 37–38.

61. Rimsky-Korsakov, *Mlada* (1981), 112.

62. Saint-Saëns, *Samson et Dalila*, Act I, trio. See also the discussion of the image of Dalila in Locke, "Constructing the Oriental 'Other'" (1991), 279.

63. Jung, *The Archetype of the Collective Unconscious* (1990), 21.

64. Freud, *Interpretation of Dreams* (1999), 11.

65. Ibid., 54. Here Freud discusses the import of the theories of Hildebrandt and Fichte for the study of dreams.

66. Ibid., 74–77.

67. See Shorter, *Historical Dictionary of Psychiatry* (2005), 73.

68. Ibid.

69. Hirstein, *Brain Fiction: Self-Deception and the Riddle of Confabulation* (2006), 56; Davis, King, and Schultz, *Fundamentals of Neurologic Disease* (2005), 196.

70. Davidson, "Psychosomatic Aspects of Korsakoff Syndrome" (1948), 1–17, 3.

71. Ovsyannikov and Ovsyannikov, "Sergei S. Korsakov and the Beginning of Russian Psychiatry" (2007), 16:58–64, 60.

72. See Brintlinger and Vinitsky, *Madness and the Mad in Russian Culture* (2007).

73. Abbate, "Jankélévitch's Singularity" (2003), xviii.

74. Jankélévitch, *Music and the Ineffable*, 95.

75. Ibid., 93.

76. The name Yarilo comes from *iaro-iaryi* (bright, white; Kirsha Danilov); the ending *ilo* is a form of endearment. In various Russian regions, the folk celebrated the ritualistic rebirth and death of Yarilo. With games, songs, and dances, the man chosen to enact Yarilo would be dressed in a colorful cloth with a medley of ribbons, a paper hat decorated with rooster's feathers, and ringing bells attached to his knees and arms. Carrying the thunder club, he walked through the drunken crowd, singing and dancing in these bacchanalias. N. I. Tolstoy,

in *Slavianskaia mifologiia* (1995), 397–99. Korinfsky writes that in "some other places, the doll of decorated Yarilo was carried through the crowd in a coffin, the women lamenting in voices (singing) and men shaking the straw god, trying to wake him." *Narodnaia Rus'*, 235.

77. Bazhenov, "Solnechnye bogi slavian," 9.
78. Act IV, Scene 6.
79. Rimsky-Korsakov, *Mlada* (1959), 336–38. See also Rimsky-Korsakov, *My Musical Biography*, 205.
80. The festival and folk gatherings, fully represented in the second act, are absent in the magical third. The folk chorus reappears in the final act.
81. From Glinka's *Ivan Susanin* and *Ruslan* to Rimsky-Korsakov's *Mlada*, *Sadko*, *Tsar's Bride*, *Kashchei*.
82. Jankélévitch, *Music and the Ineffable*, 94.
83. Filippo Taglioni's ballets *La fille du Danube* (1836) and *L'ombre* (1839), starring his daughter, had remarkable success in Russia. Marie Taglioni appeared on the Russian stage every year between 1837 and 1842.
84. Darnton, *The Great Cat Massacre* (1984), 9–73.
85. Rybakov, "Rozhdenie Bogin' i Bogov" (1993), 176.
86. Rimsky-Korsakov, *My Musical Biography*, 266–74.
87. Frolova-Walker, "On *Ruslan* and Russianness," 32–33.
88. Ivan Goncharov, *Oblomov* (2005), 2.

Chapter 8

1. Figes, *Natasha's Dance: A Cultural History of Russia* (2002), 397.
2. The full name of the champion is Solovei Budimirovich.
3. After the first known notation of the bylina, by Kirsha Danilov, dozens of collected versions about Sadko introduced typified tunes and different stories. A hundred years after Danilov, Vissarion Belinsky retold the story of Sadko with great gusto in one of his four major essays about ancient Russian poems. Belinsky, "Stat'i o narodnoi poezii," in *Polnoe sobranie sochinenii* (1959), 5:416–20; see also Propp, *Russkii geroicheskii epos* (1958), 87–109.
4. *Novgorodskaia letopis* (1959) contains information about the merchant Sotko, who is considered a historical prototype of the Sadko of Novgorod bylinas. Historical Vasily Busalaevich died in 1171. Nikiforov, *Fol'klor kievskogo perioda* (1941), 1:255.
5. In a number of bylinas, the old holy man is called Mikola of Mozhaisk; Belinsky referred to him as St. Nikolai; Boris Uspensky suggested equation of the two. Belinsky, "Stat'i o narodnoi poezii" (1973); Uspensky, *Filologicheskie razyskaniia v oblasti slavianskikh drevnostei* (1982), 18.
6. Ibid., 399.
7. The historical Sadko is believed to have erected a church to St. Boris and St. Gleb, the first martyrs of the Orthodox Church (1167).
8. *Novgorodskie byliny*, 400. Propp writes that "despite her female appearance, Cherniava, Sadko's water bride, can also be a rusalka." Propp, *Russkii geroicheskii epos*, 106.
9. Ibid. The male chorus in E-flat major opens the first scene and begins the final celebration. Rimsky-Korsakov and Bel'sky, *Sadko, The Complete Works of Nikolai Rimsky-Korsakov* (1981), 3:314–15. All musical examples in this chapter are cited from Rimsky-Korsakov, *Sadko: Opera-Bylina* (1975).

10. Morrison's clear structural analysis and intertextual investigation of *Sadko* permit one the leisure of relying on his material without repeating it. Morrison, "Semiotics of Symmetry," 266.

11. Ibid., 264–65.

12. Rimsky-Korsakov, *Letopis'*, 309–10.

13. Morrison, "Semiotics of Symmetry," 271.

14. Rimsky-Korsakov, letter to Bel'sky July 19, 1895, cited by Morrison, "Semiotics of Symmetry," 271.

15. Taruskin, "Chernomor to Kashchei: Harmonic Sorcery; or, Stravinsky's 'Angle,'" 103–4.

16. In fact the situation reminds one of Pushkin's tale about the golden fish except that the old man is not sexually engaged, serving his aged and nosy wife.

17. See solo fragments of Volkhova and Yaromir. Rimsky-Korsakov, *Mlada*, vocal score, 213; *Sadko* vocal score, 112.

18. Jankélévitch, *Music and the Ineffable*, 5.

19. Rimsky-Korsakov, *Sadko*, orchestral score, 1: 79–80.

20. Ibid., 47.

21. Jung, *Archetype of the Collective Unconscious*, 9: 24–25.

22. Lord, *The Singer of Tales* (1960), 21.

23. Rimsky-Korsakov, *Sadko*, vocal score, 224–27.

24. Ibid., 236.

25. Morrison, "Semiotics of Symmetry," 269.

26. Taruskin, "Chernomor to Kashchei," 102.

27. See a comparative table of colors associated with keys by three Russian composers, Scriabin, Rimsky-Korsakov, and Asaf'ev. Vanechkina and Galeev, "'Tsvetnoi slukh' v tvorchestve N. A. Rimskogo-Korsakova" (2003); http://synesthesia.prometheus.kai.ru/zwet-sl_r.htm.

28. Morrison, "The Semiotics of Symmetry," 270.

29. Some equate Sadko with the German Siegfried; the golden fish he nets from the lake is the treasure of the Nibelung. Propp, *Russkii geroicheskii epos*, 88–89.

30. *Novgorodskie byliny*, 407.

31. Vladimir Stasov argued a parallel between this part of the bylina and poems by Harivansa about water snakes abducting Tsar Yadu to the water kingdom, where he married the five daughters of the water ruler. *Novgorodskie byliny*, 395. Stasov, *Collected Works* (1894), 3:1062–63, 68–70.

32. Taruskin, "Sadko," *Grove Music Online*.

33. Markov, *Belomorskie byliny* (1901), 491–92.

34. *Novgorodskie byliny*, 390.

35. Balzer, *Russian Traditional Culture* (1992), 45, 78–79.

36. Kate Blakey traces his roots from Jewish ethnic Khazars, who "formed an important contingent among the Russian traders and trade caravans, passing continually to and from on the great route from Central Asia, through Central Europe on to Italy [and Spain]." Blakey, "Folk Tales of Ancient Russia" (1924), 58. The tale of Dove, existing among Russians from at least the thirteenth century, gained the attention of Russian intellectuals in the second half of the nineteenth century. Among them were painter Nikolai Roerich and poet Alexander Blok, and folklorists Petr Bessonov and Petr Kireevsky.

37. Simon Morrison identifies and discusses siren song, barcarolle, berceuse, and chantey. Morrison, "Semiotics of Symmetry," 269.

38. Ibid., 265.

39. Some believe that the ancient volkhs (or volkhvs) lived on the Danube, fighting and conquering Slavic neighbors. Others suggest that they penetrated the Slavic land as pagan priests. Thus the volkhs are known as mighty warriors, shamans, and sorcerers. Their origin is debated. See S. Tolstov, "'Nartsy' i 'volkhi' na Dunae" (1948), 2:8–38. The heroic character Volkh (Vol'ga), embodying the imagery of the ancient volkhs, is central to a body of tales and bylinas. Isabel Florence Hargood listed early published epics about Volkh dating to the late seventeenth century. Hargood, *The Epic Songs of Russia* (1886), 14.

40. Propp, *Russkii geroicheskii epos*, 134–53. The Danube is also the habitat of the first operatic rusalkas. See *Das Donauweibchen* by Kauer and Hansler (1798), discussed in Chapter Five.

41. Propp, *Russkii geroicheskii epos*, 134–53.

42. Morrison offers extensive analysis of oriental layers in the East-West, past-present depiction of three foreign musical images, in "Semiotics of Symmetry," 274–75.

43. See Vasnetsov, *Vitiaz' na rasput'e* (1882), Russian Museum, www.museum.ru/alb/image. asp?18580. See Propp on bylinas about Ilya of Murom standing at the *rasput'i* of three roads. Propp, *Russkii geroicheskii epos*, 264.

44. See Dean and Lowe, "Introduction," *Marriage in Italy, 1300–1650* (1998), 4.

45. In the bylina sung by Andrei Sorokin and recorded by Rybnikov (1860), despite Sorokin's limited geographic knowledge the hero visited far seas. *Novgorodskie byliny*, 398.

46. Morrison, "The Semiotics of Symmetry," 276–77.

47. *Novgorodskie byliny*, 399.

48. Rimsky-Korsakov, *Sadko*, vocal score, 287, 293.

49. Ibid., 48.

50. Jankélévitch, *Music and the Ineffable*, 15.

51. Rimsky-Korsakov, *Sadko*, vocal score, 393.

52. Comparing recitatives in his three operas, *Mlada*, *Christmas Eve*, and *Sadko*, Rimsky-Korsakov writes that recitatives in the first two "though correct in most cases, had been undeveloped and not characteristic, the recitative of the *bylina*-opera and especially that of Sadko himself is characteristic to an unheard degree." Rimsky-Korsakov, *My Musical Biography*, 308.

53. Ibid.

54. Gasparov, *Five Operas*, 38–39. Using Gasparov's "Farewell to the Enchanted Garden" as an essential starting point of the discussion and taking it to late-nineteenth-century operas, I paraphrased his title in creating a heading for this section.

55. Morrison, "Semiotics of Symmetry," 277.

56. Gasparov, *Five Operas*, 38.

57. Glinka, *Ruslan and Liudmila*, Act IV, Scene and Aria of Liudmila, no. 18.

58. Gogol's "Christmas Eve" is one of a collection of short stories entitled *Evenings on a Farm near Dekan'ka* (1831–32?). Tchaikovsky composed his *Vakula the Smith* on the basis of Gogol's "Christmas Eve" in 1775; ten years later he created a new version of the opera, now entitled *Cherevichki* or *The Slippers*. Another ten years passed and Rimsky-Korsakov employed the same story in his opera that bears its original literary title, *Christmas Eve* (1895).

59. The "leaves of palms" in her hands and laurels by her feet are not only the attributes of the tsarina's triumphs. They might remind one of the tropical decoration of Potemkin's palace (1791), as well as abundant depictions of Catherine against ancient Grecian backgrounds that doubled as her political goals and the equivalent of public relations.

60. Larosh, *Russkii viestnik* (1887), vol. 191, 842.

61. Rimsky-Korsakov, *Letopis'*, 313.

62. Potemkin also names Catherine's heroes, including Orlov-Chesmensky, the brother of Catherine's lover and one of the small group that brought her to the throne.

63. The sequence of dances consists of "Games and Dances of Stars," "Mazurka," "Procession of Comets," "Khorovod," "Chardash and the Rain of Falling Stars," and "Demonic Kolo."

64. Gogol, *Polnoe sobranie sochinenii* (1852), 8:82–84.

Chapter 9

1. Tchaikovsky, *Pikovaia dama* (opera in three acts), libretto by Modest Tchaikovsky, 469–75. Unless indicated otherwise, English translations are the author's.

2. Guber, *Don-Zhuanskii spisok A. S. Pushkina*; Leonid Grossman, *Pis'ma zhenshchin k Pushkinu*; Riabtsev, *113 prelestnits Pushkina*. Russian accounts provide examples of unexpected, nontraditional relationships. For one and a half decades, Peter Tchaikovsky expressed affection and intimate feelings to Nadezhda von Meck, whom he agreed never to meet in person but who gave him generous financial support. Among Pushkin's many romances, several were the age of his mother. In his case as in Gherman's, the line between love and obsession, reality and phantom blurred.

3. Pushkin, *Polnoe sobraniie khudozhestvennykh proizvedenii*, 637. The poem was not published during the poet's life.

4. Catherine II, *Nakaz kommissii o sostavlenii proekta novago ulozheniia* (1767).

5. Madariaga writes: "As the empress grew older, the favorites became younger and the disparity in age became more striking." Madariaga, *Russia in the Age of Catherine the Great*, 354. Ivan Rimsky-Korsakov, twenty four, whom fifty-year-old Catherine referred to as "Pyrrhus, king of Epirus," was followed by Alexander Lanskoi, then age twenty-two, whose untimely death brought to the empress's chamber a number of short-time favorites and then the twenty-six-year-old "Redcoat" Alexander Dmitriev-Mamonov, who resided in the imperial palace for four years, to be followed by "Blackie" Zubov.

6. Dashkova, *Zapiski*, 165.

7. Alexander, *Catherine the Great*, 226.

8. The Russian as well as English spelling of the names (Russian or Russified) varies. Gasparov offers an explanation of why Pushkin uses Germann and Tchaikovsky German. Germann is pronounced with a hard *g* in Russian; I follow a conventional spelling of the name "Gherman"—German without "h" would be read in English as the nationality "German." Gasparov, *Five Operas*, 143.

9. Taruskin, "Another World: Why the Queen of Spades Is the Great Symbolist Opera" (1995), 7:8–10, 11–13; Taruskin, *On Russian Music* (2009), 114–24; Morrison, *Russian Opera and the Symbolist Movement* (2002), 45–114.

10. Taruskin, *On Russian Music*, 115. Taruskin summarizes the plot in four sentences.

11. Among comprehensive studies of *The Queen of Spades* is Vinogradov, "Stil' *Pikovoi Damy*" (1936), 74–147. Nikolai Lerner identified Pushkin's story as an anecdote in *Rasskazy o Pushkine* (1929), 137. Russian and American literary scholars who view *Queen of Spades* as a psychological novel include Gershenzon, *Mudrost' Pushkina* (2000), 1:71–79; and Rosenshield, "Freud, Lacan, and Romantic Psychoanalysis" (1996), 1:1–26. Nathan Rosen focuses on the gambling aspect; "The Theme of Cards in *The Queen of Spades*," (1975), 3:255–75.

12. Rosenshield, "Freud, Lacan, and Romantic Psychoanalysis," 22.
13. Lotman, "The Theme of Cards and the Card Game" (1978), 473.
14. Ibid., 462.
15. Klimovitsky, "'Pikovaia dama' Chaikovskogo" (1994), 224–25.
16. Catherine's *O, times!*—a satirical comedy in the style of Beaumarchais—incidentally unfolds around a grandmother and the marital prospects of her daughters and also deals with cards and superstitions, mocked by the empress. See also O'Malley, "'How Great Was Catherine?'" (1999), 33–48.
17. See Lerner, *Rasskazy o Pushkine* (1929), 145–148. Other candidates for Pushkin's countess included Countess Natalia Zagriazhskaia and, according to Julie Buckler, Countess Iusupova. Buckler states "the end of Pushkin's story represents the beginning of a new oral legend" in *Mapping St. Petersburg* (2005), 147.
18. Vrangel' and Solov'ev, *Russkaia zhenshchina v graviurakh i litografiiakh* (1911), 20, no. 173.
19. Lotman, "Theme of Cards," 457.
20. Helfant, *The High Stakes of Identity* (2002), 51.
21. Pushkin, "Iz pis'ma k Tolstomu" (1821), *Polnoe sobranie khudozhestvennykh proizvedenii*, 1090.
22. Vsevolozhskaia, *Rod Vsevolozhskikh* (2000), 28–31.
23. Ivan Vsevolozhsky insistently pursued operatic realization of *The Queen of Spades*, engaging Modest Tchaikovsky as a librettist. While approaching several composers, he may have had his eye on the great brother. Skvirskaia, "K istorii sozdaniia opery 'Pikovaia dama'" (2003), 192–93. Vsevolozhsky offered *The Queen of Spades* to Nikolai Klenovsky and later to A. Villamov and Nikolai Solov'ev. Before engaging Modest Tchaikovsky, Vsevolozhsky discussed the libretto by V. Kandaurov.
24. April 28, 1884: "This *vint* irritates me so much, that I've been afraid that it will affect my health." Two days later: "Why do I play vint? Nothing but frustration. Again lost and hardly contained madness." May 12, 1887: "Playing vint, I got mad, not about the cards, but in general." Tchaikovsky, *Dnevniki* (2000), 18–19, 23.
25. Lerner, *Rasskazy o Pushkine*, 142. Lerner, for example, compared *The Queen of Spades* to Balzac's *La Peau de chagrin* (1830).
26. Karamzin, "Bednaia Liza," http://lib.ru/LITRA/KARAMZIN/liza.txt.
27. On the close ties between Tchaikovsky's *Queen of Spades* and the works of Karamzin, see Klimovitsky, "'Pikovaia Dama' Chaikovskogo," 222–74.
28. Karamzin's Erast is also the title character of an idyll by Salomon Gessner, whose pastorals affected European literary fashions. Making his debut as a translator of Gessner's idylls, Karamzin continued to admire his pastorals, which influenced the poetics of "Poor Liza." Perhaps the *intermède* in the middle of *Queen of Spades* echoes Gessner's idyll, while also reinforcing the Tchaikovskys' eighteenth-century time frame. See also Hammarberg, "Poor Liza, Poor Èrast, Lucky Narrator" (1987), 3:318.
29. Tosi, "Sentimental Irony in Early Nineteenth-Century Russian Literature" (2000), 2:266–86.
30. Velikopol'sky, *K Erastu* (1828).
31. Thanks to Velikopol'sky, the news about Pushkin betting on his poetic works went public.
32. Shakhovskoi staged and created fifty-six plays, including operas, among them the original *Ivan Susanin* with music by Catterino Cavos, 1815. Besides *Khrizomania*, Shakhovskoi produced two other theatrical adaptations of his protégé Pushkin's works, a magic comedy *Finn* (1824) and the trilogy *Kerim-Girei* (1825).

33. Among scholars who explore the doubles pervading *Queen of Spades* are Taruskin, "Queen of Spades," *Grove Music Online*; and Kiseleva, "Pikovye Damy' Pushkina i Shakhavskogo."

34. Ibid.

35. Shavrygin, *Tvorchestvo A. Shakhovskogo v istoriko-literaturnom protsesse* (1996), 43–47; Vinogradov, "Stil' *Pikovoi Damy*," 109. The literary club of Pushkin and Shakhovskoi waged a mighty offensive against the critics of Zagoskin's historical novel *Iury Miloslavsky, ili russkie v 1612 godu*.

36. The premiere of *La dame de pique* by Fromental Halévy (1799–1862) and Eugène Scribe (1791–1861) was announced in *Sankt-Peterburgskie vedomosti* (St. Petersburg News). See Denisenko, "Pushkinskie siuzhety i teksty na stsene v 1850–1870" (2004), 129–51, 152 (n. 16). It is believed that this and several other European operatic and theatrical adaptations of *Queen of Spades* are based on a translation of the story by Prosper Mérimée (1849).

37. Gautier, *Histoire de l'art dramatique en France depuis vingt-cinq ans*, 1858, 209–10, cited in Jordan, *Fromental Halévy* (1994), 154. Berlioz appeared less congratulatory in his reviews of the spectacle, which during the following season had forty-three performances; if nothing else, his review would likely have attracted Tchaikovsky's attention.

38. The published libretto attributes the music to M. Henri Laurent. The title page states that the English *Queen of Spades* was "adapted from La dame de pique" from Dion Boucicault, *The Queen of Spades; or, the Gambler's Secret*, 1851. The plot closely resembles the libretto of Halévy/Scribe. The published libretto is acknowledged as an adaptation by Boucicault (1838–1885), but it does not mention either its French predecessor or the Russian source. Ten years later, a German version of the story, *Die Kartenschlägerin oder Pique Dame* by Franz von Suppé (1819–1885), appeared on the stage of Treumann's Kai-Theater in Vienna.

39. Boucicault, *Queen of Spades* (1851), 30.

40. Vaidman, "Rabota P. I. Chaikovskogo nad rukopis'iu libretto opery Pikovaia dama" (1980), 156.

41. His female duets, a third or a sixth apart, remind one of the female terem scenes in Catherine's *Fevei*, a tradition linked with the musical language of the time and sustained in nineteenth-century Russian operas, and specifically characteristic of Tchaikovsky.

42. Wachtel, "Rereading *The Queen of Spades*" (2000), 14–15.

43. Tchaikovsky, *Pikovaia dama* (2001), Act I, Scene 2.

44. After entering Catherine's boudoir, Dmitriev-Mamonov "was promoted to adjutant-general with the rank of lieutenant-general, and . . . received the title of count of the Holy Roman Empire," among other titles and gifts bestowed on the young officer. Alexander, *Catherine the Great*, 224.

45. Ibid., 223–24.

46. Pushkin, *Sochineniia* (1985), 1:198.

47. Ibid., 199.

48. Gasparov, *Five Operas*, 152.

49. Tchaikovsky, *Pikovaia Dama*, 63.

50. Pushkin, *Sochineniia*, 1:196.

51. Act I, Scene 1; emphasis is mine.

52. The storm breaks out as Gherman bets on love or death. Rivaling the blissful Prince, he promises to have *her* (unidentified at this point in the opera by either of the two men).

53. Protopopov and Tumanina, *Opernoe tvorchestvo Chaikovskogo* (1957), 305.

54. Shevtsova, *Dodin and the Maly Drama Theatre* (2004), 190.

55. Meyerhold, *Pikovaia Dama* (1994), 130.

56. In Russian scholarship this theme is identified as the leitmotif of the countess's apparition. Vaidman, Korabel'nikova, and Rubtsova, *Tematiko-bibliographicheskii ukazatel' sochinenii P. I. Tchaikovskogo* (2003), 177.

57. Shevtsova, *Dodin*, 190.

58. Kramer, *After the Lovedeath: Sexual Violence and the Making of Culture* (1997). See also Kallberg, "Sex, Sexuality," *Grove Music Online.*

59. Ostrovsky, "Elena Obraztsova" (2003).

60. Vinogradov, *Slovar' iazyka Pushkina* (2000), 2:770–71.

61. This monochromatic line may signify the unearthly nature of the speaker, reminiscent of Pushkin's "machine-like" countess.

62. Vinogradov, "Stil' *Pikovoi Damy*," 89–90. According to Vinogradov, Catherine's grandee Passek, who had lost a significant amount at the card table, fell asleep and in his dream saw an old stranger whose recommendations made him wake up and win on the predicted cards. In an analysis of Pushkin, Rosen suggests that "Gherman is forgiven on condition that he marry Lizaveta, which he has not done. But there is no proof that he does not intend to marry her." Rosen, "Theme of Cards," 258. Hence the Tchaikovskys' Gherman not only disobeys the word of the deceased but also makes fulfillment impossible by pushing Liza toward her suicide before entering his last game.

63. A specific gambling expression, discussed by Vinogradov, in "Stil' *Pikovoi Damy*."

64. Rosen, "Theme of Cards," 258.

65. Vinogradov, "Stil' *Pikovoi Damy*," 78; Rosen, "Theme of Cards," 258. Rosen also writes that "few critiques have ever ventured to discuss" the "accident."

66. Rosenshield, "Freud, Lacan, and Romantic Psychoanalysis," 6.

67. Perhaps Pushkin's Richelieu is Louis François, duc de Richelieu (1696–1788), whose son Armand du Plessis de Richelieu (1766–1822) became a Russian hero in the battle at Ismail, which changed the course of the Russian-Turkish war Catherine the Great ventured in 1787. For fourteen years in the early nineteenth century, Armand de Richelieu was the governor of Odessa, a city very familiar to Pushkin.

68. Lebrun, *Memoirs of Madame Vigée Lebrun* (1903), 80.

69. One of her paintings portrayed a daughter of the assumed prototype of Pushkin's countess, Countess Ekaterina Vladimirovna Apraksin, née Princess Golitsin (1768–1854), a famous beauty known as "Venus en Courroux" (Angry Venus). Other Golitsins in Vigée Lebrun's portraits include Princess Ekaterina (Karolina) Alexandrovna Dolgorouky, née de Litsin (1758–1842), an illegitimate daughter of one of the princes Golitsin; Princess Anna Alexandrovna Golitsin, née Princess Grudzinsky; Countess Varvara Nikolaevna Golovine, née Princess Galitzine (1766–1821); Princess Praskovia Andreevna Galitzine, née Countess Shouvalov (1767–1868); and Countess Irina Ivanovna Vorontsov, née Izmailov (1768–1848), sister of the celebrated Princess Golitsin, called the "Princess de Minuit."

70. Some of Acier's porcelain sculptures are preserved in the Hermitage. Sokolov, "Rodoslovnaia Tchaikovskogo: novye imena" (2003), 4:29.

71. Parakalis, "Musical Historicism in *The Queen of Spades*" (1999).

72. Gasparov, *Five Operas*, 144.

73. Ibid. Talking about "temporal swings" in Tchaikovsky's *Queen of Spades*, Gasparov focuses on the shift from the love duet in the second scene, "comparable" to "the love duet in the

second act of *Tristan and Isolde*," to the "Mozartian sounds of the introductory chorus" of the third scene.

74. The Tchaikovskys' countess is quite different from Pushkin's. In the opera she aligns with and consumes the power of Tchaikovsky's many older female personages. Unlike most nineteenth-century Russian composers who replaced motherly figures in Catherine's operas with paternal images (fathers give their daughters away in *Ivan Susanin, Ruslan and Liudmila, Rusalka, Sadko,* and *The Tsar's Bride*), young Russian heroes are free of their domestic ties and seem to have no need for parents. Tchaikovsky's operas present a gallery of older women dominating domestic scenes and retaining power, which ranges from self-sacrificial to vengeful and seductive. All three of these old countesses are engaged in the fourth scene.

75. Gasparov points out the descending line in Polina's romance and in the song of Milovzor. Gasparov, *Five Operas*, 147.

76. Taruskin in, "Another World" also talks about the "double suicide" of Liza and Gherman.

77. Surin adds "Kakaia karga, eta grafinia!" (What a harridan, this countess!)

78. The operatic Gherman's contemporary, Dmitriev-Mamonov, Catherine's favorite, fell for her chambermaid, the age of Catherine's granddaughter. After "shedding tears," Catherine arranged the wedding and sent the two away to the estate she presented as a wedding gift. Mamonov begged her to take him back. No matrimonial bliss with a wife who was a third of Catherine's age could compensate for his position as the empress's favorite.

79. Dodin, "*Pikovaia Dama/Pique Dame*" (2005).

80. In the first sentence of her first duet with Gherman, she calls him a madman. Tchaikovsky, 103.

81. In the green notebook that contains the draft of the libretto and sketches of the themes and leitmotifs, Modest includes Batiushkov's lyrics for Liza. Tchaikovsky decided to give the romance to Polina. Vaidman, "Rabota P. I. Chaikovskogo," 169.

82. Morrison points to the similarity of the two numbers in *Russian Opera and the Symbolist Movement*, 79–80. The two pairs of musical numbers, Polina's romance and Prilepa's song, and the sarabande and the countess's song from Grétry, represent peculiar doubles. The sarabande is traditionally identified with triple meter; Tchaikovsky designed it in four beats. Likewise, a polonaise in four beats is also puzzling.

83. Their two duets, linked by the descending line in their midst (the single most evocative scalar segment of the opera), mark the appearance and disappearance of Polina from the stage.

84. Asaf'ev, *Kriticheskie stat'i, ocherki i retsenzii* (1967), 132. N. Komarova discusses the leitmotif of fear in "'Russkoe' i 'zapadnoevropeiskoe' v muzykal'nom iazyke P. I. Chaikovskogo" (1991), 109–31.

85. Taruskin, "Queen of Spades," *Grove Music Online.*

86. Taruskin and Morrison employ lowercase letters. Morrison, *Russian Opera and the Symbolist Movement*; Taruskin. "Queen of Spades." Tchaikovsky used capital X and Z.

87. The composer wrote, "Z is less painful and perhaps more substantial than X—nevertheless more unpleasant" (May 12, 1887). And a few days later, "Because of it [vint] but mostly other concerns, constituting what I call Z, I felt angry like a ferocious snake" (May 19). Tchaikovsky, Dnevniki, 26–31.

88. Komarova, "'Russkoe' i 'zapadnoevropeiskoe,'" 118–20.

89. Among the themes based on a descending scale are the two parts of Gherman's Arioso ("I don't know her name" and "You don't know me"), the theme of "three cards," the opening

of the first scene, the chorus of promenaders ("Finally, God sent us a sunny spring day"), and the chorus to the empress at the end of the third scene ("Glory to you, Catherine!").

90. Taruskin, "Another World," 12.
91. Tchaikovsky, *Pikovaia dama*, 65–66, 70–71, 73, Act I, Scene 1, Storm.
92. Vaidman, "Rabota P. I. Chaikovskogo," 171.
93. Derzhavin, *Opisanie prazdnestva*, 312.
94. Quoted by Vaidman, "Rabota P. I. Tchaikovskogo," 158.
95. Gasparov, *Five Operas*, 140. Gasparov's analysis shows that it is Pushkin's second invocation of Potemkin's ball after the magical gardens of Chernomor in *Ruslan and Liudmila*.
96. Skvirskaia, "O tretiei kartine opery Tchaikovskogo 'Queen of Spades'" (About the Third Scene of Tchaikovsky's Queen of Spades), manuscript provided by its author, July 3, 2007.
97. Derzhavin, *Opisanie prazdnestva* (1791) and *Sochineniia* (1845), 313.
98. In fact, for the host (Prince Potemkin, Catherine's morganatic husband, adviser, and supporter) this ball turned out to be the empress's farewell; departing to his army in the south, he died five months later.
99. Troyat, *Catherine the Great* (1978), 297.
100. Vaidman, "Rabota P. I. Tchaikovskogo," 174–75.
101. In his letter to Grand Duke Konstantin, Tchaikovsky refers to the choral piece "Gaily, merrily" as a cantata. Cited by Skvirskaia, "K istorii sozdaniia opery 'Pikovaia dama,'" 226.
102. In several of these processional cantatas, Derzhavin collaborated with the maître of the Russian polonaise, Jozef Kozlowski. Skvirskaia discusses two versions of Kozlowski's music for the choral "Thunder of Victory, Resound!" identifying the source of chorus in the opera. Skvirskaia, "K istorii sozdaniia opery 'Pikovaia dama,'" 202–6.
103. The Tchaikovskys borrowed only a two-line refrain from Derzhavin's "Thunder of Victory, Resound!" (Grom pobedy razdavaisia!).
104. Both Gasparov and Taruskin refer to Derzhavin's "Thunder" as an anthem. Gasparov, *Five Operas*, 38; Taruskin, "Tchaikovsky: A New View–a Centennial Essay" (1999), 45–46 and 49–50; Ogarkova, *Tseremonii, prazdnestva, muzyka*, 95.
105. Ibid., 47.
106. Klimovitsky noted that "the ending of Yeletsky's aria is an almost exact replication of the opening of Tamino's aria (both in E flat major) in *The Magic Flute*; the chorus of shepherds and shepherdess at the beginning of the *intermède* . . . is thematically related to the duet (Zerlina and Masetto) and the chorus from Act One of *Don Giovanni*; the dance . . . (Tchaikovsky called it a sarabande) reminds one of the final Andante (the same key of D major) from *The Marriage of Figaro*." Klimovitsky, "'Pikovaia dama' Tchaikovskogo," 243. The duet of Prilepa and Milovzor is also linked with the opening theme of Mozart's Piano Concerto, K503.
107. Tchaikovsky, *Pikovaia dama*, 140–41, 175–79.
108. Ibid., 145.
109. Duet of Zerlina and Don Giovanni in Act I, Scene 9 of Mozart's *Don Giovanni*.
110. This common Russian saying concurs with and is transparent in Prilepa's line: "Ia s milym sred' polei i v khizhine zhit' rada, i v khizhine zhit' rada!" (With my darling among the plains, happily will I live in a hovel, happily will I live in a hovel). Tchaikovsky, *Pikovaia dama*, 163.
111. Ibid., 162–64.

112. Numbers and lowercase letters in this table refer to Tchaikovsky's numbering; capital letters refer to keys.
113. Catherine referred to *La caprice amoureux, or Ninette à la cour* (1755), by Charles Simon Favart. Golovina, *Memuary grafini Golovinoi* (2000), 127.
114. A, vot ona, Veneroiu Moskovskoi!/Kakoi-to tainoi siloi ia s neiu sviazan rokom./Mne ot teba, tebe li ot menia....
115. Skvirskaia, "K istorii sozdaniia opery 'Pikovaia dama,'" 222. The little song is also sung in French, so it immediately establishes itself as an "inserted" piece.
116. Meyerhold, *Pikovaia Dama*, 91–92.
117. The fragments, bits of themes fastened together as Gherman begins singing, break away from sad F-sharp minor into his tonal zone, with the strings already divided into multiple sections moving through the chromatic, insolvable task.
118. Morrison, *Russian Opera and the Symbolist Movement*, 90–91.
119. Taruskin, "Tchaikovsky: A New View," 51.
120. Gukovsky, *Pushkin i problemy realisticheskogo stilia* (1957), 349; cited in Cornwell, *Pushkin's the Queen of Spades* (1993), 14.
121. Taruskin, "Tchaikovsky: A New View," 30.
122. Ibid., 27.
123. Derzhavin, *Sochineniia* (2002), 288. http://www.rvb.ru/18vek/derzhavin/01text/122.htm
124. Lotman, "Theme of Cards," 466.
125. Morrison, *Russian Opera and the Symbolist Movement*, 137.
126. In Dodin's production of *Queen of Spades*, the countess merges with the empress before appearing in Catherine's stead. Shevtsova, *Dodin*, 189.
127. Tchaikovsky's pastoral duo also relates to Levshin's pair of Prelesta and Milovzor from *Torzhestvo liubvi*, a drama in three acts.
128. One of Ségur's countrymen, Claude Carloman de Rulhière at the French Embassy in St. Petersburg, left a similar description of the young empress: "Her brow is broad and open, her nose almost aquiline." Ségur, *Zapiski grafa Segiura*, 17. See also Troyat, *Catherine the Great* (1980), 158. Lady Elizabeth Craven noted, "We have had no good likenesses of her in this country; for her nose was aquiline, ... her forehead was open, and her mouth well made." Craven, *The Beautiful Lady Craven: The Original Memoirs* (1914), 96; Cross, *Catherine the Great and the British* (2001), 5.
129. Taruskin, "Tchaikovsky: A New View," 35.

BIBLIOGRAPHY

Abbate, Carolyn. "Jankélévitch's Singularity." In Vladimir Jankélévitch, *Music and the Ineffable*. Translated by Carolyn Abbate. Princeton, NJ: Princeton University Press, 2003.

———. *Unsung Voices: Opera and Musical Narrative in the Nineteenth Century*. Princeton, NJ: Princeton University Press, 1991.

Ablesimov, Alexander. *Mel'nik, koldun, obmanshchik i svat. Komicheskaia opera v trekh dieistviiakh*. Moscow: Senatskaia Tipografiia, 1782.

———, and M. Sokolovskii. *Mel'nik—koldun, obmanshchik i svat*. Moscow: Muzyka, 1984.

Abramovsky, Georgii. *Russkaia opera pervoi treti XIX veka, v pomoshch pedagogu-muzykantu*. Moscow: Muzyka, 1971.

Abramzon, Tatiana. *Poeticheskie mifologii XVIII veka: Lomonosov, Sumarokov, Kheraskov, Derzhavin*. Magnitogorsk: Magnitogorskii Gosudarstvennyi Universitet, 2006.

Adam, Adolphe. *Giselle: ballet en deux actes*. Paris: M. Bois, 1985.

Alekseev, Mikhail. *Shekspir i russkaia kul'tura*. Leningrad: Nauka, 1965.

Alekseeva, Mariia. *Graviura petrovskogo vremeni*. Leningrad: Iskusstvo, 1990.

———. "Koronatsiia Imperatritsy Ekateriny II: risunki, zhivopis', graviury." *Proceedings of the International Conference "Catherine the Great: An Epoch of Russian History,"* edited by T. Artemieva and M. Mikeshin, 220–22. St. Petersburg: Russian Academy of Science, 1996.

Alekseevna, Natal'ia, Grand Duchess of Russia, and Il'ia Shliapkin. *Tsarevna Natal'ia Aleksieevna i teatr eia vremeni*. St. Petersburg: V. Balashev, 1898.

Alexander, John T. *Catherine the Great: Life and Legend*. New York: Oxford University Press, 1989.

Andreev, V. "Ekaterina Pervaia." In *Osmnadtsatyi vek*, edited by Petr Bartenev. Vol. 1, 1–26. Moscow: Tipografiia T. Risa, Voikova, 1869.

Andrew, Joe, and Robert Reid. *Two Hundred Years of Pushkin*. Vols. 37, 39, 40, Studies in Slavic Literature and Poetics. Amsterdam and New York: Rodopi, 2003.

Angiolini, Domenico. *Torzhestvuiushchaia Minerva ili pobezhdennoe predrazsuzhdenie*. St. Petersburg: [s.n.], 1768.

Anisimov, Evgenii. *Five Empresses: Court Life in Eighteenth-Century Russia*. Translated by Kathleen Carol. Westport, CT: Praeger, 2004.

———. *Zhenshchiny na rossiiskom prestole*. St. Petersburg: Norint, 1997.

Arapov, Pímen. *Letopis' Russkago Teatra*. St. Petersburg: Tipographiia N. Tiblena, 1861.

Ardens, Nik. *Dramaturgiia i teatr A. S. Pushkina*. Moscow: Sovetskii pisatel', 1939.

Asaf'ev, Boris. *Izbrannye trudy*. 5 vols. Vol. 1. Moskva: Izdatel'stvo Akademii Nauk SSSR, 1952.

———. *Kriticheskie stat'i, ocherki i retsenzii*. Leningrad: Muzyka, 1967.

———. "Opera." In *Ocherki sovetskogo muzykal'nogo tvorchestva*, 20–38. Moscow: Gos. muzykal'noe izd-vo, 1947.

———. "Ot redaktsii." In *Mlada* (Orchestral Score). Moscow: Gos. Muz. Izdatel'stvo, 1960.

———. *Russkaia Muzyka XIX i nachalo XX v.* Leningrad: Muzyka, 1968.

Bakhtin, Mikhail. *Literaturno-kriticheskie stat'i.* Moscow: Khudozhestvennaia Literature, 1986.

Balzer, Marjorie Mandelstam. *Russian Traditional Culture: Religion, Gender, and Customary Law.* Armonk, NY: Sharpe, 1992.

Barsukov, Alexander. *Rodoslovie Sheremetevykh.* St. Petersburg: Tipografiia M. M. Stasiulevicha, 1899.

Barsukov, Nicolai. *Zhizn' Pogodina.* Vol. 3. St. Petersburg: Tipographia M. M. Stasulevicha, 1890.

Bartenev, Petr. *Osmnadtsatyi vek: istoricheskii sbornik.* 4 vols. Vol. 3. Moscow: Tipografiia T. Risa, 1869.

Batalden, Stephen K. *Catherine II's Greek Prelate Eugenios Voulgaris in Russia, 1771–1806.* Vol. 115, East European Monographs. New York: Columbia University Press, 1982.

Bauman, Thomas. "Der Barbier von Seville." In *The New Grove Dictionary of Opera,* edited by Stanley Sadie. Grove Music Online. Oxford Music Online. http://www.oxfordmusiconline. com.turing.library.northwestern.edu/subscriber/article/grove/music/O005909 (accessed 26 Jul. 2009).

———. "The Eighteenth Century: Comic Opera." In *The Oxford Illustrated History of Opera,* edited by Roger Parker, 84–121. New York: Oxford University Press, 1994.

———. "The Eighteenth Century: Serious Opera." In *The Oxford Illustrated History of Opera,* edited by Roger Parker. New York: Oxford University Press, 2001.

———. *W. A. Mozart: Die Entführung aus dem Serail,* Cambridge Opera Handbooks. Cambridge: Cambridge University Press, 1987.

Bazhenov, Alexander. "Solnechnye bogi Slavian." In *Mify drevnikh slavian,* edited by Andrei Kaisarov, Grigorii Glinka, and Boris Rybakov, 3–16. Saratov: Nadezhda, 1993.

Beaumarchais, Pierre Augustin Caron de. *Figarova zhenid'ba, komediia v piati diestviakh.* Translated by Alexander Labzin. Moscow: v Universitetskoi Tipografii u N. Novikova, 1787.

Beaumont, Cyril W. *The Ballet Called Giselle.* London: Dance Books, 1988.

Belinsky, Vissarion. "Dushen'ka, drevniaia povest' I. Bogdanovicha." *Sobranie sochinenii v deviati tomakh.* Vol. 4. Moscow: Khudozhestvennaia Literatura, 1979. http://az.lib.ru/b/ belinskij_w_g/text_0490.shtml

———. *O drame i teatre.* Moscow: Iskusstvo, 1983.

———. *Polnoe sobranie sochinenii.* 13 Vols. Vol. 5. Moscow: Izdatel'stvo Akademii Nauk SSSR, 1959.

———. *Sochineniia Aleksandra Pushkina.* Moscow: Khudozhestvennaia Literatura, 1985.

———. *Stat'i o klassikakh.* Moskva: Khudozhestvennaia Literatura, 1973.

Bennett, Susan. "Theater History, Historiography and Dramatic Writing." In *Women, Theatre, and Performance,* edited by Maggie B. Gale and Viv Gardner, 46–59. Manchester, New York: Manchester University Press, 2000.

Berezkina, S. "Ekaterina II v stikhotvorenii Pushkina 'Mne zhal; velikiia zheny'," *XVIII vek* 21, 47–21. St. Petersburg: Nauka, 1999.

Berezovchuk, L. "Mozart." In *Muzykal'nyi Peterburg XVIII vek: Ensiklopedicheskii slovar',* edited by A. L. Porfir'eva and L. N. Berezovchuk. Vol. 2, 224–42. St. Petersburg: Kompozitor, 2001.

Bergholz, Friedrich Wilhelm von. *Dnevnik kammer-iunkera Berkhgoltsa vedennyi im v Rossii v tsarstvovanie Petra Velikogo, s 1721 po 1725 god.* 4 vols. Moscow: v Tipografii Lazarevskogo Instituta Vostochnykh Yazykov, 1858–1862.

———. *Dnevnik Kamer-Iunkera F.V. Berkhgoltsa, 1721–1725.* Novoe izdanie. Moscow: Universitetskaia tipografiia, 1902.

———. "Dnevnik kammer-iunkera Berkhgoltsa vedennyi im v Rossii v tsarstvovanie Petra Velikogo, s 1721 po 1725 god" (1723–1724 only). In *Iunost' Derzhavy*. Moscow: Fond Sergeia Dubova, 2000.

Berkov, P. "Odno iz pervykh primenenii ezopovskogo iazyka v Rossii." In *Problemy teorii i istorii literatury: pamiati A. N. Sokolova,* edited by Vasilii Kuleshov, 74–82. Moscow: Izdatel'stvo Moskovskogo universiteta, 1971.

Beskin, Emmanuil. *Krepostnoi teatr.* Moscow: Kinopechat', 1927.

Bessonov, Petr Alekseevich. *Praskov'ia Ivanovna grafinia Sheremeteva; eia narodnaia piesnia i rodnoe eia Kuskovo.* Moscow: v Univ. Tipografii, 1872.

Bilbasov, V. A. *Istoriia Ekateriny vtoroi.* Berlin: Shtur, 1890.

Biliarsky, Petr. *Materialy dlia biografii Lomonosova.* St. Petersburg: v Tip. Imp. Akademii Nauk, 1865.

Blakey, Kate. "Folk Tales of Ancient Russia." *Slavonic Review* 3, no. 7 (June 2, 1924): 52–62.

Bloom, Harold. *The Anxiety of Influence: A Theory of Poetry.* 2nd ed. New York: Oxford University Press, 1997.

Bogdanovich, Ippolit. *Dushen'ka: drevniaia poviest v volnykh stikhakh.* Moscow: v Tipografii N. S. Vsevolozhskago, 1815.

———. *Dushen'ka: drevniaia povest' v vol'nykh stikhakh.* Moscow: Ladomir, 2002.

———. *Radost' Dushin'ki.* St. Petersburg: pri Imperatorskoi Akademii Nauk, 1786.

———. *Slaviane.* St. Petersburg: pri Imperatorskoi Akademii Nauk, 1788.

———. *Stikhotvorenia i poemy,* Biblioteka Poeta. Leningrad: Sovetskii pisatel', 1957.

——— and Fedor Tolstoi. *Dushen'ka: drevniaia povest' v vol'nykh stikhakh.* Moskva: Ladomir, 2002.

Bondeson, Jan. *The Feejee Mermaid and Other Essays in Natural and Unnatural History.* Ithaca, NY: Cornell University Press, 1999.

Bonecchi, Giuseppe. *Soedinenie Liubvi i Braka.* St. Petersburg: pri Imperatorskoi Akademii Nauk, 1745.

———, and Francesco Araia. *Bellerofont opera pokazana v Sanktpeterburge na novopostroennom pridvornom teatre v den' prazdnestva vozshestvia na prestol Eia Imperatorskago Velichestva Velikiia Gosudaryni Elisavety Petrovny Samoderzhitsy Vserosskia 25 Noiabria 1750 Goda.* Translated by A. Olsuf'ev. St. Petersburg: pri Imperatorskoi Akademii Nauk, 1750.

———. *Bellerofont* opera predstavlennaia na teatre v Oranienbome po poveleniiu Ego Imperatorskago Vysochestva. St. Petersburg: Pechatana pri Imperatorskoi Akademii Nauk, 1757.

———. *Scipion.* St. Petersburg: Pechatana pri Imperatorskoi Akademii Nauk, 1745.

———. *Selevk* opera predstavlennaia pri Rossiiskom Imperatorskom dvorie v vysochaishii den' koronovaniia Eia Imperatorskago Velichestva Velikiia Gosudaryni Elisavety Petrovny Imperatritsy i Samoderzhitsy Vserossiiskiia i pri torzhestvovanii shvetskoiu koronoiu viechnago mira. Moscow: v Tipografii Imperatorskoi Akademii Nauk, 1744.

Boorsch, Suzanne. "Fireworks! Four Centuries of Pyrotechnics in Prints & Drawing." *Metropolitan Museum of Art Bulletin, New Series* 58, no. 1 (2000): 3–52.

Boucicault, Dion. *The Queen of Spades; or, the Gambler's Secret.* London: Thomas Hailes Lacy, 1851.

Bratton, Jacky. "Reading the Intertheatrical, or the Mysterious Disappearance of Susanna Centlivre." In *Women, Theatre, and Performance,* edited by Maggie B. Gale and Viv Gardner, 7–24. Manchester, New York: Manchester University Press, 2000.

Brikner, Alexander. "Angliia, Prussia i Rossia, 1787–1791." *Russkii vestnik* no. 191 (October 1887): 472–537.

——. *Istoriia Ekateriny vtoroi.* St. Petersburg: Tipografiia S. Suvorina, 1885.

Brintlinger, Angela, and Ilya Vinitsky. *Madness and the Mad in Russian Culture.* Toronto: University of Toronto Press, 2007.

Britland, Karen. *Drama and the Courts of Queen Henrietta Maria.* Cambridge, UK: Cambridge University Press, 2006.

Bucciarelli, Melania, Norbert Dubowy, and Reinhard Strohm. *Italian Opera in Central Europe.* 3 Vols. Musical Life in Europe 1600–1900. Berlin: BWV, Berliner Wissenschafts-Verlag, 2006.

——, and Berta Joncus. *Music as Social and Cultural Practice: Essays in Honour of Reinhard Strohm.* Woodbridge, Suffolk: Boydell Press, 2007.

Buckinghamshire, John Hobart, Second Earl. *The Despatches and Correspondence of John, Second Earl of Buckinghamshire, Ambassador to the Court of Catherine II of Russia 1762–1765,* edited by Adelaide D'Arcy Collyer. London, New York, Bombay: Longmans, Green, 1900.

Buckler, Julie A. *Mapping St. Petersburg: Imperial Text and Cityshape.* Princeton: Princeton University Press, 2005.

Bulkina, Inna. "'Dneprovskie rusalki' i 'Kievskie Bogatyri.'" *Pushkinskie Chteniia v Tartu* (2007), www.ruthenia.ru/document/543135.html.

Burke, Peter. *The Fabrication of Louis XIV.* New Haven: Yale University Press, 1992.

Butler, Judith. "Bodies That Matter: On the Discursive Limits of 'Sex.'" In *The Routledge Reader in Gender and Performance,* edited by Lizbeth Goodman and Jane de Gay, 282–87. London, New York: Routledge, 1998.

Castelvecchi, Stefano. "From Nina to Nina: Psychodrama, Absorption and Sentiment in the 1780s." *Cambridge Opera Journal* 8, no. 2 (1996): 91–112.

Catherine II. "Imeniny gospozhi Vorchalkina." St. Petersburg: Izdanie A.F. Marksa, 1893.

——. *Ivan Czarowitz [Tsarevich], or the Rose Without Prickles That Stings Not.* London: Robinson and Sons, 1793.

——. *Memoirs of Catherine the Great.* Translated by Dominique Maroger. London: H. Hamilton, 1955.

——. *Memoirs of The Empress Catherine II.* Translated (from French to Russian) and edited by Alexander Herzen. New York: Appleton, 1859.

——. *Nakaz kommissii o sostavlenii proekta novago ulozheniia.* Moscow: pri Senate, 1767.

——. *Novgorodskoi Bogatyr' Boeslaevich: opera komicheskaia, sostavlena iz skazki, piesnei ruskikh i inykh sochinenii.* St. Petersburg: pri Imperatorskoi Akademii Nauk, 1793.

——. *O velichii Rossii.* Edited by Igor' Losievskii. Moscow: Eksmo, 2003.

——. *Razgovory i razskazy.* St. Petersburg: v Tipografii Imperatorskoi Akademii Nauk, 1782.

——. *Rossiiskaia azbuka.* St. Petersburg: pri Imperatorskoi Akademii Nauk, 1783.

——. *Skazka o Tsareviche Khlore.* St. Petersburg: v Tipografii Akademii Nauk, 1781.

——. *Sochineniia Imperatritsy Ekateriny II.* Edited by Arsenii Vedensky. St. Petersburg: Izd. A. F. Marksa, 1893.

——. *Sochineniia imperatritsy Ekateriny II.* Edited by Alexander Pypin. St. Petersburg: Tipografiia Imp. Akademii Nauk, 1901.

——. *Zapiski Imperatritsy Ekateriny Vtoroi.* St. Petersburg: Izdanie A. S. Suvorina, 1907.

——. *Zapiski kasatel'no rossiiskoi istorii.* St. Petersburg: Pechatano v Imperatorskoi Tipografii, 1788–1794.

————, and Alexander Herzen. *Mémoires de L'imperatrice Catherine II.* Londres: Trübner & Cie., 1859.

————, Vasilii Pashkevich, Carlo Canobbio, and Giuseppe Sarti. *Nachal'noe upravlenie Olega.* St. Petersburg: Pechatano v Tip. Gornago Uchilishcha, 1791. Reprint, Moscow: P. Iurgensona, 1895.

————, and Arnošt Vančura. *Khrabroi i smieloi vitiaz' Akhrideich: opera komicheskaia.* St. Petersburg: pri Imperatorskoi Akademii Nauk, 1787.

Chernov, Konstantin. *"Ruslan i Liudmila," Opera M. I. Glinki.* Moscow: Sobstvennost' izdatelia P. Iurgensona, 1908.

Cheshikhin, Vsevolod. *Istoriia russkoi opery: s 1674 po 1903.* Moscow: P. Iurgenson, 1905.

Chizhova, Irina. *Piat' imperatrits.* St. Petersburg: Znanie, 2002.

Chudinova, I. "Sakral'noe i mirskoe v tserkovno-muzykal-noi kul'ture Peterburga XVIII veka." In *Rossiia, Evropa: kontakty muzykal'nykh kul'tur,* edited by Elena Khodorkovskaia. St. Petersburg: Rossiiskii Institute Iskusstv, 1994.

Chulkov, Mikhail. *Abevega ruskikh suevieriĭ idolopoklonnicheskikh' zhertvoprinosheniĭ svadebnykh prostonarodnykh obriadov kolkovsshva shemanstva i proch.* Moscow: F. Gippius, 1786.

————. *Peresmeshnik.* Moscow: Sov. Rossiia, 1987.

————. "Povest' o Sviatoslave." In *Prikliucheniia slavianskikh vitiazei: is russkoi belletristiki XVIII veka.* Moscow: Sovremennik, 1988.

————. *Sobranie raznykh pesen.* St. Petersburg: Izd. Imperatorskoi Akademii Nauk, 1913.

————. "Sobranie raznykh pesen." Manuscript, 17–. Boston: Houghton Library, Harvard University.

————, Mikhail Popov, Vasilii Levshin, and Evgenii Kostiukhin. *Prikliucheniia slavianskikh vitiazei: iz russkoi belletristiki XVIII veka.* Moscow: Sovremennik, 1988.

Citron, Marcia J. *Gender and the Musical Canon.* Cambridge [England] and New York: Cambridge University Press, 1993.

Clement, Catherine. *Opera: The Undoing of Women.* Minneapolis: University of Minnesota Press, 1988.

Cornwell, Neil. *Pushkin's the Queen of Spades.* Critical Studies in Russian Literature. London: Bristol Classical Press, 1993.

Craven, Baroness Elizabeth. *The Beautiful Lady Craven: The Original Memoirs.* London: John Lane, 1914.

Cross, Anthony. *Catherine the Great and the British: A Pot-Pourri of Essays.* Nottingham, England: Astra Press, 2001.

Cummings, Graham. "Reminiscence and Recall in Three Early Settings of Metastasio's 'Alessandro nell'Indie.'" *Proceedings of the Royal Musical Association* 109 (1982): 80–104.

Curtiss, Mina. *A Forgotten Empress: Anna Ivanovna and Her Era, 1730–1740.* New York: Frederick Ungar, 1974.

Dal', Vladimir. *Tolkovyi slovar' v chetyrekh yomakh.* Vol. 4. Moscow: Russkii iazyk, 1989.

Dalayrac, Nicolas. *Nina, or, the Madness of Love, Translated from the French (as Published by Mr. Le Texier) by the Author of Maria, or the Generous Rustic.* London: C. Elliot, T. Kay, 1787.

D'Angeberg, le Compte [Ghodzko]. *Recueil des traites, conventions, et actes diplomatiques concernant la Pologne 1762–1862* [A Collection of Treatises, Conventions, and Diplomatic Papers Concerning Poland, 1762–1862]. Translated by Basil Dmytryshyn. Hinsdale, IL: Dryden Press (originally published in Paris), 1862.

Danilov, Kirsha. *Drevniia rossiiskiia stichotvoreniia, sobrannyia Kirseiu Danilovym.* Izd. 3. Moscow: A. A. Torlecky, 1878.

———. *Drevniia ruskiia stikhotvoreniia.* Moscow: v Tipografii Semena Selivanovskago, 1804.

Danilova, Albina. *Ozherel'e svetleishego: plemiannitsy kniazia Potemkina.* Moskva: Eksmo, 2005.

Danina, Katia. "Art and Authority: The Hermitage of Catherine the Great." *Russian Review* 63, no. 4 (2004): 630–54.

Dargomyzhsky, Alexander. *Rusalka.* Vocal score. Moscow: Muzyka, 1975.

Darlow, Mark. *Nicolas-Etienne Framery and Lyric Theatre in Eighteenth-Century France.* Oxford: Voltaire Foundation, 2003.

Darnton, Robert. *The Great Cat Massacre and Other Episodes in French Cultural History.* New York: Vintage Books, 1984.

Dashkova, Ekaterina. *The Memoirs of Princess Dashkova.* Translated by Kyril Fitzlyon. Durham, NC: Duke University Press, 1995.

———. *Zapiski.* Moscow: Izdatel'stvo Moskovskogo Universiteta, 1987.

Davidson, G. M. "Psychosomatic Aspects of Korsakoff Syndrome." *Psychiatric Quarterly,* 2:1 (1948): 1–17.

Davis, Larry E., Molly K. King, and Jessica L. Schultz. *Fundamentals of Neurologic Disease.* New York: Demos Medical, 2005.

Dean, Trevor, and Kate Lowe. "Introduction: Issues in the History of Marriage." In *Marriage in Italy, 1300–1650,* edited by Trevor Dean and K. J. P. Lowe, 1–21. Cambridge: Cambridge University Press, 1998.

de la Messelière, Comte Louis-Alexandre Frotier. *Voyage à Pétersbourg, ou, Nouveaux mémoires sur la Russie.* Paris: Chez la Ve. Panckoucke, 1803.

Denisenko, S. "Pushkinskie siuzhety i teksty na stsene v 1850-1870." *Vremennik Pushkinskoi komissii,* 2004.

Dereza, Liudmila. *Russkaia literaturnaia skazka pervoi poloviny XIX veka.* Dnepropetrovsk: Dnepropetrovskii Nacional'nyi Universitet, 2001.

Derzhavin, Gavrila. *Anakreonticheskie Pesni.* Moscow: Nauka, 1986.

———. "Ob opere." In *Sochineniia.* St. Petersburg v Tipografii Konstantina Zhernakova, 1845: 373–376.

———. *Opisanie prazdnestva, byvshago po sluchaiu vziatiia Izmaila, u Ego Svetlosti Gospodina General-Fel'dmarshala i Velikago Getmana Kniazia Grigoriia Aleksandrovicha Potemkina-Tavricheskago, v prisutstvii Eia Imperatorskago Velichestva i Ikh Imperatorskikh Vysochestv, 1791 Goda Aprelia 28 Dnia.* St. Petersburg: Pechatano u I. K. Shpora, 1792.

———. *Sochineniia.* St. Petersburg: v Tipografii Konstantina Zhernakova, 1845.

———. *Sochineniia.* Edited by Aleksandr Smirdin. Izd. 2. ed. Vol. 2. St. Petersburg: Tipografiia. Yakova Treia, 1851.

———. *Sochineniia.* St. Petersburg: Akademik proekt, 2002.

———. *Stikhotvoreniia.* Leningrad: Sovetskii Pisatel', 1957.

Dixon, Simon. "The Posthumous Reputation of Catherine II in Russia 1797–1837." *Slavic and East European Review* 77, no. 4 (October 1999): 646–79.

Dmitriev, Ivan. *Polnoe sobranie stikhotvorenii,* Biblioteka Poeta. Leningrad: Sovetskii pisatel', 1967.

———. "Prichudnitsa." In *Polnoe Sobranie Stikhotvorenii.* Leningrad: Sovetskii. pisatel', 1967; http://www.rvb.ru/18vek/dmitriev/01text/07tales/065.htm (accessed June 2011).

————. Sochineniia, ed. A. M. Peskov and I. Surat (Moscow: Pravda, 1986); http://az.lib.ru/d/ dmitriew_i_i/text_0090.shtml.

Dmytryshyn, Basil. *Imperial Russia*. Hinsdale, IL: Dryden Press, 1974.

Dobrovol'skaia, G. N. "Angiolini." In *Muzykal'nyi Peterburg XVIII vek: Ensiklopedicheskii slovar'*, edited by A. L. Porfir'eva and L. N. Berezovchuk. Vol. 1, 40–42. St. Petersburg: Kompozitor, 2000.

Dodin, Lev. *Pikovaia Dama/Pique Dame*. Opera National de Paris, 2005 (released 2007). TDK OPPIQUE.

Dolgorukaia, Nataliia Borisovna. "Svoeruchnye Zapiski." In *Zapiski russkikh zhenshchin XVIII–pervoi poloviny XIX veka*, 41–66. Moscow: Sovremennik, 1990.

Dolgorukov, Ivan. *Kapishche moego serdtsa*. Moscow: University Press, 1874.

————. *Povest' o rozhdenii moem, proiskhozhdenii i vsei zhizni*. Vol. 1. St. Petersburg: Nauka, 2004.

Dostoyevsky, Fyodor. *Polnoe sobranie sochinenii v 30 tomakh*. Vol. 26. Leningrad: Nauka, 1984. http://www.repetitor.org/materials/dostoevsky3.html (accessed June 2010).

————, I. U. Rozenblium, and S. Chulkov. *Prestuplenie i Nakazanie; Bednye Liudi; Diadiushkin Son*. Moscow: Khudozhestvennaia Literatura, 1983.

Dreiden, Simon, and Kornei Chukovsky, eds. *Russkaia revoliutsiia v satire i iumore*. Moscow: Isvestiia TSK SSSR, 1925.

Drizen, N. *Materialy k istorii russkago teatra*. Moscow: Tip. Bakhrushina, 1905.

Druskin, Mikhail, and Iury Keldysh. *Ocherki po istorii russkoi muzyki, 1790–1825*. Leningrad: Muzgiz, 1956.

Dynnik, Tatiana. *Krepostnoi teatr*. Moscow: Akademia, 1933.

Eco, Umberto. "Horns, Hooves, Insteps." In *The Sign of Three*, edited by Umberto Eco and Thomas A. Sebeok, 198–220. Bloomington: Indiana University, 1983.

Egunov, A. N. "Nemetskaia 'Pikovaia Dama.'" *Vremennik Pushkinskoi kommissii*, no. 6 (1967–68): 111–15.

Eiges, Iosif. *Muzyka v zhizni i tvorchestve Pushkina*. Moscow: Muzgiz, 1937.

Elizabeth I, Queen. *Selected Works*. Edited by Steven W. May. New York: Washington Square Press, 2004.

Elizarova, Natalia. *Ostankino*. Moscow: Isskustvo, 1966.

————. *Teatry Sheremetevykh*. Moscow: Izd. Ostankinskogo dvortsa-muzeia, 1944.

Euripides. *Alkestis*. Translated by Gilbert Murray. London: Allen & Unwin. Ruskin House, 1924.

————. *Heracles and Other Plays*. Translated by Robin Waterfield. Oxford: Oxford University Press, 2003.

Evgenii, Metropolitan of Kiev. *Slovar' russkikh svietskikh pisatelei, sootechestvennikov i chuzhestrantsev, pisavshikh v Rossii*. Moscow: v Universitetskoi Tipografii, 1845.

Evreinov, Nikolai. *Istoriia russkogo teatra s drevneishikh vremen do 1917 goda*. New York: Izdatel'stvo Chekhova, 1955.

————. *Krepostnye aktery*. Leningrad: Izd-vo Kubuch, 1925.

Fedorov, Vasilii. *Repertuar Bol'shogo teatra SSSR, 1776–1955*. Vol. 1. New York: Norman Ross, 2001.

Fedorova, V. "Biblioteki Ekateriny II v Zimnem Dvortse." *Proceedings of the International Conference "Catherine the Great: An Epoch of Russian History,"* edited by T. Artemieva and M. Mikeshin, 60–62. St. Petersburg: Russian Academy of Science, 1996.

Feldman, Martha. "Magic Mirrors and the Seria Stage: Thoughts Toward a Ritual View." *Journal of the American Musicological Society* 48, no. 3 (1995): 423–84.

———. *Opera and Sovereignty: Transforming Myths in Eighteenth-Century Italy*. Chicago: University of Chicago Press, 2007.

Fendeizen, Nikolai. *Ocherki po istorii muzyki v Rossii s drevneishikh vremen do kontsa XVIII veka*. 2 vols. Moscow: Gosudarstvennoe izdatel'stvo, Muzsektor, 1928.

Figes, Orlando. *Natasha's Dance: A Cultural History of Russia*. New York: Metropolitan Books, 2002.

Finagin, Aleksei. "Evstigney Fomin: zhizn' i tvorchestvo." In *Muzyka i muzykal'nyi byt staroi Rossii: Materialy i issledovaniia*, 94–95. Leningrad: Akademia, 1927.

Fisher, Christine. "Self-Stylization in a Ceremonial Context: Maria Antonia Walpurgis as Talestri, Regina delle Amazzoni." In *Italian Opera in Central Europe*, edited by Norbert Dubowy, Melania Bucciarelli, and Reinhard Strohm, 202–19. Berlin: BWV, Berliner Wissenschafts-Verlag 2006.

Fomin, Evstigney, and Alexander Ablesimov. *Mel'nik—koldun, obmanshchik i svat*. Moscow: Gosudarstvennoe muzykal'noe izdatel'stvo, 1956.

Fooks, Jacquetta Beth. "The Serf Theatre of Imperial Russia." Ph.D. dissertation, University of Kansas, 1970.

Freud, Sigmund. *The Interpretation of Dreams*. Oxford: Oxford University Press, 1900, 1999.

Friedman, Rebecca. *Masculinity, Autocracy and the Russian University, 1804–1863*. New York: Palgrave Macmillan, 2005.

Frolova-Walker, Marina. "Fundamental'naia elektronnaia biblioteka: russkaia literatura i fol'klor." In *Ukazatel' istochnikov. Slovar' russkogo yazyka XVIII veka*, 1984.

———. "On *Ruslan* and Russianness." *Cambridge Opera Journal* 9, no. 1 (1997): 21–45.

———. *Russian Music and Nationalism: From Glinka to Stalin*. New Haven: Yale University Press, 2007.

Ganulich, A. "Pridvornaia karusel' 1766 goda i ee otrazhenie v literature i iskusstve." In *Proceedings of the International Conference "Catherine the Great: An Epoch of Russian History,"* edited by T. Artemieva and M. Mikeshin, 234–37. St. Petersburg: Russian Academy of Science, 1996.

Garber, Marjorie. "Dress Codes, or the Theatricality of Difference." In *The Routledge Reader in Gender and Performance*, edited by Lizbeth Goodman and Jane de Gay, 176–82. New York: Routledge, 1998.

Gasparov, Boris. *Five Operas and a Symphony: Word and Music in Russian Culture, Russian Literature and Thought*. New Haven: Yale University Press, 2005.

Gaub, Albrecht. *Die Kollektive Balett-Oper "Mlada."* Berlin: Verlag Ernst Kuhn, 1998.

Gautier, Théophile. *Gautier on Dance*. Translated by Ivor Guest. London: Dance Books, 1986.

———. *Histoire de l'art dramatique en France depuis vingt-cinq ans*. Vol. 1. Paris: Magnin Blanchard et compagnie, 1858.

Gay, Penny. "The History of Shakespeare's Unruly Women." In *The Routledge Reader in Gender and Performance*, edited by Lizbeth Goodman and Jane de Gay, 41–46. London: Routledge, 1998.

Geertz, Clifford. *Negara: The Theatre State in Nineteenth-Century Bali*. Princeton: Princeton University Press, 1980.

Geldern, James von. "The Ode as a Performative Genre." *Slavic Review* 50, no. 4 (1991): 927–39.

Gershenzon, Mikhail. *Mudrost' Pushkina*. 2 vols. Vol. 1. Moscow: Universitetskaia kniga, Jerusalem: Gesharim, 2000.

Gessner, Salomon, and Vasilii Levshin. *Idillii i pastush'i poemy*. Moscow: Pechatano v tipografii pri teatrie u Khr. Klaudiia, 1787.

Ginsburg, Judith. *Representing Agrippina: Constructions of Female Power in the Early Roman Empire*. American Classical Studies 50. Oxford: Oxford University Press, 2006.

Ginzburg, Semen. *Istoriia russkoi muzyki v notnykh obraztsakh*. Moscow: Muzyka, 1968.

———. *Russkii muzykal'nyi teatr 1700–1835*. Leningrad: Iskusstvo, 1941.

Giuntini, Francesco. "Throne and Altar Ceremonies in Metastasio's Dramas." In *Italian Opera in Central Europe*, edited by Melania Bucciarelli, Norbert Doubwy, and Reinhard Strohm, 221–33. Berlin: Berliner Wissenschafts-Verlag, 2006.

Glinka, Mikhail. *Ruslan and Liudmila*. Moscow: Muzyka, 1966.

Glinka, Sergei. *Zapiski*. St. Petersburg: Izdanie redaktsii zhurnala "Russkaia starina," 1895.

Glumov, Alexander. *Muzykal'nyi mir Pushkina*. Moscow: Gosudarstvennoe Muzykal'noe Izd-vo, 1950.

Glushkova, V. *Nikolai Aleksandrovich L'vov*, Moskva Sovremennaia. Moscow: Komitet po arkhitekture i gradostroitel'stvu goroda Moskvy (Moskomarkhitektura), 2003.

Gogol, Nikolai. *Zhizn'. Polnoe Sobranie Sochinenii*. Vol. 8. Moscow: Moscow Academy of Sciences, 1952.

Golburt, Luba. "Derzhavin's Ruins and the Birth of Historical Elegy." *Slavic Review* 65, no. 4 (2006): 670–93.

Golovina, Varvara. *Memuary grafini Golovinoi: zapiski kniazia Golitsyna*. Edited by S. Nikitina. Moscow: Tri veka istorii, 2000.

Golubov, Alexander. "Ivan Batov—russkii Stradivari." In *Mastera Krepostnoi Rossii*, edited by Vadim Safonov, 161–95. Moscow: Izd-vo TsK VLKSM Molodaia Gvardiia, 1938.

Goncharov, Ivan. *Oblomov*. Translated by David Magarshack. London: Penguin Books, 2005.

Gorbatov, Inna. *Catherine the Great and the French philosophers of the Enlightenment*. Bethesda, MD: Academica Press, 2006.

Gorin, Igor. *Igor Gorin in Opera and Song*. Sound recording. Wyastone Leys Monmouth, UK: Nimbus Records, 2006.

Gozenpud, Abram. *Muzykal'nyi teatr v Rossii: ot istokov do Glinki*. Leningrad: Gos. muzykal'noe izd-vo, 1959.

———. "Pushkin i russkaia opernaia klassika." In *Pushkin: issledovaniia i materialy*, 200–216. Leningrad: Akademiia Nauk, 1967.

———. *Stikhotvornaia komediia, komicheskaia opera, vodevil' kontsa "XVIII"—nachala "XIX" veka*. Leningrad: Sovetskii pisatel', 1990.

Graf Nikolai Petrovich Sheremetev. Moscow: Nash Dom, 2001.

Grech, Nikolai. *Zapiski o moei zhizni*. Moscow, Leningrad: Akademiia, 1930.

Greenblatt, Stephen, ed. *Representing the English Renaissance*. Berkeley: University of California Press, 1988.

———. *Shakespearean Negotiations: The Circulation of Social Energy in Renaissance England*. New Historicism: Studies in Cultural Poetics 84. Berkeley: University of California Press, 1988.

———. *Will in the World: How Shakespeare Became Shakespeare*. New York: Norton, 2004.

Grenier, Svetlana Slavskaya. *Representing the Marginal Woman in Nineteenth-Century Russian Literature: Personalism, Feminism, and Polyphony*. Contributions in Women's Studies. Westport, CT: Greenwood Press, 2001.

Groos, Arthur. "Madame Butterfly: The Story." *Cambridge Opera Journal* 3, no. 2 (1989): 125–58.

Grossman, Leonid. *Pis'ma zhenshchin k Pushkinu: s prilozheniem vospominanii o Pushkine M. N. Volkonskoi*. Moskva: Sovremennye problemy, 1928.

Grot, Iakov. *Ekaterina II i Gustav III*. St. Petersburg: Tipografiia Imperatorskoi Akademii Nauk, 1877.

Guber, Petr. *Don-Zhuanskii spisok A.S. Pushkina: glavy iz biografii s portretami*. Khar'kov: Del'ta, 1993.

———. *Liubovnyi byt pushkinskoi epokhi*. Edited by Petr Guber. Vol. 2. Moscow: Vasanta, 1994.

Guberti, Nikolai. *Materialy dlia russkoi bibliografii: chronologicheskoe obozrenie redkich i zamechatel'nych russkich knig XVIII stoletiia, napechatannych v Rossii grazdanskim shriftom. 1725–1800*. 3 vols. Moskva: Izdanie pri Mosk. Universitete, 1878–1891. Reprinted Ann Arbor: University Microfilms, 1966.

Gukovsky, G. "G. A. Petrov." In *Istoriia russkoi literatury*, 353–63. Vol. 4, part 2. Moscow: Izd-vo Akademii Nauk SSSR, 1947.

———. *Pushkin i problemy realisticheskogo stilia*. Moscow: Gos. Izd-vo Khudozhestvennoi. Literatury, 1957.

Gus'kov, N. A. "K probleme zhanrovogo svoebraziia komedii imperatritsy Ekateriny II (tsikl 1772)." In *Proceedings of the International Conference Catherine the Great: An Epoch of Russian History*, edited by T. Artemieva and M. Mikeshin, 128–30. St. Petersburg: Akademiia Nauk, 1996.

Gusliarov, E. *Vse dueli Pushkina*. Kaliningrad: Iantarnyi skaz, 2001.

Hammarberg, Gitta. "Poor Liza, Poor Èrast, Lucky Narrator." *Slavic and East European Journal* 31, no. 3 (1987): 305–21.

Hargood, Isabel Florence. *The Epic Songs of Russia*. New York: Scribner, 1886.

Harris-Warrick, Rebecca. "Ballet." In *The New Grove Dictionary of Opera*, edited by Stanley Sadie. Oxford Music Online. http://www.oxfordmusiconline.com.turing.library.northwestern.edu/ subscriber/article/grove/music/46700?q=diaghilev+and+cleopatra&search=quick&pos= 3&_start=1#firsthit (accessed December 18, 2009).

Heine, Heinrich. "Elementary Spirits." In *Collected Works*. Vol. 11, 107–211. New York: Crosup & Sterling, 1906.

Helfant, Ian M. *The High Stakes of Identity*. Evanston: Northwestern University Press, 2002.

———. "Pushkin's Ironic Performances as a Gambler." *Slavic Review* 58, no. 2, Special Issue: Alexander Pushkin 1799–1999 (1999): 371–92.

Hensbergen, Gijs van. *Antonio Gaudi, Genius Loci*. Moskva: Eksmo, 2003.

Herman, Judith Lewis, and Lisa Hirschman. *Father-Daughter Incest*. Cambridge: Harvard University Press, 2000.

Herzen, Aleksandr. "Soroka-Vorovka." In *Izbrannoe*. Moscow: Pravda, 1954.

Hirstein, William. *Brain Fiction: Self-Deception and the Riddle of Confabulation*. Cambridge, MA: MIT Press, 2006.

Hokanson, Katya. "Literary Imperialism, Narodnost' and Pushkin's Invention of the Caucasus." *Russian Review* 53, no. 3 (1994): 336–52.

———. *Writing at Russia's Border*. Toronto: University of Toronto Press, 2008.

Jordan, Ruth. *Fromental Halévy*. New York: Limelight Edition, 1994.

Howe, Elizabeth. "English Actresses in Social Context: Sex and Violence." In *Routledge Reader in Gender and Performance*, edited by Lizabeth Goodwin and Jane de Gay, 60–64. London, New York: Routledge, 1998.

Hubbs, Joanna. *Mother Russia*. Bloomington: Indiana University Press, 1993.

Iatsevich, Andrei. *Krepostnye v Peterburge*. Leningrad: Obshchestvo "Staryi Peterburg," 1933.

Ingham, Norman W. *E. T. A. Hoffmann's Reception in Russia*. Colloquium Slavicum Bd. 6. Würzburg: Jal-Verlag, 1974.

"Ivan Batov—Russkii Stradivari." In *Mastera krepostnoi Rossii*, edited by Vadim Safonov, 231–33. Moscow: Molodaya Gvardiia, 1938.

Ivanits, Linda J. *Russian Folk Belief*. Armonk, NY: Sharpe, 1989.

Ivanitsky, Alexander. "Dushen'ka I. Bogdanovicha i russkaia khvalebnaia oda." *Slavica tergestina*, no. 7 (1999): 33–63.

Ivanov, Viacheslav. *Selected Essays*. Evanston: Northwestern University Press, 2001.

Iz"iasnenie i izobrazhenie velikago feierverka kotoroi po okanchanie torzhestv velikago kniazia Petra Feodorovicha i Gosudaryni Velikiia Ekateriny Alekseevny vseia Rossii v Sansktpeterburge na Neve reke pred Imperatorskim Zimnim domom predstavlen byl avgusta 1745. St. Petersburg: pri Imperatorskoi Akademii Nauk, 1745.

James, April Lynn. "Her Highness' Voice: Maria Antonia, Music and Culture at the Dresden Court." Ph.D. dissertation, Harvard University, 2002.

Jankélévitch, Vladimir. *Music and the Ineffable*. Translated by Carolyn Abbate. Princeton, NJ: Princeton University Press, 2003.

Jonce, L. JaFran. "Tunisian Women as Professional Musicians." In *Women and Music in Cross-Cultural Perspective*, edited by Ellen Koskoff. Champaign: University of Illinois Press, 1987.

Jones, Amelia. "Acting Unnatural: Interpreting Body." In *Decomposition: Post-Disciplinary Performance*, edited by Sue-Ellen Case, Philip Brett, and Susan Leigh Foster, 10–17. Bloomington: Indiana University Press, 2000.

Jones, Nancy A., and Leslie C. Dunn, eds. *Embodied Voices*. Cambridge: Cambridge University Press, 1994.

Jones, Robert E. *Provincial Development in Russia: Catherine II and Jakob Sievers*. New Brunswick, NJ: Rutgers University Press, 1984.

———. "Urban Planning and the Development of Provincial Towns in Russia, 1762–1796." In *The Eighteenth Century in Russia*, edited by J. G. Garrard, 321–44. Oxford: Clarendon Press, 1973.

———. "Urban Planning and the Development of Provincial Towns in Russia During the Reign of Catherine II." In *The Eighteenth Century in Russia*, edited by John Gordon Garrard. Oxford: Clarendon Press, 1973.

Jordan, Ruth. *Fromental Halévy*. New York: Limelight Edition, 1966.

Jung, Carl Gustav. *The Archetype of the Collective Unconscious*. Translated by R. F. C. Hill. Princeton, NJ: Princeton University Press, 1990.

Kaisarov, Andrei. "Slavianskaia i rossiiskaia mifologia." In *Mify drevnikh slavian*, edited by Andrei Kaisarov, Grigorii Glinka and Boris Rybakov, 23–86. Saratov: Nadezhda, 1993.

Kalaidovich, Konstantin, and Kirsha Danilov. "Predislovie." In *Drevniia rossiiskiia stikhotvoreniia sobrannyia Kirsheiu Danilovym*, i–xxxvi. Moscow: v Tipografii Semena Selivanovskogo, 1818.

Kallberg, Jeffrey. "Sex, Sexuality." *Grove Music Online*, http://www.grovemusic.com.turing. library.northwestern.edu (accessed August 11, 2007).

Kamensky, Alexander. *The Russian Empire in the Eighteenth Century: Searching for a Place in the World*. Translated and edited by David Griffiths. Armonk, NY: Sharpe, 1997.

Kantor, Marvin. Introduction to *Dramatic Works of D. I. Fonvizin*, by Denis Fonvizin. Bern: Herbert Lang; Frankfurt: Peter Lang, 1974.

Kaplan, Gisela T., and Lesley J. Rogers. "Scientific Constructions, Cultural Predictions: Scientific Narratives of Sexual Attraction." In *Feminine/Masculine and Representation*, edited by Terry Threadgold and Anne Cranny-Francis, 211–30. Sydney: Allen & Unwin, 1990.

Karabanov, A. *Osnovanie Russkogo Teatra*. St. Petersburg: v Tipografii Voenno-uchebnykh zavedenii, 1849.

Karamzin, Nikolai. "Bednaia Liza." http://lib.ru/LITRA/KARAMZIN/liza.txt (accessed April 28, 2008).

———. *Izbrannye sochineniia v dvukh tomakh*. 2 vols. Vol. 1. Moscow: Khudozhestvennaia Literatura, 1964.

———. *Sochineniia*. 8 vols. Vol. 7. Moscow: v Tipografii Semena Selivanovskogo, 1803–04.

———. *Sochineniia*. Moscow: v Tipografii Semena Selivanovskago, 1894.

Karatygina, A. In *Pushkin Glazami Zhenshchin*, edited by V. M. Kirillova. Astana: Ueldora, 1999.

Karlinsky, Simon. "Russian Comic Opera in the Age of Catherine the Great." *19-Century Music* 7, no. 3 (1984): 318–25.

Kashin, N. *Teatr N. B. Usupova*. Moscow: Gos. Akademiia Khudozhestvennykh Nauk, 1927.

Keldysh, Iury. *Istoria russkoi muzyki*. 3 Vols. Vol.1. Moscow: Muzgiz, 1948.

———. *Pamiatniki russkogo muzykal'nogo iskusstva*. Moscow: Muzyka, 1972.

Kelly, George Armstrong. "The Machine of the Duc d'Orléans and the New Politics." *Journal of Modern History* 51, no. 4 (1979): 667–84.

Kern, Anna. *Vospominaniia, dnevniki, perepiska*. Moscow: Khudozhestvennaia Literatura, 1974.

Khemnitser, Ivan. *Basni i skazki I.I. Khemnitsera v trekh chastiakh*. St. Petersburg: pri Imperatorskoi Akademii Nauk, 1811.

Khodorkovskaia, E. S. "Opera Seria." In *Muzykal'nyi Peterburg*, edited by A. L. Porfir'eva. Vol. 2: 285–93. St. Petersburg: Kompozitor, 2001.

Khrapovitsky, Alexander. *Pamiatnye zapiski*. Moscow: Glavnaia redaktsiia teatral'noi literatury, 1990 (originally published 1862).

———. *Pamiatnye zapiski A.V. Khrapovitskogo*. Edited by G. N. Gennadi. Moscow: University Press, 1862.

Kikta, Valery. *Pushkinskaya muzikal'naya panorama XIX–XX vekov*. Moscow: Muzyka, 1999.

Kimbell, David. *Italian Opera*. Cambridge: Cambridge University Press, 1991.

Kiseleva, Liubov'. "Pikovye Damy' Pushkina i Shakhovskogo." In *Pushkinskie chteniia*, 183–203. Tartu: Tartuski Universitet, 2000. http://www.ruthenia.ru/document/365133.html (April, 2009).

Klimovitsky, Abram. "'Pikovaia Dama' Tchaikovskogo: kul'turnaia pamiat' i kul'turnye predchu-vstviia." In *Rossiia, Yevropa: kontakty muzykal'nykh kul'tur*, edited by Elena Khodorkovskaia, 222–74. St. Petersburg: Rossiiskii Institut Istorii Iskusstv, 1994.

Kniazhnin, Iakov. *Komedii i komicheskie opery*. St. Petersburg: Giperion, 2003.

———. *Neschast'e ot karety*. St. Petersburg: Pri Imperatorskoi Akademii Nauk, 1779.

Komarnitskaia, Ol'ga. "Drama, epos, skazka, lirika v russkoi klassicheskoi opere XIX veka." In *Russkaia opera XIX Veka*, edited by Tatiana Maslovskaia, 5–27. Moscow: Gosudarstvennyi muzykal'no-pedagogicheskii institut im. Gnesinykh, 1991.

———. "Russkaia opera XIX veka." In *Sbornik trudov*, edited by Tatiana Maslovskaia, 135. Moscow: Gosudarstvennyi muzykalno-pedagogicheskii institut im. Gnesinykh, 1991.

Komarova, N. "'Russkoe' i 'zapadnoevropeiskoe' v muzykal'nom iazyke P. I. Tchaikovskogo. 'Pikovaia Dama' i Don-Zhuan." In *Russkaia opera XIX veka*, edited by Tatiana Maslovskaia, 109–31. Moscow: Gosudarstvennyi Muzykal'no-Pedagogicheskii Institut im. Gnesinykh, 1991.

Korinfsky, Apollon. *Narodnaia Rus'*. Moscow: Moskovskii Rabochii, 1901, 1994.

Kostiukhin, Evgenii. "Drevnaia Rus' v rytsarskom oreole." In *Prikliucheniia slavianskikh vitiazei*, edited by Evgenii Kostiukhin, 5–20. Moscow: Sovremennik, 1988.

Kostomarov, Nikolai. *Russkaia istoriia v zhizneopisaniiakh ee glavneishikh deiatelei*. Vypusk 3. Moscow: OLMA-PRESS, 2003.

Kozlowski, Josef. "Grom pobedy razdavaisia!" In *Istoriia russkoi muzyki v notnykh obraztsakh*, edited by L'vovich Ginzburg Semen, 428–31. Moscow: Myzyka, 1968.

Kramer, Lawrence. *After the Lovedeath: Sexual Violence and the Making of Culture*. Berkeley: University of California Press, 1997.

———. "Little Pearl Teardrops." In *Music, Sensation, and Sensuality*, edited by Linda Phyllis Austern, 57–74. New York: Routledge, 2002.

Krasovskaia, Vera. *Ruskii baletnyi teatr*. Leningrad: Isskustvo, 1958.

Kremlev, Iulii. *Natsional'nye cherty russkoi muzyki*. Leningrad: Muzyka, 1968.

Krylov, Ivan. *Istoricheskoe opisanie vsekh koronatsii imperatorov i imperatrits*. Moscow: Universitetskoi tipografi, 1856.

———. *P'esy 1844–1944*. Moscow: Iskusstvo, 1944.

———. *Polnoe sobranie sochinenii*. 3 vols. Vol. 3. Moscow: Gos. Izd-vo Khudozh. Literatury, 1945–46.

Kukhel'bekker, Vilgel'm. "O napravlenii nashei poezii, osobenno liricheskoi, v poslednee desiatiletie," 1824; http://az.lib.ru/k/kjuhelxbeker_w_k/text_0180.shtml (accessed April 2007).

Kulikov, Roman. *Skazka ili starinnaia byval'shchina*. Boston: Houghton Library, Harvard University, 1795.

Kulikov, V. "Polabskie i pomorskie slaviane." Paper presented at Slaviane i ikh sosedi. Moscow, 1998.

Kurmacheva, Maya. *Krepostnaia intelligentsia Rossii*. Moscow: Nauka, 1983.

La Place, Pierre Antoine de. *Le Theatre Anglois*. 8 vols. Londres: [s.n.], 1746.

Larosh, German. *Russkii viestnik*. Vol. 191. Moskva: M. M. Katkov, 1887.

Lazzaroni, Lodovico, and Vincenzo Manfredini. *Le Rivali/Sopernitsy*. St. Petersburg: pri Imperatorskoi Akademii Nauk, 1765.

Le Brun, Cornelius. *Abstract of Travels Through Russia and Persia to the East Indies: Containing the Observations He Made in Russia*. 2 vols. Vol. 2. *The Present State of Russia*. London: s.n., 1722.

Lebrun, Elisabeth Vigée. *Memoirs of Madame Vigée Lebrun*. Translated by Lionel Strachey. New York: Doubleday, 1903.

Lekarstvo ot zadumchivosti: russkaia skazka v izdaniiakh 80-kh godov 18 veka. Edited by K. E. Korepova and L. G. Belikova. St. Petersburg: Pechatano u Vil'kovskago i Galchenkova, 1786. Reprint, St. Petersburg: Tropa Troianoba, 2001.

Lepskaia, Liia. *Repertuar krepostnogo teatra Sheremetevykh*. Moscow: Gos. tsentral'nyi teatral'nyi muzei im. A. A. Bakhrushina, 1996.

Lerner, Nikolai. *Rasskazy o Pushkine*. Leningrad: Priboi, 1929.

Leskov, Nikolai. *Povesti i rasskazi*. Moscow: Khudozhestvennaia Literature, 1959.

Letopisets soderzhashchii v sebe Russkuiu istoriiu. Moscow: v Sinodal'noi Tipografii, 1819.

Levashov, Evgenii. "Introduction: the Opera *Sankpeterburgskii gostinyi dvor i ee avtory*." In *Kak pozhivesh', tak i proslyvesh', ili sanktpeterburgskii gostinyi dvor* [*Sanktpeterburgskii gostinnyi dvor*]; *Opera by Pashkevich*, edited by Evgenii Levashov, 466–91. Moscow: Muzyka, 1980.

Lévi-Strauss, Claude. *The Elementary Structures of Kinship*. Boston: Beacon Press, 1969.

Levitskii, Dmitrii. *Portrait of Ekaterina Khrushcheva and Princess Ekaterina Khovanskaya*. 1773. http://www.artrussia.ru/artists/picture.php?rarity=1&pic_id=83&foa=f (accessed October 5, 2008).

Levitsky, A. A. "Obraz vody u Derzhavina i obraz poeta." In *XVIII vek*, edited by Natalia Kochetkova, 47–71. St. Petersburg: Nauka, 1996.

Levshin, A. A. *Put' k bezsmertnomu sozhitiiu angelov, ili sobranie raznoobraznykh dlia soviesti utieshitelnykh razmyshlenii*. Moscow: Pechatano v privillegirovannoi Tipografii u F. Gippiusa, 1787.

Levshin, Vasilii. *Garstlei i Florinichi: mieshchanskaia tragediia*. Moscow: v Universitetskoi Tipografii u N. Novikova, 1787.

———. *Nravouchitel'nyia basni i pritchi*. Moscow: v Tipografii teatra u Khr. Klaudiia, 1787.

———. *Ruskiia skazki, soderzhashchiia drevnieishiia povetvovaniia o slavnykh bogatyriakh*. Moscow: v Universitetskoi Tipografii u N. Novikova, 1780–1783.

———. *Torzhestvo liubvi, dramma v trekh dieistviiakh*. Moscow: v Universitetskoi Tipografii u N. Novikova, 1787.

———. *Vechernie chasy, ili drevniia skazki slavianskikh*. Moscow: v Tipografii Kompanii Tipograficheskoi, 1787.

Liria, Duke. "Pis'ma o Rossii v Ispaniiu pervago ispanskago poslannika Diuka De-Liriia." In *Osmnadtsatyi vek: istoricheskii sbornik*, edited by Petr Bartenev, 27–132. 4 vols. Vol. 3. Moscow: Tipografiia T. Risa, 1869.

Livanova, Tamara. *Glinka: tvorcheskii put'*. 2 vols. Moscow: Gos. Muzykal'noe izdatel'stvo, 1955.

———. *M. I. Glinka: sbornik materialov i statei*. Moscow: Gos. muzykal'noe izdatel'stvo, 1950.

———. *Opernaia kritika v Rossii*. Moscow: Muzyka, 1966

———. "Polemika V. V. Stasova i A. N. Serova ob operakh Glinki." In *Pamiati Glinki*, edited by Vasilii Kiselev, Tamara Livanova, and Vladimir Protasov, 399–440. Moscow: Izdatel'stvo Akademii Nauk SSSR, 1958.

———. *Russkaia muzykal'naia kul'tura XVIII veka*. 2 vols. Moscow: Gos. muzykal'noe izdatel'stvo, 1952.

Locatelli, Giovanni Battista. *Ubezhishche Bogov*. St. Petersburg: Tipografiia Akademii Nauk, 1757.

Locke, Ralph P. "Constructing the Oriental 'Other': Saint-Saëns's *Samson et Dalila*." *Cambridge Opera Journal* 3, no. 3 (November 1991): 261–302.

———. "What Are These Women Doing in Opera?" In *En Travesti: Women, Gender Subversion, Opera*, edited by Corinne E. Blackmer and Patricia Juliana Smith, 59–98. New York: Columbia University Press, 1995.

Logan, Sandra. *Text/Events in Early Modern England: Poetics of History*. Burlington, VT: Ashgate, 2007.

Lomonosov, Mikhail. *Izbrannye proizvedeniia*. Leningrad: Sovetskii pisatel', 1965 and 1986.

———. *Izbrannye sochineniia*. Moscow, St Petersburg: Sovetskii pisatel', 1965.

———. *Kratkoi Rossiiskoi Lietopisets*. St. Petersburg: Pri Imperatorskoi Akademii Hauk, 1760.

———. "Oda na torzhestvennyi den' voshestviia na Vserossiiskii prestol Eie Velichestva Imperatricy Elisavety Petrovny" (1752). In *Izbrannye proizvedeniia*. Leningrad: Sovietskii Pisatel', 1986.

———. *Polnoe sobranie socinenii*. 11 vol. Vol. 6. Moscow: Izdatel'stov Akademii Nauk SSSR, 1952.

———. *Zapiski po russkoi istorii*. Edited by Igor' Lesievsky. Moscow: Eksmo, 2003.

Lord, Albert B. *The Singer of Tales*. Cambridge, MA: Harvard University Press, 1960.

Losev, Lev. *On the Beneficence of Censorship: Aesopian Language in Modern Russian Literature*. München: O. Sagner in Kommission, 1984.

Losievsky, Igor'. "S perom i skipetrom." In *Catherine, o velichii Rossii*, 5–56. Moscow: ESKMO-AKSMO, 2003.

———. "Dushoi bluzhdaiu." *Zapiski po russkoi istorii* by Lomonosov. Moscow: EKSMO, 2003.

Lotman, Iury. *Besedy o russkoi kul'ture*. St Petersburg: Iskusstvo, 1994.

———. *Izbrannye Stat'i*. 3 vols. Vol. 3. Tallinn: Alexandra, 1992.

———. *Russkaia literatura i kul'tura prosveshcheniia*, Sobranie Sochinenii. Moscow: Ob'edinennoe gumanitarnoe izdatel'stvo, 1998.

———. "The Theme of Cards and the Card Game." *PTL: A Journal of Descriptive Poetics and Theory of Literature* 3, (1978): 455–92.

———, and Boris Uspensky. "Otzvuki kontseptsii Moskva—Tretii Rim." In *Izbrannye stat'i*, Vol. 3: 201–12. Tallinn: Alexsandra, 1992.

Lupanova, Irina. *Russkaia narodnaia skazka v tvorchestve pisatelei pervoi poloviny XIX veka*. Petrozavodsk: Gos. izdatel'stvo Karelskoi ASSR, 1959.

Lutz, Tom. *Crying: The Natural and Cultural History of Tears*. 1st ed. New York: Norton, 1999.

L'vov, Nikolai, ed. *Letopisets Russkoi ot prishestviia Rurika do konchiny tsaria Ioanna Vasil'evicha*. St. Petersburg: v Tipografii Gornago Uchilishcha, 1792.

———, ed. *Podrobnaia letopis' ot nachala Rossii do poltavskoi batalii*. St. Petersburg: u I. K. Shnora, 1798–99.

———, and Konstantin Lappo-Danilev. *Izbrannye sochineniia*. Vol. 1. Köln, Bëlau-Ferlag: Russkii khristianskii gumanitarnyi in-t, Akropol, 1994.

———, and Ivan Prach. *Sobranie russkikh narodnykh pesen s ikh golosami*. Edited by Malcolm Hamrick Brown. Introduction and appendix by Margarita Mazo, Classics of Russian Musical Folklore in Facsimile. Ann Arbor: UMI Research Press, 1987.

Madariaga, Isabel de. *Russia in the Age of Catherine the Great*. New Haven: Yale University Press, 1981.

———. *Catherine the Great: A Short History*. New Haven: Yale University Press, 1990.

Maes, Francis. *A History of Russian Music: From Kamarinskaya to Babi Yar*. Berkeley: University of California Press, 2002.

Maikov, Vasilii. *Opisanie raznykh uveselitel'nykh zrielishch, predstavlennykh vo vremia mirnago torzhestva, zakliuchennago mezhdu Rossiiskoiu Imperieiu i Ottomanskoi Portoiu: v vysochaishem prisudstvii Eia Imperatorskago Velichestva, Vseavgustieishei i Nepobiedimoi Monarkhini, Materi Otechestva Ekateriny II i Ikh Imperatorskikh Vysochestv, pri mnogochislennom sobranii naroda, bliz' Moskvy na Khodynkie, 1775 goda iiulia 16 dnia*. Moscow: Pechatano pri Gosudarstvennoi Voennoi kollegii, 1775.

Makogonenko, Georgii, and Ilia Serman, eds. *Poety XVIII veka*. 2 vols. Vol. 1. Leningrad: Sovetskii Pisatel', 1972.

Mansel, Philip. *Prince of Europe: The Life of Charles-Joseph de Ligne, 1735–1814*. London: Weidenfeld & Nicolson, 2003.

Manstein, Cristof Hermann. *Contemporary Memoirs of Russia, from the Year 1727, to the Year 1744. Translated from the Original Manuscript of the Baron de Manstein*. London: printed for T. Becket and P. A. de Hondt, 1773.

Marker, Gary. "God of Our Mothers." In *Orthodox Russia*, edited by Valerie A. Kivelson and Robert H. Greene, 193–210. University Park: Pennsylvania State University Press, 2003.

Markov, A. *Belomorskie byliny*. Moscow: Levenson, 1901.

Markova, Ol'ga. *Rossiia, zakavkazskie i mezhdunarodnye otnosheniia v XVIII veke*. Moscow: Nauka, 1958.

Marrese, Michelle Lamarche. *A Woman's Kingdom: Noblewomen and the Control of Property in Russia, 1700–1861*. Ithaca: Cornell University Press, 2002.

Matvieev, Artamon. *Kniga ob izbranii na tsarstvo Velikago Gosudaria, Tsaria i Velikago Kniazia Mikhaila Fedorovicha*. Moscow: Synodal'naia tipografiia, 1856.

McCarren, Felicia M. *The Female Form: Gautier, Mallarmé and Celine Writing Dance*. Ph.D. dissertation, Stanford University, 1992.

McClary, Susan. *Feminine Endings: Music, Gender, and Sexuality*. Minneapolis: University of Minnesota Press, 2002.

Meehan-Waters, Brenda. "Catherine the Great and the Problem of Female Rule." *Russian Review* 34, no. 3 (1975): 293–307.

———. *Autocracy and Aristocracy: The Russian Service Elite of 1730*. New Brunswick, NJ: Rutgers University Press, 1982.

Melissino, Petr. *Opisanie feierverka, pri torzhestve brakosochetaniia ikh Imperatorskikh Vysochestv Gosudaria Velikago Kniazia Aleksandra Pavlovicha i Gosudaryni Velikiia Kniagini Elisavet Alekseevny predstavlennago v Sanktpeterburge na Tsaritsynom Lugu, oktiabria dnia 1793 goda*. St. Petersburg: I. K. Shnor, 1793.

Metastasio, Pietro. *Artaksers, drama na muzyke*. Russian translation by Peter Medvedev. St. Petersburg: Pechatano pri Imperatorskoi Akademii Nauk, 1738.

Meyerhold, Vsevolod. *Pikovaia dama*. St. Petersburg: Kompozitor, 1994.

Mihailovich, Alexandar. *Tchaikovsky and His Contemporaries: A Centennial Symposium*. Contributions to the Study of Music and Dance 49. Westport, CT: Greenwood Press, 1999.

Mikhnevich, Vladimir. *Ocherk istorii muzyki v Rossii v kul'turno-obshchestvennom otnoshenii*. St. Petersburg: F. Sushchinsky, 1879.

Moiseeva, G. N, et al. *Zapiski russkikh zhenshchin XVIII—pervoi poloviny XIX veka*. Moscow: Sovremennik, 1990.

Montefiore, Simon Sebag. *Potemkin: Catherine the Great's Imperial Partner*. New York: Vintage Books, 2005.

———. *Prince of Princes: The Life of Potemkin*. New York: Thomas Dunne Books, 2000.

Mooser, Robert-Aloys. *Annales de la musique et des musiciens en russie au XVIIIe siècle*. 3 vols. Genève: Mont-Blanc, 1948–1951.

———. *L'opéra-comique français en Russie au XVIII siècle*. Genève: R. Kister, 1954.

———. *Opéras, intermezzos, ballets, cantates, oratorios joués en Russie durant le XVIIIme siècle*. Genève: Imprimerie A. Kundig, 1945.

Moracci, Giovanni. "K izucheniiu komedii Ekateriny II. Problemy avtorstva." *Study Group of Eighteenth-Century Russia* no. 30 (2002): 12–17.

Morozov, Alexander. "Introduction." *Russkaia stikhotvornaia parodiia,* 5–88. Leningrad: Sovetskii pisatel', 1960.

Morrison, Simon. *Russian Opera and the Symbolist Movement.* Berkeley: University of California Press, 2002.

———. "The Semiotics of Symmetry, or Rimsky-Korsakov's Operatic History Lesson." *Cambridge Opera Journal* 13, no. 3 (November 2001): 261–93.

Mottley, John. *The History of the Life and Reign of the Empress Catharine: Containing a Short History of the Russian Empire, from Its First Foundation to the Time of the Death of That Princess... . By John Mottley, Esq.* London: printed for William Meadows; and M. Read, 1744.

Mozart, Wolfgang Amadeus. *Idomeneo: Opera Seria in Three Acts.* New York: International Music, 1952.

Mullaney, Steven. *The Place of the Stage: License, Play, and Power in Renaissance England.* Ann Arbor: University of Michigan Press, 1988.

Murav'eva, O. *Dan' priznatel'noi liubvi: russkie pisateli o Pushkine.* Leningrad: Lenizdat, 1979.

Muzikal'nyi Peterburg. Edited by A. L. Porfir'eva. Vol. 4. St. Petersburg: Kompozitor, 2001.

Naroditskaya, Inna. "Serf Actresses in the Tsarinas' Russia: Social Class Cross-Dressing in Russian Serf Theaters of the Eighteenth Century." In *Musical Voices of Early Modern Women: Many-Headed Melodies,* edited by Thomasin LaMay, 239–70. Burlington: Ashgate, 2005.

Nazarova, L. "K istorii sozdaniia poemy Pushkina 'Ruslan i Liudmila.'" In *Pushkin: issledovaniia i materially,* 216–21. Leningrad: Akademiia Nauk, 1956.

Nikiforov, A. *Fol'klor kievskogo perioda.* Moscow: Izdatel'stvo Akademii Nauk SSSR, 1941–1956, 10 vol. Vol. 1 (1941).

Nikitina, Liudmila. *Istoriia russkoi muzyki.* Moscow: Akademiia, 2000.

Nikolaeva, S. "Ot Nikolaia L'vova do Nikolaya Gumileva: evolutziya skal'dicheskikh motivof v russkoi poezii." In *Genii vkusa,* edited by M. V. Stroganov, no. 3. 82–94. Tver': Tverskoi Gos. Universitet, 2003.

Nikolai, Andrei. *Krasota: skazka.* St. Petersburg: v Tipografii Imperatorskago Sukhoputnago Shliakhetnago Kadetskago Korpusa, 1782.

Nikolev, Nikolai. *Rozana i Lubim: dramma s golosami, v chetyrekh deistviakh.* Moscow: v Universitetskoi Tipografii u N. Novikova, 1781.

———. "Rozana i Lubim." In *Russkaia komediia i komicheskaia opera XVIII veka,* edited by Pavel Berkov. Moscow: Iskusstvo, 1950.

Nikolev, Sergei Ivanovich. *Literaturnaia kul'tura petrovksoi epokhi.* St. Petersburg: Dmitrii Bulanin Press, 1996.

Novgorodskie byliny. Edited by Iury Smirnov and Viktor Smolitskii. Literaturnye Pamiatniki. Moscow: Nauka, 1978.

Novikov, Nikolai. *Drevniaia rossiiskaia vivliofika.* 5 vols. Vol. 1. St. Petersburg: Myshkin, Tipografiia P. Anisimova, 1773–1775, reprinted 1896.

Novyi rossiiskii pesennik. St. Petersburg: u I. K. Shnora, 1791.

Obstoiatel'noe opisanie torzhestvennykh poriadkov blagopoluchnago vshestviia v tsarstvuiushchii grad Moskvu i sviashchenneishago koronovaniia Eia Avgusteishago Imperatorskago Velichestva, Vsepresvieteishiia Derzhavneishaia Velikiia Gosudaryni Imperatritsy Elisavety Petrovny, Samoderzhitsyy Vserossiskoi: ezhe byst vshestvie 28 fevralia, koronovaniee 25 aprelia 1742 goda. St. Petersburg: v Tipografii Akademii nauk, 1744.

Odessky, Mikhail. *Ocherki istoricheskoi poetiki russkoi dramy: Epokha Petra I.* Moscow: Rossiskii Gos. Gumanitarnyi Universitet, 1999.

Ogarkova, Natalia. *Tseremonii, prazdnestva, muzyka russkogo dvora XVIII–nachala XIX veka.* St. Petersburg: Rossiiskii Institut Istorii Iskusstv, Dmitrii Bulanin, 2004.

Olearius, Adam. *The Voyages and Travells of the Ambassadors Sent by Frederick, Duke of Holstein, to the Great Duke of Muscovy and the King of Persia.* London: printed for John Starkey and Thomas Basset, 1669.

Olenina, Anna. *Dnevnik; Vospominaniia.* Vol. 9, Pushkinskaia Biblioteka. St. Petersburg: Akademicheskii proekt, 1999.

Olin, V. "Moi mysli o romanticheskoi poeme g. Pushkina 'Ruslan i Liudmila.'" In *Pushkin v prizhiznennoi kritike*, edited by Vadim Erazmovich Vatsuro and S. A. Fomichev, 104–6. St. Petersburg: Komissiia, 1996.

O'Malley, Lurana Donnels. "Catherine the Great's Operatic Splendor at Court: The Beginning of Oleg's Reign." *Essays in Theater/études théâtrales* 17, no. 1 (November 1998): 33–51.

———. *The Dramatic Works of Catherine the Great: Theatre and Politics in Eighteenth-Century Russia.* Aldershot, England: Ashgate, 2006.

———. "'How Great Was Catherine?' Checkpoints at the Border of Russian Theatre." *Slavic and East European Journal* 43, no. 1 (1999): 33–48.

Opisanie allegoricheskoi illuminatsii, predstavlennoi vo vseradostneishii den' koronatsii Eia Imperatorskago Velichestva, Ekateriny Vtoryia, Samoderzhitsy Vserossiiskiia, v Moskve v Universitetskom domie, 1762 godu. Moscow: v Universitetskoi Tipografii, 1762.

Opisanie koronatsii Eia Velichestva Imperatritsy Ekateriny Alekseevny, torzhestvenno otpravlenoi v tsarstvuiushchem grade Moskve 7 Maie, 1724 godu. Moscow: v Synodal'noi Tipografii, 1725.

Opisanie koronatsii Eia Velichestva Imperatritsy, i Samoderzhitsy Vserossiiskoi, Anny Ioannovny, torzhestvenno otpravlennoi v tsarstvuiushchem grade Moskve, 28 Aprelia, 1730 godu. Moscow: v Moskve pri Senate, 1730.

Opisanie maskarada i drugikh uveselenii, byvshikh v primorskoi L'va Aleksandrovicha Naryshkina dachi, otstoiavshei ot Sanktpeterburga v 11 verstakh po Petergofskoi doroge, 29 iiulia 1772 godu. St. Petersburg: Tipografiia Akademiia Nauk, 1772.

Opisanie vseradostneishago vshestviia Blagochestiviisheia Gosudaryni Imperatritsy Ekateriny Alekseevny Samoderzhitsy Vserossiiskiia, v Sviato-Troitskiiu Sergievu Lavru. Moscow: Pechatano pri Imperatorskom Moskovskom Universitete, 1762.

Ostankino. (Author unknown.) St. Petersburg: Tipografiia M.M. Stasiulevicha, 1897.

Ostolopov, Nikolai. *Slovar' drevnei i novoi poezii. Wörterbuch der Dichtkunst.* München: W. Fink, 1971.

Ostrovsky, Alexander. "Elena Obraztsova." *Russkaia Germaniia*, no. 3 (January 20–26, 2003), http://i-love.ru/pressa/text548.html (accessed August, 2007).

Ovsyannikov, S. A., and A. S. Ovsyannikov. "Sergei S. Korsakov and the Beginning of Russian Psychiatry." *Journal of the History of Neurosciences*, 2007, 16:58–64.

Parakalis, James. "Musical Historicism in *The Queen of Spades.*" In *Tchaikovsky and His Contemporaries: A Centennial Symposium*, edited by Alexandar Mihailovic, 177–188. Westport, CT: Greenwood Press, 1999.

Pashkevich, Vasilii, and M. Matinsky. *Kak pozhivesh', tak i proslyvesh', ili sanktpeterburgskii gostinyi dvor: opera.* 2 ed. Pamiatniki Russkogo Muzykal'nogo Iskusstva Vyp. Moscow: Muzyka, 1980.

Pavlenko, Petr. *Sobranie sochinenii v shesti tomakh.* Moscow: Gos. izd-vo khudozhestvennoi lit-ry, 1953.

Pekelis, Mikhail. *Dargomyzhskii i narodnaya pesnia.* Moscow: Gos. Izdatel'stvo, 1951.

Pendle, Karin. "Marsollier des Vivetières, Benoît-Joseph." In *The New Grove Dictionary of Opera*, edited by Stanley Sadie. *Grove Music Online. Oxford Music Online.* http://www.oxfordmusiconline.com.turing.library.northwestern.edu/subscriber/article/grove/music/O006324 (accessed October 5, 2008).

Perrault, Charles. *Skazki o volshebnitsakh s nravoucheniiami.* Translated by Lev Voinov. St. Petersburg: v Senatskoi Tipografii, 1781.

Peskov, A. M. "Poet and stikhotvorets Ivan Ivanovich Dmitriev." In Ivan Dmitriev, *Sochineniia.* Edited by A. M. Peskov and I. Surat. Moscow: Pravda, 1986; http://az.lib.ru/d/dmitriew_i_i/text_0090.shtml (accessed June 2011).

Petrovskaia, Ira. "Elisaveta Petrovna." In *Muzikal'nyi Peterburg*, edited by A. L. Porfir'eva. Vol. 1. 334–42. St. Petersburg: Kompozitor, 2001.

Piatnitsky, P. *Skazanie o venchanii russkikh tsarei i imperatorov.* Moscow: Tipo-Litagrafiia O. Lashkevich, 1896.

Pikovaia dama. Leningrad: Izd. Len. Gos. Akad. Teatra, 1935.

Poggioli, Renato. "The Masters of the Past: Pushkin." In *Alexander Pushkin*, edited by Harold Bloom, 9–19. New York: Chelsea House, 1987.

Pogosian, Elena. "Lomonosov i Khimera: otrazhenie literaturnoi polemiki 1750 godov v maskarade Torzhestvuiushchaia Minerva." In *Trudy po russkoi i slavianskoi filologii*, 11–24. Tartu: Tartu Ulikooli Kirjastus, 2008 http://www.ruthenia.ru/document/543655.html (accessed August 2010).

Popovchuk, M., E. Komarnitskaia, and A. Negare. *Shkol'nyi Slovar', Russko-moldavskii i moldavsko-russkii.* Izd. 2. Kishinev: Lumina, 1975.

Porfir'eva, Anna. "Pashkevich." In *Muzykal'nyi Peterburg XVIII vek: Ensiklopedicheskii slovar'*, edited by A. L. Porfir'eva and L. N. Berezovchuk. Vol. 2, 340–44. St. Petersburg: Kompozitor, 1996.

———, and L. N. Berezovchuk, eds. *Muzykal'nyi Peterburg XVIII vek: Ensiklopedicheskii slovar'.* Vol. 4. St. Petersburg: Kompozitor, 2001.

———. "Sarti." In *Muzykal'nyi Peterburg XVIII vek: Ensiklopedicheskii slovar'*, edited by A. L. Porfir'eva and L. N. Berezovchuk. Vol. 3, 79–92. St. Petersburg: Kompozitor, 1996.

Pritsak, Omeljan. *The Origin of Rus'.* Cambridge, MA: Harvard University Press, 1981.

Propp, Vladimir. *Morphology of the Folktale.* Austin: University of Texas Press, 1968, 2003.

———. *Russkaya skazka.* Leningrad: Leningrad University Press, 1984.

———. *Russkii geroicheskii epos.* Moscow: Gosudarstvennoie Izd. Khudozhestvennoi Literatury, 1958.

Proskurina, Vera. *Mify imperii: literatura i vlast' v epokhu Ekateriny II.* Moscow: Novoe Literaturnoe Obozrenie, 2006.

Protopopov, Vladimir, and Nadezhda Tumanina. *Opernoe tvorchestvo Tchaikovskogo.* Moscow: Izdatelstvo Akademii Nauk SSSR, 1957.

Pushkareva, Natalia. *Women in Russian History: From the Tenth to the Twentieth Century.* The New Russian History. Translated by Eve Levin. Armonk, NY: Sharpe, 1997.

Pushkin, Alexander. *Polnoe sobranie khudozhestvennykh proizvedenii.* St. Petersburg: Folio, Moscow: Olma, 1999.

———. *Polnoe sobranie sochinenii.* Moscow: Rossiiskaia Akademia Nauk, 1999.

———. *Rukoiu Pushkina: nesobrannye i neopublikovannye teksty*. Edited by M. A. Tsiavlovsky, L. B. Modzalevsky, T. G. Zinger. Moscow [Leningrad]: Akademiia, 1935.

———. *Sochineniia*. 3 vols. Moscow: Khudozhestvennaia Literatura, 1985.

Pushkin, Vasilii. *Sochineniia V.L. Pushkina*, edited by V. Saitova. St. Petersburg: Izd. Evg. Evdokimova, 1893.

Pye, Christopher. "Hobbes and the Spectacle of Power." In *Representing the English Renaissance*, edited by Stephen Greenblatt, 279–301. Berkeley: University of California Press, 1988.

Pyliaev, Mikhail. *Staroe zhit'e: ocherki i rassazy o byvshikh v otshedshee vremia obriadakh i poriad-khakh*. St. Petersburg: Niva, 2000.

———. *Staraia Moskva*. St. Petersburg: Izdanie A. S. Suvorina, 1891.

Rabinovich, Alexander. *Russkaia opera do Glinki*. Moscow: Muzgiz, 1948.

Radishchev, *Puteshestvie iz Peterburga v Moskvy*. Moscow: Detskia Literatura, 1975, http://az.lib.ru/r/radishew_a_n/text_0010.shtml (accessed June 2008).

Ram, Harsha. *The Imperial Sublime: A Russian Poetics of Empire*. Madison: University of Wisconsin Press, 2003.

Reddy, William M. "Sentimentalism and Its Erasure: The Role of Emotions in the Era of the French Revolution." *Journal of Modern History* 72, no. 1 (2000): 109–52.

Reed, Phyllis Ann. *The Rusalka Theme in Russian Literature*. Ph.D. dissertation, University of California, Berkeley, 1973.

Retsepter, Vladimir, and Mihail Shemiakin. *Vozvrashcheniie pushkinskoi rusalki*. St. Petersburg: Pushkin State Theater Center, 1998.

Reyfman, Irina, and E. A. Belousova. *Ritualizovannaia agressia: duel' v russkoi kul'ture i literature*. Moskva: Novoe literaturnoe obozrenie, 2002.

Riabtsev, Evgenii. *113 prelestnits Pushkina*. Rostov-na-Donu: Feniks, 1999.

Rimsky-Korsakov, Nikolai. *Letopis' moei muzykal'noi zhizni*. St. Petersburg: Tip. Glazunova, 1909.

———. "Mlada." DVD. Kultur Films 6973074, 2005.

———. *Mlada: An Opera Ballet in Four Acts. Complete Works*. Orchestral score. Rimsky-Korsakov. Melville, NY: Belwin-Mills, 1981.

———. *Mlada. Vocal score. Polnoe sobranie sochinenii*. Vol. 32. Moscow: Gosudarstvennoe muzykal'noe izdatel'stvo, 1959.

———. *My Musical Biography*. Translated by Judah A. Joffe. New York: Knopf, 1923.

———. *Noch' pered Rozhdestvom*. Moscow: Gos. Muzykal'noe Izd-vo, 1951.

———. *Sadko: Opera-Bylina*. Leningrad: Muzyka, 1975.

———, and Vladimir Bel'sky. *Sadko. The Complete Works of Nikolai Rimsky-Korsakov*. Vols. 1–3. Melville: Belwin Mills, 1981.

Ritzarev, Marina. *Eighteenth-Century Russian Music*. Burlington, VT: Ashgate, 2006.

Rosen, Nathan. "The Theme of Cards in the Queen of Spades." *Slavic and East European Journal* 19, no. 3 (1975): 255–75.

Rosenshield, Gary. "Freud, Lacan, and Romantic Psychoanalysis: Three Psychoanalytical Approaches to Madness in Pushkin's *The Queen of Spades*." *Slavic and East European Journal* 40, no. 1 (1996): 1–26.

———. *Pushkin and the Genres of Madness: The Masterpieces of 1833*. Publications of the Wisconsin Center for Pushkin Studies. Madison: University of Wisconsin Press, 2003.

Roth, Michael S. "Remembering Forgetting: Maladies de la Mèmoire in Nineteenth-Century France." *Representations* no. 26 (1989): 49–68.

Rovinsky, D. *Russkiia narodnye kartinki*. St. Petersburg: Tipografiia Imperatorskoi Akademii Nauk, 1881.

Rubin, Maria. "Pushkin's *Gavriliada*: A Study of the Genre and Beyond." *Slavic and East European Journal* 40, no 4 (1996): 623–631.

Rushton, Julian. *Mozart*. London: Oxford University Press, 2006.

Rybakov, B. "Rozhdenie bogin' i bogov." In *Mify drevnikh slavian*, edited by Andrei Kaisarov, Grigorii Glinka, and Boris Rybakov, 3–16. Saratov: Nadezhda, 1993.

Sadie, Stanley. *Mozart and his Operas*. London: Macmillan Reference Ltd., 2000.

Said, Edward W. *Orientalism*. 1st ed. New York: Pantheon Books, 1978.

Sakhnovsky, Vasily. *Krepostnoi usadebnyi teatr*. Leningrad: Kolos, 1924.

Savchenko, S. V. *Russkaia narodnaia skazka*. Kiev, 1914. Reprint, Cleveland: Bell & Howell, 1967.

Schakovskoy, Zinaïda princesse. *The Fall of Eagles: Precursors of Peter the Great*. New York: Harcourt, Brace & World, 1964.

———. *Precursors of Peter the Great*. London: J. Cape, 1964.

Schönle, Andreas. *Authenticity and Fiction in the Russian Literary Journey, 1790–1840*, Russian Research Center Studies (Harvard University), 92. Cambridge: Harvard University Press, 2000.

Schuler, Catherine. "The Gender of Russian Serf Theatre and Performance." In *Women, Theater, and Performance: New Histories, New Historiographies*, edited by Maggie B. Gale and Vivien Gardner, 216–35. New York: Manchester University Press, 2000.

———. *Theatre & Identity in Imperial Russia*. Studies in Theatre History and Culture. Iowa City: University of Iowa Press, 2009.

Seaman, Gerald R. "Catherine the Great and Musical Enlightenment." *New Zealand Slavonic Journal* 37 (2003): 129–36.

Segal, Charles. *Euripides and the Poetics of Sorrow*. Durham, NC, and London: Duke University Press, 1993.

Ségur, Louis-Philippe. *Zapiski grafa Segiura o prebyvanii ego v Rossii v tsarstvovanie Ekateriny II (1785–1789)*. St. Petersburg: Tipografiia V. N. Maikova, 1865.

Semenkova, T. G., and O. V. Karamova. *Russkie tsaritsy i tsarevny*. Moskva: Ales, 2001.

Semibratova, Irina. "Afterwords." In *Oboroten'. Russkie Fantasmagorii*, edited by Orest Somov, 327–35. Moscow: Book Tent, 1994.

Senelick, Laurence. "The Erotic Bondage of Serf Theatre." *Russian Review* 50, no. 1 (1991): 24–34.

Serman, Ilia. "I. F. Bogdanovich." In Bogdanovich, *Stikhotvoreniia i poemy*. Biblioteka Poeta. Bol'shaia. Seriia. 2. Izd., 5–42. Leningrad: Sovetskii pisatel', 1957.

———. *Poety XVIII veka*. Edited by Georgii Makogonenko. Leningrad: Sovetskii Pisatel', 1958.

———, and Ippolit Bogdanovich. "Introduction." In *Stikhotvoreniia i Poemy*, 5–42. Leningrad: Sovetskii pisatel', 1957.

Serov, Alexander. *Izbrannye stat'i*. Edited by G. N. Khubova. 2 vols. Vol. 1. Moscow: Gosudarstvennoe Muzykal'noe izdatel'stvo, 1957.

———. *Rusalka, opera A. S. Dargomyzhskogo*. Moscow: Gos. Muzykal'noe izdatel'stvo, 1953.

Shakespeare, William. *William Shakespeare's Schauspiele*. 12 vols. Translated by Johann Joachim von Eschenburg. Neue Ausg. ed. Zurich: Orell, Gessner, Fussli, 1775.

Shamiakin, Ivan. *Etnahrafiia Belarusi: encyclopedia*. Minsk: Belaruskaia sav. entsyklapedyia imia Petrusia Brouki, 1989.

Shavrygin, Sergei. *Tvorchestvo A. Shakhovskogo v istoriko-literaturnom protsesse 1800–1840 Godov.* St. Petersburg: Dm. Bulanin, 1996.

Shcherbakova, Maria. *Muzyka v russkoi drame: 1756–pervaia polovina XIX v.* St. Petersburg: Ut, 1997.

———. "Ossian in the Late 18th and Early 19th-Century Russian Theatre." *Scotland and Russia in the Enlightenment.* The Philosophical Age. Almanac 15. St. Petersburg: Center for History of Ideas, 91–99.

———. "Puteshestvie v istoriiu." *Muzyka v biblioteke,* no. 7 (2003), http://www.bibliograf.ru/issues/2003/11/18/0/425/ (accessed July 2007).

Shepetov, K. *Krepostnoe pravo v votchinah Sheremet'evyh.* Moscow: Ostankino Museum Press, 1947.

Sheremetev, Nikolai, and Sergei Sheremetev. *Stolietnie Otgoloski, 1801 God.* Moscow: Tipo-lit. A.V. Vasil'eva, 1901.

Shevtsova, Maria. *Dodin and the Maly Drama Theatre.* London: Routledge, 2004.

Shik, Alexander. *Odesskii Pushkin.* Paris: Dom knigi, 1938.

Shliapkin, Il'ia. Introduction to *Tsarevna Natal'ia Aleksieevna i teatr eia vremeni,* by Natal'ia Alekseevna, Grand Duchess of Russia. St. Petersburg: V. Balashev, 1898.

Sholok, Edvard. *Ostankino i ego teatr.* Moscow: Moskovskii rabochii, 1949.

Shorter, Edward. *Historical Dictionary of Psychiatry.* New York: Oxford University Press, 2005.

Skvirskaia, Tamara. "K istorii sozdaniia opery 'Pikovaia Dama.'" In *Tchaikovsky: novye documenty i materialy,* 191–229. St. Petersburg: Kompozitor, 2003.

Smart, Mary Ann. "The Silencing of Lucia." *Cambridge Opera Journal* 4, no. 2 (1991): 119–41.

Smirnov-Sokol'sky, Nikolai. *Rasskazy o knigakh.* Izd. 5. ed. Moscow: Kniga, 1983.

Smith, Douglas, ed. and trans. *Love and Conquest: Personal Correspondence of Catherine the Great and Prince Grigory Potemkin.* DeKalb: Northwestern Illinois University Press, 2004.

———. *The Pearl: A True Tale of Forbidden Love in Catherine the Great's Russia.* New Haven: Yale University Press, 2008.

Smith, Marian Elizabeth. *Ballet and Opera in the Age of Giselle.* Princeton, NJ: Princeton University Press, 2000.

Sobranie nailuchshikh rossiiskikh pesen. Chasti I V. Soderzhashchaia v sebie 6 pesen. St. Peterburg: Izdannyia izhdiveniem Knigoprodavtsa F. Meiera, 1781.

Sokolov, V. "Rodoslovnaia Tchaikovskogo: novye imena." In *Tchaikovskii: novye documenty i materialy,* 7–33. St. Petersburg: Kompozitor, 2003.

Soler, Vicente Martín y, and Lorenzo Da Ponte. *L'arbore di Diana: Dramma Giocoso in Due Atti.* Edited by Leonardo Waisman. Musica Hispana. Madrid: Instituto Complutense de Ciencias Musicales, 2001.

Soloveytchik, George. *Potemkin, Soldier, Statesman, Lover and Consort of Catherine of Russia.* New York: Norton, 1947.

Sommer-Amthis, Andrea. "Opera and Ceremonial at the Imperial Court of Vienna." In *Italian Opera in Central Europe,* edited by Melania Bucciarelli, Norbert Dubowy and Reinhard Strohm, 179–90. Berlin: BWV Berliner Wissenschafts-Verlag, 2006.

Shorter, Edward. *Historical Dictionary of Psychiatry.* New York: Oxford University Press, 2005.

Staehlin, Jakob von. *Izobrazhenie iziasnenie feierverka i illuminatsi kotorye aprieli 25 dnia 1742 godu po blagopoluchno sovershivshemsia vysokom pomazani i koronovanii Eia Velichestva Vsepriesvietliehia, Derzhavnieshi, Velikai Nepobiedimyia Gosudaryni Elisavety Petrovny Imperatritsy i Samoderzhitsy Vserossiskiai.* St. Petersburg: pri Imperatorskoi Akademii Nauk, 1742.

———. *Muzyka i balet v Rossii XVIII veka.* Leningrad: Triton, 1935.

Staniukovich, Vladimir. *Domashnii krepostnoi teatr Sheremetevykh XVIII veka.* Leningrad: Izd. Gos. Russkogo Muzeia, 1926.

Starikova, Liudmila. "Chto taitsia za strokoi documenta." In *Teatral'naia zhizn' Rossii v epokhu Elizavety Petrovny.* Moscow: Nauka, 2003.

———. *Teatral'naia zhizn' Rossii v epokhu Anny Ioannovny.* Moscow: Radiks, 1995.

———. *Teatral'naia zhizn' Rossii v epokhu Elizavety Petrovny.* Moscow: Nauka, 2003.

Stasov, Vladimir. *Collected Works.* Vol. 3. St. Petersburg, 1894.

———. *Mikhail Ivanovich Glinka.* Moscow: Gos. Muzykal'noe Izdatel'stvo, 1953.

Stepanov, V. "Ob avtore *Peresmeshnika.*" In *Peresmeshnik.* Moscow: Sov. Rossiia, 1987, 326–50.

Stoletnie otgoloski. Moscow: Tipo-lit. A.V. Vasil'eva, 1801.

Stroganov, M. V. *Genii vkusa.* Tver': Tverskoi Gosudarstvennyi Universitet, 2001.

Strong, Roy C. *Art and Power: Renaissance Festivals, 1450–1650.* Berkeley: University of California Press, 1984.

Sumarokov, Alexander. *Polnoe sobranie vsekh sochinenii.* 10 vols. Vol. 9. Moscow: Novikov, 1781.

Sytova, Alla. *The Lubok: Russian Folk Pictures, 17th to 19th Century.* Leningrad: Aurora Art, 1984.

Sviiasov, E. V. "Evolutsia Pronominatsii "Ekaterina II-Minerva (Pallada)." *Proceedings of the International Conference "Catherine the Great: An Epoch of Russian History,"* edited by T. Artemieva and M. Mikeshin, 52–54. St. Petersburg: Russian Academy of Science, 1996.

Tallemant, Paul. *Iezda v ostrov liubvi.* Translated by Vasily Trediakovsky. St. Petersburg: v Tipografii Morskago Shliakhetnago Kadetskago Korpusa, 1778.

Taruskin, Richard. "Another World: Why the Queen of Spades Is the Great Symbolist Opera." *Opera News* 60, no. 7 (1995): 8–10, 12–13.

———. "Catherine II." *The New Grove Dictionary of Opera*, edited by Stanley Sadie. *Grove Music Online. Oxford Music Online* (accessed September 1, 2009).

———. "Chernomor to Kashchei: Harmonic Sorcery; or, Stravinsky's 'Angle.'" *Journal of the American Musicological Society* 38, no. 1 (1985): 72–142.

———. *Defining Russia Musically.* Princeton: Princeton University Press, 1997.

———. "'Entoiling the Falconet': Russian Musical Orientalism in Context." *Cambridge Opera Journal* 4, no. 3 (1992): 253–80.

———. "Fomin, Evstigney Ipat'yevich." In *Grove Music Online.* http://www.oxfordmusiconline.com.turing.library.northwestern.edu/subscriber/article/grove/music/09938 (accessed April 18, 2006).

———. "Glinka's Ambiguous Legacy and the Birth Pangs of Russian Opera." *19th-Century Music* 1, no. 2 (1977): 142–62.

———. "Mlada (II)." In *The New Grove Dictionary of Music and Musicians*, edited by Stanley Sadie. *Grove Music Online.* http://www.oxfordmusiconline.com.turing.library.northwestern.edu/subscriber/article/grove/music/O903247 (accessed January 19, 2008).

———. *On Russian Music.* Ahmanson Foundation Humanities Endowment Fund. Berkeley: University of California Press, 2009.

———. "Pashkevich, Vasily Alekseyevich." In *Grove Music Online.* Oxford Music Online. http://www.oxfordmusiconline.com.turing.library.northwestern.edu/subscriber/article/grove/music/21006 (accessed October 6, 2009).

———. "The Queen of Spades." In *Grove Music Online*, edited by Stanley Sadie. Oxford Music Online, http://www.oxfordmusiconline.com.turing.library.northwestern.edu/subscriber/article/grove/music/O004733 (accessed April 20, 2009).

————. "Sadko." In *Grove Dictionary of Music and Musicians*, edited by Stanley Sadie. *Oxford Music Online*, http://www.oxfordmusiconline.com.turing.library.northwestern.edu/ subscriber/article/grove/music/O002379 (accessed October 24, 2006).

————. *Stravinsky and the Russian Traditions: A Biography of the Works Through Mavra*. Berkeley: University of California Press, 1996.

————. "Tchaikovsky: A New View—A Centennial Essay." In *Tchaikovsky and His Contemporaries: A Centennial Symposium*, edited by Alexandar Mihailovic, 17–60. Westport, CT: Greenwood Press, 1999.

Tchaikovsky, Peter. *Cherevichki* [The Slippers]. Vol. 2. Moscow: Gos. Myzykal'noe izdatel'stvo, 1951.

————. *Dnevniki*. Moscow: Nash Dom-D'Age d'Homme, 2000.

————, and Modest Tchaikovsky. *Pikovaia Dama*. Moscow: Muzyka, 2001.

Teplov, Grigorii. *Mezhdu delom bezdel'e ili sobranie raznykh pesen*. 1779.

Terebenina, Rimma. "Kopia 'Zapisok Ekateriny II' iz archiva pushkina." *Vremennik Pushkin Commissii* 29 (1969): 8–22.

Tokmakov, Ivan. *Istoricheskoe opisanie vsekh koronatsii rossiiskikh tsarei, imperatorov i imperatrits*. Moscow: K. I. Tikhomirov, 1896.

Tolstov, S. "'Nartsy' i 'volkhi' na Dunae." *Sovetskaia etnografiia* 2 (1948), 8–38.

Tolstoy, Leo. *Anna Karenina*. Translated by Louise and Aylmer Maude. Oxford: Oxford University Press, 1995.

Tolstoy, N. I. *Slavianskaia mifologiia* (encyclopedia), 397–99. Moscow: Ellis Lak, 1995.

Tosi, Alessandra. "Sentimental Irony in Early Nineteenth-Century Russian Literature: The Case of Nikolai Brusilov's *Bednyi Leandr*." *Slavic and East European Journal* 44, no. 2 (2000): 266–86.

Trachevsky, Alexander. *Russkaia istoriia*. St. Petersburg: Izdatel'stvo K. L. Rikkera, 1895.

Trediakovsky, Vasily. *Izbrannye proizvedeniia*. Leningrad: Sovetskii pisatel', 1963.

————, and Paul Tallemant. *Ezda v ostrov liubvi*. St. Petersburg: v Tipografii Morskago Shliakhetnago Kadetskago Korpusa, 1778.

Troyat, Henri. *Catherine the Great*. Henley-on-Thames: Ellis, 1978.

————. *Catherine the Great*. New York: Dutton, 1980.

Trutovsky, Vasilii. *Sobranie russkikh prostykh pesen s notami, 1776–1779*. Moscow: Gosudarstvennoe muzykal'noe izdatel'stvo, 1953.

Tsvetaeva, Marina. "Pushkin and Pugachev." In *Sobranie sochinenii v semi tomakh*. Vol. 5, 498–524. Moscow: Ellis Lak, 1994.

Tsvetkova, M. V. *"Eksentrichnyi russkii genii": poeziia Mariny Tsvetaevoi v zerkale perevoda*. Moscow, Nizhnii Novgorod: Vektor-Tis, 2003.

Tyn'nianov, Iury. *Pushkin i ego sovremenniki*. Moscow: Nauka, 1969.

Udovik, Viacheslav. *Odesskie gratsii A. S. Pushkina*. Sankt-Peterburg: [S.n], 2004.

Ushakova, Elizaveta. *Al'bom Elizavety Nikolaevny Ushakovoi*. Edited by Tatiana Krasnoborod'ko. St. Petersburg: Logos, 1999.

Uspensky, Boris. *Filologicheskie razyskaniia v oblasti slavianskikh drevnostei*. Moscow: Izd-vo Moskovskogo universiteta, 1982.

————. *Semiotika istorii. Semiotika kul'tury*. In *Izbrannye trudy*, 3 vols. Vol. 1, 83–124. Moscow: Gnozis, 1994.

Vaidman, Polina. "Rabota P. I. Tchaikovskogo nad rukopis'iu libretto opery Pikovaia dama." In *P. I. Tchaikovsky i russkaia literatura*, edited by Boris Anshakov, 155–77. Izhevsk: Udmurtiia, 1980.

————, Ludmila Korabel'nikova, and Valentina Rubtsova. *Tematiko-bibliographicheskii ukaza-tel' sochinenii P. I. Tchaikovskogo*. Moscow: Muzyka, 2003.

Vanechkina, I., and B. Galeev. "'Tsvetnoi slukh' v tvorchestve N. A. Rimskogo-Korsakova." In *Russkaia muzyka XVIII-XX vekov: Kul'tura i traditsii*. Kazan: Conservatoriia, 2003, 182–195, http://synesthesia.prometheus.kai.ru/zwet-sl_r.htm (accessed November, 2008).

Vasil'ev, Vladimir. *Starinnye feierverki v Rossii*. Leningrad: Izdatel'stvo Gos. Ermitaga, 1960.

Vasil'eva, E. E., and V. A. Lapin. "Kant." In *Muzykal'nyi Peterburg XVIII vek: Ensiklopedicheskii slovar'*, edited by A. L. Porfir'eva and L. N. Berezovchuk. Vol. 2, 20–37. St. Petersburg: Kompozitor, 1998.

Vasil'eva, Larisa, and Ada Bakirova. *Zhena i muza: taina Aleksandra Pushkina*. Moscow: Atlantida-XXI vek, 1999.

Vasmer, Maks. *Etimologicheskii slovar' russkogo yazyka*. Translated by O. Trubachev. 4 vols. Vols. 3 and 4. Moscow: Progress, 1964.

Vatsuro, Vadim, and S. Fomichev. *Pushkin v prizhiznennoi kritike 1820–1827*, Pushkinskaia Prem'era. St. Petersburg: Gos. pushkinskii teatralnyi tsentr, 1996.

Velikopol'sky, Ivan. *K Erastu*. Moscow: v tipografii Avgusta Semeva, 1828.

Veresaev, Vikentii. *Pushkin v zhizni: sistematicheskii svod podlinnykh svidetel'stv sovremennikov*. Moscow: Moskovskii rabochii, 1984.

Viazemsky, Petr, and M. Gillel'son. *Sochineniia v dvukh tomakh*. Edited by M. Gillel'son. Moscow: Khudozhestvennaia Literatura, 1982.

Vigel', Filipp. *Zapiski*. Edited by S. Shtraikh. Moscow: Zakharov, 2000.

Vigor, Lady Rondeau. *Letters from a Lady, Who Resided Some Years in Russia, to Her Friend in England*. London: J. Dodsley, 1777.

Vinogradov, Viktor. *Slovar' iazyka Pushkina*. 4 vols. Moscow: Azbukovnik, 2000.

————. "Stil' Pikovoi Damy." *Pushkin: Vremmenik pushkinskoi komisii*, 74–147. Moscow: Akademiia Nauk SSSR, 1936.

Voeikov, Alexander. "Razbor poemy 'Ruslan i Liudmila.'" In *Pushkin v prizhiznennoi kritike, 1820–1827*, edited by Vadim Vatsuro and S. Fomichev, 36–68. St. Petersburg: Gos. Pushkinskii teatral'nyi tsentr, 1996.

Vrangel', Baron N., and N. Solov'ev. *Russkaia zhenshchina v graviurakh i litografiakh: vystavka portretov*. St. Petersburg: Kruzhok liubitelei russkikh iziashchnykh izdanii, 1911.

Vremennik pushkinskoi komissii. Vol. 20, 1962–1981. Moskva: Izdatel'stvo Akademii Nauk SSSR, 1963.

Vsevolodsky-Gerngross, Vsevolod. *Istoriia dramaticheskogo teatra*. Vol. 1. Moscow: Iskusstvo, 1977.

————. *Russkii teatr ot istokov do serediny XVIII veka*. Moscow: Izdatel'stvo Akademii Nauk SSSR, 1957.

Vsevolozhskaia, Liudmila. *Rod Vsevolozhskikh*. Ekaterinburg: Gazeta Shtern, 2000.

Vyzgo-Ivanova, Irina. *Opera M. I. Glinki "Ruslan i Liudmila."* St. Petersburg: Asterion, 2004.

Wachtel, Andrew Baruch. *An Obsession with History: Russian Writers Confront the Past*. Stanford: Stanford University Press, 1994.

————. *Plays of Expectations: Intertextual Relations in Russian Twentieth-Century Drama*. Seattle: Herbert J. Ellison Center for Russian, East European, and Central Asian Studies, University of Washington, 2006.

————. *Remaining Relevant After Communism*. Chicago: University of Chicago Press, 2006.

————. "Rereading *The Queen of Spades*." *Pushkin Review* no. 3 (2000): 3–21.

———, and Ilya Vinitsky. *Russian Literature*. Cambridge: Polity Press, 2009.

Waisman, Leonardo J. "Introduction." In *L'arbore di Diana. Drama giocoso in due atti*, xxi–xxxii. Madrid: Ediciones del Instituto Complutense de Ciencias Musicales, 2001.

Waliszewski, Kazimierz. *The Romance of an Empress, Catherine II of Russia*. 2 vols. London: Heinemann, 1894.

Weber, Friedrich Christian. *The Present State of Russia*. 2 vols. London: printed for W. Taylor. W. and J. Innys, and J. Osborn, 1722–23.

Wieland, Christoph Martin, and Vasilii Levshin. *Oberon, tsar' volshebnikov, poema gospodina Vilanda v chetyrnadtsati piesniakh*. Moscow: v Tipografii Kompanii Tipograficheskoi, 1787.

Wiley, John Roland. *A Century of Russian Ballet*. Oxford: Clarendon Press, 1990.

William Shakespeares Schauspiele. Translated by Johann Joachim von Eschenburg. Zurich: Orell, Gessner, Fussli, 1775–82.

Wilson, Kenneth. "*L'Olimpiade*: Selected Eighteenth-Century Settings of Metastasio's Libretto." Ph.D. dissertation, Harvard University, 1982.

Wortman, Richard. *Scenarios of Power: Myth and Ceremony in Russian Monarchy*. Studies of the Harriman Institute 1. Princeton: Princeton University Press, 1995.

Wotton, Tom S. "Drums." *Musical Times* 71, no. 1051 (1930): 792–94.

Wyngaard, Amy S. *From Savage to Citizen: The Invention of the Peasant in the French Enlightenment*. University of Delaware Press Studies in Seventeenth- and Eighteenth-Century Art and Culture. Newark: University of Delaware Press, 2004.

Yegenoglu, Meyda. *Colonial Fantasies: Towards a Feminist Reading of Orientalism*. Cambridge: Cambridge University Press, 1998.

Yorke-Long, Alan. *Music at Court: Four Eighteenth-Century Studies*. London: Weidenfeld and Nicolson, 1954.

Zabelin, Ivan. *Domashniii byt russkago naroda v XVI i XVII st*. Moscow: Tipografiia Gracheva, 1872.

Zakharova, Oksana. *Baly Pushkinskogo Vremeni*. Moscow: Zhurnalistskoe agenstvo "Glasnost'," 1999.

———. *Svetskie tseremonialy v Rossii XVIII—nachala XX veka*. Moscow: Tsentrpoligraf, 2001.

Zapadov, A. B. "Komicheskaia opera." In *Istoriia russkoi literatury*, 284–95. Moscow: Izdatel'stvo Akademii Nauk SSSR, 1947.

Zelenin, Dmitrii. *Izbrannye trudy: ocherki russkoi mifologii: umershie neestestvennoiu smert'iu i rusalki*. Moscow: Indrik, 1995.

Zhukovsky, Vasilii. "Rybak." In *Pesn' Lubvi: lyrika russkih poetov XIX i XX vekov*. Moscow: Pravda, 1988.

Zil'bershtein, Ilya. *Liubovnyi byt pushkinskoi epokhi*. Moskva: Sovremennik, 1999.

Zorin, Andrei. "Eden in Taurus: Catherine II's Journey to Crimea in 1787—Political and Cultural Intentions." Translated by Iain L. Fraser. In *Unravelling Civilisation: European Travel and Travel Writing*, edited by Hagen Schulz-Forberg, 225–244. Brussels: P.I.E. Peter Lang, 2005.

———. "Nezabvennaia Dushen'ka." In *Dushen'ka: drevniaia povest' v vol'nykh stikhakh*, 7–20. Moscow: Ladomir, 2002.

Zozulina, Natalia. "Vremia peterburgskoi tantsemanii." *St. Peterburgskii teatral'nyi zhurnal* (2003). http://ptzh.theatre.ru/2003/32/7/ (accessed January 2006).

INDEX

Abbate, Carolyn, xv, 190, 228
Ablesimov, Alexander. *See Miller—Wizard,*
    Cheat, and Matchmaker (Ablesimov)
Abramovsky, Georgii, 330*n*3, 330*n*10,
    331*n*23, 332*n*53, 332*n*54
Adam, Adolphe
    Giselle, 196, 205–06, 221, 338*n*41,
        339*n*67–68, 340*n*72–73
    La Fille du Danube, 204, 340*n*71
Adolf Frederick, King of Sweden, 46
"Aesopian language," 147, 153, 330*n*2
    See also inoskazanie
Akhrideich. See Brave and Bold Knight
    Akhrideich, The
Alekseeva, Mariia, 303*n*29
Alekseev, Mikhail, 326*n*55–56, 326*n*58,
    326*n*60
Aleksei Mikhailovich, Tsar of Russia, 31, 36
Aleksei Petrovich, Tsarevich, 8, 16
Alessandro nell'Indie (Araia, Metastasio)
    cross-textual allusions, 49
    influence on other works, 329*n*118
    links to *Slaviane,* 50, 141–43
    performances of, 42, 141, 313*n*160
    plot, 43, 50
Alexander I, Emperor of Russia
    Catherine's affection for, 35, 88
    Khlor identified with, 316*n*55
    marriage to Princess Elisabeth of Baden,
        35–36, 39, 88, 105, 309*n*74
    reign, 149
Alexander, John T., 307*n*15, 307*n*17, 307*n*30,
    308*n*49, 348*n*7, 350*n*44–45
Alexander Nevsky (film), 106
Aliabiev, Alexander, *Rusalka,* 204
Alkista, 138, 139
Amour and Psyche (la Fontaine), 51
Amour et Psyche (ballet), 35, 309*n*77

Andreev, V., 301*n*11, 302*n*21
Angiolini, Domenico
    Semira, 49
    Triumphant Minerva, 23
Anisimov, Evgenii, 36, 304*n*39, 309*n*83,
    309*n*85, 316*n*58
Aniuta operas, 53–61
    foreshadowing Liza and Nina, 61
    origins, 54
    performances, 54, 82
    reversals and social transgressions, 53–54,
        56–59
    Russian comic operas inspired by,
        53, 54, 57
    See also Aniuta (Popov); *Coffeegrounds-*
        Reader (Krylov); *Miller—Wizard,*
        Cheat, and Matchmaker,
        (Ablesimov); *Misfortune from*
        a Coach (Kniazhnin); opera, comic
Aniuta (Popov), 53–54, 57, 68
Anna, Empress of Russia
    accession to throne, 8–9, 12, 70, 303*n*25,
        304*n*45
    coronation, 29, 30, 31, 32, 34, 308*n*51
    first opera troupes invited by, 16, 29, 41
    Ice Castle wedding, 22, 26, 100, 103,
        307*n*28
    marriage to Duke of Courland, 8, 37,
        310*n*90
    masculine attributes, 11, 12,
        304*n*61
    music and theater under, 4, 16, 17, 41–42,
        44, 49, 305*n*80, 305*n*86
    parents, 303*n*23
    relationship with Biron, 14, 305*n*67
    schools for acting and music, 9, 17, 71,
        305*n*80
    weddings staged, 40, 310*n*94